VITAL RECORDS

OF

ANDOVER

MASSACHUSETTS

TO THE END OF THE YEAR 1849

VOLUME I.—BIRTHS

PUBLISHED BY THE
TOPSFIELD HISTORICAL SOCIETY
TOPSFIELD, MASS.
1912

NEWCOMB & GAUSS
Printers
Salem, Massachusetts

EXPLANATIONS

The following records of births, marriages and deaths include all entries to be found in the books of record kept by the town clerks; in the church records; in the returns made to the Salem Quarterly Court; in the cemetery inscriptions; and in private records found in family Bibles, etc. These records are printed in a condensed form in which every essential particular has been preserved. All duplication of the town clerks' record has been eliminated, but differences in entry and other explanatory matter appear in brackets. Parentheses are used when they occur in the original record; also to indicate the maiden name of a married woman.

When places other than Andover and Massachusetts are named in the original records, they are given in the printed copy. Marriages and intentions of marriage are printed under the names of both parties. Double dating is used in the months of January, February and March, prior to 1752, whenever it appears in the original and also, whenever from the sequence of entry in the original the date may be easily determined. In all records the original spelling of names is followed and in the alphabetical arrangement the various forms should be examined, as items about the same family may be found under different spellings.

The register of deaths in the South Parish, between 1710 and 1771, referred to in the Historical Manual of the South Church published in 1859, has not been found.

The town clerk's records, Book II, 1701-1800, are badly worn, and portions of many of the entries in the first hundred pages are missing, thus accounting for the frequent use of the word torn and the dash.

The gravestone records are from copies of gravestones made in October, 1864 by Alfred Poore, M. D., and now in possession of the Essex Institute.

ANDOVER

The territory within the limits of the town of Andover was originally called Cochicawick. Andover was incorporated as a town May 6, 1646, and was named for the town in Hants County, England, which had been the home of many of its settlers.

A committee was appointed by the General Court on June 1, 1652, to lay out the bounds between Andover and Cambridge, and the same day the Court granted that the five or six hundred acres laid out by Rowley, without their line near Andover town, should belong to Andover.

The bounds between Andover and Billerica were established May 26, 1658.

The bounds between Andover and Wills Hill were established May 9, 1678.

June 20, 1728, a part of Andover was included in the new town of Middleton.

April 17, 1847, a part of Andover was included in the new town of Lawrence.

April 7, 1855, a part of Andover was established as North Andover.

Feb. 7, 1879, a part of Andover was annexed to Lawrence.

The bounds between Andover and Tewksbury were established May 21, 1903.

The bounds between Andover and North Reading were established Apr. 22, 1904.

The population of Andover at different periods was as follows:

1765,	2,442.	1820,	3,889.
1776,	2,953.	1830,	4,530.
1790,	2,863.	1840,	5,207
1800,	2,941.	1850,	6,945
1810,	3,164.	1905,	6,632.

ABBREVIATIONS

a.—age.
abt.—about.
b.—born.
bef.—before.
bet.—between.
bp.—baptized.
bur.—buried.
c. c.—Copy of Essex Co. Court records, at the Clerk of Court's office, made by Alfred Kimball in 1856.
C. R. 1.—North Parish Congregational Church records.
C. R. 2.—South Parish Congregational Church records.
C. R. 3.—West Parish Congregational Church records.
C. R. 4.—Christ Church records.
C. R. 5.—North Andover Congregational Church records.
C. R. 6.—Theological Seminary Church records.
ch.—child.
chn.—children.
Co.—county.
CT. F.—court files, Essex Co. Quarterly Court.
CT. R.—court record, Essex Co. Quarterly Court.
d.—daughter; day; died.
Dea.—deacon.
dup.—duplicate entry.
G. R. 1.—gravestone record, North Parish Burying Ground.
G. R. 2.—gravestone record, South Parish Burying Ground.
G. R. 3.—gravestone record, West Parish Burying Ground.
G. R. 4.—gravestone record, Christ Church Burying Ground.
G. R. 5.—gravestone record, Theological Seminary Burying Ground.

G. R. 6.—gravestone record, Second Burying Ground, in North Andover.

G. R. 7.—gravestone record, Ridgewood Cemetery.

h.—husband; hour.

inf.—infant.

int.—intention of marriage.

jr.—junior.

m.—male; married; month.

P. R. 1.—Bible record now in possession of Miss Charlotte Helen Abbot.

P. R. 2.—Family record now in possession of Miss Ellen Richardson.

P. R. 3.—Bible record now in possession of Mrs. E. A. Higgins.

P. R. 4.—Bible records now in possession of Miss Anna B. Abbott.

P. R. 5.—Bible record now in possession of Edward Adams, North Andover.

P. R. 6.—Bible record now in possession of Frank W. Abbott, North Andover.

P. R. 7.—Bible record now in possession of Charles B. Adams, North Andover.

P. R. 8.—Bible records, now in possession of Mrs. S. H. Bailey.

P. R. 9.—Bible record now in possession of George T. Abbott.

P. R. 10.—Bible records now in possession of Mrs. William Cheever.

P. R. 11.—Bible record now in possession of Ballard Holt.

P. R. 12.—Bible record now in possession of Fred Andrews.

P. R. 13.—Family record now in possession of Miss Florence Averill, North Andover.

P. R. 14.—Account book now in possession of Miss Florence Averill, North Andover.

P. R. 15.—Record now in possession of Orrin Foster.

P. R. 16.—Bible record, now in possession of Jacob W. Barker, North Andover.

P. R. 17.—Records now in possession of Jacob W. Barker.

P. R. 18.—Bible record now in possession of Miss Emily Carter.

P. R. 19.—Bible record now in possession of George Caldwell.

P. R. 20.—Bible record now in possession of George I. Smith, North Andover.

P. R. 21.—Family record now in possession of Miss Maria D. Kimball.

P. R. 22.—Bible record now in possession of Mrs. Hannah Tucker, North Andover.

P. R. 23.—Bible record now in possession of Mary G. Carleton, North Andover.

P. R. 24.—Bible record now in possession of Mrs. Edward Butterworth, North Andover.

P. R. 25.—Bible record now in possession of Andrew J. Barker, North Andover.

P. R. 26.—Bible record now in possession of Clifton Berry, North Andover.

P. R. 27.—Bible record now in possession of Mrs. Edward Cooper, North Andover.

P. R. 28.—Bible record now in possession of Mrs. Martha A. Russell.

P. R. 29.—Bible record now in possession of Miss Angie Burtt.

P. R. 30.—Bible records now in possession of Mrs. J. W. Mooar.

P. R. 31.—Bible record now in possession of William A. Trow.

P. R. 32.—Bible record now in possession of Miss Lucretia Bailey.

P. R. 33.—Bible record now in possession of Mrs. William E. Burtt.

P. R. 34.—Bible record now in possession of Miss Mary Boutwell.

P. R. 35.—Bible record now in possession of John Bailey.

P. R. 36.—Bible record now in possession of Frank E. Bailey.

P. R. 37.—Framed record now in possession of Mrs. Charles H. Newton.

P. R. 38.—Unframed record now in possession of Mrs. Charles H. Newton.

P. R. 39.—Bible record now in possession of Mrs. Caroline S. Rea.

P. R. 40.—Bible record now in possession of Miss Laura Alden Bailey, North Andover.

P. R. 41.—Bible records now in possession of Mrs. Warren Bailey.

P. R. 42.—Bible record now in possession of Mrs. J. W. Barnard.

P. R. 43.—Bible record now in possession of Miss Ellen Abbott.

P. R. 44.—Bible record now in possession of Mrs. E. Francis Holt.

P. R. 45.—Family record now in possession of George W. Foster.

P. R. 46.—Note book record now in possession of Miss Florence Averill, North Andover.

P. R. 47.—Bible record now in possession of George L. Averill.

P. R. 48.—Bible record now in possession of Mrs. Frederick P. Hannaford, North Andover.

P. R. 49.—Framed family record now in possession of Miss Sarah Jenkins.

P. R. 50.—Bible record now in possession of Frank Eaton, North Andover.

P. R. 51.—Bible record now in possessson of Mrs. Mary H. Lacy, North Andover.

P. R. 52.—Family Register now in possession of Orrin Foster, North Andover.

P. R. 53.—Bible record now in possession of Frank Goodhue, North Andover.

P. R. 54.—Bible record now in possession of Mrs. John Barker.

P. R. 55.—Bible record now in possession of Mrs. Oliver P. Berry, Wolfboro, N. H.

P. R. 56.—Bible record now in possession of John Cochran.

P. R. 57.—Bible record now in possession of Mrs. Albert Lowe.

P. R. 58.—Bible record now in possession of B. F. Wardwell.

P. R. 59.—Bible record now in possession of N. E. Bartlett.

P. R. 60.—Family record now in possession of Miss Sara Poor.

P. R. 61.—Account book now in possession of Miss Martha Farnham, North Andover.

P. R. 62.—Bible record now in possession of Miss Eldora Ellis, North Andover.

P. R. 63.—Bible record now in possession of John Peters Clark, North Andover.

P. R. 64.—Framed record now in possession of Mrs. S. M. Wagstaff.

P. R. 65.—Bible record now in possession of Mrs. S. M. Wagstaff.

P. R. 66.—Bible record now in possession of Miss Hannah E. Giddings.

P. R. 67.—Bible record now in possession of Mrs. Daniel Fitz.

P. R. 68.—Bible record now in possession of George Goldsmith.

P. R. 69.—Bible record now in possession of Mrs. Frank Holt.

P. R. 70.—Bible record now in possession of James Jaquith.

P. R. 71.—Bible record now in possession of Miss Sarah Jenkins.

P. R. 72.—Family record now in possession of Mrs. Mary A. Davis.

P. R. 73.—Record now in possession of Ira O. Gray.

P. R. 74.—Bible record now in possession of B. F. Wardwell.

P. R. 75.—Bible record now in possession of Mrs. Lois Manning.

P. R. 76.—Bible record now in possession of Mrs. S. Jennie Marland, Griffen, Ga.

P. R. 77.—Bible record now in possession of Stillman Harnden.

P. R. 78.—Family record now in possession of George Stevens.

P. R. 79.—Bible records now in possession of Charles Johnson.

P. R. 80.—Bible record now in possession of Mrs. Andrew Smith, Lynn.

P. R. 81.—Bible records now in possession of Miss Maria D. Kimball, North Andover.

P. R. 82.—Bible record now in possession of Mrs. E. W. Moody, North Andover.

P. R. 83.—Bible record now in possession of Charles W. Tucker, Swampscott.

P. R. 84.—Bible record now in possession of Henry Keniston, North Andover.

P. R. 85.—Bible record now in possession of Mrs. Winslow, Lynn.

P. R. 86.—Bible record now in possession of David Wallwork, North Andover.

P. R. 87.—Bible record now in possession of Mrs. Robert Peterson, North Andover.

P. R. 88.—Bible record now in possession of Mrs. Mary E. Perkins, North Andover.

P. R. 89.—Bible record now in possession of Mrs. Edward Butterworth, North Andover.

P. R. 90.—Bible record now in possession of Mrs. George A. Rea, North Andover.

P. R. 91.—Bible record now in possession of Mrs. Charles H. Poor, North Andover.

P. R. 92.—Bible record now in possession of Isaac Osgood, North Andover.

P. R. 93.—Records now in possession of Clarence W. Reynolds, North Andover.

P. R. 94.—Bible record now in possession of Mrs. M. A. Russell.

P. R. 95.—Bible record now in possession of Mrs. M. Warren Tuck.

P. R. 96.—Bible record now in possession of Miss Abbie Hill.

P. R. 97.—Bible record now in possession of A. Sewell Stott.

P. R. 98.—Bible record now in possession of Augustus Upton.

P. R. 99.—Bible record now in possession of Mrs. Elmer Conkey.

P. R. 100.—Bible record now in possession of Mrs. William Gile, North Andover.

P. R. 101.—Bible record now in possession of Miss Olive Rea, North Andover.

P. R. 102.—Bible record now in possession of Mrs. J. J. Abbott.

P. R. 103.—Framed record now in possession of Mrs. John Holt.

P. R. 104.—Record now in possession of Frank Carlton.

P. R. 105.—Bible record now in possession of Mrs. Elizabeth M. Eames.

P. R. 106.—Bible record now in possession of Miss Kate Johnson, North Andover.

P. R. 107.—Record now in possession of Miss Harriet S. Tapley, Salem.

P. R. 108.—Record now in possession of C. H. A. Sanborn.

rec.—recorded.

s.—son.

sr.—senior.

T. C.—town copy.

unm.—unmarried.

w.—wife; week.

wid.—widow.

widr.—widower.

y.—year.

7 *br.*—September

8 *br.*—October.

9 *br.*—November.

x *br.*—December.

ANDOVER BIRTHS

TO THE END OF THE YEAR 1849

ABBET (see also Abbott), Benjamine, s. Georg and Hannah, Dec. 20, 1662.
Georg, s. Georg, sr. and Hanna, June 7, 1655.
Georg, s. Georg and Sara, Jan. 28 [1658].
Hanna, d. Georg and Hanna, June 9, 1650.
Hanna, d. Georg and Sara, Sept. 22, 1668.
John, s. Georg and Sara, Aug. 26, 1662.
Joseph, s. Georg and Hanna, Mar. 11, 1649.
Joseph, s. Georg and Hanna, Mar. 30, 1652.
Mary, d. Georg and Sara, Mar. 20, 1664.
Nathaniell, s. Georg and Hanna, July 4, 1671.
Sara, d. Geaorg, sr. and Hanna, Nov. 14, 1659.
Sara, d. Georg, jr. and Sara, Sept. 6, 1660.
Thomas, s. Georg and Hannah, May 6, 1666.
William, s. Georg, sr. and Hanna, Nov. 18, 1657.

ABBETT (see also Abbott), Elizabeth, d. Georg and Hanna, Jan. 29, 1673.
Nehemia, s. Georg and Sara, July 20, [16]67.
Sara, d. Thomas and Sara, Jan. 8, 1671.
Timmothy, s. Georg and Hanna, Nov. 17, 1663.

ABBOT (see also Abbott), Abel, s. Nathan, jr. and Sarah, Sept. 7, 1786.
Abel, s. Abel and Sarah, Mar. 5, 1812.
Abel, s. Capt. Abel and Mary, May 6, 1824.
Abiathar, s. Abel and Mary (Jones), May 6, 1824. P. R. 6.
Abiel, s. Nehemiah, jr. and Hannah, Sept. 4, 1760.
Abiel, s. Dr. Abiel and Phebe, Nov. 6, 1761.
Abiel, s. John [jr. C. R. 2.] and Abigail, Aug. 17, 1770.
Abigail, d. John, 5th [jr. C. R. 2.] and Abigail, Sept. 15, 1764.
Abigail, d. Capt. Moses and Elizabeth, Dec. 22, 1783.
Abigail, d. Capt. Jeduthun and Hannah, May 23, 1790.

ABBOT, Abigail B., bp. Apr. 25, 1824. C. R. 2.
Abigail W., d. Jona[than] and Abigail, bp. Nov. 7, 1825. C. R. 2.
Abigal, d. Baracias and Hannah, Aug. 25, 1751.
Abigall, d. Nemiah and Abigal, Oct. 7, 1699.
Abner, s. Stephen, jr. and Mary, Aug. 26, 1751.
Abner, s. Stephen [jr. C. R. 2.] and Mary, Jan. 29, 1761.
Adaline Alton, d. Asa and Judith, Dec. 31, 1800.
Albert Costello, s. Nathan, 5th, bp. Nov. 7, 1840. C. R. 2.
Albert Cutler, s. Albert, bp. Dec. 18, 1836. C. R. 2.
Almond, s. Nehemiah and Rebecca, Jan. 20, 1832.
Amelia, d. Caleb and Deborah, Aug. 6, 1805.
Amos, s. Jeduthun and Hannah, Sept. 7, 1786.
Amos, s. [Dea. C. R. 2.] Nathan, jr. and Sarah, Mar. 13, 1795.
Amos, s. Jacob and Betsy, Feb. 14, 1820. [Apr. 14. dup.]
Amos [Chandler. P. R. 4.], s. Capt. Job and Lucy, Feb. 15, 1823.
Amy F., d. Amos and Esther, Dec. 11, 1832.
Andrew, s. Solomon and Lucy, Aug. 8, 1808.
Angelina [E. dup.], d. William B. and Lucinda, Jan. 7, 1828. [Apr. 20. dup.]
Anna, d. Joseph, 3d and Anna, Nov. 15, 1749.
Anna, d. Zebediah [jr. C. R. 2.] and Rebecca, Aug. 30, 1767.
Anna, d. Thomas, jr. and Lydia, Feb. 28, 1769.
Anna, d. twin, Moses and Elizabeth, Sept. 8, 1776.
Anna, d. Josiah and Anna [Nov. T. C.] 30, 1790.
Anna, d. Ens. Zebadiah and Sarah, May 18, 1801.
Anne, d. Zebadiah and Anne, July 27, 1752.
Anne, d. Darias and Mary, Aug. 31, 1758.
Arthur Hale, s. Albert, trader, and Abby H., May 19, 1849.
Asa, s. Asa and Elezebith, June 14, 1749.
Asa, s. Timothy and Sarah, Nov. 15, 1770. [Nov. 11. P. R. 8.]
Asa, s. Darius, bp. Sept. 4, 1774. C. R. 2.
Asa, s. Bigsby and Hepsibah, Mar. 7, 1787.
Asa Albert, s. Asa and Judah, Mar. 29, 1799.
Asa Hart, s. Gardner and Rachael, Feb. 27, 1816.
Barachias, s. Barachias, jr. and Sarah, Dec. 20, 1771. [bp. Oct. 29, 1771. C. R. 2.]
Barachias H., s. James and Mary, June 24, 1816.
Baxbye, s. Wiliam and Experance, Nov. 24, 1750.
Belinda A., d. Joel F. and Mary, Nov. 20, 1838.
[Benjamin. C. R. 2.] ——n, s. Benjamin, jr. and Elezebith, Apr. 13, 1748.
Benjamin, s. Benjamin and Elezebith, Apr. 11, 1749.
Benjamin, s. John, 3d [jr. C. R. 2.] and Phebe, May 29, 1751.
Benjamin, s. John, 5th [jr. C. R. 2.], and Abigail, Sept. 17, 1762.

ABBOT, Benjamin, s. Dr. Abiel and Phebe, May 28, 1763.
Benjamin, s. David and Prudence, June 26, 1768.
Benj[ami]n, s. Jonathan, jr. and Mary, June 7, 1770.
Benj[amin], s. Bigsby and Hepsibah, Nov. 8, 1776.
Benjamin, s. Benjamin and Rhoda, Mar. 29, 1795.
Benjamin, s. Benjamin, jr. and Mary, July 19, 1798.
Benj[ami]n, s. Benj[ami]n, 3d and Polly, Aug. 29, 1815.
Benjamin Farrington, s. Herman and Lydia, Nov. 1, 1815.
Benjamin F[lint. C. R. 2.], s. Enoch and Nancy, June 1, 1809.
Ben Naomie, d. illegitimate, Benjamin and Naomie Lovejoy, ——, 1684.
Bete, d. John, 3d and Hannah, Nov. 9, 1758.
Betsey, d. Capt. Stephen and Sarah, Nov. 4, 1778.
Bette, d. Tho[ma]s, jr. and Lydia, June 25, 1763.
Betsy, d. Bigsby and Hepsibah, Sept. 18, 1780.
Betsy, d. Philip and Elizabeth, bp. Apr. 20, 1788. C. R. 1.
Bezaleel, s. John and Sarah, Mar. 16, 1761.
Bushrood Washington, s. Enoch and Nancy, Oct. 19, 1821.
Butler, s. Nehemiah, jr. and Susanna, Jan. 28, 1782.
Caleb, s. Asa and Elezebith, Oct. 28, 1751.
Caleb, s. Caleb and Lucy, Nov. 10, 1779.
Caleb, s. Timothy, jr. and Jerusha, Dec. 23, 1810.
Caleb O., s. Gardner and Rachel, Apr. 11, 1826.
Calvin, s. Darius, bp. May 19, 1771. C. R. 2.
Caroline, d. Gardner and Rachael, Feb. 8, 1814.
Caroline L., d. W[illia]m B. and Lucinda, Sept. 7, 1817.
Caroline M., d. Amos, bp. June 1, 1823. C. R. 2.
Castello C., s. Nathan, 3d and Mary E., Dec. 27, 1837.
Charles, s. Josiah and Ruth, Nov. 25, 1784.
Charles, s. Caleb and Lucy, Jan. 8, 1786.
Charles, s. Gardner and Rachael, Aug. 12, 1818.
Charles, s. Jona[than] and Abigail, bp. Nov. 7, 1825. C. R. 2.
Charles Adams, s. David, farmer, and Mary G., May 2, 1844.
Charles A[twood. C. R. 2.], s. Enoch, jr. and Roxanna, Sept. 26, 1836.
Charles E., s. Orlando and Lydia, June 15, 1832.
Charles Franklin, s. Charles and Dorcas, Oct. 20, 1807.
Charles Wallace, s. David and Mary G., bp. Nov. 1, 1846. C. R. 3.
Charles Warren, s. Paschal, jr., bp. Dec. 5, 1841. C. R. 2.
Charlotte N[elson. C. R. 2.], d. Enoch, jr. and Roxanna, Nov. 9, 1832.
Charlotte Sarah, bp. Apr. 27, 1828. C. R. 2.
Chloe, d. Thomas [jr. C. R. 2.] and Lydia, Nov. 4, 1771.
Clara Lucretia, d. Phebe, June 13, 1849.

ABBOT, Clarisa, d. Caleb and Deborah, Aug. 25, 1803.
Clarrissa Allen, d. Jacob and Betsy, May 12, 1822.
Daniel, s. Asa and Elezebith, June 15, 1754.
Daniel, s. Jonathan and Ruth, Oct. 20, 1770.
Daniel, s. Timothy and Sarah, Feb. 25, 1777.
Daniel, s. Caleb and Lucy, June 15, 1789.
Daniel, s. Caleb and Lucy, Feb. 19, 1799.
Daniel, s. Ezra and Hannah, Mar. 9, 1803.
Daniel C., s. Jacob and Betsy, Aug. 26, 1812.
Daniel Flint, s. Moses, jr. and Priscilla, Dec. 1, 1810.
Daniel Poor, s. Ezra, bp. Mar. 13, 1803. C. R. 2.
David, s. Jonathan [3d. C. R. 2.] and Mary, Mar. 11, 1764.
David, s. David and Prudence, Mar. 4, 1766.
David, s. David and Priscilla, Dec. 23, 1792.
David, bp. Nov. 12, 1815. C. R. 2.
David Putnam, s. Gardner and Rachel, Apr. 1, 1824.
David W[arren. C. R. 3.], s. Jonathan, jr. and Lydia, Aug. 3, 1830.
Dorcas, d. Maj. G., bp. Dec. 14, 1766. C. R. 2.
Dorcas, d. Jonathan, 4th and Ruth, Sept. 6, 1772.
Dorcas, d. David and Prudence, Dec. 5, 1773.
Dorcas, d. Jonathan, 3d and Dorcas, Mar. 26, 1782.
Dorcas, d. James and Mary, June 14, 1818.
Dorcas, bp. Apr. 25, 1824. C. R. 2.
Dorcas Hibbard, d. Jacob, Esq. and Lydia, Feb. — [bp. Feb. 29. C. R. 2.], 1784.
Dorcas J., bp. Dec. 3, 1820. C. R. 2.
Dorcas L., d. Charles and Dorcas, Mar. 28, 1814.
Dorcase, d. Josiah and Anna, Mar. 4, 1796.
Dorcis, d. Joseph, 3d and Annah, Oct. 26, 1755.
Dorcis, d. Stephan, jr. and Mary, Sept. 23, 1758.
Ebenezer, s. Ebenezer and Hannah, Jan. 1, 1720-21.
Ebenezer, s. Ebenezer, 4th [jr. C. R. 2.] and Lydea, Jan. 15, 1757.
Ebenezer, s. Isaac, jr. and Susanna, Dec. 7, 1760.
Edman, s. twin, Peter and Elezebith, June 22, 1758.
Edward F. [H. C. R. 2.], s. Dea. Zebadiah and Sarah, Dec. 24, 1816.
Elenor, d. Thom[a]s, jr., bp. Nov. 10, 1771. C. R. 1.
Elezebith, d. David and Prudance, Feb. 26, 1754.
Elezebith, d. John, 4th and Sarah [3d w. C. R. 1.], Mar. 24, 1754.
Elezebith, d. Ens. George and Hannah, July 10, 1755.
Elezebith, d. Samuel, jr. and Elezebith, Nov. 2, 1755.
Elisabeth, d. Asa and Elisabeth, May 21, 1747.

ABBOT, Eliza A., d. Noah, jr. and Eliza A., Nov. 13, 1834.
Eliza Judith, d. Henery and Judith, at Boston, June 16, 1808.
Elizabeth, d. Darius and Mary, Mar. 26, 1763.
Elizabeth, d. John, 5th [jr. C. R. 2.] and Abigail, Aug. 2, 1766.
Elizabeth, d. Stephen and Mary, Oct. 22, 1766.
Elizabeth, d. Moses and Elizabeth, May 8, 1768.
Elizabeth, d. Nehemiah and Lydia, Oct. 22, 1781.
Elizabeth, d. Barachias, jr. and Sarah, Sept. 14, 1784.
Elizabeth, d. Caleb and Lucy, July 27, 1791.
Elizabeth, d. Benjamin and Mary, Mar. 8, 1814.
Elizabeth, d. Capt. George and Ruth, Nov. 15, 1817.
Elizabeth, bp. July 12, 1829. C. R. 2.
Elizabeth H., bp. Apr. 25, 1824. C. R. 2.
Elizabeth Jaquith, d. Asa and Juda, Nov. 8, 1807.
Elizabeth Kneeland, d. Capt. Henry, bp. Jan. 12, 1783. C. R. 2.
Elizabeth W., d. Amos and Ester M., Mar. 4, 1816.
Ellen E. [Ella Elizabeth. C. R. 2.], d. Nathan B., farmer, and Elizabeth, July 23, 1848.
Emeline Jane, d. Charles and Dorcas, May 31, 1817.
Emma, d. Orlando, farmer, and Charlotte V., Aug. 2, 1845.
Enoch, s. Moses and Elizabeth, Apr. 8, 1774.
Enoch, s. Jonathan, 3d and Ruth, bp. Sept. 22, 1782. C. R. 1.
Enoch, s. Enoch and Nancy, Nov. 7, 1804.
Enos, s. Jonathan and Ruth, Feb. 7, 1769.
Ephraim, s. Ephraim [jr. C. R. 2.] and Lydia, Mar. 18, 1759.
Ezra, s. James and Abigail, Mar. 11, 1721-2.
Ezra, s. John, 5th [jr. C. R. 2.] and Abigail, Dec. 2, 1760.
Ezra, s. Ezra and Hannah, Mar. 30, 1799.
Ezra, s. Daniel [David. C. R. 2.] and Priscilla, Apr. 19, 1801.
Ezra, s. Ezra, bp. Dec. 4, 1808. C. R. 2.
Fanney, d. Jeaduthun and Hannah, Mar. 30, 1779.
Fanny, d. Josiah and Ruth, Dec. 20, 1787.
Farnum, s. Jonathan, 4th and Ruth, June 25, 1779.
Frances O., d. Gardner and Rachel, Sept. 12, 1832.
Francis Flint, s. Enoch, bp. May 7, 1843. C. R. 2.
Francis H., s. Enoch and Roxann, Dec. 17, 1842.
Gardner, s. Caleb and Lucy, Sept. 29, 1787.
George, s. Stephen, jr. and Mary, June 13, 1756.
George, s. John Lovejoy and Phebe, Apr. 25, 1785.
George, s. George and Ruth, Oct. 4, 1813.
George A., s. Orlando and Lydia, Nov. 28, 1830.
George A[lfred. C. R. 2.], s. Benj[ami]n, 3d, Aug. 11, 1831.
George Lewis, s. William and Rachel, Oct. 27, 1821.
George T[homas. P. R. 9.], s. Enoch, victualler, and Roxanna Tyler, b. Boxford, Sept. 6, 1849. [1844. P. R. 9.]

ABBOT, George Washington, s. Josiah and Anna, Dec. 24, 1799.
Hannah, d. John, 5th and Hannah, July 6, 1749.
Hannah, d. George, jr. and H[a]nnah, Oct. 15, 1749.
Hannah, d. John, 3d and Hannah, Aug. 29, 1751.
Hannah, d. Ebenezer, 4th and Lydia, Jan. 27, 1752.
Hannah, d. Wiliam and Experance, July 15, 1753.
Hannah, d. Stephen, jr. and Mary, Aug. 10, 1753.
Hannah, d. Samuel, jr. and Elezebith, Apr. 24, 1757.
Hannah, d. Solomon and Hannah, May 1, 1757.
Hannah, d. Nemiah, jr. and Hannah, Sept. 19, 1758.
Hannah, d. Thomas [jr. C. R. 2.] and Lydia, May 5, 1759.
Hannah, d. David and Prudence, Jan. 5, 1762.
Hannah, d. twin, Nehemiah [jr. C. R. 2.] and Hannah, Jan. 18, 1765.
Hannah, d. Darius, bp. Mar. 3, 1765. C. R. 2.
Hannah, d. William [3d. C. R. 2.] and Sarah, June 11, 1767.
Hannah, d. Moses, bp. Apr. 19, 1772. C. R. 2.
Hannah, d. Jeduthun and Hannah, July 10, 1773.
Hannah, d. Jonathan, 3d and Mehetable, Nov. 18, 1774.
Hannah, d. Steven, of Salem, bp. Apr. 30, 1775. C. R. 2.
Hannah, d. Lt. Jonathan [jr. C. R. 2.] and Mary, Oct. 14, 1776.
Hannah, d. John, 3d and Phebe, Oct. 15, 1777.
Hannah, d. Capt. Stephen and Sarah, Nov. 8, 1780.
Hannah, d. Jonathan and Ruth, bp. Aug. 28, 1785. C. R. 1.
Hannah, d. Capt. John Lovjoy and Phebe, Feb. 17, 1793.
Hannah, d. twin, Stephen and Hannah, Oct. 4, 1802.
Hannah, d. Ezra and Hannah, June 16, 1806.
Hannah, d. Nathan, jr. and Hannah, Sept. 9, 1807.
Hannah, bp. Aug. 31, 1817. C. R. 2.
Hannah, d. Charles and Dorcas, May 17, 1823.
Hannah, bp. June 4, 1826. C. R. 2.
Hannah Frye, d. Ezra, bp. June 22, 1806. C. R. 2.
Hannah [H. P. R. 3.], d. Noah, jr. and Eliza, Nov. 10, 1838.
Hannah J., d. Asa and Judith, Aug. 31, 1815.
Hannah J., d. Moody B. and Hannah V., Mar. 20, 1832.
Hannah J., d. Moody B. and Hannah V., Apr. 18, 1842.
Hannah L[ucelia. C. R. 2.], d. Paschal and Hannah, Sept. 27, 1830.
Hannah M., d. Asa, jr. and Hannah, Mar. 31, 1819.
Harman, s. Zebediah and Rebecca, Mar. 5, 1771.
Harriot N., d. Jona[than] and Abigail, bp. Nov. 7, 1825. C. R. 2.
Henery Woodward, s. Henery and Judith, Oct. 12, 1810.
Henrietta, d. Amos, 2d, farmer, and Lydia, May 30, 1849.
Henry, s. Darius and Mary, June 1, 1761.

ABBOT, Henry, s. Henry, jr. and Phebe, July 10, 1770.
Henry, s. Henry, jr. and Phebe, Sept. 6, 1771.
Henry, s. Capt. Henry and Phebe, Apr. 8, 1777.
Henry, s. Samuel, jr. and Rhoda, Feb. 11, 1787. T. C.
Henry, s. Lt. Moses and Elizabeth, Sept. 22, 1778.
Henry, s. Bigsby and Hepsibah, Mar. 5, 1785.
Henry, s. Enoch and Nancy, Aug. 12, 1799.
Henry Blanchard, s. Sam[ue]l, jr., bp. Aug. 8, 1790. C. R. 2.
Henry R[ussell. P. R. 1.], s. Nathan and Hannah, Apr. 19, 1815.
Hepsibah, d. Bigsby and Hepsibah, Aug. 17, 1772.
Herman, s. Herman and Lydia, Mar. 25, 1803.
Herman, s. Herman and Lydia, Dec. 28, 1808.
Hermon, s. Benja[mi]n, 3d and Polly, Dec. 3, 1809.
Hermon, s. David and Priscilla, Jan. 15, 1814.
Hipzibeth, d. Benjamin and Mary, Feb. 7, 1812.
Holten, s. Philip and Elizabeth, June 26, 1774.
Horace S[ylvester. P. R. 8.], s. Sylvester, farmer, and Rhoda Nov. 6, 1848.
Hulda, d. Joseph, jr. and Anna, Oct. 21, 1760.
Isaac, s. Ebenezer, 3d and Martha, Oct. 13, 1750.
Isaac, s. Isaac and Susanna, June 16, 1762.
Isaac, s. Isaac, jr. and Phebe, Dec. 9, 1768.
Isaac, s. Capt. Henry and Phebe, June 9, 1779.
Isaac, s. William and Rebeckah, Nov. 12, 1803.
Isaac, s. Isaac, jr. and Mary, Mar. 26, 1805.
Isaac F[oster. C. R. 2.], s. Dea. Paschal and Hannah, Apr. 3, 1834.
Isaac H. [Newton. C. R. 2.], s. Isaac and Dolly, Jan. 24, 1830.
Isaac Moody, s. Henry and Judith, Jan. 24, 1823.
Israel, s. Joseph, jr. and Mary, Jan. 29, 1771.
Jacob, s. Benjamin and Abbigaiel, Feb. 2, 1736-7.
Jacob, s. Dea. Joseph and Deborah, Feb. 9, 1745-6.
Jacob, s. John, 4th [jr. C. R. 2.] and Abigail, Aug. 25, 1771.
Jacob, s. Lt. Moses and Eliza[beth], June 30, 1781.
Jacob A., s. Jacob and Betsy, Apr. 9, 1811.
James, s. Joseph, jr. and Mary, Feb. 2, 1768.
James, s. Barachias [jr. C. R. 2.] and Sarah, Mar. 30, 1780.
James Holt, s. James and Mary, Sept. 11, 1812.
Jeaduthun, s. Jeaduthun and Hannah, June 18, 1777.
Jeduthan, s. William and Exprence, Aug. 6, 1749.
Jeremiah, s. Nathan and Sarah (Ballard), June 29, 1784. P. R. 4.
Jeremiah, s. Nathan [jr. C. R. 2.] and Sarah (Ballard), Aug. 14, 1790. P. R. 4.
Jeremiah, s. Zebadiah and Sarah, Jan. 9, 1807.
Jeremiah, s. Zebadiah and Sarah, Jan. 9, 1808.

ABBOT, Jethro, s. Ebenezer, jr. and Lydia, Apr. 18, 1761.
Job, s. Nathan, jr. and Sarah, Aug. 7, 1782.
Job, s. Job and Lucy, Sept. 15, 1813. [Dec. 13. P. R. 4.]
Job, s. Nathan B., farmer, and Elizabeth L., Aug. 23, 1845.
Joel, s. Thomas, jr. and Lydia, Nov. 22, 1765.
Joel, s. Barachias, jr. and Sarah, Apr. 29, 1775.
Joel, s. Barachias [jr. C. R. 2.] and Sarah, Oct. 17, 1776.
John, "a Legetemat Son of" Hannah, Jan. 26, 1753.
John, s. John, 5th. [jr. C. R. 2.] and Abigail, Apr. 8, 1759.
John, s. John, jr. and Hannah, Jan. 24, 1769.
John, s. Nehemiah, jr. and Susanna, July 29, 1779.
John, s. Enoch, bp. July 19, 1795. C. R. 2.
John, s. Ezra and Hannah, Mar. 17, 1801.
John, s. Ezra and Hannah, Feb. 9, 1812.
John, s. Capt. George and Ruth, May 26, 1820.
John K., s. Joseph T. and Betsy, Aug. 13, 1833.
John K., s. Joel and Mary, Aug. 4, 1836.
John L., s. George and Ruth, Mar. 9, 1822.
John Lovejoy, s. George, jr. and Hannah, Apr. 12, 1757.
John Lovejoy, s. John Lovejoy and Phebe, Nov. 29, 1783.
John Tuck, s. Mary and John Tuck, Nov. 5, 1810.
[Jonathan. C. R. 1.] ——than, s. John, 4th and Hannah, Apr. 12, 1748.
Jonathan, s. Lydia, bp. May 24, 1752. C. R. 2.
Jonathan, s. Jonathan, 3d and Mary, Mar. 3, 1760.
Jonathan, s. Jonathan, 3d and Mehetable, June 11, 1776.
Jonathan, s. David [jr. C. R. 2.] and Priscilla, June 12, 1796.
Jonathan, s. Benjamin and Rhoda, Nov. 15, 1801.
Jonathan, s. Stephen, bp. Dec. 4, 1808. C. R. 2.
Jonathan E[dward. C. R. 3.], s. Capt. Jonathan and Lydia, Jan. 5, 1828.
Joseph, s. Thomas [and Sara. CT. F.], Mar. 16, 1666-7. CT. R.
Joseph, s. Joseph, jr. and Anna, Feb. 16, 1758.
Joseph, s. John, 4th and Sarah, Dec. 7, 1758.
Joseph, s. John and Sarah, Oct. 18, 1763.
Joseph, s. Joseph, 3d and Mary, Nov. 6, 1763.
Joseph, s. Bixby, bp. June 21, 1778. C. R. 2.
Joseph, s. Herman and Lydia, Sept. 6, 1811.
Joseph [Bixby. C. R. 2.], s. Bigsby and Hepsibah, Feb. 1, 1783.
Joseph Thomson, s. Benjamin, jr. and Mary, Dec. 19, 1809.
Joseph W[arren. C. R. 2.], s. Nathan, 5th and Mary E., Sept. 18, 1836.
Joshua, s. Joseph, 3d, bp. Nov. 10, 1765. C. R. 2.
Joshua, s. Zebadiah, bp. May 2, 1773. C. R. 2.

ABBOT, Joshua, s. Jonathan, jr. and Mary, Nov. 22, 1774.
Joshua, s. Zebediah, bp. Feb. 17, 1782. C. R. 2.
Joshua, s. Capt. Jona[than] and Mary, June 9, 1784.
Joshua, s. Nathan, jr. and Sarah, June 29, 1784.
Joshua, s. Nathan, 3d, bp. July 4, 1784. C. R. 2.
Joshua, s. Dea. Nathan and Sarah, Jan. 29, 1796.
Joshua, s. Dea. Nathan and Sarah, Apr. 22, 1797.
Joshua, s. Herman and Lydia, Dec. 3, 1804.
Joshua, s. Solomon and Lucy, Feb. 6, 1805.
Joshua, s. David and Priscilla, Sept. 1, 1806.
Josiah, s. David and Prudence, Dec. 29, 1759.
Josiah, s. Isaac, jr. and Mary, Dec. 5, 1801.
Justin E., s. Benj[ami]n, 3d and Rebecca, Apr. 11, 1820.
Kneeland, s. Ephr[aim], jr., bp. May 22, 1748. C. R. 2.
Lotte, d. Sarah Peabody, Apr. 3, 1802.
Louisa Dickerman, d. Gardner and Rachel, Feb. 14, 1812.
Luce, d. William and Experience, Sept. 3, 1758.
Luce, d. Isaac and Susanna, Mar. 20, 1759.
Lucretia Ann, d. Charles A., tradesman, and Martha A., Sept. 15, 1849.
Lucy, d. Jeduthun and Hannah, Oct. 9, 1775.
Lucy, d. Caleb and Lucy, Feb. 20, 1784.
Lucy, d. Solomon and Lucy, Oct. 30, 1794.
Lucy, d. Job and Lucy, Oct. 18, 1811.
Lucy, d. Timothy and Jerusha, Apr. 11, 1816.
Lucy Flint, d. Charles and Dorcas, Sept. 17, 1811.
Luther, s. Darius, bp. May 16, 1773. C. R. 2.
Lydea, d. Henry and Mary, Feb. 10, 1722-3.
Lydea, d. Joseph, 3d and Anna, Oct. 23, 1753.
Lydea, d. Ebenezer, 4th [jr. C. R. 2.] and Lydea, June 18, 1754.
Lydea, d. Thomas, jr. and Lydea, Apr. 10, 1757.
Lydia, d. Jeduthun and Hannah [Mar.], 1781. [bp. Apr. 1. C. R. 2.]
Lydia, d. Philip and Elizabeth, bp. July 4, 1790. C. R. 1.
Lydia, d. Hermon and Lydia, Oct. 5, 1800.
Lydia, d. Nathan and Sarah (Ballard), Nov. 4, 1800. P. R. 4.
Lydia Clark, d. Lt. John L[ovejoy. C. R. 2.] and Phebe [bp. July 24. C. R. 2.], 1791.
Lydia Clark, d. Abiel and Hannah, May 13, 1797.
Marcus W., s. Caleb, cordwainer, and Frances M., b. Methuen, Mar 23, 1849.
Margaret W., d. George and Ruth, Feb. 9, 1811.
Margaret Wood, d. George and Ruth, Nov. 26, 1815.
Martha, d. Ephraim and Sarah, Mar. 30, 1733.

ABBOT, Martha, d. Jonathan, jr. and Martha, Jan. 23, 1748-9.
Martha, d. Ebenezer, 3d and Martha, Mar. 7, 1753.
Martha, d. [Maj. C. R. 2.] George, Esq. and Hannah, Oct. 17, 1764.
Martha Jenks, d. Capt. John L. and Phebe, Nov. 26, 1799.
Martha Lovejoy, d. Stephen, bp. Sept. 18, 1808. C. R. 2.
Martha M., d. Gardner and Rachel, May 30, 1828.
Martha T., d. William and Lucinda, May 1, 1830.
Martin Buxton, s. Charles and Dorcas, Feb. 28, 1821.
Mary, d. Nathanaell and Dorcas, Jan. 28, 1697-8.
Mary, d. George, jr. and Hannah, Sept. 4, 1751.
Mary, d. John, 5th and Hepzebeth, May 4, 1752.
Mary, d. George, jr. and Hannah, June 29, 1753.
Mary, d. Darius, bp. Nov. 25, 1759. C. R. 2.
Mary, d. Jonathan, 3d and Mary, Jan. 10, 1762.
Mary, d. [Lt. C. R. 2.] Henry, jr. and Phebe, Apr. 4, 1768.
Mary, d. David and Priscilla, June —, 1791. [bp. June 26, 1791. C. R. 2.]
Mary, d. Caleb and Lucy, Mar. 25, 1793.
Mary, d. Abner, bp. May 14, 1797. C. R. 2.
Mary, d. Benjamin, Nov. 16, 1809.
Mary, d. James and Mary, Nov. 4, 1810.
Mary, d. Benj[ami]n, 3d and Polly, Nov. 4, 1812.
Mary, d. Paschal and Mary, June 21, 1814.
Mary E., d. Joseph T. and Betsy, Jan. 10, 1835.
Mary Elizabeth, d. Paschal, jr., bp. Jan. 7, 1838. C. R. 2.
Mary Fisk, d. Isaac, jr. and Hepsabeth, Mar. 14, 1800.
Mary Fisk, d. the late Isaac and Hepzibah, grandd. Dea. Isaac Abbot, bp. May 10, 1807. C. R. 2.
Mary F[loyd. P. R. 10.], d. Henry and Lucy, June 7, 1831.
Mary F[rances. C. R. 2.], d. Nathan, 5th and Mary E., Feb. 3, 1835.
Mary Greenleaf, d. Benjamin, jr. and Mary, July 11, 1806.
Mary J., d. Henry and Judith, Aug. 23, 1820.
Mary Jane, d. Charles B. and Martha M., Apr. 6, 1848.
Mary M., d. Jacob and Betsy, Jan. 10, 1828.
Mary M., d. Jacob and Betsy, Jan. 10, 1829.
Mary Phillips, d. Stephen and Hannah, Jan. 5, 1807.
Mary T[yler. C. R. 2.], d. Enoch, jr. and Roxanna, Apr. 6, 1835.
Mehetabel, d. Jonathan [4th. C. R. 2.] and Mehetabel, Sept. 29, 1764.
Micah, s. Isaac, jr. and Susanna, May 15, 1766.
Milton Langstroth, s. Dea. Paschal, bp. Jan. 7, 1838. C. R. 2.
Mira Ballerd, d. David and Mary, bp. Sept. 3, 1848. C. R. 3.

ABBOT, Molly, d. Joseph, jr. and Mary, June 18, 1773.
Moody Bridges, s. Jeduthun, jr. and Betsy, May 24, 1808.
Moses, s. Moses and Elizabeth, Nov. 30, 1765.
Moses, s. Moses, jr. and Martha, Apr. 10, 1802.
Moses, s. Jacob and Betsey, Dec. 20, 1814.
Nabby, d. Jonathan, 3d and Mehetabel, July 30, 1770.
Nancy, d. Enoch and Nancy, Mar. 15, 1801.
Nathan, s. Asa and Elezebith, Nov. 18, 1756.
Nathan, s. Jonathan [3d. C. R. 2.] and Mary, May 17, 1768
Nathan, s. Nathan, jr. and Sarah, Aug. 25, 1778.
Nathan, s. Nathan, jr. and Hannah, Feb. 25, 1799.
Nathan, s. David and Priscilla, July 5, 1799.
Nathan, s. Nathan, jr. and Hannah, July 17, 1809.
Nathan B[allard. P. R. 4.], s. Capt. Job and Lucy, Nov. 18, 1816.
Nathan Chandler, s. Benjamin and Rhoda, Jan. 17, 1807.
Nathaniel, s. Nathaniel and Mercy, May 22, 17[14].
Nathaniel, s. Dea. Joseph and Deborah, Oct. 27, 1751.
Nathaniel, s. Nathaniel and Sarah, June 20, 1774.
Nathaniel Ballard, s. Jacob and Betsey, July 6, 1809.
Nehemiah, s. Bigsby and Hepsibah [Oct. T. C.] 18, 1790.
Nehemiah, s. Abiel and Hannah, Sept. 28, 1794.
Nemiah, s. John, 4th [jr. C. R. 1.] and Sarah, June 18, 1756.
Nemiah, s. Nemiah, jr. and Hannah, Mar. 10, 1757.
Noah, s. [Moses. C. R. 2.], May 11, 1770. P. R. 3.
Obadiah, s. [Dea. C. R. 2.] Joseph, jr. and Deborah, Nov. 23, 1749.
Obed, s. Abner and Ruth, Sept. 14, 1789.
Olive, d. Isaac, bp. July 9, 1758. C. R. 2.
Olive, d. David and Prudence, July 24, 1770.
Olive, d. Philip and Elizabeth, June 1, 1772.
Oramel G., s. Moses, jr. and Tryphena M., Apr. 2, 1834.
Orlando, s. Caleb and Lucy, Nov. 20, 1782.
Orlando, s. Charles and Dorcas, Sept. 21, 1809.
Pamela, d. Capt. Jeduthun and Hannah, Oct. 11, 1792.
Parker Clark, s. Nehemiah, bp. Sept. 28, 1783. C. R. 2.
Paschal, s. Nathan, jr. and Sarah, July 23, 1788.
Paschal, s. Nathan and Hannah, Apr. 13, 1819.
Paschal G., s. Paschal and Hannah, Jan. 20, 1833.
Paschal G., s. Paschal and Hannah, Apr. 25, 1836.
Paschal Job, s. Dea. Paschal, bp. Jan. 5, 1840. C. R. 2.
Patty, d. Jonathan, 3d and Dorcas, June 9, 1785.
Paul, s. Darius and Mary, Mar. 18, 1767.
Peter, s. twin, Peter and Elezibeth, June 22, 1758.
Phebe, d. [Dea. C. R. 2.] Isaac and Phebe, Nov. 14, 1746.

ABBOT, Phebe, d. Baracias and Hannah, Aug. 29, 1749.
Phebe, d. Joshua and Phebe, Aug. 20, 1750.
Phebe, d. Ebenezer, 3d and Martha, Aug. 22, 1755.
Phebe, d. Nehemiah, jr., bp. Apr. 3, 1763. C. R. 2.
Phebe, d. [Lt. C. R. 2.] Henry, jr. and Phebe, Jan. 25, 1766.
Phebe, d. Jonathan, 3d and Mary, Feb. 26, 1766.
Phebe, d. Isaac, jr. [3d. C. R. 2.] and Phebe, May 27, 1767.
Phebe, d. John [jr. C. R. 2.] and Abigail, Nov. 18, 1768.
Phebe, d. Hannah, bp. Nov. 29, 1772. C. R. 2.
Phebe, d. Capt. Stephen, bp. Dec. 14, 1783. C. R. 2.
Phebe, d. Capt. Moses and Elizabeth, Mar. [bet. 5-9.], 1786.
Phebe, d. Jonathan, 3d and Dorcas, Jan. 17, 1788.
Phebe, d. John L[ovejoy. C. R. 2.] and Phebe, June 15, 1789.
Phebe, d. Benjamin and Rhode, Nov. 27, 1798.
Phebe, d. Isaac, jr. and Mary, July 9, 1803.
Phebe, d. David and Priscilla, Aug. 5, 1803.
Phebe, d. Isaac, jr., deceased, and Mary, bp. June 21, 1807. C. R. 2.
Phebe [A. C. R. 2.], d. Henry and Judith, Dec. 19, 1814.
Phebe, d. Jacob and Betsy, Dec. 12, 1823.
Phebe Elizabeth, d. James and Mary, Nov. 7, 1820.
Phebe Foxcroft, d. Caleb and Lucy, Feb. 8, 1797.
Phebe H[utchinson. C. R. 2.], d. Stephen and Hannah, Mar. 22, 1813.
Philep, s. John, 4th and Hannah, Oct. 11, 1749.
Philip, s. Philip and Elizabeth, bp. Aug. 23, 1778. C. R. 1.
Priscilla, d. Capt. Jonathan [jr. C. R. 2.] and Mary, July 29, 1780.
Priscilla, d. David and Priscilla, June 10, 1790.
Prisey, d. Isaac, jr. and Phebe, June 1, 1770.
Prudance, d. David and Prudance, Oct. 3, 1757.
Rebeca, d. Dea. Joseph and Deborah, June 19, 1754.
Rebecca, d. Capt. Jeduthun and Hannah, Mar. 10, 1795.
Rebecca, d. Ens. Zebadiah and Sarah, June 5, 1799.
Rebecca, d. William and Rebecca, Oct. 6, 1806.
Rebecca H[olt. P. R. 2.], d. Enoch and Nancy, July 12, 1811.
Rebecca J., d. Nehemiah and Rebecca, Nov. 4, 1833.
Rebeckah, d. Moses and Elizabeth, Jan. 2, 1763.
Rhoda, d. twin, Barachias and Hannah, Apr. 23, 1747.
Rhoda, d. twin, Moses and Elizabeth, Sept. 8, 1776.
Rhoda, d. Samuel, jr. and Rhoda, Oct. —, 1788.
Rhoda, d. Benjam[in] and Rhoda, Oct. 24, 1796.
Rhoda, d. Benjamin, 3d and Polly, Apr. 16, 1818.
Rhoda Ann, d. Enoch and Nancy, Apr. 11, 1817.
Richard M[errill. C. R. 2.], s. Daniel and Sally, Mar. 29, 1832.

ABBOT, Ruben, s. John, 4th and Sarah, July 16, 1766.
Ruth Bodwell, d. Josiah and Ruth, Jan. 1, 1786.
Ruthy, d. Abner, bp. July 31, 1785. C. R. 2.
Sally, d. Zebadiah and Sarah, Feb. 24, 1798.
Salome J., d. William and Rachel, Nov. 10, 1827.
Salome Jane, d. William, bp. Nov. 3, 1833. C. R. 2.
Samuel, s. George [jr. C. R. 2.] and Hannah, June 12, 1759.
Samuel, s. [Maj. C. R. 2.] George, Esq. and Hannah, Sept. 19, 1760.
Samuel, s. Stephen [jr. C. R. 2.] and Mary, Apr. —, 1763. [bp. Apr. 17, C. R. 2.]
Samuel, s. David and Prudence, Mar. 27, 1764.
Samuel, s. Job, bp. May 20, 1781. C. R. 2.
Samuel, s. Philip and Elizabeth, bp. July 31, 1785. C. R. 1.
Samuel, s. John Lovejoy and Phebe, June 29, 1787.
Samuel, s. Bigsby and Hepsibah, Jan. 28, 1789.
Samuel, s. Abner, bp. Jan. 29, 1792. C. R. 2.
Samuel, s. Caleb and Lucy, Jan. 28, 1795.
Samuel, s. Isaac, jr., deceased, and Mary, Feb. 22, 1807.
Samuel F[lint. P. R. 2.], s. Enoch and Nancy, Aug. 3, 1814. [1813. P. R. 2.]
Samuel Kidder, s. Benjamin, jr. and Mary, Nov. 22, 1803.
Samuel Shelden, s. Samuel, jr. and Rhoda, Sept. 23, 1790.
[Sarah. C. R. 2.], d. David and Hannah, Apr. 7, 1726.
Sarah, d. Stephen [jr. C. R. 2.] and Mary, Aug. 1, 1747.
Sarah, d. [Dea. C. R. 2.] Isaac and Phebe, Jan. 2, 1749-50.
Sarah, d. Joseph, 3d and Anna, Sept. 3, 1751.
Sarah, d. [Maj. C. R. 2.] George, Esq. and Hannah, Oct. 3, 1762.
Sarah, d. William and Experience, June 16, 1763.
Sarah, d. Eben[eze]r, jr. and Lydia, Dec. 7, 1765.
Sarah, d. Jonathan, 4th and Mehetabel, June 22, 1766.
Sarah, d. John, 3d and Sarah, Dec. 30, 1768.
Sarah, d. William [jr. C. R. 2.] and Sarah, June 3, 1769.
Sarah, d. Jonathan, 4th and Ruth, Jan. 21, 1775.
Sarah, d. Stephen, bp. June 30, 1776. C. R. 2.
Sarah, d. Nathaniel and Sarah, Oct. 12, 1775.
Sarah, d. Lt. Jonathan and Mary, July 9, 1778.
Sarah, d. Barachias [jr. C. R. 2.] and Sarah, Oct. 10, 1779.
Sarah, d. Timothy and Sarah, May 22, 1783.
Sarah, d. Abner and Ruth, July 11, 1787.
Sarah, d. Josiah and Anna, Nov. 10, 1791.
Sarah, d. Nathan, jr. and Sarah, Dec. 20, 1792.
Sarah, d. James and Mary, July 23, 1814.

ABBOT, Sarah, d. Capt. Benj[ami]n and Elizabeth, Dec. 25, 1817.
Sarah Ann, d. Asa and Judith, Dec. 23, 1811.
Sarah A[ugusta. C. R. 2.], d. George L., carpenter, and Sarah M., Jan. 20, 1846.
Sarah B., d. Amos and Ester M., Apr. 10, 1814.
Sarah Emily Maria, d. Daniel and Sally, Dec. 15, 1834.
Sarah Fisk, d. Isaac, jr., deceased, and Mary, bp. June 21, 1807. C. R. 2.
Sarah Kneeland, d. Capt. John L., and Phebe, July 7, 1797.
Sarah Peabody, d. Jeduthun and Hannah, July 4, 1783.
Sarah Rachel F., d. Gardner and Rachel, Aug. 8, 1830.
Sarah Saunders, d. Jacob and Betsey, May 5, 1808.
Serena, d. David and Priscilla, July 8, 1805.
Serena, d. David and Priscilla, Sept. 8, 1808.
Simmeon, s. Isaac, jr. and Susanna, May 29, 1764.
Solomon, s. Jonathan, jr. and Mary, Nov. 1, 1772.
Solomon, s. Solomon and Lucy, Sept. 22, 1802.
Sophia, d. Josiah and Anna, Aug. 20, 1793.
Sophrona, d. Enoch and Nancy, Feb. 18, 1803.
Stephen, s. Stephen, jr. and Mary, Aug. 1, 1749.
Stephen, s. Jonathan, 3d and Dorcas, Dec. 30, 1779.
Stephen, s. Capt. Stephen and Sarah, Dec. 28, 1781.
Stephen, s. Abner, bp. Dec. 14, 1794. C. R. 2.
Stephen, s. twin, Stephen and Hannah, Oct. 4, 1802.
Stephen E., s. John B., farmer, and Caroline, Apr. 5, 1849.
Susan C., d. Henry and Judith, Dec. 13, 1827.
Susanna, d. John, 4th and Hannah, Dec. 20, 1753.
[Susanna. C. R. 1.], d. Isaac, jr. and Susanna, Feb. 17, 1756.
Sylvester, s. Asa and Judith, Feb. 3, 1803. [Feb. 26. P. R. 8.]
Tammerson, d. [Maj. C. R. 2.] George, Esq. and Hannah, Jan. 14, 1769.
Thaddeus, s. Jacob and Betsy, Feb. 13, 1818.
Theodore, s. Ebenezer and Lydia, Sept. 10, 1763.
Thomas, s. Thomas [jr. C. R. 2.] and Lydia, May 25, 1761
Timothy, s. twin, Barachias and Hannah, Apr. 23, 1747.
Timothy, s. Nathan, jr., bp. June 26, 1763. C. R. 2.
Timothy, s. Barachias, jr. and Sarah, Mar. 30, 1773.
Timothy, s. Timothy and Sarah, Sept. 28, 1774.
Timothy, s. Caleb and Lucy, Jan. 13, 1781.
Timothy, s. Phillip and Elizabeth, bp. Feb. 25, 1781. C. R. 1.
Timothy, s. Bigsby and Hepsibah, Feb. 22, 1793.
Timothy [Sereno Timothy. P. R. 8.], s. Asa and Judith, Aug. 17, 1805.
Timothy, s. James and Mary, Aug. 13, 1823.

ABBOT, Timothy, s. James and Mary, Feb. 4, 1826.
Timothy, s. James and Mary, Feb. 28, 1826.
Triphena, d. Darius and Mary, Feb. 23, 1769.
Walter, s. William and Rachel, July 17, 1825.
Walter Stuart, s. Josiah and Anna, Feb. 23, 1798.
Warren, s. Bixby, bp. July 19, 1795. C. R. 2.
Warren, s. Bigsby and Hepzibah, July 14, 1796.
William, s. Isaac [jr. C. R. 2.] and Phebe, Oct. 30, 1772.
William, s. Bigsby and Hepsibah, July 14, 1774.
William, s. Samuel, jr. and Rhoda, Oct. 18, 1792.
William, s. William, jr. and Hannah, Jan. 5, 1801.
William, s. William and Rebecca, Sept. 7, 1801.
William, s. Jeduthun, jr. and Betsey, May 27, 1805.
William, s. Benjamin, jr. and Mary, Feb. 9, 1808.
William, s. John L. and Phebe, Dec. 16, 1809.
William, s. William and Rachael, Feb. —, 1820.
William A., s. Amos and Esther M., Aug. 9, 1831.
William H., s. Abel, jr. and Apphia, Nov. 13, 1837.
William Lovejoy, s. twin, Nehemiah [jr. C. R. 2.] and Hannah, Jan. 18, 1765.
William Lovejoy, s. Capt. John Lovejoy and Phebe, Jan. 25, 1795.
William T., s. Joseph T. and Betsy, Mar. 15, 1836.
Zebadiah, s. Zebadiah and Sarah, May 20, 1805.
Zebadiah, s. Zebadiah and Sarah, Apr. 10, 1810.
Zebediah, s. Zebediah and Rebecca, June 6, 1769.
Zerviah, d. Jonathan, 4th and Mehetabel, Mar. 19, 1768.
——, ch. [Nathanie]l and Dorcass, Nov. 4, 1709.
——, s. Mr. Isaac and Phebe, Nov. 12, 1747.
——, d. Eben[e]zer and Susanna, bp. —— [1752]. C. R. 1.
[torn]a, d. Isaac, jr. and Susannah, Aug. 29, 1754.
——, s. David and Prudence, Feb. 15, 1756.
——, s. Nathan and Sarah (Ballard), June 11, 1780. P. R. 4.
——, s. Nathan and Sarah (Ballard), Mar. 2, 1781. P. R. 4.
——, s. Solomon and Lucy, Nov. 7, 1796.
——, 1st ch. Nathan and Hannah, July 13, 1803. P. R. 1.
——, 2d ch. Nathan and Hannah, Nov. 22, 1804. P. R. 1.
——, 3d ch. Nathan and Hannah, Dec. 17, 1805. P. R. 1.
——, d. wid. ——, [of] Concord, N. H., bp. Jan. 30, 1814. C. R. 2.
——, s. Jacob and Betsy, Aug. 20, 1816.
——, d. Joshua and Lydia, Sept. 23, 1821.
——, s. Amos and Esther M., Dec. 10, 1821.
——, d. Gardner and Rachel, Mar. 16, 1822.

ABBOT, ——, d. William B. and Lucinda, Feb. 9, 1826.
——, ch. Josiah F. and Hannah, Nov. 29, 1827.
——, d. Jacob and Betsy, Nov. 30, 1827.
——, s. Jonathan and Lydia, May 31, 1833.
——, s. Joel and Mary, Mar. 22, 1834.
——, d. Joel and Mary, July 11, 1840.
——, s. Samuel, farmer, and Susanna B., May 24, 1844.

ABBOTT (see also Abbet, Abbett, Abbot, Abbut, Abbutt, Abett), [Aaron, s. Thomas. C. R. 2.], ——mas and Hannah, Aug. 8, 1714.
[Aaron. C. R. 2.], s. Thomas and Elisabeth, Feb. 17, 1732-3.
Abby Dorcas, d. J. Alfred, bp. Oct. 17, 1847. C. R. 2.
Abby Elizabeth, d. Albert, trader, and Abby H., June 3, 1843.
[Abiel, s. C. R. 2.] [Jo]hn and Elizabeth, Jan. 7, 1715-16.
Abiel, s. Benjamin and Abigail, July 24, 1735.
Abiel, s. John [jr. C. R. 2.] and Phebe, Apr. 19, 1741.
Abiel, d. Ephraim, jr. ["who deceased this morning," ch. bp. Apr. 14. C. R. 2.] and Hannah, Apr. 12, 1745.
Abiell, s. Nehemiah and Abigail, Aug. 10, 1693.
Abigaiel, d. Benjamin and Abigaiel, Jan. 13, 1733-4.
[Abigail. C. R. 2.], d. James and Abigail, Jan. 1, 1714-15.
Abigail, d. Benja[min] and Abigail, Mar. 28, 1731.
Alfaretta Wentworth, d. Joel F., laborer, and Mary, Feb. 28, 1847.
Alson Baily, s. W[illia]m, bp. Sept. 7, 1845. C. R. 2.
Amos, s. James and Abigall, Feb. 18, 1725-6.
Amos Alfred, s. Amos and Esther M., May 30, 1820.
[Anna. C. R. 2.], d. Sergt. Benjamin and Abigail, Oct. 13, 1740.
[Anne. C. R. 2.], d. Zebadiah and Anne, Sept. 11, 1729.
Asie, s. Timothy [jr. C. R. 2.] and Mary, Oct. 17, 1721.
Barachias, s. Barachias and Hannah, Jan. 16, 1733-4.
Barachias, s. Barachias and Hannah, May 22, 1739.
Bathshaba, d. Joseph and Deborah, Sept. 16, 1735.
Benjamin, s. Benjamin and Sarah, July 1, 1686.
Benjamin, s. Benjamin and Mary, Oct. 21, 1723.
Benjamin, s. Ebenezer and Elisabeth, Jan. 25, 1738-9.
Benjamin, s. David and Hannah, Jan. 16, 1742-3.
Benjamin, s. Benj[ami]n and Joanna, bp. June 28, 1766. C. R 1.
[Caleb. C. R. 2.], s. Timothy and Mary, Aug. 19, 1738.
Caleb A., s. Caleb, cordwainer, and Frances M., Nov. 10, 1844.
Caroline Brown, d. Sylvester, yeoman, and Rhoda B., Sept. 23, 1846.
Caroline L., May 23, 1826.

ABBOTT, Caroline Mackey, d. Amos and Esther M., Feb. 22, 1823.
Catherine T., d. Henry W., trader, and Eliza, Jan. 9, 1847.
Charles Henry, s. Henry W., trader, and Eliza F., Feb. 8, 1845.
Charles Jonathan, s. Nathan C. and Hannah, bp. Aug. 23, 1840. C. R. 3.
Charlotte Atwood, Sept. 27, 1836. P. R. 9.
Charlotte H[elen, in pencil.], d. Henry R., carpenter, and Lydia, July 13, 1844.
Cloe, d. Zebediah and Anne, Nov. 5, 1737.
Daniel, s. Daniel and Hannah, Feb. — [1714-15].
[Daniel, s. C. R. 2.], [E]phraim and Sarah, Sept. 3, 1724.
[Daniel. C. R. 2.], ——iel, s. Benjamin and Mary, Dec. 29, 1725.
Daniell, s. George and Dorcas, Jan. 10, 1687-8.
Darcus, d. Nathaniel [jr. C. R. 2.] and Penelopy, Nov. 11, 1728.
Darcus, d. Henry and Mary, May 11, 1729.
David, s. Benjamin and Sarah, Jan. 18, 1688-9.
David, s. Jonathan and Zerviah, —— 28, ——. [bp. Jan. 6, 1717. C. R. 2.]
David, s. David and Hannah, Mar. 17, 1727-8.
David A[lbert. C. R. 3.], s. David and Mary G., Aug. 29, 1834.
Deborah, d. Joseph and Deborah, Sept. 17, 1732.
Deborah, d. twin, Joseph [jr. C. R. 2.] and Deborah, July 15, 1740.
Deborah, d. Stephen, jr. and Mary, Oct. 13, 1745.
Dorcas, d. Timothy and Hannah, Apr. 25, 1698.
Dorcas, d. Timothy and Mary, Oct. 2, 1735.
Dorcas, d. [Sergt. C. R. 2.] Benjamin and Abigail, Aug. 1, 1744.
Dorcas, d. Dea. Joseph and Deborah, Jan. 19, 1747-8.
Dorothy, d. Thomas and Sarah, Jan. 2, 1676.
Ebenezer, s. John and Sarah, Sept. 27, 1689.
Ebenezer, s. Thomas and Sarah, Nov. 23, 1689.
Ebenezer, s. Ebenezer and Hannah, Nov. 23, 1723.
Ebenezer, s. Ephraim and Sarah, Feb. 20 [1731. C. R. 2.].
Edward, s. Thomas and Hann[ah], —— [1702].
Edward A., s. William B. and Lucinda, June 20, 1825.
Edward Payson, s. Henry and Lucy, Oct. 17, 1833. P. R. 10.
Edward West, s. Amos and Esther M., Apr. 4, 1818.
Edwin, s. Isaac and Dolly, Sept. 3, 1839.
Elezebeth, d. Stephen and Sarah, Dec. 29, 1721.
Elezebeth, d. Ephraim and Sarah, June 29, 1726.
Elisabeth, d. Benjamin and Abigail, Oct. 27, 1738.
Elisabeth, d. Barachias and Hannah, Nov. 2, 1740.
Eliza, d. Isaac and Dolly, Apr. 13, 1837.
Elizabeth, d. William and Elizabeth, Apr. 29, 1683.

ABBOTT, Elizabeth, d. George and Dorcas, July 25, 1690.
Elizabeth, d. George and Elizabeth, Nov. 5, 1695.
Elizabeth, d. John and Elizabeth, bp. Oct. 28, 1711. C. R. 2.
[Elizabeth, d. C. R. 2.], [Na]thaniel and Dorcas, Feb. 1, 1713-14.
Elizabeth, d. James and Abigail, June 24, 1718.
Elizabeth, d. Daniel and Hannah [bp. July, 1719. C. R. 1.].
Elizabeth, d. George and Mary, Sept. 10, 1[726. C. R. 2.].
[Elizabeth. C. R. 1.], d. Uriah and Sarah, Aug. 3, 1728.
Elizabeth, d. David and Hannah, July 23, 1733.
Elizebeth, d. Thomas [jr. C. R. 2.] and Elizebeth, Jan. 10, 1726-7.
Elizebeth, d. George and Mary, Nov. 5, 1727.
Ellen Jenette, d. George L., carpenter, and Sarah M., Jan. 25, 1848.
Ellen Matilda, d. Henry and Nancy, July 26, 1838. P. R. 10.
Ephraim, s. Jo[h]n and Sarah, Aug. 6, 1682.
Ephraim, s. Stephen and Sarah A., —— [1710].
Ephraim, s. Ephraim and Sarah, July 22, 1718.
Ephraim, s. Ephraim [jr. C. R. 2.] and Hannah, June 22, 1739.
Ephraim, s. Ephraim, 3d [jr. C. R. 2.] and Mary, Dec. 5, 1742.
Ephraim, s. Ephraim [jr. C. R. 2.] and Hannah, May 8, 1743.
Essex Saunders, s. Charles F., cordwainer, and Louisa, July 20, 1845.
Esther Ann, d. Amos and Esther M., Feb. 6, 1826.
Eunice Tuttle, d. Joseph, painter, and Phebe [Lovejoy. C. R. 3.], Aug. 31, 1847.
Ezra, s. William and Elizabeth, July 7, 1689.
Ezra, s. John [jr. C. R. 2.] and Phebe, Sept. 27, 1737.
Frances Jerusha, d. Caleb and Maria, Dec. 25, 1837.
Franciner, d. Isaac, blacksmith, and Eliza Ann, Mar. 13, 1848.
Francis Ann, d. David and Mary G., June 3, 1840.
Francis Flint, Dec. 16, 1842. P. R. 9.
George, s. Willia[m] and Elizabeth, Mar. 19, 1686-7.
George, s. George and Elisabeth, July 28, 1691.
George, s. Willia[m] and Elisabeth, Dec. 21, 1691.
George, s. George and Dorcas, Dec. 22, 1692.
George, s. [torn] [1706].
George, s. George and Mary, Dec. 14, 1724.
George, s. George, jr. and Hannah, Feb. 9, 1747-8.
George A[lfred. C. R. 2.], s. James A[lfred. C. R. 2.], manufacturer, and Mary J., Nov. 15, 1843.
George B., s. Moses, jr., farmer, and Tryphena M., May 20, 1843.
George Warren, s. Orlando and Charlotte, June 23, 183 9.
Hannah, d. George and Dorcas, Feb. 27, 1684.
Hannah, d. Timothy and Hannah, Oct. 8, 1695.

ABBOTT, Hannah, d. Tho[ma]s and Hannah, Sept. 10, 1700.
Hannah, d. William, Apr. 5, 1701.
Hannah, d. John and Hannah, Sept. — [1711.].
Hannah, d. Stephen and Sarah, July 30, 1716.
Hannah, d. David and Hannah, Oct. 10, 1721.
Hannah, d. Ebenezer and Hannah, Dec. 29, 1721.
Hannah, d. David and Hannah, Dec. 1, 1723.
Hannah, d. Timothy [jr. C. R. 2.] and Mary, June 21, 1726.
Hannah, d. George and Mary, Dec. 14, 1733.
Hannah, d. Ephraim [jr. C. R. 2.] and Hannah, Dec. 26, 1734.
Hannah, d. James and Abigil, Jan. 21, 1734-5.
Hannah, d. Barachias and Hannah, May 18, 1737.
Hannah, d. Joseph [jr. C. R. 2.] and Deborah, June 15, 1742.
Hannah, d. Ephraim, 3d and Mary, Mar. 1, 1744-5.
Hannah B[elcher. P. R. 10.], d. Henry, 3d, farmer, and Lucy, Apr. 29, 1844.
Hannah Belcher, d. Henry, 2d, laborer, and Lucy, July 20, 1847.
Hannah F., d. Henry R., machinist, and Lydia, Sept. 2, 1846.
Hannah Maria, d. Nathan C., farmer, and Hannah, Feb. 8, 1845.
Harrit Amanda, d. Henry and Nancy, Jan. 20, 1836. P. R. 10.
Henry, s. George and Dorcas, June 12, 1696.
Henry, s. Henry and Mary, Dec. 31, 1724.
Henry G., s. Henry R., carpenter, and Lydia, Feb. 24, 1848.
Hermon A., s. twin, Joseph and Caroline, Aug. 20, 1842.
Hubbard M., s. Moses and Tryphena M., Jan. 29, 1839. T. C.
Isaac, s. George and Dorcas, Apr. 4, 1699.
Isaac, s. Ebenezer and Hannah, June 30, 1728.
Isaac, s. [Dea. C. R. 2.] Isaac and Phebe, Feb. 3, 1744-5.
Isaac Morse, s. Joel T., farmer, and Mary, Feb. 18, 1844.
Isaack, s. Thomas and Hannah, Feb. 13, 1715-16. [1716-17. C. R. 2.]
Jabez, s. Thomas and Elezabeth, Apr. 18, 1731.
Jacob, s. George and Elizabeth, Mar. 19, 1693-4.
James, s. William and Elisabeth, Feb. 12, 1694-5.
[James. C. R. 2.], s. James and Abigail, Jan. 12, 1716-17.
James, s. Ebenezer and Hannah, Apr. 14, 1736.
Jane Green, d. Amos and Esther M., July 23, 1828.
[Jeremiah. C. R. 2.], s. John [jr. C. R. 2.] and Phebe, May 14, 1743.
[Jesse. C. R. 2.], s. Thomas and Elisabeth, May 3, 1740.
Jesse, s. Thomas and Elisabeth, Oct. 4, 1741.
Joanna, d. Job and Lucy (Chandler), Nov. 4, 1828. P. R. 4.
Job, s. Jonathan and Zerviah, Oct. 3, 1724.
Job, s. Jonathan, bp. Aug. 24, 1729. C. R. 2.

ABBOTT, Job, s. Job and Lucy (Chandler), June 8, 1820. P. R. 4.
Job, s. Nathan B. and Elizabeth (Noyes), Aug. 23, 1845. P. R. 4.
Joel, s. Benjamin and Abigail, Oct. 2 [torn], 1742. [bp. Oct. 31. C. R. 2.]
John, s. John and Sarah, Nov. 2, 1674.
John, s. Thomas and Sarah, Sept. 23, 1681.
John, s. Nehemiah and Abigail, Nov. 4, 1697.
John, s. John and Elizabeth, —— [1703].
John, s. Uriah and Sarah, Mar. 10, 1724-5.
John, s. John, jr. and Phebe, Sept. 1 [1735. C. R. 2.].
John T[aylor. C. R. 2.], s. Daniel and Sally, May 17, 1842.
Jonathan, s. Jonathan and Zerviah, —— 6, ——. [bp. Dec. 12, 1714. C. R. 2.]
Jonathan, s. David and Hannah, Oct. 24, 1739.
Joseph, s. Samuell, Mar. 16, 1666. CT. R.
Joseph, s. Thomas and Sarah, Aug. 16, 1674.
Joseph, s. John and Sarah, Dec. 19, 1676.
Joseph, s. George and Dorcas, Oct. 7, 1680.
Joseph, s. John and Elizabeth, Apr. 24, 1719.
Joseph, s. Joseph and Hannah, May 31, 1724.
Joseph, s. Thomas and Elizabeth, Dec. 29, 1734.
Joseph, s. twin, Joseph [jr. C. R. 2.] and Deborah, July 16, 1740.
Joseph, s. Joseph, 3d and Hannah, Mar. 29, 1742.
Joseph, s. [Dea. C. R. 2.] Joseph and Deborah, Apr. 2, 1744.
Joseph A., s. twin, Joseph and Caroline, Aug. 20, 1842.
Joseph Farnham, s. Isaac and Dolly, July 4, 1832.
Joshua, s. Nathaniel and Dorcas [bp. Feb. 3, 1712. C. R. 2.].
[Joshua. C. R. 2.], s. Ephraim and Sarah, Sept. 25, 1722.
Joshua, s. Joseph [jr. C. R. 2.] and Deborah, Jan. 21, 1733-4.
Joshua, s. Joseph [jr. C. R. 2.] and Deborah, —— 27, 1739. [bp. Apr. 29. C. R. 2.]
Joshuah, s. John and Sarah, June 6, 1685.
Josiah, s. Ephraim and Sarah, Sept. 26, 1728.
Josiah, s. David and Hannah, —— 5, ——. [bp. Feb. 8, 1736. C. R. 2.]
Lewis Lowe, s. Albert, trader, and Abby C., Feb. 21, 1845.
Lucy, d. Orlando, farmer, and Charlotte V., Dec. 2, 1847.
Lucy Caroline, d. Henry and Nancy, May 23, 1826. P. R. 10.
Lydea, d. George and Sarah, Mar. 31, 1675.
Lydea, d. Timothy and Mary, Mar. 28, 1733.
Lydia, d. Zebadiah and Anne, July 23, 1735.
Lydia, d. Thomas and Elisabeth, Oct. 5, 1743.
Lydia, d. Barachias and Hannah, Mar. 7, 1744-5.
Martha, d. Ephraim [sr. C. R. 2.] and Sarah, July 13, 1737.

ABBOTT, Mary, d. Thomas and Sarah, July 23, 1686.
Mary, d. John and Sarah, Jan. 9, 1687-8.
Mary, d. Nehem[iah], Mar. 23, 1701.
[Mary. C. R. 2.], d. Steephen and Sarah, Aug. 4, 1713.
Mary, d. John and Hannah, May 5 [1716].
Mary, d. Timothy and Mary, Oct. 5, 1718.
Mary, d. Ephraim and Sarah, —— 9 , 1720.[bp. July 10, 1720. C. R. 2.]
Ma[ry. T. C.], d. George and Mary, Mar. 12, 1722-3.
[Mary. C. R. 2.], d. Timothy and Mary, Jan. 7, 1723-4.
Mary, d. Ebenezer and Hannah, Apr. 2, 1725.
Mary, d. Henry and Mary, Mar. 28, 1727.
Mary, d. John and Hannah, Nov. 12, 1727.
Mary, d. Benjamin and Abigael, July 21, 1732.
Mary, d. James and Abigael, Oct. 12, 1732.
Mary, d. Henry and Mary, Aug. 13, 1737.
Mary, d. Ephraim [3d. C. R. 2.] and Mary, Mar. 11, 1740-41.
Mary, d. Stephen, jr. and Mary, Mar. 8, 1743-4.
Mary Eliza, d. David and Mary G., Mar. 21, 1836.
Mary Jane, d. William and Mary, bp. Sept. 18, 1842. C. R. 3.
Mehetabel, d. Benj[ami]n and Joanna, bp. June 28, 1766. C. R. 1.
[Mehetbel. C. R. 2.] ——etbel, d. Ephraim [jr. C. R. 2.] and Hannah, Aug. 11, 1736.
Mehetebel, d. Stephen and Sarah, Mar. 17, 1727-8.
Mehitabell, d. George and Sarah, Apr. 4, 1680.
Moses, s. George and Elizabeth, Feb. 4, 1698-9.
Moses, s. Barachias and Hannah, Aug. 9, 1735.
Moses Bailey, s. William and Mary P., Dec. 5, 1842. T. C.
Myra Ballard, d. twin, David, yeoman, and Mary, Dec. 30, 1847.
Myron Grant, s. twin, David, yeoman, and Mary, Dec. 30, 1847.
Nathan, s. George and Dorcas, Feb. 12, 1682.
Nathan, s. William and Elizabeth, Dec. 10, 1692.
Nathan, s. Jonathan and Zerviah, —— 17, ——. [bp. Apr. 19, 1719. C. R. 2.]
Nathan, s. Paul and Elezebeth, Apr. 10, 1721.
Nathan, s. Daniel and Hannah, Oct. 16, 1723.
Nathan, s. Timothy [jr. C. R. 2.] and Mary, Jan. 7, 17[28-]9.
Nathan, s. Thomas and Elisbeth, Feb. 7, 1736-7.
Nathan Emerson, s. Nathan, 5th and Mary Elizabeth, Nov. 13, 1833.
Nathan F., s. Daniel and Sarah, Jan. 20, 1828.
Nathan Gilbert, s. Chandler and Hannah, bp. May. 20, 1838. C. R. 3.
Nathaniel, s. Nathaniel and Penelope, Mar. 10, 1726-7.

ABBOTT, Nathaniel, s. Joseph [jr. C. R. 2.] and Deborah, Aug. 12, 1737.
Nathaniel Frye, s. Philip and Elizabeth, bp. Sept. —, 1783. C. R. 1.
Nathaniell, s. Thomas and Sarah, Jan. 19, 1678.
Nehemiah, s. Nehemiah and Abigail, Jan. 19, 1691-2.
Nehemiah, s. Ebenezer and Hannah, Feb. 2, 1726-7.
Nehemiah, s. Zebadiah and Anne, Aug. 24, 1731.
Newton, s. Isaac and Dolly, Mar. 5, 1835.
Noah, jr., Jan. 2, 1810. P. R. 3.
Noah B., s. Noah, jr. and Eliza, Nov. 3, 1840.
Obed, s. George and Elizabeth, Mar. 16, 1696-7.
Paul, s. Willia[m] and Elizabeth, Mar. 28, 1697.
Peter, s. Ephraim and Sarah, May 8, 1734.
Phebe, d. Daniel and Hannah, Apr. 7, 1721.
Phebe, d. James and Abigaiel, Nov. 22, 1727.
Phebe, d. Ebenezer and Hannah, Jan. 3, 1731-2.
Phebe, d. John [jr. C. R. 2.] and Phebe, Apr. 14, 1733.
Pheb[e. C. R. 2.], d. Timothy and Mary, Feb. 16, 1736-7. [Feb. 28. P. R. 8.]
Phebe, d. Benj[ami]n and Joanna, bp. June 28, 1766. C. R. 1.
Philip, s. William and Elizabeth, Apr. 3, 1699.
Priscilla, d. John and Sarah, July 7, 1691.
Priscilla, d. Stephen and Sarah, Feb. 20, 1719-20.
[Priscilla. C. R. 2.], d. Barachias and Hannah, Feb. 13, 1742-3.
[Rachel. C. R. 2.], d. James and Abigall, Nov. 17, 1720.
Rebeca, d. twin, James, Aug. 13, 1730.
[Rebecca. C. R. 2.], d. Nathaniel and Dorcass, Apr. 24, 1717.
Rhoda, d. Ephraim, jr. and Hannah, June 22, 1741.
Rubin, s. James and Abigaill, Apr. 4, 1723.
Sally B. [Sarah Barnard. C. R. 2.], d. Amos and Esther M., July 10, 1838.
Sam[ue]l, s. Benjamin and Sarah, May 8, 1694.
Samuel, s. Thomas [jr. C. R. 2] and Elezebeth [bp. Nov. 7, 1725. C. R. 2.].
Samuel, s. Stephen and Sarah, June 23, 1726.
[Samuel, C. R. 2.], s. George and Mary, Feb. 25, 1731-2.
Samuel, s. Ebenezer and Elisabeth, ——, 1736.
Samuell, s. George and Sarah, May 30, 1678.
Samuell, s. Jonathan and Zerviah, Sept. 20, 1727.
Sarah, d. George and Dorcas, Aug. 26, 1679. [1678. CT. R.]
Sarah, d. John and Sarah, Nov. 26, 1680.
Sarah, d. Stephen and Sarah, Oct. — [1711].
Sarah, d. John and Hannah, Mar. 18, 1712-13.

ABBOTT, [Sarah. C. R. 2.], d. Ephraim and Sarah, Jan. 25, 1715-16.
Sarah, d. Benjamin and Elizabeth, Aug. 2 [1718. C. R. 2.].
Sarah, d. John and Hannah, Aug. 5, 1[722].
Sarah, d. George and Mary, Jan. 14, 1729-30.
Sarah, d. twin, James, Aug. 13, 1730.
Sarah, d. Timothy and Mary, May 5 [1731. C. R. 2.].
Sarah, d. Zebadiah and Anne, Aug. 3, 1733.
Sarah, d. Ephraim [jr. C. R. 2.] and Hannah, Nov. —, 1737.
Sarah, d. James and Sarah, Mar. 1, 1742-3.
Sarah Eliza, d. W[illia]m, of Amoskeag, bp. Nov. 29, 1840. C. R. 2.
Sarah Frances, d. Abel, jr. and Apphia L., Apr. 10, 1839.
Sarah Jane, d. Priscilla, May 22, 1815.
Sarah Job, d. Job and Lucy (Chandler), July 19, 1818. P. R. 4.
Sarah L[incoln. C. R. 2.], d. Albert and Abba, May 13, 1840.
Sarah Maria, d. Moody B., farmer, and Hannah V., Sept. 17, 1844.
Sarah R., d. Abel, jr. and Apphia, Aug. 11, 1842.
Sarah Stevens, d. Orlando and Charlotte, Feb. 24, 1841.
[Simeon. C. R. 2.], s. James and Abigal, Sept. 18, 1724.
[Solomon. C. R. 2.], s. David and Hannah, Feb. 14, 1730-31.
Stephen, s. John and Sarah, Feb. 14, 1678.
Stephen, s. Stephen and Sarah, Mar. 2, 1717-18.
Thomas, s. Thomas and Hannah, Jan. 3, 1698-9.
Thomas, s. Thomas and Elezebath, Apr. 4, 1729.
Timothy, s. Timothy and Hannah, June 20, 1693.
Timothy, s. Timothy and Mary, Oct. 26, 1719.
[Timothy. C. R. 2.] ——othy, s. Asa and Elisabeth, June 4, 1745.
Uriah, s. George and Elizabeth, Nov. 20, 1692.
[Uriah. C. R. 1.], s. Uriah and Sarah, Sept. 29, 1735.
Warren Grant, s. Nathan C., farmer, and Hannah B., Dec. 3, 1848.
Willia[m], s. Willia[m] and Elizabeth, Mar. 17, 1684-5.
William, s. James and Abigail, Sept. 8, 1719.
William, s. Joseph and Hannah, Dec. 3, 1730.
William, s. Uriah and Sarah, Oct. 2, 1738.
William, s. twin, Mr. Isaac and Phebe, July 21, 1741.
William, s. Clerk John [jr. C. R. 2.] and Phebe, Jan. 3, 1747-8.
William Warren, s. William and Mary, bp. Sept. 18, 1842. C. R. 3.
Zebadiah, s. [torn], — [1706].
Zebadiah, s. Thomas and Hannah,—[1708?].
Zebadiah, s. Zebadiah and Anne, Sept. 27, 1739.
Zebadiah, s. Nehemiah and Abigail, Apr. 6, 1695.
Zerviah, d. Jonathan and Zerviah [bp. Aug. 12, 1722. C. R. 2.].
——, ch. [torn], —— 15 [1701].

ABBOTT, ——, ch. [torn]h, July 27, 1701.
——, ch. [torn]beth, Mar. 17, 1702-3.
——, ch. [Geo]rge and Elizabeth, Apr. 16, 1706.
——, ch. [torn]ll and Marcy, Feb. 22, 1710-11.
——, s. twin, Thomas and [torn], Mar. 31, 1710-11.
[torn]ine, d. twin, Thomas and [torn], Mar. 31, 1710-11.
——, ch. Daniel and Hannah, Sept. 15, 1712.
——, ch. Daniel and Hannah, Dec. 16, 1713.
——, ch. [Dan]iel and Hannah, Dec. 19, 1716.
——, d. Uriah and Sarah, Dec. 7, 1726.
——, d. Edward and Darcus, Feb. 15, 1728-9.
——, s. Uriah and Sarah, Aug. 20, 1729.
——, s. Jonathan and Zerviah, Sept. 30, 1733.
——, s. Jonathan and Lydea, Apr. 10, 1839.
——, s. Mrs. Mary Ann, July 30, 1843.
——, s. Jurid, farmer, and Mary, Apr. 16, 1846.

ABBUT (see also Abbott), ——, ch. [torn] and Elizabeth, Aug. 3, 1704.
——, ch. [torn] and [D]orcas, Jan. 22, 1704-5.

ABBUTT (see also Abbott), Mary, d. Uriah and Sarah, —— 5 [1733].
Nathanael, s. Nathanael and Dorcas, June 9, 1700.
—— ch. [Tho]mas and Hannah, Dec. 1, 1704.
——, ch. [torn] and Abigail, Nov. 10, 1704.
——ch. [torn] and Eliza[beth], June 27, 1704.

ABETT (see also Abbott), Mehetabel, d. Georg and Sara, Feb. 17, 1671.

ADAMS, Abby Ann, d. John and Elizabeth, Mar. 10, 1811.
Amos, s. John, 3d and Susanna, May 24, 1801.
Amos, s. John, jr. and Susannah, Sept. 17, 1816. [Sept. 13. P. R. 7.]
Ann R., d. William, laborer, and Marion T., both b. Scotland, Dec. 6, 1848.
Charles, s. Nathan, jr. and Susannah, bp. Sept. 16, 1792. C. R. 1.
Charles, s. John [4th. P. R. 5.] and Eliza [Elizabeth A. P. R. 5.], Apr. 23, 1842.
Charlotte, d. Lt. John, jr. and Dorcas, May 29, 1796.
David, s. Israel and Tabitha, May 2, 1742.
Dolly, d. Enoch and Sarah, Nov. 17, 1784.
Elisabeth, d. Israil and Tabitha, Dec. 24, 1737.

ADAMS, Eliza Ann, d. John, 3d [4th. P. R. 5.] and Elizabeth, May 26, 1830.
Elizabeth, d. Israel, jr. and Eliz[abe]th, Nov. 4, 1761.
Elizabeth, d. Nathan and Elizabeth, Aug. 18, 1786.
Elizabeth, d. Nathan and Elizabeth, Sept. 21, 1790.
Ellen Maria, d. John, 3d [4th. P. R. 5.] and Elizabeth, Apr. 27, 1828.
Emeline Osgood, d. Maj. John, jr. and Dorcas, Jan. 31, 1808.
Emily Jane, d. John and Eliz[abeth], bp. May 16, 1813. C. R. 2.
Emily Jane, d. John and Elizabeth, Jan. 2, 1814.
Enoch, s. Enoch and Sarah, June 23, 1779.
Esther, d. Israel, jr. and Eliz[abe]th, May 26, 1770.
Evelina, d. John, jr. and Susannah, Sept. 24, 1811.
Frank, s. John, 4th and Elizabeth A. (Stevens), July 1, 1847. P. R. 5.
George, s. John, 5th [4th. P. R. 5.] and Elizabeth A., Apr. 2, 1827. [Apr. 1. P. R. 5.]
Hannah, d. John and Hannah, July 26, 1760.
Hannah, d. John and Hannah, bp. June 3, 1764. C. R. 1.
Hannah, d. John, jr. and Dorcas, Dec. 18, 1791.
Harriot, d. John, jr. and Susannah, Oct. 28, 1806.
Henry, s. Enoch and Sarah, bp. Aug. 15, 1790. C. R. 1.
Isaac, s. John and Hannah, Apr. 25, 1767.
Isaac, s. Lt. John, jr. and Dorcas, Oct. 27, 1798.
Israel, s. Israel, jr. and Eliz[abe]th, Jan. 13, 1768.
Israil, s. Israil and Tabitha, Jan. 26, 1733-4.
James, s. John, jr. and Susannah, Dec. 29, 1819.
John, s. Israïl and Tabitha, July 3, 1735.
John, s. John and Hannah, Feb. 26, 1766.
John, s. John, 3d and Susanna, Feb. 26, 1803. [Feb. 24. P. R. 5.]
John, s. John, jr. [4th. P. R. 5.] and Elizabeth A., Dec. 26, 1834.
John Emory, s. Enoch and Sarah, Dec. 5, 1780.
John Osgood, s. Maj. Jo[h]n and Dorcas, Sept. 3, 1811.
Joseph, s. John, bp. May 8, 1774. C. R. 1.
Joseph, s. Enoch and Sarah, Apr. 4, 1788.
Joseph, s. John, jr. and Dorcas, Mar. 21, 1790.
Joshua, s. Israel and Tabitha, Nov. 9, 1739.
Joshua, s. Israel, jr. and Elizabeth, Aug. 24, 1763.
Latitia, d. John, jr. and Susannah, Oct. 29, 1813.
Lewis J., s. Lewis J., shoemaker, of Lowell, and Elizabeth, Feb. 28, 1846.
Loisa, d. Lt. John, jr. and Dorcas, Dec. 28, 1803.
Loisa, d. John, 3d and Susanna, Dec. 30, 1804.
Maria, d. John, jr. and Susannah, Feb. 24, 1809.

ADAMS, Martha, d. Lt. John, jr. and Dorcas, May 28, 1801.
Martha [Stevens. P. R. 5.], d. John [4th. P. R. 5.], cordwainer, and Eliza, Sept. 16, 1843.
Mary [Mary Holt. C. R. 1.], d. Lt. John, jr. and Dorcas, Nov. 4, 1793.
Nathan, s. Nathan and Elizabeth, Jan. 28, 1788.
Phebe P[hillips. C. R. 6.], d. John and Elizabeth, July 24, 1817.
Samuel, s. Israel, jr. and Elizabeth, Nov. 7, 1765.
Sarah, d. twin, Israel and Tabitha, July 26, 1744.
Sarah, d. John and Han[na]h, bp. July 18, 1762. C. R. 1.
Sarah, d. Enoch and Sarah, Nov. 17, 1782.
Sarah, ward of Maj. John, bp. Sept. 4, 1825. C. R. 1.
Sarah Ann, d. Maj. [Capt. C. R. 1.] John, jr. and Dorcas, Feb. 2, 1806.
Sarah M[ooar. P. R. 5.], d. John, 3d [4th. P. R. 5.] and Elizabeth, Dec. 8, 1832. [Dec. 9. P. R. 5.]
Susan Cutter, d. John, jr. [4th. P. R. 5.] and Elizabeth, Mar. 15, 1837.
Susan Cutter, d. John [4th. P. R. 5.] and Elizabeth, July 20, 1839.
Susanna, d. John, 3d and Susanna, Nov. 13, 1799.
Susannah, d. Nathan and Susannah, bp. Nov. 23, 1794. C. R. 1.
——, s. James C. and Augusta, Mar. 20, 1841.

AHERN, Elizabeth, d. Eugene, laborer, and Mary, Jan. 5, 1848.

AIKEN, Georgiann Elizabeth, d. ——, bp. Feb. 22, 1834. C. R. 6.

ALLEN (see also Allin), Abigail, d. Asa, bp. July 15, 1787. C. R. 2.
Andrew, s. Andrew and Faith, May 9, 1657.
Andrew, s. Andrew and Elizabeth, Dec. 20, 1685.
Andrew, s. Andrew and Mary, July 7, 1721.
Asa, s. Asa, bp. May 24, 1789. C. R. 2.
Asa, s. Asa, bp. July 11, 1790. C. R. 2.
Charles, s. Joseph and Lucy, Aug. 13, 1826.
Charles Adam, s. Charles R. and Sarah, Aug. 18, 1837.
Eliza, d. Joseph D. and Lucy, Sept. 11, 1828.
Elizabeth, d. Andrew and Elizabeth, Oct. 1, 1682.
George Oakes, s. Joseph and Lucy, July 17, 1822.
Hanna, d. Andrew and Faith, Oct. 28, 1652.
Hannah, d. John and Mercy, Sept. 12, 1690.
Hannah E., d. John C. and Hannah, Sept. 12, 1828.
Henry V., s. Joseph V. and Lucy, Mar. 30, 1817.
Isaac, s. Asa, bp. July 15, 1792. C. R. 2.

ALLEN, James, s. Andrew and Elizabeth, Mar. 2, 1683-4.
John, s. Andrew and Faith, Mar. 16, 1661-2.
John, s. John and Mercy, Apr. 31, 1687.
John, s. John and Mercy, June 12, 1688.
John Hasket, s. Joseph V. and Lucy, June 24, 1824.
Joseph Farnum, s. Joseph V. and Lucy, Aug. 19, 1813.
Lucy Jane, d. Joseph V. and Lucy, Apr. 15, 1820.
Mary Elizabeth, d. Benjamin, laborer, and Hannah, Sept. 25, 1847.
Metilda, d. Thomas and Rachel, Feb. 3, 1817.
Samuel J., s. Joseph F., cordwainer, and Catharine, Feb. 13, 1846.
Samuel James, s. Joseph V. and Lucy, May 29, 1815.
Sarah, d. Andrew and Elizabeth, June 11, 1690.
Thomas, s. Andrew and Elizabeth, Oct. 17, 1687.
Thomas, s. Andrew and Mary, Nov. 18, 1723.
Timothy Fletcher, s. Thaddeus P., bp. Sept. 25, 1842. C. R. 2.
Walter B., s. Joseph V. and Lucy, Aug. 23, 1831.

ALLET, William H., s. Stephen and Huldah, June 9, 1828.

ALLIN (see also Allen), Andrew, s. James and Deborah, June 13, 1747.
Andrew, s. James and Deborah, Feb. 23, 1754.
Deborah, d. James and Deborah, July 14, 1738.
Elisabeth, d. James and Deborah, July 5, 1744.
James, s. Andrew and Mary, Aug. 9, 1713.
[James. C. R. 1.], s. James and Deborah, Jan. 13, 1741-2.
John, s. Andrew and Mary, Dec. 11, 1716.
[Martha. C. R. 1.], d. James and Deborah, Jan. 5, 1739-40.
[Mary. C. R. 1.], d. Andrew and Mary, May 19, 1719.
Mehetebel, d. James and Deborva, May 26, 1749.

AMBROSE, Mary Eliza, d. twin, John, cordwainer, and Mary Ann, Sept. 1, 1847.
Sarah Elizabeth, d. twin, John, cordwainer, and Mary Ann, Sept. 1, 1847.

AME (see also Ames), Cyrus [Ames. C. R. 2.], s. Prince and Unice, Jan. 2, 1809.

AMES (see also Ame, Eames, Eams, Eimes), Abigail, d. Samuel and Hannah, bp. ——, 1722. C. R. 1.
Abigail, d. Samuell and Eliz[abeth], bp. ——, 1756. C. R. 1.
Abigail, d. Benjamin and Dorcas, Oct. 4, 1779.
Alexander, s. Prince and Unice, Feb. 2, 1796.
Amos, s. Sam[ue]l and Hannah, bp. Jan. 20, 1733-4. C. R. 1.

AMES, Anna, d. Prince and Unice, Feb. 28, 1787.
Benjamin, s. Samuel and Hannah, at Lexington, June 6, 1724.
Benjamin, s. Benjamin and Hepsebeth, Nov. 9, 1749.
Benjamin, s. Benjamin, jr. and Phebe, Feb. 24, 1773.
Benjamin, s. Benjamin, jr. and Phebe, Oct. 30, 1778.
Benjamin, s. Simeon, jr. and Dorcas, Oct. 27, 1830.
Chandler, s. Benjamin and Hephzibah, Nov. 14, 1747.
Daniel, s. Spafford and Mary, Apr. 29, 1789.
Dorcas, d. Benj[ami]n and Dorcas, July 25, 1773.
Dorcas, d. Benjamin and Dorcas, July 31, 1776.
Elizabeth, d. [Ens. C. R. 2.] Benjamin and Hepsibah, Aug. 8, 1760.
Elizabeth, d. Benj[ami]n, jr. and Phoebe, Jan. 19, 1789.
Elizabeth Abbot, d. Simeon and Sarah, Jan. 3, 1794.
Eunice, d. Peter and Eunice, Oct. 22, 1800.
Ezra Chandler, s. Benja[mi]n, jr. and Phoebe, Jan. 1, 1785.
Frederick, s. Spafford and Mary, Aug. 12, 1800.
Gayton O[sgood. C. R. 3.], s. Simeon, jr. and Dorcas, Oct. 27, 1827.
George, s. Prince and Unice, July 27, 1793.
Hannah, d. Benjamin and Hepsebith, Nov. 26, 1751.
Hannah, d. Benj[ami]n, jr. and Phebe, July 19, 1781.
Hannah, d. Simeon and Sarah, Nov. 4, 1796.
Hepsebith, d. Benjamin and Hepsebith, Nov. 3, 1755.
Hepsibah, d. Benja[min], jr. and Phoebe, Jan. 20, 1777.
Isaac, s. Benjamin, jr. and [torn], Nov. 13, 1794.
Isaac, s. Benjam[in], jr. and Phebe, Nov. 13, 1795.
James, s. Prince and Unice, July 14, 1798.
Jane, d. John and Mary, Feb. 26, 1820.
John, s. Spafford and Mary, Apr. 8, 1792.
John, s. Timothy, bp. Aug. 11, 1793. C. R. 2.
Lavina, d. Prince and Eunice, Apr. 18, 1803.
Lydia, d. Samuel and Elizabeth, Aug. 22, 1767.
Mary, d. Spafford and Mary, Nov. 19, 1782.
Mary P[oor. C. R. 3.], d. Simeon, jr. and Dorcas, Mar. 18, 1829.
Mehitable, d. Simeon, jr. and Dorcas, Sept. 24, 1824.
Molly, d. Benja[min], jr. and Phoebe, July 3, 1783.
Moses B[ailey. C. R. 3.], s. Simeon, jr. and Dorcas, Jan. 30, 1826.
Nancy, d. John and Mary, Apr. 3, 1827.
Nathan, s. Benjamin, jr. and Phebe, May 7, 1787.
Nathan White, s. Spafford and Mary, Feb. 11, 1785.
Peter, s. Prince and Unice, Apr. 22, 1785.
Peter, s. Prince, bp. Apr. 19, 1789. C. R. 2.

AMES, Phillip, s. Prince and Unice, Feb. 27, 1791.
Phineas, s. Samuel and Elizabeth, Sept. 7, 1764.
Phoebe, d. Benjamin, jr. and Phoebe, Apr. 8, 1775.
Rhoda, d. Benja[min], jr. and Phebe, Jan. 12, 1792.
Rhoda, d. Simeon and Sarah, Nov. 6, 1814.
Richard, s. Benjamin and Hepsebath, Sept. 16, 1754.
Richard, s. Benj[ami]n and Hephsibah, Aug. 16, 1758.
Robert, s. Robert and Rebecca, Feb. 28, [16]67.
Robert, s. Sam[ue]ll and Hannah, bp. ——, 1737. C. R. 1.
Sally Adams, d. Timothy, bp. Apr. 12, 1789. C. R. 2.
Sampson, s. Prince and Eunice, Sept. 20, 1805.
[Sam. C. R. 1.] uel, s. Samuel, jr. and Elisabeth, Sept. 19, 1746.
Samuel, s. Timothy, bp. Nov. 6, 1791. C. R. 2.
Samuel, s. Spafford and Mary, Nov. 4, 1795.
Sarah, d. Simeon and Sarah, Aug. 14, 1790.
Sarah, d. Simeon, bp. Apr. 7, 1793. C. R. 2.
Sarah, d. Spafford and Mary, bp. Jan. 7, 1798. C. R. 1.
Simeon, s. Samuel and Hannah, June 23, 1741.
Simeon, s. Sam[ue]l, bp. Mar. 11, 1759. C. R. 1.
Simeon, s. Benj[ami]n and Dorcas, Mar. 29, 1772.
Simeon, s. Simeon and Sarah, Dec. 23, 1799.
Solomon, s. Samuel, jr. and Elezebith, Apr. 21, 1754.
Spaffard, s. Samuel, jr. and Elezebith, Mar. 23, 1752.
Stephen, s. Samuel, jr. and Elezebith, Aug. 24, 1749.
Stephen, s. Spafford and Mary, Apr. 14, 1787.
Timothy, s. Capt. Benj[amin] and Hepsibah, Sept. 26, 1765.
Timothy, s. Timothy, bp. Aug. 23, 1789. C. R. 2.
Unice, d. Prince, bp. May 17, 1801. C. R. 2.

ANDERSON, Ann L., d. Samuel, overseer in factory, and Isabell, May 5, 1845.
Charles, s. wid. Abigail, bp. Sept. 11, 1831. C. R. 2.
Edward, s. wid. Abigail, bp. Sept. 11, 1831. C. R. 2.
Francis, s. wid. Abigail, bp. Sept. 25, 1831. C. R. 2.
Henry, s. wid. Abigail, Sept. 11, 1831. C. R. 2.
Isabella Sarah, d. Samuel, factory overseer, and Isabella, Oct. 3, 1848.
Mary Jane, d. wid. Abigail, bp. Sept. 11, 1831. C. R. 2.

ANDREW (see also Andrews), Robert, s. Richard, warp twister, and Mary, Dec. 29, 1847.

ANDREWS (see also Andrew), Charlotte Martha, d. Meuzies Christopher and Martha (Griffin), July 18, 1848. P. R. 12.

ANDREWS, Ellen Maria, d. Meuzies Christopher and Martha (Griffin), Dec. 11, 1842. P. R. 12.
Payson K[irk. C. R. 2.], s. M. C. [Meuzies Christopher. P. R. 12.], carriagemaker, and Martha, Aug. 31, 1845.

ANGIER, Charles A., s. Asa A., carpenter, and Lucy T., Sept. 23, 1843.
Lucy Caroline, d. Asa, jr. and Abigail, June 4, 1838.

ANNICE (see also Annis), Abigail, d. Ezra and Sarah, Feb. 24, 1771.
James, s. Ezra and Sarah, Feb. 10, 1770.
James, s. James and Beulah, Jan. 25, 1774.

ANNIS (see also Annice), Aleanor, d. Ezra and Sarah, Aug. 12, 1760.
Bulah, d. James and Bulah, Sept. 22, 1775.
Diadama, d. James and Bulah, Apr. 22, 1771.
Hannah, d. Rolf, bp. Feb. 24, 1765. C. R. 2.
Jacob, s. Ezra and Sarah, Feb. 26, 1763.
John, s. Ezra and Sarah, Aug. 20, 1764.
Rebecca, d. Rolf, bp. Apr. 5, 1767. C. R. 2.
Ruth, d. Ezera and Sarah, Mar. 22, 1757.
Sarah, d. Ezra and Sarah, Nov. 28, 1759.

ANTRIM, John, s. Joseph, flax dresser, and Esther, both b. Ireland, July 16, 1849.

APPLETON, Charles Horatio, s. Daniel and Hannah, bp. July 5, 1819. C. R. 1.
George Swett, s. Daniel and Hannah, bp. Oct. 1, 1821. C. R. 1.
George Washington, s. Nath[anie]l, Esq., bp. Oct. 29, 1775. C. R. 2.
Sarah W., d. Thomas H. and Fidelia, June 25, 1829.
——, ch. Daniel and Hannah, bp. May 11, 1817. C. R. 1.

ARMATAGE (see also Armitage), ——, d. Moses, Jan. 1, 1826.

ARMITAGE (see also Armatage), ——, s. Mr. ——, May 13, 1822.

ASHWORTH, William E., s. James, spinner, and Sarah, Apr. 18, 1849.

ASLET (see also Aslett), John, s. John and Rebecka, Feb. 16, 1656.
Mary, d. John and Rebecka, Apr. 24, 1654.
Ruth, d. John and Rebecka, Aug. 8, 1660. [1659. CT. R.]
Sara, d. John and Rebecka, Jan. 14, 1658.
Sara, d. John and Rebecka, Aug. 14, 1662. [1661. CT. R.]

ASLETT (see also Aslet), Elizabeth, d. John and Rebecka, May 26, 1666.
Rebecca, d. John and Rebecca, May 6, 1652.

ASTEN (see also Austin), Daniel, s. Tho[mas], bp. Dec. 7, 1746. C. R. 2.
John, s. Daniel and Eunice, July 1, 1764.
Luce, d. Daniel and Eunice, Dec. 18, 1762.
Mary, d. Daniel and Eunice, Aug. 15, 1771.

ASTIN (see also Austin), Benjamin, s. Benjamin and Mary, Jan. 11, 1740-41.
Betty, d. Daniel and Eunice, June 8, 1773.
Daniel, s. Thomas and Hannah, Aug. 7, 1698.
Joan, s. Sam[ue]l and Lucy, July 13, 1697.
Mary, d. Sam[ue]l and Lucy, Feb. 28, 1700-1701.
Sam[ue]l, s. Samuel and Lucy, Aug. 27, 1694.
Samuel, s. Daniel and Eunice, Nov. 20, 1765.
Sarah, d. Sam[ue]ll and Lucy, Mar. 28, 1692.
Thomas, s. Thomas and Hannah, Jan. 23, 1691-2.

ASTINE (see also Austin), Benjamin, s. Thomas and Hannah, June 16, 1694.
Phinehas, s. Benjamin and Mary, Nov. 3, 1737.
Sarah, d. Benjamin and Mary, May 21, 1735.

ASTING (see also Austin), Nathan, s. Thomas, bp. May 9, 1725. C. R. 2.

AUSTEN (see also Austin), Daniel, s. Daniel and Prissilla, Oct. 1, 1724.
John, s. Benjamin and Mary, Jan. 25, 1729-30.
Lucy, d. Daniel and Eunice, Apr. 23, 1769.
Martha, d. Benjamin and Mary, June 1, 1725.
Priscilla, d. Daniel and Priscilla, July 26, 1723.
Ruth, d. Benjamin and Mary, —— 12 [bp. July 16, 1721. C. R. 2.].
Ruth, d. Thomas and Bula, Oct. 8, 1752.
Sarah, d. Benjamine and Mary, Dec. 13, 1731.

AUSTEN, Thomas, s. Benjamin and Mary, Apr. 24, 1727.
——, d. Benjamin and Mary, Dec. 9, 1729.

AUSTIN (see also Asten, Astin, Astine, Asting, Austen), Abiall, s. Thomas and Hannah, —— [1703].
Adalina, d. Samuel and Dorcas, May 4, 1801.
Amos P., s. David M. and Mary, May 27, 1834.
Benjamin, s. Benjamin and Mary, Feb. 12, 1722-3.
Charles, s. John and Dorcas, bp. May 24, 1812. C. R. 1.
Daniel, s. Samuel and Lucy, —— [1711].
Daniel Frye, s. John and Dorcas, bp. Nov. 24; 1805. C. R. 1.
Eliza, d. John and Dorcas, bp. Dec. 7, 1800. C. R. 1.
Eliza, d. David M., laborer, and Mary C., Sept. 10, 1845.
Emily, d. John and Dorcas, bp. Oct. 22, 1809. C. R. 1.
George W., s. David M., laborer, and Mary C., June 14, 1843.
Hannah, d. John and Dorcas, bp. Sept. 11, 1803. C. R. 1.
Harriot, d. John and Dorcas, bp. Aug. 3, 1794. C. R. 1.
Harriot James, d. Eliza, July 18, 1821.
Henery, s. Samuel and Dorcas, Nov. 21, 1803.
Henry, s. Samuel and Dorcas, Aug. 23, 1797.
Hezekiah, s. Tho[mas] and Sarah, bp. Apr. 26, 1719. C. R. 2.
Isaac Marble, s. Samuel and Dorcas, Jan. 23, 1799.
John, s. John and Dorcas, Sept. 7, 1796.
Mary, d. Benjamin and Mary, Apr. 7, 1719.
Mary, d. Jacob, bp. July 27, 1777. C. R. 2.
Mary Ann Parker, d. Samuel and Dorcas, Oct. 12, 1807.
Nathan A., s. David M. and Mary, Nov. 17, 1838.
Polly, d. John and Dorcas, bp. May 27, 1798. C. R. 1.
Rhoda, d. Jacob, bp. Jan. 14, 1776. C. R. 2.
Ruby, d. John and Dorcas, bp. July 15, 1792. C. R. 1.
Sally, d. John and Dorcas, bp. Nov. 27, 1791. C. R. 1.
Samuel H., s. David M., laborer, and Mary C., May 26, 184[7 or 8].
Sarah, d. Tho[mas] and Sarah, bp. Jan. 12, 1718. C. R. 2.
Sarah, d. Daniel and Eunice, Aug. 13, 1767.
Sophrona, d. Stephen and Sophronia, July 12, 1826.
Thomas, s. Thom[as], bp. Mar. 4, 1716. C. R. 2.
Timothy, s. Benjamin and Mary, Mar. 16, 1732-3.
——, ch. [torn]nah, July 17, 1701.
——, d. Samuell and Lucye, Apr. 3, 1706.
——, ch. [torn] and Hannah, Apr. 7, 1706.

AVERIL (see also Averill), Betsey, d. Paul and Deborah, bp. Oct. 24, 1790. C. R. 1.
Elizabeth, d. John and Betty, bp. July 21, 1805. C. R. 1.
John, s. Paul and Deborah, bp. Nov. 23, 1777. C. R. 1.

AVERILL (see also Averil), Elisabeth, Mar. 10, 1795. P. R. 13.
Elizabeth, d. Joseph and Elizabeth, Sept. 27, 1819.
George D., s. Joseph and Elizabeth, Sept. 10, 1830.
John, s. Tho[mas], bp. Oct. 25, 1741. C. R. 2.
John, s. Paul, Nov. 16, 1776. P. R. 14.
John, s. Joseph and Elizabeth, Jnly 18, 1821.
Joseph, s. Joseph and Elizabeth, Aug. 18, 1824.
Paul, Sept. 27, 1742. P. R. 13.

AVERY, Sarah, d. Tho[ma]s, bp. Nov. 3, 1751. C. R. 2.
Thomas, s. Tho[mas], bp. Sept. 27, 1747. C. R. 2.

AYER, Julia Ann, d. Samuel, Feb. 25, 1821.

B[torn], Isaack [torn], Sept. — [1702].

BACHELLER (see also Batchelder), Joseph, s. Joseph and Hannah, Feb. 9, 1766.
Judith, d. Joseph and Judith, Jan. 1, 1765.

BACHELLOR (see also Batchelder), John, s. Joseph and Judith, Mar. 21, 1761.
Judith, d. Jos[ep]h [Joseph. C. R. 1.] and Judith, Mar. 15, 1763.

BADGER, George, s. twin, Milton and Clarissa, July 2, 1834.
Milton, s. Rev. Milton and Clarissa, Feb. 1, 1831.
Milton, s. Rev. Milton and Clarissa M., Dec. 7, 1832.
William, s. twin, Milton and Clarissa, July 2, 1834.

BAILIE (see also Bailey), George Edward, s. Robert and Hannah, bp. May 1, 1831. C. R. 1.
Thomas K., s. Robert and Hanah, Aug. 4, 1831.

BAILEY (see also Bailie, Baily, Bayle, Bayley, Bayly), Abba W., s. Roderick, Dec. 15, 1837.
Abby M., d. John, laborer, and Sarah, Mar. 27, 1849.
[Abby Mary. in pencil.], d. James, farmer, and Abby F., Feb. 18, 1846.
Abby O., d. Samuel, 3d and Prudence (Farmer), Dec. 1, 1837. P. R. 36.
Andrew O., s. Roderick, Oct. 15, 1841.
Anne, d. Nathan, jr., bp. Feb. 12, 1769. C. R. 2.
Arrathusa, d. Samuel and Sally, May 21, 1803.

BAILEY, Asa A., s. Theodore and Lavina, June 12, 1829.
Betsey, d. Samuel and Sally, Apr. 10, 1808.
Charles, s. John M. and Elizabeth, Nov. 26, 1821.
Charles Henry, s. Joseph and Lucy, Mar. 27, 1841. P. R. 41.
Charles K., s. Samuel, 2d [3d. P. R. 36.] and Prudence, June 9, 1830.
Charles Pinkney, s. James and Lucy, Aug. 26, 1799. T. C.
Charles [Pinkney. C. R. 1.], s. Otis and Lucinda [A. C. R. 1.], Jan. 2, 1843.
Charles W., s. Timothy, farmer, and Lucy A., Nov. 21, 1845.
Charles Walter, s. James and Abigail F., Nov. 13, 1838.
Charlotte E., d. John T., tinman, and Orella, b. Barre, Vt., Oct. 20, 1848.
Charlotte Osgood, d. Otis and Lucinda A., Sept. 28, 1838.
Clarindia, d. Samuel and Sally, Sept. 15, 1810.
Clarissa Rebecca, d. Sam[ue]l G., cordwainer, and Clarissa R., Oct. 8, 1843.
Cynphia, d. John, deceased, and Hannah, Dec. 16, 1807.
Daniel, s. Daniel, jr. and Sophia, June 23, 1810.
Daniel, s. Daniel, jr. and Sophia, May 8, 1812.
Ebenezer, s. Timothy and Ritty, Apr. 10, 1819.
Edward, s. John T. and Orilla, Oct. 24, 1838.
Edward, s. James, farmer, and Abby, Oct. 20, 1844.
Edward Mansfield, s. John T. and Aurelia, bp. July 19, 1840. C. R. 4.
Elias P., s. Roderick, at Grasbury, Vt., Dec. 17, 1832.
Elizabeth, d. Joshua and Hipsabeth, July 4, 1802.
Elizabeth, d. Nathan and Betsey, Mar. 1, 1805.
Elizabeth, d. John M. and Hannah A., Jan. 22, 1813.
Eliza[beth], d. John M. and Lucy, Apr. 14, 1815.
Elizabeth, d. Nathan and Chloe, May 23, 1820.
Elizabeth, d. Daniel and Sophia [R. C. R. 2.], Aug. 27, 1824.
Elvy W., s. Samuel and Sally, Mar. 1, 1815.
Emily B., d. Samuel and Mary, Dec. 27, 1836.
Esther, d. Theodore and Lavina, Mar. 29, 1836.
Fanny, d. Moses, jr., bp. Oct. 14, 1792. C. R. 2.
Frederick, s. James and Abigail F., Oct. 2, 1841.
George, s. wid. Lucy, bp. June 2, 1808. C. R. 2.
George, s. James, farmer, and Abigail F., July 5, 1843.
George Albert, s. Joseph and Lucy, May 11, 1843. P. R. 41.
George J., s. John, laborer and Sarah, May 3, 1846.
George Lewis, s. Dan[ie]l and Sophia, bp. June 18, 1837. C. R. 3.
George O[tis. C. R. 1.], s. Otis and Lucinda A[lden. P. R. 40.], May 24, 1836.

BAILEY, Hannah, d. Sam[ue]ll, jr., bp. Oct. 21, 1753. C. R. 2.
Hannah, d. Sam[ue]l, jr., bp. Apr. 6, 1760. C. R. 2.
Hannah, d. William and Rebecca, Dec. 13, 1776.
Hannah, d. Lt. Moses and Elizabeth, May 3, 1779.
Hannah, d. wid. Lucy, bp. June 2, 1808. C. R. 2.
Hannah, d. William, jr. and Rebecca, Mar. 13, 1813.
Hannah Ames, d. John Moar and Elizabeth (Boynton), Jan. 22, 1813. P. R. 38.
Hannah R[ogers. C. R. 1.], d. Otis, butcher, and Lucinda, Nov. 7, 1845.
Harriott, d. John M. and Betsy, Jan. 23, 1820.
Henrietta, d. Timothy and Ritta, Oct. 5, 1816. [Nov. 5. P. R. 41.]
Henry H., Jan. 21, 1835. P. R. 41.
Hephzibah, d. Joshua and Hephzibah, Oct. 2, 1795.
James, s. Sam[uel], jr., bp. Oct. 9, 1757. C. R. 2.
James, Aug. 16, 1787. P. R. 40.
James, s. wid. Lucy, bp. June 2, 1808. C. R. 2.
James, s. Timothy and Ritta, Sept. 2, 1814.
James Henry, s. Timothy, 3d, farmer and Lucy, July 24, 1843.
James L., s. Roderick, at Merrimac, N. H., Oct. 9, 1830.
James Rogers, s. James and Abigail F., Sept. 27, 1836.
John, s. Moses, jr., bp. Oct. 14, 1792. C. R. 2.
John, s. Daniel and Sophia, Oct. 23, 1817.
John Alden, s. Otis, victualler, and Lucinda A., b. Duxbury, Oct. 15, 1849.
John B., s. Samuel, 2d and Prudence, Nov. 15, 1832.
John Mooar, s. Lt. Moses and Elizabeth, July 20, 1784.
John Moar, s. John M[ooar. P. R. 38.] and Elizabeth, Oct. 16, 1817.
John T., s. Samuel and Polly, July 12, 1812.
Joseph, s. William, jr. and Rebecca, Nov. 29, 1810.
Joseph Otis, s. Joseph and Lucy, Apr. 20, 1839. P. R. 41.
Joshua, s. Joshua and Hephzibah, May 7, 1798.
Laura Alden, d. Otis and Lucinda A[lden. P. R. 40.], Mar. 1, 1841.
Levi, s. Sam[ue]ll, jr., bp. Feb. 23, 1766. C. R. 2.
Lucretia Ann, d. Sam[ue]l G., cordwainer, and Clarissa B., Mar. 28, 1845.
Lucy, Apr. 11, 1815. P. R. 37.
Lucy Ann, d. Joseph and Lucy, July 18, 1837. P. R. 41.
Lucy Ann, d. Timothy, 3d, farmer, and Lucy Ann, b. Lawrence, June 9, 1849.
Lucy Elvira [A. P. R. 37.], d. Joseph and Lucy, Mar. 7, 1847. P. R. 41. [1848. P. R. 37.]

BAILEY, Lucy Jane, d. Theodore K. and Lavina, Feb. 23, 1826.
Lydia Abbot, d. Enoch and Lydia, Dec. 20, 1825.
Mary, d. Sam[uel], jr., bp. July 25, 1762. C. R. 2.
Mary Ann, d. Daniel and Sophia, July 28, 1820.
Mary E[lizabeth. P. R. 41.], d. Joseph, farmer, and Lucy, Dec. 17, 1845.
Mary Louisa, d. Samuel G., cordwainer, and Clarissa, Dec. 5, 1846.
Mary Palmer, d. Nathan and Betsey, June 24, 1810.
Mary Stanley, d. Samuel, jr. and Mary, Nov. 4, 1815.
Moses, s. Moses, jr., bp. Jan. 20, 1793. C. R. 2.
Moses, s. Sam[ue]l, jr. and Mary, Feb. 7, 1819.
Moses A[lbert. P. R. 38.], s. Timothy and Sally, Mar. 5, 1835.
Nathan, s. Moses and Elizabeth, Feb. 2, 1775.
Nathan, s. Moses and Elizabeth, Feb. 4, 1777.
Nathan, s. Nathan and Elizabeth, Apr. 28, 1816.
Omar, s. Samuel and Sally, Sept. 4, 1806.
Omer Roderick, s. Roderick, farmer, and Charlotte, June 3, 1843.
Otis, s. James and Lucy, Apr. 18, 1809. T. C.
Percey [Persis. P. R. 41.], d. William and Rebecca, May 25, 1783.
Phineas, s. Samuel and Sarah, June 24, 1800.
Rachel, Dec. 11, 1825. P. R. 41.
Rebecca, d. William and Rebecca, Aug. 25, 1774.
Rebecca, d. Lt. Moses and Rebecca, Apr. 10, 1781.
Rebecca, d. William, jr. and Rebecca, Nov. 19, 1804.
[Rebecka. P. R. 41.], d. Timothy and Henrietta, Apr. 16, 1821. [Apr. 10. P. R. 41.]
Rhoda, d. Lt. Moses and Elizabeth, May 7, 1789.
Roderick O., s. Roderick, June 3, 1843.
Rodrick, s. Samuel and Sally, Jan. 1, 1805.
Roxana, Jan. 26, 1833. P. R. 41.
Rufus, s. wid. Lucy, bp. June 2, 1808. C. R. 2.
Rufus R., s. Timothy and Ritta, Aug. 9, 1823. T. C.
Sally, d. Samuel and Sally, Nov. 28, 1796.
Salome, d. Daniel, jr. and Sophia, Apr. 23, 1815.
Samuel, s. Sam[ue]l, jr. [Jan. 1. P. R. 36.], 1767. C. R. 2.
Samuel, s. Samuel and Sally, Mar. 14, 1795.
Samuel G., s. Samuel, 2d [3d. P. R. 36.] and Prudence, June 7, 1827.
Samuel Gilson, June 28, 1815. P. R. 32.
Samuel Henry, s. Samuel G., shoemaker, and Clarrissa, Sept. 11, 1848.
Sarah, d. Moses and Elizabeth, Nov. 1, 1772.

BAILEY, Sarah, d. William and Rebecca, Feb. 6, 1779.
Sarah, d. Daniel and Sophia, Oct. 4, 1826.
Sarah E., d. Abner and Esther, July 13, 1830.
Sarah F[rances. C. R. 4.], d. John T. and Oressa [Aurelia. C. R. 4.], Mar. 12, 1840.
Sarah J[ane. C. R. 3.], d. Daniel and Sophia, Apr. 23, 1829.
Sarah Jane, d. John, laborer, and Sarah, Nov. 6, 1847.
Sarah L[oring. C. R. 1.], d. Otis and Lucinda [A. C. R. 1.], Apr. 22, 1834.
Theodore, s. Daniel and Molly, Oct. 13, 1798.
Theodore J., s. Theodore K. and Lavina, Aug. 31, 1827.
Thomas, s. Theodore K., brickmaker, and Lavina, Aug. 24, 1843.
Timothy, s. William and Rebecca, Jan. 20, 1786.
Timothy, s. Lt. Moses and Elizabeth, Oct. 18, 1786.
Timothy, s. Timothy and Ritta, Nov. 29, 1812.
Timothy P[almer. P. R. 38.], s. Timothy and Sally, May 25, 1828.
Tristram B., May 30, 1830. P. R. 41.
Walter, s. wid. Lucy, bp. June 2, 1808. C. R. 2.
Walter, s. John Moar and Elizabeth (Boynton), Aug. 30, 1827. P. R. 38.
Walter D., s. Roderick, Dec. 1, 1835.
Warren A., July 9, 1828. P. R. 41.
Warren Francis, s. Theodore and Lavinia, Aug. 4, 1839.
William, s. William and Rebecca, Dec. 28, 1780.
William [3d. P. R. 32.], s. William, jr. and Rebecca [Jan. 20, 1807. P. R. 32; Dec. 24, 1806. P. R. 41.].
William, s. William, jr. and Rebecca, Sept. 20, 1808.
William John, s. Robert and Hannah, bp. Jan. 1, 1833. C. R. 1.
——, d. Samuel, jr. and Mary, June 11, 1821.
——, d. Sam[ue]l, jr. and Mary, Mar. 18, 1826.
——, s. John M., jr. and Elizabeth, Aug. 30, 1827.

BAILY (see also Bailey), Joshua, grands. Samuel, bp. Nov. 1, 1778. C. R. 2.
Oliver, s. Nathan, bp. June 4, 1775. C. R. 2.

BAKER, Betty, d. Jonathan and Sarah, July 4, 1776.
Daniel, s. Simon Epes, jr. and Sarah, Mar. 12, 1803.
David, s. Symonds Epes, bp. Mar. 13, 1803. C. R. 2.
Deborah Bowers, d. Henry Gray and Deborah, Dec. 10, 1786.
George [Frost. C. R. 2.], s. David and Lucy F., Oct. 10, 1830.
Henry Gray, s. Dr. Symonds and Lydia, Apr. 1, 1767.

BAKER, Issabell Maria Jenkins, d. Jacob, physician, and Elisabeth T., Feb. 3, 1847.
Joseph W., s. Joseph and Abigail B., Mar. 13, 1831.
Lucy Caroline, d. David, bp. Mar. 22, 1840. C. R. 2.
Prisa, d. Henry Gray and Deborah, Apr. 14, 1789.
Sarah E[lizabeth. C. R. 2.], d. David and Lucy F., Feb. 18, 1834.
Simonds Eps, s. Dr. Symonds and Lydia, Jan. 17, 1779.
Susanna Sargeant, d. Dr. Symonds and Lydia, Apr. 10, 1769.
Thomas, s. Henry Gray and Deborah, Mar. 18, 1792.

BALARD (see also Ballard), Dorathy, d. Timothy and Hannah, Dec. 12, 1757.
Hannah, d. Hezekiah, jr. and Lydeah, Dec. 6, 1748.
Lydea, d. Uriah, jr. and Lydea, Aug. 9, 1756.
Mary, d. Wiliam and Hannah, May 15, 1754.
Uriah, s. Uriah, jr. and Lydea, Oct. 7, 1758.
[torn]ice, d. Wiliam and Hannah, July 7, 1757.

BALDWIN, George, s. W[illia]m, baker, and Eliza A., Dec. 16, 1845.
Lydia A., d. William, baker, and Eliza A., Oct. 5, 1848.
Mary Ellen, d. Loammi and Priscilla E., Oct. 8, 1837.

BALLARD (see also Balard, Ballerd, Ballord), Abigail, d. Uriah and Elizabeth, Aug. 17, 1718.
Anna, d. Timothy [jr. C. R. 2.] and Sarah, Nov. 15, 1762.
Benjamine, s. Joseph and Rebecka, —— [1703-4?].
Clarissa Jane, bp. May 5, 1839. C. R. 2.
Daniel, s. Jeremiah and Mary, May 1, 1728.
Dorathy, d. Joseph and Elizabeth, Nov. 8, 1679.
Dorathy, d. Josiah and Mary, June 24, 1741.
Dorcas, d. twin, Hezekiah, jr. and Mary, Dec. 17, 1793.
Dorcis, d. Dea. Hezekiah and Lydea, Oct. 16, 1757.
[Dorithy. C. R. 2.], d. Joseph and Rebecka, Jan. 26, 1714-15.
[Ebenezer. C. R. 2.], s. Joseph and Rebecka, July 2, 1713.
Edward, s. Capt. Joshua and Phebe, June 26, 1819.
Elisabeth, d. Timothy and Hannah, Nov. 29, 1746.
Elizabeth, d. John and Rebekah, June 29, 1699.
Elizabeth, d. Joseph and Rebecca, Jan. 14, 1700-1701.
Enoch, s. William and Hannah, June 3, 1685.
Gayton, s. Capt. Joshua and Phebe, July 8, 1821.
George William, s. Charles, bp. Sept. 3, 1843. C. R. 2.
Hannah, d. Joseph and Elizabeth, July 17, 1677.
Hannah, d. William and Hannah, Mar. 21, 1683.

BALLARD, Hannah, d. Hezekiah and Rebecka, June 27, 1714.
Hannah, d. Josiah and Mary, Jan. 3, 1732-3.
[Hannah. C. R. 2.], d. Timothy and Hannah, June 8, 1736.
Hannah, d. Wiliam and Hannah, May 18, 1751.
Hannah, d. Nathan and Hannah, May 12, 1764.
Hannah, d. Joseph and Hannah, Sept. 7, 1774.
Hannah Frye, d. Hezekiah, jr. and Mary, Aug. 5, 1791.
Henry Ethelbrid, s. John, carpenter, and Jane, Apr. 21, 1845.
Hepsebah, d. William and Hannah, Apr. 8, 1688.
Hezekiah, s. Joseph and Elizabeth, Mar. 22, 1682. [crossed out on original.]
Hezekiah, s. Hezekiah and Rebecka [bp. June 5, 1720. C. R. 2.].
Hezekiah, s. Dea. Hezekiah and Lydia, July 18, 1762.
Hezekiah, s. Hezekiah, jr. and Mary, Feb. 19, 1787.
Hezekiah, s. Hezekiah, jr. and Mary, Aug. 31, 1796.
Israiel, s. John and Sarah, Feb. 4, 1747-8.
James, s. Josiah and Mary, July 3, 1730.
Jeremiah, s. Joseph and Rebekah, Mar. 29, 1697.
Jeremiah, s. Jeremiah and Mary, Sept. 16, 1726.
John, s. John and Rebekah, Dec. 16, 1682.
John, s. William and Hannah, Oct. 17, 1690.
John, s. Sherebiah and Lydia, Feb. 15, 1719-20.
John, s. Timothy and Hannah, June 9, 1734.
John, s. Timothy and Hannah, Apr. 9, 1739.
John, s. Joseph and Hannah, Oct. 11, 1778.
Johnathan, s. John and Rebeckah, Dec. 9, 1686.
Jonathan, s. Sherebiah and Lydea, Nov. 25, 172[9. C. R. 2.].
Joseph, s. Joseph and Rebecca, June 2, 1699.
Joseph, s. Jose[ph], [torn] [1706-7?].
Joseph, s. Jeremiah and Mary, Oct. 6, 1732.
Joseph, s. Uriah, jr. and Sarah, Sept. 17, 1739.
[Joseph. C. R. 2.], s. Timothy and Hannah, Aug. 19, 1741.
[Joseph. C. R. 2.], s. Timothy and Hannah, Oct. —, 1749. [bp. Oct. 29. C. R. 2.]
Joseph, s. Joseph and Hannah, Sept. 12, 1776.
Joseph, s. Hezekiah and Rebeca, Dec. 5, 1724.
Joshua, s. Hezekiah and Rebeca, Mar. 24, 1727-8.
Joshua, s. Jeremiah and Mary, Aug. 3, 1730.
Joshua, s. Hezekiah and Lydea, June 28, 1753.
Joshua, s. Timothy [jr. C. R. 2.] and Sarah, Aug. 24, 1760.
Joshua, s. Hezekiah [jr. C. R. 2.] and Molly, Jan. 3, 1785.
Joshua, s. Joshua and Phebe, Jan. 28, 1813.
Josiah, s. Joseph and Rebekah, June 22, 1699.
[Josiah, s. C. R. 2.], Josiah and Mary, Aug. 14, 1721.

BALLARD, Josiah, s. William, bp. Mar. 10, 1793. C. R. 2.
Loes, d. Hezekiah [jr. C. R. 2.] and Lydia, July 19, 1746.
Luce, d. Dea. Hezekiah and Lydia, Apr. 4, 1760.
Lucy, d. W[illia]m, bp. July 10, 1757. C. R. 2.
Lucy, Apr. 4, 1760. P. R. 4.
Lydea, d. Josiah and Mary, Mar. 12, 1727-8.
[Lydia. C. R. 2.], d. Sherebiah and Lydia, Nov. 27, 1726.
[Lydia. C. R. 2.], d. Hezekiah [jr. C. R. 2.] and Lydia, July 30, 1742.
[Mary. C. R. 2.] —ary, d. Jeremiah and Mary, Dec. 27, 1722.
Mary, d. Josiah and Mary, Dec. 29, 1725.
Mary, d. Timothy and Hannah, May 1, 1732.
Mary, d. Hezekiah, jr. and Lydea, Feb. 27, 1750-51.
Mary, d. [William. C. R. 2.], Dec. 1, 1788. P. R. 31.
Mary, d. Hezekiah, jr. and Mary, Feb. 13, 1789.
Mehetabel, d. Uriah [jr. C. R. 2.] and Lydia, Mar. 26, 1761.
Nathan, s. Timothy and Hannah, Nov. 1, 1744.
Nathan, s. William, bp. Feb. 6, 1791. C. R. 2.
Nathan, s. Hezekiah [jr. C. R. 2.] and Mary, Oct. 6, 1801.
Peleg, s. William and Hannah, Sept. 20, 1694.
Pennellope, d. Joseph[torn] [1705?].
Phebe, d. Jeremiah and Mary, Oct. 1, 1724.
Phebe, d. Josiah and Mary, July 25, 1738.
Phebe, d. Timothy and Hannah, Nov. 5, 1752.
Phebe Abbot, d. Joshua and Phebe, Aug. 22, 1811.
Rebecca, d. Hezekiah, jr. and Lydia, May 16, 1744.
[Rebecca. C. R. 2.], d. Josiah and Mary [bp. June 23. C. R. 2.], 1745.
Rebeckah, d. John and Rebeckah, Jan. 28, 1684.
Ruth, d. John and Rebeckah, Feb. 18, 1693-4.
Ruth, d. Sherebiah and Lydia, Apr. 17, 1724.
Samuel, s. Joseph and Rebecka, Sept. 13, 1718.
Samuel, s. Hezekiah and Rebeca, Dec. 30, 1730.
Samuel, s. Tim[oth]y, jr., bp. Nov. 1, 1761. C. R. 2.
Sarah, d. Joseph and Rebeckah, Aug. 31, 1693.
Sarah, d. John and Rebeckah, May 6, 1696.
Sarah, d. Hezekia and Rebecka, Ju— [bp. June 16, 1717. C. R. 2.].
Sarah, d. Josiah and Mary, July 29, 1735.
Sarah, d. Uriah [jr. C. R. 2.] and Mehetable, Nov. 9, 1745.
Sarah, d. John and Sarah, Feb. 22, 1749-50.
Sarah, d. Dea. Hezekiah and Lydea, Dec. 28, 1755.
Sarah, d. Timothy, jr. and Sarah, Feb. 2, 1756.
Sarah, d. Will[ia]m and Hannah, Feb. 17, 1760.
Sarah, d. twin, Hezekiah, jr. and Mary, Dec. 17, 1793.

BALLARD, [Shebiah. C. R. 2.], s. Sherebiah and Lydia, Sept. 24, 1722.
Sherebaat, s. John and Rebekah, Nov. 14, 1688.
Sherebiah, s. John and Sarah, May 9, 1745.
Sherebiah, s. Jonathan and Priscilla, Mar. 12, 1764.
Stephen, s. Joshua and Phebe, Sept. 9, 1815.
Tabatha, d. Joseph and Elisabeth, Mar. 28, 1688.
Tabitha, d. Joseph and Elizabeth, Mar. 19, 1686-7.
Thomas, s. William and Hanah, Mar. 24, 1699-1700.
Timothy, s. Timothy and Hannah, Mar. 1, 1729-30.
Timothy, s. Timothy, jr. and Sarah, July 28, 1757.
Uriah, s. Joseph and Elizabeth, Nov. 16, 1684.
Uriah, s. Uriah and Elizabeth, Apr. 28, 171[5. C. R. 2.].
Willia[m], s. Joseph and Elizabeth, Dec. 3, 1674.
[William. C. R. 2.], s. Josiah and Mary, Oct. 2, 1723.
William, s. Timothy [jr. C. R. 2.] and Sarah, May 19, 1759.
William, s. W[illia]m, bp. June 10, 1764. C. R. 2.
William, s. William, bp. June 25, 1786. C. R. 2.
William, s. Joshua and Phebe, May 15, 1825.
——, ch. Joseph and Rebecka, —— 24 [1702].
——, ch. ——h and Rebecka, Aug. 5, 1709.
——, ch. Joseph and Rebecka, Mar. 1, 1710-11.

BALLERD (see also Ballard), Ellener, d. Joseph and Elizabeth, Aug. 24, 1672.
Hanna, d. William and Grace, Aug. 14, 1655.
John, s. William and Grace, Jan. 17, 1653.
Joseph, s. Joseph and Elizabeth, Jan. 26, [16]67.
Lidda, d. William and Grace, Apr. 30, 1657.

BALLORD (see also Ballard), Molly Smith, d. Joseph, bp. Apr. 22, 1781. C. R. 2.

BAMFORD, Charles R., s. Jesse, spinner, and Maria, Sept. 18, 1846.

BARCLAY, Daniel, s. Peter, flax-dresser, and Ellen, Feb. 25, 1848.

BARDWELL, Elizabeth H., d. Simeon, farmer, and Almira E., b. Salem, Oct. 2, 1849.
Francilia J[enette. C. R. 3.], d. Simeon, farmer, and Elmira E., [Almira P. C. R. 3.], Sept. 2, 1845.
Simeon, s. Rev. Horatio and Rachael, May 13, 1822.

BARKER, Abiel, s. Richard and Sarah, Oct. 12, 1714.
Abiel, s. Abiel and Hannah, May 14, 1736.
Abiell, s. William and Mary, July 15, 1697.
Abigael, d. Benjamin and Mehetebel, Sept. 6 [1725].
Abigail, d. Phillemon and Mary, Apr. 26, 1731.
Abigail, d. Nehemiah and Mary, Jan. 24, 1762.
Abigail, d. Joshua and Ruth, Sept. 29, 1808.
Abigail, d. Jedediah K. and Abigail, Sept. 17, 1823.
Allice, d. Benjamin and Hannah, Feb. 14, 1697-8.
Allice, d. Jonathan and Mary, Apr. 9, 1731.
Andrew, s. Philemon and Mary, Sep. 22, 1741.
Andrew Jackson, s. Samuel F. and Lydia (Meriam), May 3, 1830. P. R. 25.
Ann, d. Nathan, jr. and Ann, Mar. 21, 1743-4.
Ann, d. Richard, jr. and Mehetable, Dec. 9, 1746.
Asa, s. Timothy and Mehetable, Mar. 9, 1745-6.
Asa, s. Timothy and Mehetebel, Dec. 10, 1748.
Benjamin, s. Richard and Hannah, Oct. 23, 1691.
Benjamin, s. Benjamin and Hannah, Feb. 15, 1695-6.
Benjamin, s. Benjamin and Mehetabel, Feb. 14 [1730-31].
Benj[ami]n, s. Joseph and Mehetabel, bp. ——, 1752. C. R. 1.
Benjamin, s. Benjamin and Betty, May 16, 1777.
Benjamine, s. Richard and Joanna, Feb. 28, 1663.
Betsey, d. Benjamin and Betty, Jan. 7, 1788.
Betty, d. John and Mehetabel, May 7, 1771.
Billy, s. John, jr. and Hannah, June 28, 1780.
Bryant Parrot, s. Dr. Moses and Ruth, Aug. 10, 1785.
Caleb, s. twin, Quartermaster John and Sarah, Oct. 21, 1726.
Charles Otis, s. Stephen, jr. and Assena, Mar. 8, 1802.
Charles Otis, s. Nathan, farmer, and Mary J., b. Portland, Me., Sept. 21, 1849.
Charlotte, d. John, jr. and Phebe, Mar. 11, 1788.
Charlotte, d. Henry and Lois, Aug. 5, 1838.
Charlottee, d. Stephen and Asenath, July 26, 1812.
Daniel, s. Zebediah, bp. Feb. 14, 1725. C. R. 2.
Daniel, s. Phillemon and Mary, Oct. 6, 1728.
Daniel, s. Benjamin and Mehetabel, May 11, 1734.
Deborah, d. John and Mary, Mar. 7, 1684-5.
Deborah, d. William and Mary, Feb. 1, 1716-17.
Deborah, d. John, jr. and Mehetebel, Aug. 25, 1754.
Ebenezer, s. Richard and Joanna, Mar. 22, 1651.
Ebenezer, s. Ebenezer and Abigall, May 17, 1687.
Ebenezer, s. Philemon and Mary, Mar. 4, 1735-6.
Ebenezer, s. Philemon and Mary, Mar. 31, 173 [9. C. R. 1.].

BARKER, Edmund, s. Stephen, jr. and Ascene, Sept. 1, 1793.
Elezebith, d. Samuel 3d and Elezebith, Apr. 27, 1748.
Elezebith, d. Stephen and Sarah, Mar. 14, 1749-50.
Elezebith, d. Timothy and Mehetibel, Feb. 24, 1750-51.
Elinor, d. Isaac and Rebecca, Sept. 19, 1796.
Elizabeth, d. Richard and Hannah, Feb. 11, 1688-9.
Elizabeth, d. Samuell and Sarah, —— [1711].
Elizabeth, d. John and Sarah [Mary. C. R. 1.], July 4, 1734.
[Elizabeth. C. R. 1.], d. Abiel and Ann, July —, 1739.
Elizabeth, d. Samuel, jr. and Susanna, Aug. 2, 1776.
Elizabeth, d. John and Phebe, Feb. 25, 1801.
Elizabeth, d. Joshua and Ruth, Jan. 27, 1807.
Elizabeth, d. Capt. Stephen and Asenath [Apr. —, 1810?].
Eliza[bet]h Farnum, d. Phineas and Nabby, Aug. 13, 1790.
Emma, d. Charles, machinist, and Ann, both b. England, Aug. 27, 1848.
Enock, s. Joshua and Martha, bp. Oct. 26, 1766. C. R. 1.
Ephraim, s. John and Mary, Oct. 26, 1692.
Ephraim, s. John and Sarah [bp. Aug. —, 1719. C. R. 1.].
Ephraim, s. William and Martha, May 23, 173 [0. C. R. 1.].
Eunis, d. John, 3d and Mehetebel, Mar. 19, 1749-50.
Franklin M., s. Sam[ue]l M., farmer, and Harriet E., July 25, 1848.
[George Longley. P. R. 16.], s. John, farmer, and Mary, Apr. 15, 1848.
George W., s. Henry and Lois, Oct. 29, 1834.
Hananiah, s. David, of Rumford, bp. June 23, 1734. C. R. 1.
Hanna, d. Richard and Joanna, Oct. 21, 1656.
Hannah [Baker. CT. R.], d. Willia[m] and Mary, Sept. 5, 1681.
Hannah, d. Richard and Hannah, Mar. 11, 1686-7.
Hannah, d. Benj[amin] and Hannah, 8br 18, 1689.
Hannah, d. twin, Ben[jamin] and Mehetebel, Aug. 2, 1722.
Hannah, d. Phillemon and Mary, Mar. 29, 1733.
Hannah, d. Abiel and Hannah, —— 5 [bp. Oct. 7, 1733. C. R. 1.].
Hannah, d. Richard and Ann, of Pelham, bp. ——, 1750. C. R. 1.
Hannah, d. Abiel and Sarah, Jan. 5, 1763.
Hannah, d. John, jr. and Hannah, Apr. 3, 1775.
Hannah, d. John, jr. and Phebe, Oct. 25, 1790.
Hannaniah, s. William and Mary, Apr. 19, 1685.
Harriet, d. Henry and Lois, Apr. 4, 1836.
Harriot, s. John, jr. and Phebe, June 4, 1793.
Henery, s. Stephen, jr. and Assena, Jan. 28, 1800.
Henry Osgood, s. Samuel F. and Lydia (Meriam), Oct. 28, 1825. P. R. 25.

BARKER, [Hepsiba. C. R. 1.], d. John and Sarah, Feb. 27, 1730-31.
Hepsibah, d. William and Mary, Mar. 24, 1686-7.
Hesther, d. Richard and Hannah, Aug. 10, 1695.
Isaac, s. John, jr. and Mehetebel, July 17, 1756.
Isaac, s. Abiel and Sarah, Aug. 24, 1769.
Isaac A[llen. P. R. 25.], s. Samuel F. and Lydia, Nov. 14, 1823.
Isaac H., s. Samuel F. and Lydia, May 4, 1830.
Isaac Henry, s. Samuel F. and Lydia, July 24, 1832.
Jacob, s. Jacob, bp. Aug. 25, 1754. C. R. 2.
Jacob W., s. John, farmer, and Mary, b. Sidney, Me., May 3, 1849.
Jacob Wood, s. John and Phebe, June 14, 1795.
James, s. Stephen and Mary, Aug. 24, 1700.
James, s. Phineas and Sarah, Sept. 10, 1763.
Jedidiah Holt, s. Nathan and Sarah, Oct. 3, 1791.
Joanna, d. John and Mary, July 7, 1687.
Joanna, d. Benjamine and Hannah, —— [1706-7?].
Joanna, d. John, 3d and Mehetebel, Mar. 23, 1747-8.
Johanna, d. John and Sarah, Aug. 3, 1717.
John, s. John and Mary, Nov. 3, 1673.
John, s. William and Mary, Mar. 15, 1688-9.
John, s. William and Mary, Feb. 10, 1689-90.
[Jo]hn, s. John and Sarah, Sept. 5, 1713.
[John. T. C.], s. John and Sarah, Sept. 25, 1714.
[John. C. R. 1.], s. John and Sarah, Aug. 15, 1721.
[John. C. R. 1.], s. Stephen and Mary, Sept. 28, 1721.
John, s. Richard, jr. and Mehetab[el], Feb. 6, 1742-3.
John, s. Abiel and Ann, Nov. 4, 1743.
John, s. twin, John, jr. and Mehetebel, Sept. 27, 1752.
John, s. Stephen and Sarah, Apr. 24, 1753.
John, s. John and Mehetabel, Oct. 22, 1760.
John, s. Abiel and Sarah, Dec. 31, 1764.
John, s. John, jr. and Hannah, Nov. 19, 1770.
John, s. John and Phebe, Dec. 13, 1797. [Dec. 3. P. R. 17.]
John, s. Capt. Stephen and Asenath, Dec. 16, 1814.
John, s. John, farmer, and Mary, Apr. 7, 1845.
Jonas, s. Nathan and Ann, Jan. 24, 1737-8.
[Jonas. C. R. 1.] ——as, s. Nathan and Ann, Dec. 29, 1738.
Jonathan, s. Zebediah, bp. Apr. 28, 1723. C. R. 2.
Jonathan, s. Jonathan and Mary, Oct. 23, 1728.
Jonathan, s. Richard, jr. and Mehiteba[l], Nov. 20, 1748.
Jonathan, s. Joshua and Martha, Sept. 6, 1762.
Jonathan Tyler, s. Capt. Stephen and Assenath, May 28, 1804.
Joseph, s. Benjamin and Hannah, Feb. 20, 1699-1700.

BARKER, Joseph, s. Joseph and Prissilla, Oct. 4, 1[728. C. R. 1.].
Joseph, s. Benjamin and Betty, May 28, 1780.
Joshua, s. Quartermaster John and Sarah, Dec. 7, 1724.
Joshua, s. twin, Quartermaster John and Sarah, Oct. 21, 1726.
Joshua, s. Samuel and Sarah, jr. —— [1727. C. R. 1.].
Joshua, s. Samuel and Sarah, jr., Dec. 23, 1728.
Joshua, s. Samuel, jr. and Susanna, Sept. 20, 1782.
Judeth, d. twin, Benjamin and Mehetebel, Apr. 12, 1728.
Judith, d. Richard and Hannah, Nov. 12, 1699.
Lydia, d. Steephen and Mary, Jan. 28, 1693-4.
Lydia, d. Philemon and Mary, July 18, 1737.
Lydia, d. Joshua and Ruth, Feb. 6, 1812.
Mariah, d. Isaac and Rebekah, July 9, 1798.
Martha, d. Benjamin and Hannah, Feb. 18, 1691-2.
Martha, d. Nathan and Bethiah, — [1714].
Martha, d. twin, Ben[jamin] and Mehetebel, Aug. 2, 1722.
Mary, d. John and Mary, Sept. 3, 1679.
Mary, d. Willia[m] and Mary, May 12, 1695.
Mary, d. Stephen and Mary, Mar. 29, 1696.
Mary, d. Will[ia]m and Mary, — [1711-12?].
[Mary. C. R. 1.] d. John [jr. C. R. 1.] and Sarah, Dec. 24, 1722.
Mary, d. Phillemon and Mary, Apr. 15, 1725.
Mary, d. John, jr. and Sarah, July 10, 1726.
Mary, d. Sarah, and "Reputed" d. Israel How, May 20, 1740.
Mary, d. Nathan and Ann, June 13, 1741.
Mary, d. Nathan, jr. and Mary, Mar. 17, 1754.
Mary, d. Stephen and Sarah, Mar. 16, 1758.
Mary, d. Samuel, jr. and Susanna, Aug. 21, 1778.
Mary, d. John [jr. C. R. 1.] and Phebe, Nov. 22, 1781. P. R. 17.
Mary, d. Capt. Stephen and Assenah, July 8, 1806.
Mary Augusta, d. Henry and Louis, June 19, 1841.
Mary L., d. Nathan, yeoman, and Mary J., Jan. 23, 1847.
Mary Louisa, d. Samuel F. and Lydia (Meriam), Aug. 4, 1828. P. R. 25.
Mehetable, d. Richard, jr. and Mehetabel, Mar. 25, 1744-5.
Mehetable, d. Timothy and Mehetable, Aug. 26, 1747.
Mehetebel, d. twin, Benjamin and Mehetebel, Apr. 12, 1728.
Mehetebel, d. Richard, jr. and Mehetebel, Nov. 21, 1749.
Mehetebel, d. twin, John, jr. and Mehetebel, Sept. 27, 1752.
Mehetebel, d. twin, Samuel, 3d and Elezebith, Dec. 16, 1752.
Mehitabel, d. Samuel and Sarah, June 13, 1716.
Mehitable, d. John, jr. and Hannah, Sept. 23, 1777.
Mehitable, d. Joshua and Ruth, Dec. 21, 1815.
Moses, s. Nathan, 3d and Mary, May 22, 1745.

BARKER, Nabe, d. twin, Samuel, 3d and Elezebith, Dec. 16, 1752.
Nathan, s. Ebenezer and Abigail, Sept. 24, 1688.
Nathan, s. John and Mary, May 23, 1690.
Nathan, s. Nathan, 3d and Mary, Sept. 22, 1743.
Nathan, s. Samuel [3d. C. R. 1.] and Susanna, Aug. 12, 1768.
Nathan, s. Capt. Stephen and Assenath, May 30, 1808.
Nathan A., s., Nathan, farmer, and Mary J., June 19, 1848.
Nehemiah, s. Stephen and Mary, Feb. 17, 1691-2.
Obediah, s. Joshua and Martha, Oct. 20, 1758.
Phebe, d. Abiel and Ann, Aug. 21, 1746.
Phebe, d. Samuel, jr. and Sarah, Jan. 2, 1749-50.
Phebe, d. John, jr. and Phebe, Mar. 9, 1786.
Phebe E[lizabeth. P. R. 16.], d. John, yeoman, and Mary, July 30, 1846.
Phebee, d. Abiel and Jane, bp. Apr. —, 1756. C. R. 1.
Phelemon, s. Phelemon and Mary, Mar. 16, 1726-7.
Phenihas, s. Samuel, 3d and Elisabeth, Mar. 19, 1744-5.
Philemon, s. Ebenezer and Abigail, Apr. 22, 1695.
Phinehas, s. twin, Phinehas and Nabby, Aug. 10, 1775.
Polly, d. John, 3d and Phebe, Nov. 22, 1781.
Polly Crane, d. Dr. Moses and Ruth, Nov. 20, 1777.
Priscilla, d. Benjamin and Hannah, Feb. 25, 1693-4.
Prudence, d. John and Sarah, Feb. 7, 1736-7.
Reb[ecca, d. Isaac and Rebecca. T. C.], May 29, 1792.
Rebeccah, d. Mary and Benj[ami]n Kimball, Feb. 11, 1798.
Reuba, d. John, jr. and Mary, July 9, 1782.
Richard, s. Richard and Joanna, Apr. 10, 1654.
Richard, s. John and Mary, Feb. 20, 1675.
Richard, s. Richard and Hannah, July 24, 1698.
Richard, s. Benjamin and Mehetebel, Oct. 17, 1720.
Richard, s. twin, John, jr. and Hannah, Aug. 21, 1773.
Ruth, d. Joshua and Martha, Sept. 26, 1760.
Sally, d. John, jr. and Phebe, Oct. 11, 1783.
Sally, d. Nathan and Sarah, Mar. 25, 1798.
Samuel, s. William and Mary, Feb. 13, 1691-2.
[Sam]uel, s. Samuel and Sarah, Oct. 10, 1714.
Samuel, s. Samuel, 3d and Elisabeth, Jan. 11, 1742-3.
Samuel, s. twin, Phinehas and Nabby, Aug. 10, 1775.
Samuel, s. Nathan and Sarah, July 1, 1793.
Samuel M[eriam. P. R. 25.], s. Samuel F. and Lydia, Mar. 4, 1822.
Sara, d. Stephen and Sarah, July 16, 1756.
Sarah, d. Richard and Hannah, Nov. 23, 1684.
Sarah [Mary. C. R. 1.], d. John and Sarah, Dec. 13, 1728.

BARKER, Sarah, d. Nathan and Ann, Jan. 18, 1746-7.
Sarah, d. Samuel, jr. and Sarah, Oct. 4, 1747.
Sarah, d. Phineas and Sarah, Mar. 26, 1762.
Sarah, d. John, jr. and Mehetabell, Jan. 9, 1763.
Sarah, d. Phineas, bp. July 28, 1765. C. R. 2.
Sarah, d. Abiel and Sarah, Feb. 4, 1772.
Sarah, d. Benjamin and Betty, May —, 1784. [bp. May 23. C. R. 1.]
Sarah, d. John [jr. C. R. 1.] and Phebe, Oct. 11, 1783. P. R. 17.
Sarah, d. Stephen, jr. and Assenath, Oct. 20, 1795.
Sarah, d. Jed[edia]h and Abigail, May 6, 1831.
Solomon, s. Abiel and Sarah, May 6, 1767.
Stephen, s. William and Mary, June 20, 1683.
Stephen, s. Stephen and Mary, June 26, 1688.
Stephen, s. John, jr. and Sarah, June 15, 1724.
Stephen, s. Stephen and Sarah, Oct. 12, 1771.
Stephen, s. twin, John, jr. and Hannah, Aug. 21, 1773.
Steven, s. Richard and Joan[na], July 6, 1659.
Susanna, d. John, jr. and Mehetebel, Aug. 16, 1758.
Susanna, d. Samuel, jr. and Susanna, Aug. 30, 1770.
Susanna, d. Nathan and Sarah, Jan. 29, 1806.
Susanna F., d. Jedediah and Abigail, Aug. 15, 1826.
Thomas, s. Joseph and Prissilla, F[eb.] 26 [1730-1].
Timothy, s. William and Mary, May 10 [1714].
Timothy, s. William and Mary, Feb. 18, 1720-21.
Timothy, s. Zebediah, bp. May 21, 1721. C. R. 2.
Timothy, s. Mehetebel, wid., "6 months after his father's Death," Feb. 26, 1753.
Vesta Vinal, d. Dr. Moses and Ruth, May 11, 1782.
Wendall Randolph, s. Dr. Moses and Ruth, July 14, 1780.
William, s. Willia[m] and Mary, Jan. 22, 1677.
William, s. Stephen and Asena, Jan. 20, 1798.
Zebediah, s. Stephen and Mary, Feb. 2, 1689-90.
Zebediah, s. Zebediah and Elizabeth, bp. Oct. 5, 1718. C. R. 2.
Zebediah, s. Zebed[iah] and Elizabeth, bp. Mar. 20, 1720. C. R. 2.
——, ch. [torn] and Hannah [1701].
——, ch. [torn], May 12, 1702.
——, ch. Stephen and Mary, —— [1704].
——, ch. [torn] and Mary, Dec. 14, 1704.
——, ch. [torn] and Mary, Mar. 15, 1705-6.
——, ch. [torn] and Hannah, July 14, 1706.
——, ch. Samuell and Sarah, May 30, 1709.
——, ch. [torn]am and Mary, Nov. 12, 1709.

BARKER, ——, ch. [torn] and Sarah, May 2, 1712.
——, ch. Richard and Sarah, Oct. 6, 1712.
——, ch. John and Sarah, Oct. 26, 1715.
——, d. Richard and Sarah, Apr. 10, 1717.
——, d. Richard and Sarah, Sept. 23, 1720.
——, d. Stephen and Mary, Jan. 16, 1724-5.
——, s. twin, Abiel and Ann, Nov. 2, 1742.
——, s. Abial and [torn], Jan. 12, 1749-50.
——, d. Mehetebel, wid. [2 or 3] "months and 23 days after the Death of her father," ——, 175[1].
——, s. Henry and Lois, May 18, 1833.

BARNARD (see also Barnerd, Barnot, Barnott), Abigail, d. James and Abigail, Apr. 10, 1722.
Abigail, d. John [jr. C. R. 2.] and Allice, May 15, 1744.
Abigail, d. Stephen, bp. Apr. 1, 1764. C. R. 2.
Abigail, d. James and Sarah, Feb. 21, 1767.
Abraham [Stickney. C. R. 3.], s. Hermon and Elizabeth, July 22, 1826.
Allice, d. John, jr. and Allice, July 28, 1742.
Anna, d. Robert and Rebecka, Sept. 21, 1719.
Charles Porter, s. Hermon and Elizabeth, bp. Sept. 3, 1843. C. R. 3.
Charles Warren, s. Hermon and Elizabeth, bp. Sept. 4, 1831. C. R. 3.
Daniel, s. Stephen, jr., bp. Jan. 29, 1758. C. R. 2.
David, s. James and Sarah, Nov. 18, 1758.
David, s. John, bp. Jan. 19, 1777. C. R. 2.
David, s. James, jr. and Hannah, May 15, 1794.
David, s. John, jr. and Lydia, Jan. 7, 1797.
David, s. David and Lydia, Oct. 14, 1808.
Edward, s. Rev. John and Sarah [bp. June 15, 1720. C. R. 1.].
Edward Putman, s. Daniel and Betty, May 9, 1787.
Elezebith, d. Stephen [jr. C. R. 2.] and Elezebith, Nov. 17, 1749.
Elisabeth, d. Mr. John and Sarah, June 16 [1732. C. R. 1.].
Elisabeth, d. Rev. John and Sarah, Dec. 20, 1735.
Eliza, d. David and Lydea, Dec. 14, 1813.
Eliza Ann, d. Hermon and Elizabeth, bp. Sept. 3, 1843. C. R. 3.
Francis, s. Gilbert, trader, and Hannah, Mar. 10, 1847.
George, s. James, jr. and Hannah, June 20, 1803.
George Newton, s. Isaac and Elizabeth, bp. Sept. 18, 1842. C. R. 3.
Gilbert, s. John, jr. and Hannah, Aug. 23, 1818.
Hannah, d. Stephen and Rebekah, Mar. 7, 1677-8. [1678-9. CT. R.]

BARNARD, Hannah, d. James and Abigaell, J—— 8 [bp. July 12, 1724. C. R. 2.].
Hannah, d. Theoder and Hannah, July 28, 1724.
Hannah, d. John, jr. and Hannah, Apr. —, 1821.
Henry Francis, s. Isaac C. and Elizabeth, bp. May 6, 1849. C. R. 3.
H. J., ch. Jacob and Hannah, Mar. 21, 1815. P. R. 42.
Henry Justin, s. Jacob and Hannah [May 26. P. R. 42.], 1834. C. R. 3.
Henry O[sgood. C. R. 3.], s. Osgood and Martha [Hannah. C. R. 3.], Feb. 13, 1831.
Herman E., s. Herman and Betsy, bp. Oct. 3, 1824. C. R. 2.
Hermon, s. John, jr. and Lydia, May 9, 1794.
Horatio, s. Hermon and Elizabeth, Apr. 22, 1829.
Isaac Albert, s. Isaac O. and Eliza A., Oct. 15, 1832.
Isaac Osgood, s. John and Lydea, May 10, 1805.
Jacob, s. John and Sarah, Sept. 15, 1730.
Jacob, s. John, jr. and Alice, July 20, 1750.
Jacob, s. John, jr. and Lydia, July 9, 1791. [1792. P. R. 42.]
Jacob W[arren. C. R. 3.], s. Jacob [and Hannah. C. R. 3.], Feb. 14, 1833.
James, s. Stephen and Rebekah, Dec. 28, 1686.
James, s. James and Abigael, Sept. 24, 1727.
James, s. Stephen and Elisabeth, Aug. 7, 1745.
James, s. Stephen, bp. Oct. 31, 1762. C. R. 2.
James, s. James and Sarah, June 27, 1769.
James, s. James, jr. and Hannah, June 26, 1796.
James, s. James, jr. and Hannah, July 4, 1801.
John, s. Stephen and Rebekah, Mar. 25, 1674.
John, s. Mr. Thomas and Elizabeth, Feb. 26, 1689-90.
John, s. John and Amy, Apr. 16, 1697.
John, s. Rev. John and Sarah, Apr. 16, 1723.
John, s. John and Sarah, May 8, 1728.
John, Apr. 20, 1760. P. R. 28.
John, s. John and Sarah, Apr. 24, 1761.
John, s. John, jr. and Lydia, Sept. 26, 1789.
John, s. John, jr. and Hannah, July 20, 1816.
John H., s. Henry F., cabinet maker, and Mary A., Mar. 13, 1846.
Jonathan, s. Robert and Rebeca [bp. Mar. 6, 1721. C. R. 2.]
Joseph, s. James, jr. and Hannah, Oct. 8, 1798.
L. H., ch. Jacob and Hannah, June 19, 1826. P. R. 42.
Lydia, d. John, jr. and Allice, Jan. 23, 1745-6.
Lydia, d. David and Lydia, Feb. 5, 1806.
Lydia, d. John and Lydia, Feb. 10, 1808.
Lydia Maria, d. Isaac O. and Eliza A[nn. C. R. 3.], Apr. 8, 1835.

BARNARD, Martha, d. Robert and Rebecah, Apr. 10, 1722.
Martha A., d. Osgood and Martha, July 9, 1828.
Mary, d. Nathaniel and Ruth, June 2, 1737.
Mary, d. Nathaniel and Ruth, Dec. 4, 1739.
Mary, d. twin, John, jr. and Allice, Jan. 21, 1747-8.
Mary, d. Stephen [jr. C. R. 2.] and Elezebith, Oct. 11, 1751.
Mary Elizabeth, d. Jacob and Hannah [Sept. 21. P. R. 42.], 1831. C. R. 3.
[Mehetabel. C. R. 2.], d. James and Abigael, Feb. 3, 1730-31.
Mehetable, d. John, jr. and Alice, Dec. 17, 1740.
Molly, d. Stephen, bp. July 27, 1760. C. R. 1.
Nabby, d. Daniel and Betty, Jan. 1, 1789.
Nathaniel, s. Nathaniel and Ruth, Mar. 4, 1743-4.
Nathaniell, s. Stephen and Rebeckah, Nov. 31, 1682.
Oran [Ornan. C. R. 2.], s. John and Lydia, Sept. 9, 1803.
Osgood, s. John, jr. and Lydia, Nov. 23, 1799.
Phebe, d. John and Sarah, Feb. 20, 1767.
Phebe, d. John, bp. Jan. 28, 1781. C. R. 2.
Rebecca, d. twin, John, jr. and Allice, Jan. 21, 1747-8.
Robert, s. Stephen and Rebeckah, Mar. 28, 1689.
Ruby, d. David and Lydia, Sept. 22, 1811. [1813. P. R. 20.]
[Samuel. C. R. 2.], s. Nathaniel and Ruth, Aug. 13, 1741.
[Sarah. C. R. 1.], d. Rev. John and Sarah, Apr. 28, 1719.
Sarah, d. John and Sarah, Aug. 7 [1724. C. R. 2.].
Sarah, d. Mr. John and Sarah, Aug. 9, 1727.
[Sarah. C. R. 2.], d. John [jr. C. R. 2.] and Sarah, Feb. 12, 1731-2.
Sarah, d. John and Sarah, Mar. 20, 1758.
Sarah, d. James, bp. Aug. 2, 1761. C. R. 2.
Sarah, d. James and Sarah, June 10, 1764.
Sarah, d. James, jr. and Hannah, Sept. 22, 1792.
Sarah, d. Osgood and Martha, May 6, 1839.
Sarah E[lizabeth. C. R. 3.], d. Isaac O. and Eliza A., June 22, 1829.
Stephen, s. Stephen, bp. Mar. 1, 1767. C. R. 2.
Susanna, d. Stephen and Elisabeth, Oct. 10, 1743.
Susanna, d. Stephen [jr. C. R. 2.] and Elisabeth, Dec. 21, 1747.
Theodore, s. Mr. Thomas and Elizabeth, Feb. 16, 1691-2.
[Theodore, s. C. R. 1.], Theoder and Hannah, Oct. 22, 1722.
Theodore, s. John and Sarah, Dec. 25, 1772.
Thomas, s. Mr. Thomas and Elizabeth, Oct. 20, 1688.
Timothy, s. Nancy and Timothy Poor, Aug. 20, 1819.
——, ch. John, jr. and Hannah, Mar. 18, 1824.
——, d. Jacob and Hannah, June 19, 1826.

BARNERD (see also Barnard), [Benjamin. C. R. 2.] ——amine, s. Robert and Rebecka, Feb. 14, 1715-16.
Elizabeth, d. Theodor and Hannah, N[ov.] — [1718].
James, s. James and Abigail, June 26, 1717.
Lydia, d. Robert and Rebecka, Oct. 12, 1717.
Marcy, d. Robert and Joane, Apr. 8, 1658.
Rebecka, d. twin, Stephen and Hannah, Dec. 17, 1718.
[Robert. C. R. 2.] ——rt, s. Robert and Rebecka, Aug. 30, 1714.
[Sarah. C. R. 2.], d. John and Amy, Apr. 16, 1717.
Stephen, s. twin, Stephen and Hannah, Dec. 17, 1718.
Stephen, s. James and Abigail, July 31, 17[19. C. R. 2.].
[torn]h, d. Stephen and Hannah, Jan. 27, 1715-16.

BARNES, Mary A., d. Moses D. and Eunice, June 24, 1840.

BARNET, [torn], ch. [torn], Mar. 18, 1702-3.

BARNOT (see also Barnard), [Sarah Barnard. C. R. 2.], ch. [Robe]rt and Rebecka, Sept. 22, 1712.

BARNOTT (see also Barnard), ——, ch. [torn] and Eamy, —— [1701].

BARRETT, Ellen Augusta, d. Charles, tin-plate worker, and Mary A., July 9, 1847.

BARRON, Anna, d. Thomas and Sarah, bp. Oct. 18, 1840. C. R. 4.
Charles, s. Thomas and Sally, Nov. 3, 1830.
Charles Howarth, s. Thomas and Sarah, bp. July 21, 1839. C. R. 4.
Elizabeth Jane, d. Thomas and Sarah, bp. July 21, 1839. C. R. 4.
Ellen Arkworth, d. Thomas, flannel dresser, and Sally, May 24, 1847.
Lucy Ann, d. Thomas and Sarah, bp. July 21, 1839. C. R. 4.

BARTLETT, Daniel, s. Daniel and Hannah, Oct. 17, 1801.
Hannah, d. Daniel and Hannah, July 24, 1800.
Morris S., s. Levi, farmer, and Julia, Apr. 4, 1846.
——, d. Geo[rge] K., Nov. 17, 1826.

BARTON, Bradford Henry, s. Bradford and Sarah, Sept. 5, 1836.
Sarah Elizabeth, d. Bradford and Sarah, Dec. 31, 1838.

BATCHELDER (see also Bacheller, Bachellor, Batcheller, Batchellor), Anna Carlton, d. Joseph, jr. and Phebe, Apr. 2, 1781.
Sarah, d. Uzziel and Sarah, bp. June 6, 1779. C. R. 1.
Uzziel Ray, s. Uzziel and Sarah, bp. Nov. 5, 1780. C. R. 1.

BATCHELLER (see also Batchelder), ——, ch. Capt. Jeremiah, Feb. 1, 1818.

BATCHELLOR (see also Batchelder), Judith, d. Sam[ue]l and Judith, bp. Jan. 13, 1765. C. R. 1.

BATES, Ann Louise, d. John S., carpenter, and Mercy, Mar. 12, 1849.
Lavinia Bacon, d. ——, bp. Apr. 8, 1837. C. R. 6.
William Henry, s. ——, bp. Apr. 8, 1837. C. R. 6.

BATTLES, Helen Maria, d. Winslow and Charlotte, July 18, 1838.
Helen Maria, d. Winslow and Elizabeth, bp. Sept. 18, 1842. C. R. 3.
Otis W., s. Winslow and Charlotte, Dec. 24, 1833.
Otis Winslow, s. Winslow and Elizabeth, bp. Sept. 18, 1842. C. R. 3.

BAXBY (see also Bixby), [Daniel, s. Mephibosheth. C. R. 2.] and Mary, Dec. 31, 1713.
David, s. twin, Mephibosheth and Mary, Mar. 31, 1718-19. [*sic*]
Hannah, d. Joseph and Experiance, Aug. 19, 172[6. C. R. 2.].
Jonathan, s. twin, Mephibosheth and Mary, Mar. 31, 1718-19. [*sic*]
Martha, d. Mephibosheth and Mary Mar. 2, 1721-2.
Mary, d. Tho[ma]s and Deborah, Mar. [1710].
Mary, d. Mephibosheth and Mary [bp. Feb. 13, 1715. C. R. 2.].
[Nat[hanie]ll. C. R. 2.] —aniel, s. Mephibosheth and Mary, Mar. 24, 1718-19.
Samuel, s. Mephibosheth and Mary, Aug. 31, 1716.

BAXTER, Daniel, s. twin, illegitimate, Elezebith, Sept. 4, 1748.
Jonathan, s. William and Elisabeth, Feb. 11, 1744-5.
Samuel, s. twin, illegitimate, Elezebith, Sept. 4, 1748.
William, s. William and Elizabeth, Feb. 14, 1742-3.

BAYLE (see also Bailey), Dorathy, d. Samuel, jr. and Hannah, Jan. 25, 1756.
Enoch, s. Capt. Enock and Presila, Aug. 9, 1757.
Levi, s. Samuel and Mary, Nov. 2, 1739.

BAYLEY (see also Bailey), Anna, d. Nathan and Deborah, Feb. 10, 1769.
Chloe, d. Nathan [jr. C. R. 2.] and Deborah, Apr. 22, 1773.
Deborah, d. Nathan [jr. C. R. 2.] and Deborah, Jan. 2, 1763.

BAYLEY, Dolly, d. Nathan and Deborah, Dec. 10, 1777.
Elisabeth, d. Edward and Elisabeth, Feb. 17, 1735-6.
Elizabeth, d. Ebenezer and Elizabeth, Oct. 9, 1767.
Elizabeth, d. Moses and Elizabeth, July 6, 1768.
Hannah, d. Nathan [jr. C. R. 2.] and Deborah, Dec. 21, 1765. [bp. Dec. 23, 1764. C. R. 2.]
Joshua, s. Moses and Elizabeth, Aug. 14, 1770.
Mary, d. Nathan and Deborah, Jan. 2, 1767.
Molle, d. John and Hannah, Dec. 23, 1760.
Moses, s. Moses and Eliz[abe]th, Oct. 20, 1766.
Nathan, s. Nathan [jr. C. R. 2.], and Deborah, Apr. 2, 1771.
Obadiah, s. Nathan and Deborah, May 31, 1775.
Phebe, d. Nathan and Debor[ah], Sept. 9, 1781.
Sarah, d. Eben[eze]r and Eliz[abe]th, Jan. 7, 1770.

BAYLY (see also Bailey), James, s. James and Sarah, bp. ——, 1721. C. R. 1.

BEAN (see also Beane), Abigail V., d. Levi and Mary, Dec. 7, 1825.
Arthur N., s. Levi and Mary, Mar. 13, 1824.
George, s. Samuel, manufacturer, and Sarah, Sept. 4, 1843.
Hannah A. L., d. Joel W., mason, b. N. H., and Martha J., Oct. 25, 1849.
Henry, s. Levi and Mary, Aug. 15, 1828.
Laura C., d. Arthur M., stablekeeper, and Caroline E., Dec. 17, 1848.
Mary E., d. Levi and Mary, June 16, 1833.
——, d. Elijah, Dec. 24, 1827.

BEANE (see also Bean), Samuel G., s. Levi and Mary, Aug. 20, 1819.

BEARD, Rheuben, s. Rheuben and Clarissa, Feb. 25, 1808.

BEAUMONT, Arthur, s. William, weaver, and Susanna, both b. England, June 6, 1848.

BEAVENS (see also Bevens), Andrew, s. Edward and Mary, Dec. 31, 1746.
[M. T. C.] ary, d. Edward and Mary, Dec. 17, 1736.
Mary, d. Edward and Mary, Oct. 13, 1742.
Susanna, d. Edward and Mary, Dec. 16, 1740.

BEAVERLY (see also Beverly), John, s. David and Hannah, Nov. 22, 1737.

BECKET, John R., s. Alexander, farmer, and Charlotte, Feb. 4, 1845.

BECKFORD, Jacob O., s. Henry S. and Mary A., Nov. 26, 1830.

BELL, Anne Maria, d. William and Ann, bp. Jan. 23, 1842. C. R. 4.
George Webster, s. William and Ann, bp. Apr. 10, 1846. C. R. 4.
Isabella Jane, d. William and Ann, bp. Oct. 21, 1838. C. R. 4.
Joseph W[illiam. C. R. 4.], s. William and Anna, Sept. 18, 1839.
Joshua, s. William, manufacturer, and Ann, Nov. 9, 1845.
Robert, s. William, laborer, and Blythe, Aug. 26, 1848.
William Henry, s. William and Anne, Dec. 31, 1837.

BENNET (see also Bennett), Elias Hammond, s. Amos, bp. Nov. 17, 1782. C. R. 1.
John, s. Amos, bp. Aug. 29, 1784. C. R. 1.

BENNETT (see also Bennet), Edward Jarvis, s. Charles, spinner, and Mary Ann, Oct. 4, 1844.
Roselia Elizabeth, d. Luther S., laborer, and Mary A., June 3, 1848.

BEREY (see also Berry), Sarah, d. Ens. Benjamin and Prisala, Jan. 20, 1758.

BERRY (see also Berey), Abigail, d. Elijah and Nabby, Sept. 9, 1809.
Albert, s. Jacob and Susannah (Winchester), Nov. 18, 1830. P. R. 39.
Ambros, s. Benjamin and Hannah, Dec. 28, 1795.
Amos, s. Nathaniel and Lydia, Aug. 14, 1805.
[Anceil. P. R. 39.], s. Jacob and Susan, July 19, 1822.
Benjamin, s. Benj[ami]n, jr. and Phebe, bp. Sept. 7, 1777. C. R. 1.
Betsy, May 26, 1776. P. R. 21.
Betty, d. Benj[ami]n, jr., bp. June 25, 1780. C. R. 1.
Caroline S., d. Jacob and Susannah (Winchester), June 14, 1840. P. R. 39.
Daniel, s. Capt. Benjamin, bp. Feb. 16, 1777. C. R. 1.
Daniel, s. Israel and Serena, Feb. 8, 1818.
Daniel G., Oct. 21, 1818. P. R. 26.
Daniel P., s. Daniel [G. P. R. 26.], yeoman, and Susan, Sept. 17, 1846. [Sept. 29. P. R. 26.]

BERRY, Edward, s. Benjamin and Hannah, Feb. 5, 1789.
Elbert, s. Israel and Serena, Nov. 5, 1842.
Ellen A[ugusta. C. R. 2.], d. Israel and Serena, Mar. 31, 1840.
Eunice Hayward, d. Elijah and Nabby, Feb. 27, 1804.
Fidelia, d. Jacob and Susannah (Winchester), June 24, 1833. P. R. 39.
Hannah, d. Benj[ami]n, jr. and Mary, Nov. 3, 1761.
Hannah, d. Nath[anie]l and Lydia, Sept. 15, 1813.
Hannah Osgood, d. Nathaniel and Lydia, July 12, 1812. C. R. 1.
Harriot, d. Lt. Nathaniel and Lydia, Dec. 31, 1806.
Henery Putnam, s. Elijah and Nabby, May 13, 1806.
Henry, s. Jacob and Susannah, Sept. 21, 1828.
Herman, s. Nathaniel and Lydia, Jan. 18, 1804.
Hiram, s. Jacob and Susannah, Aug. 25, 1818.
Hiram, s. Jacob and Susan, June 25, 1820.
Hitty, d. Benj[ami]n, jr. and Mary, bp. Apr. 17, 1768. C. R. 1.
Horace, s. Amos and Rebecca, June 19, 1838.
Jacob, s. Benj[ami]n, jr. and Mary, May 7, 1766.
Jacob, s. Jacob and Susannah, Mar. 21, 1817.
Jacob W., s. Jacob and Susannah, Sept. 14, 1837. P. R. 39.
Jacob W., s. Daniel [G. P. R. 26.], farmer, and Susan, Feb. 29, 1844. [Jan. 29. P. R. 26.]
John, s. Ens. Benjamin and Priscilla, Jan. 13, 1756.
John, s. John and Unic, bp. Sept. 27, 1789. C. R. 1.
Joseph, s. Benjamin and Phebe, bp. Nov. 8, 1789. C. R. 1.
Loiza, d. Jacob and Susanna, Sept. 4, 1826.
Lucy, d. Benj[ami]n, jr., bp. July 13, 1777. C. R. 1.
Lucy, d. Elijah and Nabby, May 21, 1816.
Lydia [Abbot. C. R. 1.], d. Nathaniel and Lydia, Aug. 31, 1801.
Mariah [Fanny. C. R. 1.], d. Capt. Nathaniel and Lydia, Apr. 24, 1810. [May 24. P. R. 15.]
Mary A[nn. C. R. 1.], d. Capt. Nath[anie]l and Lydia, Mar. 4, 1823.
Molly, d. Benj[amin], jr. and Mary, bp. Aug. 17, 1760. C. R. 1.
Nancy Robinson, d. Benj[ami]n, jr., bp. Feb. 2, 1783. C. R. 1.
Nathanel, Mar. 27, 1776. P. R. 15.
Olive, d. Elijah and Nabby, Apr. 29, 1813.
Osgood, s. Benjamin and Hannah, June 30, 1792.
Phebe, d. Benjamin [jr. C. R. 1.] and Phebe, Feb. 26, 1773.
Priscilla, d. Benj[ami]n, jr. and Mary, May 20, 1760.
Rebecca, d. Capt. Nathaniel and Lydia, Nov. 4, 1808.
Rhoda, d. Benj[ami]n [jr. C. R. 1.] and Phebe, Aug. 24, 1774.
Samuel, s. Jacob and Susannah (Winchester), July 28, 1835. P. R. 39.

BERRY, Sarah, d. Benjamin, jr. and Mary, Aug. 6, 1763.
Susannah, d. Jacob and Susan, Sept. 21, 1824.
Timothy, s. Benj[ami]n, jr. and Phebe, May 30, 1771.
William, s. Capt. Nath[anie]l and Lydia, July 23, 1817.
——, s. Elijah and Nabby, Oct. 21, 1818.
——, s. Benjamin and Priscilla, July 29, 1743.

BEVENS (see also Beavens, Bevins), Edward, s. Edward and Mary, Oct. 20, 1730.
Elisabeth, d. Edward and Mary, May 26, 1744.
John, s. Edward and Mary, Feb. 15, 1734-5.

BEVERLEY (see also Beverly), Asa, s. David and Ruth, Oct. 9, 1776.
Daniel, s. David and Ruth, Aug. 21, 1775.
Martha, d. Hannah, "a Legetemat Daughter," Oct. 21, 1754.
Tabitha, d. David and Hannah, May 5, 1742.

BEVERLY (see also Beaverly, Beverley), Charlottee, d. Joel and Hannah, July 7, 1820.
David, s. David and Hannah, Feb. 12, 1733-4.
David, s. David and Hannah, Aug. 2, 1739.
David, s. David and Hannah, bp. ——, 1744. C. R. I.
David, s. David, jr. and Ruth, Aug. 3, 1767.
David Farnum, s. Daniel and Hannah, Jan. 30, 1812.
Hanah, d. David and Hannah, Sept. 11, 1731.
Hannah, d. David and Hannah, Jan. 24, 1725-6.
Hannah, d. David and Hannah, bp. ——, 1744. C. R. I.
Harriet A., d. Joel and Hannah, Aug. 12, 1827.
James, s. David and Hannah, Jan. 19, 1723-4.
James, s. Daniel and Hannah, Dec. 12, 1806.
Jédediah, s. David and Ruth, Oct. 17, 1765.
Joel, s. John and Lydia, Mar. 5, 1794.
John, s. David and Hannah, Apr. 19, 1744.
John Calvin, s. Daniel and Hannah, July —, 1818.
Jona[than] E., s. Daniel and Hannah, June 15, 1820.
Lydia, d. David and Ruth, bp. Mar. 1, 1772. C. R. I.
Lydia H., d. Daniel and Hannah, Jan. 31, 1814.
Lydia Hildrith, d. Daniel and Hannah, Jan. 10, 1809.
Margaret E., bp. July 13, 1823. C. R. 2.
Mary, d. David and Hannah, Feb. 2, 172 [8-9].
Mary, d. David, bp. ——, 1748. C. R. I.
Mary Ann, d. John and Sally, July 20, 1826.
Permelia A., d. Daniel and Hannah, Feb. 20, 1804.

BEVERLY, Phebe, d. John and Lydia, Aug. 25, 1798.
Samuel, s. David and Hannah, Aug. 8, 1748.
Samuel Dale, s. Lydia, June 21, 1800.
Tryphena Hills, d. Daniel and Hannah, Jan. 29, 1816.
William H., s. Joel and Hannah, Mar. 1, 1823.
——, ch. Daniel and Hannah, Jan. 24, 1815.

BEVINS (see also Bevens), Nathaniel, s. Edward and Mary, Jan. 16, 1731-2.

BICKNELL, Emma Amelia, d. David C., manufacturer, and Emily P., Apr. 24, 1849.

BIGSBIE (see also Bixby), Daniell, s. Daniell and Hannah, Sept. 18, 1675.
David, s. Daniel and Hannah, Feb. 15, 1687-8.
Hannah, d. Daniell and Hannah, Dec. 13, 1679.
Joseph, s. Daniel and Hannah, Mar. 5, 1695-6.
Mephibosheth, s. Daniell and Hannah, Apr. 3, 1690.
Sarah, d. Daniell and Hannah, Jan. 19, 1683.
Thomas, s. Daniell and Hannah, Dec. 18, 1681.

BIGSBY (see also Bixby), Amos B., s. Alvin, laborer, and Nancy, Dec. 10, 184 [7 or 8].
Charles M., Moses, laborer, and Vesta, Oct. 30, 184 [7 or 8].
Mary, d. Daniel and Hannah, Apr. 10, 1693.
——, ch. Thomas and Deborah, Oct. 9, 1704.

BINGHAM, Anna, d. Henry, finisher, and Anna, Sept. 19, 1846.
John Williams, s. Henry, presser, and Ann, Jan. 22, 1848.

BINNS, Jane, d. Stephen and Maria, Oct. 17, 1829.

BIRD, Luke, s. Michael, laborer, and Mary, Sept. 10, 1848.

BIRT (see also Burt), Nathan, s. Elisabeth, bp. Sept. 10, 1786. C. R. 2.

BIXBEE (see also Bixby), Experiance, d. Joseph and Experiance, Mar. 12, 172 [4. C. R. 2.].

BIXBY (see also Baxby, Bigsbie, Bigsby, Bixbee), James R., s. Alvin, laborer, and Nancy, July 2, 1846.

BLACKBURN, Belinda Pilling, June 18, 1842. P. R. 27.
Mary Ann, Mar. 5, 1840. P. R. 27.
——, d. Richard, May 28, 1820.

BLAKELY, Elizabeth, d. Charles, gardener, and Margaret, Aug. 25, 1847.

BLANCHARD (see also Blancherd), Aaron, s. Thomas [jr. C. R. 2.] and Elisabeth, July 27, 1740.
Aaron, s. Aaron and Nelly, Aug. 12, 1766.
Abiel, s. Benjamin and Mary, Sept. 25, 1737.
Abiel, s. Benjamin and Mary, Oct. 20, 1741.
Abigail, d. Josiah and Sarah, Sept. 23, 1734.
Abigail, d. Jame and Abigail, Apr. 7, 1766.
Abigail, bp. June 8, 1828. C. R. 2.
Abner, s. James and Abigail, May 23, 1764.
Alexis R., s. Amos, jr. and Clarissa, July 19, 1832.
Amos, s. Daniel and Jerusha, Jan. —, 1766. T. C.
Amos, s. Aaron and Nelly, Sept. 1, 1777.
Amos, s. Amos and Elizabeth, Mar. 7, 1807.
Anna, d. James and Abigail, June 28, 1768.
Anne, d. Johnathan and Anne, Apr. 6, 1691.
[Anne. C. R. 2.], d. Benjamin and Mary, Nov. 22, 1722.
[Annis. C. R. 2.], d. Stephen and Deborah, June 26, 1736.
Arthur C., s. Amos, jr. and Clarissa, Jan. 29, 1831.
Bathsheba, d. Nathan and Bathsheba, Apr. 20, 1754.
Benjamin, s. Johnathan and Anne, Feb. 14, 1692-3.
Benjamin, s. Benjamin and Mary, Mar. — [bp. Mar. 19, 1720-21. C. R. 2.].
Benjamin, s. Josiah and Sarah, July 3, 1750.
Benjamin, s. Aaron, bp. Jan. 6, 1793. C. R. 2.
Betty, d. Thomas, bp. Feb. 14, 1790. C. R. 2.
Caleb, s. Samuel and Ruth, Mar. 18, 1760.
Caroline Green, d. W[illia]m and Car[oline], bp. Mar. 19, 1837. C. R. 2.
Cherlotte, d. Samuel, jr. and Lucy, Oct. 9, 1785.
Cyrene, d. Amos and Lavina, Oct. 12, 1800.
Daniel, s. Joseph and Sarah, July 15, 1735.
Daniel, s. Daniel and Jerusha, Sept. 20, 1759.
Darcus, d. Benjamin and Mary, Mar. 28, 1730.
David, s. Johnathan and Anne, June 8, 1687.
David, s. Benjamin and Mary, Feb. 19, 1739-40.
David, s. Stephen and Deborah, Apr. 10, 1740.

BLANCHARD, David, s. David and Margaret, Mar. 19, 1762.
[Deborah. T. C.], d. Thomas and Rose, Apr. 18, 1712.
Deborah, d. Stephen and Deborah [Feb.] 26 [1724-5].
Deborah, d. Stephen, bp. Nov. 26, 1727. C. R. 2.
Dinah, d. Stephen and Deborah, Dec. 28, 1731.
Dorothy, d. Jeremiah, bp. Nov. 3, 1776. C. R. 2.
Eber, s. Jeremiah and Dorothy, Jan. 14, 1769.
Edmond, s. Amos and Elizabeth, bp. Nov. 13, 1814. C. R. 2.
Edward, s. Amos and Elizabeth, Nov. 1, 1814.
Elezebeth, d. Benjamin and Mary, May 17, 1734.
Eli, s. Amos, bp. Mar. 6, 1803. C. R. 2.
Elisabeth, d. Josiah and Sarah, Apr. 3, 1738.
Elizabeth, d. Thomas [jr. C. R. 2.] and Elizabeth, July 20, 1733.
[E]lizabeth, d. James and Elizabeth, Mar. 21, 1760.
Elizabeth Orne, d. W[illia]m and Caroline M., bp. July 26, 1840. C. R. 2.
Elizebeth, d. Joseph and Sarah, July 17, 1726.
Emery Chase, s. Aaron, bp. Aug. 8, 1790. C. R. 2.
Eunice, d. Josiah and Sarah, Oct. 30, 1742.
Eunice, d. Samuel and Ruth, Aug. 12, 1755.
Fredrick, s. Samuel, jr. and Lucy, Dec. 14, 1775.
Fredrick, s. Samuel, jr., bp. Oct. 25, 1778. C. R. 2.
Hannah, d. Joseph and Sarah, Oct. 8, 1728.
Hannah, d. Stephen, jr., July 20, 1752.
Hannah, d. Josiah [jr. C. R. 2.] and Lydia, Oct. 19, 1769.
Hannah, d. Daniel, bp. Feb. 4, 1776. C. R. 2.
Hannah, d. Sam[ue]ll, jr. and Lucy, Apr. 19, 1793.
Henry, s. Samuel, jr. and Rhoda, Feb. 11, 1787.
Isaac, s. Thomas and Hannah, Oct. 9, 1723.
Isaac, s. Thomas, jr. and Elisabeth, Feb. 18, 1744-5.
Isaac, s. David [Daniel. C. R. 2.] and Jerusha, Sept. 14, 1763.
Isaac, s. Josiah, jr., bp. Oct. 17, 1779. C. R. 2.
Jacob, s. Johnathan and Anne, Feb. 19, 1688-9.
Jacob, s. Benjamin and Mary, May 11, 1724.
Jacob, s. Stephen and Deborah, Mar. 28, 1743.
Jacob, s. Stephen [jr. C. R. 2.] and Hannah, June 22, 1758.
James, s. Stephen and Deborah, Dec. 5, 1733.
James, s. James and Elizabeth, Feb. 6, 1759.
James, s. James and Abigail, Mar. 16, 1763.
James P., s. James P. and Mary Ann, Sept. 29, 1833.
Jedediah, s. Samuel, jr. and Lucy, Dec. 7, 1783.
[Jeremiah. C. R. 2.], s. Joseph and Sarah, June —, 1733. [bp. June 24. C. R. 2.]
Jeremiah, s. Jeremiah and Dorothy, Oct. 10, 1759.

BLANCHARD, Jerusha, d. Daniel and Jerusha, June 24, 1761.
John, s. Joseph and Sarah, July 19, 1737.
John, s. Stephen, jr. and Hannah, Feb. 16, 1767.
John, s. Joseph and Dinah, Feb. 20, 1768.
John, s. Aaron and Nelly, June 1, 1772.
John, s. Samuel, jr. and Lucy, Mar. 17, 1787.
John, s. John and Dorcas, May 2, 1790.
Johnathan, s. Johnathan and Anne, Feb. 28, 1685-6.
Jonathan, s. Benjamin and Mary, Feb. 7, 1727-8.
Jonathan, s. Stephen and Deborah, Mar. 8, 1737-8.
Joseph, s. Thomas and Rose, Feb. 19, 1700-1701.
Joseph, s. Joseph and Sarah, Feb. 9, 1730-31.
Joseph, s. Joseph, jr. and Dinah, May 20, 1754.
Joseph, s. Joseph and Dinah, Apr. 10, 1765.
Joshua, s. Benjamin and Mary, —— 28 [bp. May 29, 1726. C. R. 2.].
Joshua, s. Sam[ue]ll and Ruth, July 25, 1769.
Joshua, s. Samuel, jr. and Lucy, Mar. 1, 1789.
[Josiah, s. T. C.] Thomas and Rose, Aug. 16, 1704.
Josiah, s. Josiah and Sarah, Oct. 10, 17[40. C. R. 2.].
Josiah, s. Josiah and Sarah, Nov. 13, 1746.
Josiah, s. Josiah, jr., bp. at Tewksbury, Sept. 8, 1771. C. R. 2.
Judith, d. Jeremiah, bp. June 13, 1779. C. R. 2.
Lois, d. Tho[ma]s, bp. Sept. 7, 1783. C. R. 2.
Lois, d. Thomas, bp. Oct. 24, 1784. C. R. 2.
Lucy, d. Daniel and Jerusha, Jan. —, 1771. T. C.
Lucy, d. Aaron and Nelle, Feb. 12, 1774.
Lucy, d. Sam[ue]ll, jr. and Lucy, June 6, 1777.
Lucy, d. Aaron and Nelly, June 10, 1780.
Lydea, d. Thomas, jr. and Elizebeth, Jan. 30, 1747-8.
Lydia, d. Josiah, jr. and Lydia, Aug. 3, 1766.
Lydia H., d. Abel and Elezabeth, Apr. 26, 1828.
Margaret J[ennett. C. R. 2.], d. Abel and Elizabeth, Jan. 25, 1831.
Mary, d. Johnathan and Anne, Dec. 2, 1696.
[Mary. C. R. 2.], d. Stephen and Deborah, June 4, 1728.
Mary, d. Stephen, jr. and Hannah, Aug. 9, 1760.
Mary, d. Samuel and Ruth, Feb. 4, 1762.
Mary, d. Aaron and Nelle, Sept. 2, 1764.
Mary, d. Aaron and Nelly, Mar. 17, 1786.
Mary Ann, d. James and Mary A., Feb. 27, 1830.
Mary Ballard, d. Sam[ue]ll and Lucy, Dec. 14, 1794.
Mary E[lizabeth. C. R. 2.], d. Abel and Elizabeth, Dec. 14, 1829.
Molly, d. Josiah, jr., bp. Mar. 16, 1783. C. R. 2.

BLANCHARD, Molly, d. twin, Thomas, bp. Dec. 21, 1788. C. R. 2.
Nathan, s. Stephen and Deborah, Mar. 30, 1730.
Nelle, d. Aaron, bp. Jan. 7, 1776. C. R. 2.
Nelly, d. Aaron and Nelly, Apr. 20, 1770.
Peter, s. Jeremiah and Dorothy, Aug. 12, 1767.
Phebe, d. Joseph and Sarah, Nov. 3, 1741.
Phebe, d. Stephen [jr. C. R. 2.] and Hannah, Dec. 15, 1762.
Phineas, s. Stephen, jr. and Hannah, June 21, 1750.
Priscy, d. twin, Thomas, bp. Dec. 21, 1788. C. R. 2.
Rebecca, d. Daniel and Jerusha, May —, 1768. T. C.
Ruth, d. Samuel, jr. and R[torn], Aug. 18, 1751.
Samuel, s. Samuel, jr. and Ruth, Nov. 7, 1753.
Samuel, s. Aaron, bp. Sept. 7, 1777. C. R. 2.
Samuel, s. Samuel, jr. and Lucy, May 11, 1779.
Samuel Jenkins, s. Josiah, bp. July 2, 1786. C. R. 2.
Sarah, d. Joseph and Sarah, July 25, 1723.
Sarah, d. Josiah and Sarah, Feb. 27, 1731-2.
Sarah, d. Stephen, jr. and Hannah, Feb. 27, 1755.
Sarah, d. Jeremiah, bp. Nov. 13, 1774. C. R. 2.
Solomon, s. Samuel and Ruth, Feb. 26, 1757.
Solomon, s. Samuel and Ruth, Feb. 2, 1765.
Solomon, s. Sam[ue]ll, jr. and Lucy, Apr. 23, 1791.
Stephen, s. Stephen and Deborah, Aug. 9, 172[6].
Stephen, s. Stephen, jr. and Hannah, Jan. 4, 1748-9.
Susanna, d. Thomas, jr. and Elisabeth, Mar. 19, 1741-2.
Susanna, d. Aaron and Nelly, May 23, 1768.
Susanna, d. Aaron and Nelly, June 18, 1782.
Susanna, d. Aaron and Nelly, Mar. 20, 1784.
Thomas, s. Thoma[s] and Rose, Jan. 15, 1699-1700.
Thomas, s. Thomas [jr. C. R. 2.] and Elisabeth, Jan. 20, 1734-5.
Thomas, s. Aaron and Nelle, Nov. 11, 1762.
Thomas, s. Tho[ma]s, bp. Oct. 1, 1786. C. R. 2.
Timothy, s. Thomas [jr. C. R. 2.] and Elisabeth,[1] Sept. 26, 1737.
Timothy, s. Samuel, jr. and Lucy, Nov. 17, 1795.
William, s. Samuel, jr. and Lucy, July 8, 1781.
——, ch. [torn] and Anne, —— [1702].
——, d. Thomas and Rose, Mar. 25, 1705-6.
——, s. Benjamin and Mary, Feb. 14, 1731-2.
——, ch. James and Mary Ann, Oct. 30, 1831.

BLANCHERD (see also Blanchard), Abiel, s. Daniel, bp. Apr. 4, 1773. C. R. 2.
Hannah, d. Thomas and Ro[se], —— [1706-7?].

BLANCHERD, Hannah, d. Samuel and Sarah, Oct. 7, 1719.
Henry, s. Jeremiah, bp. July 25, 1773. C. R. 2.
Isaac, s. Josiah, jr., bp. Dec. 17, 1775. C. R. 2.
[Lydia. T. C.], d. Thomas and Roas, Aug. 21, 1714.
Mary, d. Benjamine and Mary, Dec. — [bp. Dec. 6, 1719. C. R. 2.].
Mehetabel, d. Thomas and Hannah, Oct. 3, 1716.
[Nathaniel, s. T. C.], Thomas and Hannah, Feb. 2, 1718-19.
Pheoby, d. Samuel and Sarah, May 29, 1[715. C. R. 2.].
Roase, d. Thomas and Rose [Jan. 12, 1709-10. T. C.].
[Samuel. C. R. 2.], s. Samuel and Sarah, Jan. 14, 1716-17.
[Sarah. C. R. 2.], d. Samuel and Sarah, May 9, 1712.

BLANY, James, s. Nicholas and Ann, bp. Dec. 27, 1836. C. R. 1.

BLOOD, Albert, s. Rodgers and Martha, Apr. 9, 1818.
Albert F., s. Albert, machinist, and Elizabeth, June 17, 1844.
Barfield T., s. Rodgers and Martha, Mar. 2, 1825.
Charles, s. Rodgers and Martha, Dec. 28, 1822.
Edwin G., s. Albert, machinist, and Elizabeth, b. Tamworth, N. H., Sept. 15, 1849.
George B., s. Albert, machinist, and Elizabeth, Mar. 1, 1846.
George Warren, s. Rodgers and Martha, Dec. 11, 1839.
Hiram, s. Rodgers and Martha, June 3, 1832.
James Cochran, s. Rodgers and Martha, Dec. 23, 1827.
Jonathan K., s. Rogers and Martha, Mar. 31, 1816.
Julia, d. Rodgers and Martha, Mar. 9, 1841.
Lewis Cochran, s. Rodgers and Martha, July 22, 1820.
Martha M., d. Rogers and Martha, Mar. 6, 1829.
Nathan, s. Rodgers and Martha, Oct. 29, 1836.
Nathan, s. Rodgers and Martha, Oct. 29, 1837.
Roxanna, d. Rodgers and Martha, Aug. 4, 1834.

BLUNT (see also Blunte), Abigail, d. Isaac, bp. Oct. 11, 1761. C. R. 2.
Abigail, d. Isaac and Mary, Oct. 6, 1762.
Angelina L., d. Samuel and Perses, July 16, 1830.
Ann, d. Hamborough and Mehitabell, —— [1706-7?].
Anna, d. Isaac and Mary, May 9, 1763.
Anna, d. John, bp. Aug. 10, 1788. C. R. 2.
Anna, d. Isaac and Lois, Mar. 1, 1801.
Anne, d. Willia[m] and Elizabeth, Apr. 25, 1687.
Bathsheba, d. William and Elizabeth, Nov. 13, 1684. [Nov. 31. *sic.* CT. R.]
Charles C., s. Samuel P. and Persis, Sept. 7, 1832.

BLUNT, Charles C., s. Samuel P. and Persis, Dec. 29, 1833.
David, s. William and Sarah, Nov. 18, 1699.
David, s. David and Lydea, Mar. 9, 1728-9.
David, s. David and Mary, Jan. 11, 1740-41.
David, s. Lt. David and Polly, May 5, 1811.
Ebenezer, s. William and Sarah, Mar. 8, 1716-17.
Elezebith, d. Isaac and Mary, July 27, 1752.
Eliza, d. Isaac and Lois, July 17, 1803.
[Elizabeth. C. R. 2.] ——abeth, d. William and Sarah, Sept. 26, 1714.
Ephraim, s. Ephraim and Zerviah, bp. Aug. 9, 1747. C. R. 2.
[Ep]hraim [Ephraim. C. R. 2.], s. William and Sarah, Feb. 5, 1720-21.
Hanburrough, s. William and Elizabeth, Sept. 22, 1681. [Nov. 22. CT. R.]
Hannah, d. Hamborough and [torn], —— [1710].
[Hannah. T. C.] ——ah, d. Isaac and Marey, Sept. 25, 1748.
Hannah, d. Isaac and Lois, Nov. 11, 1798.
Henry A., s. Samuel P. and Persis, July 4, 1824.
[Isaac. T. C.], s. [William. C. R. 2.] and Sarah, Nov. 5, 1712.
Isaac, s. Isaac and Mary, Sept. 26, 1766.
Isaac, s. Isaac, jr., bp. Nov. 30, 1794. C. R. 2.
Isaac, s. Isaac, jr. and Lois, Nov. 25, 1795.
Isaac O., s. Sam[ue]l and Persis, Mar. 21, 1826.
John, s. Willia[m] and [torn], —— [1706-7?].
John, s. Isaac and Mary, Jan. 31, 1756.
John, s. John, bp. June 11, 1786. C. R. 2.
John K., s. Isaac and Lois [bp. Nov. 20, 1808. C. R. 2.]
Jonathan, s. Will[ia]m and Sarah, —— [1708?].
Joshu M., s. Samuel P. and Persis, Sept. 27, 1837.
Joshua, s. Lt. Isaac and Lois, Feb. 1, 1806.
Lydea, d. David and Lydea, Apr. 6, 1731.
Mary, d. William and Elizabeth, Sept. 28, 1679.
Mary, d. Isaac and Mary, Feb. 14, 1746-7.
Mary Harvey, d. John, bp. Mar. 28, 1784. C. R. 2.
Mary Jane, d. Isaac, jr., bp. Jan. 6, 1833. C. R. 2.
Mary Pearce, d. Lt. David and Polly, Feb. 22, 1807.
Mehetabel, d. Isaac and Mary, Jan. 4, 1769.
Persis M., d. Samuel P. and Persis, Sept. 26, 1828.
Polly, d. Isaac, jr. and Lois, Dec. 25, 1792.
Sally, d. John, bp. Nov. 2, 1783. C. R. 2.
Samuel Phelps, s. Isaac, jr. and Lois, May 19, 1796.
Samuel W., s. Samuel P. and Persis, Apr. 5, 1822.
Samuell, s. William and Elizabeth, Jan. 29, 1673.

BLUNT, Sam[ue]ll, s. William and Elisabeth, Apr. 24, 1689. [Apr. 29. CT. R.]
Sarah, d. [torn], —— [1702].
Sarah, d. Isaac and Mary, Dec. 12, 1750.
Tabbatha, d. Isaac and Mary, Feb. 7, 1765.
William, s. David and Mary, Oct. 6, 1743.
——, s. Isaac and Mary, Sept. 12, 1757.

BLUNTE (see also Blunt), William, s. William and Elizabeth, Oct. 6, 1671.

BOALMAN, Elizabeth, d. twin, John and Elizabeth, June 24, 1798.
John, s. John and Elizabeth, Feb. 6, 1796.
William, s. twin, John and Elizabeth, June 24, 1798.

BODWEL (see also Bodwell), Daniel, s. Daniel and Eliz[abeth], bp. ——, 1721-2. C. R. I.
Daniel, s. Daniel and Eliz[abeth], bp. ——, 1722. C. R. I.
Elizabeth,d. Dan and Eliz[abeth], bp. —— [1719 or 20]. C. R. I.
Stephen, s. James and Mary, bp. ——, 1720. C. R. I.

BODWELL (see also Bodwel), Abigall, d. Henery and Bethia, Jan. 15, 1686[-7].
Daniel, s. William M. and Mary, May 21, 1813.
Daniell, s. Henry and Bethia, Feb. 14, 1692-3.
George N., s. Daniel, shoemaker, and Rhoda H., July 21, 1845.
Hannah, d. Henry and Bethia, Sept. 1, 1696.
Hannah, d. W[illia]m M. and Mary, Nov. 22, 1818.
Henery, s. twin, Henery and Bethia, Jan. 27, 1685-[6].
Henry, s. Henry and Bethiah, Nov. 6, 1688. [1689. CT. R.]
Hiram, s. William M. and Mary, Aug. 17, 1815.
James, s. Henry and Bethiah, Jan. 10, 1690-91.
James, s. James and Mary, Feb. 1 [1712-13].
Josiah, s. twin, Henry and Bethia, Jan. 27, 1685[-6].
Judith, d. Henry and Bethiah, Apr. 4, 1698.
Mary, d. Henery and Bethia, Apr. 1, 1684.
Mary, d. William M. and Mary, Oct. 24, 1810.
Ruth, d. Henry and Bethiah, Dec. 2, 1699.
Sarah, d. Samuel and Bethia, Dec. 1, 1694.
——, ch. [Hen]ry and Bethia, July 10, 1701.

BOGAN, Hannah L., d. Walter and Mary, Oct. 31, 1818.

BOND, Edwin Grayham, s. William and Sally, Nov. 25, 1821.
Martha, d. William and Sarah, Oct. 3, 1819.
Sarah, d. twin, William, Dec. 14, 1826.
William, s. twin, William, Dec. 14, 1826.

BOOTH, Sarah, d. John and Sally, May 28, 1832.
Wiliam, s. George and Bete, Nov. 17, 1754.

BOUTWELL, Edward Hyde, s. George and Fanny, Dec. 22, 1832. P. R. 34.
George, jr., s. George and Fanny, Feb. 3, 1831. P. R. 34.
James P[aschal. C. R. 2.], s. James and Mary P., Feb. 6, 1840.
Louisa Wilder, d. George and Fanny, Feb. 2. 1840. P. R. 34.
Lucy Frances, d. George and Fanny, July 23, 1828. P. R. 34.
[Mary King. P. R. 34.], d. George, farmer, and Fanny, Apr. 11, 1846.
Mary Lucelia, d. J[ame]s, bp. June —, 1838. C. R. 2.
Parthenia Pelham, d. George and Fanny, Sept. 23, 1835. P. R. 34.
Samuel Hyde, s. George and Fanny, Mar. 25, 1838. P. R. 34.

BOWERS, John Frye, s. Phillip and Chloe, Dec. 21, 1796.

BOWIN, William, s. "Ebenezer Johnson's wife Sarah," Jan. 23, 1747-8.

BOWMAN, Hannah, d. John and Hannah, Jan. 25, 1797.
Isaac, s. John and Hannah, July 16, 1789.
John, s. John and Hannah, Feb. 22, 1784.
Jonathan, s. John and Hannah, Feb. 28, 1786.
Mary, d. John and Hannah, Aug. 21, 1799.
Phebe, d. John and Hannah, bp. June 6, 1802. C. R. 1.
Philip Farington, s. John and Hannah, Sept. 25, 1794.
Sarah, d. John and Hannah, bp. June 3, 1792. C. R. 1.

BOYNTON (see also Buoynton), Amos, s. Thomas and Hannah, Oct. 27, 1776.
Benjamin, s. Thomas and Hannah, July 24, 1780.
Benjamin, s. Benjamin and Belinda, July 18, 1817.
Clarissia Richardson, d. Amos and Clarissia, May 4, 1810.
David, s. Thomas and Hannah, Jan. 4, 1784.
David, s. David and Elizabeth, Feb. 10, 1826.
Elisabeth, d. Moses, bp. Mar. 5, 1780. C. R. 2.
Elizabeth, d. Thomas and Hanah, Jan. 18, 1789.
Hannah, d. Thomas and Hannah, Mar. 11, 1773.

BOYNTON, Hannah, d. Amos and Clarisia, Apr. 3, 1812.
Henry, s. Benjamin and Belinda [Lucinda. C. R. 3.], Feb. 21, 1833.
Hepzibah, d. Thomas and Mary, Nov. 18, 1792.
Isaac, s. David and Elizabeth, Aug. 28, 1821.
Louisa, d. Benjamin and Belinda, May 15, 1826.
Mary, d. Moses, bp. June 21, 1778. C. R. 2.
Mary, d. Thomas and Hannah, Aug. 1, 1778.
Mary, d. Jona[than], bp. Oct. 26, 1783. C. R. 2.
Mary, d. Thomas, jr. and Rebecca, Mar. 5, 1805.
Mary A., d. David and Elizabeth, Dec. 17, 1816.
Mary J., d. Benj[ami]n and Belinda, July 28, 1820.
Moses, s. Moses, bp. Dec. 23, 1781. C. R. 2.
Moses Hadley, s. Benj[ami]n and Belinda, May 3, 1823.
Nathan, s. Moses, bp. May 18, 1783. C. R. 2.
Phebe, d. Jona[than], bp. Mar. 25, 1787. C. R. 2.
Rebecca, d. Thomas, jr. and Rebecca, Oct. 18, 1800.
Sally, d. Jona[than], bp. Nov. 28, 1784. C. R. 2.
Samuel, s. Thomas and Hannah, Nov. 8, 1785.
Samuel, s. Thomas, bp. Sept. 11, 1791. C. R. 2.
Sarah, d. Thomas and Hannah, Jan. 30, 1782.
Thomas, s. Thomas and Hannah, Jan. 7, 1775.
Thomas, s. Thomas, jr. and Rebecca, Aug. 28, 1816.
——, s. Benj[ami]n and Belinda, Nov. —, 1818.
——, s. Benjamin and Belinda, Oct. 9, 1824.

BRADDG (see also Bragg), Dorcas [Bragg. C. R. 1.], d. Thomas and Dorathy, Feb. 4, 1746-7.

BRADGGES (see also Bragg), Anne, d. Edwar[d], Apr. 24, 1[744].

BRADGS (see also Bragg), Josiah, s. Edward and Marcy, Aug. 23, 172[6].

BRADLEE (see also Bradley), Caroline L., d. George and Louisa, Apr. 13, 1828.

BRADLEY (see also Bradlee, Bradly), Ann Whittier, d. Jonathan and Sally, Aug. 11, 1833.
Anna, d. Jonathan and Sarah, 2d w., Nov. 1, 1798.
Betsey, d. Jonathan and Sarah, June 10, 1784.
Caroline [L. P. R. 7.], d. Joseph and Charlotte, May 28, 1819.
Catharine, d. Jonathan and Sally, Dec. 21, 1830.

BRADLEY, Charles, s. Jonathan and Sarah, 2d w., Dec. 17, 1792.
Charlotte M., d. Joseph and Charlotte, Aug. 1, 1829.
George, s. Jonathan and Sarah, 2d w., Nov. 28, 1796.
George, s. Joseph and Mary, Dec. 4, 1800.
Granvill, s. Jonathan, jr. and Sally, Aug. 29, 1816.
Harison, s. Jonathan and Sarah, 2d w., Dec. 4, 1793.
Harrison, s. Jonathan and Sally, June 3, 1827.
Harriot, d. Joseph and Charlottee, Feb. 23, 1817.
James, s. Jonathan and Sarah, 2d w., July 1, 1795.
John A., s. George and Louisa, May 1, 1826.
John B., s. Joseph and Charlotte, May 28, 1831.
Jonathan, s. Jonathan and Sarah, Oct. 19, 1786.
Jonathan, s. Jonathan and Sally, Sept. 27, 1820.
Joseph Edwin, s. Joseph and Charlotte, July 3, 1814.
Joshua W., s. Jonathan and Sally, Aug. 26, 1818.
Maria H., d. Joseph and Charlotte, Feb. 9, 1826.
Mary Ann, d. Joseph and Charlotte, Sept. 6, 1812.
Polly, d. Jonathan and Sarah, May 3, 1779.
Sarah Smith, d. Jonathan, jr. and Sally, Jan. 1, 1815.
Susan Jane, d. Jonathan and Sally, Nov. 1, 1824.
Susanna, d. Jonathan and Sarah, 2d w., Feb. 17, 1801.
William, s. Jonathan and Sarah, Jan. 7, 1782.
William, s. Jonathan and Sarah, Jan. 16, 1789.
William O., s. George and Louisa, Aug. 9, 1838.
William Osgood, s. George, trader, and Susan, Dec. 30, 1843.
——, d. Joseph and Charlotte, Sept. 8, 1821.

BRADLY (see also Bradley), George L., s. George and Louisa, May 7, 1830.

BRADSTREET, Anne, d. Dudley and Anne, Nov. 5, 1681.
Dudley, s. Dudley and Ann, Apr. 27, 1678.
Eliza[beth] Ingalls, d. Elijah and Phebe, May 28, 1791.
John, s. Simon and An, July 22, 1652.
Margarett, d. Dudley and Anne, Feb. 19, 1679-80.
Samuel, s. Dudley and Mary,—— [1711].
——, ch. [torn]ley and Mary, Mar. 1, 1705-6.

BRADY, James H., s. Patrick, manufacturer, and Mary E., Jan. 24, 1846.

BRAG (see also Bragg), Dorcis, d. Thomas and Dorathy, Apr. 27, 1751.
Edward, s. Edward and Anne, June 22, 1748.

BRAG, Edward, s. Edward and Anne, June 8, 1751.
Ruth, d. Thomas and Dorathey, June 26, 1748.

BRAGG (see also Braddg, Bradgges, Bradgs, Brag, Bragges), Bridget, d. John and Sarah, Aug. 26, 1772.
Dolly, d. Ingalls and Mary [Molly. C. R. 1.], Feb. 4, 1783.
Elizabeth, d. Ingalls and Mary, Mar. 16, 1781.
Hannah, d. Thomas and Dorothy, June 14, 1767.
Ingals, s. Thomas and Dorathy, June 24, 1753.
Ingalls, s. Ingalls and Mary [Molly. C. R. 1.], July 15, 1777.
James Frye, s. Ingalls and Molly, Dec. 4, 1787.
Lydia, d. Thomas and Dorothy, June 19, 1763.
Molly, d. Ingalls and Mary [Molly. C. R. 1.], Apr. 29, 1779.
Pamela, d. Ingalls and Molly, bp. Oct. 2, 1791. C. R. 1.
Sarah, d. Thomas and Dorathy, Oct. 1, 1757.
Sarah, d. Thomas and Dorothy, June 14, 1759.
Sukey, d. Ingals and Molly, bp. Nov. 16, 1794. C. R. 1.
Susanna, d. Thomas and Dorathy, Aug. 19, 1755.
Thomas, s. Ingalls and Mary, Apr. 7, 1785.

BRAGJES (see also Bragg), [L]ydea, d. Edward and Marcy, Oct. 9, 1723.
[Thomas. C. R. 2,], s. Edward and Marcy, Mar. 2, 1720-21.

BRAIN, Patrick, s. Miclo, laborer, and Aorial, Aug. 10, 1845.

BRAINARD, John, s. James, spinner, and Mary, June 20, 1846.

BRANEN, James, s. Lawrence, flax-dresser, and Betsey, both b. Scotland, Feb. 6, 1849.

BRENNEN, Charles, s. James, spinner, and Mary, Apr. 16, 1845.
Charles, s. James, spinner, and Mary, Mar. 23, 1846.
John Augustus, s. James, spinner, and Mary, June 17, 1846.
Vincent John, s. William, spinner, and Mary, Sept. 25, 1847.

BRIDGES (see also Briges), Abiel, s. John and Mary, May 14, 1767.
Albert Kingsbury, s. Levi R. and Abigail S., bp. July 2, 1848. C. R. 3.
Anna, d. John and Mary, Aug. 26, 1765.
Bethia, d. James and Sarah, Aug. 9, 1696.
Betty, d. James, 3d and Mary, Sept. 21, 1782.
Charles Moody, s. Moody and Rebecca, June 10, 1833.

BRIDGES, Chloe, d. James and Mary, Dec. 28, 1743.
Dorcas, d. James and Mary, Mar. 15, 1767.
Dorcas, d. James and Mary, Mar. 15, 1768.
Dorcas, d. Mr. Moody and Naamah, May 23, 1769.
[Eleanor. C. R. I.], d. James and Elener, Feb. 26, 1730-31.
Elizabeth, d. John and Mary [Elizabeth. CT. R.], June 5, 1683.
Enoch, s. Moody and Naama, Aug. 23, 1762.
Enoch, s. John and Mary, bp. May 17, 1767. C. R. I.
Enoch, s. John and Mary, Oct. 5, 1774.
Fidelia, see Phidelia.
George O[sgood. C. R. I.], s. Lt. Moody and Rebecca, May 25, 1820.
Hannah, d. James and [torn], — [1702].
Hannah, d. Moody and Naamah, Sept. 17, 1764.
Hannah, d. James and Mary, June 18, 1794.
Hannah, d. James, jr. and Eliza[be]th, bp. June 22, 1794. C. R. I.
Henry G[ardner. C. R. I.], s. Col. Moody and Rebecca, Jan. 12, 1826.
Henry Gardner, s. Lt. James [jr. C. R. I.] and Elizabeth, May 11, 1789.
Isaac Cazneau, s. Moody and Rebeca, Oct. 12, 1839.
James, s. James and Sarah, Feb. 16, 1694-5.
James, s. James and Elener, June 2, 1729.
James Otis, s. Col. Boody [Moody. C. R. I.] and Rebecca, Mar. 22, 1824.
Jehiel, s. John and Mary, Dec. 17, 1768.
John, s. James and Mary, Sept. 5, 1741.
Jonathan, s. John and Mary, June 25, 1776.
Joseph Edward, s. Moody and Rebecca, bp. June 5, 1836. C. R. I.
Joseph Edward, s. Moody and Rebecca, Oct. 30, 1837.
Martha, d. Moody and Naamah, Apr. 30, 1767.
Mary, d. John and Mary, Jan. 27, 1678.
Mary, d. James and Ellener, Oct. 29, 1724.
Mary, d. James and Mary, May 13, 1761.
Mary, d. John and Mary, Oct. 19, 1763.
Mary, d. James, 3d and Mary, Sept. 21, 1786.
Mary Montgomery, d. Moody and Rebecca, Mar. 26, 1822.
Mehetabel, d. John and Mary, Feb. 12, 1770.
Mehitabell, d. John and Mary, Apr. 20, 1688.
Moode, s. James and Ellener, Jan. 19, 1722-3.
Moody, s. John and Mary, Apr. 6, 1772.
Moody, s. James, 3d and Mary, Sept.—, 1784.
Nancy, d. James, jr. and Mary [Hepzibah. C. R. I.], Dec. 14, 1791.

BRIDGES, Phebe, d. James and Mary, Jan. 21, 1765.
Phidelia, d. Lt. James [jr. C. R. 1.] and Elizabeth, Mar. 23, 1788.
Rebecca O[sgood. C. R. 1.], d. Moody and Rebecca, Mar. 14, 1829.
Rosenia Elinor, d. Capt. Isaac and Maria Barbara Louisa, Oct. 24, 1796.
Ruby, d. Moody and Naamah, Apr. 30, 1771.
Ruby, d. James [jr. and Hepzibah. C. R. 1.] and Mary, Oct. 12, 1799.
Samuell, s. John and Mary, July 19, 1681.
Sarah, d. James and Sarah, Feb. 25, 1692-3.
Sarah, d. James and Elener, Mar. 4, 1732-3.
Sarah, d. James and Mary, Dec. 21, 1739.
Sarah, d. James [jr. C. R. 1.] and Mary, June 1, 1797.
Susanna, d. Moody and Naamah, May 3, 1760.
Thomas, s. James and Mary, Dec. 12, 1758.
Tryphena, d. James, jr. [3d. C. R. 1.] and Mary, Dec. 8, 1788.
——, d. James and Elener, Dec. 12, 1726.

BRIERLY, Benjamin F., s. John and Sarah, Oct. 20, 1837.
Edward, s. John, manufacturer, and Sarah, Jan. 29, 1844.
Ellen, d. David and Alice, Apr. 15, 1834. P. R. 22.
Hannah, d. David and Alice, Jan. 13, 1836. P. R. 22.
James William, s. John and Sarah, Oct. 4, 1835.
Nancy, d. John, manufacturer, and Sarah, Nov. 25, 1845.
Sarah, d. John and Sarah, June 3, 1839.
Sarah Ann, d. David and Alice, Aug. 15, 1832. P. R. 22.
Sarah Ellen, d. John and Sally, Apr. 29, 1841.

BRIGES (see also Bridges), Abigall, d. Moodey and Nama, Sept. 25, 1756.
Elenor, d. Moodey and Nama, Oct. 8, 1758.
Isaac, s. Moodey and Nama, Feb. 3, 1753.
James, s. Moodey and Name [Naama. C. R. 1.], Nov. 4, 1751.
James, s. James and Mary, Nov. 24, 1756.
Nama, d. Moodey and Nama, Sept. 7, 1748.
Sarah, d. Moodey and Nama, June 14, 1750.
——, d. Moodey and Nama, Feb. —, 1755.

BRIGGS, Harriet S., d. William T., clergyman, and Harriet S., both b. Scituate, Mar. 7, 1849.
——, d. James and Nancy, Jan. 27, 1828.

BRISTOW, Lydia, d. ——, Dec. 26, 1765.

BRITTON, Margaret, d. William, bp. July 4, 1841. C. R. 2.

BROOKS, Amelia, d. David and Elizabeth, Jan. 14, 1846. C. R. 4.
Charles Edward, s. David, cloth finisher, and Elizabeth, May 6, 1847.
Eliza Ann, d. David, factory operative, and Elizabeth, both b. England, May 8, 1848.
Elizabeth, d. Edward, factory operative, and Mary A. [Ann. C. R. 4.], both b. England, Sept. 28, 1848.
Ellen Ann, d. Isaac and Julia, Jan. 28, 1847. C. R. 4.
Elvia Ann, d. David and Elizabeth, May 8, 1849. C. R. 4.
Helen Ann, d. Isaac, spinner, and Julia, Jan. 29, 1847.
John, s. Isaac and Julia, Dec. 24, 1844. C. R. 4.

BROWN (see also Browne), Angelina, d. Artemas and Lydia H., Feb. 8, 1832. P. R. 29.
Anstress, d. Joseph, of Tewksbury and Rachel Abbot, Apr. 25, 1812.
Benjamin, s. Jacob and Ruby, Dec. 17, 1835.
Betsy, d. Jacob and Ruby, July 4, 1838.
Caroline Maybin, d. John James and Emily Willard, Jan. 6, 1839. C. R. 4.
Charles, s. Jacob, cordwainer, and Ruby, Mar. 12, 1848.
Cynthia, d. John and Cynthia, bp. May 30, 1824. C. R. 2.
Edwin A[ugustus. C. R. 4.] B[oardman. C. R. 4.], s. John J[ames. C. R. 4.], goldsmith, and Emily F. [Willard. C. R. 4.], July 4, 1846.
Elizabeth F[iske. C. R. 4.], d. John J., trader, and Emily [W. C. R. 4.], Oct. 29, 1848.
Emeline M., d. William H., farmer, and Elizabeth, Oct. 23, [26. dup.], 1843.
Emily Fiske, d. John J. and Emily W., bp. Apr. 18, 1844. C. R. 4.
George Henry, s. Joseph and Clarissa, Apr. 31, 1839.
George Temple, s. John James and Emily W., bp. Feb. 24, 1841. C. R. 4.
Hannah, d. James and Phebe, Aug. 23, 1748.
Hannah F., d. Jacob and Ruby, July 23, 1829.
Jacob, s. Jacob and Ruby, Jan. 13, 1827.
Jacob, s. Jacob and Betsy, Feb. 13, 1827.
Jacob, s. Jacob and Ruby, Sept. 12, 1831.
Jacob Putnam, s. Hugh and Pemela, Jan. 18, 1825.
James, s. James and Phebe, May 29, 1743.
James W[illard. C. R. 4.], s. John J., watchmaker, and Emily W., Sept. 10, 1844.

BROWN, John, s. James and Phebe, July 3, 1735.
John, s. John and Lucy, Sept. 9, 1777.
Joseph Alexander, s. Hugh and Pamela, Jan. 5, 1824.
Joseph P., s. Joseph and Clarissa, Oct. 2, 1832.
Laroy S., s. Jacob and Ruby, Sept. 28, 1833.
Laura Ann, d. Jacob and Ruby, at Reading, Feb. 19, 1843.
Lucinda, d. Jacob, cordwainer, and Ruby, Oct. 3, 1844.
Martha Jane, d. William, wool-sorter, and Elizabeth, both b. England, May 22, 1849.
Martha Louisa, d. Thomas B. and Martha, Oct. 8, 1833.
Mary, d. Jacob and Ruby, July 21, 1825.
Mary, d. Jacob and Ruby, Apr. 21, 1828.
Mary E., d. William H. and Elezabeth, Mar. 14, 1840.
Mary E., d. Joseph and Clarissa, Apr. 20, 1842.
Mary F., d. Joseph, manufacturer, and Lucy E., Sept. 12, 1844.
Nancy, d. John and Cynthia, bp. May 30, 1824. C. R. 2.
Nancy E., d. Jacob and Ruby, at Lynnfield, July 17, 1840.
Phebe, d. James and Phebe, June 9, 1737.
Phebe, d. James and Phebe, Apr. 12, 1741.
Phebe A., d. William H. and Elizabeth, Mar. 23, 1847.
Roxana, May 15, 1806. P. R. 35.
Samuel, s. James and Phebe, Apr. 27, 1745.
Sarah Allen, d. Joseph, tailor, and Clarissa, Sept. 20, 1847.
Sarah Elizabeth, d. Artemas and Lydia H., Sept. 6, 1834. P. R. 29.
Susan B., d. William and Dorcas, Aug. 24, 1830.
——, twin chn. Ja[mes] and Phebe, Apr. 20, 1740.
——, ch. Joseph and Clarissa, June 26, 1837.
——, d. John and Louisa, Apr. 8, 1838.
——, s. William H., laborer, and Eliza [1846 or 1847].

BROWNE (see also Brown), George T., s. John J. and Emily, Aug. 5, 1840.

BUCKLEY, Anna Elizabeth, d. Phineas and Anna, bp. July 21, 1839. C. R. 4.
George, s. Phineas and Hannah, June 22, 1830.
James Edward, s. James, carder, and Anna, Feb. 12, 1848.
Joseph, s. Phinehas, laborer, and Hannah, June 8, 1844.
Phineas, s. Phineas and Anna, bp. Mar. 27, 1842. C. R. 4.
Sarah Ann, d. Phineas and Anna, bp. July 21, 1839. C. R. 4.

BUOYNTON (see also Boynton), Benjamin, s. Benjamin and Lucinda, bp. July 15, 1832. C. R. 3.
Joshua, s. Benjamin and Lucinda, bp. July 15, 1832. C. R. 3.

BUOYNTON, Louisa, d. Benjamin and Lucinda, bp. July 15, 1832. C. R. 3.
Mary Jane, d. Benjamin and Lucinda, bp. July 15, 1832. C. R. 3.
Moses Hadley, s. Benjamin and Lucinda, bp. July 15, 1832. C. R. 3.

BURBANK, George A., s. Jonathan and Eliza, Oct. 16, 1822.

BURCH, James, s. James and Rachil, Jan. 17, 1755.

BURCHMON, Eliza A., d. John, tailor, and Eliza A., Dec. 22, 1844.

BURNAP, Betty, d. Samuel and Bette, Feb. 22, 1771.
Samuel, s. Samuel and Betty, Nov. 24, 1773.

BURNET (see also Burnett), Ann, d. Robert and Margaret, Mar 20, 1832.
Robert, s. Robert and Margaret, Jan. 30, 1837.

BURNETT (see also Burnet), Thomas, s. Robert and Margaret, Nov. 4. 1834.

BURNHAM, Albert Prince, s. John and Diantha, May 5, 1839.
George Story, s. Zacheus and Dolly, July 9, 1813.
John A., s. John, blacksmith, and Diantha, Oct. 30, 1843.
John Augustus, s. John and Diantha, Mar. 7, 1837.
John Henry, s. Henry A., blacksmith, and Susan, Oct. 13, 1847.
——, s. John, blacksmith, and Diantha, Apr. 15, 1847.

BURNS, Hannah, d. George and Hannah, Jan. 3, 1825.
Julia Ann, d. George and Hannah, June 6, 1820.
Lydia, d. George and Hannah, June 24, 1829.
Martha, d. Elias, Mar. 12, 1826.
Mary, d. George and Hannah, Mar. 1, 1827.
Mary Jane, d. Elias, bp. June 16, 1833. C. R. 2.
Sarah, d. George and Hannah, Feb. 15, 1822.

BURR, Charles E., s. Samuel, laborer, and Eliza, Dec. 16, 1845.
——, d. Samuel, manufacturer, and Eliza, Feb. 11, 1844.

BURT (see also Birt, Burtt), Abiah, d. Joseph and Abiah, Dec. 13, 17[59].
Ben, s. Joseph, jr. and Mary, ——ry 15 [1794. T. C.]. [bp. Feb. 23, 1794. C. R. 2.]

BURT, Charles F., s. Jed[edia]h and Mary, Jan. 21, 1831.
Elizabeth, d. Joseph and Abiah, Sept. 18, 1761.
Eunice Carlton, d. Joseph, jr. and Mary, Sept. 10, 1787.
Francis Edward, s. Jedediah, bp. Nov. 2, 1834. C. R. 2.
Hannah, d. Joseph, bp. Oct. 28, 1781. C. R. 2.
Hannah, d. Jedediah, bp. Feb. 1, 1801. C. R. 2.
Henry, s. Jedediah, bp. Feb. 1, 1807. C. R. 2.
Jedediah, s. Jedediah, bp. Aug. 11, 1793. C. R. 2.
Jedidia, s. Joseph, bp. June 23, 1771. C. R. 2.
John, s. Joseph, May 6, 1770. C. R. 2.
John, s. Joseph, jr. and Mary, —— 24, 1791. [bp. Jan. 30, 1791. C. R. 2.]
Joseph, s. Joseph and Abiah, July 5, 1765.
Joseph, s. Joseph, jr. and Molly, Oct. 18, 1788.
Joseph, s. Joseph, jr., bp. Oct. 31, 1790. C. R. 2.
Joseph [M. C. R. 2.], s. Jedediah and Sarah, June 8, 1817.
Lois, d. Joseph and Abiah, June 16, 1763.
Lucy, d. Joseph, bp. June 5, 1785. C. R. 2.
Sarah, d. Joseph, bp. Dec. 4, 1774. C. R. 2.
Sarah, d. Jedediah and Sarah, Feb. 21, 1799.
Seth, s. Joseph, jr. and Molly, July 4, 1792.
Susanna, d. Joseph and Abiah, June 25, 1758.
Unice Carlton, d. Joseph, jr., bp. Oct. 31, 1790. C. R. 2.
William Henry, s. Jedediah, bp. Jan. 6, 1833. C. R. 2.

BURTT (see also Burt), Abba F[rances. C. R. 2.] C[aldwell. C. R. 2.], d. Jedediah and Mary, Jan. 12, 1836.
Elmira H., d. Henry and Hannah, Sept. 10, 1834.
Fanny Mooar, d. Joseph, bp. Oct. 17, 1779. C. R. 2.
Francis Edward, s. Jedediah and Mary, Oct. 31, 1833.
George N[elson. C. R. 2.], s. Jedediah and Mary, Apr. 1, 1832.
Hannah, d. Jedediah and Sarah, Jan. 28, 1801.
Hannah E[liza. P. R. 33.], d. Henry and Abigail, Apr. 21, 1840.
Henery, s. Jedediah and Sarah, Jan. 31, 1807.
Jedediah, s. Jedediah and Sarah, Feb. 6, 1804.
Joseph E[dward. P. R. 33.], s. Henry and Hannah, June 3, 1838.
Mary, d. John and Tryphena, Aug. 30, 1816.
Mary L[ouisa. C. R. 2.], d. Jedediah and Mary, Apr. 5, 1838.
Sarah E[lizabeth. C. R. 2.], d. Jedediah and Mary, Aug. 14, 1840.
Seth Frye, s. Seth and Hannah, Jan. 4, 1818.
Thomas H., s. Henry and Hannah, Aug. 23, 1836.
William, s. Jedediah and Sarah, July 7, 1809.
William E[dwards. P. R. 33.], s. Henry, saddle and harness manufacturer, and Abigail, Jan. 9, 1844.

BURTT, William H., s. Jedediah and Mary, Mar. 16, 1829.
——, d. John and Tryphena, Feb. —, 1818.
——, d. Jedediah, Jr. and Caroline Stickney, Aug. —, 1827.

BUSSELL (see also Buswell), Henry H., s. Gilbert H., laborer, and Nancy A., July 25, 1848.
Sarah, d. Robert and Hannah, Oct. 23, 1698.
Thomas, s. Robert and Hannah, —— [1703].

BUSWELL (see also Bussell, Buzzell), Catharine, d. Eben[eze]r, Feb. 12, 1831.
Harriet [Driver. C. R. 2.], d. Ebenezer and Catharine M., Sept. Sept. 7, 1832.
Moses, s. [torn], May —, 1701.

BUTLER, Henery, s. Mr. Benjamin and Dorcas, Nov. 27, 1754.
Mary, "reputed" d. Nicholas Butler and Mary Russ, June 25, 1688.

BUTTERFIELD, Charles H., s. Charles A. and Mary Ann, May 6, 1833.
George Henry, s. Charles A. and Mary Ann, Dec. 3, 1837.
Harriet Ann, d. Ch[ar]l[e]s A. and Mary A., June 10, 1837.
John Barker, s. Charles A. and Mary Ann, Nov. 25, 1839.
Joseph B., s. Charles and Mary A., May 1, 1842.

BUTTERS, Abigail C., d. Francis [and Betsey. C. R. 2.], Oct. 31, 1819.
Elizabeth, d. Francis and Betsey, bp. Aug. 1, 1824. C. R. 2.
Francis, s. Francis and Betsey, bp. Aug. 1, 1824. C. R. 2.
Henry A., s. Francis and Betsey, bp. Aug. 1, 1824. C. R. 2.
James, s. Francis and Betsey, bp. Aug. 1, 1824. C. R. 2.
Otis W., s. Francis and Betsey, bp. Aug. 1, 1824. C. R. 2.
——, s. Francis and Mahitable, Aug. 19, 1821.

BUTTERWORTH, Charles L[ewis. P. R. 24.], s. John, spinner, and Mary, Jan. 3, 1849. [Dec. —, 1848. P. R. 24.]

BUXTON, Mary J., d. David, Aug. 16, 1831.

BUZZELL (see also Buswell), Mary T., d. Samuel T., carpenter, and Mary J., Dec. 1, 1845.
——, d. Joseph, laborer, and Sarah, Jan. 9, 1846

CALAHAN (see also Callahan), Charles, s. twin, Robert and Dorcas, May 15, 1803.
William, s. twin, Robert and Dorcas, May 15, 1803.

CALDWELL, Albert W., s. twin, Rufus F., yeoman, and Mary, Aug. 28, 1846.
Dolly, d. John, bp. Feb. 16, 1777. C. R. I.
George, s. Rufus and Mary, Nov. 2, 1836.
Henry W., s. twin, Rufus F., yeoman, and Mary, Aug. 28, 1846.
Samuel, Apr. 19, 1776. P. R. 19.
Will[ia]m, s. John, bp. Oct. 15, 1775. C. R. I.

CALLAHAM (see also Callahan), Agustus, s. Robert and Dorcas, Mar. 12, 1815. [Apr. 12. dup.]
Edward, s. Robert and Dorcas, June 18, 1813.
Henry, s. Robert and Dorcas, Jan. 5 [1812, in pencil; 1811. C. R. I.].
James, s. Robert and Dorcas, Jan. 8, 1805.
Robert, s. Robert and Dorcas, Jan. 21, 1809.

CALLAHAN (see also Calahan, Callaham, Callehan, Callyham), Edward, s. Robert and Dorcas, Feb. 1, 1818. [Jan. 31, 1818. C. R. I.]
Edward, s. James, laborer, and Emily, b. Bradford, Aug. 11, 1848.
George A., s. Augustus and Mary, Apr. 26, 1839.
Henry, s. Robert and Dorcas, Jan. 5, 1811. C. R. I.
Lenry, s. William, watchman, and Hannah, Jan. 2, 1844.
Hydia, d. Robert and Dorcas, Jan. 27, 1807.
Mariah, d. Robert and Dorcas, Dec. 25, 1819.
Mary A., d. Augustus, farmer, and Mary, June 10, 1843.
William H., s. William, laborer, and Hannah, Nov. 23, 1849.

CALLEHAN (see also Callahan), Charles Henry, s. James and Catherin[e], Apr. 11, 1833. [Apr. 13. dup.]
James Albert, s. James, laborer, and Emily E., July 28, 1846.
Lydia Maria, d. James, stone layer, and Emily E., Aug. 6, 1844.
Martha, d. William, laborer, and Hannah, Jan. 24, 1847.

CALLYHAM (see also Callahan), Jonathan Gardner, s. Robert and Dorcas, Sept. 2, 1823.

CAMBEL (see also Campbell), Alexander, s. Alexander and Anna Gage, Mar. 2, 1781.

CAMPBELL (see also Cambel), Agnes Watson, d. James, baler of goods, and Isabella, both b. Scotland, Nov. 25, 1848.
Hannah J., d. William K., laborer, b. N. H., and Pamelia, b. Frankfort, Me., Dec. 12, 1849.
James, s. John, factory operative, and Margaret, Feb. 27, 1849.
James, s. John, dyer, and Margaret, both b. Ireland, June 27, 1849.
John Knox, s. James, laborer, and Issabella, Oct. 10, 1846.

CARELTON (see also Carleton), Christopher, s. John and Hannah, June 2, 1692.

CAREY, James Henry, s. John, farmer, and Mary A., both b. England, Sept. 18, 1849.

CARLETON (see also Carelton, Carlton, Caurlton, Cuarlton), Abigail, d. Joseph and Abigail, May 23, 1696.
Amos Dearborn, s. Daniel and Phebe, Jan. 3, 1839.
Charles Wheaton, s. Isaac and Desire, bp. June 11, 1843. C. R. 4.
Conrad, s. Isaac, bp. June 12, 1814. C. R. 2.
Edward, s. Isaac and Desire, bp. June 11, 1843. C. R. 4.
George, s. John D., farmer, and Hannah, Dec. 11, 1843.
Hannah, d. John and Hannah, July 10, 1694.
Hannah Emery, d. Edward and Phebe, of Bluehill, bp. May 17, 1795. C. R. 2.
Henry C., s. Isaac, hatter, and Desire, May 27, 1845.
James G., s. James C. and Mary D., May 4, 1839. P. R. 23.
James W., s. Joseph, carpenter, and Mary J., Feb. 22, 1846.
John, s. John and Hannah, Feb. 27, 1689-90.
Josiah B., s. Deborah, Apr. 5, 1840.
Mary, d. John and Hannah, Apr. 7, 1700.
Mary A. P., d. Daniel and Phebe K., Nov. 10, 1840.
Octavia A., d. James C. and Mary D., Sept. —, 1837. P. R. 23.
Samuel, s. John and Hannah, June 3, 1696.
Susan Elizabeth, d. Ja[me]s C. and Mary D., Oct. 17, 1843.
——, s. Daniel, farmer, and Phebe, Jan. 25, 1844.

CARLILE, John, grands. Mr. Mullington, bp. Mar. 20, 1836. C. R. 4.

CARLTON (see also Carleton), Abiah A., d. Amos and Abiah, May 19, 1829.
[Abigail. C. R. 1.], d. John and Hannah, jr., June 29, 1728.
Abigal, d. Isaac and Abigal, Jan. 14, 1752.
Abraham, s. Nathaniel and Mary, bp. ——, 1722. C. R. 1.

CARLTON, Almira, d. Frederick and Ema, Nov. 20, 1817.
Amos, s. Daniel, 3d and Mary, Jan. 25, 1779.
Amos, s. Amos [jr. C. R. 1.] and Hannah, Apr. 25, 1802.
Amos P., s. Capt. Amos and Abiah, Dec. 26, 1831.
Ann Maria, d. James F. and Ann Maria, June 27, 1833
Anne, d. Ezekiel and Marcy, Feb. 9, 1748-9.
Asa, s. Asa and Hannah, Dec. 5, 1764.
Asie, s. Christopher and Martha, Jan. 4, 1728-9.
Assenath, d. Benjamin and Sarah, Oct. 1, 1803.
Benjamin, s. Christopher and Martha, Mar. 8, 1725-6.
Benjamin, s. Joshua and Mary, Oct. 23, 1751.
Benjamin, s. Christefor and Elezebith, Jan. 22, 1756.
Benjamin, s. Benjamin and Sarah, bp. Mar. 23, 1783. C. R. 1.
Benjamin Farnum, s. John, jr. and Chloe, Mar. 23, 1817.
Betty, d. Ezekiel and Dorcas, Mar. 26, 1781.
Catharine, d. Jacob and Phebe, Apr. 13, 1816.
Charles, s. Phineas and Joanna, July 6, 1806.
Charles S., s. Amos, jr. and Sarah H., May 16, 1827.
Christopher, s. Christopher and Mary, Apr. 17, 1810.
Conrad, s. Isaac, jr. and Mary, Apr. 26, 1802.
Cristefor, s. Cristefor and Elezebith, Nov. 7, 1749.
Cristefor, s. Cristefor and Elezebith, May 2, 1751.
Dane [Dean. C. R. 1.], s. Dane [Dean. C. R. 1.] and Deborah, Dec. 28, 1787.
Daniel, s. Daniel and Priscila, Mar. 6, 1736-7.
Daniel, s. Daniel and Mercy, May 22, 1760.
Daniel, s. Daniel, 3d and Mary, June 17, 1780.
Daniel, s. Amos and Hannah, bp. Mar. 13, 1808. C. R. 1.
David, s. Christopher and Elizabeth, Feb. 15, 1763.
David, s. Christo[phe]r and Elizabeth, Dec. 24, 1764.
David, s. James and Eliz[abe]th, Sept. 15, 1768.
Dean, s. Peter and Elezebith, Oct. 28, 1758.
Debora, d. Samuel and Debora, Mar. 10, 1728-9.
Deborah, d. Dean and Deborah, Feb. 6, 1796.
Dorcas, d. Asa and Hannah, Dec. 27, 1762.
Dorcas, d. Ezekiel, jr. and Dorcas, Oct. 3, 1769.
Elbridge G [erry. C. R. 1.], s. Christopher and Mary, May 4, 1820.
Elezebith, d. Cristefor and Elezebith [July or Aug., 1753.].
Elisabeth Stevens, d. Christopher and Mary, June 22, 1812.
Eliza Ann, d. Maj. Dean and Martha, Sept. 26, 1817.
Eliza K., d. Jacob and Phebe, July 12, 1818.
Eliza Kimball, d. Jacob and Phebe, Oct. 24, 1814.
Elizabeth, d. Michael and Elizabeth, Dec. 11, 1761.

CARLTON, Elizabeth, d. James and Eliz[abe]th, July 22, 1766.
Elizabeth, d. Enoch and Eliz[abet]h, Sept. 4, 1815.
Elizabeth Adams, d. Michael and Hannah, Aug. 15, 1803.
Enoch, s. Ezekiel and Dorcas [Sarah. C. R. 1.], Apr. 20, 1783.
Enoch, s. Benjamin and Sarah, Sept. 29, 1785.
Eunice, d. Ezekiel and Marcy, Feb. 23, 1750-51.
Ezekiel, s. Ezekiel and Marcy, Nov. 22, 1742.
Ezekiel, s. Ezekiel and Dorcas, Apr. 10, 1776.
Ezekiel, s. Ezekiel, jr. and Phebe, Mar. 15, 1815.
Fanney Marble, d. Benja[min] and Sarah, July 6, 1798.
Fanny, d. Ezekiel, jr. and Elizabeth, bp. Dec. 12, 1773. C. R. 1.
Fanny, d. Ezekiel, jr. and Dorcas, Dec. 5, 1774.
Frederic Asa, s. Fredrick and Ema, May 5, 1815.
Frederick, s. Benjamin and Sarah, May —, 1788. [bp. June 1. C. R. 1.]
George E[dward. C. R. 1.], s. John, jr. and Chloe, May 24, 1823.
George R., s. Rev. George J. and Joanna, Aug. 26, 1838.
Guy, s. Isaac and Martha, Jan. 8, 1822.
Guy, s. Isaac and Martha, Apr. 2, 1830.
[Hannah. C. R. 1.] —ah, d. John and Hannah, Apr. 28, 1720.
Hannah, d. John and Hannah, Jan. 9, 1721-2.
Hannah, d. Ezekiel and Marcy, May 26, 1741.
Hannah, d. Joshua and Mary, Dec. 11, 1744.
Hannah, d. Asa and Hannah, Oct. 14, 1757.
Hannah, d. Ezekiel and Dorcas, Aug. 11, 1778.
Hannah, d. Daniel, 3d and Mary, Mar. 21, 1784.
Hannah, d. Dean and Deborah, bp. Sept. 28, 1794. C. R. 1.
Hannah, d. Dean and Deborah, bp. Jan. 5, 1800. C. R. 1.
Hannah C., d. James C., trader, and Mary D., June 9, 1846.
Hannah Farnum, d. Amos and Hannah, Sept. 24, 1803.
Hannah Ingalls, d. Dean and Deborah, July 18, 1806.
Harriot F., s. Enoch and Betsy, July 21, 1819.
Harriott Lovejoy, d. Isaac and Martha, Jan. 17, 1820.
Hazen K., s. Kimball and Betsy, Aug. 12, 1830.
Helen [S. P. R. 23.], d. James C., trader, b. Methuen, and Mary D., May 29, 1848.
Henry, s. Christopher and Mary, June 10, 1818.
Henry E., s. Enoch and Betsey, Aug. 9, 1824.
Henry P[utnam. C. R. 1.], s. John, jr. and Chloe, May 30, 1821.
Hiram A., s. Enoch and Betsy, Aug. 18, 1821.
Isaac, s. Isaac and Abigal, Mar. 24, 1753.
Isaac, s. Asa and Hannah, Oct. 27, 1772.
Isaac, s. Samuel and Sarah, Oct. 1, 1777.
Isaac, s. Samuel and Sarah [Dorcas. C. R. 1.], Apr. 28, 1783.

CARLTON, Isaac, s. Christopher and Mary, Sept. 26, 1813.
Israel, s. Michael and Eliz[abe]th, July 30, 1763.
Jacob, s. twin, Daniel, 3d and Molly [Mary. C. R. 1.], Feb. 26, 1792.
John Farnum, s. John, jr. and Chloe, July 18, 1813.
James, s. John and Hannah, Mar. 2, 1729-30.
James, s. James and Eliz[abe]th, June 6, 1762.
James Farnum, s. Amos and Hannah, Feb. 7, 1805.
James S., s. Amos, jr. and Sarah H., Mar. 4, 1829.
Jedidiah, s. Dane and Deborah, Feb. 1, 1790.
Jeremy, s. Samuel and Sarah, Mar. 20, 1782.
[John. C. R. 1.], s. Christephor and Martha, ——, 1720.
John, s. Ezekiel and Marcy, Sept. 19, 1744.
John, s. Isaac and Abigal, Dec. 17, 1754.
John, s. Asa and Hannah, Mar. 10, 1768.
John, s. Peter and Sarah, Mar. 30, 1778.
John, s. Samuel and Sarah, bp. Sept. 14, 1788. C. R. 1.
John, s. Samuel and Sarah, Dec. 13, 1789.
John, s. John and Chloe, Oct. 13, 1811.
John Dean, s. Maj. Dean and Martha, Feb. 1, 1816.
John Dean, s. Dean, bp. Feb. 8, 1846. C. R. 1.
John Farnum, s. Christ[ophe]r and Mary, Nov. 5, 1815.
John Ingalls, s. Dane and Deborah, Mar. 31, 1792.
John Kimball, s. Ezekiel, jr. and Phebe, Mar. 8, 1803.
John Walter, s. John Dean and Hannah, bp. Feb. 8, 1846. C. R. 1.
Jonathan, s. Isaac and Abigail, Jan. 28, 1760.
Jona[than] [Frye. C. R. 1.], s. Ezekiel, jr. and Phebe, Jan. 17, 1805.
Joseph, s. Isaac and Abigail, Sept. 18, 1761.
Joseph, s. Samuel and Sarah, Feb. 7, 1780.
Joseph, s. Michael and Hannah, July 18, 1801.
Joseph W[arren. C. R. 1.], s. Ezekiel, jr. and Phebe, Feb. 14, 1817.
Julia Ann, d. Kimball and Betsy, Dec. 10, 1832.
Kimbal, s. Daniel, jr. and Molly, Dec. 18, 1796.
Lydea, d. Joshua and Mary, Aug. 6, 1746.
Lydea, d. Joshua and Mary, July 29, 1749.
[Lydia. C. R. 1.], d. Joshua and Mary, Aug. 7, 1747.
Lydia Kimball, d. Ezekiel, jr. and Phebe, Sept. 29, 1809.
Marcy, d. Ezekiel and Marcy, June —, 1736. [bp. June 13. C. R. 1.]
Marcy, d. Ezekiel and Marcy, Nov. 21, 1739.
Maria [Mira. C. R. 1.], d. Dean and Deborah, May 11, 1801.
Martha, d. Christopher and Martha, June 12, 1722.

CARLTON, Martha, d. Isaac and Abigal, Jan. 21, 1758.
Martha, d. Benja[min] and Sarah, April 18, 1791.
Mary, d. John and Hannah, Aug. 15, 17[23].
Mary, d. Christopher and Martha, July 29, 1724.
Mary, d. Ezekiel and Marcey, Apr. 16, 1755.
Mary, d. Asa and Hannah, Mar. 2, 1761.
Mary, d. Michael and Hannah, Sept. 1, 1805.
Mary [G. P. R. 23.], d. James C. and Mary Deane, May 12, 1841. [May 21. P. R. 23.]
Mary Kimball, d. Amos, deceased, and Hannah, Feb. 4, 1810.
Mercy, d. Daniel, jr. and Mercy, May 3, 1776.
Mercy, d. Daniel, 3d and Mary, Mar. 22, 1782.
Michael, s. Michael and Elizabeth, Nov. 29, 1760.
Michal, s. Ezekiel and Marcy, Nov. 22, 1737.
Molley, d. Joshua and Mary, at Reading, July 26, 1741.
Molly, d. Ezekiel, jr. and Dorcas, Aug. 30, 1771.
Molly, d. Daniel, 3d and Molly [Mary. C. R. 1.], May 24, 1788.
Molly, d. twin, Daniel, 3d and Molly [Mary. C. R. 1.], Feb. 26, 1792.
Molly, d. Daniel, 3d and Molly, Sept. 26, 1794.
Nabby, d. Amos and Abigail, Jan. 27, 1800.
Oliver Osgood, s. Eze[kie]l, jr. and Phebe, Mar. 29, 1812.
Osgood Loring, s. Capt. Amos and Abiah, Feb. 29, 1836.
Pamela, d. Benjamin and Sarah, Sept. 9, 1793.
Pamela Gardner, d. Molly, bp. Aug. 23, 1795. C. R. 1.
[Peter. C. R. 1.], s. Ezekiel and Marcy, Dec. 14, 1734.
Peter, s. Peter and Elezebith, Apr. 24, 1757.
Peter, s. Dean and Deborah, bp. Jan. 21, 1798. C. R. 1.
Peter, s. John, jr. and Chloe, June 22, 1808.
Peter, s. John, jr. and Chloe, July 15, 1815.
Phebe, d. John and Hannah, Jan. 7, 1724-5.
Phebe, d. Christo[phe]r and Elizabeth, Sept. 8, 1760.
Phebe, d. Christo[phe]r and Eliz[abe]th, Sept. 4, 1767.
Phebe, d. Daniel, 3d and Mary, Mar. 3, 1786.
Phebe, d. Edward, of Blue Hill, bp. June 17, 1792. C. R. 2.
Phebe, d. Ezekiel, jr. and Phebe, Aug. 24, 1801.
Phebe, d. Ezekiel and Phebe, bp. Dec. 1, 1805. C. R. 1.
Phineas, s. Christefor and Elezebith, Mar. 28, 1758.
Phineas Verry, s. Phineas and Joanna, July 17, 1810.
Putnam, s. Amos and Hannah, Dec. 30, 1806.
Rebecca White, d. Robert E., carpenter, and Maria E., Apr. 26, 1847.
Ruben, s. Michael and Elizabeth, June 19, 1772.
Samuel, s. Ezekiel and Marcy, Mar. 10, 1745-6.

CARLTON, Samuel, s. Samuel and Sarah, Aug. 6, 1773.
Samuel, s. Samuel and Sarah, Sept. 20, 1776.
Sarah, d. Asa and Hannah, Apr. 8, 1759.
Sarah, d. James and Elizabeth, June 4, 1764.
Sarah, d. Peter and Sarah, July 29, 1774.
Sarah, d. Benjamin and Sarah, Dec. 19, 1780.
Sarah, d. Samuel and Sarah, Oct. 27, 1785.
Sarah A., d. Charles and Mary, May 13, 1832.
Sarah Holten, d. Ezekiel and Phebe, Apr. 21, 1807.
Sarah I[ngalls. C. R. I.], d. John, jr. and Chloe, Feb. 15, 1820.
Sophia, d. John, jr. and Chloe, Dec. 20, 1809.
Susan Ann, d. Daniel and Lucinda, Apr. 7, 1824.
Susanna, d. John and Hannah, Nov. 8, 1731.
Theoder, s. Christopher and Martha, Sept. 14, 1731.
Theoder, s. Christopher and Martha, Mar. 18, 1733-4.
Timothy, s. Ezekiel and Marcy, Nov. 9, 1752.
Timothy, s. Daniel, 3d and Molly [bp. June 21. C. R. I.], 1789.
William, s. Ezekiel and Dorcas, bp. Feb. 25, 1787. C. R. I.
William A., s. Kimball and Betsy, June 3, 1827.
——, s. John and Hannah, jr., Oct. 27, 1726.
——, s. Ezekiel and Marcy, Aug. 31, 1732.
——, ch. Joshua, bp. ——, 1749. C. R. I.
——, twin sons Hannah and Orlando Abbot, Aug. 21, 1812.
——, twin chn. Ezekiel, jr. and Phebe, Feb. 27, 1814.
——, s. Col. Dean and Martha, Feb. 21, 1821.
——, ch. Kimball and Betsy, Feb. 18, 1826.
——, ch. Isaac and Mary Ann, Oct. 1, 1831.
——, s. Isaac and Mary Ann, June 30, 1833.
——, s. Isaac and Mary Ann, Aug. 3, 1834.

CARNEY, Martha J., d. Bartholomew and Jane, Aug. 9, 1838.
Mary A., d. Bartholomew and Jane, May 19, 1840.
——, s. Bartholomew, laborer, and Jane, Oct. 11, 1843.

CARPENTER, John, s. Nelson, laborer, and Sarah, Sept. 29, 1843.

CARR, ——, ch. Samuel, manufacturer, Feb. 17, 1844.

CARRIER, Andrew, s. Thomas and Martha, May 7, 1677.
Elizabeth, d. Richard and Elisabeth, June 3, 1695.
Hannah, d. Thomas and Martha, July 12, 1689.
Hannah, d. Tho[mas] and [torn], —— 20, 1708-9.
John, s. Richard and Elizabeth, Mar. 16, 1696-7.

CARRIER, Richard, s. Richard and Martha, July 17, 1674.
Thomas, s. Thomas and Susannah [bp. Feb. 7, 1714. C. R. 2.].
——, ch. [Tho]mas and Susannah, Mar. 6, 1705-6.
——, ch. Th[om]as and Susanna, Oct. 21, 1710.
——, d. Thomas and Susanna, July 2, 1712.

CARRUTH (see also Caruth), Charles Henry, s. Isaac and Ann D., bp. July 7, 1844. C. R. 3.
Sumner, s. Isaac and Ann D., bp. July 7, 1844. C. R. 3.

CARTER, Abigail B[uck. C. R. 2.], d. Richard and Abigail, June 9, 1824. P. R. 18.
Albert A[lonzo. C. R. 2.], s. Richard and Abigail, Oct. 23, 1840. P. R. 18.
Edward, s. Richard and Abigail, Oct. 29, 1829.
Edwin, s. Richard and Abigail, Jan. 29, 1821. [1822. P. R. 18.]
Emily, d. Richard and Abigail, Aug. 6, 1838. P. R. 18.
Ephraim, s. Thomas and Thankfull, Dec. —, 1782.
Henry J[aques. C. R. 2.], s. Richard and Abigail, May 31, 1833.
Justin, s. Richard and Abigail, Apr. 27, 1820.
Mary Sophia, d. Justin, farmer, and Mary R., Feb. 16, 1848.
Nancy, d. Thomas and Thankfull, Jan. 1, 1781.
Richard [Brooks. C. R. 2.], s. Richard and Abigail, Jan. 29, 1822.
Sophia B[lanchard. C. R. 2.], d. Richard and Abigail, July 12, 1826. P. R. 18.
William R[ich. C. R. 2.], s. Richard and Abigail, July 15, 1836.
——, d. Richard, July 12, 1826.

CARUTH (see also Carruth), Francis W[hipple. C. R. 3.], s. Isaac and Ann D., Aug. 2, 1837.
Isaac S[mith. C. R. 3.], s. Isaac and Ann D., Mar. 11, 1840.

CARYLE, Thomas, s. Michael, laborer, and Brageat, both b. Ireland, May 16, 1848.

CASWALL, Mary Elizabeth, d. Rev. Henry and Mary Chase, Nov. 1, 1833. C. R. 4.

CATING, Thomas C., s. Thomas, laborer, and Eliza, Sept. 11, 1845.

CAURLTON (see also Carleton), [Christo]pher, s. Christopher and Martha, Dec. 31, 1717.

CAURLTQN, Daniell, s. John and Hannah, J—— [1707?].
Hanah, d. Joseph and Abigaill, Nov. 28, 1699.
Isaack, s. Christopher and Martha, Nov. — [1716].
Joseph, s. Joseph and Abigail, Nov. 9, 1698.
Joshuah, s. John and Hannah, Mar. 18 [1714-15].
Priscilla, d. John and Hannah, —— [1711].
Priscilla, d. John and Hannah, Aug. 28, 1717.
——, d. John and Hannah, Feb. 7, 1718-19.

CAVENDER, Barney, s. Thomas, laborer, and Ann, July 7, 1848.

CHADWICK, David, s. David and Sarah, Jan. 9, 1752
Joshua, s. David and Sarah, Jan. 4, 1755.
Obed, s. Joseph and Anna, Nov. 13, 1776.
Zebediah, s. Joseph and Anna, Jan. 26, 1771.

CHAMBERLAIN, Martha Ann, d. Charles W., machinist, and Mary A., Sept. 4, 1846.

CHANDLER, Abby Jane, d. Joseph, jr. and Lucy R. (Gates), May 21, 1840. T. C.
Abial, s. Abial and Hephzibah, —— [1711].
[Abiel. C. R. 2.], s. twin, John and Hannah, Nov. 24, 1717.
Abiel, s. Abiel and Rebecca, June 27, 1742.
Abiel, s. Joshua and Hannah, Aug. 28, 1760.
Abiel, s. Timothy, bp. June. 13, 1773. C. R. 2.
Abiell, s. John and Hannah, Jan. 9, 1686-7.
Abigaiel, d. Philemon and Elizebeth, Mar. 7, 17[25. C. R. 2.].
Abigail, d. Isaac [2d. C. R. 2.] and Abigail, Dec. 13, 1781.
Abigal, d. Isaac and Abigal, Sept. 3, 1794.
Abijah, s. Josiah and Sarah, Mar. 24, 1718-19.
Adela, d. Hepzabeth and James, Aug. 15, 1826.
Albert Ballard, s. Hermon, yeoman, and Phebe A., Oct. 18, 1847.
Alice, d. Stevens, bp. Oct. 2, 1803. C. R. 2.
Amanda, d. James, jr. and Hepzebeth, July —, 1823.
Amos, s. Timo[thy], bp. Dec. 15, 1777. C. R. 2.
Amos, grands. Zebediah, bp. Aug. 5, 1804. C. R. 2.
Amos, s. Fanney, Apr. 4, 1807.
Anngenett, d. James, jr. and Hepzebeth, Apr. 4, 1830.
Ann Elizabeth, d. J., bp. Sept. 28, 1845. C. R. 2.
Ann Maria, d. Ralph H., bp. July 3, 1836. C. R. 2.
Annis, d. Thomas and Mary, Mar. 24, 1689.
Asa, s. Tho[ma]s, bp. Apr. 29, 1759. C. R. 2.
Ballard, s. [Ens. C. R. 2.] David and Mary, Jan. 23, 1765.

CHANDLER, Benjamin, s. Isaac, bp. July 24, 1768. C. R. 2.
Benjamin, s. James and Phebe, June 27, 1790.
Benjamine, s. Josiah and Sarah, —— [1707?].
Bridget, d. Thomas, jr. and Elisabeth, Apr. 2, 1744.
Bridgett, d. Joseph and Mehitabel, Sept. 19, 1719.
[Bridgit. C. R. 2.], ch. Thomas, jr. and Mary, Sept. 2, 1712.
Chloe, d. Nathan, jr. and Phebe, June 30, 1771.
Clarissa, d. John and Abigail, Oct. 8, 1799.
Cloe, d. Timothy, jr., bp. Sept. 1, 1771. C. R. 2.
Damon, d. Flora, bp. July 5, 1778. C. R. 2.
Daniel, s. Josiah and Sarah, Aug. 8 [1727. C. R. 2.].
Daniel, s. David and Mary, July 9, 1754.
Daniel, s. Daniel, bp. Mar. 9, 1777. C. R. 2.
Darcus, d. [Ens. C. R. 2.] John and Hannah, July 18, 1[727. C. R. 2.].
David, s. Thomas and Mary, Jan. 11, 1698-9.
David, s. Josiah and Sarah, Dec. 15, 1724.
[David. C. R. 2], s. David, jr. and Mary, June 10, 1751.
David Walker, s. Tim[oth]y, jr., bp. Aug. 6, 1769. C. R. 2.
Deborah, d. Zebadiah, jr. and Deborah, Apr. 26, 1757.
Deborah, d. Zebadiah and Lucy, Apr. 11, 1783.
Dolly, d. John and Dorothy, July 28, 1783.
Dorcas, d. James and Phebe, Jan. 13, 1800.
Dorcas Ballard, d. Nathan and Lucy, Oct. 2, 1797. P. R. 4.
Dorcas Ballard, d. Joshua, jr. and Dorcas, Apr. 1, 1800.
[Ebenezer. C. R. 2.], s. Thomas, jr., May 18, 1749.
Edward, s. Jonathan and Hannah, July —, 1818.
Elenor, d. Willia[m] and Elenor, Jan. 23, 1687-8.
Elezebeth, d. Philemon and Elezebeth, July 18, 1721.
Elezebeth, d. William and Elizebeth, Feb. 19, 1729-30.
Elezebith, d. Phileman, jr. and Ketura, Jan. 29, 1748-9.
Elezebith, d. Wiliam and Mary, Oct. 4, 1749.
Elisabeth, d. Thomas [jr. C. R. 2.] and Eli[torn], Dec. 17, 1739.
Elisabeth, d. Thomas, jr. and Elisabeth, Mar. 13, 1741-2.
Elisabeth, d. Philimon [jr. C. R. 2.] and Ketura, May 12, 1744.
Eliza, s. Thomas and Elezebith, Aug. 6, 1753.
Eliza, d. Joseph, bp. June 20, 1802. C. R. 2.
Eliza C., d. Joshua, jr. and Eliza, Aug. 30, 1827.
Elizabeth, d. Thomas and Mary, July 13, 1693.
Elizabeth, d. Thomas [jr. C. R. 2.] and Mary, May 15, 1718.
Elizabeth, d. Philemon and Elizab[eth], June 30, 1719.
Elizabeth, d. William and Elizabeth, June 10, 1734.
Elizabeth, d. Nathan [jr. C. R. 2.] and Phebe, May 15, 1763.
Elizabeth, d. Tim[oth]y, jr., bp. Sept. 6, 1767. C. R. 2.

CHANDLER, Elizabeth, d. William, jr. and Elizabeth, June 10, 1777.
Elizabeth, d. Zebadiah and Lucy, May 19, 1796. [bp. Apr. 24. C. R. 2.]
Elizabeth, d. James and Phebe, Nov. 17, 1797.
Elizabeth, d. Joseph and Mary, June 13, 1802.
Elizabeth C., d. Joshua and Susan, Nov. 11, 1824.
Elizebeth, d. Zebadiah and Sarah, M— [1720-21.]. [bp. Apr. 2, 1721. C. R. 2.]
Emily Jane, d. Ralph H. and Phebe, Nov. 15, 1825.
Emma, d. John, bp. May 6, 1849. C. R. 2.
Ephraim, s. Thomas and Mary, Oct. 2, 1696.
[Eunice. C. R. 2.], d. Thomas, jr. and Elisabeth, Feb. 12, 1745-6.
Ezra, s. Nathan [jr. C. R. 2.] and Phebe, June 20, 1761.
Ezra, s. Nathan and Lucy, Oct. 8, 1794. P. R. 4.
Ezra, s. Zebadiah and Lucy, June 27, 1785.
Ezra, s. Nathan and Lucy, Sept. 26, 1792. P. R. 4.
Fanney, d. Zebadiah and Lucy, June 18, 1781.
Francis E., d. Ralph H. and Mary, Oct. 11, 1838.
George, s. John and Abigail, Oct. 16, 1805.
George G[ates. C. R. 3.], s. Joseph, jr. and Lucy R., Dec. 18, 1837.
George H., s. John and Phebe, Feb. 18, 1842. T. C.
George Warren, s. John, bp. June 5, 1842. C. R. 2.
Hannah, d. William and Mary, Feb. 5, 1673.
Hannah, d. John and Hannah, May 12, 1690.
Hannah, d. Thomas and Mary, Aug. 23, 1700.
Hannah, d. John and Hannah, —— [1709?].
Hannah, d. Henry and Lydia, Mar. —, 1711-12.
[Hannah. C. R. 2.], d. Thomas and Mary, Dec. 15, 1714.
Hannah, d. Joseph, bp. Feb. 2, 1724. C. R. 2.
Hannah, d. Nathan and Priscilla, May 20, 1735.
Hannah, d. David [sr. C. R. 2.] and Abiel, June 21, 1755.
Hannah, d. Wiliam and Rebeca, Aug. 29, 1756.
Hannah, d. Joshua and Hannah, Oct. 13, 1764.
Hannah, d. Isaac, bp. Jan. 13, 1771. C. R. 2.
Hannah, d. James and Phebe, Dec. 28, 1785.
Hannah, d. Zebadiah and Lucy, June 17, 1787.
Hannah, d. John, bp. Oct. 2, 1791. C. R. 2.
Hannah, d. Joshua, bp. Oct. 13, 1793. C. R. 2.
Hannah, d. Isaac and Abigal, Jan. 10, 1798.
Harriot, d. Joseph, jr. and Mary, Dec. 13, 1811.
Henry, s. Thomas and Hanna, May 28, [16]67.
Henry, s. Henry and Liddia, Sept. 3, 1696.
Henry, s. Isaac, bp. July 27, 1766. C. R. 2.

CHANDLER, Henry, s. John, bp. Mar. 30, 1788. C. R. 2.
Henry, s. James and Phebe, June 23, 1802.
Henry Flint, s. Joshua and Eliza, Sept. 26, 1835.
[Hephsibah. C. R. 2.] ——ah, d. Timothy and Hephzebah, Apr. 7, 1726.
Hephzibah, d. David and Abiel, at Rumford, Oct. 16, 1743.
Hepzibath, d. James, jr. and Hepzibath, June 24, 1816.
Hermon, s. James, bp. July 21, 1805. C. R. 2.
Hermon G[eorge. C. R. 3.], s. Hermon and Phebe A., Mar. 28, 1832.
Hermon Phelps, s. Nathan and Lucy, Dec. 19, 1801. P. R. 4.
Holbrook, s. Ralph H. and Phebe, July 12, 1815.
Holbrook, s. Ralph H. and Phebe, May 27, 1820.
Huldah, d. David and Abiel, at Suncook [N. H.], Aug. 16, 1740.
Isaac, s. [Ens. C. R. 2.] John and Hannah, Feb. 22 [1725. C. R. 2.].
Isaac, s. Philemon and Elesibeth, Sept. 24, 1727.
Isaac, s. Nathan and Prissilla, Apr. 8, 173[2. C. R. 2.]
Isaac, s. Wiliam and Rebeca, Oct. 4, 1754.
Isaac, s. Isaac and Hannah, Jan. 28, 1758.
Isaac, s. Isaac [2d. C. R. 2.] and Abigail, June 11, 1784.
Isaac, s. James and Phebe, Feb. 25, 1795.
Isaake, s. Joseph and Sarah, Aug. 24, 1696.
Jacob, s. twin, Phillemon, May 23, 1731.
Jacob, s. William, jr. and Elizabeth, Apr. 23, 1774.
James, s. William and Mary, Dec. 13, 1736.
James, s. Isaac and Hannah, Nov. 28, 1761.
James, s. James and Phebe, May 16, 1788.
James F., s. Oscar, machinist, and Ann, May 4, 1848.
James [Rodney. C. R. 3.], s. James, jr. and Hepzibeth, July 13, 1820.
Jemima, d. [torn], May 2, 1701.
Joanna, d. Zebadiah and Sarah, —— [1710].
Joanna, d. Daniel and Joanna, Aug. 8, 1774.
John, s. John and Hannah, Oct. 23, 1677.
John, s. John and Hannah, Mar. 14, 1679-80.
John, s. John and Hannah, —— [1702].
John, s. Thomas and Mary, Feb. 13, 1716-17.
John, s. Joseph and Mehetebel, Jan. 19, 1721-2.
John, s. Thomas and Mary, Dec. 14, 1723.
John, s. John and Tabitha, Aug. 15, 1730.
John, s. Philemon [jr. C. R. 2.] and Keturah, Apr. 26, 1740.
John, s. John and Hannah, July 18, 1750.
John, s. Isaac and Hannah, Nov. 21, 1759.

CHANDLER, John, s. William, jr. and Eliz[abe]th, Nov. 7, 1768.
John, s. [Ens. C. R. 2.] David and Mary, July 4, 1771.
John, s. John, bp. Sept. 11, 1785. C. R. 2.
John, s. John Blanchard and Elizabeth, Feb. 5, 1789.
John, s. John and Abigail, Dec. 28, 1797.
John, s. John and Abigail, Dec. 28, 1799.
John, s. Joshua, jr. and Hannah, June 20, 1806.
John, s. John and Hannah, July 7, 1848.
John H[enry. C. R. 2.], s. John and Phebe, Feb. 15, 1840.
John N[ewton. C. R. 2.], s. Ralph H. and Phebe, Mar. 10, 1833.
[Jonathan, s. C. R. 2.] [T]homas and Mary, Oct. 20, 1712.
Jonathan, s. Josiah and Sarah, Feb. 21 [1721-2.].
Jonathan, s. Joseph and Mary, Feb. 6, 1793.
Jonathan F., s. Jonathan and Hannah, Oct. 9, 1816.
Joseph, s. Thomas and Hannah, Aug. 3, 1669.
Joseph, s. William and Bridget, July 17, 1682.
Joseph, s. Joseph and Sarah, June 29, 1694.
Joseph, s. Joseph and Mehitabel, Feb. 13, 1716-17.
Joseph, s. Joseph and Sarah, Apr. 1, 1743.
Joseph, s. Joseph, jr. and Mary, June 8, 1743.
Joseph, s. John and Hannah, Jan. 30, 1753.
Joseph, s. Thomas and Elezebith, Dec. 22, 1756.
Joseph, s. Zebadiah and Deborah, May 2, 1759.
Joseph, s. Joseph and Mary, Dec. 18, 1783.
Joseph, s. James and Phebe, Dec. 18, 1792.
Joseph, s. Joseph, jr. and Mary, June 10, 1808.
Joseph, s. twin, Ralph H. and Phebe, May 30, 1818.
Joseph, s. Holbrook and Phebe, Sept. 3, 1827.
Joseph Henry, s. Joseph and Lucy, bp. Aug. 28, 1836. C. R. 3.
Joshua, s. Joshua and Sarah, July 23, 1732.
Joshua, s. Joshua and Hannah, Aug. 18, 1758.
Joshua, s. Abiel and Mary, May 15, 1785.
Joshua, s. Joseph and Mary, Jan. 13, 1789.
Joseph, s. Joshua, jr. and Dorcas, Mar. 19, 1803.
Joshua, s. Joshua and Susan, Oct. 5, 1821.
Joshua Herbert, s. Joshua, jr. and Eliza, Sept. 2, 1831.
Joshuah, s. John and Hannah, —— [1705?].
Josiah, s. William and Sarah, Dec. 28, 1683. [Dec. 29. CT. R.]
Josiah, s. David and Mary, Jan. 20, 1762.
Laura Maria, d. Ralph H., farmer, and Mary H., Oct. 5, 1844.
Leonard, s. Reben Guliver and Elizabeth, ——, 1785.
Lois, d. Stevens, bp. Oct. 2, 1803. C. R. 2.
Luce, d. Nathan, jr. and Phebe, June 26, 1758.
Lucy, d. Zebediah, jr. and Lucy, Feb. 8, 1775.

CHANDLER, Lucy, d. Nathan [jr. C. R. 2.] and Lucy, Nov. 30, 1785.
Lucy J[ohnson. C. R. 3.], d. Joshua and Susan, Jan. 23, 1827.
Lucy King, d. Joseph and Mary, Aug. 28, 1795.
Lydia, d. Tho[ma]s and Mary, —— [1709-10].
Lydia, d. John and Hannah, Aug. 10, 1720.
Lydia, d. David and Abiel, May 29, 1746.
Lydia, d. Zebadiah, jr. and Deborah, May 18, 1761.
Lydiah, d. Henery and Lydia, Nov. 27, 1699.
Malvina, d. James and Hepsabeth, bp. May 24, 1829. C. R. 3.
Martha, d. Joseph and Mary, July 4, 1804.
Martha Foster, d. Joshua, jr. and Eliza, July 6, 1829.
Martha Hurd, d. Joshua and Susan, bp. Aug. 28, 1831. C. R. 3.
Mary, d. William [and Mary. CT. F.], July 5, 1659. CT. R.
Mary, d. Thomas and Mary, Feb. 18, 1686-7.
Mary, d. Thomas, jr. and Mar[y], Mar. 8, 1701-2.
[Mary. C. R. 2.], d. John and Hannah, May 7, 1712.
Mary, d. Mary, d. Tho[mas], sr., bp. Oct. 19, 1712. C. R. 2.
Mary, d. Joseph and Mehitabell, Mar. 4, 1712-13.
Mary, d. Henery and Lydia, Mar. 14, 1712-[13].
Mary, d. David and Abiel, Aug. 8, 1734.
Mary, d. Philemon and Elisabeth, Jan. 15, 1735-6.
Mary, d. Nathan and Priscilla, June 15, 1740.
Mary, d. William and Mary, Feb. 8, 1740-41.
Mary, d. William and Mary, May 3, 1745.
Mary, d. [Lt. C. R. 2.], Zebediah, jr. and Deborah, Apr. 4, 1764.
Mary, d. Nathan, jr. and Phebe, May 18, 1766.
Mary, d. Timothy, jr. and Mary, bp. May 17, 1767. C. R. 2.
Mary, d. Isaac, bp. Nov. 28, 1773. C. R. 2.
Mary, d. Isaac [2d. C. R. 2.] and Abigal, June 5, 1786.
Mary, d. twin, Ralph H., and Phebe, May 30, 1818.
Mary, d. Joshua and Susan, Aug. 10, 1828.
Mary Ann, d. Ralph H. and Phebe, Oct. 27, 1823.
Mary Ballard, d. Joseph, jr. and Mary, Apr. 25, 1810.
Mary K., d. Joshua and Susan, Aug. 10, 1829.
Matilda Eliza, d. Joshua, jr. and Eliza, Aug. 30, 1827.
Mehetabel, d. William and Rebeckah, Apr. 28, 1761.
Mehetebel, d. Henry and Lydia, June 23, 1720.
Mehitabel, d. Joseph and Sarah, Feb. 27, 1698-9.
Mehitabel, d. Zebadiah and Sarah, ——, 1717. [bp. Oct. 27, 1717. C. R. 2.]
Melvina, d. James and Hepzibeth, Nov. 17, 1828.
Molly, d. David and Mary, Oct. 27, 1773.
Nabby, d. Isaac, 3d, bp. Dec. 3, 1786. C. R. 2.

CHANDLER, Nancy, d. John and Abigail, Oct. 17, 1795.
Nathan, s. Nathan and Prisscilla, Feb. 19, 1729-30.
Nathan, s. Nathan, jr. and Phebe, June 16, 1756.
Nathan, s. Nathan and Lucy, Mar. 29, 1788. P. R. 4.
Nathan, s. Joseph and Mary, July 2, 1797.
Nathan, s. Joshua and Dorcas, Feb. 1, 1812.
Nathan, s. Ralph H. and Phebe, Apr. 11, 1829.
Nathan [Wallace. P. R. 30.], s. Joshua, farmer, and Eliza, Sept. 13, 1843.
Nathaniell, s. Joseph and Sarah, —— [1703].
Nehemiah, s. Henery and Lydia, —— [1703].
Oscar, s. James, jr. and Hepzabeth, Oct. 17, 1824.
Peter, s. Thomas and Elezebith, Mar. 25, 1755.
Phebe, d. Willia[m] and Bridget, Sept. 17, 1680.
[Phebe. C. R. 2.], d. John and Hannah, Jan. 2, 1714-15.
[Phebe. C. R. 2.], d. Phillemon and Elizabeth, July 3, 1729.
Phebe, d. Nathan and Prisc[illa], June 4, 1742.
Phebe, d. Nathan, jr. and Phebe, Oct. 18, 1754.
Phebe, d. Zebadiah and Lucy, Aug. 29, 1776.
Phebe, d. James and Phebe, Aug. 28, 1783.
Phebe A., d. Ralph H. and Phebe, Nov. 9, 1816.
Phebe M[aria. C. R. 3.], d. Hermon P. and Phebe A., Nov. 18, 1838.
Pheoby, d. Thomas and Mary, —— [1708?].
Philemon, s. William and Mary, Aug. 24, 1667.
Philemon, s. William and Mary, Sept. 4, 1671.
Philemon, s. William and Sarah, May 15, 1690.
Philemon, s. Philemon and Elizabeth, Oct. 7, 1717.
Philemon, s. William and Rebecca, Dec. 30, 1765.
Philemon, s. William, jr., bp. Dec. 21, 1783. C. R. 2.
Polly, d. Joseph and Polly, Mar. 27, 1787.
Priscilla, d. Zeabadiah and Sarah, Apr. 26, 1713.
Priscilla, d. Nathan [jr. C. R. 2.] and Phebe, June 31, 1768. [bp. June 5. C. R. 2.]
Ralph Holbrook, s. Joseph and Mary, Feb. 17, 1791.
Rebecca, d. Joseph and Mary, Oct. 29, 1816.
Rebeckah, d. William and Rebeckah, Mar. 3, 1759.
Rebekah, d. Nathan and Lucy, July 17, 1790. P. R. 4.
Reubin, s. Joseph [sr. C. R. 2.] and Sarah, Dec. 6, 1744.
Rhoda, d. Joseph and Sarah, —— [1705?].
Rhoda, d. Nathan, jr. and Phoebe, Mar. 2, 1774.
Rhoda, d. Zebadiah [Jedediah. C. R. 2.] and Lucy, July 1, 1793.
Roas, d. William and Elizabeth, Apr. 12, 1728.
Rodah, d. William and Bridgett, Sept. 26, 1684.

CHANDLER, [Samuel, s. C. R. 2.] Josiah and Sarah, July 2, 1713.
Samuel, s. twin, John and Hannah. Nov. 24, 1717.
Samuel, s. [Ens. C. R. 2.] John and Hannah, —— 22. [bp. Aug. 25, 1723. C. R. 2.]
Samuel, s. David, jr. and Mary, Nov. 4, 1757.
Samuel, s. Isaac and Hannah, Jan. 25, 1764.
Samuel, s. John and Abigail, Dec. 7, 1803.
Sam[ue]ll, s. Henry and Lydia, Oct. 11, 1698.
Sara, d. Thomas and Hanna, Dec. 20, 1661.
Sara, d. William and Mary, Jan. 29, 1662.
Sarah, d. Joseph and Sarah, Mar. 10, 1692-3.
Sarah, d. William and Sarah, Mar. 13, 1692-3.
Sarah, d. John and Hanah, Oct. 8, 1693.
Sarah, d. Josiah and Sarah [bp. Nov. 18, 1716. C. R. 2.].
Sarah, d. Josiah and Sarah, May 3, 1736.
Sarah, d. Zebadiah, jr. and Deborah, May 8, 1751.
Sarah, d. David and Sarah, May 12, 1761.
Sarah, d. Jeremiah and Martha, July 17, 1773.
Sarah, d. Joseph and Mary, Mar. 10, 1800.
Sarah Ann, d. Isaac, jr. and Sarah, Sept. 3, 1813.
Sarah Eliza, d. Ralph H. and Phebe, Jan. 9, 1836.
Stephan, s. Zebadiah, jr. and Deborah, Oct. 26, 1754.
Stephen, s. Zebadiah and Lucy, Oct. 22, 1790.
Stevens, s. William and Mary, Dec. 15, 1738.
Susan, d. Joshua and Susan, Apr. 16, 1818.
Susan, d. Joshua and Susan, Feb. 9, 1820.
Thomas, s. Thomas and Hanna, Oct. 2, 1652.
Thomas, s. Thomas and Hanna, Oct. 9, 1664.
Thomas, s. William and Mary, Mar. 2, 1668.
Thomas, s. William and Mary, Dec. 5, 1676.
Thomas, s. Thomas and Mary, June 4, 1691.
Thomas, s. William and Elezebeth, Oct. 3 [1726. C. R. 2.].
Thomas, s. Thomas [jr. C. R. 2.] and Elezebith, Oct. 22, 1751.
Timothy, s. Thomas and Mary, Mar. 29, 1694-5.
Timothy, s. David and Abiel, at Suncook [N. H.], Apr. 5, 1738.
Timothy, s. Timothy, bp. Sept. 10, 1775. C. R. 2.
William, s. Thomas and [Hanna. CT. F.], May 28, 1659.
William, s. Willi[am] and Mary, Jan. 31, 1661.
William, s. Philemon and Elezebeth, Apr. 29, 1723.
William, s. William and Elezabeth, Jan. 25, 1731-2.
William, s. William and Mary, Mar. 18, 1746-7.
William, s. William, jr. and Eliz[abe]th, May 16, 1770.
William Henry, s. Hermon and Phebe, bp. July 21, 1839. C. R. 3.

CHANDLER, Zachariah, s. William and Sarah, May 1, 1695.
Zachariah, s. twin, Phillemon, May 23, 1731.
Zebadiah, s. Joshua and Sarah, Dec. 23, 1729.
Zebadiah, s. Zebadiah, jr. and Deborah, Nov. 11, 1752.
Zebadiah, s. Zebadiah and Lucy, Sept. 8, 1779.
Zebediah, s. John and Hannah, Apr. 1, 1683.
——, ch. [torn] and Mary, —— [1702].
——, ch. Thomas and Mary, July 14, 1704.
——, ch. [Thom]as and Mary, Oct. 9, 1704.
——, ch. [torn] and Lydia, Dec. 25, 1704.
——, ch. [torn], June 10, 1706.
——, d. Henery and Lydia, July 9, 1709.
——, ch. [torn] and ——abel, Dec. 10, 170[9].
——, ch. Josiah and Sarah, June 7, 1710-11.
——, ch. Thomas and Mary, Feb. 16, 1710-11.
——, ch. [torn] and Mehittebell, Apr. 22, 1711.
——, d. Henery and Lydia, Dec. —, 1716.
——, s. Henery and Lydia, Apr. 19, 1718.
——, s. Thomas and Mary, jr., Nov. 23, 1720.
——, s. Joseph and Mehetebel, Sept. 10, 1726.
——, d. John and Tabitha, July 10, 1728.
——, ch. Timothy, bp. Sept. 1, 1771. C. R. 1.
——, s. Joseph and Mary, July 10, 1815.

CHAPMAN, John, s. Nathaniell and Mary, Feb. 13, 1685-6.
——, ch. [torn] and Anne, Dec. 5, 1709.

CHASE, Abigail M., d. John and Anna, May 2, 1824.
Andrew, s. Samuel, laborer, and Harriet, Mar. 9, 1846.
Andrew Jackson, s. Capt. John and Anna, May 9, 1815.
Caroline Augusta, d. John and Anna, Feb. 15, 1829.
Eliza Ann, d. John and Anna, Aug. 8, 1811.
Enoch Bartlett, s. John and Anna, Oct. 4, 1822.
Eunice A., d. Capt. John and Anna, May 15, 1820.
Fanny Evelina, d. John and Anna, Sept. 14, 1826.
Franklin A., s. Samuel, laborer, and Harriet T., Dec. 3, 1848.
Franklin Newton, s. John and Anna, Sept. 3, 1833.
John Edwards, s. John and Anne, Dec. 9, 1817.
Mehetabel, d. Emery and Mehetabell, Dec. 12, 1768.
Sally, d. wid. Mehitabel, bp. Nov. 9, 1788. C. R. 2.
Samuel Milton, s. John and Anna, Apr. 30, 1831.
Sarah S., d. John and Anna, Oct. 2, 1813.
Seth, s. John and Anna, July 28, 1809.
Susan Rebecca, d. Seth, cordwainer, and Charlotte, at Lowell, Feb. 1, 1847.

CHEEVER, Benjamin, s. Samuel and Mary, May 28, 1827.
Frances Ann, d. James and Lydia, Aug. 15, 1830.
James Osgood, s. James, bp. Oct. 12, 1834. C. R. 2.
Samuel, s. Samuel and Sarah, Apr. 11, 1824.
Samuel, s. Benjamin, farmer, and Betsey, Sept. 8, 1848.
Sarah M., d. Benjamin, yeoman, and Betsy, Dec. 30, 1846.
William, s. James and Henrietta, June 30, 1835.
——, s. James and Lydia, Nov. 20, 1828.

CHENY (see also Cheyne, Chyene), George A., s. Ariel, cordwainer, b. Georgetown, and Emily, b. Weare, N. H., Dec. 14, 1848.

CHEYNE (see also Cheny), William, s. William, tailor, and Margarett, May 26, 1845.

CHECKERIN (see also Chickering), Hannah, d. Samuel and Hannah, July 13, 1730.
Zechariah, s. Samuel and Hannah, May 13, 1729.

CHICKERING (see also Checkerin, Chickren, Chickring), Augusta, d. Jacob and Sarah J., Mar. 11, 1842.
Benjamin, s. Susannah, bp. Feb. 17, 1760. C. R. 1.
Caroline, d. J., bp. June 8, 1845. C. R. 2.
Caroline Amanda, d. Charles and Priscilla, Mar. 8, 1835.
Charles, s. Dean and Sarah, Dec. 23, 1803.
Charles J., s. Charles and Priscilla, Dec. 18, 1836.
Cloe, d. Zachariah and Sarah, Oct. 15, 1785.
Ceree, s. Zachariah and Mary O., Aug. 10, 1815.
Daniel, s. Samuel, jr. and Mary, Nov. 25, 1776.
Daniel, s. Daniel and Susanna, Nov. 26, 1805.
Daniel Osgood, s. Daniel and Susanna, Aug. 1, 1811.
Dean, s. Dean and Sarah, Mar. 20, 1788.
Dorcas, d. Samuel and Hannah, July 14, 1742.
Edward, s. Daniel and Susanna, July 24, 1800.
Elisabeth, d. Samuel and Hannah, Jan. 25, 1736-7.
Elizabeth, d. John, bp. Sept. 19, 1773. C. R. 1.
Elizabeth, d. Samuel, jr. and Esther, Oct. 14, 1789.
Emily, d. Jacob and Sarah J., July 5, 1840.
Esther, d. Samuel, jr. and Esther, May 29, 1788.
Fanny M., d. W[illia]m and Fanny, Nov. 8, 1838.
Farnum, s. Dean and Sarah, May 17, 1786.
Frederick, s. Zachariah and Sarah, Dec. 20, 1776.

CHICKERING, George, s. Samuel, jr. and Esther, Sept. 29, 1798.
George E., s. William, carpenter, and Fanny, June 29, 1843.
George Osgood, s. Zachariah and Sarah, Sept. 18, 1782.
Hannah, d. Samuel and Mary, July 1, 1762.
Hannah, d. Zachariah and Sarah, Aug. 8, 1773.
Hannah, d. Samuel, jr. and Mary, July 6, 1779.
Hannah [Maria. C. R. 1.], d. Zach[ariah] and Mary O., Sept. 15, 1819.
Henry, s. Daniel and Susanna, Aug. 11, 1813. [Sept. 9, 1813. dup.]
Horace Dean, s. Charles and Priscilla, July 14, 1838.
Isaac, s. Samuel [jr. C. R. 1.] and Mary, Aug. 5, 1770.
Isaac, s. Dean and Sarah, Feb. 10, 1793.
Jacob, s. Zachariah and Mary O., Aug. 2, 1806.
Jefferson, s. Dean and Sarah, Feb. 14, 1802.
John, s. Samuel and Hannah, Aug. 15, 1744.
John, s. Dean and Sarah, Oct. 4, 1790.
Joseph, s. Samuel, jr. and Mary, Aug. 30, 1772.
Joseph, s. Dean and Sarah, Oct. 25, 1797.
Joseph, s. Daniel and Susanna, Dec. 10, 1797.
Joseph, s. Daniel and Susannah, bp. Oct. 6, 1811. C. R. 1.
Lydia, d. twin, Zachariah and Sarah, Aug. 10, 1780.
Mary, d. Zachariah and Sarah, bp. Sept. 23, 1787. C. R. 1.
Mary Dane, d. Daniel and Susana, Jan. 14, 1816.
Mary F., d. John and Mary, July 9, 1813.
Mary Gordon, d. Isaac and Susan, bp. Apr. 12, 1818. C. R. 1.
Mary Osgood, d. Zachariah and Mary O., Oct. 26, 1804.
Milton, s. Jacob and Sarah J., Oct. 5, 1838.
Molly, d. Sam[ue]ll, jr. and Mary, May 19, 1758.
Otis, s. Jacob, carpenter, and Sarah J., Nov. 27, 1846.
Rebeccah, d. Zachariah and Sarah, Mar. 1, 1775.
Sally, d. Dean and Sarah, June 23, 1795.
Samuel, s. Samuel and Hannah, Sept. 28, 1732.
Samuel, s. Samuel, jr. and Mary, Feb. 4, 1756.
Samuel, s. Samuel, jr. and Esther, Apr. 13, 1787.
Samuel, s. Samuel and Esther, Oct. 10, 1792.
Samuel, s. Dean and Sarah, Oct. 13, 1799.
Samuel, s. Jacob, carpenter, and Sarah J., b. Derry, N. H., July 5, 1849.
Sarah, d. Samuel and Hannah, Mar. 5, 1734-5.
Sarah, d. John and Sarah, July 11, 1771.
Sarah, d. Sam[ue]ll, jr. and Mary, May 23, 1766.
Sarah, d. twin, Zachariah and Sarah, Aug. 10, 1780.
Sarah, d. Daniel and Susanna, Mar. 26, 1807.

CHICKERING, Sarah, d. Daniel and Susanna, May 21, 1809.
Sarah Abbot, d. Zachariah and Mary O., Oct. 9, 1808.
Sarah G., d. Isaac and Susannah, Sept. 16, 1814.
Sarah Jane, d. Isaac and Susan, bp. Apr. 12, 1818. C. R. I.
Sophia, d. Samuel jr. and Esther, Feb. 12, 1803.
Susan, d. Isaac and Susan, bp. Apr. 12, 1818. C. R. I.
Susanna, d. Samuel and Hannah, Jan. 25, 1738-9.
Susanna, d. Daniel and Susanna, Jan. 25, 1802.
Susanna, d. Daniel and Susanna, Aug. 19, 1803.
Susannah, d. Isaac and Susannah, Dec. —, 1812.
William, s. Zachariah and Mary, bp. Sept. 1, 1811. C. R. I.
William H., s. William and Fanny, July 3, 1837.
William W[allace. C. R. 2.], s. William and Fanny, July 9, 1841.
William Wallace, s. Charles, farmer, and Priscilla, Nov. 4, 1843.
Zachariah, s. Samuel and Hannah, Mar. 29, 1747.
Zachariah, s. Zachariah and Sarah, Aug. 16, 1778.
Zachariah, s. Samuel jr. and Esther, Jan. 29, 1795.
——, ch. John and Mary, Nov. 9, 1815.
——, d. John and Mary, Nov. 30, 1816.

CHICKREN (see also Chickering), Mary, d. Samuel and Hannah, Jan. 17, 1749-50.
Phebe, d. Samuel and Hannah, Nov. 9, 1751.

CHICKRING (see also Chickering), Dane, s. Sam[ue]ll, jr. and Mary [bp. June 26, 1768. C. R. I.].
Dean, s. Samuel, jr. and Mary, Feb. 8, 1760.
Elezebith, d. Capt. John and Mehetebel, Apr. 9, 1758.
John, s. Capt. John and Mehetebel, Oct. 22, 1754.
Zachariah, s. Sam[ue]ll, jr. and Mary, May 19, 1764.

CHOISE, Hannah Johnson, d. Emery, bp. May 28, 1780. C. R. 2.

CHRISTIE, James, s. George, flax-dresser, and Margaret, Apr. 5, 1845.

CHURCHILL, Arabella Louisa, d. Samuel and Eliza Ann, bp. Mar. 14, 1847. C. R. 4.
Gilbert Willett, s. Samuel and Eliza Ann, bp. Mar. 14, 1847. C. R. 4.
Harriet Sophia, d. Samuel and Eliza Ann, bp. Mar. 14, 1847. C. R. 4.
Melinda Vanola Shaw, d. Samuel and Eliza Ann, bp. Mar. 14, 1847. C. R. 4.

CHYENE (see also Cheny), Mary, d. John, operative, and Margaret, Aug. 29, 1844.
Sarah, d. W[illia]m, tailor, and Margaret, Apr. 26, 1844.

CLARK (see also Clarke, Clerck, Clerk), Abba Ann, d. Thomas and Sarah Ann, May 1, 1837.
Abijah, s. Abijah and Hannah, Aug. 3, 1780.
Amasa, s. Dr. Francis and Sarah F., Jan. 14, 1844.
Andrew, s. Andrew and Betsy, at Pomfret, Conn., May 25, 1814.
Angeline True, d. Benj[amin] and Almira H., bp. Sept. 6, 1840. C. R. 3.
Ballard, s. William and Rebecca, Mar. 7, 1773.
Benjamin, s. Joseph and Sarah [Mary. C. R. 2.], Aug. 11, 1720.
Benjamin, s. Joseph, jr. and Elisabeth, Mar. 28, 1743.
Betty, d. John and Jenney, Apr. 14, 1777.
Caroline, d. W[illia]m and Mary, bp. July 10, 1814. C. R. 2.
Catharine B. [Cradal. C. R. 1.], d. Hobart and Elizabeth, Oct. 11, 1827.
Charles, s. Samuel and Sarah, Aug. 10, 1783.
Charles, s. Capt. Samuel, bp. Apr. 27, 1794. C. R. 2.
Charles Henry, s. Benj[amin] and Almira H., bp. Sept. 6, 1840. C. R. 3.
Deliverence, d. Joseph and Sarah [Mary. C. R. 2.], July 24, 1715.
Dorothy, d. Hobart and Elizabeth, Nov. 10, 1829.
Ebenezer, s. Timothy and Elezebith [Sarah. C. R. 1.], Feb. 28, 1753.
Elezebith, d. Timothy and Elezebith, Mar. 30, 1748.
Elisabeth, d. Joseph, jr. and Elisabeth, Nov. 17, 1740.
Elisabeth, d. Timo[thy] and Elizabeth, bp. Apr. —, 1746. C. R. 1.
Elisabeth, d. Dr. Parker and Lydia, Apr. 18, 1746.
Eliza Ann, d. Thomas and Sarah A., May 29, 1834.
Elizabeth, d. Andrew and Betsy, at Woodstock, Conn., Nov. 30, 1816.
Elizabeth S., d. Hobart and Elizabeth, Dec. 11, 1825.
Elizabeth Smith, d. Hobart and Elizabeth, May 20, 1817.
Emma, d. Robert, flax-dresser, b. Scotland, and Mary, b. Sudbury, Nov. 30, 1849.
Ephriam, s. Joseph, jr. and Elisabeth, July 20, 1745.
Ezra, s. Ezra and Hannah, Dec. 28, 1805.
George T[homas. C. R. 1.], s. Hobart [jr. C. R. 1.] and Elizabeth, June 26, 1818.
Gideon Foster, s. Samuel, jr. and Elizabeth, Jan. 29, 1797.
Hannah, d. Joseph and Sarah, May 31, 1723.

CLARK, Hannah, d. Dr. Parker and Lydia, Apr. 2, 1743.
Hannah, d. William and Rebecca, July 24, 1776.
Hannah, d. Abijah and Hannah, Aug. 12, 1778.
Henry Newton, s. Tho[ma]s and Sarah Ann, Aug. 8, 1839.
Hobart, s. John H., butcher, and Emily, Apr. 22, 1848.
Isaac, s. John and Jenney, July 13, 1775.
James, s. John and Mary, May 25, 1736.
Jefferson, s. Lemuel, bp. June 15, 1800. C. R. 2.
Jeremiah, s. John and Jenny, Nov. 23, 1791.
Jeremy, s. John and Jenney, Aug. 23, 1786.
Jesse, s. Thomas, painter, and Sarah Ann, Aug. 7, 1844.
John, s. John and Mary, June 10, 1734.
John, s. John and Mary, Oct. 8, 1738.
John, s. Timothy and Elisabeth, Mar. 6, 1741-2.
John, s. Timothy and Elisabeth, Dec. 10, 1744.
John, s. John and Jenney, July 2, 1782.
John, s. Abijah and Hannah, July 20, 1782.
John, s. Micah and Abigail, June 27, 1783.
John Hubbard [Hobart. C. R. 1.], s. Hobort [jr. and Elizabeth. C. R. 1.] and Elazt., Jan. 21, 1816.
Jonathan, s. Joseph and Elisabeth, Oct. 14, 1736.
Joseph, s. Joseph and Elisabeth, Apr. 20, 1735.
Joseph, s. Joseph [jr. C. R. 2.] and Elisabeth, Mar. 31, 1739.
Joseph, s. John and Jenney, May 20, 1784.
Joseph, s. W[illia]m and Mary, bp. Aug. 8, 1813. C. R. 2.
Joseph [Farwell. C. R. 1.], s. Hobart [jr. C. R. 1.] and Elizabeth, Jan. 18, 1820.
Lucy Farwell, d. Hobart and Elizabeth, bp. June 3, 1838. C. R. 4.
Lydia, d. Dr. Parker and Lydia, Aug. 16, 1744.
Lydia, d. Abijah and Hannah, July 17, 1788.
Lydia F., d. Andrew and Betsy, Feb. 13, 1821.
Marcellus, s. Benjamin and Elmira, Nov. 24, 1837.
Martha Ann, d. Nathan and Persis, June 28, 1828. [July 5. dup.]
Mary, d. Abijah and Hannah, Nov. 25, 1790.
Mary, d. Robert, flax-dresser, and Mary, Dec. 11, 1843.
Mary Helen Maria, d. James R., machinist, and Helen, both b. Scotland, at Boston, May 18, 1848.
Micha, s. Micha and Abigal, Apr. 5, 1789.
Nathan, s. Abijah and Hannah, May 16, 1784.
Nathan [Franklin. C. R. 2.], s. Nathan and Persis, May 3, 1824.
Parker, s. Dr. Parker and Lydiah, Apr. 3, 1748.
Peter, s. Hobart [jr. C. R. 1.] and Elizabeth, Mar. 16, 1822.
Rebecca Ray, d. William and Rebecca, Nov. 12, 1770.

CLARK, Samuel, s. Micah and Abigail, July 8, 1781.
Sarah, d. Joseph and Sarah [Mary. C. R. 2.], —— [1713]. [bp. May 31, 1713. C. R. 2.]
Sarah, d. Timothy and Elezebith, Sept. 9, 1749.
Sarah, d. John and Jenney, Feb. 7, 1789.
Sarah Elizabeth, d. Hobart, jr. and Elizabeth, bp. May 5, 1827. C. R. 1.
Sarah F., d. Thomas and Sarah Ann, July 13, 1842.
Susan S., d. W[illia]m and Mary [Jan. ? 1816].
Susannah, d. Joseph and Sarah, July 31, 1725.
Thomas, s. Timothy and Elezebith, Jan. 13, 1752.
Thomas, s. Ezra and Hannah, June 27, 1807.
Thomas H [enry. C. R. 2.], s. Thomas and Sarah Ann, Oct. 1, 1832. [1833. dup.]
[Timothy. C. R. 1.] ——y, s. Timothy and Elisbth, Oct. 5, 1740.
William, s. Joseph, jr. and Elisabeth, Aug. 27, 1747.
William, s. William and Rebecca, Feb. 15, 1769.
W[illia]m, s. W[illia]m and Mary, bp. Aug. 8, 1813. C. R. 2.
William Hovey, s. Hobart, jr. and Elizabeth, bp. May 5, 1827. C. R. 1.
Zebadiah Chandler, s. Ezra and Hannah, Aug. 8, 1809.
——, s. Hobart and Elizabeth, Feb. 14, 1824.
——, d. John and Margaret, Mar. 10, 1827.
——, d. Hobart and Elizabeth, Sept. 30, 1833.
——, s. John and Margaret, Nov. 10, 1834.
——, ch. Thomas and Sarah Ann, Jan. 8, 1836.
——, d. Thomas, painter, and Sarah, Aug. 11, 1846.

CLARKE (see also Clark), Frank Darricott, s. Dr. Francis, manufacturer, and Sarah F. [(Marland). C. R. 4.], Oct. 21, 1846.
Sarah F [rancis. C. R. 4.], d. Francis, M. D. and Sarah, June 8, 1840.

CLEGG, James A., s. Thomas, harness and reed maker, Jan. 9, 184 [7 or 8].
Mary E., d. Edward, wool-sorter, and Mary A., both b. England, Dec. 3, 1849.

CLEMENT (see also Clements), Abby F., d. Moses and Caroline, Dec. 21, 1839.
[Anna J. in pencil.], d. Moses, carpenter, and Caroline, Dec. 16, 1845.
Benja[min] Franklin, s. Moses, carpenter, and Caroline, Apr. 16, 1848.

CLEMENT, Caroline L., d. Moses and Caroline, June 21, 1836.
Catharine, d. Benj[ami]n and Mary, Aug. —, 1819.
Elizabeth, d. Benjamin and Mary, Dec. 20, 1830.
George G., s. Moses and Caroline, Oct. 9, 1837.
John P., s. Jonathan and Phebe F., Mar. 3, 1825.
Martha [Hemenway. c. r. 6.], d. Jonathan and Martha, Dec. 17, 1822.
Mary F., d. Moses and Caroline, Sept. 26, 1842.
Moses W., s. Moses and Caroline, June 5, 1834.
Sarah M., d. Moses, carpenter, and Caroline, Feb. 6, 1844.
——, s. Benj[ami]n and Mary, Feb. 21, 1821.
——, s. Benjamin and Mary, Sept. 1, 1827.
——, d. Moses and Caroline, Dec. 2, 1839.

CLEMENTS (see also Clement), Benjamin, s. Benjamin and Mary, Feb. 20, 1815.
Hannah, d. Benj[ami]n and Mary, Apr. 15, 1817.
Mary Ann, d. Benjamin and Mary, Mar. 10, 1813.
Moses, s. Benjamin and Mary, Aug. 12, 1811.

CLERCK (see also Clark), Mary, d. Joseph and Sarah [Mary. c. r. 2.], —— [1710]. [bp. May 31, 1713. c. r. 2.]

CLERK (see also Clark), Benjamin, s. Joseph and Sarah [Mary. c. r. 2.], Feb. 27, 1716-17.
Joseph, s. Joseph and Sarah [Mary, bp. May 31, 1713. c. r. 2.].
Lydia, d. Joseph and Sarah [Mary. c. r. 2.], May —, 1718. [bp. June 1, 1718. c. r. 2.]

CLOUGH (see also Clow), Catherine Ruth, d. Josiah B. and Dorcas, Mar. 15, 1843.
Elizabeth, d. Josiah G. and Dorcas, Oct. 8, 1837.
William Ebenezer, s. Josiah B. and Dorcas [Dec. 27?], 1840.

CLOW (see also Clough), Joseph, s. Nathan, bp. Feb. 19, 1786. c. r. 2.

COAL (see also Cole), Isaac, s. Solomon and Mehitable, June —7 [27. t. c.], 1769.
John, s. Solomon and Mehitable, Mar. 19, 1768.
Timothy, s. Solomon and Mehitable, Jan. 29, 1767.

COCHRAN (see also Cochren), Abigail, d. Samuel and Mary, Apr. 13, 1812.

COCHRAN, Almira, d. Capt. Henry and Eunice S., Mar. 6, 1816.
Elizabeth W., d. Capt. Samuel and Mary, Feb. 10, 1816.
Emeline, d. John and Mary, Mar. 5, 1822.
George L., s. John and Mary, May 3, 1827.
Henry, s. Samuel and Mary, Mar. 29, 1814.
Henry, s. Henry and Eunice S., Aug. 30, 1814.
James, s. John and Mary, Sept. 17, 1829.
James Calvin, s. James H. and Sarah S., Jan. 17, 1845. P. R. 56.
Johial, s. Samuel and Mary, Oct. 29, 1810.
John W., s. James H. and Sarah S., Apr. 2, 1841. P. R. 56.
Justin, s. Capt. Henry and Eunice C., Mar. —, 1818.
Mary, d. Samuel and Mary, Oct. 17, 1808.
Parker E[merson. P. R. 56.], s. James H., blacksmith, and Sarah S., Jan. 19, 1845. [Jan. 20, 1843. P. R. 56.]
Rufus H., s. James H., blacksmith, b. Reading, and Sarah S., Oct. 16, 1849.
Samuel, s. Samuel and Hannah, Jan. 16, 1805.
Samuel, s. Samuel and Hannah, Jan. 16, 1815.
Sarah F., d. John and Mary, Jan. 15, 1826.
——, s. John, by —— Merrill, Mar. 2, 1822.
——, s. Capt. Samuel, July 16, 1830.
——, s. James H. and Sarah S., Oct. 10, 1847. P. R. 56.

COCHREN (see also Cochran), James, s. James and Sarah, Oct. 6, 1735.

COFFERING (see also Coffrin), Elisabeth, d. James and Sarah, Jan. 20, 1737-8.

COFFIN, James Dudley, s. wid. Mary, bp. May 15, 1831. C. R. 2.
Mary Gerrish, d. wid. Mary, bp. May 15, 1831. C. R. 2.
Nathaniel Wheeler, s. wid. Mary, bp. May 15, 1831. C. R. 2.
——, d. William and Experience, of Boston, bp. ——, 1719. C. R. 1.

COFFRIN (see also Coffering), James, s. James and Sarah, bp. Dec. 7, 1735. C. R. 1.
Jenny, d. James, Feb. 3, 1773.

COGSWELL, Benjamin P[unchard. C. R. 4.], s. twin, Francis, lawyer, and Mary S. [Marland. C. R. 4.], Mar. 16, 1845. [bp. Oct. 27, 1844. C. R. 4.]
Elizabeth, d. Sam[ue]ll and Eliz[abe]th, Apr. 18, 1770.
James, s. Samuel, bp. Jan. 30, 1780. C. R. 2.

COGSWELL, Joseph, s. Sam[ue]ll and Eliz[abe]th, Jan. 8, 1765.
Lucy, d. Samuel, bp. Mar. 23, 1777. C. R. 2.
Lucy, d. Samuel, jr. and Mary, Aug. 25, 1810.
Mary, d. Samuel, jr. and Mary, Dec. 14, 1807.
Samuel, s. Samuel and Eliz[abe]th, Oct. 22, 1768.
Samuel, s. Samuel, jr., bp. Dec. 31, 1797. C. R. 2.
Sarah, d. Samuel, jr., bp. Apr. 30, 1797. C. R. 2.
Thomas, s. Samuel, jr., bp. Nov. 3, 1799. C. R. 2.
Thomas, s. Samuel, jr. and Mary, Aug. 16, 1801.
Thomar M[arland. C. R. 4.], s. twin, Francis, lawyer, and Mary S. M[arland. C. R. 4.], Mar. 16, 1845. [bp. Oct. 27, 1844. C. R. 4.]

COLBE (see also Coolebe), Hannah, d. Daniel and Hannah, Oct. 22, 1735.
Sarah, d. Daniel and Hannah, Dec. 26, 1742.

COLE (see also Coal), Caroline F., d. James R., laborer, b. Bradford, and Sarah A., b. N. H., Aug. 27, 1849.
George S[amuel. C. R. 3.], s. Job T., machinist, and Hannah, Jan. 3, 1844.
Hannah Jane, d. Job Thomas and Hannah, June 28, 1838.
Thomas Morton, s. Job Thomas and Hannah, Apr. 24, 1836.

COLEMAN, Alexander, s. Cochran and Mary Jane, bp. Nov. 29, 1841. C. R. 4.
Sophia R., d. William, watchman, and Susan, Dec. 21, 1845.
Stephen, s. Cochran and Mary Jane, bp. Nov. 29, 1841. C. R. 4.
William Raymond, s. William, watchman, and Martha, May 29, 1843.

COLLINS, John Henry, s. John A., bp. July 27, 1837. C. R. 6.

CONANT, Hannah Kilham Fish, d. Nathaniel and Elizabeth K., Aug. 27, 1822.

CONNER, Abijah, s. Ann, Aug. 7, 1743.

CONSTANTINE, Emma Midgely, d. John and Eliza, Oct. 22, 1848. C. R. 4.

COOLEBE (see also Colbe), Daniel, s. Daniel and Hannah, June 16, 1731.

COOPER, Caroline L[ucinda. C. R. 4.], d. Samuel [Thatcher. C. R. 4.] and Caroline [Lucinda. C. R. 4.], Oct. 16, 1842.
Margaret E[lizabeth. C. R. 2.], d. Samuel E. and Elezabeth, Oct. 23, 1830.
[Samuel G. C. R. 2.], s. Samuel and Betsy, Sept. 16, 1826.
William [P. C. R. 2.], s. Sam[ue]l and Elizabeth, Feb. 4, 1828.

CORBETT, Harriet F., d. Benj[min] S., clergyman, and Harriet, at Dedham, June 24, 1843.

CORNELIUS, Jeremiah Evarts, s. Mary, bp. Apr. 22, 1832. C. R. 6.
Sarah Edwards, d. Rev. E., bp. ——, 1830. C. R. 6.

CORY, Hannah, d. Ephraim, bp. May 20, 1787. C. R. 2.

COULIE, ——, d. James, factory overseer, and Grace, both b. Scotland, Dec. 2, 1849.

COWDERY (see also Cowdry), Mary E., d. William S., machinist, b. Chester, N. H., and Eliza J., b. Methuen, Jan. 11, 1849.

COWDRY (see also Cowdery), Frances Agnes, d. William S., machinist, and Eliza J., Apr. 10, 1847.

COWENS, William, s. William and Jane, bp. Aug. 18, 1776. C. R. 1.

COX, Jonathan French, s. twin, Lem[ue]l, bp. Dec. 15, 1777. C. R. 2.
Mary E., d. Francis R., blacksmith, and Lydia C., July 1, 1844.
Sally Hickling, d. twin, Lem[ue]l, bp. Dec. 15, 1777. C. R. 2.

CRAGIN, Thomas, s. Dennis, labourer, and Mary K., Mar. 18, 1848.

CRAMM, Benjamin, s. John, bp. May 6, 1722. C. R. 2.
Elizabeth, d. John, bp. May 6, 1722. C. R. 2.
Huldah, d. John and Sarah, bp. Aug. 7, 1715. C. R. 2.
John, s. John and Sarah, bp. Aug. 4, 1717. C. R. 2.
Sarah, d. John, bp. May 6, 1722. C. R. 2.

CRAWFORD (see also Croford), Elizabeth A., d. James, moulder, b. Scotland, and Sarah, b. England, Sept. 25, 1848.
George Eli, s. Joseph, machinist, and Amelia, both b. Scotland, May 21, 1848.

CROCKETT, Augustus N., s. Bartlett D., machinist, and Betsy, Aug. 12, 1843.
Geo[rge] Bartlett, s. B. D. and Betsy, Nov. 12, 1841.
George E., s. Bartlett, machinist, and Betsy, June 12, 1845.

CROFORD (see also Crawford), Sarah, d. Jane, Oct. 15, 1751.

CROMBIE, Anna, d. James and Mary, bp. Aug. 28, 1768. C. R. 1.
Benjamin, s. twin, James and Sarah, Nov. 19, 1765.
Joseph, s. twin, James and Sarah, Nov. 19, 1765.
Molly, d. James and Sarah, Jan. 28, 1761.
Sarah, d. James and Sarah, July 25, 1762.
Suse, d. James and Sarah, Jan. 27, 1764.

CROSBY, Amos, s. John and Hannah, June 22, 1801. [bp. June 29, 1800. C. R. 2.]
Benjamin, s. John, bp. Apr. 18, 1802. C. R. 2.
Benjamin, s. John and Hannah, May 27, 1803.
Ebenezer, s. Timo[thy], bp. Apr. 13, 1777. C. R. 2.
Geo[rge] Hodges, s. Josiah, farmer, and Hannah, May 27, 1844.
Hannah, d. John and Hannah, Mar. 7, 1797.
Jedediah, s. Timo[thy], bp. July 4, 1779. C. R. 2.
John, s. John and Hannah, July 15, 1793.
Josephine, d. Josiah and Hannah K., Oct. 10, 1839.
Mary, d. Michal, bp. Nov. 3, 1799. C. R. 2.
Mary, d. Timothy and Polly, June 6, 1801.
Mary Manning, d. Josiah, merchant, b. Billerica, and Hannah K., b. Salem, Dec. 4, 1848.
Rachel, d. Michael, bp. Oct. 26, 1797. C. R. 2.
Samuel Boynton, s. John, bp. Sept. 6, 1795. C. R. 2.
Simon, s. Simon, bp. June 12, 1814. C. R. 2.
Solomon, s. John and Hannah, Sept. 18, 1799. [Sept. 23, 1798. C. R. 2.]
Thomas, s. Timo[thy], bp. May 17, 1778. C. R. 2.
——, d. Josiah and Hannah H., Feb. 17, 1842.

CROSS, Joseph, s. Samuel and Martha, Apr. 26, 1753.
Martha, d. Samuel and Martha, Feb. 8, 1749-50.
Mary, d. John, bp. ——, 1727. C. R. 1.

CROWLEY, Robert E., s. Michael, spinner, and Mary, Feb. 13, 1844.
Thomas P., s. Michael, spinner, and Mary, Dec. 26, 1845.

CROWTHER, Ellen Elizabeth, d. Elijah and Mary, bp. July 19, 1840. C. R. 4.
Frances Howarth, ch. Elijah and Mary, bp. May 30, 1841. C. R. 4.
James Ashworth, s. Elijah and Mary, bp. July 19, 1840. C. R. 4.
Mary Elanor, d. Elijah and Mary, bp. July 19, 1840. C. R. 4.
William E., s. Elijah, manufacturer, and Mary, Apr. 25, 1845.

CRYER, John E., s. George, manufacturer, and Alice, Oct. 4, 1843.

CUARLTON (see also Carleton), ——, ch. John and Hannah, Mar. 21, 1705-6.

CUMINGS (see also Cummings), Marcy, d. twin, John and Mary, Dec. 28, 1745.

CUMMINGS (see also Cumings, Cummins), Abiathar, s. Amos, of Norway, bp. Jan. 27, 1805. C. R. 2.
Abiather, s. Jonathan and Mary, Sept. 22, 1786.
Amos, s. Jonathan and Mary, July 2, 1781.
Ann, d. Joseph and Mary, June 27, 1820.
Asa, s. Asa and Hannah, Apr. 4, 1784.
Asa, s. Asa and Hannah, Sept. 29, 1790.
Assena, d. Samuel and Lucy, Mar. 19, 1805.
Betty, d. Jonathan and Mary, Oct. 13, 1783.
Charles, s. Stephen and Deborah, Mar. 29, 1787.
Charles, s. Samuel and Lucy, Jan. 15, 1804.
Charles, s. Charles and Hannah, Jan. 14, 1812.
Charles Osgood, s. Joseph and Mary, June 29, 1818.
Daniel, s. Jonathan, jr. and Mary, Dec. 6, 1776.
Daniel, s. Jonathan, jr. and Mary, Sept. 2, 1778.
Daniel, s. Daniel and Mary, Feb. 26, 1783.
Daniel, s. Daniel and Hannah, Apr. 21, 1804.
Deborah, d. Stephen and Deborah, bp. Nov. 27, 1785. C. R. 1.
Deborah Gould, d. Stephen and Deborah, Oct. 19, 1794.
Elizabeth, d. [Capt. C. R. 2.] Daniel and Hannah, May 20, 1808.
Elizabeth [Wainwright. C. R. 2.], d. Dr. James and Sarah, Sept. 28, 1836.
Enoch, s. Asa and Hannah, Dec. 24, 1782.
Francis, s. Asa and Hannah, Apr. 25, 1793.

CUMMINGS, Hannah, d. Asa and Hannah, Oct. 23, 1785.
Hannah, d. Daniel, bp. Oct. 27, 1805. C. R. 2.
Henry, s. Joseph and Mary, May 24, 1822.
Joseph, s. Stephen and Deborah, Dec. 6, 1792.
Joseph H., s. Joseph and Mary, June 15, 1816.
John, s. Asa and Hannah, Mar. 9, 1792.
Lucy, d. Samuel and Lucy, Nov. 19, 1802.
Lydia, d. Asa and Lydia, May 27, 1798.
Martha T., d. Joseph, bp. Jan. 2, 1825. C. R. 2.
Mary Eastman, d. Daniel and Hannah, Dec. 22, 1811.
Mary Elizabeth, d. Samuel and Lucy, Mar. 8, 1812.
Mehitable, d. Samuel and Lucy, Mar. 4, 1806. [May 4. dup.]
Phebe, d. David and Anne, bp. May 30, 1756. C. R. 2.
Sally, d. Peter and Abigal, Aug. 25, 1781.
Samuel, s. Samuel and Lucy, Oct. 29, 1801.
Sam[ue]l J., s. John and Abigail, Dec. 13, 1828.
Sarah, d. Asa and Hannah, Oct. 12, 1794.
Stephen, s. Stephen and Deborah, Mar. 14, 1784.
Stephen Osgood, s. Charles and Hannah, Feb. 21, 1810.
Susanna, d. Asa and Hannah, Apr. 29, 1789.
Susannah, d. Stephen [wid. Deborah. C. R. 1.], Aug. 25, 1797.
Will[ia]m Peabody, s. Stephen and Deborah, July 28, 1782.
——, Charles, farmer, and Mary R., Oct. 3, 1843.

CUMMINS (see also Cummings), Aaron, s. Asa and Hannah, bp. Sept. 20, 1789. C. R. 1.
Elizabeth, d. Joseph and Mary, Jan. 11, 1826.
Jonathan, s. Jonathan [jr. C. R. 2.] and Mary, Feb. 5, 1771.
Mary, d. Jonathan and Mary, Aug. 25, 1768.
Mary, d. Jonathan, jr. and Mary, Nov. 1, 1774.
Sarah, d. Jonathan, jr. and Mary, May 21, 1767.
Stephen, s. Jonathan, jr. and Mary, Jan. 12, 1773.

CUNNINGHAM, James, s. John, laborer, and Margeret, Aug. 9, 1847.
John, s. Luke, laborer, and Mary, both b. Ireland, Nov. 1, 1848.
Margaret, d. John, laborer, and Margaret, both b. Ireland, Dec. 9, 1849.

CURNEEL, Rachell, d. Mary, bp. ——, 1727. C. R. 1.

CURTICE (see also Curtis), Hannah, d. Thomas and Pheoby, June 16, 1714.
Israel, s. Thomas and Pheoby, Apr. 28, 1719.

CURTICE, John, s. Thomas and Pheoby, ——, 1709-10.
Pheoby, d. Thomas and Pheoby [1711-12?].
Rebecka, d. Thomas and Pheoby, June ——, 1717.
Thomas, s. Thomas and Pheoby, J—— [1707?].

CURTIS (see also Curtice), David, s. Thomas and Phebe [Jan.] — [1721-2].
Luetta, d. Markwell T., machinist, and Lydia, Jan. 22, 1849.
Maria, d. Putnam and Susan, Apr. 16, 1830.
Martha, d. Putnam and Susan, Dec. 28, 1834.
Mary W., d. Putnam and Sophia, Apr. 12, 1832.
Samuel, s. Putnam and Susan, Apr. 22, 1828.
Will[ia]m, s. John and Molly, bp. Apr. 24, 1768. C. R. I.
——, s. Thomas and Phebe, Sept. 21, 1724.
——, d. Putnam, Mar. 22, 1826.
——, s. Thomas and Phebe, June 8, 1727.

CUSHING, Elisha James, s. Elisha and Lucy, June 26, 1818.
John, s. John and Mehitable, bp. Jan. 27, 1771. C. R. I.

CUTLER, Charles, s. William, farmer, and Amelia [(Holten) in pencil.], May 21, 1846.

DALAND, Abigail, d. George and Abigail, Jan. 23, 1822.
Clarence Goldsmith, s. Geo[rge], bp. Nov. 4, 1827. C. R. 2.
Clarissa, d. George and Mary C., July 27, 1827.
George, s. George and Mary, Oct. 7, 1829.
John, s. George and Mary B., May 15, 1833.
Mary G., d. George and Mary, July 23, 1826.
William [Bachelder. C. R. 2.], s. George and Mary B., Apr. 13, 1832.
William B[atchelder. C. R. 2.], s. George and Mary C., Jan. 6, 1831.

DALE, Ebenezer, s. Ebenezer and Serena P., bp. July 5, 1812. C. R. I.
Emma, d. Archelaus, bp. July 28, 1782. C. R. 2.
Eunice, d. Archelaus, bp. Dec. 17, 1786. C. R. 2.
James Green, s. Eb[e]n[eze]r and Serena P., bp. Oct. 17, 1819. C. R. I.
Lydia, d. Archelaus, bp. July 25, 1784. C. R. 2.
Martha, d. Eben[ezer] and Serena P., bp. Dec. 7, 1817. C. R. I.
Serena Parker, d. Ebenezer and Serena P., bp. May 22, 1814. C. R. I.
William Johnson, s. Ebenezer and Serena, bp. May 12, 1816. C. R. I.

DALEY (see also Daly), Charles, s. Patrick, laborer, Mar. 11, 184[7].

DALY (see also Daley), Charles, s. Patrick, laborer, and Margaret, both b. Ireland, Apr. 29, 1848.
Charles, s. Patrick, laborer, and Margaret, both b. Ireland, Mar. 25, 1849.

DANE (see also Dean), Abbot Kimball, s. Peter O. and Lucy, Mar. 3, 1807.
Abiah Mooar, d. W[illia]m, jr., bp. Apr. 1, 1792. C. R. 2.
Amos, s. Henry and Elizabeth, Feb. 24, 1812.
Anna, d. Joseph and Allice, Nov. —, 1782. [bp. Nov. 24. C. R. 2.]
Benjamin, s. John, jr. and Elezebith, July 18, 1748.
Benjamin, s. Philemon and Priscilla, July 10, 1776.
Benjamin, s. William, jr., bp. Oct. 31, 1790. C. R. 2.
Benj[ami]n A., s. Benj[ami]n, jr. and Lydia, Dec. 21, 1815.
Daniel, s. Francis and Hannah, Apr. 24, 1698.
Daniel, s. Daniel and Elizebeth, Mar. 7, 1725-6.
Daniel, s. John and Sarah, Nov. 10, 1735.
David, s. Francis, bp. May 24, 1789. C. R. 2.
Deborah, d. John, jr. and Deborah, June 27, 1784.
Deliverance, d. Nathaniel and Deliverance, Feb. 20, 1692-3.
Dorcas, d. Joseph and Eliz[abe]th, Apr. 14, 1769.
Dorcas, d. William and Phebe, Apr. 22, 1771.
Dorcis, d. Joseph and Dorcis, Jan. 15, 1752.
Elezebeth, d. Daniel and Elezebeth [Aug. —, 1724.].
Elezebith, d. Dea. John and Elezebith, Dec. 3, 1756.
Elisabeth, d. John, jr. and Elisabeth, Aug. 6, 1745.
Elizabeth, d. Moses and Priscilla, Oct. 18, 1801.
Elizabeth, d. Henery and Elizabeth, Feb. 22, 1810.
Eunice, d. Daniel and Prudence, Apr. 27, 1773.
Eunice Pilsbery, d. James and Rebecca, Sept. 28, 1813.
Francies, s. Francies and Hannah, Mar. 31, 1[715. C. R. 2.].
Francis, s. Francis and Elizabeth, Dec. 8, 1656.
Francis, s. Francis and Hannah, Aug. 19, 1690.
Francis, s. John and Sarah, Dec. 21, 1725.
Francis, s. Francis and Abiah, May 1, 1782.
Fransis, s. John, jr. and Elezebith, Feb. 18, 1750-51.
George, s. Chandler and Susan (Wallace), Jan. 19, 1840. T. C.
George, s. William, bp. May 14, 1797. C. R. 2.
Hannah, d. John and Sarah, Dec. — [bp. Dec. 14. C. R. 2.], 1718.
Hannah, d. Daniel and Elizabeth, Mar. 4, 1733-4.
Hannah, d. Joseph and Eliz[abe]th, Nov. 1, 1764.

DANE, Hannah, d. William and Phebe, Nov. 14, 1776.
Hannah, d. Moses and Priscilla, July 6, 1799.
Harriot Elizabeth, d. Benjamin and Sally, Sept. 28, 1822.
Henry, s. Philemon and Priscilla, Aug. 6, 1772.
Henry, s. Henry and Elizabeth, Jan. 16, 1797.
Henry, s. illegitimate, Persis and Henry Melcoy, Aug. 13, 1826.
James, s. Moses and Priscilla, Aug. 6, 1804.
James, s. Moses and Priscilla, May 17, 1806.
James, s. Benjamin and Sarah, Sept. 12, 1811.
James Moody, s. John, jr. and Deborah, Dec. 13, 1788.
Jedediah, s. Francis, bp. Mar. 7, 1784. C. R. 2.
John [Dean. dup.], s. Francis and Hannah, 9br. 18, 1692.
John, s. John and Sarah, Nov. 26, 1716.
[John. C. R. 2.], s. John, jr. and Elisabeth, May —, 1740. [bp. May 4. C. R. 2.]
John, s. Lt. William and Phebe, Nov. 16, 1779.
John, s. John, jr. and Deborah, Nov. 20, 1786.
John, s. Francis, bp. Apr. 9, 1786. C. R. 2.
John, s. Moses and Priscilla, June 27, 1812.
John, s. Benjamin and Sally, June 4, 1825.
John O., s. Benj[ami]n, jr. and Lydia, Nov. 28, 1820.
Joseph, s. Francis and Hannah, Apr. 5, 1696.
Joseph, s. Joseph and Lydia, Nov. —, 1718. [bp. Nov. 16. C. R. 2.]
Joseph, s. John and Sarah, Aug. 16, 1723.
Joseph, s. Joseph and Dorcis, Jan. 22, 1754.
Joseph, s. Benjamin and Sarah, Jan. 15, 1815.
Joseph, s. Benj[ami]n, jr. and Lydia, May 14, 1819.
Joseph Burt, s. William, jr. and Susanna, Jan. 25, 1785.
Joseph N., s. Moses Nute and Priscilla, July 25, 1816.
Loisa, d. James and Rebecca, Aug. 1, 1810.
Lydia, d. William and Phebe, July 13, 1769.
Lydia, d. Moses and Priscilla, Jan. 26, 1810.
Lydia, d. Benj[ami]n, jr. and Lydia, Aug. 15, 1817.
Martha Louisa, d. Hermon, bp. July 26, 1835. C. R. 2.
Mary, d. Nathaniell and Deliverance, Feb. 7, 1686-7.
Mary, d. Francis and Hanah, Apr. 22, 1699.
Mary, d. Daniel and Elizebath, Nov. 24, 1727.
Mary, d. John and Sarah, Apr. 27, 1731.
[Mary. T. C.], d. John and Sarah, Sept. 27, 1733.
Mary, d. William and Mary, Aug. 14, 1761.
Mary, d. William, bp. June 29, 1794. C. R. 2.
Mary, d. Benjamin and Sarah, July 14, 1813.
Mary E[lizabeth. C. R. 3.], d. John and Sally, Aug. 29, 1833.
Mary Moody, d. Moses and Priscilla, Oct. 12, 1813.

DANE, Moody, s. Moses and Priscilla, Sept. 6, 1803.
Moses, s. Moses and Priscilla, Sept. 10, 1797.
Moses, s. Moses and Priscilla, July 10, 1815.
Nathaniel, s. Daniel and Elezebeth, Jan. 31 [1721. C. R. 1.].
Osgood, s. William, jr. and Susanna, July 15, 1787.
Peter Osgood, s. Joseph, jr. and Allice, Nov. 3, 1784.
Phebe, d. John and Sarah, May 21, 1721.
Phebe, d. Joseph and Elizabeth, May 14, 1762.
Philemon, s. John, jr. and Elisabeth, Feb. 2, 1741-2.
Polly Moody, d. Moses and Priscilla, Oct. 31, 1793.
Priscilla, d. Philemon and Priscilla, July 27, 1774.
Priscilla, d. Moses and Priscilla, Sept. 26, 1795.
Rebekah, d. Henry and Elizabeth, Sept. 23, 1798.
Sally, d. Henery and Elizabeth, Oct. 30, 1802.
Sally P[illsbury. C. R. 3.], d. John and Sally, Nov. 6, 1829.
Sarah, d. John and Sarah, Nov. 9, 1714.
Sarah, d. William and Mary, Mar. 12, 1763.
Sarah, d. Benjamin and Sarah, Mar. [Apr. dup.] 23, 1809.
Susanna, d. William, jr. and Susanna, Dec. 23, 1782.
Timothy, s. William and Phebe, May 9, 1773.
Wiliam, s. Wiliam and Mary, Oct. 17, 1753.
Wil[liam. C. R. 2.], s. John and Sarah, Mar. 15, 1727-8.
William, s. William [jr. C. R. 2.] and Susanna [Mar.], 1781. [bp. Aug. 19. C. R. 2.]
——, s. Benjamin, jr. and Lydia, Dec. 17, 1822.

DANFORTH, Cusiah, d. Joshua and Cusiah, Aug. 11, 1757.
[Elizabeth. T. C.] ——bith, d. John and Elezebeth, Oct. [22?], 1755. [bp. Oct. 26. C. R. 2.].
Hannah, d. John and Elezebith, June 26, 1757.
John, s. Joshua and Cusiah, July 23, 1756.

DARBE (see also Derby), William, s. William and Hannah [of Boston. C. R. 2.], Aug. 25, 1745.

DARLIN (see also Darling), Sarah, d. Jonathan and Sarah, May 20, 1745.

DARLING (see also Darlin), Amos, s. Eliakim and Martha, Jan. 16, 1766.
Eliakim, s. Eliakim, bp. Aug. 2, 1767. C. R. 2.
Jonathan, s. Jonathan and Hannah, Nov. 25, 1763.
William, s. Eliakim, bp. Aug. 13, 1769. C. R. 2

DARRACOTT (see also Darricott), Julia Marland, d. Franklin, engineer, and Julia [M. (Marland). C. R. 4.], Sept. 29, 1847.

DARRICOTT (see also Darracott), Eliza M., d. Franklin, civil engineer, b. Boston, and Julia M., Nov. 10, 1849.

DASCOMB, Fanny E. [Frances Elizabith. C. R. 3.], d. Jacob and Fanny, May 30, 1828.
Lucretia O [sgood. C. R. 3.], d. Jacob and Fanny, Jan. 28, 1839.
Mary Rebecca, d. Jacob and Fanny, bp. July 8, 1832. C. R. 3.
Osgood Johnson, s. Jacob and Fanny, bp. July 8, 1832. C. R. 3.

DAVICE (see also Davis), Aaron, s. Mark and Abigaiel, June 26, 1738.
Asa, s. Mark and Abigail, Oct. 6, 1742.
John, s. Mark and Abigail, Jan. 15, 1740-41.
Moses, s. Mark and Abigail, Oct. 13, 1735.
——, twin chn. Mark and Abigail, Jan. 2, 1726-7.

DAVIDSON, Mary J., d. Alexander, Jan. 28, 1841.

DAVIS (see also Davice), Ann E., d. Edmund, founderer, and Sarah, June 12, 1844.
Caroline, d. Levi, jr. and Mary, Dec. 14, 1829.
Charles H., s. Edmond, iron founder, b. Greenland, N. H., and Sarah, b. Gilmanton, N. H., Aug. 25, 1848.
Eliza, d. Levi and Rebecca, Mar. 25, 1808.
Elizabeth F., Dec. 19, 1780. P. R. 63.
Ellen Lewzette, d. Joseph, manufacturer, and Eveline, Jan. 25, 1848.
Ellen Maria, d. George L., machinist, Nov. 17, 1847.
Ephraim, s. Ephraim and Mary, Mar. 9, 1688-9.
George H., s. George L., machinist, and Harriet R., Aug. 30, 1844.
Hannah, d. Robert and Prudence, Dec. 5, 1769.
Hannah, d. Maria, at the almshouse, Dec. 29, 1819.
Hannah J., d. Daniel A., carpenter, b. Vt., and Martha J., May 6, 1849.
Harriet Elizabeth, d. George L., machinist, b. Oxford, and Harriet, Sept. 21, 1849.
Henry, s. Edward, laborer, and Elizabeth, Aug. 27, 1848.
James, s. Rōbert, bp. May 2, 1762. C. R. 1.
James, s. Alexander and Jane, bp. Dec. 27, 1836. C. R. 1.
James H., s. George L., machinist, and Harriet F., Apr. 18, 1846.

DAVIS, John, s. Levi, jr. and Mary, Feb. 2, 1823.
Lucy, d. Eben, Mar. 8, 1835.
Lucy Abbot, d. James and Mercy, Apr. 16, 1806.
Mariah Higgins, d. Mariah, Mar. 9, 1838.
Mark, s. Mark and Abigail, June 2, 1734.
Mary, d. Ephraim and Mary, May 27, 1691.
Mary, d. Levi, jr. and Mary, Apr. 7, 1821.
Nathan, s. Levi and Rebecca, Feb. 9, 1806.
Nathaniel, s. Robert and Prudence, Oct. 13, 1765.
William, s. Robert and Prudence, Sept. 18, 1760.
——, s. Levi, jr. and Mary, Aug. 22, 1827.

DAWHURST, Betsy, d. James and Betsy, Mar. 7, 1830.
Mary A., d. James and Betsy, July 15, 1832.

DAY, Betty, d. Robert, bp. May 14, 1780. C. R. 2.
Joseph, s. Robert, bp. June 29, 1777. C. R. 2.

DEAN (see also Dane, Deane), Abiell, s. Francis and Hannah, Sept. 17, 1686.
Benjamin, s. Benjamin and Sally, May 5, 1804.
Chandler, s. Henery and Elizabeth, Oct. 16, 1804.
Daniell, s. Nathaniell and Deliverance, Mar. 26, 1684.
Hannah [Dane. CT. R.], d. Nathaniell and Deliverance, Sept. 29, 1680.
Hannah, d. Francis and Hannah, 9br. 6, 1687.
Herman, s. Henery and Elizabeth, Feb. 21, 1807.
John, s. Henery and Elizabeth, Sept. 24, 1801.
Joseph Mooar, s. Peter O. and Lucy, Oct. 4, 1808.
Joshua, s. Moses and Priscilla, July 9, 1807.
Mary, d. James and Rebeckah, Oct. 3, 1800.
Nathaniell, s. Nathaniell and Deliverance, June 18, 1674.
Peter, s. Peter Osgood and Lucy, Dec. 3, 1805.
Phebe [Dane. C. R. 2.], d. William and Phebe, Dec. 18, 1767.
Phebe, d. James and Rebecca, July 14, 1807.
Rebecca, d. James and Rebecca, Mar. 9, 1803.

DEANE (see also Dean), Abigail, d. Nathaniel and Deliverance, Dec. 27, 1698.
Abigall, d. Francis and Elizabeth, Oct. 13, 1652.
Francis [Dane. CT. R.], s. Nathaniell and Deliverance, Oct. 1, 1678.
Frances [Dearborn. CT. R.], s. Francis and Hannah, Apr. 22, 1683.
Nathaniell, s. Nathaniel and Deliverance, Dec. 1, 1675.

DEARBORN, Clara, Alvahretta, d. Alvah, laborer, and Elizabeth, Dec. 13, 1848.
Dorothy A., d. Nathaniel, laborer, and Eliza, Aug. 12, 1848.
John S., s. Nathaniel, laborer, and Eliza, Nov. 7, 1844.

DELANO, Louisa M., d. Henry F., yeoman, and M. C., Sept. 25, 1846.
Maria Louisa, d. H. F. and Elizabeth, bp. Aug. 28, 1847. C. R. 4.
Mary Ann Carter Warland, d. Henry F. and Elizabeth, bp. Sept. 5, 1841. C. R. 4.

DELAP (see also Dunlap), Anna, d. John and Elizabeth, Nov. 25, 1772.
Betty, d. John and Elizabeth, Jan. 12, 1776.
Hannah, d. John, bp. Feb. 20, 1791. C. R. 2.
James, s. John and Elizabeth, Dec. 7, 1760.
John, s. John and Elizabeth, Feb. 25, 1779.
Jonathan [Boynton. C. R. 1.], s. Jonathan Boynton and Polly, May 5, 1797.
Mary [Dunlap. C. R. 2.], d. John and Anna, Mar. 29, 1739.
Robert [Dunlop. C. R. 2.], s. John and Anne, Aug. 10, 1743.
Sarah, d. John and Elizabeth, Aug. 10, 1783.

DENES (see also Dennis), Elizabeth, d. Nathan and Demaros, Sept. 29 [1726].

DENIS (see also Dennis), Elezebith, d. Luis [Lewis. C. R. 1.] and Annah, Aug. 12, 1755.

DENISON, Hellen, d. John, laborer, and Mary, both b. Ireland, Sept. 19, 1849.

DENNET (see also Dennett), Horatio W., s. Horatio, machinist, and Maria S., Mar. 19, 1845.

DENNETT (see also Dennet), Horatio B., s. Horatio, carpenter, b. Amesbury, and Mary J., b. Newmarket, May 15, 1849.

DENNIS (see also Denes, Denis), John, s. Lewis, bp. Apr. 26, 1761. C. R. 1.
Moses, s. Moses, bp. Apr. 6, 1783. C. R. 2.
Sally, d. Moses, bp. Nov. 20, 1785. C. R. 2.

DENVIR, George, s. Robert and Abigail, Dec. 23, 1828.
John, s. Robert and Abigail, June 15, 1827.
Mary Ann, d. Robert and Abigail, Oct. 24, 1829.

DERBY (see also Darbe), Benja[min] Punchard, s. John and Rebecca P., July 4, 1826.
Caroline, d. John and Rebecca P., Nov. 7, 1828. [Dec. 1. dup.]
Maria, d. John and Rebecca P., Jan. 10, 1834.
Martha Punchard, d. John and Rebecca P., Sept. 3, 1831.
Mary Stone, d. John and Rebecca, Nov. 24, 1835.

DILAWAY (see also Dillaway), John, s. Samuel and Dorathy, Jan. 27, 1756.

DILLAWAY (see also Dilaway), Abigal, d. Samuel and Dorathy, Mar. 18, 1753.
Benjamin, s. Samuel and Dorathy, Sept. 1, 1754.
Elezebith, d. Samuel and Dorathy, Dec. 29, 1749.
Martha, d. Lydia, "Reputed" d. Matthew Hardey, Aug. 11, 1746.
Olive, d. John and Olive, Oct. 10, 1778.
Wiliam, s. Samuel and Dorathy, July 7, 1751.

DINSMORE (see also Dunsmore), Mary, d. John, bp. Mar. 28, 1736. C. R. 1.

DIXON, Edward, s. Henry, laborer, and Ann, Feb. 14, 1846.

DOBBIN (see also Dobbins), Mason, s. John, bp. Sept. 8, 1799. C. R. 2.
Thomas, s. John, bp. Nov. 8, 1795. C. R. 1.

DOBBINS (see also Dobbin, Dobin), Sarah Brown, d. John, bp. Oct. 3, 1790. C. R. 2.

DOBIN (see also Dobbins), John, s. John and Sarah, June 17, 1788.
Mary Osgood, d. John and Sarah, July 24, 1792.
Sarah [Brown. C. R. 2.], d. John and Sarah, May 18, 1790.

DODD, James, s. Jona[than] M. and Abigail, May 17, 1833.

DODGE, Elizabeth, d. Enos and Lydia, Mar. 17, 1813.
Enos, s. Enos and Lydia, July —, 1820.
Eveline, d. Amos, hostler, and Angeline, at Boston, Oct. 24, 1846.
Hepzabeth, d. Zadock and Lydia, Dec. 11, 1806.
Jona[than] Beverly, s. Enos and Lydia, Feb. 11, 1811.
Lydia, d. Enos and Lydia, Feb. 2, 1806.
Sarah Haskel, d. Enos and Lydia, July 12, 1809.
Tammy Sawyer, d. Enos and Lydia, Nov. 12, 1807.
——, ch. Tammy, Oct. 18, 1827.

DOE, Almira, d. Bradstreet and Eliza, Dec. 16, 1830.
Roxana, d. Bradstreet and Eliza, Dec. 13, 1827.

DOLLOFF, John Milton, s. John, painter, and Caroline [T. C. R. 2.], June 16, 1848.

DOLTON, ——, s. Philemon and Bethia, of Hampton, N. H., Jan. 31, 1723-4.

DONALD, Elijah W., s. William, laborer, and Agnes, July 31, 1848
Mary Jane, d. William, fireman, and Agnes, Oct. 5, 1844.
William Alexander, s. William C., engine tender, and Agnes, July 30, 1846.

DONIVAN, Bridget, d. Patrick, laborer, and Bridget, Sept. 10, 1848.
Dennis, s. Thomas, laborer, and Mary, Nov. 1, 1848.

DOVE, Claralyl [Clara Lyul. C. R. 3.], d. John, manufacturer, and Ellen C. [Hellen Mc. C. R. 3.], Aug. 5, 1844.
Ellen Christina, d. John and Ellen [Helen. C. R. 3.] M., Aug. 21, 1838.
Geo[rge] W[illia]m Webster, s. John and Ellen [Helen. C. R. 3.]. M., June 4, 1835.
Issabella Cragie, d. John and Ellen M., in Scotland, Dec. 15, 1831.
Laura Smith, d. John and Ellen, bp. Oct. 23, 1842. C. R. 3.
Marcy Alexander, d. John and Ellen, bp. Sept. 13, 1840. C. R. 3.

DOW, Charles E., s. David, mason, and Susan, Feb. 8, 1847.
Ebenezer, s. Ebenezer and Elizabeth, Feb. 21, 1761.
Edmund, s. Eben[ezer], bp. June 24, 1770. C. R. 2.
Jacob, s. Ebenezer, bp. Apr. 14, 1776. C. R. 2.
John, s. Ebenezer and Elizabeth, Jan. 27, 1763.
Joseph, s. Eben[eze]r, bp. June 19, 1768. C. R. 2.

Dow, Moody, s. Eben[eze]r, bp. Sept. 28, 1766. C. R. 2.
Rhoda, d. Ebenezer and Elizabeth, Apr. 30, 1772.
Sarah, d. Ebenezer and Elizabeth, Feb. 19, 1765.

DOWNES (see also Downs), Isaac H., s. Benjamin R. and Fanny, Sept. 7, 1829.
Joel P., s. Benja[min] R. and Fanny, May 29, 1838.
Paschal G., s. B. R. and Fanny, June 2, 1835.
Sarah F[rances. C. R. 2.], d. Benjamin R. and Fanny, Nov. 16, 1827.
——, s. Robert and Abigail, Jan. 27, 1826.

DOWNING, Abigail, d. Sam[ue]ll and Abigail, Sept. 29, 1768.
Allise [Alice. C. R. 2.], d. Samuel and Abigail, July 8, 1778.
Amos, s. Samuel and Abigail, July 13, 1783.
Ann, d. John and Nancy, Apr. 6, 1829.
Anne, d. Richard and Temperance, Oct. 28, 1755.
Augusta, d. Sam[ue]l and Ruby, bp. Nov. 21, 1830. C. R. 3.
Deborah Shelden, d. Palfry and Lydia, Aug. 10, 1796.
Eben Bailey, s. Samuel, jr., shoemaker, and Rebecca H., Aug. 1, 1847.
Elisabeth, d. Samuel, jr., bp. Jan. 24, 1790. C. R. 2.
Eliza R., d. Samuel, jr., shoemaker, and Rebecca, Apr. 13, 1846.
Emily, d. Sam[ue]l and Ruby, bp. Aug. 24, 1834. C. R. 3.
Experance, d. Richard and Temperance, July 20, 1753.
Frederick Fry, s. Sam[ue]l and Ruby, bp. Jan. 6, 1828. C. R. 3.
George O., s. Samuel and Ruby, May 22, 1835.
Hannah, d. Richard and Temperance, Dec. 12, 1746. [bp. Nov. 30, 1746. C. R. 2.]
Hannah, d. Samuel and Abigail, Aug. 20, 1780.
Hannah F., d. Palfrey W. and Hannah, July 9, 1820.
John, s. Richard and Anstis [Atta. C. R. 2.], June 14, 172[0. C. R. 2.].
John, s. Samuel and Abigail, Feb. 1, 1766.
John, s. Paulfry [Palfry. C. R. 2.] and Lydia, Aug. 25, 1801.
John, s. John and Nancy, Feb. 11, 1826.
John Newton, s. Samuel and Ruby, Nov. 13, 1837.
Lucreacha, d. Richard and Temperance, June 9, 1751.
Lydia, d. Palfry, bp. Sept. 12, 1790. C. R. 2.
Mary, d. Palfrey W. and Hannah, May 13, 1818.
Mary Jane, d. Palfrey W. and Hannah, Mar. 10, 1825.
Molly, d. Samuel and Abigail, Aug. 13, 1774.
Oliver, s. Sam[ue]l and Ruby, bp. Jan. 6, 1828. C. R. 3.
Palfray, s. John and Nancy, Oct. 2, 1832.

DOWNING, Palfrey, s. Richard, bp. Apr. 12, 1761. C. R. 2.
Palfry, s. Richard and Anstis, —17. [bp. Oct. 23, 1726. C. R. 2.]
Palfry Ward, s. Palfry and Lydia, [June] 5, 1791. [bp. July 3, 1791. C. R. 2.]
Richard, s. Richard and Temperance, Mar. 31, 1758.
Richard Derby, s. Samuel and Abigail, May 13, 1785.
Ruby Eliza, d. Sam[ue]l and Ruby, bp. July 6, 1828. C. R. 3.
Samuel, s. Samuel and Abigail, Jan. 3, 1765.
Samuel, s. Palfry and Lydia, Sept. 1, 1794.
Samuel, s. Lt. Palfry and Lydia, Dec. 15, 1798.
Samuel, s. Samuel and Ruby, Nov. 3, 1821.
Sarah, d. Richard and Tempranc, Mar. 28, 1749.
Sarah, d. Samuel and Abigail, Oct. 9, 1772.
Temperance Derby, d. Palfry, bp. Sept. 12, 1790. C. R. 2.
Thomas, s. Samuel and Abigail, July 24, 1770.
Waldo P., s. Palfry, jr., bp. Oct. 3, 1824. C. R. 2.
——, s. Palfry W. and Hannah, July 18, 1822.
——, d. Samuel and Ruby, Feb. 14, 1840.

DOWNS (see also Downes), Charles Carroll, s. B., bp. Aug. 28, 1831. C. R. 2.
Fanny, d. Benjamin and Fanny, Nov. 25, 1824.
Joel Parker, s. Benjamin R. and Anna, May 16, 1835.
——, s. Benjamin R. and Fanny, Aug. 1, 1826.

DRAKE, Amos, s. George and Lucy, June 4, 1832.
Eleanor, d. George and Lucy, Aug. 13, 1829.
Lucy L., d. George and Eunice, Dec. 13, 1820.
Orin, s. George and Lucy, July 14, 1826.

DRESER (see also Dresser), Jonathan, s. Jonathan and Sarah, Sept. 14, 1757.

DRESSER (see also Dreser), Benj[ami]n, s. Jonathan and Sarah, Jan. 6, 1768.
Chloe, d. Jonathan and Sarah, Dec. 15, 1765.
Elezebith, d. Jonathan and Sarah, July 23, 1752.
Levi, s. Jonathan and Sarah, Feb. 24, 1761.
Mary, d. Jonathan and Sarah, Nov. 1, 1762.
Sarah, d. Jonathan and Sarah, Sept. 17, 1750.
Simmeon, s. Jonathan and Sarah, Feb. 21, 1759.
Stephan, s. Jonathan and Sarah, Oct. 25, 1754.

DRUMMOND, Charles F., s. John, cabinetmaker, and Harriet G., Oct. 21, 1843.

DULAP (see also Dunlap), Molly, d. John and Elizabeth, Apr. 11, 1770.

DUNCAN, James, s. James, laborer, and Cristern, Aug. 2, 1848.

DUNCKLEE (see also Dunclee), Andrew Willson, s. Andrew Wilson and Rebekah, Feb. 28, 1796.
Dolly [Ballard. C. R. 2.], d. Andrew Willson and Rebekah, Sept. 18, 1797.

DUNCLEE (see also Duncklee, Duntlin), Cadwallador F. [Ford. C. R. 1.], s. Nath[anie]l and Sarah, Mar. 16, 1799.
Elizabeth L., d. Nath[anie]l and Sarah, Oct. 17, 1802.
Hannah, d. Nath[anie]l and Sarah, Feb. 2, 1791.
Isaac, s. Nathaniel and Sarah, Dec. 3, 1814.
Jacob, s. Andrew W. and Rebecca, July 4, 1802.
John, s. Nath[anie]l and Sarah, Jan. 18, 1797.
Martha, d. twin, Andrew W. and Rebecca, Sept. 12, 1805.
Martha, d. Nathaniel and Sarah, Dec. 30, 1805.
Mary, d. twin, Andrew W. and Rebecca, Sept. 12, 1805.
Mary Ford, d. Nath[anie]l and Sarah, Apr. 11, 1792.
Mary Ford, d. Nathaniel and Sarah, Nov. 22, 1811.
Nancy, d. Nath[anie]l and Sarah, Apr. 5, 1795.
Nathaniel, s. Nath[anie]l and Sarah, Mar. 25, 1793.
Rebecca, d. Andrew W. and Rebecca, Sept. 8, 1807.
Rebecca, d. Nathaniel and Sarah [Nov. or Dec., 1808].
Sarah, d. Nath[anie]l and Sarah, Apr. 9, 1789.

DUNFE, Joseph, s. Joseph and Mary, Feb. 29, 1761.

DUNLAP (see also Delap, Dulap), Almira, d. Henery Ames and Sarah, Sept. 10, 1800.

DUNN, George H., s. Aaron and Martha, July 5, 1840.

DUNSMORE (see also Dinsmore), Elizabeth, d. John and Janet, bp. Aug. 26, 1733. C. R. 1.

DUNTLIN (see also Dunclee), John [Dunckley. C. R. 2.], s. Andrew W. and Rebecca, Sept. 4, 1799.
Martha, d. Nathaniel, bp. Feb. 17, 1805. C. R. 2.
Mary Ford, d. Nath[anie]l, bp. Apr. 24, 1791. C. R. 2.
Nancy, d. Nat[hanie]l, bp. Apr. 5, 1795. C. R. 2.
Sarah, d. Nath[anie]l, bp. Aug. 22, 1790. C. R. 2.

DURANT, Amos, s. Amos, bp. Nov. 24, 1793.
Benjamin, s. Amos, bp. Dec. 2, 1798. C. R. 2.
Hannah, d. Amos, bp. Nov. 24, 1793. C. R. 2.
John Willard, s. Willard, stonecutter, and Mary W., Dec. 31, 1847.
Mary B., May 25, 1786. P. R. 64.
Mary Butler, d. Amos, bp. Nov. 24, 1793. C. R. 2.
Phebe, d. Amos, bp. Dec. 13, 1795. C. R. 2.
Sarah, d. Amos, bp. Nov. 24, 1793. C. R. 2.
——, d. William and Mary, Jan. —, 1819.
[Josephine S. P. R. 67.], d. Willard, stonecutter, b. Billerica, and Mary W., b. Denmark, Me., Nov. 3, 1849.

DWINNELL, Jacob G., s. David and Sally, Sept. 25, 1811.

EAMES (see also Ames), Bethiah, d. [Ens. C. R. 2.] Benj[ami]n and Hephsibah, July 22, 1762.
Elisabeth [Ames. C. R. 1], d. Samuel and Elisabeth, Jan. 14, 1744-5.
Priscilla, d. Thomas and Lucy, Sept. 3, 1763.
Simon, s. Samuel and Elizabeth, Oct. 28, 1761.
Timothy W., s. Benjamin, yeoman, and Lavinia D., Dec. 18, 1846.

EAMS (see also Ames), Sarah, d. Thomas and Lucy, Dec. 2, 1766.

EATON, John, ——, 1775. P. R. 50.
Joseph, ——, 1820. P. R. 50.
Mary, d. John and Mary, bp. Oct. 2, 1814. C. R. 2.
Sophronia, d. John and Mary, bp. Oct. 2, 1814. C. R. 2.
——, s. John, bp. Nov. —, 1822. C. R. 2.

EDES, Bette, d. Thomas and Abigail, Oct. 10, 1764.
Hannah, d. Thomas, bp. Oct. 4, 1789. C. R. 2.
Jacob, s. Thomas and Abigail, Nov. 8, 1768.
Micajah, s. Thomas and Abigail, Sept. 17, 1766.
Thomas, s. Thomas and Abigail, Jan. 28, 1763.
Thomas, s. Thomas, bp. Oct. 4, 1789. C. R. 2.
Susanna, d. Thomas and Abigail, July 28, 1761.

EDMONDS, Elizabeth, d. William and Mary, bp. June 29, 1735. C. R. 1.

EDSON, Dolly O[phelia. C. R. 3.], d. Nath[anie]l and Dolly, Aug. 31, 1828.
Edmund B., s. Elijah and Persis, Jan. 17, 1834.
Elizabeth, d. Nathaniel and Dolly, Sept. 27, 1829.
Nancy H., bp. June 18, 1826. C. R. 2.

EDSON, Nathan W., s. Elijah and Persis, Apr. 27, 1830.
——, s. Nathaniel and Dolly, Oct. 30, 1832.

EDWARDS, Elizabeth, d. Rev. Justin and Lydia, Nov. 12, 1824.
George Carlton, s. Ivory and Elizabeth, Jan. 9, 1837.
Geo[rge] H., s. Prof. B. B. and J. B., bp. Nov. 6, 1842. C. R. 6.
Jona[than], s. Rev. Justin and Lydia, July —, 1820.
Julia Maria, d. Fred[eric]k A. and Triphena, June 28, 1839.
[Justin A., C. R. 2.], s. Rev. Justin and Lydia, Jan. —, 1819.
Lydia, d. Rev. Justin and Lydia, Mar. 6, 1826.
Newton, s. Rev. Justin and Lydia, Mar. 13, 1822.
Sarah B., d. Ivory and Elizabeth, May 21, 1839.
Sarah Billings, d. Rev. B. B., bp. [bet. July 27 and Dec. 31.], 1837. C. R. 6.

EIMES (see also Ames), Daniell, s. Robert and Rebeckah, Apr. 7, 1663. [Oct. 11. CT. R.]
Dorothy, d. Robert and Rebeckah, Dec. 20, 1674.
Hannah, d. Robert and Rebeckah, Dec. 18, 1661.
Jacob, s. Robert and Rebeckah, July 20, 1677.
John, s. Robert and Rebeckah, Oct. 11, 1670.
John, s. John and Pricilla, Aug. 12, 1693.
Joseph, s. Robert and Rebeckah, Oct. 9, 1681.
Lydia, d. twin, Daniell and Lydia, Jan. 24, 1683-4.
Nathan, s. Robert and Rebeckah, Nov. 19, 1685.
Rebeckah, d. twin, Daniell and Lydia, Jan. 24, 1683-4.

ELISHA, Rufus, s. Mary, June 8, 1834.

ELLENWOOD (see also Ellingwood), Charles Cheever, s. Eben[eze]r and Sarah, July 12, 1841.

ELLES (see also Ellis), Augustus Hilton, s. K. S., bp. Nov. 11, 1832. C. R. 2.
Frederick Hilton, s. K. S., bp. Mar. 15, 1835. C. R. 2.

ELLINGWOOD (see also Ellenwood), Charles Cheever, s. Eben[eze]r [carpenter. dup.], and Sally [Sarah. dup.], Feb. 19, 1843.
Gayton B., s. Eben[eze]r, laborer, and Sarah, Feb. 13, 1848.
George E., s. Ebenezer, farmer, and Sarah, Apr. 4, 1845.
Henry Osgood, s. Eben[eze]r and Sally, in Maine, June 8, 1832.
Sarah Frances, d. Eben[eze]r and Sally, in Maine, June 25, 1834.
Zeruah A., d. Eben[eze]r and Sally, Feb. 21, 1839.

ELLIOT (see also Elliott), John, s. John, manufacturer, and Ann, Jan. 26, 1845.
Lydia Downing, d. Andrew and Abigail, Nov. 5, 1806.
Naby, d. Andrew and Abigail, Mar. 22, 1804.

ELLIOTT (see also Elliot), Margery, d. John and Ann, Apr. 15, 1847.

ELLIS (see also Elles), Abba, d. Glida and Abba, Dec. 11, 1828.
Elizabeth A., d. Arno, blacksmith, and Ann, May 6, 1845.
Susanna, d. Arno, blacksmith, Sept. 1, 184[7 or 8].

ELVA, Anna, d. Elvey, laborer, Nov. 10, 184[7 or 8].

ELVY, Ann, d. John, bp. Jan. 1, 1848. C. R. 4.

EMERSON, Charlotte, d. Prof. Ralph and Eliza R., Apr. 21, 1838.
Ebenezer Porter, s. Ralph and Eliza R., Aug. 14, 1834.
[Edward Davis, in pencil.], s. Joseph, clergyman, and Sarah H., Nov. 9, 1845.
Elizabeth, d. [Rev. C. R. 6.] Ralph and Eliza R., Feb. 15, 1836.
Julia F., d. James, laborer, May 15, 184[7-8].
Mary E., d. Isaac and Mary, Nov. 6, 1822.
Mary P[amela. C. R. 6.], d. Joseph, clergyman, b. Dartmouth, and Sarah H., b. Oxford, June 26, 1848.
Ralph, s. Ralph and Eliza R., May 3, 1831.

EMERY (see also Emory, Emry), Abigail, d. Joseph and Elizabeth, —— [1705?].
Abigail, d. Joseph and Abigail, Nov. 19 [1734].
Elizabeth, d. Joseph and Elizabeth, 7br. 28, 1698.
Elizabeth, d. Joseph and Abigaiel, Jan. 2, 1732-3.
Jacob, s. Joseph and Abigail, Dec. 11, 1737.
Jacob, s. Joseph, jr. and Hannah, July 18, 1768.
Joseph, s. Joseph and Elizabeth, Apr. 19, 1696.
Joseph, s. Joseph and Abigail [Elizabeth. C. R. 1.], Oct. 7, 1736.
Joseph, s. Joseph and Abigail, June 3, 1739.
Joseph, s. Joseph, jr. and Hannah, Dec. 19, 1764.
Samuel, s. Joseph, and Abigail [June or July, 1742].
Samuel, s. Joseph, jr. and Hannah, Aug. 19, 1766.
Samuel, s. Briggs Hollowell and Sarah, bp. Apr. 3, 1796. C. R. 1.
——, d. Joseph and Elizabeth, Dec. 10, 1710.

EMORY (see also Emery), Benjamin Farnum, s. Briggs Hallowel and Sarah, bp. Feb. 23, 1800. C. R. I.

EMRY (see also Emery) [Priscilla. C. R. I.], d. Thomas and Priscilla, Aug. 4, 1739.

ENGOLLS (see also Ingalls), Francis, s. Henry and Mary, Sept. 23, 1663.
Henry, s. Henry and Mary, Dec. 8, 1656. [Dec. 10. CT. R.]
James, s. Henry and Mary, Sept. 24, 1669.
John, s. twin, Henry and Mary, May 21, 1661.
Mary, d. Henry and Mary, Jan. 28, 1659.
Moses, s. Henry and Mary, June 26, [16]66.
Samuell, s. Henry and Mary, Oct. 3, 1654.
Sara, d. Henry and Mary, Sept. 7, 1672.
Steven, s. twin, Henry and Mary, May 21, 1661.

ENGOLS (see also Ingalls), Mary, d. [torn], Mar. 10, 1701.

EVANS, ——, d. Samuel, farmer, and Abigail, June 20, 1848.

EVERSON (see also Everton), Rhoda Gleason, d. Ephraim, machinist, and Rhoda, May 14, 1846.

EVERTON (see also Everson), Emily Frances, d. Ephraim and Rhoda, Aug. 21, 1836.
Emily Frances, d. Ephraim and Rhoda, Aug. 20, 1843.
George Ephraim, s. Ephraim and Rhoda, Dec. 10, 1834.
Rhoda Gleason, d. Ephraim and Rhoda, Feb. 23, 1839.

FAIRBANKS, Hollis W., s. Hollis W., painter, and Caroline P., Dec. 1, 1845.

FALKNER (see also Faulkner), Elbridg[e] Carlton, s. Elace, bp. Nov. 17, 1811. C. R. I.

FARINGTON (see also Farrington), Affa, d. John and Sarah, Mar. 8, 1756.
Anne, d. Daniel and Elisabeth [July or Aug., 1741].
Benjamin, s. John and Sarah, Sept. 20, 1737.
Benjamin S[umner. C. R. I.], s. Benja[min] and Harriot, Dec. 18, 1830.
Ebenezer, s. Daniel, jr. and Hannah, June 27, 1754.
Ebenezer, s. Daniel and Hannah, Oct. 10, 1757.
Edward, s. Edward and Martha, July 9, 1699.

FARINGTON, Edward, s. John and Sarah [Nov.? 1745].
Elezebith, d. Daniel, jr. and Hannah, Feb. 3, 1759.
Elisabeth, d. Daniel and Elisabeth, May 14, 1739.
Hannah, d. twin, John and Sarah, Feb. 20, 1747-8.
Jabez, s. Anna, bp. May 27, 1759. C. R. I.
Jacob, s. Dan[ie]l, bp. Mar. 16, 1734-5. C. R. I.
[John. C. R. I.], s. John and Sarah, Nov. 4, 1731.
John, s. Daniel and Elezebith, Apr. 11, 1754.
John, s. Daniel and Eliza[beth], Apr. —, 1755.
John, s. John, jr. and Phebe, Oct. 12, 1779.
John Elbridge, s. Benj[amin] and Mary, bp. Dec. 7, 1834. C. R. I.
Lucinda Frances, d. Benj[amin] and Mary, bp. Apr. 2, 1837. C. R. I.
Lydia, d. John and Sarah, Oct. 24, 1735.
Lydia, d. Benja[min] and Sarah, Sept. 26, 1776.
Martha, d. John and Sarah, Oct. 5, 1741.
Mary [Sarah. C. R. I.], d. Daniel and Elezebith, Sept. 30, 1751.
Mehetabel, d. John, bp. ——, 1741. C. R. I.
Meribah, d. Mary, bp. Sept. 16, 1733. C. R. I.
Phebe, d. twin, John and Sarah, Feb. 20, 1747-8.
Phebe Varnum, d. John, bp. Apr. 1, 1781. C. R. 2.
Philip, s. Daniel and Elezebith, Apr. 9, 1749.
[Phineas. C. R. I.], —— ihas, s. Daniel and Elisabeth, Mar. 7, 1737-8.
Polly, d. John, jr. and Phebe, Dec. 19, 1777.
[Putnam. C. R. I.], s. Daniel and Elisabeth, Oct. —, 1746.
Putnam, s. Daniel, jr. and Hannah, Jan. 17, 1756.
Ruth, d. Daniel and Elisabeth, May 10, 1744.
Sarah, d. John and Sarah, Feb. 2, 1739-40.
Sarah, d. John and Sarah, Dec. 30, 1743.
Sarah, d. John, bp. Jan. 9, 1785. C. R. 2.
Stephen, s. John and Sarah, Apr. 24, 1751.
——, s. Daniel and Elisabeth, May ——, 1733.
——, d. John and Sarah, July 8, 1733.
——, s. Daniel and Elisabeth, Mar. 8, 1735-6.

FARLEY, Elizabeth, d. Samuel and Eliz[abe]th, Aug. 11, 1766.
Mary, d. Samuel and Elizabeth, May 11, 1771.
Samuel, s. Samuel and Eliz[abe]th, Jan. 2, 1769.

FARMER, Abigail N., ——, 1761. P. R. 36.
Andrew, s. Joseph, bp. Jan. 25, 1784. C. R. 2.
Dorcas, d. Joseph, bp. Oct. 8, 1785. C. R. 2.
Life, Mar. 21, 1760. P. R. 36.
Prudence, Jan. 15, 1797. P. R. 36.

FARNAM (see also Farnham), Debora, d. James and Johanna, Jan. 13, 1728-9.
[Ebenezer. C. R. 1.], s. [Josiah. C. R. 1.] and Mary, Aug. 4, 1754.
Epharam, s. Josiah and Mary, Oct. 13, 1751.
Isarel, s. Thomas, jr. and Lydea, June 14, 1758.
James, s. John, jr. and Sarah, Aug. 8, 1750.
Joanna, d. Josiah and Mary, Sept. 27, 1757.
John C., s. Benjamin, jr. and Ruth, Apr. 11, 1815.
Lydea, d. Thomas, jr. and Lydea, Nov. 10, 1756.
Mary, d. Thomas and [E]lizabeth, Mar. 24, 1666.
Moses, s. Dan[ie]l and Lydia, bp. Jan. 24, 1779. C. R. 1.
Peter, s. John, jr. and Sarah, May 8, 1752.
Phebe, d. Ebenezer and Precila, Dec. 15, 1750.
Simeon, s. Capt. John and Sarah, Oct. 9, 1756.
Susanna, d. Asa and Susanna, Nov. 12, 1758.
Theoder, s. Josiah and Mary, Jan. 24, 1748-9.
——, d. John, jr. and Sarah, Aug. 14, 1754.

FARNAUM (see also Farnham), Abiah, d. Timothy and Dinah, Sept. 15, 1729.
Abigail, d. Barachias and Hephzibah, May 27, 1734.
[Ann. C. R. 1.], d. Jonathan and Elizabeth, Sept. 10, 1729,
Anne, d. Jonathan and Elizabeth, Apr. 25, 1728.
Barachias, s. Barachias and Hephzibah, Mar. 11, 1728-9.
Barrachias, s. Barachias and Hephzibah, Apr. 8, 1736.
Eliphelet, s. Henry and Phebe, Mar. 25, 1725.
[Elizabeth. C. R. 1.], d. James and Johannah, Jan. 19, 1727-8.
Hannah, d. Stephen and Hannah, Jan. 17, 1728-9.
Hannah, d. Ebenezer and Priscilla, Sept. 9, 1733.
Jeremiah, s. Samuel and Mary, July 29, 1735.
Johanna, d. James and Johanna, May 22, 1725.
Jonathan, s. David and Dorathy, Oct. 14 [1725].
Joshua, s. Stephen and Hannah, July 24, 1[727].
J] osiah, s. Josiah and Mary, Dec. 19, 1736.
Mary, d. Ephraim and Mary, Sept. 16, 1729.
Mary, d. Barachias and Hephzibah, Apr. 29, 1732.
Mary, d. Josiah and Mary, Sept. 28, 1734.
[Phebee. C. R. 1.], d. Timothy and Dinah, Oct. 10, 1731.
Rachel, d. Barachias and Hephzebah, Jan. 31, 1726-7.
Sarah, d. Barachias and Hephzebah, Mar. 22, 1724-5.
Sarah, d. David and Dorathy, Mar. 30, 1728.
Susanna, d. Barachias and Hepzibah, Apr. 9, 1730.
[Susanna. C. R. 1.], d. Ebenezer and Priscilla, Aug. 31, 1735.
Tabitha, d. James and Johannah, Mar. 18, 1729-30.

FARNAUM, Timothy, s. Timothy and Dinah, Feb. 8, 1734-5.
Timothy, s. Timothy and Dinah, Sept. 18, 1736.
——, d. James and Johanna, Nov. 18, 1726.
——, d. Stephen and Hannah, Jan. 22, 1730-31.
——, s. Samuel and Mary, Jan. 22, 1732-3.

FARNEM (see also Farnham), Bridgett, d. Samuel and Hannah, May 28, 17[14].
Dinah, d. Thomas and Hannah, —— [1703].
Ebenezer, s. Thomas and Hannah,——[1711].
Elizabeth, d. Sam[ue]ll and Hannah, Mar. —, 1710.
Elizabeth, d. Jonathan and Elizabeth, Nov. 9, 1711.
Elizabeth, d. John and Johanna, June — [1717].
Elizabeth, d. Ephraim and Priscilla, —— [1718].
Henery, s. Henery and Phoebe, Apr. 8, 171[5. C. R. 2.].
James, s. Ephraim, ——[1705?].
Johannah, d. John and Johanna, ——, [1712].
Joseph, s. Ephraim and Priscilla, —[1714-15].
Mannasseh, s. Henery and Pheobie, Feb. 15, 1716-17.
Mary, d. John and Joannah, May 21 [1714].
[Phebe. C. R. 2.], d. Henery and Pheobe, July 4, 1713.
Rebecka, d. Thomas and Hannah, ——[1705?].
Rebecka, d. Jonathan and Elizabeth, Mar. 14, 1715-16.
Tabitha, d. [torn], —— [1706].
Timothy, s. Ephraim, May 4, 1702.
Zebadiah, s. Realph and Sarah, —— [1705?].
——, ch. [torn] and [H]annah, Feb. 28, 1702-3.
——, ch. [torn] and ——h, Mar. 16, 1702-3.
——, ch. [E]phraim and Priscilla, Mar. 25, 1708-9.
——, s. Thomas and Hannah, May 16, 1709.
——, ch. [torn] and Joanna, Apr. 1, 1711.
——, ch. Sam[ue]ll and Hannah, May 4, 1712.
——, s. Ephraim and Priscilla, July 19, 1712.

FARNHAM (see also Farnam, Farnaum, Farnem, Farnom, Farnum), Abba Ann [Abby Anne. C. R. 2.], d. John C. and Dorcas, Feb. 15, 1838.
Albert Warren, s. Samuel, mason, and Sarah, Feb. 20, 1845.
Amlet Augusta, d. Jere and Elizabeth, Mar. 24, 1835.
Benjamin [Armstrong. C. R. 3.], s. Edwin and Susan B., Oct. 11, 1835.
Benjamin H., s. Jacob and Rebecca, Oct. 23, 1836.
Caroline, d. Joseph and Maria, Dec. 21, 1832. P. R. 61.
Clara, d. John C., printer, and Sarah T., Dec. 4, 1848.

FARNHAM, Deborah C., d. Joseph and Mariah, Aug. 28, 1830.
George Haskell, s. Susan W., bp. June 13, 1841. C. R. 3.
Hannah Ingalls, d. Joseph and Maria, Aug. 28, 1830. P. R. 61.
Harriet Lavinia, d. Edwin and Susan, bp. Oct. 21, 1837. C. R. 3.
Harriett, d. Jesse and Sarah, Aug. 7, 1838.
Harriot Lavina [Harriet Lavinia. C. R. 3.], d. Edwin and Harriot [Harriet. C. R. 3.], Sept. 26, 1828.
Henry S[idney. C. R. 3.], s. Edwin and Susan B., Apr. 18, 1833.
Hiram Putnam, s. John and Almira, Dec. 2, 1838.
Jacob, s. Jacob and Rebecca, Sept. 15, 1832.
Jacob L., s. Jacob and Rebecca, Nov. 2, 1829.
John E., s. Edwin and Harriot, Dec. 21, 1826.
John Henry, s. John and Almira, Apr. 30, 1832.
John Ingalls, s. Joseph and Maria, Sept. 10, 1837.
John Lewis, s. John P., mason, and Abby Ann, Aug. 28, 1847.
John Osgood, s. Isaac and Sarah, July 23, 1835.
John P., s. Timothy and Nancy, July 3, 1822.
Joseph H., s. Seth, farmer, and Sarah, Jan. 14, 1845.
Julia Ann, d. Tim[oth]y and Nancy, Apr. 11, 1825.
Martha Ellen [Allen. C. R. 1.], d. twin, Joseph and Maria, Aug. 5, 1835.
Mary Almira, d. John and Almira, Sept. 9, 1835.
Mary Frances, d. twin, Joseph and Maria, Aug. 5, 1835.
Olive, d. Samuel, mason, b. N. H., and Sarah, b. Sudbury, Sept. 26, 1849.
Orrin Lewis, s. Jere and Sarah, June 24, 1835.
Sarah, d. William and Elizabeth, July 29, 1816.
Sarah Elizabeth, d. John and Almira, Nov. 19, 1829.
Sarah J., d. Leonard and Sarah, Dec. 27, 1831.
Sarah Maria, d. John C. and Dorcas, Nov. 18, 1839.
Sarah M., d. Seth and Sarah, Nov. 17, 1840.
Sarah Maria, d. Isaac and Sarah, May 29, 1842.
Sarah Maria, d. Joseph and Maria, Nov. 29, 1828. P. R. 61.
Seth T., d. Seth and Sarah, May 6, 1838.
Susan Berry, d. Jere and Sarah, Aug. 30, 1837.
Susan F., d. Jacob and Rebecca, Feb. 11, 1835.
William Wallace, s. John and Almira, Feb. 5, 1828.
William Wallis, s. John and Almira, bp. Aug. 1, 1841. C. R. 1.
——, d. Benjamin, jr. and Ruth, Feb. 18, 1823.

FARNOM (see also Farnham), Sarah, d. John and Elizabeth, Oct. 23, 1700.

FARNUM (see also Farnham), Abiah, d. Timothy and Dina, Oct. 15, 1742.
Abiah, d. Ebenezer and Priscilla, Feb. 13, 1746-7.
Abiah, d. Benj[ami]n and Dolly, May 6, 1770.
Abiah, d. Benjamin, jr. and Ruth, Jan. 23, 1796.
Abigail, d. Ralph and Sarah, May 3, 1692.
Abigall, d. Thomas and Elizabeth, Dec. 29, 1682.
Abigial J., d. Timothy and Nancy, Dec. 24, 1827.
Augustus, s. Peter and Chloe, May 20, 1805.
Alfred, s. Daniel and Lydia, bp. Aug. 17, 1783. C. R. I.
Am[os, s. Israel and Phebe. T. C.], May 17, 1792.
Anne, d. John and Rebekah, Dec. 11, 1677.
Anne, d. John and Mary, Jan. 18, 1695-6.
Asa, s. Thomas and Phebe, May 11, 1736.
Asa, s. Asa and Susanna, May 27, 1760.
Asa, s. Asa and Lucindia, Mar. 25, 1788.
Barachias, s. Ralph and Sarah, Mar. 16, 1696-7.
Becca, d. Jedediah and Becca, Oct. 12, 1776.
Benjamin, s. Ralph and Sarah, Mar. 14, 1698-9.
[B]enjamin, s. Timothy and Dinah, Sept. 16, 1738.
Benjamin, s. Timothy and Dinah, Dec. 16, 1746.
Benj[ami]n, s. Asa, bp. Apr. 1, 1764. C. R. I.
Benj[ami]n, s. Benjamin and Dolly [Dorata. C. R. I.], Mar. 1, 1772.
Benj[ami]n, s. Daniel and Lydia, bp. Apr. 28, 1776. C. R. I.
Benjamin, s. Asa and Lucindia, Aug. 21, 1794.
Benjamin, s. Benjamin, jr. and Ruth, Apr. 23, 1801.
Benja[min] Armstrong, s. Capt. Jedediah and Susana, Apr. 29, 1811.
Betsey, d. John and Mary, Dec. 10, 1787.
Charles, s. Isaac and Mary [Molly. C. R. I.], Sept. 21, 1787.
Charles Hazen, s. Benj[ami]n, jr. and Ruth, Aug. 12, 1817.
Charlotte, d. John and Mary, June 1, 1786.
Charlottee, d. Isaac and Mary, Feb. 22, 1793.
Chloe, d. Peter and Chloe, Apr. 5, 1792.
Clefford, s. Wil[lia]m and Elizabeth, July 12, 1805.
Cloe, d. Capt. Benjamin and Dorothy [Dolly. C. R. I.], Nov. 21, 1783.
Daniel, s. Ralf and Sarah, Jan. [21. T. C.], 1690-91.
Daniel, s. John and Sarah, June 15, 1741.
Daniel, s. Daniel and Lydia [Mercy. C. R. I.], Apr. 13, 1770.
David, s. John and Rebekah, Oct. 7, 1681.
David, s. John and Rebeckah, Apr. 4, 1690.
David T., s. Samuel P. and Olive T., Nov. 25, 1835.

FARNUM, Debora, d. Thomas and [E]lizabeth, May 17, 1668.
Dolly, d. Benj[ami]n and Dolly, Aug. 18, 1768.
Dolly, d. Benjamin, jr. and Ruth, Mar. 31, 1799.
Dolly, d. Benjamin, jr. and Ruth, June 8, 1808.
Doratha, d. Samuel and Dorcas, bp. Jan. 20, 1793. C. R. 1.
Dorothy, d. Ebenezer and Priscilla, Jan. 21, 1744[-5].
Dorcas, d. Tho[ma]s [jr. C. R. 1.] and Lydia, Dec. 27, 1766.
Dorcas, d. Samuel and Dorcas, Mar. 14, 1778.
Ebenezer, s. Ebenezer and Priscilla, Nov. 13, 1737.
Edwin, s. Jedediah, jr. and Susannah, Aug. 4, 1800.
Elisabeth, d. Josiah and Mary, Sept. 4, 1746.
Elizabeth, d. Thomas and El[torn], Feb. 19, 1661.
Elizabeth, d. John and Elizabeth, June 7, 1687.
Elizabeth, d. W[illia]m and Elizabeth, July 17, 1801.
Elizabeth, d. Peter and Chloe, Dec. 7, 1807.
Elizabeth Brandon, d. Jacob and Elizabeth Foster, Apr. 3, 1800.
Enoch, s. Capt. John and Sarah, Aug. 2, 1766.
Enoch, s. Jedediah and Becca, Feb. 28, 1789.
Enoch, s. Peter and Chloe, July 19, 1799.
Ephraim, s. Ralph and Elizabeth, Oct. 1, 1676.
Ephraim, s. Ephriam and Pricilla, Oct. 12, 1700.
Ephraim, s. Josiah and Mary, July 3, 1744.
Fanney [Maria. C. R. 1.], d. Timothy and Susanna, May 31, 1810.
Frederick, s. James and Rebecca, Aug. 25, 1781.
Frye, s. James and Rebecca, Nov. 1, 1783.
Frye, s. Peter and Chloe, July 21, 1801.
Gemima, d. Henry and Phoebe, bp. Mar. 22, 1719. C. R. 2.
Hanna, d. Ralfe and Elizabeth, Dec. 7, 1668.
Hannah, d. John and Elisabeth, Dec. 31, 1693.
Hannah, d. Thomas and Hannah, Jan. 24, 1694-5.
Hannah, d. Nathaniel and Hannah, Jan. 19, 1721-2.
Hannah, d. Jonathan and Elezebeth, Jan. 5, 1724-5.
Hannah, d. James and Rebecca, Apr. 28, 1777.
Hannah, d. Samuel and Dorcas, bp. Aug. 23, 1789. C. R. 1.
Hannah, d. Capt. Benja[min] and Dolly, Oct. 27, 1789.
Hannah, d. Timothy and Susanna, Sept. 30, 1804.
Hariot, d. Wiliam and Elizabeth, Mar. 7, 1809.
Henery, s. Ralph and Sarah, Sept. 15, 1687.
Henry, s. Ralfe and Elizabeth, Dec. 7 [16]66.
[Hephsibah. C. R. 2.], d. Barachias and Hephzibah, Oct. 3, 1723.
Ira, s. James and Rebecca, Aug. 12, 1790.
Isaac, s. John, jr. and Sarah, Dec. 19, 1742.
Isaac, s. Isaac and Mary, Mar. 3, 1773.
Isaac, s. Isaac, jr. and Percis, Mar. 19, 1804.

FARNUM, Israel, s. Israel and Phebe, June 8, 1790.
Jacob, s. Benjamin and Dolly, Oct. 14, 1774.
Jacob, s. Elizabeth Foster, wid. Jacob, "who was drowned in the great Pond, Aug. 19, 1801," b. Jan. 8, 1802.
Jacob, s. Benjamin, jr. and Ruth, May 31, 1803.
James, s. John and Elisabeth, Oct. 17, 1691.
James, s. James and Johanna, A[pr.] 24 [1723].
James, s. Capt. John and Sarah, Aug. 8, 1750. P. R. 61.
James, s. James and Rebecca, Aug. 24, 1779.
James, s. Peter and Chloe, Sept. 29, 1802.
Jedediah, s. John, jr. and Sarah, Jan. 10, 1744-5.
Jedediah, s. Jedediah and Becca, Apr. 31, 1772.
Jedidiah, s. Wiliam and Elezabeth, Dec. 17, 1807.
Jemima, d. David and Dorathy, Mar. 21, 1729-30.
Jemima, see also Gemima.
Jere, s. Timothy and Susanna, Mar. 17, 1797.
Jeremiah s. Jere and Sarah, June 27, 1828.
Jeremy, s. James and Rebekkah, bp. Nov. 20, 1785. C. R. I.
Jesse, s. Timothy and Susannah, Feb. 4, 1793.
John, s. Ralfe and Elizabeth, Apr. 1, 1664.
John, s. John and Rebecca, Jan. 20, 1670.
John, s. John and Rebecca, Apr. 13, 1672.
John, s. John and Elizabeth, Feb. 13, 1684.
John, s. John and Mary, Dec. 25, 1697.
John, s. John and Sarah, Apr. 15, 1740.
John, s. Jedediah and Becca, Mar. 26, 1774.
John, s. Peter and Chloe, Dec. 5, 1794.
John, s. John and Mary, Sept. 4, 1796.
John Cooledge, s. Benja[min], jr. and Ruth, Mar. 11, 1815.
John E[dward. C. R. I.], s. Maj. Jedediah and Susanah [Susan. C. R. I.], July 6, 1819.
John Osgood, s. Isaac and Mary, Mar. 24, 1781.
John P., s. Timothy and Nancy, July —, 1820.
Johnathan, s. John and Rebekah, Apr. 27, 1684.
[J]onathan, s. twin, Jonathan and Elezebeth, Nov. 21, 1720.
Joseph, s. Ralph and Sarah, Feb. 4, 1700-1701.
Joseph, s. Thomas and Phebe, June 18, 1745.
Joseph, s. Samuel and Dorcas, Jan. 3, 1781.
Joseph, s. Peter and Chloe, July 6, 1797.
Joseph Holt, s. Benj[amin], jr. and Ruth, Oct. 12, 1810. C. R. I.
[Joshua. C. R. 2.] ——a, s. Henry and Phebe, Mar. 29, 1723.
Josiah, s. Josiah and Mary, Aug. 4, 1739.
Lavina, d. Jedediah, jr. and Susanna, Aug. 16, 1806.
Leonard, s. Isaac, jr. and Persis, June 9, 1802.

FARNUM, Levi, s. Timothy and Susanna, Oct. 26, 1787.
Lucinda, d. Asa and Lucinda, Mar. [bet. 3-5], 1786.
Lucy, d. Asa and Lucindia, Mar. 23, 1786.
Lucy, d. Timothy and Susanna, Mar. 23, 1789.
Lydia, d. Samuel and Hannah, Oct. 15, 1699.
Lydia, d. Jedidiah and Becca, July 14, 1780.
Lydia, d. Daniel and Lydia, bp. Mar. 25, 1781. C. R. I.
Lydia, d. Timothy and Susanna, Feb. 28, 1795.
Lydia, d. Moses and Submit, June 2, 1802.
Lydia Ann, d. Jere and Sarah, July 28, 1830.
Maria, d. William and Elizabeth, Aug. 26, 1818.
Martha, d. Thomas and Elizabeth, Apr. 15, 1680.
Martha, d. James and Johanna, May 16, 1724.
Martha, d. Isaac and Mary, Mar. 12, 1779.
Martha, d. Isaac, jr. and Percis, Sept. 17, 1809.
Mary, d. John and Mary, Mar. 16, 1693-4.
Mary, d. Rebeca, and "Reputed," d. Edward Farington, jr., Jan. 31, 1722-3.
Mary, d. Samuel and Mary, Aug. 13 [1731. C. R. I.].
Mary, d. Thom[a]s, jr., bp. May 27, 1770. C. R. I.
Mary, d. Isaac and Mary, Feb. 24 [25. dup.], 1775.
Mary, d. Mr. John and Mary, Mar. 5, 1785.
Mary, d. John, bp. Sept. 28, 1806. C. R. I.
Mary, d. Timothy and Susannah, Aug. 3, 1808.
Mary, d. Isaac, jr. and Percis, May 7, 1812.
Mary Ann, d. Enoch and Mary, Nov. 4, 1808.
Mary Marble, d. Jedediah, jr. and Susanna, July 16, 1803.
[Mehetable. C. R. I.], d. John and Joanna, Nov. —, 1720.
Mehetable Porter, d. Daniel and Lydia, bp. Dec. 18, 1785. C. R. I.
Mehittabell, d. Thomas and Elizabeth, Feb. 25, 1673.
Molley, d. Capt. Benjamin and Dolley, Oct. 18, 1780.
Moses, s. Moses and Submit, July 3, 1804.
Nancy, d. Timothy and Susanna, Mar. 13, 1791.
Nathan, s. John, jr. and Sarah, May 19, 1739.
Nathan, s. Capt. John and Sarah, May 2, 1761.
Nathan, s. Daniel and Lydia, Apr. 12, 1772.
Nathanael, s. Nath[anae]ll and Hannah, bp. May 15, 1720. C. R. 2.
Nathaniel, s. Ralph and Sarah, July 25, 1695.
Nathaniel, s. Capt. John and Sarah, May 2, 1761.
Nathaniel, s. Samuel and Dorcas, Feb. 6, 1783.
Olive L., d. Samuel and Olive, July 10, 1839.
Pamela, d. Sam[ue]l and Dorcas, bp. Dec. 9, 1787. C. R. I.
Peeter, s. David and Dorathy, Jan. 3, 1723-4.

FARNUM, Percis, d. Isaac, jr. and Percis, Mar. 6, 1799.
Peter, s. Timothy and Dinah, Nov. 8, 1740.
Peter, May 8, 1752. P. R. 61.
Peter, s. David and Damaras, Aug. 30, 1763.
Peter, s. Peter and Sarah, Nov. 6, 1785.
Peter, s. Isaac and Percis, bp. May 10, 1812. C. R. I.
Phebe, d. John and Elisabeth, June 24, 1698.
Phebe, d. Tho[ma]s, bp. —— [1749-50]. C. R. I.
Phebe, d. Thomas and Lydia, July 25, 1762.
Phebe, d. Capt. Benjamin and Dolley [Dorota. C. R. I.], Feb. 3, 1779.
Phebe, d. Israel and Phebe, Mar. 31, 1788.
Phebe, d. Timothy and Susanna, Nov. 21, 1800.
Phebe [Johnson. C. R. I.], d. Maj. Jedidiah and Susannah, May 15, 1816.
Phoebe, d. Benjamin and Dorothy, June 18, 1776.
Polly Saltmarsh, d. Benja[min], jr. and Ruth, June 4, 1795.
Priscilla, d. Ebenezer and Priscilla, Mar. 24, 1740-41.
Putnam Ingalls, s. James and Rebekah, bp. Mar. 23, 1788. C. R. I.
Ralfe, s. Ralfe and Elizabeth, June 1, 1662.
Ralph, s. Ralph and Sarah, May 25, 1689.
Rebecca, d. James and Rebecca, June 4, 1774.
Rebecca, d. Jacob and Rebecca, Dec. 26, 1827.
Rebecca Poor, d. Jedediah, jr. and Susanna, Sept. 25, 1808.
Rhoda, d. Capt. Benjamin and Dolly, July 27, 1787.
Rube, d. Timothy and Susanna, bp. Mar. 23, 1806. C. R. I.
Ruby Foster, d. Wil[lia]m and Elizabeth, May 2, 1814.
Sally, d. John and Mary, Feb. 5, 1790.
Samuel, s. John, jr. and Sarah, Aug. 8, 1747.
Samuel, s. Samuel, jr. and Dorcas, Sept. 25, 1776.
Samuel, s. Asa and Lucindia, July 7, 1792.
Samuel P., s. Samuel P. and Olive T., May 25, 1837.
Sara, d. Ralfe and Elizabeth [Jan. 14, 1661. CT. R.].
Sarah, d. Ralph and Sarah, May 5, 1686.
Sarah, d. Ebenezer and Priscilla, Oct. 21 [1742. C. R. I.].
Sarah, d. Thomas and Lydia, Sept. 21, 1764.
Sarah, d. David and Damaras, Nov. 10, 1767.
Sarah, d. Isaac and Mary, Mar. 10, 1771.
Sarah, d. Peter and Sarah, Sept. 4, 1784.
Sarah Descomb, d. Peter and Chloe, Apr. 6, 1790.
Sarah Frye, d. James and Rebeca, Sept. 2, 1795.
Sarah Frye, d. Enoch and Mary, July 11, 1806.
Sary [Sarah. C. R. I.] Jane, d. Jere and Sarah, Apr. 7, 1827.
Seth, s. Benjamin, jr. and Ruth, Sept. 15, 1805.

FARNUM, Simeon, s. Capt. John and Sarah, Oct. 9, 1756. P. R. 61.
Simeon, s. Jedidiah and Becca, Mar. 1, 1783.
Sophia, d. Daniel and Lydya, bp. Jan. 25, 1789. C. R. 1.
Stephen, s. Jo[h]n and Rebeckah, Oct. 19, 1674.
Sukey, d. Timothy and Susanna, Jan. 14, 1799.
Susan, d. Benjamin, jr. and Ruth, Dec. 7, 1812.
Susan Berry, d. Jere and Sarah, Aug. 29, 1832.
Susana, d. Wiliam and Elizabeth, Apr. 12, 1812.
Susanna, d. Asa, bp. June 2, 1765. C. R. 1.
Susanna, d. Isaac and Mary, Jan. 2, 1784.
Susanna, d. Samuel and Dorcas, Mar. 13, 1785.
Susanna, d. Asa and Lucinda, Mar. 30, 1790.
Susanna Bowman, d. Benj[amin], jr. and Ruth, bp. Dec. 13, 1812. C. R. 1.
Susannah, d. Jedediah and Susannah, Oct. 30, 1798.
Tabitha, d. Thomas and Elizabeth, Oct. 17, 1678.
Theoder, s. Josiah and Mary, Apr. 13, 1742.
Thomas, s. Ralfe and Elizabeth, July 14, 1670.
Thomas, s. Thomas and Eliz[abeth], June 15, 1672.
Thomas, s. John and Rebekah, Aug. 11, 1687.
[Thomas. C. R. 1.], s. David and Dorathy, May 14, 1720.
Thomas, s. Thomas and Phebe, Sept. 6, 1734.
Timothy, s. Thomas [jr. C. R. 1.] and Lydia, May 13, 1759.
Timothy, s. Jedidiah and Becca, Dec. 17, 1784.
William, s. Ralph and Sarah, Aug. 5, 1693.
William, s. Jedediah and Becca, Sept. 19, 1778.
Wil[lia]m, s. Wil[lia]m and Elizabeth, Apr. 17, 1803.
William Frye, s. John and Mary, Aug. 7, 1798.
Zechariah, "a child Wm. Barachias Farnum undertoook ye Education of," bp. Sept. 10, 1732. C. R. 2.
——, ch. [torn and] Hannah, —— [1701].
[torn]iell, s. Nathaniell and Hannah, May —, 1720.
——, d. twin, Jonathan and Elezebeth, Nov. 21, 1720.
——, s. John, jr. and Sarah, May 23, 1746.
——, d. Capt. Benja[min] and Dolly, Dec. 3, 1782.
——, ch. Levi, Mar. 31, 1820.

FARREL (see also Farwell), Francis Henry, s. Henry, blacksmith, and Mary, June 13, 1844.

FARRINGTON (see also Farington), Anna, d. Phinehas and Anna, bp. Mar. 30, 1766. C. R. 1.
Benjamin, s. Benj[ami]n and Sarah, Oct. 8, 1771.

FARRINGTON, Daniel, s. Daniel and Elizabeth, ——, 1731. [1732. P. R. 63; bp. June 4, 1732. C. R. 1.]
Daniel, s. Phinehas and Anna, bp. Jan. 13, 1771. C. R. 1.
Elisabeth Putnum, d. John, bp. Jan. 26, 1783. C. R. 2.
Elizabeth, d. Edward and Martha, Dec. 10, 1690.
Hannah, d. Daniel and Hannah, July 9, 1765.
Harriet S[ophia. C. R. 1.], d. Benja[min] and Harriet, Dec. 31, 1828.
Jacob, s. Edward and Martha, Jan. 26, 1695-6.
John, s. Edward and Martha, July 29, 1693.
John, s. Benjamin and Sarah, bp. Dec. 25, 1774. C. R. 1.
John, s. Benjamin and Sarah, Dec. 20, 1775.
Martha, d. Edward, —— [1702].
Mary, d. Edward and Martha, Mar. 5, 1712-13.
Putnam, s. Phinehas and Anna, bp. Oct. 16, 1768. C. R. 1.
Rheuba, d. Benjamin and Sarah, May 7, 1798.
Sally, d. Benjamin and Sally, Mar. 13, 1796.
Sam[ue]l, s. Phinehas and Anna, bp. Dec. 18, 1763. C. R. 1.
Sarah, d. Benjamin and Sarah, Apr. 6, 1773.
Sarah Matilda, d. Benjamin and Harriet, Mar. 8, 1833.
——, ch. [torn]ha, Jan. 29, 1704-5.
——, ch. Edward and Martha, Aug. 26, 1710.

FARWELL (see also Farrel), Hannah Sexton, d. Asa, teacher, and Hannah S., Aug. 27, 1848.
William Holden, s. Asa, teacher, and Hannah S., May 6, 1847. [May 16. dup.]

FAULKNER (see also Falkner), Abiel, s. Joseph and Damaris, Oct. 30, 1728.
Abiel, s. Abiel and Mary, Sept. 4, 1755.
Abiel, s. Abiel and Hannah, Mar. 6, 1778.
Abigall, d. Francis and Abigall, Aug. 12, 1683.
Abijah, s. Hannah, bp. Sept. 4, 1768. C. R. 1.
Ammiruhamah, s. Francis and Abigail, Mar. 20, 1692-3.
Benjamin, s. Paul and Hannah, May 6, 1736.
Betty, d. wid. Mary, bp. Sept. —, 1761. C. R. 1.
Damaris, d. Abiel and Mary, Nov. 3, 1753.
Daniel, s. Joseph and Mary, May 11, 1734.
Daniel, s. Daniel and Phebe, Dec. 10, 1760.
Daniel, s. Daniel and Phebe, July 17, 1765.
Daniel, s. Lovel and Dorcas, bp. July 17, 1814. C. R. 2.
Daniell, s. John and Sarah, Jan. 15, 1685-6.
Dorathy, d. Paul and Hannah, Jan. 30, 1725-6.

FAULKNER, Dorcas, d. Joseph, jr. and Hannah, Sept. 24, 1766.
Dorothy, d. Francis and Abigall, Feb. 15, 1680.
Edmond, s. Paul and Hannah, June 24, 1730.
Edmund, s. Francis and Abigall, Apr. 2, 1688.
Edward Y., s. Lovel and Dorcas, Mar. 30, 1820.
Elbridge Carleton, s. Lovel and Martha, Mar. 31, 1810.
Elezebeth, d. Edmond and Elezebeth, —21 [1720-21. C. R. 1.].
Elizabeth, d. Francis and Abigall, July 4, 1676.
Elizabeth, d. Francis and Abigall, Dec. 7, 1678.
Elizabeth, d. Edmond and Elizabeth, June 2, 17[15].
Elizabeth, d. Paul and Hannah, Mar. 27, 1728.
Enoch, s. Daniel and Phebe, Nov. 8, 1767.
Frances, d. Francis and Abigall, Apr. 29, 1686.
Francis, s. Ammi Ruhamah and Hannah, Sept. 16, 1728.
Hanna, d. Edmond and Dorathy, May 8, 1658.
Hannah, d. John and Sarah, Mar. 4, 1698-9.
Hannah, d. Ammi Ruhama and Hannah, Mar. 12, 1726-7.
Hannah, d. Paul and Hannah, Mar. 11, 1738-9.
Hann[a]h, d. Joseph and Mary, Jan. 22, 1742-3.
Hannah, d. Abiel and Hannah [bp. July 25. C. R. 2.], 1779.
Hannah Abbot, d. John and Hannah, Apr. 14, 1814.
James, s. Ammi Ruhamma and Hannah, Oct. 25, 1730.
John, s. Edmond and Dorathy, May 16, 1654.
John, s. Edmond and Elizabeth, Sept. 9, 1718.
John, s. Daniel and Phebe, Feb. 9, 1770.
John, s. Joseph, bp. Feb. 11, 1770. C. R. 1.
John, s. Abiel and Hannah, Mar. 7, 1785.
John H., s. Lovell and Betsy Holmes, Jan. 31, 1832.
John Sullivan Abbot, s. John and Hannah, June 7, 1823.
John W., s. Elbridge C., farmer, and Martha, May 27, 1845.
Jonathan, s. Daniel and Phoebe, Nov. 12, 1775.
Joseph, s. John and Sarah, Mar. 1, 1695-6.
Joseph, s. Joseph and Mary, July 15, 1732.
Joseph, s. Abiel and Mary, Sept. 24, 1752.
Joseph, s. Abiel and Hannah, July 30, 1783.
Joseph Warren, s. Joseph and Lydia, Oct. 27, 1812.
Julia Ann, d. John and Hannah, Feb. 22, 1820.
Louisa J., d. John and Hannah, Feb. 12, 1817.
Lovel, s. Lovel and Dorcas, Sept. 2, 1812.
Lydia Abbot, d. Joseph and Lydia, Mar. 22, 1810.
Mary, d. John and Sarah, May 2, 1693.
Mary, d. Joseph and Mary, Feb. 5, 1736-7.
Mary, d. Timothy and Deborah, May 25, 1746.
Mary, d. Abiel and Hannah, July —, 1781. [bp. July 8. C. R. 2.]

FAULKNER, Mary, d. Lovel and Dorcas, Mar. 2, 1814.
Mary E., d. Timothy P., machinist, and Elizabeth, Jan. 18, 1847.
Mary Poor, d. Joseph and Lydia, July 10, 1817.
Nathaniel, s. Paul and Hannah, Apr. 13, 1729.
Nathaniell, s. [torn], —— 18 [1701].
Paul, s. Paul and Hannah, June 30, 1737.
Peter, s. Timothy and Deborah, Nov. 5, 1743.
Phebe, d. Daniel and Phebe, Jan. 27, 1772.
Samuel, s. Paul and Hannah, Oct. 8, 1724.
Samuel Foster, s. Lovell and Dorcas, Mar. 25, 1816.
Sarah, d. John and Sarah, Mar. 31, 1688.
Sarah, d. John and Sarah, June 29, 1690.
Sarah, d. Timothy and Debrah, May 3, 1742.
Sarah, d. Joseph and Mary, Apr. 13, 1748.
Sarah, d. Daniel and Phebe, Oct. 19, 1762.
Sarah J., d. Elbridge C., farmer, and Martha, Sept. 14, 1843.
Thomas, s. Abiel and Hannah, Feb. 5, 1787.
Timothy, s. Lovel and Dorcas, Dec. 27, 1817.
Timothy, s. Timothy and Deborah, Sept. 14, 17[30. C. R. 1.].
William, s. Lovel and Mary, Mar. 30, 1822.
W[illia]m Alfred, s. Alacy and Lucy, Nov. 27, 1824.
——, ch. [torn], —— 23 [1701].
——, s. John and Sarah, May 10, 1704.
——, d. Paul and Sarah, Dec. 2, 1715.
——, d. Edmond and Elezebeth, Jan. 1, 1724-5.
——, d. Paul and Hannah, June 27, 1734.
[torn]ris, d. Joseph and Mary, May —, 1740.
——, ch. Joseph and Lydia, Jan. 21, 1815.
——, ch. Joseph and Lydia, Dec. 2, 1824.

FAWDRY, Elizabeth, d. John, laborer, and Susan, Nov. 20, 1844.

FAY, Anna Austin, d. Samuel and Hannah, Mar. 9, 1843. [d. wid. Hannah, bp. July 16. C. R. 2.]

FEAVER (see also Lefaver), Hannah, d. Jacob and Hannah, May 31, 1743.
Mary, d. Jacob and Hannah, Mar. 1, 1738-9.
Willebe, s. Jacob and Hannah, July 31, 1737.

FELLOWS, Deborah, d. William J., cordwainer, and Mary A., June 15, 1845.
George, s. William and Sarah, July 14, 1835.
Horace, s. William, cordwainer, b. Salem, and Mary A., May 17, 1849.

FELLOWS, Martha, d. William, May 25, 1833.
William Albert, s. William, cordwainer, and Mary Ann, Jan. 9, 1848.

FELT, Joshua, s. Joshua, bp. Apr. 26, 1747. C. R. 2.

FERGUSON, see Furguson.

FIELD (see also Fields), Mastin, s. Mastin and Hannah, Aug. 14, 1772.
Rebecca, d. Henry and Rebecca, Apr. 21, 1771.

FIELDING, Rebecca, d. John, operative, and Esther, Aug. 17, 1844.

FIELDS (see also Field), Henry, s. Samuel and Sarah, Nov. 17, 1743.
John, s. Samuel and Sarah, Mar. 9, 1756.
Joshua, s. Samuel and Sarah, Feb. 9, 1747-8.
Mastin, s. Samuel and Sarah, Apr. 6, 1745.
Mastin, s. Samuel and Sarah, Mar. 29, 1746.
Samuel, s. Samuel and Sarah, July — [1719].
Samuel, s. Samuel and Sarah, Feb. 13, 1752.
Sarah, d. Samuel and Sarah, Dec. 8, 1750.
Sarah, d. Samuel and Sarah, Apr. 26, 1754.
Sarah, d. Samuel and Sarah, Jan. 20, 1758.
——, twin sons, Samuel and Sarah, Dec. 2, 1749.

FIFE, James, s. James, flax-dresser, and Margaret, Oct. 22, 1843.

FIFIELD, Francis Abner, s. Abner and Abigail, Jan. 18, 1838.
——, s. Abner and Abigail, Jan. 11, 1840.

FINDLAY, Eliza, d. John and Catherine A., of Scotland, June 14, 1839.
Issabella, d. John and Catherine Annet, Feb. 28, 1841.
John Sherret, s. John and Catherine R., bp. Sept. 3, 1843. C. R. 3.

FISH, Amos, s. Benjamin and Mary, Feb. 10, 1767.
Andrew J., s. Isaac and Sophronia, Aug. 9, 1832.
Artemus, s. Benja[min], jr. and Lydia, Nov. 6, 1811.
Artemus, s. Benj[amin] and Mary C., bp. Sept. 30, 1832. C. R. 1.
Benjamin, s. Benjamin and Mary, June 9, 1745.
Benjamin, s. Benjamin and Martha, Jan. 17, 1775.
Benjamin Cobourn, s. Benja[min] and Mary C., Dec. 3, 1821.
Betty, d. David and Betty, bp. Nov. 28, 1779. C. R. 1.

FISH, Catharine M[iranda. C. R. I.], d. Benj[ami]n and Mary, Feb. 22, 1828.
Charles A., s. Ebenezer, laborer, and Sarah E., Nov. 13, 1848.
David, s. Benjamin and Mary, ——, 1751.
David, s. David and Betty, bp. Dec. 3, 1780. C. R. I.
Ebenezer, s. Benjamin and Mary, Mar. 11, 1748.
Ebenezer, s. Benj[amin], Mar. 18, 1748.
Ebenezer, s. Ebenezer and Phebe, Mar. 31, 1772.
Ebenezer, s. Ebenezer, farmer, and Sarah E., June 30, 1844.
Eliza, d. Nahum A., farmer, and Almira A., May 11, 1848.
Eliza L., d. Augustus, laborer, and Almira, May 11, 1848.
Ephraim, s. Benjamin, jr. and Lydia, Feb. 28, 1818.
Fanney, d. Benjamin and Martha, May 25, 1779.
Frederick E., s. Eben[eze]r and Sarah E., Sept. 8, 1840.
Harriet [Matilda. C. R. I.], d. Benjamin and Mary, Apr. 2, 1840.
Harriet Newell, d. Benj [amin] and Mary Coburn, Apr. 2, 1841.
Isaac, s. Benjamin, jr. and Lydia, June 11, 1802.
Jonathan, s. David and Betty, bp. Mar. 30, 1783. C. R. I.
Jonathan H., s. Isaac and Sophronia, Nov. 17, 1830.
Loisa Maria, d. Benj[amin] and Mary C., bp. Apr. 4, 1830. C. R. I.
Lucy A., d. Isaac and Sophronia, Aug. 23, 1834.
Lydia, d. Benjamin, jr. and Lydia, Dec. 7, 1807.
Maria L., d. Benjamin and Mary, Mar. 15, 1830.
Martha, d. Benj[ami]n and Martha, Feb. 11, 1777.
Martha A. [Ann. C. R. I.], d. twin, Benjamin, jr. and Mary [C. C. R. I.], Nov. 11, 1823.
Martha E., d. Isaac and Sophronia, May 21, 1829.
Mary E[lisabeth. C. R. I.], d. twin, Benjamin, jr. and Mary [C. C. R. I.], Nov. 11, 1823.
Mary E., d. Ebenezer, yeoman, and Sarah, Sept. 15, 1846.
Molley, d. Benjamin and Mary, Dec. 29, 174[4. C. R. I.].
Molly, d. David and Betty, bp. May 15, 1785. C. R. I.
Nanne, d. Benjamin and Mary, Jan. 6, 1758.
Rachel, d. Benjamin, bp. May 16, 1762. C. R. I.
Samuel A., s. Isaac and Sophronia, Mar. 26, 1837.
Sarah, d. Benj[ami]n and Mary, Mar. 12, 1760.
Sarah E., d. Ebenezer, jr. and Sarah E., June 27, 1842.
Sarah Jane, d. Benj[ami]n, jr. and [Mary C. C. R. I.], Aug. 13, 1825.
Sophia M., d. Isaac and Sophronia, May 14, 1839.
Sophronia, d. Isaac and Sophronia, Jan. 19, 1827.
Susan Frances, d. Benj[amin] and Mary, bp. June 7, 1835. C. R. I.
Susanna, d. Benjamin and Mary, Nov. 2, 1754.
William Edwin, s. Benj[amin] and Mary C., July 15, 1837.
——, s. Benjamin, jr. and Mary, Dec. 23, 1821.

FISK, Asa, s. William and Sarah, Feb. 28, 1738-9.
Charles, s. Rev. Charles and Hannah, Aug. 5, 1831.
Deborah, d. Jonathan and Deborah, Jan. 10, 1769.
Ebenezer, s. Ebenezer and Susannah, — 21 [173—].
Ephraim, s. Ebenezer and Susannah, —30, 173–. [1739. C. R. 1.]
Hephsibah, d. John, jr. and Hephsibah [d. wid. Hephsibah, bp. Oct. 24. C. R. 2], Apr. 21, 1773.
John, s. John and Mary, July 15, 1751.
John, s. John, jr. and Hepsa, Apr. 15, 1771.
[Joseph. C. R. 1.], s. William and Sarah, Jan. 19, 1735-6.
Josiah, s. John and Mary, Dec. 21, 1760.
Mary, d. William and Sarah, Apr. 28, 1730.
Mary, d. John and Mary, Jan. 5, 1753.
Mary, d. Jona[than], bp. Sept. 24, 1775. C. R. 2.
Rachel, d. William and Sarah, Dec. 7, 1733.
Susannah, d. Ebenezer and Susannah, —— 13 [bp. Oct. 22, 1732. C. R. 1.].
William, s. William and Sarah, Apr. 1, 1731.
——, ch. William and Mary, Jan. 3, 1710-11.
——, ch. [Wi]lliam and Marah, May 31, 1713.
——, d. William and Mary, Sept. 19, 1724.
——, ch. Ebenezer and Susanna, Apr. 14, 1731.
——, d. Ebenezer and Susanna, Mar. 17, 1740-41.

FLAGG, Caroline, d. Timothy and Hannah, Oct. 16, 1825.
Hannah Trow, d. Timothy, bp. Nov. 11, 1832. C. R. 2.
James H[icks. C. R. 2.], s. Timothy and Hannah, July 5, 1829.
John D[alton. C. R. 2.], s. Timothy and Hannah, Apr. 2, 1823.
Martha S[wan. C. R. 2.], d. Timothy and Hannah, July 15, 1821.
Sarah H[icks. C. R. 2.], d. Timothy and Hannah, Nov. 7, 1819.
Timothy, s. Capt. Timothy and Hannah, July 29, 1827.

FLANDERS, David, s. Simon and Mary, Nov. 28, 1831.
Elisebeth, d. Simon and Mary, Dec. 25, 1834. P. R. 62.
Emaline N., d. Simon and Mary, Apr. 24, 1823.
Hannah L., d. Simon and Mary, Dec. 27, 1818.
James, s. Simon and Mary, Feb. 6, 1830.
Julia Ann, d. Simon and Mary, Sept. 25, 1825. [Oct. 27, 1825. P. R. 62.]
Mary B., d. Simon and Mary, Aug. 4, 1814.
Ruth, d. Simon and Mary, Apr. 27, 1828. [Mar. 28. P. R. 62.]
Sarah, d. Simon and Mary, Feb. 20, 1821.
Simon, s. Simon and Mary, Nov. 30, 1816.

FLEMING (see also Flemming), Catherine, d. Robert and Ellen, Oct. 7, 1841.
Ellen, d. Robert and Ellen, Dec. 29, 1837.
John, s. Robert and Ellen, Feb. 26, 1835.
Martha, d. Robert and Martha, Apr. 19, 1840.
Mary, d. David, laborer, and Ellen, both b. Ireland, Apr. 7, 1849.
William, s. Robert and Ellen, June 17, 1833.

FLEMMING (see also Fleming), Ann, d. Robert and Ellen, bp. Nov. 20, 1839. C. R. 4.
Catharine, d. David, laborer, Dec. 10, 184[7 or 8].

FLETCHER, George, s. George and Hannah, Nov. 4, 1829.

FLINT, Addison [Augustine. C. R. 2.], s. twin, Alanson and Hannah, Nov. 17, 1831.
Alanson, s. John and Ruth, Oct. 19, 1806.
Alanson [Augustus. C. R. 2.], s. twin, Alanson and Hannah, Nov. 17, 1831.
Amos, s. Amos and Abigail, Nov. 9, 1803.
Ann Eliza, d. John and Lydia O. [Clark. C. R. 4.], Mar. 13, 1835.
Asseneth, d. Amos and Abigail, Apr. 10, 1806.
Charles Leavitt, s. James, bp. Sept. 26, 1841. C. R. 2.
Charles William, s. Alanson and Hannah, bp. July 21, 1839. C. R. 3.
Elizabeth [Eliza. C. R. 2.], d. John and Ruth, Dec. 9, 1803.
Emily Elizabeth, d. John and Lydia C[lark. C. R. 4.], Nov. 26, 1828.
George E., s. Miles, farmer, and Catherine (Hardy), Feb. 24, 1845.
Hannah Griffin, d. Alanson and Hannah, bp. Oct. 17, 1841. C. R. 3.
Hannah M[aria. C. R. 4.], d. John and Lydia [Clark. C. R. 4.], Nov. 9, 1838.
Hannah Mariah, d. John and Lydia, Sept. 20, 1824.
Harriot, d. Caleb and Sarah, bp. Oct. 9, 1825. C. R. 2.
Henry, s. John and Ruth, at Danvers, May 4, 1794.
Henry K[irk. C. R. 2.], s. Alanson and Hannah, Feb. 7, 1834.
James M., s. Caleb and Sarah, bp. Oct. 9, 1825. C. R. 2.
John, s. John and Ruth, at Danvers, Feb. 21, 1792.
John H[enry. C. R. 4.], s. John and Lydia [Clark. C. R. 4.], Mar. 6, 1842.
John W[arren. C. R. 2.], s. Alanson and Hannah, July 14, 1836.

FLINT, Joseph, s. Caleb and Sarah, bp. Oct. 9, 1825. C. R. 2.
Loring, s. Caleb and Sarah, bp. Oct. 9, 1825. C. R. 2.
Lucinda, d. John and Ruth, Oct. 30, 1796.
Lydia, d. John and Lydia, Nov. 2, 1828.
Lydia L[ucretia. C. R. 4.], d. John and Lydia [Clark. C. R. 4.], May 14, 1831.
Maria H[enrietta. C. R. 2.], d. Alanson and Hannah, Oct. 11, 1829.
Martha Russell, d. John and Lydia [Clark. C. R. 4.], July 11, 1833.
Milton, s. Miles, carpenter, and Catherine, Nov. 28, 1846.
Nancy, Sept. 19, 1777. P. R. 45.
Phebe, d. Amos and Abigail, Nov. 7, 1810.
Sarah Abbott, d. John and Lydia [Clark. C. R. 4.], Sept. 12, 1826.
Sarah F., d. Miles, carpenter, and Catherine, May 5, 1849.
Sarah J., d. Caleb and Sarah, bp. Oct. 9, 1825. C. R. 2.
Sarah Maria, d. John and Lydia, Sept. 12, 1826.
Sophrona, d. Amos and Abigail, Sept. 15, 1808.
Warner, s. Caleb and Sarah F., bp. Oct. 9, 1825. C. R. 2.

FLOOD, Clarisa, d. William and Lydia, Mar. 1, 1799.
Michael, s. Philip, laborer, and Susan, Apr. 15, 1847.
William, s. William and Lydia, Aug. 16, 1800.

FOLLANSBEE, Ella P., d. Paul B., farmer, b. West Newbury, and Eliza A., July 24, 1849.
John, s. Bailey P., farmer, and Eliza A., May 28, 1845.

FOLLEN, Mary, d. Patrick, laborer, and Catherine, both b. Ireland, July 8, 1848.

FOOT (see also Futt), Clarissa, d. Daniel and Phebe, bp. Aug. 1, 1824. C. R. 2.
Daniel, s. Daniel and Phebe, bp. Aug. 1, 1824. C. R. 2.
Enock, s. Enock and Ruth, June 11, 1748.
Harriot, d. Daniel and Phebe, bp. Aug. 1, 1824. C. R. 2.
John, s. Sarah, bp. ——, 1752. C. R. 1.
Phebe, d. Daniel and Phebe, bp. Aug. 1, 1824. C. R. 2.

FORSTER (see also Foster), Lucy, d. John and Sarah, Nov. 23, 1793.
Pricella, d. Gideon and Eliza[beth], Apr. 5, 1778.
Rebecca, d. William, jr. and Rebecca, Jan. 11, 1778.
Sarah, d. Gideon and Elizabeth, June 14, 1775.

FOSS, Charles W., s. Drew and Mary, Feb. 20, 1818.

FOSTER (see also Forster), Aaron, s. Phinehas and Sarah, Dec. 27, 1808.
Abiel, s. Asa and Elisabeth, Aug. 8, 1735.
Abigael, d. Joseph and Deliverance, Nov. 15, 1723.
Abigael, d. Joseph and Deliverance, Nov. 19, 1730.
Abigail, d. Andrew and Mary, May 18, 17[38. C. R. 1.].
Abigail, d. Gideon and Elizabeth, Jan. 13, 1771.
Abigail, d. Daniel and Hannah, Sept. 19, 1798.
Abigail, d. Daniel, 2d and Mehitable, Nov. 20, 1837.
Abigail Caroline, d. Thomas C. and Abigail, June 14, 1814.
Abigal, d. Jacob and Abigal, July 8, 1756.
Abigal, d. Nathan and Susannah, July 28, 1796.
Abraham, s. twin, Andrew [Abraham. CT. R.] and Mary, May 25, 1677.
Abraham, s. Abraham and Ma[ry], —— [1705 ?].
Abraham, s. Abraham [jr. C. R. 2.] and Sarah, Dec. 1, 1730.
Abraham, s. Jacob and Abigail, Oct. 4, 1760.
Abraham, s. Andrew, jr. and Hannah, May 30, 1762.
Abraham, s. twin, Andrew and Hannah, June 20, 1766.
Abraham, s. Peter and Lydia, July 3, 1797. [bp. July 2. C. R. 1.]
Addaline G., d. Jacob, jr. and Elizabeth, Dec. 4, 1806.
Albert H., s. Phebe and James Dunn, Mar. 5, 1831.
Alice, d. Charles W., carpenter, and Dorcas, July 26, 1845.
Amy, d. Davis, bp. Oct. 6, 1799. C. R. 2.
Andrew, s. Abraham and Esther, July 22, 1696.
Andrew, s. Andrew and Mary, Aug. 29, 1731.
Ann, d. Jacob and Abigal, Nov. 18, 1758.
Ann Maria, d. Capt. Tho[ma]s C. and Abigail, Oct. 16, 1822.
Ann Maria, d. Capt. Thom[a]s C. and Abigail, May 18, 1827.
Annie, d. J. Plumer, farmer, and Sarah A., Sept. 28, 1848.
Aron, s. Ephraim and Hannah, Apr. 21, 1699.
Asa, s. Will[ia]m and Sarah, —— [1710].
Asa, s. Asa and Elizabeth, Aug. 29, 1733.
Asie, s. Moses and Elezebeth, Apr. 15, 1721.
Augusta, s. Ebenezer and Sarah, Nov. 2, 1815.
Benjamin, s. Joseph and Deliverance, —— 27 [bp. July 10, 1720. C. R. 2.].
Benj[ami]n, s. Asa and Eliza[beth], bp. ——, 1747. C. R. 1.
Betsey, d. Abraham and Sarah, Oct. 31, 1790.
Betsey Abbot, d. Peter and Lydia, Sept. 27, 1792.
Caroline, d. Charles W. and Dorcas A., July 30, 1841.
Catharine [H. C. R. 2.], d. Daniel, 3d and Bethiah, Sept. —, 1819.

FOSTER, Charles Brown, s. William E. and Margarett, Aug. 31, 1841.
Charles E., s. Dane and Mary S., Oct. 7, 1841.
Charles Prescott, s. John P. and Harriet F., Nov. 26, 1839.
Charles Samuel, s. Nathan and Harriet, Dec. 13, 1833.
Charles William, s. Charles and Mehitable, June 9 [Sept. 27. dup.], 1815.
Charlotte A[ugusta. C. R. 3.], d. Timothy and Lydia, July 25, 1825.
Clara Augusta [L. dup.], d. Isaac [farmer. dup.] and Frances B., Oct. 24, 1843.
Clarissa, d. Moses and Sarah, Apr. 8, 1823.
Dane, s. Ebenezer and Sarah, Jan. 19, 1814.
Daniel, s. Moses and Elezebeth, Jan. 7, 1725-6.
Daniel, s. Asa and Elisabeth, Sept. 25, 1737.
Daniel, s. Abraham, jr. and Sarah, Oct. 13, 1741.
Daniel, s. Joshua and Lydia, Mar. 10, 1759.
Daniel, s. Daniel and Hannah, bp. June 26, 1763. C. R. 1.
Daniel, s. Stephen and Abigail, Apr. 26, 1765.
Daniel, s. Daniel and Polly, Jan. 15, 1792.
Daniel, s. Daniel and Hannah, June 26, 1800.
Daniel B., s. Daniel, 3d and Bethiah, Feb. 2, 1816.
Daniel Peters, s. Daniel, 2d and Mehitable, Dec. 22, 1835.
David, s. Ephraim and Hannah, Apr. 18, 1694.
[David. T. C.], s. David and Lydia, Nov. 29, 1717.
David, s. Abraham [jr. C. R. 2.] and Sarah, May 31, 1737.
David, s. Asa and Elisabeth, May 7, 1740.
David, s. Asa and Elisabeth, Dec. 24, 1741.
David, s. Stephen and Abigail, Mar. 5, 1744-5.
David [Smith. C. R. 1.], s. Moses and Sarah, May 25, 1826.
Debora, d. John, 3d and Deborah, Feb. 2, 1752.
Deborah Lotrop, d. Jacob, jr. and Ruth, June 12, 1798.
Deliverance, d. Joseph and Deliverance, May 22, 171[5. C. R. 2.].
Dorcas, d. John, jr. and Deborah, Aug. 26, 1747.
Dorcas, d. Obediah, bp. June 29, 1777. C. R. 2.
Dorcis, d. Jacob and Abigal, Feb. 14, 1749-50.
Easter, d. Andrew and Mary, Feb. 11, 1734-5.
[Ebenezer. T. C.], s. David and Elizabeth, Nov. 23, 1715.
Ebenezer, s. Phineas and Sarah, Sept. 5, 1805.
Edward H., s. Israel, laborer, and Sarah, Sept. 16, 1845.
Elezebith, d. Andrew, jr. and Hannah, Sept. 14, 1754.
Elezebith, d. Stephen and Abigal, Aug. 9, 1757.
Elijah, s. Aaron and Martha, Apr. 11, 1727.
Elisabeth, d. Moses and Mary, Mar. 8, 1739-40.

FOSTER, Elisabeth, d. Asa and Elisabeth, Apr. 14, 1744.
Elisabeth, d. Andrew and Mary [Sarah. C. R. 1.], Feb. 20, 1745-6.
Eliza, d. Daniel, bp. Jan. 16, 1803. C. R. 2.
Elizabeth, d. Joseph and Deliverance, Fe[b.] 8 [1729. C. R. 2.].
Elizabeth, d. Gideon and Elizabeth, Feb. 23, 1769.
Elizabeth, d. Timothy and Elizabeth, Sept. 25, 1782.
Elizabeth, d. Daniel and Polly, Jan. 11, 1803.
Elizabeth, d. Charles and Lucy, Feb. 28, 1803.
Eliza[beth] Barker, d. Nathan and Susanna, Dec. 10, 1792.
Elizabeth D., d. Timothy and Lydia, Apr. 28, 1823.
Ellen J., d. John, jr. and Sarah, Nov. 12, 1838.
Emma F., d. John Prescott, farmer, and Harriet F., Jan. 3, 1845.
Ephraim, s. Ephraim and Hannah, Mar. 12, 1687-8.
Ephraim, s. Moses and Mary, Aug. 30, 1731.
Ephraim, s. John and Debrah, Nov. 13, 1745.
Esther, d. Andrew and Mary, Jan. 14, 1680.
Esther, d. Joseph and Deliverance [bp. Nov. 4, 1716. C. R. 2.].
Francis, s. Daniel and Polly, Dec. 29, 1800.
Frederick, s. Obediah and Hannah, July 20 [29. dup.], 1775.
George, s. Daniel and Polly, June 21, 1810.
George Cutler, s. W[illia]m H., printer, and Rhoda J., Sept. 30, 1847.
George Edwin, s. twin, John Prescott and Harriet, May 20, 1843.
George Otis, s. Eben and Sally, Feb. 21, 1833.
George Whitfield, s. George, expressman, and Rebecca, May 21, 1847.
Georgiette, d. George and Rebecca, Apr. 21, 1836.
Gideon, s. Ephraim and Hannah, May 13, 1692.
Gideon, s. John and Mary, Aug. 21 [1739. C. R. 2.].
Gideon, s. Obediah, bp. June 27, 1779. C. R. 2.
Hanna, d. Andrew and Mary, July 16, 1668.
Hannah, d. Ephraim and Hannah, May 28, 1682.
Hannah, d. Ephraim and Hannah, May 25, 1684.
Hannah, d. Abraham and Mary, June 13, 1[716. C. R. 2.].
Hannah, d. Ephraim and Abigael, Aug. 2, 1725.
[Hannah. C. R. 2.], d. Joseph and Deliverance, June 22, 1727.
Hannah, d. Ephraim and Abigael [Hannah. C. R. 1.], Mar. 23, 1729-30.
[Hannah. C. R. 1.] ——ah, d. Joshua and Mary, Apr. 9, 1739.
Hannah, d. Andrew and Mary, Oct. 30, 1739.
Hannah, d. Jacob and Hannah, Sept. 4, 1744.
Hannah, d. Jacob and Abigal, July 23, 1754.
Hannah, d. Wiliam and Hannah, June 20, 1756.

FOSTER, Hannah, d. Daniel and Hannah, bp. Feb. 13, 1763. C. R. 1.
Hannah, d. Obediah and Hannah, Sept. 15, 1773.
Hannah, d. Jonathan, bp. May 2, 1784. C. R. 1.
Hannah, d. John and Sarah, Dec. 22, 1795.
Hannah, d. John and Sarah, Nov. 25, 1797.
Hannah, d. Daniel and Hannah, Oct. 28, 1805.
Hannah, d. Daniel and Mehitable, May 14, 1843.
Hannah A., d. Thomas C. and Abigail, Aug. 8, 1817.
Hannah Berry, d. Peter and Lydia, May 27, 1799.
Hannah W., d. Daniel, trader, and Mehitable, May 14, 1843.
Harriet, d. Nathan, jr. and Harriet, Dec. 3, 1837.
Harriet C., d. William E., farmer, and Margaret, May 20, 1843.
Harriet C. K., d. Henry, wheelwright, and Sarah J., Jan. 24, 1847.
Harriet Maria, d. Eben[eze]r and Sally, Apr. 23, 1830.
Harriet O., d. Dane, farmer, and Mary S., Oct. 9, 1845.
Harriot, d. Daniel and Polly, Feb. 22, 1806.
Henry, s. Moses and Mary, July 23, 1733.
Henry, s. Ebenezer and Sarah, Apr. 22, 1819.
Henry W., s. William E., laborer, and Margarett, Oct. 26, 1845.
Herman, s. John, jr. and Polly, Oct. 31, 1800.
Hester, d. Abraham and Hester, June 8, 1683.
Hitty, d. David and Ruth, Aug. 28, 1776.
[Isaac, s. C. R. 2.] Abraham and Mary, June 26, 1712.
Isaac, s. Joshua and Mary, May 25, 17[36].
Isaac, s. John and Mary, Apr. 28, 1737.
Isaac, s. Joshua and Mary, Feb. 10, 1744-5.
Isaac, s. Jacob and Abigal, Dec. 23, 1751.
Isaac, s. twin, Andrew and Hannah, June 20, 1766.
Isaac, s. Peter, bp. Aug. 8, 1790. C. R. 2.
Isaac, s. John and Sally, July 7, 1806.
Isaac Mooar, s. Timothy and Lydia, Oct. 23, 1821.
Israel, s. Aaron and Martha, July 17, 1729.
Jacob, s. Abraham and Mary, June — [1718].
Jacob, s. Jacob and Abigail, Nov. 20, 1747.
Jacob, s. W[illia]m and Mehitable, Apr. 29, 1775.
Jacob, s. Jacob, jr. and Phebe, Oct. 15, 1777.
James, s. Abraham, jr., deceased, and Sarah, Sept. 29, 1743
Jane, d. Daniel and Polly, Dec. 26, 1808.
Jane H., d. Jacob, jr. and Elizabeth, Mar. 2, 1809.
Jedidiah, s. Ephraim and Abigail, Oct. — [1717].
Jedidiah, s. Ephraim and Abigael, Oct. 10 [1726].
Jemima, d. Ephraim and Hannah, Feb. 23, 1685-6.
Jemima, d. John, jr. and Deborah, Nov. 22, 1741.
Jemina, d. John and Rebecka, —— [1717].

FOSTER, Joanna Chandler, d. Dea. Charles and Mehitable, Sept. 9, 1808.
Job, s. Joseph and Deliverance, Aug. 22, 1725.
John, s. Ephraim and Hannah, Mar. 26, 1690.
John, s. John and Mary, Mar. 22, 1728-9.
John, s. John and Mary, Feb. 14, 1732-3.
John, s. John, 3d and Deborah, Jan. 8, 1749-50.
John, s. Stephen and Abigail, Dec. 10, 1759.
John, s. John and Deborah, Oct. 24, 1760.
John, s. Obediah and Hannah, Mar. 3, 1770.
John, s. John and Hannah, Feb. 10, 1773.
John, s. William and Mehetable, Sept. 8, 1782.
John, s. John, bp. Jan. 14, 1787. C. R. 2.
John, s. John and Sarah, July 23, 1802.
John, s. Daniel and Hannah, Sept. 8, 1813.
John [Edwin. C. R. 3.], s. Timothy and Lydia, Dec. 14, 1833.
John Edmond, s. twin, John Prescott and Harriet, May 20, 1843.
John J., s. Phinehas and Sarah, Apr. 27, 1811.
John Plumer, s. Dea. Charles and Mehitable, Oct. 28, 1817.
John Prescott, s. John, 3d and Mary, July 26, 1818.
John W., s. John and Sarah, Mar. 11, 1840.
John W., s. John Plummer, yeoman, and Sarah A., Nov. 21, 1846.
Jonathan, s. Joseph and Deliveranc, Mar. 21, 1721-2.
[Jonathan. C. R. 2.], s. Abraham [jr. C. R. 2.] and Sarah, Apr. 24, 1734.
Jonathan, s. Asa and Elisabeth, July 28, 1747.
Joseph, s. Abraham and Esther, Apr. 6, 1690.
Joseph, s. Joseph and Deliverance, Aug. 5, 1718.
Joseph, s. Joseph and Mary, July 9, 1751.
Joseph, s. Andrew, jr. and Hannah, Feb. 11, 1760.
Joseph, s. Job and Hannah, Jan. 17, 1762.
Joseph, s. Hannah, bp. Mar. 9, 1788. C. R. 2.
Joseph William, s. Tho[ma]s C. and Abigail, July 31, 1824.
Joshua, s. Joshua and Mary, M[ay] 19 [1731. C. R. 1.].
Joshua, s. Abraham and Sarah, July 17, 1732.
Joshua, s. Joshua, jr. and Lydia, July 5, 1757.
Joshuah, s. Ephraim and Hannah, —— [1701-2].
Judeth, d. John, 3d and Debora, July 29, 1755.
Julia Ann, d. William E. and Margaret G., Mar. 26, 1832.
Laura, d. Jacob, 3d and Elizabeth, Oct. 25, 1803.
Louisa Ann, d. Jacob, jr. and Elizabeth, Sept. 3, 1812.
Lucy, d. Capt. Asa and Lucy, Feb. 1, 1765.
Lucy, d. Charles and Lucy, Nov. 17, 1800.
Lucy, d. Peter and Lydia, July 21, 1801.

FOSTER, Lucy, d. Charles W., farmer, and Dorcas [A. dup.], July 12, 1843.
Lyddea, d. David and Lyddea, July 21, 1720.
Lydia, d. William and Sarah, —— [1707?].
Lydia, d. Andrew and Mary, July 24, 1733.
Lydia, d. Joshua and Lydia, Dec. 30, 1761.
Lydia, d. Peter and Lydia, Nov. 16, 1794.
Lydia Louisa, d. Timothy and Lydia A., Nov. 11, 1818.
Marcy [Mary. CT. R.], d. Andrew and Mary, June 10, 1673.
Margaret W[ood. C. R. 3.], d. Timothy and Lydia A., Nov. 15, 1830.
Martha, d. Aaron and Martha, Mar. 12, 1724-5.
Martha, d. Ebenezer and Sarah, Aug. 7, 1817.
Martha, d. Eben[ezer] and Sarah, bp. Sept. 6, 1835. C. R. 1.
Mary, d. Andrew and An, July 9, 1652.
Mary, d. Andrew and Mary, Nov. 28, 1670.
[Mary. C. R. 1.], d. Andrew and Mary, Jan. 21, 1727-8.
Mary, d. Joseph and Deliverance, Nov. 16, 1732.
Mary, d. John and Mary, Jan. 12, 1734-5.
Mary, d. Moses and Mary, Mar. 21, 1735-6.
Mary, d. Moses and Mary, Dec. 27, 1737.
Mary, d. Joshua and Mary, Nov. 23, 1741.
Mary, d. Isaac, bp. Aug. 26, 1744. C. R. 2.
Mary, d. Jacob and Abigail, Apr. 18, 1746.
Mary, d. Joseph and Mary, Aug. 20, 1753.
Mary, d. William and Hannah, July 21, 1763.
Mary, d. Job and Hannah, Feb. 5, 1775.
Mary, d. Jacob, jr. and Phebe, Mar. 5, 1789.
Mary Bridges, d. Nathan and Susanna, Aug. 19, 1807.
Mary Chandler, Aug. 6, 1844. P. R. 45.
Mary E[lizabeth. C. R. 2.], d. Capt. Thom[a]s C. and Abigail, Apr. 23, 1829.
Mary Elizabeth, d. John Prescott and Harriet F., Sept. 1, 1841.
Mary Jane, d. Ebenezer and Sarah, Dec. 2, 1826.
Mary Jane, d. William E. and Margaret G., May 23, 1835.
Mary O., d. William P., harness-maker, and Lucinda, b. N. H., Dec. 5, 1849.
Mary Osgood, d. John and Sarah, Sept. 29, 1812.
Mary Peabody, d. Moses and Sarah, Jan. 16, 1814.
[Mehitable. C. R. 1.] ——bel, d. David and Lidea, May 21, 1730.
Mehitable, d. Dudly and Rachel, Sept. 17, 1772.
Mehitable G., d. Charles and Mehitable, Apr. 7, 1813.
Moses, s. Ephraim and Hannah, Sept. 27, 1696.

FOSTER, Moses, s. Moses and Elizabeth, Mar. 26, 1728.
Moses, s. David and Ruth, Aug. 6, 1780.
Moses, s. Moses and Sarah, Sept. 8, 1815.
Moses, s. Moses and Sarah, Aug. 29, 1821.
Nabbe, d. Stephen and Abigal, Aug. 23, 1749.
Nancy, d. Davis, bp. Jan. 4, 1801. C. R. 2.
Nathan, s. Joshua and Mary, Aug. 11, 1733.
Nathan, s. Stephen and [Abi]gail, Nov. 23, 1761.
Nathan, s. Nathan and Susannah, Sept. 4, 1798.
Nathaniel, s. John, bp. July 7, 1734. C. R. 1.
Newell H., s. John and Sarah, Apr. 13, 1834.
Obadiah, s. John and Mary, May 25, 1741.
Obediah, s. Obediah and Hannah, Nov. 28, 1771.
Orin, s. Phineas, laborer, and Huldah, Mar. 18, 1846.
Orman, s. Daniel, trader, and Mehitable, Nov. 15, 1845.
Orrin Nathan, s. Nathan, jr. and Harriet, Apr. 7, 1843.
Osgood, s. John and Mary, Nov. 10, 1745.
Pamelia, d. Peter and Lydia, Aug. 20, 1806.
Paulina, d. Ebenezer and Sarah, Jan. 6, 1821.
Paulina, d. Ebenezer and Sarah, Feb. 20, 1822.
Paulina, d. Israel and Sarah, Jan. 10, 1843.
Penelope, d. Aaron and Martha, Jan. 6, 1722-3.
Peter, s. Andrew, jr. and Hannah, Dec. 30, 1757.
Peter, s. Andrew and Hannah, May 31, 1764.
Phebe, d. Andrew and Mary, Jan. 25, 17[28-9].
Phebe Hall [Holt. C. R. 2.], d. Jacob, jr. and Phebe, Apr. 16, 1785.
Phebe Holt, d. Israel and Sarah, June 8, 1840.
Phinehas, s. Phinehas and Sarah, Feb. 28, 1807.
Polly, d. Joseph and Polly Mar. 11, 1785.
Polly, d. Daniel and Polly, Feb. 26, 1794.
Priscilla, d. Gideon, bp. Apr. 12, 1778. C. R. 2.
Rebecah, d. David and Lydea, July 25, 1732.
Rebecca, d. John and Dorcas, Nov. 30, 1735.
Rebecca, d. Andrew and Mary, Oct. 2, 1736.
Rebecca, d. Stephen and Abigail, Mar. 11, 1745-6.
Rebecca, d. Charles and Lucy, June 12, 1797.
Rebecca, d. Nathan and Susanna, Aug. 9, 1804.
Rebeckah Georgette, Apr. 21, 1836. P. R. 45.
Roderick, s. Charles W[illia]m and Dorcas, Apr. 23, 1839.
Rose, d. Ephraim and Hannah, May 9, 1679. [1678. CT. R.]
Roxby Moody, d. Jacob, jr. and Elizabeth, Dec. 9, 1810.
Rube, d. John and Sally, Oct. 19, 1791.
Ruth, d. Ephraim and [torn], [1703-4?].

FOSTER, [Ruth. C. R. 1.], d. David and Lydea, Oct. 31, 1722.
Ruth, d. Jacob and Abigail, Sept. 4, 1761.
Sabara, d. John, jr. and Polly, May 31, 1802.
Sally, d. Daniel and Polly, Apr. 30, 1797.
Sally, d. Nathan and Susanna, Oct. 14, 1800.
Sally, d. Peter and Lydia, June 12, 1804.
Samuel, s. Andrew and Mary [Sarah. C. R. 1; July or Aug.], 1741.
Samuel, s. Peter and Lydia, Oct. 22, 1787.
Samuel, s. Nathan and Susannah, May 10, 1794.
Samuel, s. Moses and Sarah, Mar. 20, 1812.
Samuel, s. Phinehas and Sarah, Mar. 9, 1813.
Sarah, d. twin, Andrew [Abraham. CT. R.] and Mary, May 25, 1677.
Sarah, d. Abraham and Mary, July — [1707?].
Sarah, d. Abraham [jr. C. R. 2.] and Sarah, Sept. 28, 1739.
Sarah, d. Asa and Elezebeth, Feb. 15, 1749-50.
Sarah, d. Joseph and Marey, Dec. 31, 1755.
Sarah, d. William and Hannah, Sept. 9, 1765.
Sarah, "ch. given to Job," bp. July 14, 1771. C. R. 2.
Sarah, d. Gideon, bp. June 25, 1775. C. R. 2.
Sarah, d. John and Sarah, Aug. 18, 1799.
Sarah, d. John, jr. and Elizabeth, Dec. 27, 1799.
Sarah, d. Ebenezer and Sarah, June 3, 1812.
Sarah Augusta, d. Israel and Sarah, Aug. 17, 1841.
Sarah B., d. Moses and Sarah, May 12, 1811.
Sarah Banks, d. Timothy and Elizabeth, July 12, 1784.
Sarah E[meline. C. R. 3.], d. Timothy and Lydia, Oct. 17, 1827.
Sarah E. S., d. John, harness-maker, and Sarah, Nov. —, 1845.
Sarah F., d. Phineas and Sarah, Oct. 17, 1815.
Sarah Jane, d. Thomas C. and Abigail, Dec. 13, 1815.
Sarah W., d. Moses and Sarah, Dec. 25, 1817.
Simeon, s. Stephen and Abigal, Aug. 14, 1755.
Solomon, s. John and Mary, Apr. 14, 1743.
Stephan, s. Stephan and Abigal, July 3, 1751.
Stephen, s. John and Rebecka, Aug. 14, 1720.
Stephen, s. John and Sally, Feb. 15, 1798.
Susan Frye, d. Daniel, 2d and Mehitable, Oct. 18, 1839.
Susan S., d. Lt. Moses and Sarah, Nov. 18, 1819.
Susanna, d. Sam[ue]l, bp. Apr. 29, 1764. C. R. 1.
Susanna, d. Nathan and Susanna, Apr. 4, 1791.
Susannah, d. Joshua and Mary, Dec. 17, 1747.
Tamisen, d. Gideon and Eliza[beth], May 1, 1773.
Thomas Chandler, s. Timothy, bp. Oct. 4, 1789. C. R. 2.

FOSTER, Thomas E., s. Thomas C. and Abigail, Dec. 16, 1820.
Timothy, s. Timothy and Elizabeth, Feb. 16, 1781.
Timothy, s. Timothy and Elizabeth, July 12, 1786.
Tirza, d. Davis, bp. Sept. 12, 1802. C. R. 2.
Unis, d. Stephen and Mary, Apr. 15, 1753.
William, s. John and Mary, Sept. 24, 1727.
William, s. John and Mary, Mar. 4, 1729-30.
William, s. John, 3d and Deborah, Oct. 3, 1743.
William, s. Wiliam and Hannah, June 1, 1758.
William, s. John and Sarah, Jan. 12, 1806.
Wil[lia]m, s. John and Mary, Apr. 10, 1815.
William H., s. Daniel and Bethiah, bp. July 18, 1824. C. R. 2.
William P[hillips. C. R. 2.], s. William and Sarah W., Jan. 21, 1830.
William P[itt. C. R. 2.], s. John and Hannah, Jan. 22, 1779.
——, ch. [torn] and Sarah, Sept. 27 [1701].
——, d. Abraham and Mary, Sept. 24, 1704.
——, d. Abraham and Mary, Oct. 3, 1710.
——, s. John and Rebecka, Feb. 17, 1715-16.
——, ch. Abraham and Mary, bp. June 8, 1718. C. R. 2.
——, d. Moses and Elezebeth, Mar. 25, 1723.
——, d. Andrew and Mary, Nov. 24, 1726.
——, s. John and Mary, Jan. 13, 1731-2.
——, s. Joseph and Deliverance, Mar. 29, 1737.
——, d. Joshua and Mary, Mar. 22, 1749-50.
——, ch. El[torn], ——, 1789.
——, ch. Phinehas and Sarah, Oct. 17, 1815.
——, s. Phineas and Sarah, Jan. 31, 1820.
——, s. John and Sarah, May 28, 1832.
——, s. John and Sarah, Feb. 11, 1833.
——, ch. Eben[eze]r and Ellen H., Jan. 4, 1836.
——, ch. Israel and Sally, bp. Dec. 5, 1847. C. R. 1.

FOULER (see also Fowler), Sarah, d. Philip, bp. Apr. 11, 1773. C. R. 2.

FOWLER (see also Fouler), George M., s. Isaac and Elmira, Oct. 29, 1835.
Joseph, s. Abigail, bp. Sept. 22, 1776. C. R. 2.
Josiah, s. Philip, bp. July 1, 1770. C. R. 2.
Philip, s. Philip, bp. July 1, 1770. C. R. 2.
William, s. Philip, bp. Oct. 14, 1770. C. R. 2.

FOX, Clarisa, d. Daniel and Phebe, Mar. 10, 1809.
Daniel, s. Daniel and Phebe, Mar. 17, 1806.

Fox, Harriott, d. Daniel and Phebe, Nov. 25, 1813.
Hulda, d. Asa Kieth and Sally Fox, Sept. 15, 1800.
Phebe, d. Daniel and Phebe, Jan. 8. 1811.

FO[torn], Hannah, d. [torn] [1704].

FRANKS, Martha, d. Joseph and Rachel, Dec. 4, 1780.
Rachael, d. Joseph and Rachael, Mar. 23, 1778.

FRASER (see also Frazier), Elezebith, d. Nathan and Elezebith, Oct. 24, 1757.

FRAZER (see also Frazier), Rebeckah, d. Nathan and Elizabeth, Jan. 27, 1760.

FRAZIER (see also Fraser, Frazer), Elizabeth, d. Nathan and Eliz[abe]th, Feb. 25, 1764.
Nathan, s. [Nathan. C. R. 1.] and [E]lizabeth, Dec. 15, 1761.
Nathan, s. Nathan and Eliz[abe]th, Mar. 11, 1766.
Rebecca, d. Nathan and Eliz[abe]th, Feb. 26, 1768.

FREEMAN, Frederic, s. illegitemate, Mary, at Boston, May 5, 1838.
Jane Wright, d. Lydia and Peter Wright, Aug. 1, 1805.
——, s. James H. and Deborah, Aug. 14, 1824.

FRENCH, Abigail, d. Rev. Jonathan and Abigail, May 29, 1776.
Ann Elizabeth, d. Ziba, laborer, and Jane, Dec. 18, 1846.
Ann Maria, d. George W. and Maria M., Mar. 21, 1831.
Asa, s. Asa, bp. Nov. 13, 1785. C. R. 2.
Benjamin O[tis. C. R. 2.], s. Benjamin and Ellis, Dec. 19, 1829.
Charles, s. Peter and Elizabeth, Feb. 26, 1815.
Charles Albert, s. Charles, farmer, and Charlotte [E. C. R. 3.], Mar. 29, 1845.
Elizabeth, d. Peter and Elizabeth, Sept. 1, 1796.
Frances Ann, d. George, jr. and Mary, Oct. 3, 1833.
Francis W., s. George, jr. and Mary, June 4, 1829.
Frank Jackson, s. Charles, yeoman, and Charlotte [E. C. R. 3.], Sept. 13, 1846.
George, s. Peter and Elizabeth, Apr. 11, 1803.
George Henry, s. George and Mary, Feb. 2, 1825.
Harriot, d. Peter and Elizabeth, Mar. 16, 1801.
Henery, s. Lt. Peter and Elizabeth, Oct. 29, 1810.
Hyram Woodruff, s. Lt. Peter and Elizabeth, May 29, 1821.
Jonathan, s. Jona[than] and Abigail, Aug. 16, 1778. C. R. 2.

FRENCH, Joseph Jaquith, s. Peter and Elizabeth, Sept. 6, 1808.
Mary, d. Asa, bp. June 27, 1784. C. R. 2.
Mary A[ugusta. C. R. 3.], d. George, jr. and Mary, May 25, 1827.
Mary Holyoke, d. Jona[than] and Abigail, Aug. 6, 1781. C. R. 2.
Oratio Otis, s. Benj[amin], bp. Nov. 3, 1833. C. R. 2.
Peter, s. Peter and Elizabeth, Jan. 4, 1793.
Sarah, d. Rev. Jonathan and Abigail, Nov. 18, 1774.
Sarah, d. Rev. Jonathan and Abigail, Dec. 13, 1784.
Sarah D., d. Peter and Elisabeth, July 18, 1812.
Uriah, s. Jacob, bp. June 9, 1793. C. R. 2.
——, twin chn., Peter, jr. and Hannah, May 1, 1821.

FRETTS, Harriot, d. Henry and Joanna, Apr. 15, 1817.

FREY (see also Frye), Althina, d. Andrew and Mary, bp. Sept. 10, 1837. C. R. 3.
Andrew Milton, s. Andrew and Mary S., bp. Sept. 12, 1841. C. R. 3.
Ira, s. Mary, bp. Feb. 3, 1839. C. R. 3.
James Harvey, s. James and Elsa, bp. Oct. 7, 1827. 1827. C. R. 3.
Josephine Housten, d. James and Elsa, bp. Aug. 21, 1836. C. R. 3.
Louisa, d. Sam[ue]l and Mary, bp. Jan. 6, 1828. C. R. 3.
Lydia More, d. Enoch and Lydia, bp. Oct. 24, 1841. C. R. 3.
Mary Ann, d. Sam[ue]l and Mary, bp. Jan. 6, 1828. C. R. 3.
Sam[ue]l Charles, s. Sam[ue]l and Mary, bp. Jan. 6, 1828. C. R. 3.

FRIE (see also Frye), [Abiah. C. R. 1.], d. Nathan and Sarah, Mar. 11, 1731-2.
Abiel, s. Abiel and Abigail, Nov. 8, 1734.
Abigaiel, d. Abiel and Abigaiel, Feb. 19 [1732-3. C. R. 1.].
Abigail, d. Abiel and Abigail, Nov. 16, 1740.
Alfred, see Olford.
Benjamin, s. Samuel and Mary, Oct. 8, 1698.
Benjamin, s. John [3d. C. R. 1.] and Ruth, Apr. 5, 1721.
Benjamin, s. Timothy and Elezebith, Jan. 12, 1748-9.
Benjamin, s. Wiliam and Mary, Nov. 26, 1752.
[Bethia. C. R. 1.], d. Nathan and Sarah, June 13, 1727.
Daniel, s. Samuel and Sarah, Apr. 14, 1738.
Daniel, s. Wiliam and Mary, Sept. 29, 1756.
Darcus, d. Isaac and Naamah, Mar. 1, 1732 [-3. C. R. 1.].
David, s. Ebenezer and Elisabeth, Mar. 17, 1746-7.
Deborah, d. Sam[ue]ll and Mary, Feb. 26, 1690-91.
Deborah, d. Ebenezer and Elezebeth, Apr. 20, 1722.

FRIE, Dorathy, d. Isaac and Naamah, Jan. 23, 1730-31.
Dorcis, d. Capt. James and Elezebith, June 3, 1750.
Ebenez[e]r, s. Sam[ue]ll and Mary, Feb. 16, 1685-6.
Ebenezer, s. Ebenezer and Elisabeth, Sept. 17, 1745.
Elezebith, d. Ebenezer and Elezebith, May 17, 1749.
Elezebith, d. Timothy and Elezebith, June 14, 1751.
Elezebith, d. Samuel, jr. and Elezebith, June 2, 1755.
Elisabeth, d. James and Elisabeth, Dec. 7, 1735.
Hannah, d. Samuell and Mary, Apr. 12, 1683.
Hannah, d. Ebenezer, deceased, and Elezebeth, July 4, 1725.
Hannah, d. James and Elisabeth, Sept. 12, 1744.
Hannah, d. Capt. Joseph and Mehetebel, Mar. 23, 1748-9.
Hepsebah, d. Benjamin and Mary, Nov. 2, 1686.
Hester, d. Benjamin and Mary, July 5, 1683.
Huldah, d. Isaac and Namah, May 13, 1737.
Isaac, s. Abiel and Abigail, Feb. 6, 1747-8.
Isaac, s. Isaac and Elizabeth, bp. Dec. 17, 1769. C. R. 2.
Isack, s. John and Tabitha, Mar. 11, 1698-9.
James, s. James and Lydia, Dec. 23, 1682.
James, s. Samuel and Sarah, Sept. 13, 1731.
James, s. James and Elizebeth, Jan. 9 [1740-41. C. R. 1.].
James, s. James, jr. and Sarah, May 20, 1761.
Johannah, d. James and Elisabeth, Feb. 19, 1736-7.
John, s. Benjamin and Mary, Mar. 28, 1682.
John, s. John and Tabitha, Feb. 18, 1696-7.
John, s. Ebenezer and Elezebeth, Apr. 7, 1719.
John, s. John and Tabitha, July 28, 1720.
John, s. Sam[ue[ll and Sarah, bp. ——, 1739. C. R. 1.
John, s. Samuel and Sarah, Jan. 23, 1740-41.
John, s. Joshua and Sarah, May 9, 1750.
John, s. Timothy and Elezebith, Mar. 8, 1754.
John, s. Ebenezer and Elezebith, Aug. 16, 1754.
John, s. Timothy and Elezebith, Dec. 23, 1757.
Jonathan, s. Joshua and Mary, Mar. 6, 1728-9.
Jonathan, s. James and Elisabeth, Dec. 4, 1742.
Joseph, s. Benjamin and Mary, Feb. 11, 1684.
Joseph, s. James and Lydia, Nov. 11, 1687.
[Joseph. C. R. 1.], s. Joseph and Mehetabel, July 17, 1733.
Joseph, s. Joseph and Mehetable, July 10, 1743.
[Joshua. C. R. 1.], s. Joshua and Mary, June 10, 1727.
Joshua, s. Joshua and Sarah, Dec. 28, 1738.
Joshua, s. Joshua and Sarah, June 27, 1748.
Lydea, d. Nathan and Sarah, Mar. 3, 1724-5.
Lydea, d. Ebenezer and Elezebith, May 23, 1752.

FRIE, Lydea, d. Timothy and Elezebith, Apr. 12, 1756.
Lydia, d. James and Lydia, Feb. 10, 1680.
Marcey, d. Jonathan and Sarah, Feb. 29, 1756.
Martha, d. Isaac and Naamah, Nov. 10, 1728.
Mary, d. Samuell and Mary, Feb. 22, 1677.
Mary, d. Benjamin and Mary, Feb. 28, 1679.
Mary, d. Wiliam and Mary, Oct. 3, 1758.
Mehetable, d. Joseph and Mehetab[le], Apr. 16, 1738.
Mehetable, d. Joseph and Mehetable, May 12, 1739.
Mehetable, d. Joseph and Mehetable, Apr. 8, 1741.
Mehitabel, d. Benjamin and Mary, July 22, 1693.
Molley, d. Capt. James and Elezebeth, Mar. 9, 1752.
Nathan, s. Samuel and Mary, June 15, 1688.
Nathan, s. Nathan and Sarah, Oct. 2, 1736.
Nathan, s. Wiliam and Mary, Jan. 9, 1755.
Nathaniel, s. Benjamin and Mary, Apr. 1, 1691.
Nathaniel, s. Capt. [Maj. C. R. 1.] Joseph and Mehetebel, Apr. 22, 1753.
Olford [Alfred. C. R. 1.], s. Joshua and Sarah, Aug. 14, 1737.
Peeter, s. Samuel and Sarah, Jan. 3, 1722-3.
Phebe, d. Samuell and Mary, May 28, 1680.
Phebe, d. Nathan and Sarah, Mar. 19 [1720-21].
Phebe, d. Jonathan and Sarah, Feb. 10, 1746-7.
Phebe, d. Col. James and Sarah, Aug. 6, 1758.
Philep, s. Wiliam and Mary, Mar. 12, 1750-51.
Phiniahs, s. Joshua and Sarah [bp. Mar. 30. C. R. 1.], 1735.
Phoebe, d. James and Lydia, Mar. 29, 1693.
Prissilla, d. Nathan and Sarah, May 8, 1729.
Richard, s. Capt. Joseph and Mehetebel, Aug. 5, 1751.
Sam[ue]l, s. Sam[ue]l and Mary, Apr. 26, 1694.
Samuel, s. Samuel and Sarah, Dec. 22, 1729.
Samuel, s. Joseph and Mehetabl, Jan. 1, 1735-6.
Samuel, s. Col. Joseph and Mehetebel, July 5, 1758.
Samuel, s. Sam[ue]l, bp. Sept. 10, 1769. C. R. 2.
Samuell, s. Samuell and Mary, May 1, 1675.
Sarah, d. James and Lydia, Feb. 27, 1684.
Sarah, d. Samuel and Sarah, Mar. 25 [1721. C. R. 1.].
Sarah, d. James and Elisabeth, Mar. 8, 1738-9.
[Sarah. C. R. 1.], d. Abiel and Abigail, May —, 1743.
Sarah, d. Jonathan and Sarah, July 7, 1745.
Sarah, d. James, jr. and Sarah, Nov. 19, 1754.
Simon, s. Abiel and Abigail, Sept. 29, 1737.
Susanna, d. Samuel and Sarah, May 4, 1728.
Susanna, d. Isaac and Naamah, June 18, 1735.

FRIE, Tabitha, d. Isaac and Naamah, Mar. 31, 1740.
Tabitha, d. [Lt. C. R. 1.] Joseph and Mehetable, Oct. 11, 1746.
Theophiles, s. Samuel, jr. and Elezebith, Oct. 12, 1753.
Timothy, s. James and Lydia, Feb. 17, 1688-9.
Timothy, s. James and Lydia, Dec. 11, 1690.
Timothy, s. Samuel and Sarah, May 8, 1735.
Wiliam, s. Wiliam and Mary, July 20, 1749.
——, d. John and Tabitha, Mar. 13, 1722-3.
——, d. Nathan and Sarah, Apr. 2, 1723.
——, s. Samuel and Sarah, Sept. 15, 1724.
——, d. Joshua and Mary, Feb. 16, 1724-5.
——, d. Samuel and Sarah, Oct. 18, 1726.
——, d. Isaac and Naamah, Nov. 10, 1726.

FRIEND, Mary Ann, d. John and Mary, July 16, 1827.

FROST, Benja[min] Prescot, s. Lt. W[illia]m and Sarah, Nov. 17, 1799.
Benja[min] Prescot, s. Lt. William and Sarah, Nov. 17, 1800.
Betsey, d. Lt. William and Sarah, Aug. 21, 1781.
Beulah, Mar. 3, 1816. P. R. 65.
Doratha Clifford, d. Lt. Will[ia]m and Sarah, Mar. 1, 1785.
George S., s. Sam[ue]l A. and Mary, Jan. 1, 1825.
Hannah Holt, d. W[illia]m and Sarah, Mar. 29, 1791.
James, s. Joseph, Aug. 10, 1735. C. R. 2.
Joshua, s. Joseph, bp. Apr. 25, 1779. C. R. 2.
Lucy, d. William and Sarah, Nov. 28, 1798.
Lucy, d. Dea. William and Lucy, Sept. 29, 1835.
Lucy, d. Dea. William and Lucy, Sept. 29, 1837.
Lucy Ann, d. Sam[ue]l A. and Mary, Dec. 24, 1827.
Nathan Holt, s. William and Sarah, Sept. 4, 1778.
Nathan Holt, s. W[illia]m and Sarah, —— 11 [bp. Jan. 11. C. R. 1.], 1789.
Polly, d. Lt. William and Sarah, Jan. 18, 1787.
Sally, d. William and Sarah, Dec. 28, 1779.
Sam[u]el Abbot, s. Lt. William and Sarah, June 11, 1795.
Sarah M., d. Sam[ue]l A. and Mary, at Eden, Me., July 30, 1822.
William, s. Lt. William and Sarah, Apr. 28, 1783.
William, s. Lt. Will[ia]m and Sarah, June 12, 1793.
William, s. William and Martha W., Jan. 14, 1841.
William P., s. Sam[ue]l A. and Mary, at Eden, Me., July 11, 1823.

FRY (see also Frye), Abiall, s. John and Tabitha, —— 30 [1703].

FRY, Amos, s. Samuel, bp. Sept. 24, 1775. C. R. 2.
Anne, d. John and Tabitha, June 29, 1718.
Ebenezer, s. Ebenezer and Elizabeth, Oct. 2, 1714.
Enoch, s. Sam[ue]l, bp. Aug. 8, 1773. C. R. 2.
James, s. James and Dolly, bp. Oct. 20, 1811. C. R. 1.
Jams, s. John and An, Jan. 5, 1652.
John, s. Samuell and Mary, Sept. 16, 1672.
John, s. James and Dolly, bp. Oct. 20, 1811. C. R. 1.
Mary, d. Ebenezer and Elizabeth, —— [1712].
Nathan, s. Nathan and Sarah, Apr. 7, 1719.
Samuel, s. Samuel and Sarah, Jan. 9, 1719-20.
Sarah, d. Nathan and Sarah, May — [1717].
Timothy, s. John and Ruth, May 3, 1714.
——, d. John and Tabitha, Sept. 5, 1714.
——, s. twin, Ebenezer and Elizabeth, Mar. 3, 1716-17.

FRYE (see also Frey, Frie, Fry), Abiel, s. Simon and Hannah, Dec. 24, 1766.
Addington, s. Samuel, 3d and Mary, Nov. 4, 1808.
Amos, s. Samuel, bp. Oct. 19, 1777. C. R. 2.
Andrew, s. Enoch and Mary, Feb. 18, 1807.
Andrew Lovejoy, s. Ens. Enoch and Mary, Oct. 4, 1811.
Ann Eliza, d. James and Elsy, Sept. 26, 1829.
Anson H[ouston. C. R. 3.], s. James and Elsy Houston, July 13, 1827.
Artemus, s. Timothy and Persis, May 20, 1815.
Bctsey, d. Timothy and Betsey, Apr. 20, 1789.
Betty, d. James, jr. and Sarah, Oct. 22, 1768.
Betty, d. Benjamin and Elizabeth, Apr. 29, 1777.
Betty, d. John, 3d and Betty, Mar. 22, 1784.
Calvin [Augustine. C. R. 3.], s. Enoch, 3d, shoemaker, and Lydia, Aug. 24, 1845.
Caroline, d. John, 4th, June 4, 1812. C. R. 1.
Caroline, d. John and Jerusha, June 10, 1812.
Caroline, d. Phillip and Sarah S., June 20, 1813.
Charles, s. Amos, bp. Aug. 7, 1808. C. R. 2.
Charles Gilbert, s. Gilbert, farmer, and Hanny B., Feb. 13, 1844.
Charles Horatio, s. Nathan and Amanda, June 25, 1835.
Charles W., s. Cyrus and Phebe, July 1, 1834.
Charlotte, d. Peter and Hannah, Aug. 14, 1797.
Charlotte, d. Timothy and Percis, Feb. 13, 1804.
Chloe, d. John and Hannah, Aug. 2, 1771.
Cyrus, s. Timothy and Persis, June 21, 1805.
Cyrus H., s. Cyrus and Phebe, Oct. 2, 1832.

FRYE, Daniel Mackey, s. Lt. Frederick and Margret, Mar. 4, 1792.
Deborah A., d. Nath[anie]l and Priscilla, Jan. 8, 1821.
Dolly, d. John, jr. and Lydia, Oct. 15, 1786.
Eben, s. John, 4th and Deborah, Nov. 7, 1830.
Eliza Ann, d. wid. Priscilla, bp. Sept. 26, 1824. C. R. 2.
Eliza Ann, d. Andrew L. and Mary, Mar. 23, 1838.
Elizabeth, d. Ebenezer and Elizabeth, —— [1711].
Elizabeth, d. Jonathan and Sarah, July 24, 1772.
Elizabeth, d. Lt. Theophilus and Lucy, Mar. 25, 1797.
Elizabeth, d. Joshua and Betty, Apr. 27, 1798.
Elizabeth, d. Joseph and Susanna Sergeant, Nov. 16, 1803.
Elizabeth, d. Enoch and Mary, Sept. 18, 1818.
Ellen Jane, d. George A., carpenter, and Eliza, Dec. 26, 1847.
Elsy Ett, d. James and Elsy, Feb. 16, 1832.
Elthine, d. Andrew and Mary, May 26, 1836.
Enoch, s. Theophilus and Lucy, Aug. 29, 1776.
Enoch, s. Capt. John [3d. C. R. 1.] and Bettey [Elizabeth. C. R. 1.], Mar. 23, 1798.
Enoch, s. Enoch and Mary, Jan. 22, 1799.
Enoch H., s. Enoch, 2d and Mary, Sept. 24, 1831.
Enoch Osgood, s. Enoch, 3d and Lydia, Nov. 7, 1837.
Ezra, s. wid. Elizabeth, bp. June 5, 1768. C. R. 1.
Fanney, d. John [jr. C. R. 1.] and Lydia, Apr. 23, 1782.
Fanney, d. Theophilus, jr. and Fanney, Feb. 17, 1804.
Fidelia, d. John, 3d and Deborah, Mar. 4, 1833.
Frederick, s. Col. James and Sarah, June 9, 1760.
Frederick La Layette [*sic*], s. Rhuben and Hannah, Oct. 22, 1824.
Frederick Lucius Quintus Cincinatus, s. Lt. Frederick and Margret, Apr. 15, 1790.
Gates Ford, s. Theophilus and Fanney, June 29, 1810.
George, s. Cyrus and Phebe, June 19, 1836.
George A., s. Zachariah and Sally, Oct. 10, 1819.
Gilbert, s. Timothy and Persis, Mar. 10, 1811.
Hannah, d. twin, William and Mary, Sept. 3, 1760.
Hannah, d. John and Hannah, Apr. 25, 1762.
Hannah, d. Simon and Hannah, Aug. 18, 1763.
Hannah, d. James, jr. and Sarah, Feb. 22, 1764.
Hannah, d. Jonathan and Sarah, Aug. 15, 1764.
Hannah, d. Samuel and Anna, July 6, 1791.
Hannah, d. Samuel, jr. and Anna, Oct. 4, 1792.
Hannah, d. Ens. John and Betty [Elizabeth. C. R. 1.], Feb. 2, 1797.
Hannah, d. James and Dolly, bp. Nov. 1, 1812. C. R. 1.

FRYE, Hannah, d. Reuben and Hannah, Jan. 1, 1814.
Hannah Doliver, d. Peter and Hannah, Sept. 25, 1804.
Hannah Eliza, d. John, 3d and Deborah, Mar. 11, 1836.
Harriet Abby, d. Enoch, farmer, and Mary B., Feb. 17, 1844.
Harriet L., d. Cyrus and Phebe, Mar. 18, 1840.
Harriot, d. Capt. John and Betty [Elizabeth. C. R. 1.], Oct. 2, 1799.
Harrison, s. Stephen and Mary E., June 13, 1832.
Henry, s. Ens. Theophilus and Lucy, June 23, 1787.
Henry, s. Samuel, 3d and Mary, Oct. 4, 1810.
Herman, s. Enoch and Mary, Apr. 4, 1803.
Hiram, s. Samuel, 3d and Mary, Sept. 4, 1812.
Isaac, s. William and Deborah, Aug. 29, 1769.
Isaac, s. Ens. Enoch and Mary, Mar. 31, 1809.
James, s. Lt. Theophilus and Lucy, Feb. 23, 1792.
James D., s. Zachariah and Sally [Sarah. C. R. 2.], Apr. 16, 1822.
Jeduthan A., s. Samuel, 3d and Mary, Oct. 11, 1815.
John, s. John and Hannah, bp. Oct. 29, 1769. C. R. 1.
John, s. Lt. John and Hannah, Oct. 18, 1775.
John, s. John, 3d and Betty, Sept. 30, 1782.
John, s. Samuel, jr. and Anna, Jan. 8, 1796.
John, s. Peter and Hannah, Dec. 2, 1800.
John, s. Joshua and Elizabeth, Apr. 5, 1801.
John, s. Dolly and Jonathan P. Chapman, Oct. 7, 1805.
John, s. wid. Priscilla, bp. Sept. 26, 1824. C. R. 2.
John, s. Enoch and Mary B., May 4, 1833.
John E., s. Zachariah and Sarah, July 1, 1828.
Jonathan, s. twin, Ebenezer and Elizabeth, Mar. 3, 1716-17.
Jonathan, s. Theophalus and Lucy, June 18, 1794.
Jonathan, s. Samuel, 3d and Mary, June 26, 1805.
Joseph, s. John and Tabitha, Mar. —, 1711-12.
Joseph, s. Benjamin and Elizabeth, Nov. 6, 1767.
Joseph, s. Ens. John, 3d and Betty, Apr. 19, 1793.
Joshua, s. Joshua and Betty, June —, 1781. [bp. July 1. C. R. 1.]
Joshuah, s. John, Apr. 10, 1[701].
Julia Ann, d. John E., machinist, and Martha Ann, at Methuen, Jan. 7, 1847.
Lucy, d. Theophilus and Lucy, July 4, 1778.
Lucy, d. Phillip and Sarah Smith, Aug. 14, 1803.
Lucy, d. Joseph and Susanna Sergant, Feb. 26, 1807.
Lucy, d. Reuben and Hannah, Mar. 13, 1816.
Lucy Maria, d. William and Susan, Dec. 29, 1838.
Lydia, d. Samuel and Elizabeth, Mar. 10, 1767.
Lydia, d. Theophilus and Lucy, May 3, 1782.
Lydia Clark, d. Joseph and Susannah Sargent, July 9, 1801.

FRYE, Martha, d. twin, William and Mary, Sept. 3, 1760
Martha [Patty. C. R. 1.], d. Lt. John and Hannah, Mar. 27, 1789.
Martha, d. Moses, jr. and Martha, Mar. 16, 1800.
Martha, d. twin, Phillip and Sarah S., Sept. 17, 1809.
Martha Jenkins, d. Joshua and Elizabeth, May 29, 1807.
Martha Poor, d. Zachariah, bp. Nov. 3, 1833. C. R. 2.
Mary, d. John [jr. C. R. 1.] and Ruth, Apr. 12, 1719.
Mary, d. Jonathan and Sarah, July 26, 1759.
Mary, d. Samuel and Elizabeth, May 5, 1765.
Mary, d. John, 3d and Betty [Elizabeth. C. R. 1.], Mar. 12, 1788.
Mary, d. Enoch and Mary, May 16, 1801.
Mary, d. twin, Phillip and Sarah S., Sept. 17, 1809.
Mary, d. John, 4th and Deborah, Oct. 12, 1831.
Mary Baldwin, d. Peter and Hannah, Mar. 1, 1799.
Mary Coburn, d. Joshua and Betty, Oct. 24, 1795.
Mary E., d. Enoch and Mary B., Dec. 18, 1838.
Mary Frances, d. Stephen and Mary E., Mar. 1, 1838.
Mary Montgomery, d. Samuel, 3d and Mary, Apr. 12, 1807.
Mary S., d. Gilbert, miller, and Hannah B., Mar. 5, 1846.
Mehittabell, d. John and Tabitha, —— [1705?].
Miranda, d. Peter and Hannah, June 18, 1806.
Moses, s. William and Deborah, Feb. 17, 1771.
Nancy, d. Samuel, jr. and Anna, Feb. 6, 1789.
Nathan, s. Amos, bp. Jan. 1, 1809. C. R. 2.
Nathan W., s. Brooks, bp. June 1, 1823. C. R. 2.
Nathanael, s. Benjamin, bp. June 12, 1774. C. R. 1.
Nathaniel, s. Timothy and Eliz[abe]th, Nov. 17, 1759.
Nathaniel, s. Nathaniel and Elizabeth, June 5, 1774.
Nathaniel, s. John, 3d and Betty, Mar. 23, 1786.
Nathaniel, s. Timothy and Percis, Feb. 12, 1801.
Newton, s. Stephen, mechanic, and Emily G., June 17, 1844.
Noah Brooks, s. Timothy and Betsey, May 19, 1787.
Orin, s. Theophilus, jr. and Fanny, July 23, 1802.
Oscar Alden, s. Enoch, 3d, farmer, and Lydia B., Nov. 4, 1848.
Pamelia, d. Col. James and Sarah [Phebe. C. R. 1.], May 23, 1764.
Pamelia, d. Capt. John and Betsey [Elizabeth. C. R. 1.], Jan. 5, 1805.
Patty, d. Benj[amin], sr. and Eliz[abe]th, Mar. 23, 1772.
Persis, d. Benjamin and Eliz[abe]th, Oct. 2, 1769.
Persis, d. Timothy and Persis, Feb. 9, 1798.
Peter, s. William and Mary, June 11, 1762.
Peter, s. John and Hannah, Sept. 11, 1767.
Phebe, d. Samuel and Elizabeth, Apr. 4, 1762.
Phebe, d. Sam[ue]ll, bp. Oct. 13, 1771. C. R. 2.

FRYE, Phebe, d. William and Deborah, Oct. 3, 1772.
Phebe Frances, d. John, 3d and Deborah, Feb. 7, 1840.
Phebe Shattuck, d. Enoch and Mary, Nov. 2, 1804.
Pheoby, d. John and Tabitha, —— [1709?].
Phillip, s. William and Deborah, Mar. 25, 1774.
Phillip, s. Phillip and Sarah S., Apr. 1, 1805.
Rebeckah, d. Jonathan and Sarah, Sept. 8, 1762.
Reuben, s. Theophilus, bp. Aug. 9, 1789. C. R. 2.
Reuben, s. Reuben and Hannah, May 5, 1818.
Rheuby, d. Capt. John and Betsey, Apr. 4, 1802.
Rhoda Eliza, d. Stephen, cordwainer, and Emily, May 13, 1846.
Ruben, s. Ens. Theophilus and Lucy, Aug. 7, 1789.
Ruth, d. John and Ruth, Sept. 28, 1717.
Sally, d. Ens. John and Betty, Oct. 6, 1794.
Samuel, s. John and Hannah, May 24, 1765.
Samuel, s. Theophilus and Lucy, May 22, 1784.
Samuel, s. Samuel, jr. and Anna, Jan. 14, 1798.
Samuel, s. the late Samuel and Anna, bp. Sept. 9, 1804. C. R. 1.
Samuel, s. Samuel, 3d and Nancy, Dec. 15, 1822.
Samuel Massey, s. Joshua and Betty, June 20, 1792.
Sam[ue]l Osgood, s. John and Hannah, bp. Mar. 4, 1764. C. R. 1.
Sarah, d. Samuel and Elizabeth, May 27, 1759.
Sarah, d. John and Hannah, Sept. 9, 1773.
Sarah, d. Lt. John and Hannah, Jan. 12, 1779.
Sarah, d. Joshua and Betty, July 1, 1785.
Sarah, d. John, 3d and Elizabeth, bp. Oct. 19, 1794. C. R. 1.
Sarah, d. Joshua and Elizabeth, May 27, 1804.
Sarah, d. Phillip and Sarah Smith, May 19, 1807.
Sarah, d. Zachariah and Sarah, Sept. 17, 1814.
Sarah E., d. Zachariah and Sally, June 25, 1816.
Sarah Louisa, d. Reuben and Hannah, Feb. 1, 1838.
Sarah Lovejoy, d. Theophilus, bp. Dec. 1, 1799. C. R. 2.
Sarah M., d. William and Susan, Aug. 31, 1836.
Sephrona [Sophronia. C. R. 2.], d. Timothy and Persis, July 25, 1795.
Sophronia, d. Enoch, bp. Feb. 20, 1803. C. R. 2.
Stephen W., s. Stephen and Mary, July 9, 1830.
Susan C., d. William and Susan, Sept. 29, 1842.
Susan F., d. Enoch and Mary B., Mar. 16, 1835.
Susana Emmory, d. John [4th. C. R. 1.] and Jerusha, July 17, 1810.
Susanna, d. Lt. John and Hannah, Mar. 7, 1782.
Susanna, d. Joseph and Susanna Sargent, Mar. 29, 1800.
Susanna, d. Peter and Hannah, Dec. 21, 1802.
Susannah, d. Simon and Hannah, Jan. 16, 1765.

FRYE, Theophilus, s. Theophilus and Lucy, May 23, 1780.
Theophilus, s. Enoch and Mary, Apr. 13, 1815.
Thomas, s. Joshua and Betty, bp. Mar. 9, 1783. C. R. 1.
Timothy, s. John, 3d [jr. C. R. 1.] and Betty [Jan.] 16, 1791. [bp. Jan. 23. C. R. 1.]
Timothy, s. Timothy and Percis, Dec. 13, 1807.
Timothy, s. Noah and Abigail, bp. May 1, 1825. C. R. 2.
Tryphenia, d. Samuel, jr. and Mary, Aug. 9, 1818.
William, s. Phillip and Sarah S., Oct. 26, 1801.
William, s. Amos, bp. Aug. 7, 1808. C. R. 2.
Zachariah, s. James, jr. and Sarah, June 7, 1766.
——, ch. [torn] and Lydia, —— [1701].
——, ch. [torn] and Lydia, July 5, 1704.
——, ch. [torn]er and Elizabeth, Sept. 14, 1709.
——, ch. [torn] and Ruth, Dec. 18, 1715.
——, s. John and Tabitha, Feb. 18, 1716-17.
——, s. Nath[anie]l and Lucy, Mar. 1, 1819.
——, ch. Reuben and Hannah, July —, 1820.
——, d. Nath[anie]l and Priscilla, Jan. 9, 1821.
——, ch. Zachariah and Sally, Apr. 13, 1821.
——, Reuben and Hannah, July 20, 1822.
——, ch. John Hinchcliff and Susan, May 28, 1824.
——, s. Capt. Reuben and Hannah, Nov. 17, 1826.
——, s. Zachariah and Sarah, May 12, 1827.
——, d. Zach[ariah] and Sally, Feb. 18, 1835.
——, s. Nathan and Amanda, Feb. 12, 1840.

FULLER, Abijah, s. Daniel Page and Rebecca, Jan. 16, 1829.
Catherine T., d. Dan[ie]l Page, farmer, and Rebecca, Feb. 1, 1845.
Charles Austin, s. Sumner, bp. July 6, 1834. C. R. 2.
Edward F., s. Daniel P. and Rebecca, Apr. 20, 1831.
Edwin, s. Sumner and Mary, bp. Sept. 4, 1831. C. R. 2.
Hannah Moar, d. Dan[ie]l P. and Rebecca, Nov. 30, 1835.
Martha Morse, d. Dan[ie]l P. and Rebecca, July 13, 1838.
Rebecca E., d. Daniel P. and Rebecca, Feb. 5, 1827.
Sarah Eliza, d. Sumner, bp. July 3, 1836. C. R. 2.
Sarah Elizabeth, d. Daniel P. and Rebecca, Oct. 16, 1833.
Simeon G. [Simon Greenleaf. C. R. 4.], s. Rev. Samuel and Charlotte [Kingsman. C. R. 4.], Sept. 11, 1838.

FURBER, Samuel Henry, s. Samuel S. and Susan, Sept. 9, 1832.
John A., s. Samuel S. and Susan, July 14, 1838.

FURBUSH, Amelia, grandd. Capt., bp. Sept. 19, 1792. C. R. 2.
Anna, d. Charles, bp. Oct. 16, 1768. C. R. 2.
Betsey, d. wid. Hannah, bp. Sept. 6, 1789. C. R. 2.
Charls, s. Charls and Margerat, May 10, 1736.
Charles, s. Charles and Sarah, July 22, 1764. C. R. 2.
Dorcas, d. Charles, bp. Oct. 12, 1766. C. R. 2.
Hannah, d. wid. Hannah, bp. Sept. 6, 1789. C. R. 2.
Jedadiah, s. Charles, bp. July 1, 1770. C. R. 2.
Lucy, d. Charles, bp. Oct. 14, 1764. C. R. 2.
Margaret, d. Charles and Margaret, bp. Feb. 29, 1736. C. R. 2.
Mary, d. Charls and Margerat, —— 2, [173-]. [bp. Feb. 29, 1736. C. R. 2.]
Mary, d. Charles and Sarah, July 22, 1764. C. R. 2.
Rachel, d. Simeon and Rachel, Nov. 6, 1786.
Sarah, d. Charles and Sarah, bp. July 22, 1764. C. R. 2.
Simeon, s. Charles and Sarah, July 22, 1764. C. R. 2.
——, d. Charles, and Margerat, Apr. —, 1732.

FURGUSON, John, s. W[illia]m and Lucretia, Nov. 17, 1826.
William, s. William and Lucretia, July 29, 1824.

FUTT (see also Foot), Caleb [Foot. C. R. 1.], s. Eanock and Ruth, May 6, 1750.
Samuel [Foot. C. R. 1.], s. Enoch and Ruth, Mar. 2, 1759.

GAGE, Abby Gardner, d. Daniel K. and Mary, Aug. 8, 1827.
Betsey Kimball, d. Nathaniel and Betsey, Mar. 7, 1793.
Charlotte, d. Nathaniel and Betsey, June 18, 1806.
Daniel Kimball, s. Nathaniel and Betsey, Jan. 4, 1803.
Daniel Tenney, s. Daniel K. and Mary, Mar. 24, 1831.
Dorcas, d. Joseph and Anna, Jan. 3, 1748-9.
Ebenezer, s. Joseph and Ann, bp. ——, 1750. C. R. 1.
Ebenezer, s. Joseph and Anna, Jan. 1, 1751.
Eben[eze]r Webster, s. Isaac and Mary, Dec. 21, 1770.
Herman Kimball, s. Daniel K. and Mary, Nov. 26, 1833.
John Carlton, s. John and Betsey, Dec. 6, 1817.
John Gilman, s. Daniel K. and Mary, Nov. 7, 1835.
Jonathan Tyler, s. John and Betsey, Feb. 6, 1816.
Louisa, d. Nathaniel and Betsey, Sept. 8, 1798.
Maria, d. Nathaniel and Betsy, Aug. 18, 1796.
Martha Clark, d. John and Betsey, Mar. 13, 1820.
Mary Elizabeth, d. John and Betsey, Apr. 1, 1823.
Metilda, d. Nathaniel and Betsy, Nov. 4, 1794.
Nathaniel, s. Nathaniel and Betsey, July 15, 1800.

GAGE, Nathaniel, s. Daniel K. and Mary, Dec. 23, 1828.
Richard, s. James and Rebeckah, Nov. 28, 1758.
Sophia, d. Nathaniel and Betsey, Sept. 30, 1804.
Susanna, d. Joseph and Anna, Jan. 1, 1746-7.

GALLISHAN, Charles A[tkinson. C. R. 4.], s. George K. W. and Elizabeth, May 25, 1840.
Elizabeth [Atkinson. C. R. 4.], d. George K. W. and Elizabeth, Mar. 2, 1839.
Elizabeth A., d. G. K. W., bp. Aug. 14, 1845. C. R. 4.
Frank Willis, s. G. K. W., trader, and Ruth A[nn. C. R. 4.], June 2, 1849.
George L[ewis. C. R. 4.], s. G. K. W. and Elizabeth, May 28, 1836.
Mary L[ittle. C. R. 4.], d. Geo[rge] K. W. and Elizabeth E., Oct. 31, 1832.
Moses Henry, s. G. K. W. and Elizabeth, July 10, 1837.

GAULEY, George N., s. James, farmer, and Sarah, Sept. 26, 1843.

GENNISS, Hannah, d. Benjamin and Elizabeth, Sept. 30, 1796.

GERRISH, Moses, s. Moses and Eliz[abe]th, July 8, 1768.

GERRY, Hannah, d. Thom[a]s, bp. Dec. 5, 1761. C. R. 1.

GIBSON, [torn]th, d. William and Martha, Sept. 17, 1754.

GIDDINGS, Hannah, May 17, 1805. P. R. 66.
Hannah Elizabeth, d. Isaac and Hannah B. (Goldsmith), May 27, 1843.
Isaac, May 22, 1795. P. R. 66.
Isaac E., s. Isaac and Hannah, Feb. 9, 1840. [Feb. 15. P. R. 66.]
[James H. P. R. 66.], s. Isaac and Hannah, Feb. 28, 1839.

GILBERT, George Henry, s. George H. and Phebe J., Apr. 24, 1841.

GILCHRIST (see also Gilcreast), David B., s. Samuel and Betsy, Feb. 1, 1837.
John, s. Samuel and Betsy, July 1, 1833.
Samuel Francis, s. Sam[ue]l and Mary, Apr. 19, 1839.
Sarah J., d. Amos and Hannah, May 3, 1826.

GILCREAST (see also Gilchrist), Caroline, d. Amos and Hannah, Apr. 30, 1834.
Ellen E., d. Samuel, laborer, and Betsey, July 5, 1846.
Emily L., d. Amos and Hannah, Aug. 3, 1828.
Hannah E., d. Amos and Hannah, Oct. 8, 1822.
Lydia, d. Amos and Hannah, Aug. 1, 1824.
Lydia Ann, d. Samuel, laborer, and Betsy, June 30, 1843.
Margaret J., d. Samuel and Betsy, July 25, 1829.
Mary A., d. Amos and Hannah, Dec. 5, 1836.
Mary C., d. Samuel and Betsy, June 17, 1831.
Olive, d. Amos and Hannah, Jan. 21, 1831.

GILE (see also Guile), Amanda G[eorget. dup.], d. Erastus [Arastus. dup.], manufacturer [laborer in mills. dup.], and Amanda G. [Sarah G. dup.], Sept. 1, 1843. [Sept. 4. dup.; Sept. 15. dup.]
Caroline, d. John, clothier, and Mary Ann, Feb. 20, 1844.
Clara D., d. Erastus, mason, b. Lee, N. H., and Amanda G., b. Tewksbury, Apr. 23, 1849.
Ellen, d. William, mason, and Ellen, Apr. 9, 1845.
Phebe N[oyes. dup.], d. William, mason, and Eleanor C. [Ellena O. dup.], May 10, 1843.
William, s. John, finisher, b. Greenland, N. H., and Mary A., b. Newbury, Mar. 28, 1849.

GILL, Mary, d. James, laborer, Nov. 24, 184[7 or 8].

GILLILAND, Ruth Ann, d. John, weaver, b. Ireland, and Ann, b. England, at Woonsocket, R. I., Sept. 28, 1848.

GILLION (see also Gilyon), Easter, d. Peter and Mary, Oct. 29, 1759.

GILMAN, Charlotte, d. James, laborer, and Hannah, Oct. 18, 1844.
Emily, d. James and Hannah, May 8, 1842.
Hannah, d. William and Hannah, Apr. 24, 1838.
Hannah, d. James and Hannah, bp. Sept. 13, 1838. C. R. 1.
Harriet, d. James and Hannah, Apr. 10, 1836.
Sarah Frances, d. James and Hannah, bp. Sept. 13, 1838. C. R. 1.
William H. H., s. James and Hannah, July 8, 1840.

GILYON (see also Gillion), Peter, s. Peter and Mary, bp. May 4, 1760. C. R. 1.

GINKINS (see also Jenkins), Benjamin, s. Samuel and Rebeca, Aug. 15, 1752.

GLEASON, Albert [B. C. R. 2.], s. Capt. Joseph and Lucy, Sept. 28, 1816.
Allanda [Amanda. C. R. 2.], d. Jonathan and Sarah, Oct. 14, 1807.
Benjamin Franklin, s. Benjamin W. and Louisa, Aug. 26, 1838.
Benj[amin] G., s. Gamaliel, mason, and Hannah, Feb. 28, 1844.
Charles Whitney, s. Benjamin W. and Louisa, Apr. 9, 1841.
Damaris, d. Benjamin and Rhoda, Sept. 15, 1810.
Eliza Jane, d. John and Tameson, Nov. 3, 1830.
Ellen Augusta, d. Benj[amin] W. and Louiza, June 18, 1834.
Foster, s. Jonathan and Sally, Apr. 28, 1816.
Gamalial, s. Benjamin and Rhoda, Apr. 26, 1812.
George, s. John and Tameson, Sept. 19, 1827.
Gilman C., s. Joseph and Lucy, Nov. 5, 1809.
Gorden, s. Jonathan and Sarah, Sept. 6, 1818.
Hannah Virginia, d. Gamliel and Hannah M., July 14, 1839.
Hobart, s. Benjamin and Rhoda, Mar. 29, 1814.
Horatio, s. Jonathan and Sarah, Jan. 10, 1810.
John William, s. Joseph and Lucy, Dec. 10, 1811.
Joseph, s. Benja[min] W., machinist, and Louisa, Feb. 28, 1846.
Joseph H[arrison. C. R. 2.], s. Capt. Joseph and Lucy, July 5, 1814.
Justin, s. Jonathan and Sarah, July 29, 1812.
Justus, s. Benj[ami]n and Rhoda, July 5, 1806.
Levina, d. Jonathan and Lettice, Sept. 23, 1800.
Moses, s. Benjamin and Rhoda, July 26, 1816.
Rhoda, d. Benjamin and Rhoda, Oct. 31, 1804.
Rhoda, d. Benjamin and Rhoda, Mar. 27, 1808.
Rhoda Matilda, d. Gamaliel and Hannah M., Jan. 1, 1838.
Sarah, d. Jonathan and Sarah, Dec. 8, 1805.
Sarah E., d. Horatio and Sarah, July 23, 1837.
Stilman A., s. Benja[min] W., machinist, and Louisa, Aug. 2, 1843.
Wyman, s. John and Tameson, Dec. 3, 1816.
——, twins d. John and Tameson, Feb. 23, 1819.
——, d. John and Tameson, Mar. 29, 1821.
——, s. Capt. Joseph, Nov. 4, 1821.

GLEDHILL, Ann Amelia, d. William, laborer, and Catharine [H. C. R. 4.], June 28, 1845.
John N[ewill. C. R. 4.], s. William, manufacturer, and Catherine [H. C. R. 4.], at Norway, Me., Aug. 11, 1843.

GLEDHILL, Mary Marland, d. William [A. C. R. 4.], manufacturer, and Catharine [H. C. R. 4.], July 24, 1847.
Rachel Emma, d. William and Catherine H., bp. Apr. 10, 1846. C. R. 4.
William Francis, s. Edward, cloth finisher, and Mary, Aug. 20, 1847.

GOFF (see also Goffe), Henry, s. Henry and Lucy A., Jan. 12, 1827.

GOFFE (see also Goff), Lucy Ann, d. Henry and Lucy, Apr. 25, 1829.

GOING (see also Gowin, Gowing), Elizabeth, d. Joseph and Elizabeth, Feb. 1, 1822.

GOLD (see also Gould), James, s. Ambros and Elisabeth, Feb. 27, 1731-2.

GOLDEN, Sarah E., d. Dennis, tailor, and Ellen, Oct. 3, 1844.

GOLDSMITH, Amanda E., d. Daniel P. and Rebecca, July 17, 1844. P. R. 30.
Aphia, d. Jeremiah and Sarah, Feb. 24, 1801.
Asa, s. Isaac and Martha, Aug. 24, 1821.
Augusta Susanna Cordelia, d. John, jr. and Mary H., Aug. 16, 1836.
Benja[mi]n, s. Benja[mi]n and Hannah, Jan. 3, 1777.
Benjamin, s. John and Hannah, July 23, 1800.
Benjamin, s. Isaac and Martha, Aug. 9, 1806.
Benjamin F., s. Daniel P. and Rebecca, Nov. 14, 1847. P. R. 30.
Caroline, d. Joseph C., cordwainer, and Phebe, Jan. 13, 1847.
Caroline Louisa, d. John, jr. and Mary H., Nov. 27, 1826.
Charles F[rancis. C. R. 3.], s. William and Jane M., May 22, 1836.
Charles Sumner, s. John, jr. and Mary H., June 2, 1830.
Charlott, d. John and Hannah, May 21, 1816.
Clarissa, d. Jeremiah and Sarah, Apr. 11, 1797.
David, s. Isaac and Martha, Feb. 15, 1825.
Elbridge, s. John and Hannah, Jan. 25, 1811.
Eldesta C., ch. Daniel P. and Rebecca, Aug. 9, 1838. P. R. 30.
Elizabeth, d. Jeremiah and Sarah, Aug. 29, 1791.
Elizabeth, d. Jeremiah, jr. and Elizabeth, Dec. 23, 1834.
Elizabeth C., d. John and Hannah, Aug. 2, 1812.
Granville W., s. Daniel P. and Rebecca, May 29, 1841. P. R. 30.

GOLDSMITH, George Washington, s. John and Hannah [bp. Apr. 2, 1809. C. R. 2.].
Hannah, d. Will[ia]m, bp. July 21, 1776. C. R. 2.
Hannah, d. John and Hannah, July 4, 1798.
Hannah, d. Jeremiah and Sarah, May 17, 1805.
Hannah, d. Isaac and Marth[a], May 3, 1812.
Hannah [Burnham. C. R. 2.], d. Benjam[i]n [jr. C. R. 2.] and Hannah, Aug. 10, 1783.
Henery, s. John and Hannah, Nov. 23, 1802.
Henry Cornelius, s. John, jr. and Mary H., Mar. 2, 1834.
Henry Lowder, s. John, bp. Nov. 28, 1802. C. R. 2.
Henry Lowder, s. John and Hannah, Feb. 21, 1806.
Isaac, s. Isaac, bp. Nov. 8, 1772. C. R. 2.
Isaac, s. William, bp. Jan. 11, 1778. C. R. 2.
Isaac, s. Isaac and Martha, Feb. 25, 1803.
Jeremiah, s. Jeremiah, bp. Oct. 28, 1798. C. R. 2.
Jeremiah, s. Jeremiah and Sarah, Oct. 24, 1799.
John, s. Will[ia]m, bp. July 21, 1776. C. R. 2.
John, s. John and Hannah, Mar. 18, 1797.
Joseph, s. Joseph and Phebe, Apr. 26, 1831.
Joseph C[onvers. C. R. 2.], s. Jeremiah and Sarah, Apr. 1, 1803.
Joshua, s. Jeremiah and Sarah, Mar. 27, 1807.
Joshua, s. Jeremiah, farmer, and Eliza, Apr. 3, 1845.
Julia Augusta, d. John, jr. and Mary H., Sept. 15, 1828.
Lozina, d. Jeremiah and Sarah, Jan. 27, 1813.
Lydia, d. Isaac and Martha, May 6, 1815.
Lyman, s. John, laborer, and Mary, Dec. 27, 1845.
Martha, d. Isaac and Martha, Apr. 4, 1808.
Mary, d. Will[ia]m, bp. July 21, 1776. C. R. 2.
Mary, d. John and Hannah, June 11, 1814. [July 11. P. R. 68.]
Mary Convers, d. Jeremiah and Sarah, Feb. 17, 1795.
Mary J., d. William and Mary A., Nov. 1, 1832.
Mary Jane, d. wid. Jane M., bp. July 14, 1839. C. R. 3.
Melvin H., s. John, jr. and Mary H. S., Apr. 28, 1839.
Nathan, s. Isaac and Martha, Apr. 25, 1818.
Phebe, d. Benjamin and Hannah, Oct. 4, 1793. P. R. 70.
Polly, d. Benja[mi]n and Hannah, Apr. 15, 1787.
Samuel Abbot, s. Benja[min] and Hannah, May 24, 1780.
Sanford K., s. Daniel P. and Rebecca, Jan. 22, 1842. P. R. 30.
Sarah, d. Will[ia]m, bp. July 21, 1776. C. R. 2.
Sarah, d. Jeremiah and Sarah, Nov. 1, 1789.
Solomon, s. John and Hannah, May 10, 1804.
Thomas, s. Isaac and Martha, Aug. 19, 1809.
Unice, d. Will[ia]m, bp. July 21, 1776. C. R. 2.

GOLDSMITH, Washington, s. John and Hannah, Aug. 9, 1807.
William, s. Jeremiah and Sarah, Mar. 19, 1793.
William, s. Isaac and Martha, May 24, 1804.
William G., s. Jeremiah and Elizabeth, Nov. 28, 1832.
William O., s. William and Mary A., Nov. 2, 1830.
William Otis, s. wid. Jane M., bp. July 14, 1839. C. R. 3.

GOODHUE, Aseneth, d. Moses and Rebecca, Aug. 14, 1820. P. R. 53.
Charles H., s. John and Rebecca, Apr. —, 1839.
E. Rebecca, d. John and Rebecca, May 26, 1829.
Frank H., s. Moses, farmer, and Louisa, Nov. 2, 1848.
George A., s. John and Rebecca, Oct. 25, 1833.
John, s. John and Rebecca, Aug. 17, 1820.
Leonard, s. Moses and Rebecca, Aug. —, 1829. P. R. 53.
Levi, s. Moses and Rebecca, Jan. 13, 1827. P. R. 53.
Moses, s. Moses and Rebecca, Oct. 23, 1818.
Olive, d. Moses and Rebecca, July —, 1822. P. R. 53.
Rebecca, d. twin, Moses and Rebecca, Apr. 7, 1815.
Rebecca, d. Moses and Rebecca, Nov. 3, 1816.
Rosina, d. William, farmer, and Caroline D., Aug. 1, 1847.
Sena, d. Moses and Rebecca, Aug. 14, 1820.
Sarah, d. twin, Moses and Rebecca, Apr. 7, 1815.
[William. P. R. 53.], s. Moses and Rebecca, Aug. 16, 1821.
——, s. Benjamin, jr., Apr. 8, 1826.

GOODRICH (see also Goodridge), Henry F., changed by authority to Henry Peter French, s. Oliver and Olive, June 6, 1842.
Mary J., d. Theodore, machinist, and Mary J., Dec. 19, 1845.
Serenel Chamberlain, changed by authority to Mary Elisabeth French, d. Oliver and Dolly, Aug. 24, 1839.

GOODRIDGE (see also Goodrich), Jesse, s. Levi, bp. June 10, 1781. C. R. 2.
Mary, d. Levi, bp. Apr. 4, 1779. C. R. 2.
Sarah, d. Levi, bp. Nov. 2, 1783. C. R. 1.
Sarah, d. Levi, bp. Feb. 20, 1785. C. R. 1.

GOODWIN, Lucy Sarah, d. Sylvester, super[intenden]t of the almshouse, and Lucy Ann, Feb. 22, 1848.

GOODWIN, Moses F., s. David, laborer, and Susan R., Apr. 26, 1848.
William J., s. Sylvester, farmer, and Lucy Ann, Sept. 19, 1844.

GORDEN (see also Gordon), Hannah, d. Henry and Sarah, Aug. 20, 1771.

GORDIN (see also Gordon), George, s. Henery and Sarah, June 7, 1748.
Hannah, d. Hugh and Mary, Mar. 10, 1748-9.
Hugh, s. Henery and Sarah, July 19, 1751.
Jane, d. Henery and Sarah, Apr. 27, 1749.
Peggy, d. Henry and Sarah, Dec. 11, 1773.
Sarah, d. Henery and Sarah, Aug. 8, 1756.
Wiliam, s. Henery and Sarah, Jan. 13, 1754.

GORDING (see also Gordon), Mary, d. Henery and Sarah, Aug. 5, 1758.

GORDON (see also Gorden, Gordin, Gording), Bekky, d. Henry and Jane, bp. Dec. 12, 1773. C. R. 1.
Bethiah, d. Henry and Sarah, Dec. 25, 1762.
Bette, d. Henry and Sarah, May 2, 1765.
Hannah, d. Hugh, bp. Nov. 15, 1747. C. R. 2.
Henry, s. Henry and Sarah, Feb. 3, 1768.
John, s. Henry and Sarah, Sept. 27, 1760.
Mary, d. Hugh and Mary, July 17, 1745.

GORMON, George, s. Patrick, laborer, and Rosey, Dec. 10, 1848.

GOULD (see also Gold), Abraham J[ones. C. R. 2.], s. Abraham J. and Zeruiah, May 7, 1821.
Barzilla, ch. Cornelius and Lydia, bp. Jan. 30, 1825. C. R. 2.
Charles G., s. George and Olive, Dec. 26, 1838.
Edward Brown, s. Abraham, jr. and Mary B., July 27, 1839.
Ellen, d. George W., painter, and Olive, June 17, 1843.
Emerson, s. Cornelius and Lydia, bp. Jan. 30, 1825. C. R. 2.
Emily, d. George B. and Olive, Dec. 9, 1840.
Ester M[aria. C. R. 2.], d. Abra[ha]m J. and Zeruiah, June 28, 1819.
George, s. Abraham J. and Mary B., June —, 1830.
George, s. George W., painter, b. Hanover, N. H., and Olive, b. Norwich, Vt., Jan. 6, 1849.
Henry, s. George W., painter, and Olive, Oct. 15, [1845].
Henry A., s. Cornelius and Lydia, bp. Jan. 30, 1825. C. R. 2.
Henry Jones, s. Abra[ha]m J. and Zeruiah, Sept. 28, 1816.

GOULD, Humphrey, s. Zacheus and Anna H., Oct. 13, 1829.
Julia Anne, d. Abraham J., bp. Apr. 3, 1831. C. R. 2.
Mark, s. Henry A., farmer, and Sarah, Apr. 3, 1849.
Mary B[allard. C. R. 2.], d. Abr[aha]m J. and Mary B., Aug. 24, 1827.
Theodore F., s. Henry A., farmer, and Sarah B., Mar. 20, 1846.
Timothy B., s. Abraham J. and Mary, Aug. 2, 1825.
Walter, s. Walter B., laborer, and Louisa, June 1, 1846.
Zeruiah Elizabeth, d. Abraham J., bp. Apr. 3, 1831. C. R. 2.
——, ch. Thomas and Hannah, June 18, 1818.
——, d. Abraham J. and Zeruiah, Dec. 6, 1822.
——, ch. Abraham J. and Mary, Mar. 24, 1834.

GOWEN (see also Going), Cynthia, d. Joseph, bp. Oct. 26, 1834. C. R. 2.

GOWIN (see also Going), Hannah, d. Hannah, bp. Dec. 7, 1777. C. R. 1.

GOWING (see also Going), Elizabeth [Gowan. C. R. 2.], d. Joseph and Elizabeth, Oct. 15, 1820.
Esther [Gowan. C. R. 2.], d. Joseph and Elizabeth, July 2, 1828.
Sarah [Gowan. C. R. 2.], d. Joseph and Elizabeth, July 19, 1826.

GOWLIE, William Morrison, s. James, flax dresser, and Grace M., Aug. 12, 1847.

GRAINGER (see also Grandger, Granger, Graunger), Daniel, s. Samuel and Martha, Dec. 2, 1731.
Farnum, s. Jacob and Sarah, Aug. 14, 1770.
Hannah, d. Jacob and Sarah [Mary. C. R. 1.], Nov. 30, 1775.
Jacob, s. Samuel and Martha, Aug. 7, 1735.
John, s. Samuel and Martha, May 23, 1734.
Joseph, s. Samuel and Marth[a], Sept. 26, 1737.
Joseph, s. Jacob and Sarah, Dec. 7, 1765.
Martha, d. Samuel and Martha, Nov. 19, 1730.
Samuel, s. Samuel and Martha, Mar. 14, 1732-3.
Sarah, d. Jacob and Sarah, May 4, 1760.
Sarah, d. Jacob and Sarah, May 3, 1772.

GRANDGER (see also Grainger), Daniell, s. John and Martha, June 16, 1687.

GRANGER (see also Grainger), Daniel, s. Jacob and Sarah, Mar. 2, 1762.
Jacob, s. Jacob and Sarah, Feb. 9, 1759.
Samuel, s. Jacob and Sarah, Feb. 19, 1768.
Samuell, s. John, Apr. 12 [1701].
Samuell, s. illegitimate, Mary, Feb. 21, 1705-6.

GRANT, Charles, Aug. 18, 1783. P. R. 31.
Charles H[enry. C. R. 3.] s. Charles C., farmer, and Salome [V. C. R. 3.], July 8, 1845.
Eliza, d. Charles and Mary, June 26, 1812. P. R. 31.
Hannah B., d. Charles and Mary, Sept. 19, 1815. P. R. 31.
Josiah A., s. Charles and Mary, Feb. 1, 1829. P. R. 31.
Louisa Caroline, d. Charles C., farmer, and Salome [V. C. R. 3.], Oct. 1, 1843.
Lucy Ann, d. Benjamin P. and Fanny, Apr. 24, 1839.
Margaret, d. Charles and Mary, July 26, 1818. P. R. 31.
Mary, d. Charles and Mary, Sept. 25, 1810. P. R. 31.
Phoebe Chandler, d. Charles and Mary, July 30, 1826. P. R. 31.
William B., s. Charles and Mary, July 12, 1824. P. R. 31.
——, ch. Benja[min] P. and Fanny, May 13, 1838.

GRAUNGER (see also Grainger), Elizabeth, d. John and Martha, Jan. 30, 1695-6.
Johannah, d. John and Martha, Feb. 4, 1691-2.
John, s. John and Martha, Dec. 1, 1683.
Martha, d. John and Martha, May 17, 1682.
Mary, d. John and Martha, Sept. 27, 1680.

GRAVES, [Abraham. C. R. 2.], s. Eliazer and Sarah, Aug. 6, 1713.
[Abra]ham. C. R. 2.] [torn]aham, s. Eleazer and Sarah, Oct. 25, 1714.
Amy, d. Mark and Elizabeth, June 20, 1659.
Elieazer, s. Abraham and Anne, Mar. 10, 1688-9.
Esther, d. Abraham and Sarah, June 11, 1739.
John, s. Abraham and Anne, June 11, 1691.
John, s. Eleazer, bp. Sept. 30, 1722. C. R. 2.
Margarett, d. Marke and Elizabeth, Jan. 15, 1672.
Mark, s. Mark and Amy, Aug. 8, 1664.
Marke, s. Marke and Elizabeth, Feb. 16, 1671.
Mary, d. Thomas and Urssillah, July 21, 1723.
Ruth, d. Mark and Amy, Jan. 6, 1661.
Samuell, s. Abraham and Anna, Dec. 23, 1682. [Jan. 3, 1683. dup.]

GRAVES, Sara, d. Marke and Amy, Mar. 9, 1662-3.
Sarah, d. Elezear and Sarah [bp. July 17, 1720. C. R. 2.].
Sarah, d. Abraham and Sarah, Sept. 18, 1740.
Thomas, s. Mark and Elizabeth, May 7, 1675.
Thomas, s. Abraham and Anne, Dec. 19, 1685.

GRAY (see also Grey), [Aaron, s. Henry. C. R. 2.] and Mary, Oct. 15, 1712.
Aaron, s. Henery and Mary, Mar. 24, 1715-16.
[Aa]ron [Aaron. C. R. 2.], s. Aaron and Bethiah, June 3, 1745.
Aaron, s. Aaron and Bethiah, Oct. 16, 1747.
Abiah, d. Thomas, jr. and Mary, Apr. 20, 1786.
[Abiel, s. C. R. 2.], Robert and Mirriam, Jan. 26, 1714-15.
Amos, s. Thomas, jr. and Mary, Nov. —, 1781.
Amos, s. Amos and Lucy, Mar. 1, 1820.
Ann, d. Isaac and Rebecca, Mar. 30, 1743.
Ann Maria, d. Amos and Lucy, Sept. 30, 1822.
Benjamin, s. Daniel and Tabitha, Apr. 12, 1795.
Benjamin O., s. Benjamin and Hannah, June 9, 1829.
Braviter, s. Braviter and Dorithy, July 19, 1717.
Bridgett, d. Robert and Lydia, Apr. 5, 1737.
Catharine, d. Cornelius and Marietta, June 14, 1826.
Cornelious, s. Robert and Lydia, Dec. 11, 1738.
Cornelius, s. Robert, bp. June 10, 1759. C. R. 2.
Cornelius, s. David and Rebecca, Oct. 29, 1765.
Cornelus, s. Daniel and Tabitha Allen, Apr. 29, 1799.
Daniel, s. Thomas and Lydia, Nov. 29, 1760.
Daniel, s. Daniel and Tabby, Aug. 15, 1789.
Daniel, s. Cornelius and Marietta, Feb. 6, 1831.
[David, s. C. R. 2.] [torn]ert [Robert. C. R. 2.] and Miriam, Oct. 22, 1717.
David, s. David and Rebeckah, Dec. 8, 1762.
David, s. David and Rebecca, Mar. 15, 1798.
Deborah, d. Robert and Lydiah, Oct. 8, 1744.
Deborah, d. Dea., bp. Jan. 25, 1778. C. R. 1.
Dorathy, d. Timothy and Eleanor, Oct. 26, 1763.
[Dorithy. C. R. 2.], d. Braviter and Dorathy, June 5, 1712.
Eben T., s. Samuel A., tinman, b. Boston, and Henrietta, b. Me., Oct. 5, 1849.
Edward, s. Robert and Hannah, Sept. 12, 1679.
Edward, s. Edward and Sarah, Nov. — [1705?].
Edward, s. Edward, jr. and Sarah, Oct. 6, 1742.
Edward, s. Edward, jr. and Sarah, Nov. 17, 1756.
Elenor, d. Timothy and Elenor, Mar. 16, 1753.

GRAY, Eliza, d. Amos and Lucy, Oct. 14, 1807. [1808. dup.]
[Elizabeth. C. R. 1.], d. Edward and Hannah, Nov. —, 1720.
Elizabeth, d. Joseph, bp. Aug. 9, 1730. C. R. 2.
Elizabeth McGerry, d. Abigail, at the almshouse, July 4, 1827.
Elizabeth W. [Alice. C. R. 6.], d. Alonzo and Sarah H., Jan. 11, 1841.
Emily, d. David, jr. and Emily, Feb. 11, 1826.
Esther, d. Jacob and Betsy, May 30, 1828.
George, s. Samuel A., tinplate worker, and Henriette, at Bangor, Me., July 9, 1847.
[Hannah, d. C. R. 2.], Henery and Mary, Jan. 4, 1714-15.
Hannah, d. Thomas and Lydia, June 10, 1767.
Hannah, d. Thomas, bp. May 16, 1784. C. R. 1.
Hannah M., d. Benjamin and Hannah, Sept. 26, 1831. [Oct. 26, dup.]
Harriet N., d. Cornelius and Martha, Dec. 8, 1832.
Harriet Newell, d. Cornelius and Mary, Feb. 7, 1835.
Henry, s. Henry [jr. C. R. 2.] and Allice, Feb. 1, 1737-8.
Henry, s. Daniel and Tabatha, Feb. 3, 1797.
Henry [Jenkins. C. R. 2.], s. David and Rebecca, Dec. 17, 1806.
Henry A. J., s. Cornelius and Marietta, Mar. 22, 1829.
Henry Peters, s. David, jr. and Sarah, Feb. 7, 1836.
Hiram, s. Jacob and Betsy, Apr. 25, 1825.
Israel, s. Daniel and Tabitha, Apr. 4, 1793.
Israel, s. Israel and Lydia, Sept. 6, 1820.
Jacob, s. Thomas [jr. C. R. 2.] and Mary, Nov. 16, 1792.
James Best, s. Timothy and Elenor, Jan. 29, 1750-51. [bp. Jan. 27. C. R. 2.]
Jesse, s. David, jr. and Maria, May 15, 1840.
John, s. Benjamin Webster's wife, bp. ——, 1728. C. R. 1.
John, s. Edward, jr. and Sarah, Dec. 26, 1745.
Jonathan, s. Robert and Miriam, Mar. 21, 1715-16.
Jonathan, s. Timothy and Elenor, Mar. 18, 1755.
Joseph, s. Braviter and Dorathy, Mar. 28, 1714-15.
Joseph, s. Aron and Bethiah, Dec. 10, 1755.
Joseph, s. Timothy and Eleanor, Mar. 9, 1761.
Lucy, d. Amos and Lucy, Oct. 6, 1812.
Lydia, d. Edward and Sarah, Aug. 22, 1716.
Lydia, d. Robert and Lydea, Nov. 14, 1732.
Lydia, d. Henery and Allis, May 29, 1748.
Lydia, d. Thomas and Lydia, June 3, 1759.
Lydia, d. Daniel and Tabitha, Oct. 7, 1807.
Margaret Elizabeth, d. adopted Sam[ue]l and Martha L., bp. Sept. 5, 1841. C. R. 4.

GRAY, Martha, d. Daniel, jr. and Abigail, Jan. 18, 1813.
Mary, d. Henery and Mary, —— [1703].
Mary [Sarah. C. R. 2.], d. Braveter and Dorothy, Feb. 6 [bp. Feb. 23, 1724. C. R. 2.].
Mary, d. Isaac and Rebecca, Sept. 18, 1737.
Mary, d. Aron and Bethiah, Sept. 9, 1751.
Mary, d. Timothy and Elenor, Feb. 19, 1757.
Mary, d. Amos and Lucy, Oct. 16, 1814.
Mary Ann, d. Benj[ami]n and Hannah, Aug. 10, 1819.
Mary Eastman, d. David, bp. Apr. 1, 1791. C. R. 2.
Mary Jane, d. Cornelius and Maretta, June 14, 1825.
Meriam, d. Robert and Lydia, June 23, 1742-3.
[Miriam. T. C.], d. Robert and Mirriam, Sept. 4, 1713.
Mirriam, d. Robbert and Mirriam, —— [1708?].
Moses, s. Robert and Lydea, J[an. —, 1746-7]. [bp. Jan. 11, 1747. C. R. 2.]
Noah, s. Thomas and Mary, Jan. 31, 1797.
Noah, s. Noah and Elizabeth, Mar. 2, 1818.
Patty, d. Daniel and Tabitha, Apr. 18, 1791.
Phebe, d. Thomas and Lydia, Jan. 13, 1765.
Phebe, d. Thomas, jr. and Mary, Mar. 20, 1783.
Priscilla, d. Edward and Sarah, Jan. 10 [1712-13].
Rebecah, d. Isaac and Rebecah, Aug. 31, 1734.
Rebecca, d. David, jr. and Emily, Feb. 29, 1828.
Rebecka, d. Henery and Mary, —— [1708?].
Rebekah, d. David, bp. Mar. 24, 1799. C. R. 2.
Rob[er]t, s. R[torn], ——[1706-7?].
[Robert. C. R. 2.], s. Robert and Lydea, July 9, 1729.
Robert, s. Robert and Abigail, June 2, 1761.
Sally, d. Thomas and Mary, July 26, 1788.
Samuel, s. Henery and Mary, July 1– [1711].
Samuel, s. Samuel and Sarah, Jan. 11, 1736-7.
Samuel, s. David and Rebecca, Jan. 30, 1803.
Sarah, d. Henry and Mary, Mar. 5, 1722-3.
Sarah, d. Edward and Hannah, Mar. 18, 1722-3.
Sarah, d. Thomas and Elisabeth, Mar. 13, 1739-40.
Sarah, d. Edward, jr. and Sarah, at Hatfield, Jan. 17, 1753.
Sarah, d. Timothy and Eliner, Mar. 2, 1759.
Sarah, d. David and Rebeckah, May 9, 1759.
Sarah, d. David, jr. and Maria, Nov. 18, 1838.
Tabby, d. Daniel and Tabby [Tabitha. C. R. 1.], Dec. 1, 1787.
Thomas, s. Thomas and Lydea, Mar. 23, 1758.
Timothy, s. Braveter and Dorathy, July 19, 1721.
Timothy, s. Timothy and Elenor, Feb. 19, 1748-9.

GRAY, Walter B. G., s. Hiram, shoemaker, and Mary Ann (Dolan), b. Ireland, Apr. 18, 1846.
Wiliam, s. Aron and Bethiah, Dec. 27, 1753.
[William. C. R. 2.], s. Henery and Mary, Jan. 16, 1717[-18. C. R. 2.].
William, s. Henry [jr. C. R. 2.] and Allice, June 25, 1741.
William, s. Henry and Allice, Nov. 19, 1744.
William, s. Jacob and Betsy, Apr. 23, 1823.
——, ch. [torn] and [M]ary, Aug. 28, 1701.
——, ch. [E]dward and Sarah, June 22, 1709.
——, ch. [torn] and Mirriam, Sept. 16, 1709.
——, ch. [torn] and [S]arah, Mar. 6, 1711.
——, ch. [torn] and Dorathy, Apr. 3, 1711.
——, ch. [torn] and Miriam, July 31, 1712.
——, d. Edward and Sarah, Aug. 13, 1714.
——, s. Edward and Sarah, Apr. 2, 1718.
——, ch. Cornelius and Mary, Feb. 18, 1823.
——, d. Jacob and Betsy, July 3, 1826.
——, d. David, jr. and Emily, Aug. 26, 1833.
——, d. Alonzo and Sarah, Jan. 11, 1841.

GRA[torn], Hannah, d. [torn] [1705-6].

GREEN, Rosena, d. Olive, b. Maine, July 12, 1849.

GREENBANK, Elizabeth S., d. John and Ann, June 19, 1830.
Laura A., d. Thomas, operative, Dec. 17, 184[7 or 8].
——, ch. Tho[ma]s and Elizabeth, Nov. 20, 1837.

GREENLEAF, Charles, s. Daniel and Mary, June 9, 1792.

GREGG, David A., s. Nath[anie]l B., root-beer manufacturer, and Cecilia, Oct. 5, 1843.

GREY (see also Gray), Aron, s. Robert and Hannah, Apr. 14, 1692.
Braviter, s. Robert and Hannah, Sept. 29, 1685.
Elizabeth, d. Henry and Mary, Mar. 28, 1700.
Thomas, s. Robert and Hannah, Sept. 16, 1681. [crossed out on original.]
Sarah, d. [torn] [1703-4].

GRIFFEN (see also Griffin), Abigail, d. twin, James and Phebe, Oct. 7, 1764.
Ebenezer, s. James and Phebe, June 5, 1771.
Elizabeth, d. James and Phebe, July 7, 1758.
Hannah, d. James and Phebe, Mar. 5, 1754.
Jonathan, s. Shemuel and Abigail, June 23, 1774.

GRIFFEN, Lydia, d. James and Phoebe, Mar. 26, 1761
Martha, d. Shemuel and Abigail, Sept. 23, 1771.
Mary, d. James and Phebe, Apr. 20 [29. T. C.; 1756.].
Mary, d. James and Phoebe, Aug. 7, 1768.
Phebe, d. James and Phebe, Oct. 1, 1751.
Sarah, d. twin, James and Phebe, Oct. 7, 1764.
Thomas, s. Shemuel and Abigail, Feb. 2, 1770.

GRIFFIN (see also Griffen), Alpheus Boyd, s. Eldad and Mary, bp. Sept. 27, 1829. C. R. 2.
Anna, d. Shemuel, bp. July 28, 1782. C. R. 2.
Berthshebah, d. Daniel and Ama, Aug. 15, 1808.
Bulah, d. Daniel and Ama, Nov. 19, 1799.
Charles, s. Jonathan and Zeruiah, Aug. 3, 1802.
Charles Lee, s. Eldad and Mary, bp. Sept. 27, 1829. C. R. 2.
Cyrus, s. Jonathan and Zeruiah, Nov. 9, 1800.
Daniel, s. Daniel and Ama, Oct. 31, 1806.
Fanny Poor, d. William, bp. Sept. 16, 1792. C. R. 2.
George, s. Jonathan and Zeruiah, Mar. 15, 1807.
Hannah, d. Joshua and Hannah, Sept. 25, 1811.
Henry, s. Jonathan and Zeruiah, Feb. 3, 1810.
Hermon [Herman. C. R. 2.], s. Jonathan and Zeruiah, Sept. 30, 1805.
Isabella, d. James M., laborer, and Mary, July 17, 1848.
John Adams, s. Eldad and Mary, bp. Sept. 27, 1829. C. R. 2.
Jonathan, s. Jonathan and Zerviah, Feb. 16, 1795.
Jonathan L., s. Jonathan and Mary, July 31, 1817.
Joseph, s. Nathaniell and Elizabeth, July 4, 1672.
Joseph, s. Jonathan and Zeruiah, Nov. 8, 1798.
Josephine Kittredge, d. Eldad and Mary, bp. Sept. 27, 1829. C. R. 2.
Joshua, s. Shimuel and Abigail, Nov. 1, 1779.
Mahaly, d. Daniel and Ammy, July 12, 1802.
Maria, d. Joshua and Hannah, July 4, 1813.
Martha, d. Joshua and Hannah, Apr. 13, 1815.
Mary, d. Samuel and Mary, June 2, 1755.
Mary Wood, d. Eldad and Mary, bp. Sept. 27, 1829. C. R. 2.
Minerva, d. Daniel and Amia, Oct. 10, 1804.
Moses Porter, s. Eldad and Mary, bp. Sept. 27, 1829. C. R. 2.
Oliver, s. Shimuel and Abigail, Mar. 25, 1785.
Roxanna, d. Jonathan and Zeruiah, Dec. 27, 1803.
Sarah, d. Shimuel and Abigail, Dec. 16, 1777.
Zeruiah, d. Jonathan and Zeruiah, Feb. 6, 1797.
——, s. Jonathan and Mary, June 8, 1821.

GRINTON, Isabella, d. Alexander, laborer, and Jennett, Dec. 12, 1848.

GROSVENOR, Elizabeth H. [Kendall. C. R. 4.], d. James, ticket-master, and Elizabeth, Dec. 18, 1845.
Harriet Ely, d. James, ticket-office, R. R., b. England, and Elizabeth, b. Connecticut, Aug. 14, 1849.
Mary Hannah, d. James and Elizabeth, Apr. 10, 1841.

GROW, Hannah, d. Thomas and Rebecah, Nov. 8, 1723.
James, s. Thomas and Rebecah, Oct. 25, 1727.
John, s. Eliz[abeth] Nichols "and servant to Nath[ll] Frie," bp. ——, 1728. C. R. 1.
Joseph, s. Thomas and Rebecka, Oct. 16 [1717. C. R. 2.].
Ruth, d. Thomas and Rebecka, Aug. 2, 1720.
[Thomas. T. C.], s. Thomas and Rebecka, Nov. 7, 1714.
——, ch. Thomas and Rebecka, Apr. 21, 1712.

GUILE (see also Gile), Francis, s. John, finisher, and Mary A., July 25, 1846.

GUILFORD, Levi S., s. Levi and Sarah F., Nov. 17, 1837.

GUNNERSON (see also Gunnison), Mary Jane, d. Samuel and Sally, Mar. 18, 1833.

GUNNISON (see also Gunnerson), Abiah, d. Samuel and Sally, Jan. 24, 1825.
John, s. Samuel and Sarah, July 7, 1826.
Susanna, d. Samuel and Sarah, Aug. 11, 1823.

GUTTERSON (see also Gutturson), Abigail, d. John and Abigail, Aug. 11, 1695.
Abigall, d. John and Abigall, Oct. 27, 1689.
Abner, s. Samuel and Lydia, Mar. 27, 1768.
Elizabeth, d. John and Abigail, —— [1703].
John, s. John and Abigall, Nov. 17, 1692.
John, s. Samuel and Lydia, Aug. 27, 1766.
Lydia, d. Samuel and Lydia, Oct. 17, 1772.
Samuel, s. John and Abigail, June 10, 1700.
Samuel, s. Samuel and Lydia, Feb. 28, 1765.
Sarah, d. John and Abigail, —— [1705?].
Sarah, d. Samuel and Lydia, Sept. 3, 1774.
Simeon, s. Samuel and Lydia, Dec. 8, 1769.
William, s. John and Abigail, Oct. 31, 1697.
——, ch. Abigail, —— 13 [1701].

GUTTURSON (see also Gutterson), William, s. W[illia]m, bp. Nov. 21, 1725. C. R. 2.

HACKET, Abby Elizabeth, d. John, farmer, and Abby, Sept. 29, 1847.
Eliza Ann, d. Joseph and Eliza, Feb. 7, 1829.

HADLEY, Charles K[imball. C. R. 1.], s. Joseph and Phebe, Sept. 8, 1818.
Edward Gardner, s. Joseph and Phebe, Oct. 23, 1812. [1813. dup.]
Joseph, s. Joseph and Sarah, Sept. 27, 1780.
Joseph K., s. Joseph and Phebe, Apr. 17, 1804.
Mary Carlton, d. Joseph and Phebe, Feb. 2, 1809.
Mercy G. [Carlton. C. R. 1.], d. Joseph and Phebe, Dec. 23, 1810.
Sarah [Farnam. C. R. 1.], d. Joseph and Phebe, Mar. 27, 1816.
Susannah, d. Lydia, bp. Apr. 3, 1796. C. R. 1.

HAGGET (see also Haggett), Hannah, d. Jesse and Hannah, Oct. 26, 1789.
Isaac Sterns, s. Thomas, 3d and Mary, Feb. 3, 1775.
Jesse, s. Thomas and Susanna, Jan. 23, 1765.
John, s. Jesse and Hannah, Sept. 20, 1791.
Jonathan, s. Thomas and Susanna, May 28, 1761.
Martha, d. Moses and Martha, Jan. 31, 1700[-1].
Olive, d. Thomas and Susanna, July 24, 1768. [bp. July 10. C. R. 2.]
Phebe, d. Jacob and Deborah, May 7, 1767.
Rhoda, d. Jacob and Deborah, Sept. 30, 1765.
Thomas, s. Thomas, 3d and Mary, June 3, 1776.

HAGGETT (see also Hagget, Haggit, Haggith, Haggitt, Hagitte, Heiget, Heigett), Daniel, s. Moses [jr. C. R. 2.] and Sarah, Feb. 11, 1738-9.
Jacob, s. Moses and Sarah, Feb. 9, 1742-3.
Thomas, s. Moses and Johannah, Oct. 10, 1684.
Thomas, s. Thomas and Susanna, Jan. 19, 1747-8.
Timothy, s. Moses and Johannah, Jan. 26, 1681.
Molley, d. Moses and Sarah, May 8, 1745.
Susanna, d. Thomas and Susanna, June 13, 1746.

HAGGIT (see also Haggett), Daniel, s. Moses, jr., bp. Aug. 3, 1735. C. R. 2.

HAGGIT, Daniel, s. Moses and Sarah, Sept. 22, 1752.
Isaac, s. Moses and Sarah, June 11, 1750.
Isaac, grands. Tho[ma]s, bp. Oct. 23, 1781. C. R. 2.
Lydea, d. Thomas and Susanna, Mar. 2, 1755.
Mary, d. Tho[ma]s, bp. Jan. 8, 1764. C. R. 2.
Phebe, d. Moses, jr., bp. July 7, 1734. C. R. 2.
Susannah Adams, d. Jesse, bp. Sept. 15, 1793. C. R. 2.
Wiliam, s. Thomas and Susanna, Mar. 27, 1752.

HAGGITH (see also Haggett), Phoebe, d. Moses, bp. Mar. 6, 1726. C. R. 2.

HAGGITT (see also Haggett), Abigal, d. Thomas and Susanna, Jan. 30, 1749-50.
Lydia, d. Moses [jr. C. R. 2.] and Sarah, Sept. 12, 1736.
Moses, s. Moses [jr. C. R. 2.] and Sarah, Mar. 16, 17[32. C. R. 2.].
Sarah, d. Moses and Sarah, —— 12 [bp. Apr. 19, 1730. C. R. 2.].

HAGITTE (see also Haggett), [Thomas. T. C.] [torn]as, s. William and Mary, —— 2, 172–. [bp. July 1, 1722. C. R. 2.]

HALL, Benjamin, s. Benjamin and Rebecca, Jan. 29 [1741-2. C. R. 1.]
Benjamin, s. William and Barbara, June 1, 1779.
Edward K., s. Samuel K. and Mary D., Jan. 27, 1834.
[Eliza]beth, d. Benjamin and Rebecca, Dec. 3, 1737.
Ellen Eliza, d. Rev. Samuel, bp. Jan. 13, 1833. C. R. 6.
Henry, s. William and Christiana Babara, July 29, 1772.
Jacob, s. William and Barbara, Aug. 20, 1777.
John, s. William and Barbara [Christiana Babara. dup.], Feb. 18, 1771.
John William, s. John, bp. Oct. 7, 1842. C. R. 2.
Mary Descomb, d. S. R., bp. Feb. 24, 1837. C. R. 6.
Mary Hume, d. John, bp. Sept. 15, 1841. C. R. 2.
Mary L., d. Samuel K. and Sarah K., Nov. 15, 1836.
[Mehetable.. C. R. 1.] ——ble, d. Benjamin and Rebecca, Jan. –0, 1739-40.
Rebecca, d. Benjamin and Rebecca, Dec. 26, 1743.
Richard, s. Benjamin and Rebeca, May 11, 1748.
Sarah [Hughes. C. R. 2.], d. John, spinner, and Mary, Dec. 31, 1843.
Sarah Frances, d. Rev. [J. C. R. 2.] and Sarah Frances, Jan. 23, 1842.
Stephen A., s. Benjamin and Hannah, Mar. 17, 1817

HALL, Susanna, d. Benjamin and Rebecca, May 25, 1747.
William, s. William and Barbara [Christiana Babara.. dup.], May 13, 1768.
——, twin chn., Benjamin and Rebecca, June 6, 1746.

HALLEY, Mary, d. W[illia]m, bp. June 13, 1802. C. R. 2.

HALLIDAY, Susan, d. William, laborer, and Jane, Mar. 23, 1847.

HAMMOND, George L., s. George F., laborer, and Julia, Apr. 2, 1849.

HANTY, Joseph, s. Edward, laborer, and Ann, Sept. 27, 1848.

HARDEY (see also Hardy), Ezekiel, s. Ezekiel and Sarah, Mar. 7, 1777.

HARDING, Catherine, d. John and Sarah, June 20, 1807.
Charlott Stroud, d. John and Sarah, June 16, 1802.
James Friend, s. John and Sarah, Aug. 12, 1810.
John, s. John and Sarah, June 27, 1804.
Josephine, d. John and Hannah, July 11, 1837.
Mary Ann, d. John and Sarah, Dec. 25, 1798.
Samuel Houghton, s. John and Sarah, May 10, 1814.
Sarah Hickson, d. John and Sarah, Mar. 16, 1800.
Thomas Houghton, s. John and Sarah, Feb. 13, 1797.

HARDY (see also Hardey), Abby J., d. twin, Stephen, farmer, and Mary A., Aug. 7, 1845.
Abby Josephine, d. Henry, farmer, and Abigail W., Dec. 6, 1843.
Abiather C., s. Ezekiel and Elizabeth, June 29, 1806.
Alfred Madison, s. Hiram and Charlotte, Sept. 30, 1839.
Amelia, d. Ezekiel, jr. and Hannah, Aug. 5, 1804.
Andrew N., s. Henry, farmer, and Abigail, May 12, 1848.
Charles Henry, s. Elbridge, farmer, and Abigail, Nov. 24, 1844.
Charles William, s. Abiathar and Mary, Dec. 14, 1831.
Charlotte Augusta, d. Isaac N. and Sybel, July 28, 1834.
Daniel, s. Ezekiel and Sarah, Sept. 15, 1771.
Elbridge, s. Aaron and Sarah, Aug. 24, 1805.
Elbridge Gerry, s. Stephen, yeoman, and Mary Ann, May 19, 1847.
Elizabeth, d. Ezekiel and Sarar, Sept. 18, 1769.
Elizabeth, d. Ezekiel, jr. and Hannah, Nov. 21, 1800.
Elizabeth, d. twin, Stephen, farmer, and Mary A., Aug. 7, 1845.

HARDY, Elmira, d. Aaron and Sarah, Nov. 8, 1807.
Frances Adelade, d. Simeon, yeoman, and Mary, May 3, 1847.
Franklin, s. Ezekiel and Elizabeth, Nov. 12, 1808.
George, s. Samuel and Mary, May 6, 1806.
George Horace, s. Abiathar and Mary, Oct. 24, 1833.
Hannah Frances, d. Abiathar and Mary, July 30, 1838.
Henry Harrison, s. Simeon, farmer, and Mary, Sept. 1, 1844.
Hiram, s. Ezekiel and Elizabeth, Dec. 6, 1810.
Isaac Mooar [Moars. C. R. 2.], s. Ezekiel, jr. and Hannah, Nov. 23, 1802.
John, s. Isaac N. and Sybel, May 7, 1838.
Laura A., d. Hiram and Charlotte, Jan. 12, 1843.
Leander Foss, s. Hiram and Charlotte, Mar. 15, 1836.
Levina, d. Ezekiel, jr. and Elizabeth, July 14, 1799.
Lewis R. T., s. William, sash and blind maker, b. Tewksbury, and Susan, b. Vassalborough, Me., May 15, 1849.
Martha, d. Ezekiel, bp. May 29, 1774. C. R. 2.
Martha, d. Ezekiel and Sarah, May 27, 1775.
Martha J., d. Hiram, cordwainer, and Charlotte, Mar. 25, 1847.
Mary Elizabeth, d. Abiathar and Mary, Dec. 2, 1835.
Micajah, s. James and Jemimah, Oct. 4, 1786.
Phebe, d. Ezekiel, bp. Feb. 2, 1766. C. R. 2.
Phebe, d. Ezekiel and Sarah, Jan. 1, 1767.
——, s. Abiather and Mary B., Nov. 24, 1830.
——, s. Henry, farmer, and Abigail W., both b. Tewksbury, Dec. 8, 1849.

HARNDEN, George W., s. Jesse, farmer, and Dorothy, Aug. 12, 1843.
Laura A., d. Jesse, farmer, and Dorothy, Sept. 4, 1845.
Sarah, d. John and Sarah of Reading, bp. July 21, 1717. C. R. 2.
Sarah E., d. Jesse, farmer, and Dorothy, both b. N. H., Sept. 3, 1849.
Stilman H., s. John and Mary, July 30, 1830.

HARPER, Jane, d. William, manufacturer, and Ester, Apr. 1, 1849.
Mary Jane, d. John, manufacturer, and Mary, Dec. 1, 1848.
Robert Lawrence, s. John, manufacturer, and Mary, Oct. 14, 1846.

HARRIMAN, Almira Elizabeth, d. David, farmer, and Almira, Sept. —, 1847.

HARRIS, Elizabeth, d. George, engineer, and Maria, Aug. 10, 1845.
Joseph Harison, s. Daniel and Hannah, July 5, 1810.

HARRISON, Anastatia, d. Richard, tinman, and Mary A., both b. St. Johns, July 23, 1849.

HARTSHORN, Jonathan, s. James, bp. Jan. 22, 1775. C. R. 1.

HARVEY, Isabel, d. William, bp. Feb. 3, 1740. C. R. 2.
Mary, d. W[illia]m and Isabel, bp. ——, 1741. C. R. 1.

HASLETINE, Lucy, d. Elijah and Elizabeth, Apr. 13, 1775.

HATCH, Betsey Jane, d. Jeremiah and Betsy, Feb. 27, 1829.
Calvin P., s. Lewis G., shoemaker, b. Maine, and Martha M., Aug. 25, 1849.
Charles Gardner, s. Ezra, Aug. 12, 1818.
Enoch Mason, s. Jeremiah and Betsy, Apr. 14, 1822.
George F., s. Jeremiah and Betsy, Sept. 3, 1838.
James Horatio, s. Ezra, May 18, 1820.
Jeremiah S., s. Jeremiah and Betsy, Jan. 12, 1831.
Joel Holt, s. Ezra and Susannah, Nov. 8, 1812.
Julia Ellen, d. Enoch, cordwainer, and Lucy P., at Middleton, Apr. 19, 1845.
Justin Harrison, s. Jeremiah and Betsy, July 27, 1824.
Lucy Ann, d. Jeremiah [cordwainer. dup.] and Betsy, Dec. 10, 1843.
Martha Jane, d. Enoch M., cordwainer, and Lucy (Adams), at North Reading, June 13, 1847.
Martha M., d. Jeremiah and Betsy, Aug. 9, 1833.
Mary Elizabeth, d. Ezra, Mar. 16, 1822.
Phebe M., d. Jeremiah and Betsy, Jan. 20, 1827.
Ruth, d. Ezra and Susanna, Jan. 31, 1821.
Sarah, d. Ezra and Susannah, Dec. 22, 1814.
Sarah O., d. Jeremiah and Betsy, Aug. 27, 1835.
Sidney E., s. Enoch M., shoemaker [laborer. dup.], and Lucy P., b. Boxford, Jan. 12, 1849.
Susanna, d. Ezra and Susanna, Jan. 4, 1818.
Theophilus P. S., s. Jeremiah and Betsy, June 8, 1840.

HATHAWAY, Herbert H., s. Hiram, farmer, and Dorothy M., Nov. 18, 1843.
——, s. Hiram, laborer, and Marantha, Apr. 30, 1846.

HATHORN, Anne, d. Eben[eze]r, bp. July 10, 1768. C. R. 2.
Eliza, s. Eben[eze]r, bp. Nov. 26, 1769. C. R. 2.
Icabod, s. Elezer and Hephsibah, Oct. 30, 1761.
Margaret, d. Eben[eze]r, bp. Sept. 15, 1765. C. R. 2.

HAWARD (see also Hayward), Augustus Alonzo, s. Jabez, jr. and Hannah, Mar. 1, 1814.

HAWLEY, Betsy, d. Samuel and Hannah, Jan. 4, 1789.
Elizabeth, d. William and Chloe, Oct. 17, 1808.
Hannah, d. Sam[ue]l, bp. Sept. 15, 1793. C. R. 2.
Hannah, d. William and Cloe, June 5, 1795.
Hitty [Mehitabel. C. R. 2.] Manning, d. William and Chloe, Sept. 13, 1797.
Joseph, s. Samuel and Hannah, Sept. 15, 1791.
Martha [Patty. C. R. 2.], d. William and Chloe, July 7, 1799.
Mary, d. William and Chloe, July 15, 1801.
Mary, d. William and Chloe, Feb. 25, 1806.
Mehitable [Manning. C. R. 2.], d. W[illia]m and Chloe, July 4, 1793.
William, s. William and Chloe, Apr. 13, 1812.
——, d. William and Chloe, Nov. 15, 1817.

HAY, ——, s. Aaron, flax-comber, and Mary, Mar. 5, 1848.

HAYES, Benjamin F., s. Dudley, machinist, and Martha, Aug. 29, 1846.

HAYWARD (see also Haward), Bethia, d. twin, Jabez and Elizabeth, Apr. 22, 1759.
Betsy Osborne, d. Nehemiah and Sally, July 9, 1799.
Charles B., s. Benjamin and Eliza, July 15, 1834.
Charles W[arren. C. R. 2.], s. Henry E., farmer, and Polly S., Sept. 18, 1843.
Eliza Jane, d. Benjamin and Eliza J., Sept. 24, 1813.
Eunice, d. twin, Jabez and Elizabeth, Apr. 22, 1759.
George E., s. Benjamin H. and Eliza J., July 15, 1836. T. C.
George Edward, s. Henry E. and Polly S. C., Feb. 13, 1842. P. R. 99.
Harriet Eliza, d. Henry E[dward. C. R. 2.] and Polly S., Feb. 3, 1839.
Hellen E[lizabeth. P. R. 99.], d. Henry E. and Polly, Jan. 29, 1838. [1835. P. R. 99.]
Henry Albert, s. Henry E. and Polly S. (Curtis), Jan. 6, 1841.

HAYWARD, Nehemiah, s. Jabez and Elizabeth, Feb. 21, 1765.
Polly Osborn, d. Nehemiah and Sally, Oct. 18, 1787.
Rebecca, d. Jabez and Eliz[abe]th, Jan. 12, 1762.
Sally Whiting, d. Nehemiah and Sally, Aug. 23, 1785.
——, d. Henry and Eliza, Apr. 14, 1821.

HEARN, John, s. Patrick, laborer, and Mary, both b. Ireland, Dec. 4, 1848.

HECTER, Brabra, d. James, shoemaker, and Euphenia, Dec. 25, 1845.
James, s. James, cordwainer, and Euphemia, both b. Scotland, June 16, 1849.

HEIGET (see also Haggett), ——, ch. Moses and Martha, Aug. 21, 1709.

HEIGETT (see also Haggett), Abigail, d. Will[ia]m and Mary [Martha. C. R. 2.], —— 8 [bp. May 23, 1714. C. R. 2.].
Deborah, d. Moses and Martha, Apr. 26, 1719.
Henery, s. Moses and Martha, July 20 [1714. C. R. 2.].
Joanah, d. Moses and Marth[a], —— [1705?].
[Jonathan. C. R. 2.], s. William and Mary, Apr. 8, 1716.
Margarett, d. William and Mary, Apr. 19, 1719.
Mary, d. [torn], —— [1702].
Moses, s. Moses and Martha, —— [1703-4?].
Sarah, d. Moses and Martha, Aug. 8, 1715.
Timothy, s. Timothy and Mary, —— [1707?].
——, ch. [torn] and Mary, Oct. 15, 1709.
——, ch. Moses and Martha, Feb. 18, 1710-11.
——, ch. [torn] and Mary, Feb. 22, 1710-11.
[torn]y, s. Will[ia]m and Mary, July 15, 1713.

HEMENWAY, Cyrus Holmes, s. Rev. D., bp. Apr. 19, 1829. C. R. 6.
John Adams, s. Rev. D., bp. July 13, 1828. C. R. 6.

HENDERSON, Ellen H., d. Walter and Ellen, July 25, 1830.
Helen Howarth, d. Walter, bp. Oct. 10, 1830. C. R. 2.
John H[oward Brown. C. R. 6.], s. Samuel and Frances, July 17, 1829.

HENDRY, Charles A[lexander. C. R. 3.], s. James, flax-dresser, and Catharine, Dec. 26, 1843.
David Howe, s. James, flaxdresser, and Catharine, Nov. 18, 1847.
Mary Byers, d. James and Catherine, June 22, 1840.

HENIMAN, David G., s. David P., farmer, and Elmira, May 30, 1843.

HENLEY, James G., s. John S. and Ruth, Jan. 15, 1816.

HENRY, Charles Taylor, s. John A., cordwainer, b. Meredith, N. H., and Hannah D., Sept. 14, 1848.

HERON, Michael, s. Patrick, laborer, Dec. 22, 184[7-8].

HERRICK, Edward, s. Elijah L. and Hannah, Apr. 7, 1822.
Eliza L., d. Elijah and Hannah, Sept. 30, 1820.
Ephraim Abbot, s. Elijah L. and Hannah, Apr. 25, 1817.
George, s. Elijah L. and Hannah, Mar. 7, 1824.
Hannah [Jane. C. R. 3.], d. Elijah [L. C. R. 3.] and Hannah, May 21, 1825.
John, s. John and Mary, June 3, 1783.
John Henry, s. Jona[than] A., yeoman, and Lydia S., Mar. 19, 1848.
John W[illiam. C. R. 3.], s. Elijah L. and Hannah, Feb. 24, 1819.
Martha, d. Elijah L. and Hannah, June —, 1829.
Oliver P., s. Oliver and Sally, July 17, 1832.
Phebe Abbot, d. Elijah L. and Hannah, Mar. 25, 1816.
Samuel, s. Elijah L. and Hannah [Phebe. C. R. 3.], Nov. 11, 1835.
Sarah, d. Elijah L. and Hannah, bp. Jan. 6, 1828. C. R. 3.

HERVEY, Abby S., d. Albert, trader, and Ann W., Apr. 13, 1844.
Albert Greenough, s. Albert and Ann M., Sept. 23, 1839.
Harriet P., d. Albert, trader, and Ann W. [1846 or 1847].
Samuel Clement, s. Albert and Ann W., Apr. 17, 1835.
Sarah Cole, d. Albert and Ann M., May 14, 1837.

HIBBARD (see also Hibbord), Dorathy, d. John and Dorathy, Apr. 20, 1720.

HIBBORD (see also Hibbard), Joseph, s. John and Dorathy, July 5, 1726.
Martha, d. John and Dorathy, Mar. 17, 1721-2.
Mary, d. John and Dorathy, June 16, 1724.

HIDDEN, David Isaac Chandler, s. David and Mary C., Aug. 15, 1823. T. C.
Mary Elizabeth, d. David and Mary C., Feb. 13, 1818. T. C.

HIGGINS, Albert H. [S. C. R. 2.], s. Ebenezer and Rebecca, Apr. 3, 1838.
Charles, s. Eben P. and Rebecca H., June 27, 1840.
Eliza, d. David, flax-dresser, and Ann, both b. Scotland, Sept. 20, 1848.
Ellen, d. Solomon H. and Phebe H., Sept. 19, 1831.
George, s. Solomon H. and Phebe H., Apr. 18, 1833.
Mary A., d. Solomon H. and Phebe, Mar. 28, 1830.
Robert H[enry. dup.], s. Eben[eze]r P., painter, and Rebecca A. [H. dup.], May 5, 1843.
Sarah E., d. James H., trader, and Sarah A., Apr. 17, 1845.

HIGHLAND, Hannah, d. John and Ann, Nov. 22, 1827.

HILL, Abbie Ann, d. Joshua F. and Abigail (Merrill), Apr. 28, 1838. P. R. 96.
Abbie Ann, d. Joshua F. and Abigail (Merrill), July 3, 1841. P. R. 96.
Ann Eliza, d. Richard and Hannah, Mar. 25, 1842.
Anstrus, d. Richard and Deborah, May 28, 1814.
Benjamin, s. Benjamin Symonds and Lucy, June 18, 1840.
Eliza, d. Richard and Deborah, Jan. 9, 1807.
Elizabeth, d. William and Phebe, Mar. 19, 1820.
George O., s. William and Phebe, Feb. 26, 1831.
Hannah, d. William and Phebe, Aug. 2, 1822.
Harriet, d. William and Phebe, Nov. 16, 1837.
John M. K. [McKinley. C. R. 1.], s. John, laborer, and Mary M., Jan. 11, 1845.
Joshua F., s. Richard and Deborah, July 4, 1812.
Joshua F., s. Richard and Deborah, Apr. 6, 1816.
Leonard G., s. Richard and Deborah, July 30, 1810.
Martha Ann, d. W[illia]m and Phebe, Mar. 19, 1826.
Mary F., d. William and Phebe, Nov. 4, 1828.
Mary Frances, d. Joshua F., laborer, and Abigail, Sept. 25, 1847. [Sept. 24, 1846. P. R. 96.]
Phebe Jane, d. William, jr. and Phebe, Nov. 5, 1817.
Richard, s. Richard and Deborah, Nov. 6, 1808.
Richard Darby, s. William and Elizabeth, June 21, 1787.
Richard W., s. Richard and Hannah, Oct. 6, 1840.
Thomas, s. William and Phebe, June 27, 1829.
Tobias Cruff, s. William and Phebe, July 25, 1824.
William, s. William and Elizabeth, Sept. 15, 1794.
William J., s. William, jr. and Phebe, Aug. 30, 1816.
——, ch. Richard D. and Deborah, Mar. 19, 1820.

HILL, ——, d. Richard D. and Debrah, Nov. 23, 1821.
——, d. Richard and Deborah, Aug. 25, 1826.

HILTON, Catharine R[ichardson. C. R. 2.], d. William, merchant, and Althine K., Oct. 15, 1845.

HIRST, Ann, d. James, laborer, and Sarah, June 3, 1849.
David, s. James, dyer, and Sarah, Apr. 3, 1848.

HITCHINGS, Benjamin G., s. Capt. Benj[ami]n, Oct. 22, 1813.
Elizabeth, d. Capt. Benjamin, Aug. 14, 1815.
George F., s. Eliz[abeth], bp. June 5, 1825. C. R. 2.
Mary Ann, d. twin, Capt. Benj[ami]n, Dec. 4, 1817.
——, ch. twin, Capt. Benj[ami]n, Dec. 4, 1817.

HODGES, Benjamin, s. Capt. George and Betsey, Sept. 19, 1831.
Catharine Craddock, d. George and Sarah E., bp. May 30, 1847. C. R. 4.
Edward L., s. Samuel, manufacturer, and Martha, Mar. 11, 1846.
Martha, d. Samuel, manufacturer, and Martha, Dec. 7, 1844.
——, d. George and Betsey, Sept. 30, 1828.

HOGAN, Ann Maria, d. George, manufacturer, and Anne, July 22, 1843.
George E., s. George, laborer, and Ann, Feb. 28, 1846.
——, s. George and Anne, Sept. 19, 1841.

HOLBROOK, Abiel, s. Ralph and Sarah, Mar. 16, 1775.
Ralph, s. Ralph and Sarah, Aug. 5, 1773.

HOLMAN, Robert, s. Lucy, bp. June 1, 1783. C. R. 1.

HOLMES, Andrew Stimpson, s. Laurence, machinist, and Ann, May 1, 1848.
Ann, d. Laurence, laborer, and Ann, Aug. 22, 1846.
Benjamin, s. Henry B., clergyman, b. England, and Harriet, b. New York, June 21, 1849.
Ellen, d. twin, James, laborer, and Mary, Mar. 5, 1849.
James, s. twin, James, laborer, and Mary, Mar. 5, 1849.

HOLNY, Henry William, s. John, spinner, and Mary, Dec. 9, 1845.

HOLT (see also Hoult), Abiah [Abiel, s. C. R. 2.], d. Joshua, jr. and Phebe, Apr. 16, 1761.
Abial, s. Thomas and Allice, Apr. 25, 1718.
Abiather, s. Solomon and Mary, Jan. 31, 1813.
Abiel, s. Thomas, jr. and Hannah, Apr. 3, 1746.
Abiel, s. Daniel and Hannah, June 8, 1765.
Abiel, s. Abiel, bp. Jan. 21, 1770. C. R. 2.
Abiel, s. Asa and Dinah, Nov. 23, 1773. [bp. Oct. 24. C. R. 2.]
Abiel, s. Darius, bp. Aug. 9, 1789. C. R. 2.
Abiell, s. Nicholas and Mary, June 28, 1698.
Abigail, d. Paul and Abigaill, Aug. 21, 1716.
Abigail, d. Robert and Rebecka, Aug. 12 [1719. C. R. 2.].
Abigail, d. Joseph and Abigael, Jan. 16, 1726-7.
Abigail, d. James [jr. C. R. 2.] and Susanna, Feb. —. [bp. Feb. 22, 1736. C. R. 2.]
Abigail, d. twin, Samuel and Abigail, May 19, 1767.
Abigail, d. Simeon, bp. Nov. 18, 1781. C. R. 2.
Abigail, d. Joseph, jr. and Elizabeth, Feb. 2, 1828.
Abigail Maria Temple, d. Amos, bp. Nov 3, 1833. C. R. 2.
Abigal, d. Fifield and Abigel, Apr. 11, 1748.
Abigal, d. James, jr. and Sarah, June 18, 1758.
Abigall, d. Nicholas and Mary, Nov. 23, 1688.
Abner, s. Joseph and Ruth, Oct. 6, 1771.
Adeline, d. Thomas and Ruth, Mar. 14, 1819.
Albert, s. Eliphalet M. and Mary Ann, Oct. 19, 1837.
Albert N., s. Jonas and Pamela, Nov. 10, 1841.
Albion Francis, s. Jonas, farmer, and Permelia P., May 3, 1845.
Alfred, s. Alfred, laborer, and Clara, Nov. 26, 1848.
Allice, d. Benjamin [jr. C. R. 2.] and Lydia, Nov. 13, 1742.
Amasa, s. Zebadiah and Sarah, Dec. 30, 1785.
Amasa, s. Zebediah, bp. Jan. 11, 1789. C. R. 2.
Ambros, s. Samuel and Jemima, Sept. 20, 1742.
[Amos. C. R. 2.], s. John [jr. C. R. 2.] and Mary, May 9, 1740.
Amos, s. Jeremiah and Hannah, Feb. 16, 1760.
Amos, s. David and Hannah, Apr. 25, 1777.
Amos, s. George and Nancy, June 5, 1787.
Amos, s. Amos and Martha, July 21, 1804.
Amos, s. George and Rebecca, Nov. 2, 1818.
Amy, d. Jonathan, 3d and Ruth, July 25, 1776.
Anna, d. Isaac and Tabathy, Nov. 1, 1790.
[Anne. C. R. 2.], d. Humphry and Abigail, Apr. 29, 1719.
Anne, d. Fyfield and Abigaiel, Sept. 26, 1742.
Anne, d. Henry, jr. and Rebecca, Jan. 3, 1746-7.
Aron, s. twin, John and Sarah, June 7, 1686.

HOLT, [Asa. C. R. 2.], s. Oliver [jr. C. R. 2.] and Susanna, Aug. 4, 1736.
Asa, s. Thomas, jr. and Hannah, May 3, 1742.
Asa, s. Asa and Dinah, Mar. 26, 1768.
Asa, s. William and Elizabeth, May 5, 1794.
Asa Lewis, s. Zebadiah and Sarah, June 1, 1791.
Asenath, d. Ephraim and Phebe, Mar. 31, 1743.
Augusta, d. Stephen and Sophronia, July 9, 1826.
Ballard, s. twin, Dean, jr. and Mary, Nov. 21, 1800.
Barachias, s. Jer[emiah], bp. Feb. 19, 1758. C. R. 2.
Barzillai, s. James and Susannah, Oct. 25 [1716. C. R. 2.].
Benjamin, s. Henry and Sarah, July 8, 1696.
Benjamin, s. Benjamin [jr. C. R. 2.] and Lydia, Apr. 4, 1737.
Benjamin, s. Benjamin [jr. C. R. 2.] and Lydia, Dec. 6, 1746.
[Benjamin. C. R. 2.], s. Benjamin, jr. and Lydea, May ——, 1749. [bp. May 21. C. R. 2.]
Bethia, d. Benjamin, jr. and Lydia, Aug. 3, 1744.
Bethiah, d. Ephraim and Phebe, bp. Mar. 20, 1743, C. R. 2.
Betsey, d. Jacob, jr., bp. June 13, 1790. C. R. 2.
Betsy, d. Edmund and Betsy, Mar. 7, 1829.
Betty, d. Jonathan, 3d and Ruth, Aug. 25, 1767.
Betty Kimball, d. Simeon, bp. Nov. 21, 1779. C. R. 2.
Betty Kimble, d. twin, Simeon, bp. July 25, 1773. C. R. 2.
Bridget, d. James, bp. Jan. 16, 1737. C. R. 2.
Bridget, d. Zela, bp. Mar. 9, 1777. C. R. 2.
Bulah, d. Oliver, jr. and Susanna, Apr. 12, 1744.
Caroline Charlottee, d. Jonas and Pamela P., May 4, 1826.
Charles, s. Zebadiah and Sarah, Apr. 30, 1797.
Charles, s. Nathaniel and Mehitable, June 17, 1806.
Charles, s. Jonathan and Mary, May 27, 1817.
Charles Abbee, s. Jonas, farmer, and Permelia, Apr. 22, 1848.
Charles C[arroll. C. R. 2.], s. Joseph, jr. and Elizabeth, Aug. 5, 1831.
Charles G[alen. C. R. 2.], s. Jonas and Pamela, June 28, 1829.
Charles P., s. Timothy P. and Mary, Apr. 11, 1835.
Charlotte M., d. Thomas and Ruth, Oct. 7, 1824.
Chloe, d. Nat[hanie]ll, bp. Sept. 21, 1766. C. R. 2.
Chloe, d. Abiel, bp. Apr. 10, 1768. C. R. 2.
Clarissa, d. Amos and Martha, Aug. 15, 1806.
Clarissa J., d. Thomas and Ruth, Mar. 1, 1820.
Cleavland Beard, s. Joseph and Eliza[beth], July 9, 1799.
Cloe, d. Joshua, bp. June 4, 1775. C. R. 2.
Dane, s. Timothy [jr. C. R. 2.] and Hannah, Apr. 1, 1740.
Dane, s. Dane and Lydia, Mar. 11, 1768.

HOLT, [Daniel, s. C. R. 2.] Thomas and Allis, Sept. 18, 1723.
Dan[iel. T. C.], s. Nicholas and Darcus, Feb. 10, 1732-3.
Daniel, s. Thomas, jr. and Hannah, Sept. 11, 1740.
Daniel, s. John, jr. and Mary, Jan. 10, 1745-6.
Daniel, s. Daniel, bp. Dec. 27, 1761. C. R. 2.
Daniel, s. [Ens. C. R. 2.] John and Rachel, Dec. 11, 1762.
Daniel, s. Abiel, bp. Sept. 30, 1781. C. R. 2.
Daniel Kimball, s. Daniel, jr., bp. Feb. 25, 1781. C. R. 2.
Daniell, s. Nickolice and Mary, —— [1705?].
Dan[ie]ll, s. Benj[ami]n and Sarah of Suncook, bp. ——, 1744. C. R. 1.
Darcus, d. Nichalos and Darcus, Sept. 4, 1727.
Darius, s. David and Hannah, Mar. 6, 1765.
David, s. Samuel [jr. C. R. 2.] and Jemima, Aug. 28, 1737.
David, s. David and Sarah, July 4, 1740.
David, s. Jacob and Margret, July 13, 1749.
[David. C. R. 2], s. Jacob and Margret, —4, [17]51. [bp. Oct. 6. C. R. 2.]
David, s. David and Hannah, Oct. 16, 1768.
David, s. Jacob and Rhoda, Aug. 21, 1783.
David, s. David Lee and Hannah, Sept. 5, 1786.
David, s. Capt. Amos and Martha, Feb. 3, 1818.
David G., s. David and Sarah, July 21, 1820.
Dean, s. Dean, jr. and Mary, Mar. 16, 1799.
Deborah, d. Nicholas and Mary, Nov. 16, 1700.
Deborah, d. John, 3d and Deborah, Nov. 17, 1747.
Deborah, d. John, bp. Nov. 22, 1801. C. R. 2.
Dinah, d. Henery and Sarah, May 23, 1681.
Dinah, d. George and Elizabeth, —— [1710].
Dinah, d. Samuel [jr. C. R. 2.] and Jemima, Nov. 6, 1744.
[Dolley. C. R. 1.], d. Mr. Joseph and Dorithy, Aug. [19. P. R. 104.], 1747. [bp. Aug. 9. C. R. 1.]
[Dorcas. C. R. 2.], d. David and Sarah, Jan. 31, 1735-6.
Dorcas, s. David and Sarah, July —, 1737. [bp. July 31. C. R. 2.]
Dorcase, d. David, jr. and Rebekah, Nov. 20, 1781.
Dorcase, d. Ezra and Dorcase, Sept. 24, 1797.
Dorcis, s. Thomas, jr. and Dorcis, Mar. 19, 1753.
Dorcis, d. James, jr. and Sarah, May 6, 1756.
Dorothy, d. James, 3d and Dorothy, Apr. 22, 1764.
Dudley Foster, s. Nath[anie]l, jr. [and Mehetabel. P. R. 103.], Dec. [6. P. R. 103.], 1791. C. R. 2.
Easter, d. Joseph and Mary, Mar. 22, 1760.
Ebenezer, s. Ebenezer and Mehetable, Sept. 7 [1730. C. R. 2.].
Ebenezer L., s. Amos and Martha, Aug. 14, 1808.

HOLT, Ede, d. Timothy [jr. C. R. 2.] and Ede, Jan. 14, 1777.
Edward B., s. Jona[than] and Mary, May 2, 1819.
Edward B., s. Jonathan and Polly, Apr. 27, 1822.
Edward F[rancis. C. R. 3.], s. Solomon and Phebe, May 19, 1831. [bp. Sept. 11. C. R. 3.]
Edward Frances, s. Solomon and Phebe [May 6. P. R. 44.], 1834. C. R. 3.
Edwin, s. Thomas and Ruth, June 10, 1830.
Elen, d. Dean, Apr. 14, 1834. P. R. 11.
Elezebith, d. Timothy, 3d and Elezebith, Nov. 25, 1748.
Elezebith, d. Humphery, jr. and Mary, Oct. 29, 1750.
Elezebith, d. James, 3d and Sarah, Mar. 10, 1750-51.
Elezebith, d. Nathaniel and Elezebith, Nov. 14, 1752. [bp. Nov. 5. C. R. 2.]
Eli, s. Timothy [jr. C. R. 2.] and Ede, Apr. 6, 1786.
Elisabeth, d. Henry, jr. and Rebecca, June 8, 1743.
Eliphalet [Martin. C. R. 2.], s. Nathaniel and Mehitable, July 15, 1797.
Elisabeth, d. Timothy, 3d, bp. Sept. 24, 1775. C. R. 2.
Elisabeth Goold, d. Zebadiah and Sarah, June 13, 1795.
Eliza, d. Henry and Mehitable, Sept. 5, 1797.
Eliza Ann, d. Asa and Alethenia, Aug. 22, 1822.
Eliza Ann, d. Eliphalet M. and Mary Ann, Apr. 24, 1830.
Elizabeth, d. Henry and Sara, Dec. 29, 1670.
Elizabeth, d. George and Eli[sabeth], —— [1703].
Elizabeth, d. John and Mehitabel, June — [1718].
Elizabeth, d. Henry, jr., bp. July 10, 1743. C. R. 2.
Elizabeth, d. twin, Samuel and Abigail, May 19, 1767.
Elizabeth, d. William and Elizabeth, Mar. 12, 1790.
Elizabeth, d. Nathaniel [jr. C. R. 1.] and Mehitable, Jan. 7, 1804.
Elizabeth, d. Amos and Martha, Oct. 8, 1813.
Elizabeth, d. Joseph, jr. and Elizabeth, May 5, 1826.
Elizabeth D., d. George, jr. and Rebecca, Oct. 12, 1806.
Elizabeth S[awyer. C. R. 2.], d. Thomas and Ruth, Apr. 11, 1832.
Elizebeth, d. Moses and Elizebeth, Mar. 12, 1719-20.
Elizebeth, d. Jacob and Margret, Jan. 24, 1747-8.
Ellen Augusta, d. Moses, bp. Oct. 11, 1840. C. R. 2.
Ellen F., d. Tim[oth]y P., cordwainer, and Mary H. [F. dup.], Sept. 5, 1843.
Ellinor, d. Joseph and Ruth, Nov. 3, 1777.
Emeline Eaton, d. Eliphalet M. and Mary Ann, July 6, 1832.
Emily Burnap, d. Michael, bp. Nov. 10, 1811. C. R. 1.
Enoch, s. Jeremiah and Hannah, Mar. 20, 1762.

HOLT, Enoch, s. David and Hannah, Sept. 12, 1770.
Enoch, s. Darius, bp. Aug. 20, 1786. C. R. 2.
Enoch, s. George and Nancy, Sept. 5, 1795.
Enoch, s. twin, Dean, jr. and Mary, Nov. 21, 1800.
Ephraim, s. Henery and Martha [bp. May 31, 1713. C. R. 2.].
Ephraim, s. Ephraim and Phebe, Jan. —, 1736-7.
Ephraim, s. Ephraim and Phebe, bp. Mar. 20, 1743. C. R. 2.
Ephraim, s. Ephraim and Zerviah, July 12, 1747.
Ephraim, s. Jacob and Rhoda, Mar. 19, 1769.
Esther, d. Nehemiah, of Salem, bp. July 9, 1775. C. R. 2.
Esther A., d. James, laborer, and Mary A., Nov. 7, 1844.
Eunice, d. David and Sarah, May 22, 1747.
Ezekiel, s. twin, Ebenezer and Mehetable, July 7, 1741.
Ezra, s. Timothy and Hannah, Mar. 16, 1762.
Ezra, s. Timo[thy], jr., bp. May 17, 1789. C. R. 2.
Ezra, s. Ezra and Dorcase, Aug. 9, 1795.
Frederick Reed, s. Simeon and Sarah, Jan. 23, 1768.
Fyfeild, s. Humfry and Abigail, July 28, 17[17. C. R. 2.].
Fyfield, s. Fyfield and Abigail, Oct. 29, 1744.
George, s. Henry and Sarah, Mar. 17, 1676-7.
George, s. George and Elizabeth, Jan. 2 [1713. C. R. 2.].
George, s. Jonathan, jr. and Shuah, Feb. 21, 1756.
George, s. George and Nancy, Feb. 21, 1781.
George, s. George, jr. and Rebecca, Dec. 4, 1804.
Hamborough, s. Sam[ue]ll, jr., bp. Oct. 3, 1742. C. R. 2.
Hannah, d. James and Hannah, Aug. 10, 1677. [Aug. 12. CT. R.]
Hannah, d. Sam[ue]l and Hannah, Feb. 11, 1693-4.
Hannah, d. Olliver and Hannah, —— [1708?].
Hannah, d. Henry and Martha, bp. Aug. 16, 1719. C. R. 2.
Hannah, d. Obadiah and Rebecca, bp. Nov. 19, 1727. C. R. 2.
Hannah, d. Oliver and Susanna, Aug. 29, 172[8. C. R. 2.].
Hannah, d. Thomas, jr. and Hannah, Feb. 11, 1738-9.
Hannah, d. Timothy, jr. and Hannah, Sept. 17, 1741.
Hannah, d. Nicholas, jr. and Hannah, Nov. 16, 1741.
Hannah, d. Jonathan and Lydia, Dec. 19, 1745.
Hannah, d. Ebenezer and Mehetebel, Oct. 27, 1749.
Hannah, d. Benjamin [sr. C. R. 2.] and Elezebith, Nov. 15, 1749.
Hannah, d. Timothy, 3d and Elezebith, Jan. 18, 1754.
Hannah, d. Joshua and Ruth, Mar. 17, 1764.
Hannah, d. Nathaniel, bp. Mar. 25, 1764. C. R. 2.
Hannah, d. David and Hannah, Sept. 13, 1765.
Hannah, d. Asa and Dinah, June 20, 1766.
Hannah, d. Dane and Lydia, Apr. 16, 1771.

HOLT, Hannah, d. Ens. Joshua, jr., bp. June 9, 1771. C. R. 2.
Hannah, d. Abial, bp. Jan. 19, 1772. C. R. 2.
Hannah, d. Timothy, 3d and Hannah, July 29, 1773.
Hannah, d. Joseph and Ruth, Sept. 28, 1775.
Hannah, d. James, jr., bp. June 29, 1777. C. R. 2.
Hannah, d. Timothy and Ede, Apr. 8, 1781.
Hannah, d. Jacob and Rhoda, July 17, 1781.
Hannah, d. Isaac, bp. Aug. 3, 1783. C. R. 2.
Hannah, d. Joseph and Ruth, Apr. 7, 1787.
Hannah, d. Nathaniel [jr. C. R. 1.] and Mehitable, Sept. 16, 1801.
Hannah, d. Capt. Dean and Mary, June 15, 1805.
Hannah, d. Joseph and Lydia, Oct. 19, 1805. P. R. 102.
Hannah Aplin, d. Moses, bp. Oct. 11, 1840. C. R. 2.
Hannah B[roadstreet. C. R. 1.], d. Nathaniel and Mehetabel, Nov. 11, 1816. P. R. 103.
Hannah [Kimble. C. R. 2.], d. Abiel and Lydia, June 4, 1792.
Harmon, s. Henry and Mehitable, Dec. 24, 1793.
Harriott, d. Thomas and Ruth, Nov. 16, 1815.
Harriott, d. Thomas and Ruth, July 3, 1817.
Henery, s. [torn] ——, [1706-7 ?].
Henry, s. Henry and Sara, Jan. 24, 1673.
Henry, s. Henry [jr. C. R. 2.] and Rebecca, Oct. 1, 1736.
Henry, s. Joseph, jr., bp. Sept. 4, 1763. C. R. 2.
Henry, s. Henry and Mehitable, Feb. 28, 1791.
Henry, s. Capt. Joseph and Lydia, Apr. 5, 1819.
Hepsebeth, d. Ebenezer and Mehetebel, June 13, 1748.
Herman, s. Henry, bp. Dec. 28, 1794. C. R. 2.
Hermon, s. Hermon and Nancy, at Dracut, N. H., May 11, 1825.
Hipzabah, d. Peter and Hipzabah, Sept. 30, 1778.
Hiram, s. wid. Abigail, "Father is supposed to be Nathan Jones," bp. May 12, 1799. C. R. 2.
Horace Prescott, s. Jonas, bp. Aug. 7, 1836. C. R. 2.
Humphery, s. Henry and Sarah, Sept. 22, 1693.
Humphrey, s. Humphrey [jr. C. R. 2.] and Mary [Jan. or Feb., 1753]. [bp. Feb. 18. C. R. 2.]
Humphry, s. Humphry, bp. May 19, 1723. C. R. 2.
Humphry, s. triplet, Simeon, bp. July 27, 1777. C. R. 2.
Isaac, s. John and Mehetebel, J— 22. [bp. July 23, 1721. C. R. 2.]
Isaac, s. Obadiah and Rebeca, Oct. 30 [1729. C. R. 2.].
Isaac, s. Joshua and Ruth, May 15, 1752.
Isaac, s. Samuel and Abigail, Jan. 21, 1764.
Isaac, s. Isaac, jr., bp. July 7, 1793. C. R. 2.
Isaac, s. Isaac [jr. C. R. 2.] and Tabitha, Oct. 22, 1794.

HOLT, Israel, s. Jos— [Joshua. C. R. 2.], and Ruth. [bp. May 19, 1754. C. R. 2.].
Jacob, s. Oliver and Hannah, Mar. — [1714. C. R. 2.].
Jacob, s. Jacob and Mary, Mar. 29, 1739.
Jacob, s. Jacob and Rhoda, Feb. 15, 1765.
Jacob, s. Dane and Lydia, June 7, 1780.
Jacob, s. William and Elizabeth, Dec. 13, 1784.
Jacob, s. [Simeon. C. R. 2.] and Sarah, Mar. 7, 1787.
James, s. Henery and Sarah, Sept. 3, 1675.
James, s. Nicholas and Mary, July 23, 1693.
James, s. James and Susannah, —— [1707?].
James, s. Timothy and Rhoda, Dec. — [bp. Dec. 16, 1711. C. R. 2.].
James, s. Nichalos and Darcus, Jan. 13, 1722-3.
[James. C. R. 2.], s. James [jr. C. R. 2.] and Susanna, Dec. 29, 1738.
James, s. James, 3d and Sarah, Apr. 16, 1749.
James H., s. Isaac, jr. and Hannah, May 7, 1832.
James Hervey, s. Isaac and Tabathy, Oct. 31, 1809.
Jedadiah, s. Beulah, bp. Aug. 16, 1767. C. R. 2.
Jedeadiah, s. Nicholas, jr. and Loais, Mar. 12, 1754.
Jedediah, s. Nicholas, jr. and Hannah, Apr. 19, 1740.
Jedediah, s. twin, Ens. Stephen and Mary, at Suncook, Feb. 23, 1743-4.
Jedediah, s. Jedediah, bp. Feb. 12, 1804. C. R. 2.
Jemima, d. Samuel [jr. C. R. 2.] and Jemima, Nov. 16, 1739.
[Jeremiah. C. R. 2.], s. John [jr. C. R. 2.] and Mary, Mar. 31, 1734.
Jeremiah, s. Jeremiah and Hannah, June 8, 1756.
Jesse, s. James, sr., bp. Feb. 12, 1744. C. R. 2.
Jesse, s. James and Mehetebel, Oct. 8, 1755.
Joanna, d. Peter S., carpenter, and Louisa, Sept. 19, 1845.
Job, s. Obadiah and Rebecca, May 25, 1735.
Job, s. Obadiah and Rebecca, Feb. 28, 1738-9. [s. Obadiah, deceased, bp. July 1, 1739. C. R. 2.]
Joel, s. James, jr. and Sarah, Aug. 7, 1753.
Joel, s. John [jr. C. R. 2.] and Rachel, July 4, 1764.
Joel, s. Peter and Hipzabah, Aug. 29, 1787.
John, s. Nicholas and Hannah, Jan. 11, 1663.
John, s. John and Mehittabel, May — [bp. May 24, 1713. C. R. 2.].
John, s. John and Mary, Mar. 16, 173[2. C. R. 2.].
John, s. John, 3d and Debora, Apr. 29, 1749.
John, s. John, 4th and Lydia, Apr. 16, 1754.

HOLT, John, s. [Ens. C. R. 2.] Joshua, jr. and Phebe, Jan. 12, 1765.
John, s. David and Hannah, Feb. 22, 1769.
John, s. David, 1st, bp. Feb. 24, 1771. C. R. 2.
John, s. Peter and Hepzabah, July 15, 1796.
John Calvin, s. Peter, carpenter, and Louisa, Dec. 11, 1843.
John F[rancis. C. R. 3.], s. Abiather and Eliza [Elizabeth. C. R. 3.], Apr. 28, 1838.
John O., s. Isaac, 3d and Hannah, Oct. 26, 1820.
Jonas, s. Isaac, jr. and Tabathy, Dec. 8, 1800.
Jonathan, s. Oliver and Hannah, Aug. — [1711].
Jonathan, s. George and Mary, Dec. [bp. Dec. 28, 1718. C. R. 2.]
Jonathan, s. Thomas and Allis, May 18 [1726. C. R. 2.].
Jonathan, s. Samuel and Jemima, Feb. 5, 1728[-9].
Jonathan, s. Jonathan and Lydia, Sept. 29, 1738.
Jonathan, s. Jonathan, jr. and Shua, June 28, 1762.
Jonathan, s. Jonathan, 3d and Ruth, June 29, 1763.
Jonathan, s. triplet, Simeon, bp. July 27, 1777. C. R. 2.
Jonathan, s. Simeon, bp. Jan. 11, 1784. C. R. 2.
Jonathan, s. Zebadiah and Sarah, June 17, 1793.
Jonathan, s. George and Nancy, May 1, 1798.
Jonathan Abbott, s. Solomon and Phebe, Mar. 1, 1841. [Apr. 7. P. R. 44.]
Joseph, s. James and Hannah, Mar. 5, 1686.
Joseph, s. twin, Timothy and Rhoda [bp. Apr. 18, 1714. C. R. 2.].
[Joseph. C. R. 2.] ——ph, s. Thomas and Allice, Feb. 28, 1715-16.
Joseph, s. Timothy and Rhoda, Feb. 14, 1717-18.
[Joseph, s. C. R. 2.] Joseph and Abigail, Feb. 7, 1728-9.
Joseph, s. Benjamin [jr. C. R. 2.] and Lydia, Aug. 20, 1740.
Joseph, s. Mr. Joseph and Dorathy, Sept. 28, 1745.
Joseph, s. Thomas [jr. C. R. 2.] and Dorcas, Sept. 29, 1766.
Joseph, s. Joseph and Ruth, Apr. 16, 1769.
Joseph, s. Humphry and Phebe, July 7, 1778.
Joseph, s. Joseph and Ruth, Nov. 5, 1780.
Joseph, s. Joseph and Abigail, Jan. 20, 1790.
Joseph, s. William and Elizabeth, Jan. 28, 1792.
Joseph, s. Ezra, bp. Mar. 20, 1803. C. R. 2.
Joseph Franklin, s. Joseph and Elizabeth, Sept. 1, 1822.
Joseph Stillman, s. Joseph and Lydia, Feb. 5, 1808. P. R. 102.
Joseph S., s. T. P., cordwainer, and Mary F., May 3, 1845.
Josephine, d. Joseph S. and Lucy, Feb. 21, 1836.
Joshua, s. John and Mehetebel, June 11, 1724.
Joshua, s. Nichalos and Darcus, June 30, 1730.

HOLT, Joshua, s. Joshua, jr. and Phebe, Jan. 17, 1758.
Joshua, s. Joseph, 3d and Mary, Nov. 5, 1765.
Joshua, s. Solomon and Mary, Mar. 6, 1804.
Joshua Lovejoy, s. Abial, bp. July 25, 1784. C. R. 2.
Joshua, s. Nickolice and Mary, —— [1703].
Josiah, s. Henery and Sarah, Dec. 13, 1679.
Josiah, s. George and Mary, July 2, 1721.
Josiah, s. John, 4th and Lydea, Mar. 1, 1756.
Judeth, d. Oliver [sr. C. R. 2.] and Mary, Apr. 9, 1731.
Keturah, d. Henry and Sarah, Dec. 15, 1690.
Keturah, d. Henery and Bethiah, Feb. — [1714-15].
Keturah, d. Henry and Martha, bp. Feb. 27, 1715. C. R. 2.
Larkin, s. Isaac and Tabatha, Jan. 29, 1797.
Lemuel, s. James, bp. Jan. 24, 1748. C. R. 2.
Levi, s. Joseph and Lydia, Nov. 20, 1814. P. R. 102.
Levina, d. George and Nancy, Aug. 2, 1800.
Lewis G[arrison. C. R. 2.], s. Jonas and Pamela, Nov. 15, 1839.
Loammi, d. Simeon, bp. July 23, 1775. C. R. 2.
Loes, d. David and Sarah, June 28, 1743.
Lowis, d. Thomas and Dorcas, Oct. 29, 1760.
Lucey, d. Nath[anie]ll, bp. Nov. 15, 1761. C. R. 2.
Lucy Josephine, d. Joseph S. [jr. C. R. 2.] and Lucy, Feb. 21, 1836. P. R. 102.
Lucy L., d. Hannah, Sept. 13, 1813.
Lydia, d. James and Hannah, Sept. 27, 1681.
[Lydia, d. Thomas. C. R. 2.] and Allice, Jan. 2, 1713-14.
Lydia, d. Benjamin [jr. C. R. 2.] and Lydia, Dec. 18, 1735.
Lydia, d. Jonathan and Lydia, Mar. 7, 1735-6.
Lydia, d. Jonathan and Lydia, Mar. 16, 1739-40.
Lydia, d. Daniel [Dane. C. R. 2.] and Lydia, Aug. 12, 1765.
Lydia, d. Joseph and Ruth, Apr. 18, 1767.
Lydia, d. Jonathan, 3d and Ruth, May 15, 1770.
Lydia, d. Thomas, bp. July 12, 1778. C. R. 2.
Lydia, d. Darius, bp. Oct. 7, 1787. C. R. 2.
Lydia, d. Joseph and Lydia, Oct. 27, 1803. P. R. 102.
Lydia, d. William and Sarah, Nov. 30, 1809.
Lydia, d. William and Sarah, Apr. 9, 1811.
Marcus Morton Temple, s. Amos, bp. Nov. 3, 1833. C. R. 2.
Marey, d. Humphery and Mary, June 11, 1755.
Maria, d. Thomas and Ruth, Feb. 20, 1822.
Marth[a], d. Benjamin, jr. and Lydea, Oct. 15, 1754.
Martha, d. Amos and Martha, Jan. 31, 1803.
Martha A[nn. C. R. 2.], d. Thomas and Ruth, Mar. 24, 1828.
Mary, d. Nicholas and Mary, Feb. 13, 1680.

HOLT, Mary, d. Nicholice and Mary, Aug. — [1711].
Mary, d. George and Mary, Mar. 4, 1716-17.
Mary, d. Henery and Martha, Mar. 25, 1716-17.
Mary, d. Oliver and Mary, July 29, 1720.
Mary, d. Moses and Elezebeth, July 4, 1[722].
Mary, d. Samuel [jr. C. R. 2.] and Jemima, Nov. 5, 1727.
Mary, d. James, bp. May 18, 1735. C. R. 2.
Mary, d. John [jr. C. R. 2.] and Mary, Apr. 12, 1737.
[Mary. C. R. 2.]——y, d. Henry, jr. and Rebecca, Apr. 30, 1739.
Mary, d. Ens. Stephen and Mary, at Suncook, Dec. 15, 1741.
Mary, d. Jacob, bp. Mar. 25, 1744. C. R. 2.
Mary, d. Jacob, bp. Sept. 1, 1745. C. R. 2.
Mary, d. Benjamin [jr. C. R. 2.] and Lydea, Sept. 19, 1751.
[Mary. C. R. 2.], d. Joseph and Mary, Nov. 24, 1755.
Mary, d. Thomas, jr. and Darcos, Mar. 11, 1758.
Mary, d. Darius and Mary, Nov. 22, 1759.
Mary, d. Joshua and Phebe, Dec. 5, 1759.
Mary, d. David and Hannah, Feb. 4, 1767.
Mary, d. Jacob and Rhoda, Apr. 21, 1777.
Mary, d. George and Nancy, July 7, 1791.
Mary, d. Isaac, jr. and Tabathy, Aug. 18, 1798.
Mary, d. Solomon and Mary, Mar. 8, 1801.
Mary, d. Dean and Lydia, Dec. 28, 1802. [1803. P. R. 77.]
Mary, d. George, jr. and Rebecca, Dec. 31, 1802.
Mary, d. Capt. Solomon and Mary, Feb. 20, 1806.
Mary A., d. Timothy P. and Mary, May 12, 1837.
Mary Ann, d. Capt. Amos and Martha, Oct. 14, 1815.
Mary Ann, d. Nathan and Abigail, bp. Apr. 13, 1834. C. R. 3.
Mary Augusta, d. Eliphalet, Jan. 11, 1842. P. R. 85.
Mary Jones, d. Joseph and Lydia, Mar. 18, 1811. P. R. 102.
Mary Kimball, d. Henery and Mehitable, Apr. 9, 1802.
Mary Louisa, d. Jacob and Rachel, bp. May 14, 1809. C. R. 1.
Mary Osgood, d. Jacob, bp. Apr. 27, 1777. C. R. 2.
Mastin, s. Ephraim and Phebe, Aug. 13, 1747.
Mehetabel, d. Ebenezer and Mehetabel, Sept. 3, 1733.
Mehetable, d. Thomas [jr. C. R. 2.] and Hannah, Feb. 8, 1743-4.
Mehetebel, d. Obadiah and Rebeca, Aug. 21 [1728].
Mehitabel, d. John and Mehittabel, Oct. —. [bp. Oct. 23, 1715. C. R. 2.]
Mehitabel, d. Isaac, jr., bp. Apr. 28, 1805. C. R. 2.
Mehitabel, d. Humphrey, bp. Feb. 7, 1725. C. R. 2.
Micah, s. Joshua and Ruth, Mar. 31, 1768.
Molly, d. Jedidiah and Phebe, July 2, 1773.
Molly, d. twin, Simeon, bp. July 25, 1773. C. R. 2.

HOLT, Moses, s. twin, John and Sarah, June 7, 1686.
Moses, s. Moses and Elizabeth, Oct. 21 [1716. C. R. 2.].
[Moses. C. R. 2.], s. Jonathan and Lydia, Jan. 19, 1743-4.
Moses, s. Jonathan, 3d, bp. Sept. 20, 1772. C. R. 2.
Moses, s. Jonathan, 3d and Ruth, Sept. 3, 1773.
Moses Stillman, s. Moses, bp. Oct. 11, 1840. C. R. 2.
Nancy, d. Jona[than], 3d and Ruth, July 22, 1779.
Nancy, d. George and Nancy, Sept. 26, 1782.
Nancy, grandd. Isaac, bp. June 13, 1813. C. R. 2.
Nancy, d. Hermon and Nancy, Feb. 5, 1818.
Nathan, s. Nicholas and Darcus, Feb. 28 [1725. C. R. 2.].
Nathan, s. Thomas [jr. C. R. 2.] and Hannah, July 17, 1735.
Nathan, s. Daniel and Hannah, July 13, 1767.
Nathan, s. Capt. [Corpl. T. C.] Solomon and Mary, Apr. 18, 1808.
Nathan Abbot, s. Zela, bp. Aug. 15, 1773. C. R. 2.
Nathan Kimbel, s. Abiel, bp. Aug. 30, 1778. C. R. 2.
[Nathaniel. C. R. 2.], s. Oliver and Susanna, Nov. 23, 1725.
Nathaniel, s. Nath[anie]ll and Elizabeth, Dec. 19, 1[759]. [bp. Dec. 23, 1759. C. R. 2.]
Nathaniel, s. Humphrey, bp. Sept. 27, 1767. C. R. 2.
Nathaniel, s. Nathaniel and Elizabeth, Apr. 6, 1769.
Nathaniel, s. Nathaniel and Mehitable, Aug. 6, 1793.
Nath[anie]l, s. Nath[anie]l and Sally, at the almshouse, Dec. 12, 1820.
Nathaniel F., s. Timothy P. and Mary H., Feb. 15, 1842.
Nehemiah, s. George, bp. Apr. 7, 1723. C. R. 2.
[Nehemiah. C. R. 2.]— iah, s. Jacob and Mary, Oct. 24, 1740.
Nehemiah, s. Jacob, bp. Dec. 28, 1766. C. R. 2.
Nehemiah, s. Jacob and Rhoda, Dec. 25, 1767.
Nehemiah, s. Timothy and Edy, Apr. 1, 1773.
Nehemiah, s. Timothy [jr. C. R. 2.] and Ede, Jan. 28, 1779.
Nelle [or Eleanor. C. R. 2.], d. John, jr. and Mary, June 27, 1743.
Nemiah, s. John, 4th and Rachil, Jan. 23, 1758.
Newton, s. Joseph, jr. and Elizabeth, Feb. 13, 1830.
Nicholas, s. Lt. and Lois, bp. ——, 1756. C. R. 1.
Nickolas, s. Nickolas and Mary, Dec. 21, 1683.
[N]ickolice, s. Nickolice and Mary, Feb. 29, 1715-16.
Noah, s. Joseph, "resident, from Reading," bp. Dec. 27, 1801. C. R. 2.
Obadiah, s. Samuel and Hannah, Dec. 8, 1700.
Obadiah, s. Obadiah and Rebecca, May 6 [1731. C. R. 2.].
Obed, s. Joseph and Ruth, Nov. 25, 1773.
Oliver, s. Oliver and Hannah, Dec. 26, 1698.

HOLT, Oliver, s. Oliver and Susanna, June 1, 1722.
Oliver, s. Oliver, jr. and Susanna, Jan. 24, 1739-40.
Oliver, s. Oliver, bp. Sept. 5, 1762. C. R. 2.
Patty, d. triplet, Simeon, bp. July 27, 1777. C. R. 2.
Paul, s. Henery and Sarah, Feb. 7, 1684.
Paul, s. Joseph and Ruth, Jan. 11, 1783.
Persis, d. Samuel and Abigail, Nov. 21, 1775.
Persis, d. Isaac [jr. C. R. 2.] and Tabathy, Jan. 3, 1792.
Peter, s. Ens. Stephen and Mary, Feb. 8, 1749-50.
Peter, s. John, 3d and Deborah, Sept. 30, 1752.
Peter, s. Joshua [jr. C. R. 2.] and Phebe, June 12, 1763.
Peter, s. Peter and Hipzabeth, Dec. 5, 1776.
Peter, s. Peter and Hipsabah, June 10, 1783.
Phebe, d. Timothy and Rhoda, June 1, 1722.
Phebe, d. Ephraim and Phebe [Apr. —, 1735].
Phebe, d. Ephraim and Phebe, bp. Mar. 20, 1743. C. R. 2.
Phebe, d. Nickless, jr. and Lois, Jan. 29, 1752.
Phebe, d. Joshua, jr. and Phebe, Nov. 28, 1756.
Phebe, d. John, 3d and Deborah, Feb. 3, 1757.
Phebe, d. Jonathan, jr. and Shua, Jan. 31, 1761.
Phebe, d. Jedediah and Phebe, Feb. 18, 1771.
Phebe, d. Tho[mas], bp. June 11, 1780. C. R. 2.
Phebe, d. Peter and Hipzabah, July, —, 1785.
Phebe, d. George and Nancy, July 28, 1789.
Phebe, d. Timothy [jr. C. R. 2.] and Ede, Jan. 8, 1793.
Phebe Cummings, d. Capt. Solomon and Mary, Apr. 30, 1810.
Phebe D., d. George, jr. and Rebecca, Sept. 7, 1812.
Phebe Elizabeth, d. Dea. Solomon and Phebe, Dec. 17, 1835.
Phebe Foster, d. Nathaniel and Mehitable, July 27, 1795.
Phineas, s. Moses and Prudence, Mar. 3, 1741. [Only child. Deposition of wid. Mercy How, midwife, on Sept. 13, 1748.]
Phoebe, d. Humphrey [jr. C. R. 1.] and Phoebe, Oct. 14, 1775.
Polly, d. Daniel, bp. Aug. 17, 1783. C. R. 2.
Polly, d. Nathaniel and Mehitable, June 2, 1799.
Priscilla, d. James and Hannah, Aug. 13, 1679.
Priscilla, d. twin, Ebenezer and Mehetable, June 15, 1737.
Prissilla, d. Nicholas and Elizabeth, June 20, 1653.
Prissilla, d. George and Mary, Sept. 4 [1725. C. R. 2.].
Rachael Eunice Timandra Bartlett, d. Amos, bp. Nov. 3, 1833. C. R. 2.
[Rachel. C. R. 2.], d. twin, Ebenezer and Mehetable, June 15, 1737.
Rachel, d. twin, Ebenezer and Mehetable, July 7, 1741.
Rachel, d. Jonathan, of Lunenburg, bp. May 5, 1754. C. R. 2.

HOLT, Rachil, d. Ens. John [4th. C. R. 2.] and Rachel, Jan. 25, 1759.
Rebeca, d. Jonathan, jr. and Shuah, Feb. 5, 1755.
Rebecca, d. Samuel, jr., bp. Oct. 31, 1725. C. R. 2.
Rebecca, d. Obadiah and Rebecca, June 22, 1736.
Rebecca, d. Henry, jr. and Rebecca, May 5, 1741.
Rebecca, d. David jr. and Rebecca, Dec. 10, 1770.
Rebecca, d. David, jr. and Rebecca, Aug. 25, 1776.
Rebecca, d. George and Nancy, May 25, 1793.
Rebecca, d. Georg, jr. and Rebecca, Mar. 20, 1801.
Rebecka, d. Nicholas and Hanna, Nov. 14, 1662.
Rebecka, d. Sam[ue]ll and Hannah [bp. May 31, 1713. C. R. 2.].
Rebekah, d. James and Hannah, Mar. 29, 1688.
Rebekah, d. Nathaniel and Mehitable, Nov. 29, 1813. [Dec. 2. P. R. 103.]
Reubin, s. John, jr. and Mary, June 27, 1744.
Reubin, s. Ebenezer and Mehetable, Ju[ne] 27 [1744. C. R. 2.].
Rhoade, d. Mr. Joseph and Dorathy, at Rumford, July 17, 1750.
Rhoda, d. James, jr. and Susanna, Feb. 18, 1741-2.
Rhoda, d. Mr. Joseph and Dorathy, Dec. 30, 1753.
Rhoda, d. Joseph and Mary, Oct. 16, 1757.
Rhoda, d. Jacob and Rhoda, July 5, 1772.
Rhoda, d. Jacob and Rhoda, July 13, 1773.
Robert, s. Nicholas and Mary, Jan. 30, 1695-6.
[Rose. C. R. 2.], d. Jonathan and Lydia, Jan. 5 [1741-2. C. R. 2.].
Ruth, d. Joshua, bp. July 25, 1756. C. R. 2.
Ruth, d. Joshua [sr. C. R. 2.] and Ruth, May 11, 1758.
Ruth, d. Joseph [jr. C. R. 2.] and Ruth, Feb. 25, 1765.
Ruth, d. Abner and Ruth, July 26, 1785.
Ruth Kimball, d. Johna[than], 3d and Ruth, Apr. 18, 1782.
Rutha Octavia Eames, d. Amos, bp. Nov. 3, 1833. C. R. 2.
Ruthy W., d. Thomas, bp. Jan. 2, 1825. C. R. 2.
Sally, d. Timothy and Ede, Aug. 16, 1783.
Sally Lewis, d. Zebadiah and Sarah, Apr. 5, 1789.
Samuel, s. Samuel [jr. C. R. 2.] and Jemima, Dec. 18, 1730.
Samuel, s. John, jr., bp. May 7, 1749. C. R. 2.
[Samuel. C. R. 2.], s. Joshua and Ruth [Mar. C. R. 2.] 18, 1749-50.
Samuel, s. Samuel and Abigail, Sept. 7, 1761.
Samuel, s. Jedidiah and Phebe, Jan. 24, 1778.
Samuel, s. Isaac, jr. and Tabathy, Nov. 1, 1802.
Sam[ue]l, s. George and Rebecca, Feb. 10, 1813.
Samuel Blanchard, s. Joseph, jr. and Eliz[abe]th, Aug. 3, 1824.

HOLT, Samuel F., s. Peter and Eliza, May 9, 1838.
Samuel Madison Evans, s. Amos, bp. Nov. 3, 1833. C. R. 2.
Samuel W., s. Isaac, jr. and Hannah, Feb. 28, 1828.
Samuell, s. Samuell and Sara, Aug. 3, 1670.
Sarah, d. Henery and Sarah, June 17, 1678. [Aug. 17. CT. R.]
Sarah, d. Nicholas and Mary, Mar. 10, 1690-91.
Sarah, d. Henery and Martha, —— [1708?].
Sarah, d. Robert and Rebeacka, Jan. 18, 1720-21.
Sarah, d. Moses and Elezebeth [bp. Mar. 22, 1724. C. R. 2.].
Sarah, d. Humphy, bp. Nov. 13, 1726. C. R. 2.
Sarah, d. Obadiah, bp. Feb. 25, 1733. C. R. 2.
Sarah, d. David and Sarah, Nov. 20 [1733. C. R. 2.].
Sarah, d. Timothy, jr. and Hannah, Aug. 11, 1746.
Sarah, d. James, 3d and Sarah, Mar. 7, 1746-7.
Sarah, d. Jonathan, jr. and Shua, Feb. 3, 1757.
Sarah, d. Timothy, 3d and Elezebith, May 31, 1757.
Sarah, d. Nathan and Sarah, Oct. 29, 1758.
Sarah, d. Jedediah and Phebe, Jan. 16, 1768.
Sarah, d. David, jr. and Rebecca, Sept. 12, 1773.
Sarah, d. David and Hannah, Dec. 27, 1775.
Sarah, d. David and Rebekah, July 12, 1779.
Sarah, d. Timo[thy], jr., bp. Oct. 5, 1783. C. R. 2.
Sarah, d. Jacob and Rhod[a], May 19, 1786.
Sarah, d. William and Sarah, May 26, 1807.
Sarah, d. Amos and Martha, June 16, 1810.
Sarah Abbot, d. Ezra and Dorcas, Sept. 1, 1800.
Sarah Abbot, d. David and Sarah, Oct. 17, 1824.
Sarah E., d. Timothy P. and Mary H., June 2, 1839.
Sarah Hubbard, d. Moses, bp. Oct. 11, 1840. C. R. 2.
Sarah M., d. Isaac, 3d and Hannah, Jan. 17, 1819.
Sarah M[aria. P. R. 85.], d. Eliphalet and Mary Ann, Mar. 14, 1840.
Shuah, d. Humphrey and Abigail, Mar. 21, 1728-9.
Silence D., d. George, jr. and Rebecca, Oct. 22, 1810.
Simeon, s. Humphery [jr. C. R. 2.] and Elisabeth, Jan. 26, 1746-7.
Simeon, s. Joseph and Dorothy, at —ford, N. H., May 22, 1752.
Simeon, s. Simeon and Sarah, May 18, 1771.
Solomon, s. Ens. John, bp. Dec. 14, 1760. C. R. 2.
Solomon, s. Ens. Joshua, bp. Dec. 18, 1768. C. R. 2.
Solomon, s. Solomon, bp. Nov. 6, 1814. C. R. 2.
Solomon, s. Solomon and Phebe, Feb. 6, 1826. P. R. 44.
Solomon Augustus, s. Solomon and Phebe, Jan. 12, 1829. P. R. 44.
Sophronia, d. Stephen, jr. and Sophronia, July 21, 1827.
Stephen, s. Nicholice [jr. C. R. 2.] and Mary, Apr. 14, 1713.

HOLT, Stephen, s. twin, Ens. Stephen and Mary, at Suncook, Feb. 23, 1743-4.
Stephen, s. Jacob and Rhoda, June 7, 1771.
Stephen, s. Joshua, bp. May 2, 1773. C. R. 2.
Stephen, s. Tho[ma]s, bp. Apr. 27, 1777. C. R. 2.
Stephen, s. Asa and Lydia, May 26, 1782.
Stephen, s. Jedidiah and Phebe, Feb. 4, 1786.
Stephen, s. William and Elizabeth, Apr. 11, 1786.
Stephen, s. Timothy, bp. Sept. 2, 1798. C. R. 2.
Stephen, s. Ezra and Elizabeth G., Apr. 10, 1813.
Stephen, s. Capt. Solomon and Mary, Feb. 12, 1816.
Stephen, s. Peter and Louisa, Oct. 23, 1841.
Stephen C., s. Nathan, laborer, and Abigail, Nov. 17, 1846.
Stephen Dexter, s. Stephen and Polly, July 19, 1822.
Stephen G., s. Stephen and Sophronia, Jan. 31, 1830.
Susan L., d. Abiel and Lucinda, Mar. 19, 1838.
Susan Louisa, d. Peter and Louisa, Jan. 16, 1840.
Susan Peters, d. Eliphalet M. and Mary Ann, Dec. 28, 1834.
Susanna, d. Oliver [jr. C. R. 2.] and Susanna, "between Apr. 6 and 7," 1731.
Susanna, d. James [jr. C. R. 2.] and Susanna, Apr. 18, 1737.
Susanna, d. Nathaniel and Elezebith, May 11, 1755.
Susanna, d. James, jr. and Sarah, Oct. 27, 1760.
Susanna, d. Peter and Hipzabah, Oct. 12, 1790.
Susanna, d. Nathaniel and Mehitable, Aug. 23, 1808. [Aug. 13. P. R. 103.]
Tabitha, d. Jacob and Margret, May 19, 1753.
Tabitha, d. Joseph and Ruth, May 22, 1785.
Tabby, d. Joshua and Ruth, Feb. 25, 1770.
Tabby, d. Jacob and Rhoda, Aug. 11, 1779.
Thomas, s. Nickolas and Mary, Aug. 16, 1686.
Thomas, s. Thomas and Allies, Mar. —, 1711-12. [bp. Mar. 9. C. R. 2.]
Thomas, s. Oliver and Mary, Aug. 23 [1717. C. R. 2.].
Thomas, s. Thomas, jr. and Dorcis, June 15, 1750.
Thomas, s. Peter, bp. Sept. 10, 1780. C. R. 2.
Thomas, s. Abiel and Lydia, Jan. 15, 1790.
Thomas [A. C. R. 2.], s. Thomas and Ruth, Sept. 25, 1812.
Timothy, s. James and Hannah, Jan. 25, 1683.
Timothy, s. twin, Timothy and Rhoda [bp. Apr. 18, 1714. C. R. 2.].
Timothy, s. Nichalus and Darcus, Jan. 17, 1720-21.
Timothy, s. Timothy [jr. C. R. 2.] and Hannah, Sept. 8, 1744.
Timothy, s. Timothy, 3d and Elisabeth, May 19, 1746.
Timothy, s. Ens. Josh[u]a, bp. Apr. 5, 1767. C. R. 2.

HOLT, Timothy, s. Timothy [jr. C. R. 2.] and Edy, Feb. 22, 1775.
Timothy, s. Timothy, 3d, bp. Sept. 7, 1777. C. R. 2.
Timothy A., s. Clark and Mary, Oct. 29, 1832.
Timothy K., s. Abiel, jr. and Sally, Apr. 25, 1816.
Timothy Parker, s. Nathaniel and Mehitable, Feb. 27, 1811.
Uriah, s. Oliver [jr. C. R. 2.] and Susanna, Dec. 1, 1[733. C. R. 2.].
Uriah, s. Nathaniel and Elezebith, Sept. 13, 1757.
Uriah, s. Jacob and Rhoda, May 25, 1775.
Uzziel, s. Joshua, bp. Mar. 1, 1761. C. R. 2.
Uzziel, s. Joshua and Ruth, Apr. 12, 1766.
Valentine, s. Joseph, bp. Jan. 1, 1764. C. R. 2.
Varnum, s. Jacob, jr., bp. Oct. 5, 1788. C. R. 2.
Warren, s. Joseph, bp. Nov. 19, 1775. C. R. 2.
Warren, s. Isaac and Tabathy, Aug. 19, 1807.
Warren Ugene [Eugene. C. R. 2.], s. Jonas and Pamelia, Apr. 17, 1833.
William, s. Thomas [jr. C. R. 2.] and Dorcas, Sept. 7, 1763.
William, s. Henery and Sarah, Feb. 3, 1686-7.
William, s. Thomas and Allice, Dec. 10, 1720.
William, s. Humphry, bp. June 11, 1721. C. R. 2.
William, s. Oliver [sr. C. R. 2.] and Mary, Apr. 1, 1727.
William, s. Jonathan, jr. and Shua, Dec. 21, 1763.
William, s. George and Nancy, May 27, 1785.
William, s. William and Elizabeth, Mar. 6, 1788.
William C[larence. P. R. 85.], s. Eliphalet, carpenter, and Mary, Jan. 6, 1846.
William F., s. Thomas and Ruth, Mar. 9, 1814.
William F., s. William F., confectioner, and Vashti, Aug. 5, 1844.
William P., s. Isaac, jr. and Hannah, Aug. 18, 1830.
Zebadiah, s. Samuel and Jemima, June 1, 1733.
Zebadiah, s. Zebadiah and Sarah, Apr. 5, 1787.
Zebediah, s. [torn] ——[1705-6].
Zebediah, s. Jonathan and Shua, July 28, 1759.
Zelah, s. James, bp. Sept. 16, 1739. C. R. 2.
Zeruiah, d. Henery and Sarah, Mar. 24, 1688-9.
Zerviah, d. James and Susannah, Mar. —, 1711-12.
——, ch. Hannah, May 14, 1701.
——, ch. [Hen]ery and Martha, Nov. 28, 1702.
——, ch. [torn] and Hanah, Dec. 30, 1702.
——, ch. [torn] and [Mart]ha, Jan. 27, 1704-5.
——, ch. James and Susannah, Mar. 20, 1705-6.
——, ch. [S]amuell and Hannah, Apr. 8, 1706.
——, ch. [torn]thy and Rhoda, Apr. 30, 1706.
——, ch. [Ni]ckolice and Mary, July 23, 1709.

HOLT, ——, ch. [T]homas and Allice, Sept. 5, 1709.
——, ch. [torn]h, Mar. 15, 1710-11.
——, ch. John and Mehittabel, bp. June 8, 1718. C. R. 2.
——, d. Moses, bp. July 8, 1722. C. R. 2.
——, s. George and Mary, Apr. 3, 1723.
——, d. Samuel and Jemima, Nov. 28, 1825.
——, d. Obadiah and Rebeca, May 24, 1727.
——, d. Obadiah and Rebecca, Feb. 18, 1732-3.
——, d. Samuel [jr. C. R. 2.] and Jemima, Nov. 7, 1735.
——, twin sons, Loammi B. and Mary, Mar. 12, 1816.
——, ch. Loammi B. and Mary, Aug. 1, 1817.
——, d. Abiel, jr. and Sally, at the almshouse, Feb. 20, 1818.
——, d. Capt. Amos and Eunice, Apr. 12, 1820.
——, s. Hermon and Nancy, July 20, 1821.
——, ch. Capt. Amos and Eunice, Apr. —, 1822.
——, s. Isaac, jr. and Hannah, Apr. 17, 1822.
——, d. Thomas and Ruth, Sept. 9, 1823.
——, s. twin, Capt. Amos and Elizabeth, Apr. 27, 1824.
——, d. twin, Capt. Amos and Elizabeth, Apr. 27, 1824.
——, s. David and Sarah, May 14, 1827.
——, ch. Isaac, jr. and Hannah, Oct. 16, 1827.
——, s. Joseph S. and Lucy, June 19, 1837. P. R. 102.
——, [d. P. R. 102.] Joseph S. and Lucy, Nov. 22, 1838. [Nov. 24. P. R. 102.]
——, s. Timothy P., cordwainer, and Mary, Apr. 9, 1847.

HOLTON, James, s. James and Jerusha, Jan. 6, 1758.

HOPKINS, George E., s. John F., farmer, b. Wilmington, and Rebecca, June 29, 1849.

HOPKINSON, David, s. Jonathan and Margret, Aug. 21, 1751.

HOUGHTON, Charity, d. Eucled and Elizabeth, Mar. 27, 1798.
Charles, s. Euclid, bp. Mar. 4, 1798. C. R. 2.
Elizabeth, d. Eucled and Elizabeth, Mar. 18, 1794.
Eucled, s. Eucled and Elizabith, Feb. 28, 1792.
James, s. James, bp. June 20, 1756. C. R. 2.
John James, s. John and Julia, Jan. 22, 1807.
Nathanael, s. Eucled and Elizabeth, Apr. 8, 1796.
Sarah, d. Mercy Lovejoy and Thomas, Feb. 14, 1798.
Sarah, d. Euclid and Elizabeth, Feb. 14, 1802.
Sophia, d. Euclid, bp. Mar. 4, 1798. C. R. 2.
Thomas, s. Euclid and Elizabeth, Feb. 1, 1800.

HOULT (see also Holt), [Elias. C. R. 2.], s. George and Priscilla, Jan. 16, 1715-16.
Oliver, s. Henry and Sara, Jan. 14, 1671.
Zebadiah, s. George and Eliz[abe]th, Jan. 5, 1699-1700.

HOVEY, Catharine, d. James and Mary, Sept. 5, 1819.
Charles, s. James and Mary, Apr. 25, 1824.
Eliza, d. James and Mary, July 29, 1834.
Elizabeth, d. Martha, bp. June 25, 1769. C. R. 1.
Henry M., s. James and Mary, Nov. 24, 1821.
John C. M., s. James and Mary, Sept. 1, 1836.
Martha, d. James and Mary, Jan. 31, 1828.
Sarah J., d. James and Mary, Jan. 25, 1831.

HOW (see also Howe), Achsa, d. Daniel, jr. and Sarah, Dec. 29, 1769.
Charles, s. Nicholas and Cyntha, Mar. 3, 1832.
Daniel, s. Isral and Marcy, May 1, 1719.
Daniel, s. Daniel and Sarah, Apr. 30, 1740.
Hannah, d. [Dr. C. R. 2.] Israell and Marcy, Apr. 5, 1724.
Israel, s. Daniel and Sarah, Oct. 6, 1741.
Israel, s. Dr. Daniel and Sarah, Sept. 19, 1749.
Marcy, d. Dr. Daniel and Sarah, Nov. 1, 1744.
Martha, d. Dr. Daniel and Sarah, Aug. 2, 1746.
Mary, d. Dr. Daniel and Sarah, May 12, 1752.
Phebe, d. [Dr. C. R. 2.] Daniel and Sarah, Apr. 4, 1762.
Presilla, d. Dr. Daniel and Sarah, Apr. 2, 1755.
Priscilla, d. Daniel, jr. and Sarah, Apr. 10, 1768.
Prissilla, d. [Dr. C. R. 2.] Israel and Mercy, June 24, 1726.
[Sarah. C. R. 2.], d. [Dr. C. R. 2.] Israel and Marcy, ——ber —, 1720. [bp. Sept. 25. C. R. 2.]
[Sarah. C. R. 2.], d. [Dr. C. R. 2.] Israel and Marcy, Feb. 7, 1721-2.
Sarah, d. Daniel and Sarah, Jan. 15, 1742-3.
Sarah, d. Daniel, jr. and Sarah, Mar. 28, 1766.
Stephen, s. Timothy and Ede, July 22, 1798.
Wiliam, s. Dr. Daniel and Sarah, Mar. 5, 1754.
Wiliam, s. Dr. Daniel and Sarah, Mar. 29, 1757.

HOWARD, Hannah Mariah, d. Thomas P., carpenter, and Huldah B., Sept. 25, 1847.
Helen Elizabeth, d. Edward, bp. May 20, 1838. C. R. 2.

HOWARTH, Austin Thompson, s. James and Sarah F. F., Feb. 22, 1837.
Hannah E., d. James, jr. and Hannah B., Oct. 15, 1825.
James W., s. James and Hannah, Aug. 17, 1831.
Joseph, s. James and Hannah B., Dec. 14, 1821.
Joseph N., s. James, jr. and Hannah B., Jan. 2, 1829.
Oberlin Beaumon, s. James and Sarah F. F., Aug. 14, 1839.
Sarah Ann F., d. James, jr. and Hannah B., Oct. 1, 1823.

HOWE (see also How), Harriet M., d. Nicholas, cordwainer, and Wealthy, July 20, 1843.

HOWGATE, Sarah Ann, d. William, machinist, and Ellen, both b. England, Aug. 11, 1849.

HOWLAND, ——, s. Nathan, Apr. 17, 1826.

HOYT, Joseph, s. Samuel and Mehetebel, Feb. 5, 1758.
Molly, d. Samuel and Mehetabel, Oct. 8, 1761.

HUBBARD, Betsey, d. John and Betsy, June 26, 1793.
Leavitt, s. James M. and Lydia, Mar. 7, 1835.
Minerva, d. James M., farmer, and Lydia, June 1, 1845.

HUCHERSON (see also Hutchinson), Sarah, d. Jonathan and Elezebith, July 3, 1753.

HUCHINSON (see also Hutchinson), Phebe, d. Dan[ie]ll, bp. Jan. 6, 1740. C. R. 2.

HUMPHRIES (see also Humphry), Sally Catharine Hayward, d. William and Sally Whiting of Dorchester, Dec. 12, 1808.

HUNT, Amos, s. Paul, jr. and Mary B., Oct. 29, 1816.
Edward Buckley, s. George and Sarah, bp. Nov. 4, 1849. C. R. 4.
Edwin, s. Paul, jr. and Mary Butler, July 9, 1812.
Elizabeth, d. Paul and Elizabeth, July —, 1781.
Elizabeth, d. Paul and Elizabeth, Aug. 2, 1789.
[Hannah. P. R. 64.], d. Paul, jr. and Mary [B. P. R. 64.], Oct. 20, 1821.
Isaac, s. Paul, jr. and Mary B., July 28, 1814. [June 28. P. R. 64.]
John, s. Paul and Elizabeth, Feb. 1, 1786.
John Abel, s. George, finisher, and Sarah, Oct. 30, 1846.
John W., s. twin, Paul and Mary B. (Durant), Aug. 19, 1819. P. R. 64.

HUNT, Mary B., d. twin, Paul and Mary B. (Durant), Aug. 19, 1819. P. R. 64.
Moses Edwin, s. Isaac and Sarah Center (Worthly), May 28, 1847. P. R. 65.
Paul, s. Paul and Elizabeth, July 24, 1783.
Sarah Maria, d. Isaac and Sarah Center (Worthly), Oct. 31, 1842. P. R. 65.
Sewall Paul, s. Isaac and Sarah Center (Worthly), Jan. 19, 1845. P. R. 65.
William Amos, s. Amos, finisher, and Betsy W., Apr. 29, 1847.
——, ch. Amos, finisher, and Betsey, Apr. 29, 1847.

HUSSEY, Charles Greenleaf, s. Elijah, mechanic, and Rosina, Apr. 28, 1845.
Elijah Walter, s. Elijah and Rosina, Mar. 6, 1833.
Elvinh Augusta, d. Elijah and Rosina, July 7, 1830.
George Dexter, s. Elijah and Rosena, Feb. 18, 1832.
Harriet Moar, d. Elijah and Rosina, Aug. 20, 1835.
Luther Gayton, s. Elijah and Lucina, Feb. 22, 1837.
Mary Mooare, d. Elijah and Rosina, bp. Sept. 26, 1841. C. R. 3.
Rosina Angeline, d. Elijah and Rosina, May 3, 1828.
William Hartwell, s. Elijah, cabinet-maker, b. Rochester, N. H., and Rosena, Oct. 4, 1848.
Wyman Dwight, s. Elijah and Rosina, Feb. 13, 1843.

HUTCHENSON (see also Hutchinson), Elisabeth, d. John and Mary, May 30, 1743.

HUTCHINS, Daniel, s. Dan[ie]ll, bp. Oct. 6, 1734. C. R. 2.
Hannah, d. Dan[ie]ll, bp. July 31, 1737. C. R. 2.

HUTCHINSON (see also Hucherson, Huchinson, Hutchenson), Abigail, d. Dan[ie]ll and Judith, bp. Feb. 18, 1732-3. C. R. 1.
Charles, s. Samuel K. and Susan, June 9, 1832.
Charles Frye, s. Tho[ma]s and Pheb[e], bp. Nov. 14, 1784. C. R. 1.
Dan[ie]ll, grands. Sam[ue]ll, bp. ——, 1720. C. R. 1.
Diah, s. twin, Jona[than], bp. Nov. 3, 1776. C. R. 2.
Ebenezer, s. Thomas and Phebe, Sept. 22, 1782.
Elisabeth, d. John and Sarah, Aug. 4, 1715.
Hannah, d. Elijah and Hannah, bp. Aug. 31, 1766. C. R. 1.
Levi, s. Jona[than], bp. Aug. 19, 1781. C. R. 2.
Mary, d. Samuel K. and Susan, July 14, 1834.
Osgood, s. Thomas and Phebe, June 4, 1780.
Phebe, d. Elijah and Hannah, bp. May 8, 1768. C. R. 1.
Phebe, d. Thomas and Phebe, Feb. 23, 1779.

HUTCHINSON, Ruth, d. Samuel and Elisabeth, Nov. 20, 1694.
Samuel, s. Daniel and Judeth, Sept. 23 [1731. C. R. 1.].
Sarah, d. John and Sarah, Sept. 24, 1719.
Solomon, s. twin, Jona[than], bp. Nov. 3, 1776. C. R. 2.
Susan, d. Samuel K. and Susan, July 15, 1830.
——, d. John and Sarah, Apr. 24, 1717.

ILLSLEY, Mary, d. Enoch and Mary, bp. ——, 1755. C. R. 1.

INGALLS (see also Engolls, Engols, Ingals, Ingols), Aaron, s. David and Priscilla, May 17, 1767.
[Abiah. C. R. 1.], d. James and Mary, Oct. 18, 1731.
Abigail, d. Henry and Abigail, Jan. 15, 1692-3.
Amos, s. David and Prissilla, Mar. 14, 1763.
Ann, d. Moses and Meriah, Nov. 12, 1734.
Anna, d. twin, Daniel and Sarah, June 11, 1760.
Asa, s. Isaac and Rebeccah, June 4, 1764.
Asa, s. Francis and Eunice, Jan. 17, 1766.
Benjamin, s. John and Sarah, Nov. 8 [1716].
Benjamin, s. Moses and Meriah, Aug. 1 [1728. C. R. 1.].
Benj[ami]n Pearson, s. Benj[ami]n and Rebeckah, June 24, 1763.
Betty, d. Abijah and Elizabeth, Aug. 21, 1775.
Charles Nathan, s. Francis and Elizabeth, July 9, 1820.
Cyrus, s. Francis and Eunice, Dec. 13, 1768.
Daniel, s. Samuel and Sarah, July 30, 1689.
Daniel, s. Sam[ue]l and Sarah, Oct. 13, 1696.
David, s. Henry and Hannah, Jan. 3, 1725-6.
Deborah, d. Samuel and Sarah, Apr. 1, 1691.
Deborah, d. Sam[ue]l and Sarah, July 21, 1694.
Deborah, d. James and Mary, Apr. 29, 1722.
Deborah, d. John and Deborah, Mar. 24, 1763.
Dolly, d. Ezra and Dolly, Oct. 29, 1802.
Ebenezer, s. Josiah, jr. and Eunice, No [v.]1 [1745. C. R. 1.].
Ebenezer, s. Ebenezer and Sarah, June 11, 1759.
Ebenezer, s. Ebenezer and Sarah, Nov. 11, 1760.
Eleanor, d. Ebenezer and Sarah, Sept. 12, 1771.
Elijah, s. Daniel and Sarah, Apr. 5, 1767.
Elisabeth, d. Joseph and Phebe, Aug. 21, 1739.
Elizabeth, d. Joshua and Eliz[abe]th, Sept. 2, 1762.
Ephraim, s. James and Mary, Nov. 26, 1723.
Ezra, s. Abijah and Elizabeth, Apr. 12, 1773.
Ezra, s. Ezra and Dolly, Jan. 7, 1804.
Francis, s. Henry and Abigail, Dec. 20, 1694.

INGALLS, Francis, s. Francis and Lydea, Aug. 26, 17[21].
Francis, s. Francis and Lidea, Jan. 26, 1730 [-1].
Francis, s. Francis and Unice, May 30, 1760.
George F[rancis. P. R. 79.], s. Capt. Francis and Elizabeth, Mar. 4, 1818.
[Habijah. C. R. 1.], s. Francies and Lydia, Dec. ——, 1737.
Hannah, d. James and Hannah, Jan. 2, 1696-7.
Hannah, d. twin, Henry and Hannah, June 4, 1721.
Hannah, d. [Lt. C. R. 1.] John and Deborah, June 1, 1765.
Harriott, d. Ezra and Dolly [Dorothy. C. R. 2.], Mar. 12, 1814.
Henry, s. Henry and Abigall, Apr. 2, 1689.
Henry, s. Henry, jr. and Sarah, Apr. 20, 1746.
Henry Franklin, s. Francis and Elisabeth B. (Foster), Apr. 19, 1830. P. R. 79.
Henry Putnam, s. Putnam and Fanny, July 21, 1813.
Hiram Augustus, s. Francis and Elisabeth B. (Foster), Aug. 10, 1822. P. R. 79.
Hutchinson, s. Abijah and Elizabeth, May 6, 1769.
Ira, s. Jonathan and Sarah, Apr. 21, 1797.
Isaac, s. Henry and Hannah, Sept. 2, 1733.
Isaiah, s. Francis and Lydea, June 6, 1723.
Isaiah, s. Francis and Lydea, May 27, 1729.
Isaiah, s. Francies and Lydia, Sept. 11, 1742.
James, s. James and Hannah, Aug. 9, 1695.
James, s. James and Mary, Aug. 30, 1720.
[James. C. R. 1.], s. James, jr. and Mary, Aug. —, 1747.
James, s. Ebenezer and Sarah, July 1, 1768.
Jedediah, s. [Lt. C. R. 1.] John and Deborah, July 26, 1768.
Jemima, d. Francies and Lydia, July 27, 1740.
Jeremiah, s. Abijah and Elizabeth, Mar. 1, 1764.
John, s. John and Sarah, Mar. 23, 1696-7.
John, s. Henry and Hannah, Apr. 25, 1728.
[John. C. R. 1.], s. Moses and Moriah, July 9, 1739.
John, s. John and Deborah, Sept. 11, 1760.
Jonathan, s. Francis and Eunice, Feb. 25, 1762.
Jonathan, s. Abijah and Eliz[abe]th, Sept. 16, 1765.
Joseph, s. Henry and Mary, Mar. 2, 1674-5.
Joseph, s. Henry and Abigail, Apr. 17, 1697.
Joseph, s. Joseph and Phebe [Jan.]— [1721-2].
Joseph, s. Joseph and Phebe, Aug. 9 [1723].
Joseph, s. Nathan, bp. Apr. —, 1789. C. R. 1.
Joseph, s. Simeon and Betty, bp. Dec. 20, 1789. C. R. 1.
Joshua, s. Joseph and Phebe, Jan. 30, 1[728-9].
[Joshua. C. R. 1.], s. Joseph and Phebe, Aug. 13, 1732.

INGALLS, Josiah, s. Henery and Mary, Feb. 28, 1676.
Josiah, s. Josiah and Eunice, Oct. 31, 1747.
Judieth, d. twin, Henry and Hannah, June 4, 1721.
Judith, d. Capt. Henry and Sarah, Mar. 4, 1760.
La deme, d. Stephen and Lydia, Oct. 30, 1789.
Lucy Foster, d. Ezra and Dolly, Sept. 18, 1807.
Lydia, d. James and Hannah, Dec. 18, 1698.
Lydia, d. Francis and Lydia, May 11, 1727.
[Lydia. C. R. I.], d. Francis and Lydea, Aug. 13, 1732.
Lydia, d. Abijah and Eliz[abe]th, Oct. 7, 1767.
Lydia, d. Stephen and Lydia, Nov. 11, 1787.
Marcy, d. David and Priscilla, Apr. 29, 1761.
Maria C., d. Ezra and Dolly, Apr. 3, 1817.
Mary, d. Henry and Abigail, Feb. 25, 1690-91.
Mary, d. James and Mary, Sept. 7, 1727.
Mary, d. James, jr. and Mary, Dec. 1, 1745.
Mary, d. Ezra and Dolly, Sept. 9, 1819.
Mehetabel, d. Isaac and Rebeckah, Oct. 22, 1762.
Mehitable, d. Jonathan and Sarah, Nov. 3, 1800.
Micajah, s. Benjamin and Rebeccah, Nov. 10, 1764.
Moses, s. Sam[ue]ll and Sarah, May 30, 1687.
Moses Kimball, s. Hutchinson and Molly, Dec. 7, 1801.
Nathaniel, s. David and Priscilla, May 24, 1765.
Olive, d. Isaac and Rebeckah, Apr. 15, 1760.
Olive, d. twin, Daniel and Sarah, June 11, 1760.
Peter, s. Joseph and Phebe, Oct. 28, 1741.
Peter, s. Joshua and Eliz[abe]th, Jan. 14, 1766.
Peter, s. Simeon and Betty, bp. Nov. 18, 1787. C. R. I.
Phebe, d. Joseph and Phebe, July 7, 1725.
Phebe, d. Joshua and Eliz[abe]th, Dec. 30, 1768.
Polly, d. Daniel and Mary, bp. Oct. 8, 1786. C. R. I.
Putnun, s. Capt. Henry and Sarah, Dec. 18, 1763.
Rebeca, d. Henry and Hannah, Jan. 15, 1[730. C. R. I.].
Rob[er]t Fletcher, s. Daniel and Sarah, Sept. 26, 1763.
Ruben, s. Ebenezer and Sarah, Dec. 19, 1769.
Ruth, d. Samuel and Sarah, Feb. 19, 1698-9.
Sally, d. Jonathan and Sarah, Sept. 22, 1795.
[Samuel. C. R. I.], s. Moses and Meriah, Nov. 11, 1722.
Samuel, s. Daniel and Sarah, Aug. 13, 1747.
Samuel, s. Francis, bp. Nov. 24, 1765. C. R. I.
Samuel, s. Ebenezer and Sarah, Nov. 29, 1765.
Samuell, s. Sam[ue]ll and Sarah, May 7, 1683.
Sarah, d. Henery and Mary, Jan. 22, 1679.
Sarah, d. Sam[ue]ll and Sarah, Mar. 21, 1684-5.

INGALLS, Sarah, d. John and Sarah, Nov. 29, 1698.
Sarah, d. Francies and Lydia, Apr. 8, 1736.
Sarah, d. Henry and Hannah, Nov. 23, 1738.
Sarah, d. Henry, jr. and Sarah, Jan. 14 [1744-5. C. R. 1.].
Sarah, d. Daniel and Sarah, Aug. 24, 1745.
Sarah, d. David and Priscilla, June 5, 1771.
Sarah, d. Solomon and Mercy, Nov. 27, 1782.
Sarah Elizabeth, d. Charles N., carpenter, and Hannah A., Nov. 8, 1846.
Sarah Foster, d. Francis and Elisabeth B. (Foster), Mar. 28, 1824. P. R. 79.
Simeon, s. James and Mary, Jan. 12, 1735-6.
Simmeon, s. Joshua and Elizabeth, Sept. 3, 1764.
Solomon, s. Solomon and Mercy, July 5, 1781.
Stephen, s. Joseph and Phebe, Apr. 23, 1737.
Stephen, s. Joshua and Elizabeth, June 17, 1761.
Stephen, s. Stephen and Lydia, bp. July 28, 1793. C. R. 1.
Stephen W[illiam. P. R. 79.], s. Francis and Elizabeth [B. P. R. 79.], Jan. 1, 1834. [1833. P. R. 79.]
Susanna, d. Capt. Henry and Sarah, June 4, 1762.
Susanna, d. William and Susanna, Apr. 27, 1763.
Tabitha, d. Joseph and Phebe, Mar. 23, 1726-7.
Tabitha, d. Joseph and Phebe, Mar. 14, 1734-5.
Theodore, s. Francis and Eunice, Mar. 30, 1764.
Unice, d. Francis and Eunice, Oct. 16, 1770.
William, s. Moses and Meriah, Apr. 7, 1730.
William, s. Moses and Moriah, June 28, 1737.
William, s. Benj[ami]n and Rebecca, Sept. 19, 1768.
Wilson, s. Ezra and Dolly, Mar. 25, 1809.
Zebadiah, s. James and Mary, Nov. 3, 1729.
——, d. James and Hannah, Sept. 11, 1714.
——, d. Henry and Hannah, Sept. 12, 1723.
——, s. Francis and Lydea, Jan. 27, 1724-5.
——, d. Moses and Meriah, Oct. 5, 1725.
——, s. James and Mary, Nov. 6, 1725.
——, d. Joseph and Phebe, Aug. 10, 1730.
——, d. Francis and Lidea, June 27, 1734.

INGALS (see also Ingalls), Abigail Carlton, d. Solomon and Mercy, May 28, 1780.
Abigal, d. Ebenezer and Sarah, Oct. 14, 1749.
Abijah, s. Abijah, bp. Apr. 28, 1771. C. R. 2.
Abijah, s. Hutchinson and Molly [Polly. C. R. 1.], Sept. 21, 1798.
Augustus, s. Capt. Francis and Elizabeth, Aug. 10, 1822.

INGALS, Caleb, s. Josiah and Eunice, Feb. 22, 1756.
Daniel, s. Daniel and Sarah, June 9, 1754.
Daniel, s. Capt. Henery and Sarah, Jan. 13, 1758.
Daniel, s. Daniel and Sarah, Feb. 9, 1758.
David, s. David and Prescila, Feb. 19, 1750-51.
Deborah, d. Jos[eph] and Phebe, bp. ——, 1728. C. R. 1.
Deborah, d. James and Mary, May 28, 1753.
Deborah, d. John and Deborah, Jan. 22, 1758.
Dorcis, d. James and Mary, Feb. 18, 1750-51.
Edman, s. David and Presila, July 3, 1757.
Francis, s. Jonathan and Sarah, Aug. 18, 1793.
Hannah, d. James and Mary, Dec. 27, 1748.
Hannah, d. David and Presila, Feb. 20, 1759.
Henery, s. Henery and Sarah, Nov. 22, 1752.
Hipzibah, d. Isaac and Mary, Dec. 10, 1774.
Isaac, s. Isaac and Rebeca, Nov. 8, 1754.
Isaac, s. Isaac and Mary, May 12, 1770. [bp. May 6, 1770. C. R. 2.]
Isaiah, s. Francis, jr. and Eunes, July 13, 1756.
Isarel, s. David and Prisala, Dec. 26, 1754.
Jacob, s. Isaac and Rebeca, Feb. 24, 1757.
Jacob, s. Isaac and Mary, Aug. 27, 1772.
James, s. James and Mary, June 19, 1755.
John E[dward. P. R. 79.], s. Capt. Francis and Elizabeth, Apr. 29, 1826.
Jonathan, s. Josiah, jr. and Eunice, Dec. 4, 1753.
Molle, d. Ebenezer and Sarah, Nov. 24, 1751.
Moriah, d. Daniel and Sarah, Dec. 14, 1749.
Moses, s. Daniel and Sarah, Feb. 23, 1756.
Nabby, d. Henry, jr. and Abigail, June 17, 1778.
Nathan, s. Francis, jr. and Eunis, June 12, 1755.
Nathaniel, s. Josiah and Unice, Sept. 19, 1751.
Pheb[e] Abbot, d. Nathan and Lydia, bp. Apr. 15, 1787. C. R. 1.
Phineas, s. Francis, jr. and Unis, Nov. 14, 1758.
Precilla, d. David and Precilla, Feb. 1, 1753.
Rebeca, d. Henery and Sarah, July 4, 1754.
Rebecca, d. Isaac and Mary, June 16, 1766.
Ruth, d. Daniel and Sarah, July 26, 1752.
Sarah, d. Henery, jr. and Sarah, July 25, 1748.
Sarah, d. Ebenezer and Sarah, Nov. 6, 1753.
Sarah F., d. Capt. Francis and Elizabeth, Mar. 28, 1824.
Sarah Putnam, d. Daniel, bp. Apr. 18, 1790. C. R. 1.
Simeon, s. Josiah, jr. and Eunice, Aug. 24, 1749.
Solomon, s. Henery and Sarah, June 16, 1750.

INGALS, Susanna, d. Ebenezer and Sarah, Jan. 26, 1756.
——, ch. [torn] and Hannah, Dec. 18, 1704.
——, s. Ebenezer and Sarah, Apr. 21, 1758.

INGOLS (see also Ingalls), Abigail, d. Josiah and Mary, ——, [1709-10].
Anne, d. Josiah and Esther, June 6 [1717].
Daniel, s. Moses and Moriah, Feb. — [1713-14.].
Elizabeth, d. twin, Sarah, July 24 [1710].
Henery, s. Henery and Hannah, Apr. 13, 1719.
Hephzibah, d. James and Hannah, —— [1711].
Martha, d. John and Sarah, Feb. 9, 1712-13.
Nathaniell, s. Samuell and Sarah, —— [1703].
Pheoby, d. Josiah and Mary, —— [1707?].
Priscilla, d. [torn] [1706].
Rachell, d. Josiah and Mary, Sept. 3, 1713.
[Ruth. c. r. 1.], d. Moses and Moriah, Jan. 1, 1719-20.
Stephen, s. twin, [torn] and Sarah, July 24 [1710].
——, ch. John and Sarah, June 22, 1701.
——, ch. [torn] and Hannah, —— 13 [1701].
——, d. John and Sarah, Mar. 27, 1705-6.
——, ch. Josiah and Mary, May 15, 1706.
——, d. James and Hannah, May 31, 1709.
——, ch. [torn] and Mary, May 22, 1712.
——, ch. [Mos]es and Moriah, Dec. 18, 1716.

JACKSON, Caleb, s. Caleb and Hannah, June 14, 1786.
Caroline R[ebecca. c. r. 3.], d. Rev. Samuel C. and Caroline [T. c. r. 3.], Jan. 5, 1830.
Mary Angeline, d. Samuel C., clergyman, and Caroline T., May 28, 1847.
Nathan, s. Joseph and Cesiah, Sept. 7, 1748.
Samuel, s. Caleb and Hannah, Oct. 25, 1790.
Samuel Charles, s. Rev. Samuel C. and Caroline [T. c. r. 3.], May 28, 1841.
Samuel W[illiam. c. r. 3.], s. Rev. Sam[ue]l C. and Caroline [T. c. r. 3.], May 1, 1838.
Sarah Hale, d. Caleb and Hannah, Aug. 5, 1788.
Susanna Elizabeth, d. Sam[ue]l C. and Caroline T., July 28, 1833. c. r. 3.
William [True. c. r. 3.], s. Rev. Samuel C. and Caroline T., Nov. 17 [19. dup.], 1843.

JAMES, Abby H[arriet. c. r. 2.], d. Woodbridge L. and Phebe, Jan. 3, 1843.

JAMES, Caroline Frances, d. Woodbridge L., student in theology, of Bangor, Me., and Phebe G., Apr. 1, 1845.

JAQUITH, Abigail Ann, d. James and Phebe, June 28, 1824. P. R. 70.
Benjamin Franklin, s. James and Phebe (Goldsmith), Feb. 14, 1822. P. R. 70.
Caroline Augusta, d. James and Phebe [Jan. 14. P. R. 70.], 1839. C. R. 2.
Dorcas Jane, d. James and Phebe, Oct. 10, 1826. P. R. 70.
Edwin, s. James and Phebe, Oct. 2, 1833. P. R. 70.
Eliza Ann, d. Henry and Eliza, Apr. 14, 1829.
Ellen Crosby, d. James and Phebe, May 11, 1836. P. R. 70.
Hannah A[bbott. P. R. 70.], d. James and Phebe, Mar. 10, 1816.
Henry, s. twin, James and Phebe, May 15, 1829.
Henrietta, d. twin, James and Phebe, May 15, 1829.
Henrietta Maria, d. James and Lydia, Aug. 29, 1848. P. R. 70.
James, s. James and Phebe, Mar. 15, 1818.
Mary, d. James and Phebe, Dec. 5, 1819.
Mary C., d. Nathaniel and Eleanor, Aug. 31, 1808.
Newton, s. James and Phebe, Oct. 9, 1831. P. R. 70.
Phebe [Goldsmith. P. R. 70.], d. James and Phebe, Mar. 29, 1814.
Sarah Elizabeth, d. Henry and Eliza, Mar. 5, 1843.
William H[enry. C. R. 2.], s. Henry and Eliza, Feb. 25, 1831.
——, s. James and Phebe, Feb. 14, 1822.
——, s. James and Phebe, May 25, 1824.
——, d. James and Phebe, Oct. 10, 1826.

JENKINGS (see also Jenkins), Samuel W., s. Samuel, jr. and Servier, Apr. 13, 1813.

JENKINS (see also Ginkins, Jenkings), Anna, d. Samuel, jr. and Anna, Dec. 17, 1766.
Benjamin, s. Samuel and Rebeca, Dec. 7, 1756.
Benjamin, s. Benjamin and Peggy, Apr. 4, 1786.
Benjamin, s. William, bp. May 24, 1835. C. R. 2.
Benjamin Flint, s. Capt. Benj[ami]n, jr. and Eliz[abe]th, July 3, 1822.
Benjamin O., s. Samuel, jr. and Servier, July 2, 1815.
Charles, s. Joel and Phebe, Mar. 20, 1820.
Damon, s. Samuel, jr. and Mary, Sept. 19, 1836.
Ebenezer, s. Samuel and Lydia, Apr. 28, 1807.
Ebenezer, s. Ebenezer and Sally, June 5, 1831

JENKINS, Edward K., s. Capt. Benja[min] and Betsey, Oct. 14, 1831.
Eliab, s. Joel and Patty, Jan. 11, 1793.
Elizabeth, d. Lt. Samuel and Anna, Jan. 23, 1777.
Elizabeth, d. Benja[min], jr. and Betsy, Dec. 22, 1826.
Emily A., d. Albert H., farmer, and Nancy A., Sept. 3, 1845.
Emily E., d. Jacob, cordwainer, and Elizabeth P., Oct. 11, 1845.
Farnham, s. Samuel, jr. and Mary, Nov. 2, 1833.
Francis H., s. Albert H., farmer, and Nancy A., July 4, 1848.
Hanna[h], d. Joel and Patty [Oct?] 3, 1787.
Henry, s. Joel and Phebe, Aug. 14, 1809.
Isabel M. H., d. Jacob, laborer, and Elizabeth, June 18, 1848.
Jacob, s. Joel and Phebe, Aug. 17, 1812.
Joel, s. Samuel and Rebeca, Apr. 29, 1751.
Joel, s. Samuel and Rebeca, June 4, 1754.
Joel, s. Joel and Patty, Oct. 23, 1780.
Joel, s. Joel and Phebe, at Albany, Me., Sept. 15, 1807.
Jonn B., s. Capt. Benj[ami]n and Betsey, Oct. 7, 1829.
Jonathan, s. Joel and Patty, June 4, 1782.
Joseph, s. Benjamin, jr. and Elizabeth, Jan. 10, 1802.
Lydea, d. Samuel and Rebeca, Nov. 9, 1746.
Lydia, d. Joel and Patty, Nov. 2, 1783.
Lydia, d. Samuel and Lydia, June 14, 1801.
Lydia, d. Ebenezer and Sally, Mar. 3, 1833. P. R. 49.
[Lydia D. P. R. 100.], d. Samuel, farmer, and Mary K., Nov. 1, 1847.
Margret Flint, d. William and Polly, Apr. 17, 1819.
Margret Flint, d. W[illia]m and Polly, Jan. 15, 1825.
Mary, d. Samuel, jr. and Mary, Mar. 26, 1839.
Mary Farnum, d. William and Polly, July 23, 1821.
Matilda H., d. Ebenezer and Sally (Russell), Jan. 14, 1842. P. R. 49.
Matilda H., d. Ebenezer and Sally (Russell), Apr. 5, 1847. P. R. 49.
Micah, s. Joel and Patty, July 26, 1786.
Milon S[cott. P. R. 101.], s. Benjamin F., farmer, and Abigail F., Sept. 19, 1848.
Milton, s. William, bp. Dec. 9, 1832. C. R. 2.
Milton, s. Ebenezer and Sally, Mar. 29, 1835.
Molly, d. Samuel, jr. and Anna, July 23, 1768.
Nabby, d. Joel and Patty, Nov. 26, 1778.
Nancy, d. Ebenezer and Sally, Mar. 19, 1838.
Nathan, s. Joel and Patty, Oct. 7, 1789.
Noah, s. Joel and Phebe, Sept. 8, 1814.
Omer, s. Ebenezer and Sally (Russell), Jan. 9, 1840. P. R. 49.

JENKINS, Patty, d. Joel and Pattey, June 26, 1777.
Polly, d. Joel and Patty, Apr. 24, 1791.
Putnam, s. Samuel and Mary K., Oct. 8, 1841. P. R. 100.
Rebecca, d. Samuel, jr. and Anna, Feb. 23, 1773.
Samuel, s. Samuel and Anna, Jan. 3, 1775.
Samuel, s. Benjamin and Peggy [Elizabeth. C. R. 1.], June 4, 1790.
Samuel, s. Samuel and Lydia, Apr. 9, 1803.
Samuel, s. Eben, farmer, and Sally, July 15, 1845.
Samuel C., s. Samuel, jr. and Mary, Mar. 1, 1832.
Samuel Flint, s. Benjamin and Elizabeth, bp. Feb. 14, 1796. C. R. 1.
Sarah, d. Samuel, jr. and Anna, Oct. 21, 1770.
Sarah Barns, d. Benjamin and Elizabeth, bp. Nov. 25, 1798. C. R. 1.
Wendell Phillips, s. Eben[eze]r, farmer, and Sally, Jan. 25, 1849.
William, s. Lt. Benjamin and Peggy, June 31, 1795.
William, s. William, bp. June 12, 1831. C. R. 2.
William, s. Albert H., yeoman, and Nancy A., Nov. 15, 1846.
William Geo[rge], s. Joel and Phebe, Sept. 11, 1826.
William S., s. Benja[min], jr. and Elizabeth, July 5, 1824.
William T., s. Joel and Phebe, Sept. 10, 1826.
——, d. Samuel and Rebeca, Mar. 26, 1748.
——, 1st ch. Ebenezer and Sally (Russell), Aug. 6, 1829. P. R. 49.
——, s. Ebenezer and Sally, Feb. 9, 1840.

JENNINGS, David, s. Joseph and Elezebith, Dec. 19, 1750.
Jonathan, s. Joseph and Elezebeth, Mar. 7, 1753.

JENNESS, see Genniss.

JEWIT (see also Jewitte), James, s. Rose, Mar. 7, 1816.

JEWITTE (see also Jewit), Levina, d. Rose, Mar. 28, 1819.

JOANES (see also Jones), Benjamin, s. Wiliam and Rebeca, Nov. 16, 1747.
James, s. Wiliam and Rebeca, Jan. 11, 1749-50.

JOCELYN, Cassendana Arabella, d. Leavitt and Hannah E., bp. May 24, 1840. C. R. 3.
Georgianna Albedina, d. Leavitt and Hannah E., bp. May 24, 1840. C. R. 3.
Oscar Fitzalon, s. Leavitt and Hannah E., bp. May 24, 1840. C. R. 3.

JOHNSON, Abbigall, d. Stephen aad Elizabeth, May 22, 1675.
Abiah, d. Asa and Dolly, Sept. 20, 1795.
Abiall, s. [torn], —— [1702].
Abigail, d. Stephen and Mary, Feb. 21, 1759.
Abigail, d. Elizabeth, bp. July 17, 1763. C. R. 2.
Abigail, d. David, bp. Sept. 17, 1797. C. R. 2.
Abigal, d. Obed and Abigel, Apr. 19, 1756.
Abigall, d. [St]ephen and Elizabeth, Mar. 16, 1681-2. [Mar. 8. CT. R.]
Abraham, s. Hannah, "Reputed" s. Abraham Dor, Jan. 5, 1742-3.
Adam, s. Francis and Sarah, June 1, 1699.
Adam, s. Samuel and Anne, Sept. 27, 1742.
Addam, s. Samuel and Anne, July 20, 173[2. C. R. 1.].
Adeline, d. Edmond and Anna, Mar. 8, 1800.
Alfred Osgood, s. F., bp. June 18, 1837. C. R. 6.
Andrew, s. Jam[es], Oct. —, 1695.
Andrew, s. Andrew and Hannah, Jan. 16, 1723-4.
[Andrew. C. R. 2.], s. Andrew and Hannah, Feb. 1, 1724-5.
Ann, d. Steven and Elizabeth, Feb. 25, 1668.
Ann Maria, d. Edmond and Anna, June 18, 1812.
Anna, d. Sam[ue]ll, jr. and Anna, Mar. 27, 1771.
Anne, d. Samuel and Anne, Sept. 21, 1728.
Anne, d. Asa and Anne, at Charlestown, June 21, 1737.
Anne, d. Samuel and Anne, Apr. 16, 173[9. C. R. 1.].
Anne, d. Capt. Samuel [jr. C. R. 1.] and Anne, Dec. 31, 1777.
Annis, d. twin, James and Annis, Dec. 3, 1772.
Asa, s. Asa and Anne, Dec. 23, 1738.
Asa, s. Capt. Samuel and Elezebith, June 6, 1758.
Asa, s. Capt. Samuel and Elizabeth, Nov. 27, 1762.
Asa, s. Asa and Dolly, Oct. 22, 1797.
Benjamin, s. twin, Stephen and Elizabeth, Aug. 12, 167[7].
Benjamin, s. Willia[m] and Sarah, Dec. 3, 1689.
Benjamin, s. Benjamine and Sarah, July 5, 1715.
Benjamin, s. Caleb and Lydia, Nov. 2, 1727.
Benjamin, s. Francis and Mary, Mar. 10, 1728-9.
Benjamin, s. William and Susanna, at Sheepscot, Feb. 6, 1739-40.
Benjamin, s. Asa and Anne, May 24, 1744.
Benjamin, s. John, 3d and Este, Sept. 22, 1755.
Benjamin, s. Benjamin and Sarah, June 6, 1800.
Betsey, d. Capt. Samuel and Anna, Feb. 28, 1782.
Betsey, d. Ebenezer and Elinor, Dec. 8, 1789.
Betty, d. Phineas and Hannah, June 21, 1778.
Betty, d. John and Hannah, Sept. 1, 1779.

JOHNSON, Caleb, s. William and Sarah, Oct. 19, 1694.
[Caleb, s. C. R. 2.], Caleb and Mary, Nov. 22, 1717.
Catharine, d. Capt. Joshua and Martha, Oct. 31, 1803.
Charles Bickford, s. Solon L. and Louisa, bp. Aug. 16, 1840. C. R. 3.
Charles Frederick, s. John and Hannah [P. P. R. 79.], May 16, 1823.
Charles H[enry. C. R. 1.], s. Dr. Samuel and Susanna, Nov. 14, 1840.
Charles Henry, s. Isaac A., machinist, and Julia, Apr. 12, 1848.
Clara A., d. John G., laborer, and Sarah N., July 15, 1846.
David, s. Josiah and Anness, Aug. 20, 1715.
David, s. Andrew and Hannah, June 1, 1729.
David, s. Francis and Mary, Mar. 5, 1730-31.
David [Daniel. C. R. 1.], s. Francis and Mary, Feb. 23, 1732-3.
David, s. John, bp. Sept. 22, 1771. C. R. 2.
David, s. Jacob and Sarah, July 11, 1772.
David, s. Peter, bp. May 26, 1793. C. R. 2.
Dean, s. Phineas and Hannah, Feb. 20, 1785.
[Deborah. C. R. 2.], d. Obadiah and Debrah [July?] 5, 1642.
Deborah, d. Obadiah, jr., bp. Jan. 13, 1760. C. R. 2.
Dolivar, s. Jacob, bp. Sept. 11, 1774. C. R. 2.
Dolley Kimbal, d. Capt. Samuel and Anne, Mar. 21, 1780.
Dolly, d. Peter, bp. June 9, 1782. C. R. 2.
Dolly, d. Asa and Dolly, Feb. 2, 1800.
Dorathy, d. John and Pheoby, May 3, 1719.
Ebenezer, s. Francis and Mary, Oct. 10, 1724.
Ebenezer, s. Ebenezer and Sarah, Feb. 6, 1749-50.
Ebenezer, s. Ebenezer and Eloner, bp. Jan. 3, 1773. C. R. 1.
Ebenezer, s. Ebenezer and Eleanor, Mar. 14, 1774.
Edmond, s. Eben[eze]r and Eleanor, May 14, 1770.
Edmond, s. Lt. Sam[ue]ll [jr. C. R. 1.] and Anne, Mar. 23, 1775.
Edward, s. John and Lydia, June 28, 1805.
Edward Francis, s. Theron, farmer, and Sarah Jane, Nov. 4, 1844.
Elisabeth, d. Andrew and Hannah, Apr. 18, 1737.
Elisabeth, d. Samuel and Elisabeth, May 31, 1745.
Eliner, d. Zebadiah and Hannah, June 10, 1738.
Elinor Edmunds, d. Stephen, jr. and Sally, Dec. 14, 1806.
Elizabeth, d. James and Elizabeth, Jan. 17, 1692-3.
Elizabeth, d. Capt. Sam[ue]ll and Elizabeth, Oct. 17, 1760.
Elizabeth, d. Jacob, bp. Oct. 29, 1769. C. R. 2.
Elizabeth, d. Capt. Joshua and Martha, Apr. 2, 1801.
Elizabeth, d. Samuel, jr. and Mary, Oct. 12, 1808.
Elizabeth, d. W[illia]m, jr. and Betsey, Sept. 28, 1819

JOHNSON, Elizabeth, d. John and Hannah, bp. Oct. 17, 1819. C. R. 1.
Elizebath, d. twin, Obadiah and Hannah, Feb. 27, 1728-9.
Ellenor, d. John and Ellenor, Dec. 26, 1697.
Ephraim, s. Andrew and Hannah, Dec. 21, 1739.
Ephraim, s. Andrew and Hannah, Mar. 31, 1742.
Eunice, d. Peter, bp. June 9, 1782. C. R. 2.
Fanny, d. Peter, bp. June 9, 1782. C. R. 2.
Fanney, d. Osgood and Fanney, Nov. 8, 1804.
Frances E[lizabeth. C. R. 6.], d. Osgood and Lucretia, May 17, 1830.
Francis, s. Steven and Elizabeth, Mar. 15, 1666.
Francis, s. Francis and Sarah, Feb. 28, 1695-6.
Frederick, s. Phinehas and Hannah, bp. Aug. 10, 1788. C. R. 1.
George P. [Spofford. P. R. 79.], s. John and Hannah P., Nov. 7, 1828.
Hanah, d. John and Phebe, Sept. 22, 1726.
Hannah, d. Francies and Hannah, Mar. 3, 1717-18.
Hannah, d. Zebadiah and Hannah, Mar. 31, 17[24. C. R. 2.].
[Hannah. C. R. 2.], d. twin, Obadiah and Hannah, Feb. 27, 1728-9.
Hannah, d. John and Lydia, July 25, 1739.
Hannah, d. Obadiah and Dorathy, Feb. 8, 1753.
Hannah, d. Obadiah, jr., bp. Sept. 19, 1762. C. R. 2.
Hannah, d. Phineas and Hannah, May 12, 1772.
Hannah, d. twin, James and Annis, Dec. 3, 1772.
Hannah, d. John, jr. and Hannah, Feb. 26, 1774.
Hannah, d. Peter, bp. July 6, 1783. C. R. 2.
Hannah Blanchard, d. Jacob, bp. June 20, 1782. C. R. 2.
Hannah Fuller, d. William, jr. and Eliza[beth], Sept. 21, 1802.
Hannah P[arker. C. R. 1.], d. John and Hannah P., Jan. 16, 1827.
Horatio, s. Solon L. and Louisa, bp. Aug. 16, 1840. C. R. 3.
Isaac, s. Josiah and Annes, July 17, 1724.
Isaac, s. wid. Anna [Asa and Anna. C. R. 1.], Mar. 15, 1748-9.
Isaac, s. Jacob and Sarah, July 28, 1763.
Isaac, s. Samuel, jr. and Anna, July 6, 1769.
Isaac, s. Isaac and Alice, bp. Feb. 18, 1781. C. R. 1.
Isaac, s. Asa and Dolly, June 22, 1804.
Isaac, s. Isaac, spinner, and Sarah A., Nov. 4, 1845.
Jacob, s. Obadiah and Hannah, May 19, 1727.
Jacob, s. Jacob and Sarah, July 28, 1759.
James, s. Thomas and Mary, Feb. 4, 1672.
James, s. James and Elisabeth, Feb. 4, 1693-4.

JOHNSON, James, s. James and Sarah, —— [1718]. [bp. May 25, 1718. C. R. 2.]
James, s. Asa and Anne, Sept. 13, 174[0. C. R. 1.].
James, s. Andrew and Hannah, Oct. 15, 1743.
James, s. Obadiah, jr., bp. Aug. 25, 1765. C. R. 2.
James, s. James and Annis, Mar. 26, 1769.
James, s. Lt. William and Mary, Mar. 3, 1783.
James, s. Osgood and Lucretia, June 3, 1833.
James E., s. Samuel K., machinist, and Lucy A., b. Methuen, Jan. 15, 1849.
James H[arris. P. R. 79.], s. John and Hannah [P. P. R. 79.], Apr. 17, 1820.
Jane G[ardner. P. R. 79.], d. John and Hannah P., May 4, 1835.
Jemima, d. Thomas and Mary, Jan. 1, 1678.
Jenny, d. Ebenezer and Elinor, May 24, 1792.
Jesse K., s. John G., laborer, and Sarah N., June 10, 1848.
John, s. Thomas and Mary, Feb. 28 [16]67.
John, s. Timothy and Rebecca (Aslett), June 29, 1677.
[John. T. C.], s. John and Elenor, Feb. 24, 1690-91.
John, s. John and Pheoby, —— [1711-12?].
John, s. John and Lydia, Apr. 9, 1744.
John, s. Zebadiah, bp. June 28, 1747. C. R. 2.
John, s. John, 3d and Lydea, July 28, 1748.
John, s. John, bp. June 4, 1769. C. R. 2.
John, s John and Hannah, Dec. 8, 1777.
John, s. Ebenezer and Elinor, Apr. 12, 1786.
John, s. Benja[min] and Sarah, Sept. 7, 1793.
John, s. Benjamin and Sarah, Dec. 6, 1797.
John, s. Dr. Samuel and Susan, Oct. 10, 1833.
John Abbot, s. John and Hannah, July 21, 1810.
[John Aslebe. C. R. 1.], ——lebe s. John and Lydia, Apr. 27, 1738.
John E[dmund. P. R. 79.], s. John and Hannah [P. P. R. 79.], Sept. 17, 1818.
John Edmunds, s. William, jr. and Eliza[beth], Feb. 13, 1804.
John Gardner, s. Stephen and Sarah, Dec. 23, 1818.
Jonathan, s. Frances and Sarah, —— [1705?].
Jonathan, s. Andrew and Hannah, Jan. 27, 1731-2.
Joseph, s. twin, Stephen and Elizabeth, Aug. 12, 167[7].
Joseph, s. James and Sarah [bp. May 19, 1717. C. R. 2.].
Joseph, s. Jacob and Sarah, Apr. 1, 1765.
Joseph, s. Peter, bp. May 24, 1789. C. R. 2.
Joshua, s. Samuel, jr. and Elezebith, Feb. 13, 1752.
Joshua, s. Capt. Samuel and Elezebith, June 8, 1756.

JOHNSON, Joshua, s. Capt. [Lt. C. R. 1.] Joshua and Martha, Mar. 17, 1799.
Josiah, s. Thomas and Mary, Oct. 29, 1683.
Josiah, s. Josiah and Anness, Apr. 2, 1722.
Josiah, s. Andrew and Hannah, Aug. 31, 1734.
Josiah, s. Obadiah, jr. and Lydea, Dec. 18, 1751.
Leonard, s. Edmond and Anna, Mar. 22, 1803.
Leonard, s. John and Hannah, Jan. 16, 1812.
Louisa Peabody, d. Mary, June 22, 1828.
Lucretia O., d. Osgood and Lucretia, Jan. 30, 1835.
Lydea, d. Obadiah, jr. and Lydea, Aug. 30, 1754.
Lydia, d. John and Elenor, May 26, 1695.
Lydia, d. Caleb and Lydia, Sept. 4 [1719. C. R. 2.].
[Lydia. C. R. 2.], d. Zabadiah and Hannah, Nov. 14, 1725.
Lydia, d. Zebediah and Hannah, Feb. 27, 1735-6.
Lydia, d. John, jr. and Lydia, Feb. 23, 1745-6.
Lydia, d. Zebediah, jr. and Lydia, Aug. 4, 1764.
Lydia, d. John and Hannah, Dec. 8, 1775.
Lydia, d. Stephen and Mary [Abigail. C. R. 1.], Sept. 24, 1778.
Martha, d. Capt. Samuel, jr. and Anna, Mar. 28, 1784.
Martha, d. Lt. Joshua and Martha, Mar. 23, 1797.
Mary, d. Thomas and Mary, Feb. 11, 1659.
Mary, d. Stephen and Elizabeth, Mar. 21, 1673.
Mary, d. Returne and Mary, Oct. 9, 1678.
Mary, d. Timothy and Rebecca (Aslett), Feb. 3, 1682.
Mary, d. James and Elizabeth, Feb. —, 1701-2.
Mary, d. Josiah and Anness, Nov. 10, 17[19. C. R. 1.].
Mary, d. Caleb and Lydea, June 26, 172[1. C. R. 2.].
Mary, d. Zebed[iah], bp. May 25, 1729. C. R. 2.
Mary, d. Obadiah, jr., bp. Oct. 3, 1756. C. R. 2.
Mary, d. John and Margaret, bp. Nov. 20, 1768. C. R. 2.
Mary, d. Samuel, jr. and Mary, Feb. 27, 1805.
Mary, d. Stephen, jr. and Sarah, June 12, 1811.
Mary, d. Col. Theron and Sarah Jane, Jan. 18, 1840.
Mary E. [Allen. C. R. 1; Ellen. P. R. 79.], d. John and Hannah P., Aug. 10, 1833.
Mary E[lizabeth. C. R. 1.], d. Samuel, jr. and Susanna, Mar. 28, 1835.
Mehetabell, d. James and Elizabeth, ——ber —, 1701.
Mehetebel, d. Caleb and Lydea, Jan. 27, 1725-6.
Mehitabel, d. Willia[m] and Sarah, July 12, 1686.
Mercy, d. Timothy and Rebecca (Aslett), Nov. 18, 1687.
Molly, d. William and Mary, Mar. 9, 1774.
Moses H., s. Henry H., mason, b. Vt., and Phebe A., Aug. 12, 1849.

JOHNSON, Nabe, d. Asa and Anne, Oct. 7, 1747.
Nancy, d. Asa and Dolly, June 2, 1809.
Nancy, d. Nancy, July 4, 1834.
Nathan, s. Wiliam and Bethiah, Jan. 10, 1749-50.
Nathan, s. William, jr. and Betsy, Mar. 8, 1809.
Nath[anie]ll, s. Zebediah, jr. and Lydia, July 8, 1766.
Obadiah, s. James and Elizabeth [after 1695].
[Obadiah. C. R. 2.], s. Obadiah and Hannah, Nov. 20, 1725.
Obadiah, s. Obadiah, jr. and Lydea, Nov. 14, 1749.
Obed, s. Obed and Abigal, Dec. 18, 1750.
Obediah, s. Peter, bp. Oct. 8, 1785. C. R. 2.
Osgood, s. Jacob and Sarah, June 24, 1777.
Osgood, s. Osgood and Fanney, Sept. 9, 1803.
Osgood, s. Jacob and Fanny, July 9, 1826.
Osgood, s. Osgood, bp. Oct. —, 1831. C. R. 6.
Pamela, d. Peter, bp. June 26, 1796. C. R. 2.
Penelope, d. Timothy and Rebecca (Aslett), Feb. 13, 1680.
Penelope, d. John and Pheobe, Mar. 7, 1715-16.
Peeter, s. James and [torn] [after 1695].
Peter, s. Thomas and Mary, Aug. 8, 1675.
Peter, s. Timothy and Rebecca (Aslett), Jan. 31, 1685-6.
Peter, s. James and Sarah, Sept. 9, 1719.
Peter, s. twin, Obediah and Dorathy, July 26, 1749.
Peter, s. Samuel, jr. and Elezebith, Aug. 26, 1749.
Peter, s. Peter, bp. June 9, 1782. C. R. 2.
Peter, s. Asa and Dolly, July 6, 1811.
Phebe, d. Thomas and Mary, Jan. 3, 1664.
Phebe, d. John and Elenor, Feb. 2, 1699-1700.
Phebe, d. Zebadiah and Hannah, Mar. 16, 1733-4.
Phebe, d. John and Easter, Mar. 24, 1759.
Phebe, d. Stephen and Mary, Dec. 27, 1760.
Phebe, d. Capt. William and Mary, Jan. 4, 1790.
Phebe, d. Benjamin and Sarah, May 22, 1803.
Pheoby, d. John and Pheoby, June 10, 1714.
Phineas, s. twin, Obediah and Dorathy, July 26, 1749.
Phineas, s. Jacob and Sarah, Sept. 1, 1761.
Phineas, s. Phineas and Hannah, Oct. 30, 1775.
Phinehas, s. Samuel, jr. and Elisabeth, May 28, 1747.
Polly Blanchard, d. Peter, bp. June 9, 1782. C. R. 2.
Rebecca, d. Benjamin and Sarah, May 26, 1805.
Rebecca, d. Osgood and Fanney, Mar. 11, 1806.
Rebeccah, d. John and Hannah, Oct. 24, 1783.
Rebeccah, d. Edmond and Anna, Oct. 12, 1817.
Rebeccah Abbot, d. Osgood, bp. Mar. 23, 1806. C. R. 2.

JOHNSON, Rebeckah, d. John and Easter, Nov. 5, 1761.
Rebeckah, d. Wil[lia]m [jr. C. R. 1.] and Betsey, Feb. 18, 1813.
Rebekah, d. Asa and Dolly, Feb. 21, 1814.
Richard Henry, s. Solon L. and Louisa, bp. Aug. 16, 1840. C. R. 3.
Rooxbe, d. Ens. Joshua and Martha, Dec. 8, 1792.
Sally, d. John and Hannah, bp. Sept. —, 1781. C. R. 1.
Samuel, s. Timothy and Rebecca (Aslett), July 25, 1684.
Samuel, s. Timothy and Katherine, Mar. 23, 1712-13.
Samuel, s. Samuel and Anne, June 18, 1730.
Samuel, s. Samuel and Anne, Nov. 6, 1740.
Samuel, s. John, jr. and Lydia, Apr. 17, 1742.
Samuel, s. Samuel and Elisabeth, Apr. 5, 1743.
Samuel, s. Asa, bp. ——, 1744. C. R. 1.
Samuel, s. Obed and Abigal, Dec. 30, 1753.
Samuel, s. Zebediah, jr. and Lydia, July 1, 1762.
Samuel, s. John and Esther, Aug. 20, 1767.
Samuel, s. Samuel, jr. and Anna, Mar. 17, 1773.
Samuel, s. Capt. Samuel and Hannah, bp. July 20, 1788. C. R. 1.
Samuel, s. Ens. Joshua and Martha, Dec. 18, 1790.
Samuel, s. Peter, bp. Feb. 27, 1791. C. R. 2.
Samuel, s. Samuel, jr. and Mary, Mar. 10, 1800.
Samuel, s. Edmond and Anna, May 10, 1821.
Samuel, s. Dr. Sam[ue]l and Susanna, Apr. 20, 1831.
Samuell, s. Francies and Sarah, —— [1703].
Sam[ue]ll Marble, s. Capt. William and Mary, May 23, 1792.
Sarah, d. William and Sarah, Apr. 18, 1681.
Sarah, d. Francis and Sarah, Oct. 30, 1693.
Sarah, d. Timothy and Catharine, Nov. —[1719. C. R. 1.].
Sarah, d. Caleb and Lydea, May 19, 1724.
Sarah, d. Zebadiah and Hannah, Dec. 18, 1731.
Sarah, d. Francies and Mary, Oct. 31, 1737.
Sarah, d. Wiliam and Bethiah, Aug. 22, 1752.
Sarah, d. Ebenezer and Sarah, Sept. 1, 1752.
Sarah, d. Jacob and Sarah, Feb. 29, 1767.
Sarah, d. [Capt. C. R. 1.] Samuel, jr. and Eliza[beth], Apr. 15, 1768.
Sarah, d. Lt. William and Mary, Sept. 23, 1780.
Sarah, d. Phineas and Hannah, Nov. 12, 1782.
Sarah, d. Ebenezer and Elinor, Mar. 27, 1784.
Sarah, d. Capt. William and Mary, Aug. 16, 1787.
Sarah, d. Benj[ami]n and Sarah, Sept. 6, 1795.
Sarah, d. Asa and Dolly, bp. Feb. 19, 1804. C. R. 1.
Sarah, d. Asa and Dolly, June 7, 1807.
Sarah A., d. Isaac, manufacturer, and Sarah A., Aug. 31, 1843.

JOHNSON, Sarah Bowen, d. William, jr. and Betsey, Apr. 25, 1807.
Serena Parker, d. Lt. William and Mary, July 25, 1785.
Sidin Harris, d. Nancy, Oct. 24, 1828.
Solon, s. Solon L. and Louisa, bp. Aug. 16, 1840. C. R. 3.
Stephen, s. Stephen and Elizabeth, Dec. 7, 1679.
Stephen, s. Francies and Mary, Jan. 1, 1735-6. [bp. Jan. 5, 1734-5. C. R. 1.]
Stephen, s. Samuel and Anne, Mar. 1, 1735-6.
Stephen, s. Francies and Mary, Jan. 13, 1740-41.
Stephen, s. William and Susanna, at Sheepscot, Oct. 17, 1742.
Stephen, s. Samuel and Anne, Aug. 29, 1745.
Stephen, s. Ebenezer and Elinor, Sept. 25, 1780.
Steven, s. Steven and Elizabeth, Feb. 4, 1672.
Susan E., d. Isaac, laborer, July 7, 184[7 or 8].
Susan Maria, d. Samuel, jr., physician, and Susanna, Aug. 14, 1843.
Susanah, d. Asa and Dolly, Mar. 2, 1802.
Susanna, d. Thomas and Mary, Oct. 4, 1662.
Susanna, d. Francies and Sarah, — [1713-14].
Susanna, d. William and Mary, June 28, 1776.
Susannah, d. William and Sarah, Dec. 30, 1682.
Susannah, d. William and Sarah, Mar. 7, 1683-4.
Tabitha, d. John and Elenor, Apr. 4, 1693.
Theron, s. Capt. William and Mary, Sept. 6, 1794.
Thomas, s. Thomas and Mary, Oct. 19, 1670.
Thomas, s. Andrew and Hannah, Apr. 23, 1727.
Timothy, s. Timothy and Rebeckah, Mar. 25, 1679.
Timothy, s. Timothy and Rebecca (Aslett), Mar. 25, 1697.
Timothy, s. Timothy and [torn], —— [1705-6].
Timothy, s. Asa and Anne, Aug. 10, 1742.
Timothy, s. Samuel, jr. and Elezebith, July 16, 1754.
Timothy, s. Lt. Joshua and Martha, Jan. 14, 1795.
Wiliam, s. Wiliam and Bethiah, Feb. 25, 1747-8.
Wiliam, s. Wiliam and Bethiah, May 3, 1756.
William, s. William and Sarah, May 23, 1692.
William, s. Francies and Sarah,—— [1708?].
[William. C. R. 2.], s. Caleb and Lydea, Nov. 5, 1722.
William, s. Asa and Anna, Dec. 7, 1745.
William, s. Ebenezer and Elinor, Jan. 5, 1778.
William, s. William and Mary, June 19, 1778.
William Mitchell, s. Col. Theron and Sarah Jane, Aug. 16, 1842.
Zebadiah, s. Zebadiah and Hannah, Sept. 20, 1742.
Zebediah, s. Zebediah and Lydia, Mar. 25, 1769.
——, ch. [torn] and Sarah, —— [1701].

JOHNSON, ——, ch. [torn] and Elener,—— [1702-3].
——, ch. [torn] and Hannah, Jan. 13, 1704-5.
——, ch. [J]ohn and Mary, Oct. 5, 1709.
——, ch. [T]imothy and Katherine, Mar. 27, 1711.
——, d. Francies and Sarah, June 21, 1712.
——, d. Josiah and Annes, Aug. 29, 1712.
——, d. Timothy and Katherine, Jan. 16, 1714-15.
——, s. Timothy and Katherine, Mar. 27, 1716.
——, d. Josiah and Anness, Dec. 17, 1717.
——, d. Timothy and Catherine, Dec. 27, 1717.
——, d. John and Phebe, Aug. 23, 1721.
——, d. Francis and Mary, Apr. 20, 1726.
——, s. Charles, Jan. 18, 1827.
——, ch. John and Hannah P., bp. June 7, 1835. C. R. 1.
——, s. John G., farmer, and Sarah N., June 10, 1848.
——, ch. Francis and Sarah, [torn].

JONES (see also Joanes), Abbot, s. Ebenezer and Elizabeth, July 4, 1789.
Abigail, d. Elizabeth, of Woburn, bp. Nov. 30, 1729. C. R. 2.
Abigail, d. Jacob, bp. Oct. 29, 1786. C. R. 2.
Alford, s. Jacob and Hannah, at Lyndboro, N. H., Jan. 19, 1813.
Almira, d. Ebenezer and Mary, May 25, 1837.
Ann, d. Tho[ma]s and Sarah, b. Bradford, bp. Oct. 26, 1845. C. R. 4.
Anna, d. Nathan and Dorcas, July 17, 1801.
Anna E[liza. C. R. 2.], d. Eben[eze]r, jr. and Mary K., Oct. 17, 1830.
Betsey, d. Eben[eze]r and Elizabeth, at Wilmington, Oct. 4, 1780.
Charles E., s. Reuben and Rachel, Mar. 13, 1832.
Dorcas, d. Nathan and Dorcas, Oct. 24, 1803. [d. wid. Dorcas, bp. Sept. 30, 1804. C. R. 2.]
Dorcas, d. Hermon and Sally, Jan. 6, 1820.
Ebenezer, s. Ebenezer and Elizabeth, Jan. 31, 1792.
Eliab, s. Jacob and Hannah, Mar. 17, 1809.
Elias, s. Jewett and Susanna, Nov. 15, 1827.
Elizabeth, d. Elizabeth, of Woburn, bp. Nov. 30, 1729. C. R. 2.
Elizabeth, d. Josiah and Rebecca, Feb. 28, 1770.
Elizabeth Abbot, d. Jewett and Susanna, Feb. 7, 1812.
Elizabeth S[ettle. C. R. 4.], d. Thomas, flaxdresser, and Sarah, Jan. 9, 1847.
Elmira, d. Ebenezer, bp. Aug. 20, 1837. C. R. 2.
Gardiner, s. Hermon and Sally, Dec. 8, 1823.

JONES, Gardner, s. Nathan and Dorcas, Oct. 3, 1798.
Hannah Burt, d. Nathan and Hannah, Apr. 18, 1815.
Hannah Mehitable, d. Ebenezer, bp. Nov. 17, 1833. C. R. 2.
Harriot [Maria. C. R. 2.], d. Jewett and Susanna, Mar. 27, 1824.
Hermon, s. Nathan and Dorcas, Oct. 27, 1793.
Hermon, s. Hermon and Sally, July 6, 1831.
Hezekiah Wynn, s. Ebenezer and Elizabeth, Feb. 14, 1794.
Jacob, s. Ebenezer and Elizabeth, Aug. 13, 1782.
Jacob, s. Nathan and Dorcas, May 8, 1789.
Jacob, s. Jacob and Hannah, Sept. 3, 1807.
James W., s. Joab, farmer, and Elizabeth, both b. Reading, Aug. 13, 1849.
Jesse, s. Josiah and [M]ary, Oct. 2, 1757.
Jesse, s. Josiah and Sarah, Feb. 18, 1782.
Jewett, s. Ebenezer and Elizabeth, June 15, 1784.
Jewett, s. Jewett and Susannah, Oct. 16, 1810.
Joanna, d. Jacob, bp. Oct. 29, 1786. C. R. 2.
Jonathan, s. Josiah and Rebecca, Apr. 15, 1766.
Josiah, s. Josiah and Marey, Sept. 5, 1755.
Lemuel Howe, s. Samuel and Mary, of Passamaquoddy, bp. June 26, 1791. C. R. 2.
Lucy, d. Abiel and Lucy, Dec. —, 1818.
Lydia, d. Nathan and Dorcas, Oct. 25, 1790.
Maria, d. Jacob and Hannah, Feb. 11, 1811.
Martha [Ann. C. R. 2.], d. Jewett and Susannah, Sept. 16, 1814.
Martha M[aria. C. R. 2.], d. Reuben and Rachel, Feb. 9, 1835.
Mary, d. Josiah and Rebbecca, Jan. 20, 1768.
Mary, d. Ebenezer and Elizabeth, July 29, 1786.
Mary, d. Phillip, Mar. 28, 1842.
Mary E[lizabeth. C. R. 2.], d. Eben[eze]r, jr. and Mary K., Sept. 21, 1828.
Mary Jane, d. Jewett and Susanna, Jan. 27 [28. dup.], 1816.
Nancy [Maria. C. R. 2.], d. Nathan and Hannah, May 8, 1820.
Nathan, s. Nathan and Dorcas, Mar. 8, 1792.
Nathan Frye, s. Nathan and Hannah, July 12, 1812.
Phebe, d. Elizabeth, of Woburn, bp. Nov. 30, 1729. C. R. 2.
Phebe, d. Jacob, bp. Oct. 29, 1786. C. R. 2.
Phebe, d. Nathan and Dorcas, Sept. 22, 1795.
Phebe, d. Nathan and Dorcas, Apr. 16, 1799.
Phebe Ann, d. Hermon and Sally, Nov. 23, 1828.
Phebe Ann, d. Reuben, farmer, and Rachael, Dec. 27, 1844.
Rebeca, d. Wiliam and Rebeca, May 11, 1752.
Rebeccah, d. Josiah and Rebeccah, Feb. 7, 1765.
Reuben A[bbot. C. R. 2.], s. Reuben and Rachel, Aug. 23, 1829.

JONES, Sarah, d. Hermon and Sally, Aug. 12, 1821.
Sarah Abbot, d. Jewett and Susanna, Nov. 5, 1817.
Sarah Jane, d. Ebenezer and Mary, June 8, 1835.
Susanna, d. Jewett and Susanna, Sept. 1, 1819.
Wallace S., s. Charles F., trader, and Sarah B., both b. Boston, Sept. 10, 1849.
Willard, s. Jewett and Susanna, Aug. 11, 1821.
William, s. William and Rebecca, at Wilmington, Oct. 30, 1745.
William, s. Thomas, flax-dresser, and Sarah, both b. Scotland, July 7, 1848.
——, s. Jacob, Apr. 6, 1821.
——, ch. David and Ruth, Feb. 7, 1823.
——, s. Ebenezer, farmer, and Mary J., Dec. 10, 1843.

JORDAN (see also Jordon), Caleb S[tevens. P. R. 48.], s. Russell and Maria, Aug. 13, 1832.
Emma A[ugusta. P. R. 48.], d. Russell B. and Maria, Aug. 9, 1835.
Sarah M[aria. P. R. 48.], d. Russell B. and Maria, Feb. 27, 1834.
Williard R[ussell. P. R. 48.], s. Russell B. and Maria, July 14, 1838.

JORDON (see also Jordan), Clara L[ouisa. P. R. 48.], d. Russell B., cordwainer, and Maria, Sept. 27, 1846.

JOYCE, William, s. James, laborer, and Catherine, both b. Ireland, Dec. 7, 1849.

KEATING (see also Cating), Teresa, d. Thomas, manufacturer, and Eliza, July 23, 1843.

KEILEY, Mary E., d. John, tailor, and Anstice, Dec. 26, 1846.

KELLEY (see also Kelly), Mary Jane, d. Daniel, carpenter, and Elizabeth, Apr. 5, 1847.
——, d. Daniel and Hannah, Apr. —, 1822.

KELLY (see also Kelley), Daniel, s. Samuel, laborer, and Judith, Sept. 24, 1847.
Hannah B., d. Daniel and Mary, Nov. 29, 1819.
Thomas, s. Daniel, laborer, and Elizabeth, Apr. 9, 1849.

KEMBALL (see also Kimball), [Mehetable. C. R. 1.] ——le, d. Daniel and Mehit[abel], May 4, 1738.

KEMP (see also Kempe), Henrietta O., d. Enoch N., laborer, and Abby, May 4, 1848.
Sarah, d. Samuell and Sarah, Apr. 18, 1679. [1678. CT. R.]
Zerubbabel, s. Samuel and Sarah, May 23, 1677.

KEMPE (see also Kemp), Ann, d. Samuell and Sara, May 16, 1671.

KENAN, John, s. John, flannel-dresser, and Bridget, Apr. 16, 1847.

KENDAL (see also Kendall), Ephraim, s. Ephraim and Molly, June 17, 1786.
Harriot, d. Ephraim and Molly, Aug. 24, 1796.
Herman, s. Ephraim and Mary, July 18, 1804.
Thomas, s. Ephraim and Mary, Nov. 16, 1799.

KENDALL (see also Kendal), Joseph, s. Ephraim and Molly, Oct. 10, 1788.
Lydia H., d. Thomas P. and Lydia, Mar. 23, 1824.
Samuel, s. Ephraim and Molly, Aug. 12, 1790.
Samuel, s. Ephraim and Molly, Nov. —, 1794.
Susan P[ierce. C. R. 2.], d. Isaac and Susan [Susanna. C. R. 2.] P., Mar. 13, 1813.
Walter, s. Ephraim and Molly, Oct. 18, 1792.

KENISTON (see also Kenniston), Prescott N., s. Noah, carpenter, and Mary E., July 29, 1846.

KENNETT, Caroline Maria, d. William, manufacturer, and Frances, Feb. 9, 1844.
Eliza J., d. Thomas, laborer, and Catherine, Apr. 20, 1849.
George, s. John, carpenter, and Elizabeth, Oct. 19, 1848.
Harriet F., d. William, laborer, and Frances, Jan. 28, 1849.

KENNEY (see also Kinney), William H., s. William, laborer, Oct. 14, 184[7 or 8].

KENNISTON (see also Keniston), Emma L[adorah. P. R. 84.], d. Henry, mason, b. Effingham, N. H., and Sarah, b. Epping, N. H., July 13, 1849.

KENT, Abby Maria, d. Justin, blacksmith, and Harriet, Mar. 11, 1848.
Charles, s. Hathaway, laborer, and Maria M., Mar. 25, 1849.

KENT, David D., s. David and Mary, Mar. 10, 1828.
Eadah Frances, d. Micajah and Roxana, July 30, 1838.
Maria Augusta, d. Micajah and Roxana, Jan. 3, 1836.
Mary E. B., d. David and Mary, Jan. 18, 1830.
Mary L., d. Micajah and Roxana, Feb. 15, 1830.
——, s. Justin and Harriet, Apr. 28, 1846.

KERSHAW, James Franklin, s. Edward, spinner, and Elizabeth, both b. England, Sept. 1, 1849.
John A., s. Edward, spinner, and Elizabeth, Jan. 19, 1847.
Maria, d. James, manufacturer, and Ruhamah, Jan. 8, 1844.

KEYES, James, s. Edward, farmer, and Eliza, both b. Ireland, May 6, 1849.

KIDDER, Sarah Dix, d. Francis and Nancy, July 1, 1825.
Susan K. [Haywood. C. R. 2.], d. Francis and Nancy, Nov. 4, 1827.

KIMBAL (see also Kimball), Abiel, s. Daniel, jr. and Mary, Mar. —, 1782. [bp. Mar. 31. C. R. 1.]
Abraham, s. Moses and Jane, Mar. 8, 1773.
Alford [Alfred. C. R. 1.], s. Daniel and Mary, Aug. 29, 1791.
Andrew, s. Moses and Doratha, Nov. 18, 1780.
Daniel, s. Daniel and Mary, May 10, 1787.
Dolly Stevens [Dolly Martain. C. R. 1.], d. Daniel and Mary, May 8, 1795.
Eliza, d. Andrew and Mary, Nov. 30, 1811.
Hiram, s. Andrew and Mary, Mar. 17, 1810.
Jacob, s. Daniel and Mary, June 12, 1798.
John, s. John, jr. and Hannah, Nov. 19, 1771.
Jeremiah, s. Daniel and Mary, July 1, 1789.
Mary, d. Jacob and Sarah, Dec. 12, 1727.
Mary, d. Daniel and Mary, Oct. 18, 1785.
Mary, d. Andrew and Mary, Aug. 30, 1806.
Mehitabel, d. Joseph and Lucy, Sept. 8, 1790.
Mehitable, d. Daniel, jr. and Mary, Sept. 6, 1780.
Moses, s. Moses and Jane, Feb. 14, 1775.
Phebe, d. Moses and Doratha, Mar. 2, 1779.
Phebe, d. Moses, jr. and Hannah, Feb. 1, 1794.
Salley, d. Moses and Jane, Mar. 29, 1779.
Sarah, d. Daniel and Mary, May 6, 1793.
Sarah, d. Andrew and Mary, Mar. 17, 1805.
William, s. Moses and Jane, Apr. 10, 1777.
William, s. Joseph and Lucy, Oct. 7, 1793.
——, d. Daniel and Hester, Oct. 8, 1723.

KIMBALL (see also Kemball, Kimbal, Kimbel, Kimbol, Kimboll), Aaron, s. Aaron and Susanna, Sept. 12, 1747.
Abraham, s. William and Elizabeth, July 26, 1808.
Adeline Rebecca, d. Jesse and Lydia, Jan. 12, 1843.
Alonzo, s. Hiram, Apr. 3, 1843. P. R. 46.
Andrew, s. twin, Moses and Dorothy, Aug. 4, 1776.
Anna, d. Richard, bp. May 6, 1759. C. R. 1.
Anna, d. Sam[ue]l, bp. Jan. 13, 1760. C. R. 1.
Anna, d. Sam[ue]l, bp. June 8, 1766. C. R. 1.
Asa, s. Jacob and Sarah, June 15, 1738.
Asa, s. [torn] h, Nov. 16, 1767.
Benjamin, s. Jacob and Sarah, Mar. 22, 173[3-4].
Benjamin, s. twin, Moses and Dorothy, Aug. 4, 1776.
Benjamin, s. Benj[ami]n, Nov. 5, 1813.
Benjamin F[ranklin. C. R. 1.], s. William and Elizabeth, Nov. 14, 1805.
Betsey, d. Moses and Dorothy, Sept. 15, 1782.
Bettey, d. Moses and Jane, Aug. —, 1781.
Caroline, d. Seth and Rosina, Dec. 4, 1837.
Catharine, d. Thomas and Betsy, May 7, 1816.
Catherine K[ittredge. C. R. 1.], d. William and Elizabeth, May 3, 1811.
[Charles. P. R. 81.], s. Tho[ma]s and Betsey, Apr. 20, 1819.
Charles, s. Hiram, June —, 1830. P. R. 46.
Charles, s. Benj[amin] Franklin and Sarah J., Oct. 10, 1836.
Charles Gilbert, s. Seth and Rosena, Nov. 13, 1838.
Charles H., s. Tho[ma]s H. and Damaris, Feb. 13, 1835.
Charlotte, d. B. F., laborer, and Sarah D., Aug. 14, 1845.
Charlotte Gleason, d. Thomas H. and Damaris, Jan. 9, 1841.
Daniel, s. Daniel and Mehitable, July 6, 1741.
Daniel J., s. Jacob and Hannah, Feb. 7, 1837.
Deborah Lowthrop, d. Peter and Ruth, bp. Aug. 11, 1793. C. R. 1.
Dolly, d. Moses and Dorothy, June 8, 1765.
Dudley, s. Moses and Dorothy, Feb. 13, 1763.
Dudley, s. Moses and Dorathy, Sept. 9, 1784.
Edward, s. Benj[ami]n, June 10, 1816.
Elbridge E., s. Elbridge, cordwainer, and Deborah L., Apr. 12, 1847.
Eliza, d. Thomas and Betsy (Berry), Sept. 11, 1806. P. R. 81.
Eliza [Ann. P. R. 81.], d. Thomas and Betsey, Sept. 20, 1810.
Elizabeth, d. Benj[amin] F. and Sarah J., Apr. 10, 1839.
Ephraim, s. William and Elizabeth, Nov. 16, 1816.
Ephraim, s. Benjamin F. and Sarah D., Feb. 9, 1842.
Esther, d. Daniel, jr. and Mehetable, Mar. 25, 1743.

KIMBALL, Esther, d. —— and Esther (Barker), June 29, 1754. P. R. 51.
Ezra, s. Jessey and Susanna, Nov. 14, 1775.
Frank H. [A. P. R. 81.], s. Thomas H., blacksmith, and Damaris, July 20, 1849.
George, s. Benjamin F. and Sarah D., Aug. 13, 1830.
[Hannah. C. R. 1.], d. Daniel, jr. and Mehetebell, Oct. —, 1744.
Hannah, d. John, bp. May 26, 1776. C. R. 1.
Hannah, d. Moses and Jane, Nov. 25, 1786.
Hannah, d. William and Elizabeth, July 7, 1813.
Hannah [F. P. R. 81.], d. Thomas and Betsy, Mar. 16, 1801.
Henry G[orden. C. R. 1.], s. William and Elizabeth, July 6, 1819.
Henry G., s. Thomas H. and Damaris, Dec. 24, 1831.
Henry T., s. Thomas H. and Damaris, Dec. 24, 1830.
Hiram, s. Hiram, May —, 1838. P. R. 46.
Isaac F., s. Benj[ami]n, Dec. 13, 1811.
Israel, s. Asa and Huldah, Nov. 27, 1769.
Jacob, s. Moses and Dorothy, Mar. 22, 1764.
Jacob, s. Moses and Dorothy, Aug. 25, 1774.
Jane, d. Richard and Anna, Mar. 4, 1768.
Jedediah, s. Jesse and Susanna, May 25, 1766.
Jedediah, s. Asa and Huldah, Sept. 29, 1771.
Jeferson, s. Thomas and Betsey, July 12, 1808.
Jenne, d. Moses and Jane, July 25, 1789.
Jeremiah, s. Jesse and Susanna, Nov. 20, 1764.
Jese, s. Thomas and Betsey, Apr. 19, 1812.
Joel, s. Andrew and Mary, Feb. 23, 1814.
John, s. Moses and Dorothy, Jan. 14, 1771.
John, s. Daniel and Elizabeth, May 28, 1784.
John D., s. Thomas and Betsy, Apr. 11, 1821. [1822. P. R. 81.]
Josephine Eldora, d. illegitimate, Elizabeth, b. Lancaster, Ohio, Nov. 16, 1849.
Levina, d. Thomas and Betsy, July 19, 1814.
Lottie G., d. Thomas H. and Damaris (Gleason), Jan. 9, 1841. P. R. 81.
Lusey, d. Hiram, Nov. 12, 1840. P. R. 46.
Lydia, d. —— and Esther (Barker), Dec. 21, 1757. P. R. 51.
Lydia, d. Andrew and Easter, Mar. 9, 1761.
Lydia, d. John and Hannah, bp. Mar. 25, 1781. C. R. 1.
Lydia Angelia, d. Walter S., cordwainer, and Jane, Aug. 28, 1847.
Maria D., d. Thomas H. and Damaris, July 30, 1832.
Mariah [T. P. R. 81.], d. Thomas and Betsey, Jan. 18, 1803.
Mary, d. Moses and Jane, June 19, 1784.
Mary F., d. Jesse, farmer, and Lydia, Jan. —, 1848.

KIMBALL, Mehitable, d. —— and Esther (Barker), Mar. 13, 1752. P. R. 51.
Molly, d. Richard and Anna, bp. Dec. 20, 1761. C. R. 1.
Molly, d. Moses and Dorothy, Aug. 5, 1772.
Moses, s. Jacob and Sarah, Jan. 18, 1735-6.
Moses, s. Moses and Dorothy, Nov. 16, 1768.
Moses, s. William and Elizabeth, Jan. 13, 1803.
Nathan, s. Jesse and Susanna, Mar. 29, 1771.
Patty, d. John and Hannah, bp. June 24, 1787. C. R. 1.
Patty [Martha. P. R. 81.], d. Thomas and Betsey, May 9, 1796.
Peggy, d. Jesse and Susanna, May 16, 1769.
Phebe, d. Jacob and Sarah, Dec. 14, 1744.
Phebe, d. Daniel and Unice, bp. Apr. 23, 1769. C. R. 1.
Phebe, d. John and Hannah, bp. Mar. 14, 1779. C. R. 1.
Phebe, d. Moses and Jane, Oct. 30, 1791.
Philip, s. Sam[ue]l, bp. June 24, 1764. C. R. 1.
Pollina, d. Andrew and Mary, Mar. 13, 1808.
Putnam, s. Peter and Ruth, bp. Aug. 11, 1793. C. R. 1.
Rebecca, d. Josiah and Elizabeth, May 15, 1744.
Rheuba, d. William and Elizabeth, Oct. 14, 1800.
Rhoda, d. Richard, bp. Feb. 19, 1764. C. R. 1.
Richard, s. Jacob and Sarah, July 11, 1740.
Richard, s. Richard and Anna, Jan. 12, 1760.
Richard, s. Asa and Hulda, Jan. 24, 1764.
Ruby S., d. Thomas and Betsy, Jan. 21, 1818.
Ruth, d. Richard, bp. Feb. 9, 1766. C. R. 1.
Ruth, d. Jesse and Susanna, May 7, 1773.
Samuel, s. Asa and Hulda, Jan. 26, 1761.
Samuel, s. Peter and Ruth, bp. Aug. 11, 1793. C. R. 1.
Sarah, d. —— and Esther (Barker), Jan. 20, 1750. P. R. 51.
Sarah, d. Moses and Dorothy, Mar. 20, 1767.
Sarah, d. John and Hannah, bp. May 22, 1785. C. R. 1.
Sarah Elizabeth, d. Jesse and Lydia, Apr. 12, 1841.
Sarah J., d. Benj[amin] Franklin and Sarah J., July 1, 1832.
Susan Kittredge, d. Amos and Susannah, July 1, 1829. P. R. 52.
Susannah, d. Richard, bp. Apr. 15, 1770. C. R. 1.
Susannah, d. Moses and Jane, June 8, 1794.
Thomas, s. Thomas and Betsy (Berry), Nov. 25, 1798. P. R. 81.
Thomas, s. John and Hannah, Nov. 26, 1773.
Thomas, s. Jacob, Aug. —, 1841. P. R. 46.
Tho[ma]s Holton, s. Tho[ma]s and Betsey, Dec. 24, 1804.
Turner, s. Peter and Ruth, bp. Aug. 11, 1793. C. R. 1.
William, s. Moses, bp. Apr. 13, 1777. C. R. 2.
William G[ray. C. R. 1.], s. William and Betsey, Jan. 10, 1799.

KIMBALL, William Henry, s. Benj[amin] Franklin and Sarah J., May 21, 1834.
——, d. Jacob and Sarah, Aug. —, 1742.
——, d. Andrew and Mary, Aug. 30, 1824.
——, d. Seth and Rozena, Dec. 14, 1833.

KIMBEL (see also Kimball), Phebe, d. Thomas and Penelopy, July 5, 1743.

KIMBOL (see also Kimball), Beckee, d. Thomas and Penelopy, July 31, 1750.
Bette, d. Samuel and Ruth, Sept. 26, 1754.
Daniel, s. Daniel, jr. and Mehetebel, Oct. 6, 1750.
Ester, d. Andrew and Ester, June 29, 1754.
Hannah, d. Jacob and Sarah, Apr. 1 [1730].
Isaac, s. Andrew and Esther, June 20, 1748.
John, s. Thomas and Penelope, Mar. 26, 1748.
Marcy, d. Jacob and Sarah, Apr. 10, 1747.
[Mehit. C. R. 1.]ebel, d. Andrew and Easter, Mar. 13, 1752.
Nanne, d. Richard and Anne, June 12, 1756.
Peter, s. Samuel and Ruth, Nov. 26, 1752.
Ruth, d. Samuel and Ruth, Feb. 3, 1757.
Sarah, d. Jacob and Sarah, Aug. 2, 1725.
Sarah, d. Andrew and Easter, Jan. 21, 1749-50.
Thomas, s. Daniell and Esther, July 29, 1716.
Thomas, s. Thomas and Penelopy, July 17, 1753.
Wiliam, s. Richard and Anna, Dec. 16, 1757.
——, Jacob and Sarah, Feb. 26, 1731-2.

KIMBOLL (see also Kimball), Andrew, s. Daniel and Esther, Sept. 13, 1719.
——, s. Daniel and Esther, June 29, 1713.

KING,——, s. Zenas, Sept. 2, 1826.

KINNEY (see also Kenney), Amos, s. Tho[ma]s, bp. Oct. 6, 1782. C. R. 2.

KIRK, Robert, s. James, factory overseer, and Caroline, both b. Scotland, Oct. 17, 1849.

KITREG (see also Kittredge), Elezebith, d. Dr. John and Sarah, Apr. 30, 1751.
Mary, d. [Dr. C. R. 1.] John and Sarah, June 21, 1749.

KITTERIDG (see also Kittredge), Thomas, s. John and Sarah, July 13, 1746.

KITTERIDGE (see also Kittredge), Jacob, s. Dr., bp. —[1757]. C. R. 1.

KITTLE, Fidelia, d. Elias W. and Fidelia, Apr. 16, 1809.

KITTREDGE (see also Kitreg, Kitteridg, Kitteridge, Kittreg, Kittridg, Kittridge), Anna, d. Joseph, physician, and Henrietta F., b. Belfast, Me., Dec. 23, 1848.
George H[odges. C. R. 1.], s. Dr. Joseph and Hannah, Nov. 20, 1820.
Hannah M., d. Joseph and Hannah, July 17, 1834.
Joseph, s. Dr. Joseph and Hannah, May 25, 1822.
Maria, d. Dr. Thomas and Susanna, Dec. 26, 1792.
Mariah Franklin, d. John and Mary, bp. June 23, 1816. C. R. 1.
Martha L., d. Dr. Joseph and Hanah, Sept. 8, 1831.
Susan [Osgood. C. R. 1.], d. [Dr. C. R. 1.] and Hannah, Aug. 6, 1830.

KITTREG (see also Kittredge), Hannah, d. Dr. John and Sarah, Feb. 4, 1753.
John, s. Dr. John and Sarah, July 1, 1755.
Solomon, s. Solomon and Tabitha, Aug. 3, 1755.

KITTRIDG (see also Kittredge), John, s. Dr. Thomas and Susanna, Dec. 15, 1775.
Patty Osgood, d. Dr. Tho[ma]s and Susanna, Oct. 31, 1778.

KITTRIDGE (see also Kittredge), Allice, d. Samuel, bp. Feb. 6, 1791. C. R. 2.
Catherine, d. Dr. Thomas and Susanna, Nov. 15, 1788
David, s. Samuel, bp. Feb. 6, 1791. C. R. 2.
Hannah, d. Samuel, bp. Feb. 6, 1791. C. R. 2.
Hannah Armstrong, d. Dr. Joseph and Hannah, bp. Dec. 25, 1842. C. R. 1.
James, s. James and Mary, July 12, 1761.
Jeremiah, s. Samuel, bp. Feb. 6, 1791. C. R. 2.
John, s. Dr. Joseph and Hannah, July 10, 1826.
Joseph, s. Dr. Thomas and Susanna, Oct. 25, 1783.
Joseph, s. Dr. Joseph and Hannah, bp. Dec. 25, 1842. C. R. 1.
Mary Hodges, d. Dr. Joseph and Hannah, bp. Dec. 25, 1842. C. R. 1.
Sally [Sarah. C. R. 1.], d. Dr. Thomas and Susanna, Apr. 27, 1781.

KITTRIDGE, Samuel, s. Samuel, bp. Feb. 6, 1791. C. R. 2.
Sarah, d. Samuel, bp. Feb 6, 1791. C. R. 2.
Sarah, d. Dr. Joseph and Hannah, bp. Dec. 25, 1842. C. R. 1.
Sukey [Susanna. C. R. 1.], d. Dr. Thomas and Susanna, Aug. 10, 1772.

KNIGHTS, Elizabeth F., d. George W. and Elizabeth, Feb. 16, 1818.

KNOWLES, Lucy Ann, d. Jonathan, farmer, b. Concord, N. H., and Amanda, b. Hudson, N. H., May 10, 1849.

KNOWLTON, ——, ch. Mr. ——, Sept. 5, 1825.

LACE (see also Lacy), Joanna, d. Ephraim and Martha, Aug. 20, 1761.

LACEY (see also Lacy), Abigal, d. twin, Epharam and Martha, July 26, 1755.
Ephraim E., s. Ephraim, farmer, and Mary H., Aug. 17, 1847.
Wiliam, s. twin, Epharam and Martha, July 26, 1755.

LACIE (see also Lacy), Dorathy, d. Ephraim and Anne, May 20, 1716.

LACY (see also Lace, Lacey, Lacie, Lahorse, Lahorsey, Lasey), Andrew Kimbal, s. Epraim and Mehe[e]tabel, Oct. 16, 1792.
Betsey, d. Ephraim and Mehitable, Oct. 21, 1787.
David, s. Ephraim and Martha, Apr. 15, 1759.
Dorothy, d. Laurence and Mary, Aug. 6, 1677.
Ephraim, s. Ephraim and Mehitable, June 17, 1797.
Ephriam Everett, s. Ephriam, bp. Sept. 5, 1847. C. R. 1.
Hannah, d. John and Hannah, Dec. 31, 1797.
John, s. John and Hannah, June 4, 1801.
Laurence, s. Laurence and Mary, May 8, 1683.
Lydia, d. Ephraim and Mehitable, Nov. 13, 1789.
Mary, d. Laurence and Mary, May 25, 1674.
Mehitable, d. Ephraim and Mehitable, May 25, 1784.
Phebe, d. John and Hannah, July 22, 1806.
Sarah, d. Laurence and Mary, Oct. 1, 1686.
Thomas, s. John and Hannah, Mar. 9, 1787.
Thomas, s. John and Hannah, Jan. 6, 1804.
——, ch. [torn] and Anne, Dec. 10, 1713.
——, d. Andrew K. and Lydia, July 30, 1824.

LADD, Joseph J., s. Joseph and Eliza, Apr. 28, 1835.

LAHORSE (see also Lacy), [Ephraim Lacy. C. R. 1.], s. Ephraim and Anne, Mar. 13, 1720-21.
——, d. Ephraim and Anne, Jan. 25, 1723-4.

LAHORSEY (see also Lacy), [Ep]haram, s. Epharam and Martha, Dec. 20, 1750.

LAITON, Mary J., d. George and Phebe, Oct. 29, 1829.

LAMSON, Emelinah B[laney. C. R. 6.], d. Asa, boardinghouse keeper, and Sarah [D. C. R. 6.], Aug. 23, 1846.
John S[awyer. C. R. 2.], s. Samuel and Sarah A., Apr. 12, 1833.

LANDER, ——, s. Benjamin and Lydia, July 2, 1822.

LANE, Jeremiah, s. Patrick, laborer, and Bridget, Apr. 4, 1845.

LANGSTROTH, James Tucker, s. L. L., bp. Sept. 3, 1837. C. R. 2.

LASEY (see also Lacy), Elezebith, d. Epharam and Martha, Aug. 5, 1753.
Lydia, d. John and Hannah, Nov. 27, 1789.

LAWSON, William L., s. George, laborer, b. England, and Isabella, b. Scotland, Oct. 13, 1849.

LEAVITT (see also Leavetts), George Ayer, s. Jonathan, bp. Oct. 30, 1825. C. R. 6.
Mary Elizabeth, d. Jonathan, bp. Oct. 30, 1825. C. R. 6.
——, s. Jonathan and Joan, May 13, 1822.

LEAVETTS (see also Leavitt), Jonathan E[dwards. C. R. 2.], s. Maj. Jonathan and Loiza, July 24, 1827.

LeBARON (see also LeBarron), Frances, d. W[illia]m and Sarah, bp. July 10, 1842. C. R. 1.
William, s. Dr. Lemuel and Martha, Oct. 18, 1814.

LeBARRON (see also LeBaron), William, s. William, farmer, and Sarah J., Oct. 2, 1843.

LEE, Elizabeth Ann, d. William, dyer, and Eliza, both b. England, Oct. 8, 1849.
Hannah S., d. David, deceased, Feb. 15, 1818.
John, s. David and Deborah, Mar. 14, 1815.
Julia Anna, d. Joseph, cloth-dresser, and Ellen, Sept. 29, 1847.

LEFAVER (see also Feaver), Anne, d. Jacob and Hanah, Nov. 1, 1747.

LEGGET (see also Leggett), Anna, d. twin, James, spinner, and Elizabeth, both b. England, Nov. 28, 1849.
Sarah, d. twin, James, spinner, and Elizabeth, both b. England, Nov. 28, 1849.

LEGGETT (see also Legget, Leggit, Liggett), Mary E[lizabeth. C. R. 4.], d. James, manufacturer, and Elizabeth, Feb. 15, 1844.

LEGGIT (see also Leggett), James Isaac, s. James, bp. Aug. 2, 1846, a. 8 w. C. R. 4.

LEMAN (see also Lemon), Sarah E., d. Augustus F. and Hannah B., Dec. 2, 1839.

LEMON (see also Leman), Ebenezer Gile, s. William, book-binder, and Elizabeth, Sept. 13, 1847.
Mary Ellenwood, d. Augustus F., book-binder, and Hannah B., Oct. 29, 1848.
William Henry, s. William, book-binder, and Elizabeth, Nov. 10, 1845.

LEW, Barzilla, s. Barzilla and Dorcas, Aug. 28, 1805.
Zimry, s. Barzilla and Dorcas, Nov. 13, 1809.
——, s. Relief, July 17, 1825.

LEWIS (see also Lewiss), Elizabeth, d. Rhodnia A., laborer, and Lydia A., July 20, 1845.
Hellen G., d. Enoch, laborer, and Charlotte S., Dec. 13, 1848.
John B., s. John, bp. May 1, 1842. C. R. 2.
Sarah Matilda, d. Horace, farmer, b. New Boston, N. H., and Caroline, b. Malden, Sept. 5, 1849.
Stephen, s. Rodney, laborer, and Lydia A., at Lawrence, Mar. 11, 1849.

LEWISS (see also Lewis), Anne, d. Joanna, and "Reputed" d. Samuel Flood, June 13 [1738. C. R. 1.].

LIGGETT (see also Leggett), Hannah, d. twin, James, spinner, and Elizabeth, both b. England, Nov. 28, 1849.
Sarah, d. twin, James, spinner, and Elizabeth, both b. England, Nov. 28, 1849.

LINSEY, Mehetable Hardy, d. Sam[ue]l and Mehetable, bp. June 30, 1782. C. R. 1.
Rachel, d. Sam[ue]l and Rachel, bp. July 25, 1779. C. R. 1.
Samuel, "a Servant child to Benjamin Poor," ——, 1754. C. R. 1.

LISCOMB (see also Luscomb), Aaron N., s. Richard and Rhoda, Jan. 13, 1815.
Daniel Trow, s. Samuel and Jerusha, June 10, 1811.
Loisa, d. Samuel and Jerusha, Jan. 18, 1813.
Lucy Trow, d. Samuel and Jerusha, Nov. 23, 1806.
Lydia O., d. Richard and Rhoda, Feb. 6, 1819.
Martha, d. Samuel and Jerusha, Sept. 19, 1801. [1802. P. R. 94.]
Phebe M., d. Richard and Rhoda, Oct. 25, 1812.
Sally, d. Samuel and Jerusha, Mar. 13, 1804.
Susannah, d. Samuel and Jerusha, May 31, 1809.

LITTLE, John, s. Stephen W., machinist, and Abigail, Apr. 17, 1847.

LONG, Addeline, d. John and Mary, May 22, 1809.
Alfred, s. John and Mary, Apr. 28, 1814.
Augustus, s. Elijah, laborer, and Elisabeth, Dec. 4, 1844.
Benjamin, s. Josiah and Mary, Aug. 5, 1771.
Charles, s. Elijah and Elizabeth, Apr. 15, 1821.
Charlotte, d. Joshua and Rachel, bp. June 1, 1789. C. R. 1.
Darius, s. Josiah and Mary, Mar. 31, 1776.
Elijah, s. John and Hannah, Nov. 15, 1777.
Elijah, s. John, jr. and Mary, Mar. 29, 1807.
Elizabeth, d. John, bp. Sept. 14, 1806. C. R. 1.
Emily, d. Elijah, laborer, and Elizabeth, Jan. 22, 1847.
Hannah, d. Daniel and Hannah, bp. Sept. 18, 1774. C. R. 1.
Hannah, d. Josiah and Mary, Oct. 1, 1778.
Harriet A., d. William B., farmer, and Sarah, b. Boxford, May 17, 1849.
Harriot E., d. John and Mary, Oct. 5, 1820.
Henry, s. Elijah and Elizabeth, Aug. 8, 1819.

LONG, Henry, s. William and Sarah H., Dec. 5, 1842.
Jedediah, s. Daniel and Hannah, bp. Sept. 18, 1774. C. R. I.
Jeremiah, s. John, jr. and Mary, June 29, 1797.
John, s. John and Mary, bp. May 8, 1763. C. R. I.
John, s. John and Molly, Mar. 12, 1768-9. [*sic*]
John, s. John, jr. and Mary, Dec. 15, 1802.
Joshua, s. Josiah and Mary, July 24, 1760.
Josiah, s. Josiah and Mary, Apr. 24, 1766.
Lucretia, d. Joshua and Rachel, Jan. 14, 1780.
Marcy, d. John, jr. and Mary, May 5, 1805.
Mary, d. John, bp. Sept. 14, 1806. C. R. I.
Mehitable, d. John, jr. and Mary, Aug. 26, 1799.
Molly, d. John and Mary, bp. Sept. 20, 1767. C. R. I.
Nathaniel, s. John, jr. and Mary, May 30, 1760.
Rubee, d. Joshua and Rachel, bp. Oct. 30, 1785. C. R. I.
Ruth, d. Daniel and Hannah, bp. Sept. 18, 1774. C. R. I.
Sally [Sarah. C. R. I.], d. Josiah and Mary, May 24, 1763.
Samuel, s. Daniel and Hannah, bp. Sept. 18, 1774. C. R. I.
Sarah Hubbard, d. Joshua and Rachel, Feb. 28, 1784.
Sarah J., d. William, farmer, and Sarah, Apr. 3, 1845.
Stephen, s. John and Sarah, Sept. 18, 1751.
William B., s. Elijah and Elizabeth, Mar. 31, 1818.
——, d. Sarah, wid., Sept. 5, 1749.

LONGA, Betsy, d. Will[ia]m and Abigail, bp. Sept. 14, 1783. C. R. I.

LORD, Julia Maria, d. wid. Mary, bp. May 22, 1831. C. R. 2.
Mary Elizabeth, d. wid. Mary, bp. May 22, 1831. C. R. 2.
Thomas, s. John, laborer, and Betsy, Sept. 28, 1844.

LOREING (see also Loring), Gayton Pickman, s. Rev. Bailey and Sally P., Dec. 6, 1822.

LORING (see also Loreing), George Bailey, s. Rev. Bailey and Sally P., Nov. 8, 1817.
George B[ailey. C. R. I.], s. J. Osgood, farmer, and Ellen M[aria. C. R. I.], b. Danvers, Sept. 3, 1848.
Isaac O[sgood. C. R. I.], s. Rev. Bailey and Sally P., June 20, 1819.
John Alden, s. Rev. Bailey and Sally P., Aug. 12, 1824.
Mary Ann, d. Tho[ma]s and Sally, Sept. 25, 1813.

LOUEJOY (see also Lovejoy), Abigall, d. John and Mary, Aug. 20, 1669.
Ann, d. John and Mary, Dec. 21, 1659.
Benjamine, s. John and Mary, Dec. 4, 1664.
Christopher, s. John and Mary, Mar. 1, 1661-2.
Debora, d. John and Mary, Nov. 4, 1671.
Ebenezer, s. John and Mary, Jan. 22, 1673.
Frances, d. John and Naomie, Nov. 24, 1678.
Joseph, s. John [Thomas. CT. R.] and Mary, Feb. 8, 1662.
Mary, d. John and Mary, Apr. 11, 1652.
Nathaniell, s. John and Mary, May 29, [16]67.
William, s. John and Mary, Apr. 21, 1657.

LOUJOY (see also Lovejoy), Deborah, d. Nath[anie]ll, and Dorathy, —— [1703?].
[Deborah. C. R. 2.], d. Samuel and Hannah, Feb. 17, 1718-19.
Ezekiell, s. Nath[anie]ll and Dorathy, —— [1705?].
——, ch. John and Bathsheba, June 28, 1709.

LOVEJOY (see also Louejoy, Loujoy, Lovjoy), Abia, d. Bodwell and Sally, bp. Oct. 3, 1824. C. R. 2.
Abiah, d. Orlando and Abiah, Mar. 26, 1817.
Abial, s. Christopher and Mary, May 21, 1724.
Abiel, s. Henry and Sarah, Feb. 24 [1731. C. R. 2.].
Abiel, s. Hezekiah and Hannah, Dec. 16, 1731.
[Abiel. C. R. 2.] s. Henry [jr. C. R. 2.] and Phebe, July 25, 1737.
Abiel, s. Abiel and Mary, Aug. 3, 1784.
Abiga, s. Benjamin and Susannah, Jan. 19, 1725-6.
Abigail, d. Willia[m] and Mary, June 11, 1695.
Abigail, d. Nemiah and Abigail, Oct. 7, 1699. [the Christian names of these parents are probably incorrectly recorded as they repeat the preceding entry.]
Abigal, d. twin, Isaac and Deborah, Apr. 18, 1755.
Abner, s. Joseph and Mary, Feb. 14, 1783.
Albert, s. Henry and Betsey, May 17, 1821.
Alfred Warren, s. Ebenezer and Delinda, bp. July 26, 1835. C. R. 3.
Allice, d. William and Mary, Aug. 23, 1687.
Amos, s. Joseph and Mary, Sept. 24, 1780.
Amos, s. Amos and Elizabeth, Aug. 20, 1804.
Andrew, s. John and Hannah, Mar. 3, 1728-9.
Andrew, s. Joshua, jr. and Sarah, June 18, 1772.
Anna Pottle, d. Isaac, 3d and Mary, Jan. 19, 1796. [Feb. 19, dup; bp. Jan. 24. C. R. 2.]

LOVEJOY, Anne, d. Christopher and Anne, May 26, 1743.
Annis, d. Jonathan, bp. Jan. 31, 1725. C. R. 2.
Asa, s. John and Hannah, Dec. 19, 1733.
[Asa. C. R. 1.], s. Joseph and Mehetable, Feb. —, 1745-6.
Asa, s. Joseph and Mehetebel, Feb. 11, 1749-50.
Asa, s. Asa and Sarah, Nov. 22, 1774.
Augustus, s. Isaac, 3d and Nabby, Apr. 30, 1818.
Aulinder [Allander. C. R. 2.], s. Isaac, jr. and Mary, June 11, 1762.
Bailey, s. William B., carpenter, and Mary Ann (Clement), Oct. 5, 1846.
Ballard, s. James B. and Hannah, bp. July 17, 1814. C. R. 2.
Barilla E[sther. C. R. 3.], d. Eben[eze]r, jr., farmer, and Belina [Delinda. C. R. 3.], May 28, 1845.
Benjamin, s. Joseph and Sarah, Nov. 21, 1690.
Benjamin, s. Benjamin, jr. and Mary, Nov. 10, 1747.
Benj[ami]n, s. Abiel and Mary, Sept. 15, 1776.
Benjamin C., s. William B. and Mary Ann (Clement), Jan. 10, 1842.
Betty, d. Asa and Sarah, May 31, 1791.
Bodwell, s. Isaac, 3d and Mary, Mar. 4, 1782.
Caleb, s. William and Mary, Mar. 29, 1691.
Cathrine, d. Bodwell and Sarah, Oct. 30, 1812.
Chandler, s. Henry, jr. and Phebe, Jan. 23, 1741-2. [bp. Jan. 17, C. R. 2.]
Charles, s. Asa and Sarah, bp. Dec. 16, 1781. C. R. 1.
Charles, s. Isaac, 3d and Abigail, June 21, 1815.
Charles, s. Henry and Betsy, Apr. 13, 1827.
Charles, s. Josiah and Mary, bp. May 3, 1829. C. R. 3.
Christopher, s. Christopher and Sarah, Feb. 16, 1687-8.
Christopher, s. Christopher [jr. C. R. 2.] and Mary, July, ——. [bp. July 23, 1721. C. R. 2.]
Christopher, s. Christopher and Mary, July 11, 1[722.].
Cloe, d. Joshua and Lydea, Mar. 26, 1753.
Daniel, s. Sylvester, farmer, and Clarissa, Nov. 16, 1843.
Daniel, s. Augustus, cordwainer, and Mary, Apr. 11, 1845.
Daniel Bodwell, s. Bodwell and Sarah, Dec. 27, 1817.
Daniel Fox, s. Sylvester and Clarisa, bp. Sept. 13, 1840. C. R. 3.
David, s. Wiliam, jr. and Hannah, Sept. 8, 1755.
David, s. Nathan, bp. Nov. 17, 1782. C. R. 2.
David Boynton, s. Nathan, bp. Dec. 8, 1776. C. R. 2.
Deborah, d. Isaac and Deborah, Apr. 1, 1752.
Delina, d. Eben[eze]r, jr. and Delina, May 7, 1821.
Dorathy, d. Ezekiel and Elisabeth, May 22, 1735.

LOVEJOY, Dorathy, d. Ezekiel and Elisabeth, Sept. 15, 1740.
Dorcas, d. Henry [jr. C. R. 2.] and Phebe, Sept. 10, 1739.
[Dorcas. C. R. 2.] Do—, d. Daniel and Mary, Apr. 16, 1762.
Dorcas Elizabeth, d. Ebenezer and Delinda, bp. June 19, 1836. C. R. 3.
Dorcis, d. Joshua and Lidea, Aug. 8, 1749.
Dorcis, d. Wiliam, jr. and Hannah, June 7, 1752.
Dorothy, d. Nathaniel and Dorothy, May 24, 1697.
Dorothy, d. Daniel and Mary, Sept. 26, 1764.
Dorothy, d. Jeremiah and Dorothy, Apr. 12, 1765.
Ebenezer, s. Ebenezer and Mary, Nov. 22, 1696.
Ebenezer, s. Ebenezer [jr. C. R. 2.] and Mary, Jan. 17, 1730-31.
Ebenezer, s. Jeremiah and Dorothy, Feb. 16, 1773.
Ebenezer, s. Ebenezer and Phebe, Feb. 7, 1795.
Ebenezer, s. Isaac, 4th, bp. Apr. 12, 1795. C. R. 2.
Ebenezer Frances, s. Ebenezer and Delinda, bp. July 26, 1835. C. R. 3.
Elezebeth, d. Samuel and Hannah, Aug. 8, 1720.
Elisabeth, d. wid. Elisabeth, bp. Aug. 29, 1806. C. R. 2.
Elizabeth, d. Jonathan, bp. July 23, 1721. C. R. 2.
Elizabeth, d. Ezekiel and Elizebeth, Mar. 31, 1731.
Elizabeth, d. Mr. Nathaniel and Eliz[abe]th, May 29, 1773.
Elizabeth, d. Amos and Elizabeth, July 19, 1806.
Elizabeth, d. Stephen, cordwainer, and Lydia, Oct. 23, 1845.
Elizabeth C., d. Henry and Betsy, Feb. 29, 1820.
Elizabeth Forster, d. Capt. Nathaniel and Eliza[beth], Aug. 6, 1780.
Elizebath, d. Ezekiel and Elizabeth, Mar. 9, 1728-9.
Enoch, s. Abiel and Mary, Sept. 11, 1781.
Enoch, s. Asa and Sarah, Jan. 27, 1783.
Esther, d. Peter, bp. Sept. 20, 1789. C. R. 2.
Ezekiel, s. Ezekiel and Elisabeth, Oct. 8, 1737.
Francis, s. Hezekiah and Hannah, Oct. 30, 1734.
Frye, s. Asa and Sarah, Mar. 27, 1776.
George, s. Ebenezer and Phebe, Sept. 4, 1798.
George, s. twin, Stephen, shoemaker, and Lydia, Aug. 24, 1848.
[Habijah. C. R. 1.], s. Benjamin and Susanna, Oct. 5, 1740.
Hannah, d. Joseph and Sarah, Feb. 11, 1692-3.
Hannah, d. John and Hannah, Dec. 27, 1724.
Hannah, d. William and Hannah, Aug. 12, 1747.
Hannah, d. Jeremiah and Dorothy, May 30, 1770.
Hannah, d. Daniel, jr. and Abigail, bp. Sept. 13, 1772. C. R. 1.
Hannah, d. Joseph and Mary, Oct. 17, 1778.
Hannah, d. Nathan, bp. Oct. 18, 1778. C. R. 2.

LOVEJOY, Hannah, d. Jeremiah, jr., bp. Oct. 11, 1789. C. R. 2.
Hannah, d. James B. and Hannah, bp. July 17, 1814. C. R. 2.
Hannah Frye, d. Asa and Sarah, Jan. 2, 1785.
Harriot, d. James B. and Hannah, bp. July 17, 1814. C. R. 2.
Henery, s. William and Mary, Nov. 27, 1683.
Henery, s. William, jr. and Hannah, Nov. 23, 1753.
[Henry. C. R. 2.], s. Henry, jr. and Phebe, Oct. 19, 1744.
Henry, s. Joshua, jr. and Sarah, Dec. 7, 1775.
Henry, s. Isaac, 3d [jr. C. R. 2.] and Mary, Apr. 22, 1793.
Hezekiah, s. Hezekiah and Hannah, Oct. 29 [1729. C. R. 2.].
Isaac, s. Samuel and Hannah, F[eb.] 9 [bp. Feb. 23, 1724.] C. R. 2.].
[Isaac. C. R. 2.], s. Christopher and Mary, Apr. 13, 1731.
Isaac, s. Isaac and Deborah, Mar. 16, 1757.
Isaac, s. Isaac and Mary, Jan. 27, 1760.
Isaac, s. Asa and Sarah, Jan. 25, 1778.
Isaac, s. Isaac, 3d [jr. C. R. 2.] and Mary, Feb. 13, 1780.
Isaac, s. Isaac, 4th, bp. May 5, 1793. C. R. 2.
Isaac Foster, s. Asa and Sarah, Aug. 1, 1788.
James, s. Samuell and Hannah, Dec. 28, 1727.
James, s. Ebenezer [jr. C. R. 2.] and Mary, Mar. 22, 1[734. C. R. 2.].
James Ballard, s. Jeremiah and Dorotha, Mar. 17, 1778.
Jane M., d. Eben[eze]r, jr. and Delina, July 21, 1829.
Jeremiah, s. Ebenezer [jr. C. R. 2.] and Mary, Mar. 15, 1738-9.
Jeremiah, s. Jeremiah and Dorothy, Oct. 29, 1761.
Jeremiah, s. Ebenezer and Phebe, bp. Nov. 20, 1814. C. R. 2.
Jerry, s. Jeremiah, jr. and Hannah, Jan. 17, 1787.
Jerusha, d. Henry and Sarah, July 5, 1725.
John, s. John and Mary, Feb. 9, 1655.
John, s. John and Naomi, Sept. 3, 1680. [1681. CT. R.]
John, s John and Hannah, Nov. 5, 1723.
John, s. Hezekiah, bp. Dec. 30, 1739. C. R. 2.
John, s. Hezek[iah], bp. July 24, 1743. C. R. 2.
John, s. Joseph, jr. and Mary, Mar. 24, 1773.
John, s. Abiel and Mary, June 25, 1779.
John, s. Jeremiah and Doratha, July 25, 1780.
John, s. Asa and Sarah, Dec. 9, 1786.
John, s. Ebenezer and Phebe, bp. Nov. 20, 1814. C. R. 2.
John Phillips, s. Nath[anie]ll, Esq. and Elizabeth, Apr. 3, 1782.
Jonathan, s. Jonathan, bp. May 23, 1742. C. R. 2.
Jonathan, s. Nathaniel, jr. and Elezebith, Apr. 22, 1748.
Jonathan, s. Joshua, jr., bp. Mar. 26, 1780. C. R. 2.
Joseph, s. Joseph and Sarah, Feb. 21, 1688-9.

LOVEJOY, Joseph, s. Joseph and Sarah, Oct. 16, 1699.
Joseph, s. Benjamin and Susanna, Mar. 26, 1731.
Joseph, s. Joseph and Mehetable, Mar. 2, 1739-40.
Joseph, s. Joseph and Mehetable, May 5, 1744.
Joseph, s. Joseph and Mary, Oct. 15, 1775.
Joseph, s. Ebenezer and Phebe, June 25, 1816.
Joseph Thompson, s. Ebenezer, jr. and Delina (Lynch), June 16, 1840.
Josephine, d. W[illia]m B. and Mary Ann, Mar. 16, 1836.
Joshua, s. Benjamin and Susannah, July 10, 1723.
Joshua, s. Benja[min] and Susannah, June 11, 1724.
Joshua, s. Joshua and Lydia, Jan. 8, 1743-4.
Joshua, s. Joshua, jr. and Sarah, Apr. 26, 1771.
Josiah Ballard, s. Ebenezer and Phebe, bp. Nov. 20, 1814. C. R. 2.
Josiah Johnson, s. Jeremiah, jr. and Hannah, Mar. 6, 1785.
Josiah Otis, s. Josiah [and Mary. C. R. 3.], Feb. 9, 1829.
Judah, d. Nathan, bp. Oct. 13, 1776. C. R. 2.
Julia, d. twin, Stephen, shoemaker, and Lydia, Aug. 24, 1848.
Laura Ann, d. Samuel and Harriot, Apr. 7, 1829.
Lemuel, s. Isaac and Deborah, Apr. 13, 1763.
Lemuel [Samuel. C. R. 2.], s. Isaac, 3d [jr. C. R. 2.] and Mary, Jan. 28, 1789.
Leusa [Lucey. C. R. 2.], d. Joshua and Lydea, Aug. 4, 1755.
Lois, d. W[illia]m, jr., bp. June 14, 1752. C. R. 2.
Lois, d. Daniel, jr. and Abigail, bp. June 6, 1773. C. R. 1.
Lucinda, d. Bodwell and Sally, bp. Oct. 3, 1824. C. R. 2.
Lucretia, d. Isaac, 3d and Ruth, Nov. 19, 1784.
Lucy, d. Isaac, jr. and Mary, Aug. 3, 1757.
Lucy, d. Isaac, 3d [jr. C. R. 1.] and Ruth, Sept. 1, 1780.
Lydia, d. Joseph and Sarah, June 2, 1697.
Lydia, d. William and Mary, Apr. 29, 1699.
Lydia, d. Joshua and Lydia, July 21, 1747.
Lydia, d. Isaac and Deborah, Nov. 19, 1764.
Lydia, d. Peter, bp. Sept. 20, 1789. C. R. 2.
Marcy Frances, d. John and Mary, bp. Sept. 13, 1840. C. R. 3.
Margaret M., d. William and Phebe, Feb. 22, 1826.
Mariah Jane, d. Ebenezer and Delinda, bp. July 26, 1835. C. R. 3.
Martha, d. Henry and Sarah, Nov. 2, 1720.
Martha, d. Isaac and Ruth, Oct. 19, 1797.
Martha Brandon, d. Capt. Nath[anie]ll and Eliza[beth], July 24, 1779.
Mary, d. Willia[m] and Mary, Nov. 15, 1685.
Mary, d. Ebenezer [jr. C. R. 2.] and Mary, Mar. 21, 1724-5.

LOVEJOY, Mary, d. Christopher, jr., bp. July 13, 1729. C. R. 2.
Mary, d. Samuel and Hannah, July 23, 1730.
Mary, d. Timothy and Mary, May 24 [1731].
Mary, d. Joshua and Lydia, Aug. 13, 1745.
Mary, d. Jeremiah and Dorothy, July 21, 1763.
Mary, d. Isaac, 4th, bp. June 19, 1791. C. R. 2.
Mary, d. Marcy, bp. Oct. 13, 1793. C. R. 2.
Mary Ann, d. Henry and Betsy, Dec. 10, 1818.
Mary Booby, d. Mercy, Aug. 17, 1783.
Mary Elizabeth, d. Ebenezer and Delinda, bp. July 26, 1835 C. R. 3.
Mary Frances, d. John and Mary F., July 28, 1837.
Mary H., d. Abiah and Orlando, Sept. 24, 1811.
Mary Osgood, d. William, bp. Mar. 5, 1797. C. R. 2.
Mehetabel, d. Ebenezer [jr. C. R. 2.] and Mary, Sept. 21, 1736.
Mehetable, d. Joseph and Mehitable, Apr. 27, 1738.
Mehetable, d. Joseph and Mehetab[le], May 20, 1742.
Mehitabel, d. Asa and Sarah, Sept. 21, 1795.
Mercy, d. Isaac, jr. and Mary, Aug. 21, 1764.
Miriam, d. Christopher and Sarah, Aug. 11, 1686.
Molly, d. Joseph, jr. and Mary, Feb. 19, 1771.
Molly, d. Nathan, bp. Oct. 13, 1776. C. R. 2.
Moody, s. Samuel and Harriet, July 28, 1827.
Moses, s. Moses and Dorcas, bp. Mar. 3, 1776. C. R. 1.
Moses, s. Orlando and Abiah, July8, 1821.
Moses Thomas, s. Moses, shoemaker, and Charlotte, Sept. 22. 1844.
Nancy, d. Isaac, 3d and Abigail, Oct. 26, 1820.
Nancy Jane, d. Isaac, 3d and Abigail, Feb. 2, 1826.
[Naomi. C. R. 2.], d. Ebenezer [jr. C. R. 2.] and Mary, Feb. 9, 1728-9.
Nathan, s. Christopher [jr. C. R. 2.] and Mary, Aug. 22 [1726. C. R. 2.].
Nathan, s. Nathan, bp. Jan. 9, 1785. C. R. 2.
Nathanael, s. Nathanael and Dorothy, Feb. 7, 1698-9.
Nathanael, s. Asa and Sarah, Apr. 21, 1793.
Nathaniel, s. Nathaniel, jr. and Elisabeth, Apr. 29, 1744.
Nathaniel, s. Mr. Nathaniel and Eliz[abe]th, Jan. 13, 1775.
Nathaniel, s. Capt. Nath[anie]ll and Elizabeth, July 20, 1776.
Nathaniel, s. Nath[anie]ll, Esq. and Elizabeth, Jan. 13, 1784.
Nelson Albert, s. Moses, cordwainer, and Charlotte, Nov. 16, 1847.
Obadiah, s. Benjamin and Susanna, Mar. 31, 1733.
Orlando, s. Isaac, 3d and Ruth, Nov. 23, 1782.

LOVEJOY, Orpah, d. James B. and Hannah, bp. July 17, 1814. C. R. 2.
Patty, d. Isaac, 4th, bp. May 24, 1789. C. R. 2.
Patty, d. Isaac, 4th, bp. Oct. 22, 1797. C. R. 2.
Persis, d. Isaac and Deborah, June 15, 1761.
[Peter, s. C. R. 2.], ch. Samuel and Hannah, Nov. 5, 1725.
Peter, s. Benjamin and Susanna, Mar. 30, 1728.
Phebe, d. Hezekiah and Hannah, Nov. 29, 1727.
[P]hebe, d. Samuel and Hannah, Mar. 8, 1734-5.
[Phebe. C. R. 2.], d. Henry [jr. C. R. 2.] and Phebe, Sept. 20, 1735.
Phebe, d. Hezek[iah], bp. June 26, 1737. C. R. 2.
Phebe, d. Hezekiah and Hannah, Oct. 24, 1737.
Phebe, d. Jeremiah and Doretha, Feb. 5, 1775.
Phebe, d. Daniel, bp. July 9, 1775. C. R. 2.
Phebe, d. Isaac, 3d and Mary, Dec. 5, 1790.
Phebe, d. Ebenezer and Phebe, bp. Nov. 20, 1814. C. R 2.
Phebe, d. Bodwell and Sally, Oct. 28, 1820.
Phebe A[manda. C. R. 3.], d. Eben[eze]r, jr. and Delina, Aug. 31, 1833.
Phebe Ballard, d. Sylvester and Clarissa, bp. July 5, 1846. C. R. 3.
Phebe F., d. William and Phebe, Jan. 16, 1829.
Phebe Francis, d. Orlando and Abiah, Mar. 3, 1826.
Phoebe, d. Joshua, jr., bp. June 14, 1778. C. R. 2.
Phinehas, s. Ezekiel and Elezabeth, Feb. 18, 1732-3.
Polly, d. Isaac, 3d and Mary, June 8, 1784.
Polly, d. Isaac, of Louden, bp. Nov. 13, 1785. C. R. 2.
Polly, d. Abiel and Mary, bp. July 31, 1791. C. R. 1.
[Rebecca. C. R. 2.], d. Ebenezer [jr. C. R. 2.] and Mary, Nov. 14, 1726.
Rebecca, d. Jeremiah and Dorothy, Mar. 5, 1767.
Sally, d. Asa and Sarah, Feb. 2, 1780.
Sally, d. Ebenezer and Phebe, bp. Nov. 20, 1814. C. R. 2.
Sally Kimball, d. Bodwell and Sally, July 26, 1810.
Sam[ue]l, s. William and Mary, Apr. 10, 1693.
Samuel, s. Samuel and Hannah, —2 [bp. Feb. 4, 1722. C. R. 2.].
Samuel, s. W[illia]m, jr., bp. Sept. 23, 1750. C. R. 2.
Samuel, s. Isaac and Deborah, Sept. 11, 1753.
Samuel, s. Isaac, 4th, bp. Mar. 6, 1796. C. R. 2.
Samuel, s. Isaac, 3d and Ruth, Feb. 10, 1800.
Sara, d. John and Mary, Apr. 11, 1654.
Sarah, d. Joseph and Sarah, Feb. 21, 1685-6.
Sarah, d. Christopher and Sarah, Mar. 9, 1689-90.

LOVEJOY, Sarah, d. W[illia]m and Sarah, bp. June 26, 1720. C. R. 2.
Sarah, d. Jonathan, bp. Mar. 3, 1723. C. R. 2.
Sarah, d. twin, Isaac and Deborah, Apr. 18, 1755.
Sarah, d. William, jr. and Hannah, Nov. 28, 1758.
Sarah, d. Jeremiah and Dorothy, Aug. 28, 1768.
Sarah, d. Joshua, jr. and Sarah, Dec. 16, 1773.
Sarah, d. Nathan, bp. Oct. 1, 1780. C. R. 2.
Sarah, d. Mercy and Thomas Houghton, Feb. 14, 1798.
Sarah, d. Mary, bp. Oct. 26, 1802. C. R. 2.
Sarah, d. Orlando and Abiah, Apr. 5, 1813.
Sarah [Emeline. C. R. 3.], d. Eben[eze]r, jr. and Delina, July 4, 1838.
Stephen, s. Henry and Sarah, June 7, 1724.
Stephen, s. Abiel and Mary, July 10, 1787.
Stephen, s. Orlando and Abiah, Apr. 20, 1807.
Stephen A., s. William and Phebe, May 25, 1835.
Stephen A[bbott. C. R. 3.], s. Eben[eze]r, jr. and Delina, Nov. 13, 1831.
Sukey, d. Isaac, 3d and Ruth, Feb. 27, 1787.
Susanna, d. Isaac and Ruth, Feb. 29, 1787.
Sylvester, s. Orlando and Abiah, Oct. 12, 1809.
Sylvester, s. Sylvester and Clarissa, bp. Sept. 3, 1837. C. R. 2.
Tabitha, d. Abiel, jr. and Tabitha, Jan. 10, 1774.
Timothy, s. twin, [torn] and Dorothy,— 5 [1701].
[Timothy. C. R. 1.], s. Timothy and Mary, Aug. 20, 1732.
Warren, s. Isaac, 3d and Abigail, May 30, 1823.
Warren, s. Stephen and Lydia L., May 10, 1838.
Wiliam, s. William, jr. and Hannah, June 24, 1749.
William, s. William and Mary, Nov. 22, 1681.
William, s. Henry and Sarah, [Jan.] 31, [1721-2.]. [bp. Feb. 4, 1722. C. R. 2.]
[William. C. R. 2.], s. Henry and Sarah, Apr. 16, 1723.
William, s. Samuel and Hannah, Oct. 19, 1732.
William, s. William, jr. and Hannah, Dec. 26, 1745.
William, s. Isaac and Deborah, July 6, 1759.
William, s. Isaac, 3d and Mary, Sept. 5, 1786.
William, s. Henry and Elizabeth, [June] 1, [1791].
William, s. William, bp. Nov. 23, 1794. C. R. 2.
William, s. Orlando and Abiah, Feb. 28, 1805.
William Bailey, s. James B. and Hannah, bp. July 17, 1814. C. R. 2.
William H., s. William and Phebe, May 30, 1833.
Wiliam Russel, s. Ebenezer and Phebe, Sept. 26, 1796.
——, ch. Ebbenezer and Mary, June 12, 1704.

LOVEJOY, ——, ch. [torn], Dec. 19, 1709.
——, s. Andrew, July 7, 1821.
——, d. Eben, jr. and Delina, July 26, 1827.
——, d. Sylvester, farmer, and Clarissa, Sept. 1, 1845.

LOVERING, Franklin, s. Jonas, wheelwright, and Rebeca H., May 31, 1846.
George, s. Jonas, mechanic, and Rebecca, Apr. 14, 1844.

LOVJOY (see also Lovejoy), Anne, d. John and Bathsheba, ——, [1711].
Anne, d. William and Sarah [bp. Nov. 4, 1711. C. R. 2.].
[Caleb, s. C. R. 2.] [H]enery and Sarah, Dec. 28, 1716.
Daniel, s. Nath[anie]ll and Dorathy —— [1710].
David, s. Henery and Sarah, Oct. 10, 171[5. C. R. 2.].
Dorcas, d. twin, Dorothy, —5 [1701].
[Elizabeth. C. R. 2.], d. David and Elizabeth, ——, 1741-2. [bp. Jan. 10. C. R. 2.]
Hannah, d. Samuel and Hannah, Mar. 1, 1717-18.
[Henry, s. Henry. C. R. 2.] —ery and Sarah, Aug. 14, 1714.
Hezekiah, s. Christop[her] and [torn], —— [1701].
John, s. Ebenezer and Mary, May 14, 1698.
[Jo]hn [John. C. R. 1.] s., Benjamin and Susannah, Jan. 5, 1719-20.
Jonathan, s. Jonathan and Elizabeth [bp. July 5, 1719. C. R. 2.].
Joshuah, s. Henery and Sarah, Dec. 2 [1719. C. R. 2.].
[Mary. C. R. 2.], d. Henery and Sarah, Dec. 17, 1718. [bp. Dec. 14. C. R. 2.]
[Phebe. C. R. 2.], d. William and Sarah, Jan. 20, 1715-16.
Sarah, d. Henery and Sarah, Nov. —— [bp. Nov. 30, 1712. C. R. 2.].
William, s. W [torn], ——[1706-7?].
——, ch. [torn] and Mary, —— 6, 1701.
——, ch. [torn]hn and Bathshebah, Apr. 4, 1706.
——, s. Benjamin and Susanna, May 2, 1718.

LOW, Caroline A., d. Joseph and Sally, July 5, 1819.
Daniel, s. Joseph L. and Sally, at Boxford, May 28, 1806.
Emily W., d. Maj. Joseph L. and Sally, July 25, 1821.
Harriet Barker, d. Maj. Joseph L. and Sarah, Nov. 30, 1824.
Lucy L., d. Joseph L. and Sally, at Billerica, Feb. 24, 1808.
Mary Ann, d. Joseph L. and Sally, at Billerica, Jan. 9, 1814.
Nathan W., s. Joseph L. and Sally, at Billerica, Jan. 23, 1812.

Low, Sarah Jane, d. Joseph L. and Sally, at Billerica, Sept. 15, 1815.
Susan M., d. Joseph L. and Sally, at Billerica, Jan. 3, 1810.
William W., s. Joseph L. and Sally, Aug. 23, 1817.

LUCIUS, Richard, s. Charles, finisher, b. Germany, and Jane, b. England, May 24, 1849.

LUFKIN, Dorcas, d. wid. Mehitebal, bp. May 23, 1779. C. R. 2.
Jonathan, s. wid. Mehitebal, bp. May 23, 1779. C. R. 2.
Mehetebel, d. wid. Mehitebal, bp. May 23, 1779. C. R. 2.
Sarah, d. wid. Mehitebal, bp. May 23, 1779. C. R. 2.

LUKE, Daniel A., s. Daniel and Emily, May 11, 1830.
Hannah J., d. Daniel and Emily, Oct. 7, 1831.
John A., s. Daniel and Emily, June 22, 1833.

LUMLEY, Mary, d. James, butcher, and Harriett, June 18, 1846.

LUMMIS (see also Lummus), ——, s. Joseph and Sally, Aug. 5, 1796.

LUMMUS (see also Lummis), Benjamin, s. Joseph and Sarah, Dec. 2, 1799.
Charles, s. Samuel and Elizabeth, Sept. 11, 1811.
John, s. Joseph and Sarah, Nov. 4, 1797.
Joseph, s. Joseph and Sarah, Aug. 5, 1795.
Margaret, d. Joseph and Sarah, May 15, 1804.
Mary, d. Samuel and Elizabeth, Aug. 5, 1813.
Mary, d. Samuel and Elizabeth, Mar. —, 1815.
Michael, s. Joseph and Sarah, Sept. 6, 1793.
William, s. Joseph and Sarah, Jan. 8, 1802.

LUND, John Benson, s. John, flax-dresser, and Ellen, Apr. 11, 1848.

LUSCOMB (see also Liscomb), Aaron Edward, s. Aaron and Margaret, bp. Oct. 18, 1840. C. R. 3.
Eliza O[sgood. C. R. 3.], d. Richard and Rhoda, Oct. 14, 1827.
Hannah C., d. Rich[ar]d and Rhoda, Jan. 8, 1817.
Harriet F., d. Richard and Lydia A., July 10, 1840.
Henery, s. Henery and Hannah, July 14, 1800.
Jonathan, s. Richard and Rhoda, May 10, 1830.
Lydia, d. Richard and Rhoda, Oct. 6, 1821.

LUSCOMB, Mary, d. Henery and Hannah, Aug. 27, 1801.
Mary Ann, d. Aaron and Margaret, bp. Sept. 3, 1843. C. R. 3.
Rhoda Jane, d. Richard and Rhoda, Feb. 26, 1824.
Richard W., s. Richard and Rhoda, Mar. 29, 1826.
Samuel [Liscomb. C. R. 2.], s. Samuel and Jerusha, Aug. 18, 1815.
Sarah Julia, d. Aaron N., cordwainer, and Margaret, Oct. 6, 1846.

LYON, Charles, s. David and Fanny, June 11, 1826.
David H., s. David and Fanny, Sept. 25, 1828.
——, ch. David and Fanny, Sept. 23, 1824.

MABURY, Helen C., d. Thomas E., carpenter, b. Maine, and Hannah L., b. Ipswich, Nov. 7, 1849.

McALPINE, James, s. James, May 12, 1824.

McCANN, James, s. Michael, spinner, and Rosena, both b. Ireland, Oct. 30, 1848.

McCARREL (see also Mecarrel), Elizabeth, d. John, bp. ——, 1737. C. R. 1.

MacCARTNEY, John, s. Sarah, bp. Sept. 16, 1744. C. R. 2.

McCARTY, Bridgeat, d. Patrick, laborer, and Mary, both b. Ireland, July 22, 1848.

McCOY, Sarah E[lizabeth. dup.], d. John, farmer, and Mary, Aug. 21 [Aug. 30. dup.], 1843.

McDONALD (see also McDoniel), Harriet A., d. James P., harness-maker, b. Belfast, and Harriet, Oct. 5, 1848.
James W., s. James P., harness-maker, and Harriet, June 1, 1845.
Robert, s. John and Hannah, Mar. 20, 1824.
——, s. John and Hannah, Sept. 1, 1825.

McDONIEL (see also McDonald), ——, ch. John and Hannah, Apr. 15, 1822.

MACE, Ebenezer, s. Jonathan and Martha, June 23, 1798.
Isaac, s. twin, Isaac and Sarah, June 12, 1771.
Isaac, s. Jonathan and Martha, July 28, 1792.

MACE, Jonathan, s. Isaac and Sarah, Apr. 8, 1767.
Lydia, d. Jonathan and Martha, June 9, 1795.
Rebecca, d. twin, Isaac and Sarah, June 12, 1771.
Samuel A. Collins, s. Lydia, Apr. 30, 1821.
Sarah, d. Isaac and Sarah, Oct. 25, 1765.
Solomon, s. Jonathan, bp. July 10, 1803. C. R. 2.

McFARLAND, Jane, d. James, laborer, and Margaret, Sept. 14, 1848.

McGAHAY, Hannah, d. Thomas, manufacturer, and Hannah, July 5, 1848.

McGEE, Ellen, d. Samuel and Mary, Dec. 24, 1826.
——, ch. ——, at the factory, June 22, 1822.

McGLAGHLAN, Mary, d. W[illia]m, bp. Nov. 12, 1749. C. R. 2.

McGOWEN, Francis, s. Michael, laborer, and Mary, both b. Ireland, July 22, 1848.

McINTIRE (see also Mackentire), Jacob, s. Phineas and Mary, July 18, 1757.
Pearley, s. Phineas and Mary, Oct. 12, 1754.

McINTOSH, Martha E., d. George, laborer, and Mary, Aug. 5, 1848.

MACKENTIRE (see also McIntire, Mackintire), Edee, d. Phineas, bp. —— [1752]. C. R. 1.
Lucy, d. Phineas, bp. —— [1752]. C. R. 1.
Sarah, d. Phineas, bp. —— [1752]. C. R. 1.

MACKINTIRE (see also Mackentire), Phineas, s. Phineas and Mary, June 15, 1752.

McLATHLIN (see also McLoughlin), Joseph, s. Laurance and Mary, May 23, 1794.
Rachel Allen, d. Laurance and Mary, Sept. 14, 1792.

McLAUTHLEN (see also McLoughlin), Richard, s. Laurance and Mary, Feb. 24, 1796.

McLAUTHLIN (see also McLoughlin), Benjamin, s. Laurance and Mary, Dec. 18, 1797.

McLOUGHLIN (see also McLathlin, McLauthlen, McLauthlin), Mary Jane, d. James, wool-scourer, and Bridget, both b. Ireland, Nov. 12, 1848.

McNAMARA, Elizabeth Ann, ward W[illla]m and Ab[i]g[ai]l, bp. Apr. 16, 1843. C. R. 4.
Susanna, d. William and Abigail, June 19, 1839.
William H[enry. C. R. 4.], s. William, manufacturer, and Abigail (Smith), June 5, 1845.

McNEAL (see also McNeill), Elizabeth, d. John and Jane C., Jan. 24, 1823.
Jane C., d. John and Jane C., May 8, 1826.
John Stuart, s. John and Jane C., Feb. 17, 1824.

McNEILL (see also McNeal), John, s. Edmond and Abigail, Oct. 21, 1830.

McREA, Charlotte, d. Hector, overseer, and Charlotte, July 26, 1847.
Hector, s. Hector, laborer, b. England, and Charlotte, b. Scotland, June 26, 1849.

McROBEA (see also McRobie), Sarah, d. William and Mary, Sept. 24, 1799.

McROBIE (see also McRobea), Daniel, s. William and Mary, Sept. 21, 1809.
Isaac, s. William and Mary, July 3, 1804.
Robert, s. William and Mary, Aug. 15, 1814.
William, s. William and Mary, Aug. 27, 1806.

McWHIRK, William, s. William, farmer, b. Milton, and Mary, b. Ireland, July 19, 1849.

MAGEE, Eliza Ann, d. Samuel and Mary, Feb. 20, 1830.
Henry, s. Samuel and Mary, Feb. 27, 1838.
James, s. Samuel and Mary, Jan. 12, 1840.
John L., s. John and Martha M., Aug. 28, 1848.

MAHAN (see also Mahen), Catherine, d. twin, Patrick, spinner, and Sarah, Dec. 23, 1846.
Ellen, d. twin, Patrick, spinner, and Sarah, Dec. 23, 1846.

MAHEN (see also Mahan), Rose, d. twin, Patrick, spinner, and Sarah, Dec. 23, 1846.

MAKPACE, Charles Otis, s. Alson, laborer, b. Norton, and Jane A., b. England, Oct. 28, 1849.

MALCOY, John, s. Margaret, bp. Oct. 16, 1763. C. R. 2.
Margaret, d. Margaret, bp. Oct. 16, 1763. C. R. 2.

MALONE, Charles, s. Patrick, laborer, b. Waltham, and Catherine, b. Scotland, at Waltham, Sept. 13, 1849.

MANN, Asa, s. Lilborn Andrews' wife, by Andrew Mann, Mar. 25, 1784.
Martha W., d. Z. H., engineer, and E. H., Feb. 10, 1846.

MANNING, Albert, s. Elbridge G., machinist, and Harriet, Feb. 2, 1846.
Benjamin S., s. Samuel B. and Mary, Jan. 4, 1832.
Bridget, d. James, wheelwright, and Hanora, both b. Ireland, May 3, 1849.
Chloe, d. Thomas and Mehetable, Jan. 19, 1772.
Edward A[ugustus. P. R. 75.], s. Thomas, jr. and Sally, June 12, 1807.
Elbridge G., s. Elbridge G., machinist, and Hannah, Oct. 23, 1843.
Elizabeth H., d. Samuel and Betsy, Dec. 20, 1837.
Eri C., s. Samuel and Betsy W., Aug. 7, 1834.
Francis H., s. Elbridge and Harriet, July 21, 1840.
George, s. Samuel and Betsy W., at Dover, N. H., July 28, 1829.
Harriet E., d. Elbridge G., machinist, b. Tewksbury, and Harriet, Aug. 24, 1848.
John Hart, s. Thomas and Sarah, Feb. 8, 1824. P. R. 75.
John W., s. Samuel and Betsy W., Oct. 6, 1832.
Joseph M., s. Thomas and Sarah, Aug. 11, 1819. P. R. 75.
Mark S., s. Samuel and Betsy W., at Brentwood, N. H., May 2, 1831.
[Mary Antoinette. P. R. 75.], d. Thomas, jr. and Sally, Jan. 23, 1821.

MANNING, Mary J., d. Samuel and Betsy W., Mar. 1, 1836.
[Mary K. P. R. 75], d. Thomas, jr. and Sally, Mar. 26, 1817. [Mar. 11. P. R. 75.]
Mehetabel, d. Tho[ma]s and Mehetabel, Dec. 30, 1769.
Patty, d. Tho[ma]s, bp. Jan. 19, 1777. C. R. 2.
Rebecca Jane, d. Thomas and Sarah, Mar. 23, 1827. P. R. 75.
Sarah, d. Thomas and Mehetable, May 29, 1774.
Sarah [Ann. P. R. 75.], d. Thomas, jr. and Sarah, Dec. 2, 1809.
Sarah E., d. Samuel and Betsy W., May 11, 1839.
Sarah F., d. Samuel and Betsy, Mar. 1, 1841.
Thomas, s. Tho[ma]s and Mehitable, Apr. 30, 1780.
Thomas, s. Thomas and Mehitable, Apr. 25, 1781.

MANOCK, Olive M., d. David, laborer, and Mary, Jan. 11, 1847.

MANSUR, [John. C. R. 2.], s. John and Hannah, June 21, 1734.

MANWELL, Mary, d. Anthony, "a Frenchman who came from Louisburg," and Mary, bp. ——, 1749. C. R. 1.

MARBEL (see also Marble), Isaac, s. Noah and Mary, June 9, 1740.
Mary, d. Job and Phebe, Oct. 25, 1750.

MARBLE (see also Marbel), Allice, d. Joseph and Mary, Jan. 1, 1693-4.
Benjamin, s. Job and Phebe, May 3, 17[30. C. R. 1.].
Benjamin, s. Job and Phebe, July 12, 1739.
Caroline, d. Natha[nie]l and Lucy, bp. July 22, 1804. C. R. 1.
Cyrus, s. Noah and Mary, May 5, 1738.
[Daniel. C. R. 1.], s. Noah and Mary, Feb. 5, 1743-4.
Daniell, s. Samuel and Rebekah, Feb. 5, 1692-3.
Dorathy, d. Joseph and Mary, June 16, 1672.
Dorcas, d. Cyrus and Hannah, Feb. 24, 1762.
Edmund, s. Joseph and Mary, Jan. 8, 1684.
Elezebeth, d. Noah and Mary, Aug. 10 [1723].
Elizabeth, d. Samuell and Rebekah, Apr. 25, 1677.
Enoch, s. Sam[ue]ll and Rebekah, Mar. 27, 1686.
Enoch, s. Noah and Mary, Jan. 30, 1725-6.
Enoch, s. Cyrus and Hannah, bp. Apr. 26, 1772. C. R. 1.
Fanny, d. Cyrus and Hannah, bp. Apr. 11, 1779. C. R. 1.
Freegrace, s. Samuell and Rebekah, June 15, 1682.
Hanah, d. Joseph and Hanah, Dec. 13, 1697.
Hannah, d. Sam[ue]ll and Rebekah, May 5, 1684.

MARBLE, Hannah, d. Noah and Mary, Apr. 28, 1732.
Isaac, s. Lt. Cyrus and Hannah, bp. Feb. 24, 1782. C. R. I.
[Jer. C. R. I.]usha, d. Noah and Mary, Apr. 11, 1734.
Jesse, s. Noah and Mary, Apr. 25, 1728.
Job, s. twin, Sam[ue]l and Rebeckah, Feb. 10, 1694-5.
Johnathan, s. Joseph and Mary, Jan. 7, 1682.
Jonathan, s. Job and Phebe, July 1, 1735.
Joseph, s. Joseph and Mary, July 28, 1673.
Joseph, s. Joseph and Hannah, Aug. 15, 1699.
Joseph, s. Noah and Mary, Jan. 11, 1721-2.
Mary, d. Samuell and Rebekah, Aug. 31, 1678.
Mary, d. Joseph and Mary, June 1, 1691.
Mary, d. Noah and Mary, Dec. 20, 1724.
Mary, d. Cyrus and Hannah, bp. May 19, 1765. C. R. I.
Nabby, d. Lt. Cyrus and Abigail, bp. Nov. 3, 1776. C. R. I.
Naoma, d. Cirus, bp. Sept. 6, 1767. C. R. I.
Noah, s. Sam[ue]ll and Rebekah, Mar. 12, 1688-9.
Perses, d. Cyrus, bp. Oct. 9, 1774. C. R. I.
Phebe, d. Job and Phebe, Dec. 24, 1727.
Phebe, d. Job and Phebe, J[une. T. C.], 18 [1744. C. R. I.].
Priscilla, d. Job and Phebe, Dec. 18, 1736.
[Rebecca. C. R. I.], d. Job and Phebe, Feb. 23, 1728-9.
Rebeckah, d. twin, Sam[ue]l and Rebeckah, Feb. 10, 1694-5.
Samuel, s. Job and Phebe, Mar. 12, 1741-2.
Samuell, s. Samuell and Rebekah, Mar. 17, 1679-80.
Sarah, d. Sam[ue]ll and Rebekah, Apr. 6, 1688.
Sarah, d. Cyrus and Hannah, bp. Sept. 18, 1763. C. R. I.
Susanna, d. Job and Phebe, Dec. 22, 1732.
——, d. Joseph and Hannah—— [1]702.
——, Jacob, s. [torn], —— [1705-6].
——, d. Noah and Mary, Aug. 11, 1730.
——, s. Noah and Mary, Apr. 7, 1736.

MARLAND, Abba Northey, d. William S. and Sally, June 8, 1836.
Abraham, s. Abraham and Mary Sykes, Oct. 18, 1821. P. R. 76.
Abraham, s. William S. and Sarah N., Jan. 18, 1841.
Andrew Stewart, s. John, manufacturer, and Lucretia, Dec. 3, 1846.
Ann B., d. Abraham and Mary, Dec. 12, 1810.
Charles Hitchcock, s. William S. and Sarah N., Apr. 5, 1843.
Cynthia, d. John and Delia, July 19, 1819.
Elizabeth [Caroline. P. R. 76.], d. Abraham and Mary, July 25, 1819.
Hannah [Jane. P. R. 76.], d. Abraham and Mary, Mar. 20, 1815.

MARLAND, Harriott [Fletcher. P. R. 76.], d. Abraham and Mary, Feb. 18, 1813.
Julia Maria, d. Abraham and Mary Sykes, July 30, 1823. P. R. 76.
Martha Punchard, d. John [manufacturer. dup.], and Lucretia, Feb. 21, 1844.
Mary S[ykes. C. R. 4.], d. William S., gentleman, and Sarah, Aug. 29, 1844.
Sarah Fisher, d. Abraham and Mary Sykes, Mar. 17, 1817. P. R. 76.
Sarah Helen, d. William S. and Sarah, Feb. 1, 1838.
Thomas, s. Abraham and Mary, Oct. 18, 1821.
William, s. William S. and Sarah, Mar. 11, 1839.
William, s. John, manufacturer, and Lucretia, Dec. 19, 1848.
William Sykes, s. Abraham and Mary, May 21, 1808.

MARSH, Caroline, d. Daniel and Lucy, Mar. 13, 1804.
Lucy, d. Daniel and Lucy, July 17, 1805.

MARSHAL (see also Marshall), Sarah, d. James and Sarah, Oct. 23, 1775.

MARSHALL (see also Marshal), Abraham, s. James and Deborah, Mar. 24, 1787.
David, s. Jacob and Sarah, July 23, 1786.
George F., s. Alonzo and Elizabeth C., Mar. 11, 1837.
George Franklin, s. Moses and Irene, Nov. 20, 1837.
George M., s. Alonzo, shoemaker, and Elizabeth C., Apr. 8, 1845.
Horatio H., s. Horatio, blacksmith, and Lucy, Aug. 11, 1843.
Jacob, s. Jacob and Sarah, Aug. 13, 1780.
James, s. Jacob and Sarah, Apr. 29, 1784.
James Gilbert, s. Horatio and Lucy, July 27, 1838.
John, s. Jacob and Sarah, Aug. 17, 1774.
Lucinda Hutchings, d. Alonzo and Elizabeth, Dec. 21, 1839.
Lucy, d. Jacob and Sarah, Oct. 10, 1779.
Mehitable E., d. Alonzo and Elizabeth, May 27, 1838.
Moses Newell, s. Moses and Irene, Jan. 20, 1835.
Royall, s. Thomas and Phebe, Oct. 6, 1835.
Sarah, d. Jacob and Sarah, Oct. 27, 1776.
Susan F., d. Alonzo, cordwainer, and Elizabeth C., Aug. 11, 1843.
William, s. Jacob and Sarah, Aug. 21, 1782.
——, s. Moses and Irene, Jan. 11, 1840.
——, s. Thomas, car builder, and Phebe S., Jan. 18, 1844.

MARSTEN (see also Marston), Charles, s. Amos and Lydia, Dec. 23, 1813.
John, s. John and Mary, Jan. 27, 1748-9.
Samuel, s. John and Mary, Aug. 17, 1751.

MARSTON (see also Marsten, Marstone, Mastin, Mastine, Maston), Mary, d. Jacob and Mary, Jan. 28, 1726-7.
——, ch. [torn] and Eliza[beth], June 6, 1704.
——, s. Jacob and Mary, Sept. 24, 1724.

MARSTONE (see also Marston), Benjamin, s. John and Martha, Jan. 11, 1677.
Daniel, s. Jacob and Elizabeth, Nov. 27, 1698.
Elizabeth, d. Jacob and Elizabeth, Feb. 16, 1686-7.
Ephraim, s. John and Martha, Mar. 14, 1673-4.
Hannah, d. John and Mary, Apr. 9, 1692.
Jacob, s. Jacob and Elizabeth, Mar. 30, 1688.
Jacob, s. Jacob and Elisabeth, Jan. 23, 1692-3.
John, s. John and Mary, Sept. 11, 1693.
John, s. John and Mary, Sept. 22, 1696.
John, s. Jacob and Elizabeth, 7br. 17, 1700.
Martha, d. John and Martha, Jan. 28, 1679.
Martha, d. Jacob and Elisabeth, Jan. 23, 1694-5.
Mary, d. Jacob and Elisabeth, Mar. 7, 1688-9.
Mary, d. John and Mary, Mar. 17, 1689-90.
Mary, d. Jacob and Elisabeth, Mar. 22, 1691-2.
Sarah, d. Jacob and Elisabeth, Oct. 25, 1696.

MARTAIN (see also Martin), Abigal, d. Nathaniel and Hannah, Apr. 5, 1758.
Abraham, s. Joseph and Elisabeth, Sept. 15, 1736.
Amos, s. Samuel and Elizabeth, Oct. 5, 1761.
Christefor, s. Samuel and Elezebith, May 31, 1757.
Daniel, s. Nathaniel and Hannah, May 21, 1756.
Elezebith, d. Samuel and Elezeb[eth], July 16, 1753.
Elisabeth, d. Joseph and Elisabeth, Oct. 7, 1738.
Elizabeth, d. Joseph and Phebe, Jan. 17, 1761.
Hannah, d. John, jr. and Hannah, May 14, 1755.
Hephzebith, d. John, jr. and Hannah, Mar. 22, 1757.
John, s. John and Hannah, Mar. 24, 1759.
Jonathan, s. John and Hannah, Dec. 15, 1735.
Joseph, s. Joseph and Rachel, Oct. 31, 1[729].
Mary, d. Samuel and Elizebath, June 22, 1760.
Mary, d. Joseph and Phebe, May 4, 1763.

MARTAIN, Molly, d. John and Hannah, Apr. 2, 1762.
Nathan, s. Samuel and Eliz[abe]th, Apr. 3, 1763.
Nathaniel, s. Solomon and Dorathy, Aug. 29, 1726.
Peter, s. Samuel and Elizabeth, Feb. 22, 1759.
Phebe, d. Samuel and Elezebith, Feb. 24, 1756.
Phebe, d. Joseph, jr. and Phebe, Sept. 3, 1756.
Rachil, d. Joseph and Phebe, July 3, 1758.
Samuel, s. Samuel and Elezebith, Aug. 31, 1754.
Solomon, s. Nathaniel and Hannah, Aug. 14, 1753.
William, s. Jonathan and Phebe [Hannah. C. R. 1.], Mar. 31, 1763.

MARTIN (see also Martain), Abigail, d. Solomon and Dorathy, Aug. 14, 1731.
Abigall, d. Samuell and Abigall, Mar. 29, 1676.
Benjamin, s. Joseph and Phoebe, Nov. 16, 1774.
Charles, s. Solomon and Phebe, Dec. 19, 1793.
Clarisa, d. Solomon and Phebe, July 20, 1801.
Clarissa, d. Peter and Hannah, Feb. 27, 1798.
Clarissa, d. Phebe, bp. Sept. 4, 1814. C. R. 1.
Daniel, s. Solomon and Dorathy, Jan. 13, 1733-4.
Daniel, s. Jonathan and Phebe, Mar. 30, 1768.
Daniel, s. Solomon and Phoebe, Feb. 12, 1798.
Dorcas, d. Peter, bp. May 22, 1796. C. R. 2.
[Dorothy. C. R. 1.] ——y, d. Solomon and Dorathy, Feb. 27, 1728-9.
Elizabeth, d. Joseph and Phebe, Apr. 30, 1771.
Elizabeth Wyman, d. Peter and Hannah [June or July] 9, [1791 ?]. [bp. Apr. 1, 1792. C. R. 2.].
Hannah, d. John and Hannah, Apr. 11, 1738.
Hannah, d. Sam[ue]ll and Eliz[abe]th, Sept. 18, 1764.
Hannah, d. John and Hannah, Mar. 30, 1767.
Hannah, d. Peter and Hannah, Aug. 17, 1789.
Hannah, d. Solomon and Phebe, June 11, 1790.
Harriet E., d. John J., laborer, and Mariah B., June 16, 1848.
[Henry. C. R. 1.], s. John and Hannah, Jan. 30, 1739-40.
Isaac, s. John and Hannah, June 26, 1774.
James, s. John and Hannah, Mar. 23, 1733-4.
John, s. Sam[ue]ll and Abigall, July 3, 1685.
[John. C. R. 1.], s. John and Hannah, June 4, 1730.
John, s. John and Hannah, Sept. 21, 1764.
Jonathan, s. Jonathan and Phebe, Sept. 3, 1766.
Joseph, s. Joseph and Phebe, Dec. 17, 1766.
Lydia, d. John, bp. ——, 1738. C. R. 1.

MARTIN, Lydia, d. Sam[ue]l, bp. Mar. 12, 1769. C. R. 2.
Lydia, d. Samuel and Elizabeth, Mar. 6, 1773.
Mary, d. Samuell and Abigall, June 9, 1678.
Mary, d. Solomon and Dorathy, Aug. 27, 17[37. C. R. 1.].
Micajah, s. Samuel and Eliz[abe]th, Sept. 6, 1767.
Nathaniel, s. Solomon and Phebe, Oct. 28, 1783.
Nathaniell, s. Samuel and Abigall, Aug. 19, 1687.
Pamelia, d. twin, Solomon and Phebe, Feb. 14, 1796.
Phebe, d. Jonathan and Phebe, July 14, 1764.
Phebe, d. Joseph and Phebe, Mar. 19, 1769.
Phebe, d. Solomon and Phebe, Feb. 28, 1785.
Peter, s. Peter and Hannah, Mar. 25, 1787.
Samuel, s. John and Hannah, May 19, 1732.
Samuell, s. Samuell and Abigall, Feb. 14, 1680. [Feb. 19. CT. R.]
Sarah, d. Sam[ue]ll and Abigal, at Ipswich, Oct. 16, 1689.
Sarah, d. John and Hannah, Apr. 22, 1747.
Sarah, d. Solomon and Phebe, Apr. 3, 1792.
Sarah Abbot, d. Joseph, jr. and Sarah, Dec. 29, 1799.
Stephen, s. Joseph and Elezabeth, J — 2 [bp. July 7, 1734. C. R. 1.].
Susanna, d. John and Hannah, Mar. 27, 1742.
Susanna, d. John and Hannah, Apr. 6, 1743.
Susanna, d. Solomon and Phebe, Aug. 7, 1788.
Susannah, d. twin, Solomon and Phebe, Feb. 14, 1796.
Timothy, s. Joseph and Rachel, Oct. 18, 1732.
Timothy, s. John and Hannah, June 26, 1769.

MASON (see also Mayson), Abigail Sophia, d. Daniel and Martha T., bp. Oct. 12, 1828. C. R. 3.
Abijah, s. Robert and Phebe, Oct. 30, 1808.
Adaline S[ewall. C. R. 3.], d. Daniel and Martha F., May 10, 1821. P. R. 97.
Alfred Lee, s. Daniel and Martha F., Feb. 8, 1812.
Alonzo Sewell, s. Daniel and Martha F., Jan. 31, 1810.
Amanda L[ouisa. C. R. 3.], d. Daniel and Martha F., Apr. 28, 1828. P. R. 97.
Augustus E[ugene. C. R. 3.], s. Daniel and Martha F. [T. C. R. 3.], Aug. 10, 1818.
Daniel R., s. Daniel and Martha F., Apr. 25, 1816.
Edwin A., s. Daniel and Martha F., Apr. 22, 1830.
Eliza, d. Thomas S. and Phebe, Jan. 22, 1813.
Ellen Augusta, d. Willard and Emeline, Jan. 29, 1840.
Emeline H[elen. C. R. 3.], d. Daniel and Martha F., Oct. 3, 1825. P. R. 97.

MASON, George F., s. Frederic and Mary, Sept. 28, 1839.
Georgianna M., d. Willard, cordwainer, and Sarah J., Feb. 22, 1848.
John, s. Thomas S. and Phebe, July 13, 1814.
Josiah, s. Thomas C. and Phebe, May 20, 1822.
Lucy Ann, d. Willard and Emeline, May 3, 1838.
Martha M., d. Daniel and Martha F., June 10, 1814.
Ozro, s. Thomas C. and Phebe, July 6, 1820.
Rosabelle, d. John R., carpenter, and Eunice, Dec. 20, 1848.
Sarah C., d. Frederic and Mary, Aug. 11, 1838.
Sophia A., d. Daniel and Martha F. (Sewell), July 3, 1823. P. R. 97.
Willard, s. Thomas C. and Martha, Mar. 11, 1817.
——, d. Willard, cordwainer, and Sarah J., Feb. 25, 1847.

MASTERS, John, s. Abraham and Susanna, Aug. 20, 1754.
Susana, d. Abraham and Susana, Oct. 23, 1752.

MASTIN (see also Marston), Hannah, d. John and Mary, Jan. 22, 1746-7.

MASTINE (see also Marston), Benjamin, s. Jacob and Mary, — 13 [bp. Feb. 15, 1735-6. C. R. 1.].

MASTON (see also Marston), Bethia, d. John and Martha, July 7, 1671.
Hanna, d. John and Martha, Feb. 16, [16]67.
John, s. Jacob and Mary, July 8, 1720.
Mary, d. Jacob and Mary, June 24, 1723.
Samuell, s. Jacob and Elizabeth, —— [1705?].

MATTHEWS, David, s. James, bp. ——, 1738. C. R. 1.

MAYNARD (see also Mayward), Charles W., s. George W., laborer, and Rhoda F., Jan. 18, 1846.

MAYO, Helen L., d. Aaron D. and Sarah, Nov. 1, 1831. [Ellen Louise, d. A. A., bp. Mar. 31, 1832. C. R. 2.]
Henry Allen, s. Gideon, merchant, and Martha Ann, Aug. 29, 1846.
Matilda Elizabeth, d. Aaron D. and Sally, June 4, 1822.
Sarah Ann, d. Aaron D. and Sally, Feb. 15, 1821.
Sarah Day [Augusta. C. R. 2.], d. Aaron D. and Sarah, Jan. 8, 1828.
Susan H[untington. C. R. 2.], d. Aaron D. and Sarah, Jan. 6, 1834.
Thomas Henry, s. Aaron D. and Sarah, May 28, 1824.
Thomas Henry, s. Aaron D. and Sarah, June 28, 1826.

MAYSON (see also Mason), Warren, s. Tho[ma]s C. and Phebe, May 15, 1824.

MAYWARD (see also Maynard), Rhoda Elizabeth, d. George, farmer, and Rhoda, Feb. 25, 1845.

MEARIL (see also Merrill), Richard, s. Stephen and Keziah, Dec. 4, 1744.
——, s. Stephen and Kezia, Dec. 31, 1738.

MEARS (see also Miers), Abby Jane, d. Warren, laborer, and Abigail, Feb. 3, 1848.
Augusta, d. Moses, laborer, and Rebecca, Mar. 6, 1849.
Clarissa B., d. Zebadiah and Sarah, Feb. 11, 1834. T. C.
Louiza, d. Zebediah and Rhoda, Apr. 28, 1829.
Lucretia, d. Daniel and Mary, Oct. 2, 1848.
Martha J., d. Warren and Abigail, Jan. 29, 1834.
Rhoda, d. Daniel and Maria, Apr. 6, 1830.
Thomas W., s. Warren, jr., laborer, and Frances, b. Scotland, Feb. 16, 1849.
Walter, s. Walter, laborer, and Amelia, Apr. 10, 1846.
Warren, s. Warren and Abigail, Aug. 8, 1829.
William, s. Zebadiah and Rhoda, Sept. 23, 1831.
——, d. Zebadiah, jr. and Rhoda, Sept. 20, 1819.
——, d. Zebadiah, and Sarah, Jan. 11, 1822.
——, s. Daniel and Sarah, Jan. 14, 1826.
——, d. Daniel, farmer, and Mary, Apr. 28, 1844.
——, s. Walter, laborer, and Amelia, Feb. 29, 1848.

MECARREL (see also McCarrel), Hannah, d. John and Margaret, Apr. 21, 1737.
John, s. John and Margerate, Mar. 21, 1738-9.
Sarah, d. John and Margerat, Dec. 11, 1740.

MEEDER, Charles E., s. James and Phebe, July 1, 1838.
James, s. James and Phebe, Mar. 6, 1822.
James H[enry. C. R. 1.], s. James and Phebe, June 7, 1825.
John W., s. James and Phebe, July 21, 1840.
Mary L., d. James and Phebe, June 6, 1836.
Pamelia Clark, d. James and Phebe, Oct. 28, 1819.
Phebe E[meline. C. R. 1.], d. James and Phebe, Jan. 11, 1824.
Sarah E[lizabeth. C. R. 1.], d. James and Phebe, Dec. 17, 1830.
William Otis, s. James and Phebe, Sept. 22, 1832.
——, d. James and Phebe, Dec. 14, 1827.

MERCHANT, ——, s. Crowel, housewright, Oct. 24, 1843.

MERRIL (see also Merrill), Abigail, d. Enoch and Patty, Nov. 6, 1789.
Benjamin, s. John and Mary, May 1, 1775.
Daniel, s. Enoch and Patty, Apr. 17, 1784.
Edmond, s. Enoch and Patty, Feb. 4, 1779.
Elizabeth, d. John and Mary, Aug. 5, 1781.
Enoch, s. Enoch and Patty, Oct. 22, 1780.
Mary, d. John and Mary, Sept. 10, 1777.
Nathaniel, s. Thomas and Lydia, Nov. 21, 1782.
Patty, d. Enoch and Patty, Aug. 7, 1782.
Polly [Molly. C. R. 2.], d. Enoch and Paty [bet. July 28-Aug. 16, 1787].
Rebecca, d. Enoch and Patty, Apr. 9, 1792.
Sarah, d. John, bp. May 22, 1774. C. R. 2.
Sarah, d. John and Mary, Aug. 29, 1779.
Thomas Abbot, s. Thomas and Lydia, Jan. 18, 1780.

MERRILL (see also Mearil, Merril), Abby, d. Edward S., innholder, and Sarah, Dec. 19, 1848.
Abby Francettor Ardele, d. James, yeoman, and Susan G., Apr. 2, 1847.
Abigail, d. John, bp. Sept. 5, 1824. C. R. 2.
Alfred, s. Isaiah and Mary, Mar. 25, 1820.
Amos, s. Amos C. and Eliza, Nov. 15, 1820.
Augusta, d. Amos C. and Elizabeth, May 18, 1826.
Augusta, d. Amos and Elizabeth, May 11, 1832.
Caroline, d. Amos C. and Elizabeth, Apr. 3, 1830.
Charles Henry, s. William, farmer, and Phebe [A.], Sept. 17, 1843.
Daniel Trow, s. Daniel, jr. and Sarah, May 9, 1811.
Edward C., s. Edward S. and Sarah, Mar. 18, 1838.
Elisabeth Moody, d. Enoch, bp. Sept. 17, 1797. C. R. 2.
Eliza, d. John, bp. Sept. 5, 1824. C. R. 2.
Elizabeth, d. Amos C. and Elizabeth, July 16, 1822.
Elizabeth Jane, d. James and Susan, Jan. 19, 1840.
Francis S., s. Sylvester and Nancy, Apr. 25, 1838.
George William, s. William and Phebe A., July 30, 1839.
Harriott, d. Daniel and Sarah, Nov. —, 1818.
Hollis, s. Isaiah and Mary, Jan. 31, 1832.
James, s. Edward S. and Sarah, Dec. 10, 1842.
John, s. John and Mary, July 8, 1771.
John, s. Enoch and Patty, July 13, 1795.

MERRILL, John N., s. John and Susan, Dec. 29, 1831.
Joseph C., s. Amos C. and Elizabeth, Mar. 16, 1828.
Joseph Shattuck, s. William, farmer, and Phebe A., May 9, 1849.
Levina, d. Amos C. and Eliz[abe]th, Mar. 23, 1824.
Nancy Jane, d. Sylvester, trader, and Nancy, at Woburn, Dec. 22, 1847.
Phebe A., d. William and Phebe, Aug. 30, 1836.
Polly Ann, d. John and Susan, July 19, 1829.
Polly F., d. Jonathan and Eliza, June 20, 1832.
Priscilla, d. E. S., innholder, and Sarah, Sept. 22, 1844.
Samuel F., s. Edward S. and Sarah, May 15, 1840.
Sarah, d. Enoch, bp. May 15, 1800. C. R. 2.
Sarah, d. Daniel, jr. and Sarah, Dec. 17, 1815.
William, s. John, bp. Sept. 5, 1824. C. R. 2.
William Cross, s. James, laborer, b. Newbury, and Susan G., b. Methuen, Mar. 11, 1849.
——, s. Timo[thy] Bailey, jr. and Rebecca, Sept. 5, 1819.

MESSER, Anna, d. Stephen and Anna, Mar. 17, 1775.
Betty, d. Stephen and Anna, Mar. 19, 1771.
Joanna, d. Stephen and Anna, Mar. 14, 1769.
Sarah, d. Stephen and Anna, Sept. 7, 1777.

MIDDLETON, Agnes F., d. David, bleacher of flax, and Margaret, Oct. 22, 1843.

MIDGELEY, James, s. James and Hannah, bp. Dec. 1, 1841. C. R. 4.
Joseph, s. James and Hannah, bp. Aug. 17, 1845. C. R. 4.
Mary Alice, d. James and Hannah, bp. Apr. 16, 1843. C. R. 4.

MIERS (see also Mears), Charles, s. Daniel and Mary, Feb. 2, 1835.
Eliza, d. Warren and Abigail, June 8, 1831.
Henry, s. Daniel and Mary, Oct. 27, 1832.

MILLER, Abel, s. Abel and Catherine, May 16, 1830.
Eliza Ann, d. William, Sept. 26, 1827.
Lavina, d. William, Jan. 5, 1831.
Lucy A., d. George, machinist, and Mary A., Jan. 16, 1847.

MILLET (see also Millett), Eliza M[arland. C. R. 4.], d. William P., tailor, and Martha M., Mar. 16, 1845.
James Stephen, s. Jeremiah, laborer, and Mary, Feb. 28, 1847.

MILLET, John, s. Jeremiah and Mary, Oct. 20, 1830.
William Henry [Hardy. C. R. 4.], s. William P. and Martha [M. C. R. 4.], Apr. 7, 1841.
——, s. Jeremiah, Feb. 26, 1840.

MILLETT (see also Millet), Frank E[aton. C. R. 4.], s. William P., merchant tailor, and Martha M., Apr. 24, 1847.
Martha Punchard, d. W[illia]m P. and Martha M., bp. Mar. 12, 1843. C. R. 4.
Samuel V., s. Joseph R., carpenter, and Elizabeth, Feb. 22, 1848.

MILLS, George N., s. James and Sarah, Oct. 21, 1843.
James H., s. James H., laborer, and Sarah, Oct. 28, 1848.
Mary Annah, d. John, railroad contractor, and Mary R., at Boston, Aug. 7, 1847.

MITCHEL (see also Mitchell), George, s. John and Mary, Mar. 3, 1816.
Henry, s. John and Mary, Feb. 9, 1814.

MITCHELL (see also Mitchel), George William, s. John, dresser in factory, and Sarah, June 20, 1846.
Maria C., d. John and Mary, Nov. 10, 1812.

MOAR (see also Moore), Andrew J., s. Andrew and Abiah, May 26, 1831.
Charles J., s. Joshua and Mary, Apr. 1, 1842.
Daniel, s. Abraham and Priscilla, May 9, 1697.
George Albert, s. Joshua, farmer, and Mary E., Nov. 22, 1847.
Jacob B., s. Andrew and Abiah, May 23, 1833.
[John. C. R. 2.], s. Timothy, jr. and Elisabeth, June —, 1745. [bp. June 16. C. R. 2.]
Loes, d. Benjamin and Abiah, Nov. 10, 1747.

MOARE (see also Moore), [Abraham. C. R. 2.], s. Daniel and Martha, Jan. 14, 1727-8.
[Daniel. C. R. 2.], s. Daniel and Martha, Feb. 18, 1724-5.
[Isaac], s. twin, Daniel and Martha, May 2, 1730.
Isaac, s. Daniel and Martha, June 25, 1731.

MOARS (see also Moore), Martha Josephine, d. Andrew, cordwainer, and Abiah, Oct. 26, 1843.

MONAGEN (see also Monaghaghn), Elizabeth Ann, d. Owen and Catharine, Dec. 16, 1840.

MONAGHAGHN (see also Monagen), Vicena Jane, d. Owen, manufacturer, and Catharine, Aug. 10, 1847.

MONHAGEN (see also Munigen), John Stephen, s. Andrew, laborer, and Catherine, Nov. 4, 1846.

MONTGOMERY (see also Mountgomery), Catharine, d. Alexander and Mary [Sarah. C. R. I.], Feb. 17, 1814. [bp. Feb. 28, 1813. C. R. I.]
Charlotte, d. Alexander and Mary, Aug. 29, 1818.
Charlotte M., d. John P. and Hannah, Dec. 8, 1836.
Eliza Abbot, d. Alexander and Sarah, bp. Sept. 5, 1813. C. R. I.
George Knox, s. Alexander and Mary [Sarah. C. R. I.], June 16, 1815. [bp. June 26, 1814. C. R. I.]
James Alexander, s. Alexander and Mary [Sarah. C. R. I.], Mar. 13, 1817. [bp. Mar. 17, 1816. C. R. I.]
John Porter, s. Alexander and Mary [Sarah. C. R. I.], Dec. 26, 1812. [bp. Jan. 5, 1812. C. R. I.]
Mary, d. Alexander and Mary [Sarah. C. R. I.], Sept. 11, 1811. [bp. Sept. 28, 1810. C. R. I.]
Rebecca P[eabody. C. R. I.], d. Alexander and Mary [Sarah. C. R. I.] Mar. 21, 1809. [bp. [after Apr. 3] 1808. C. R. I.]
Sarah Ann, d. Alexander and Mary [Sarah. C. R. I.], May 10, 1810. [bp. [May 14?] 1809. C. R. I.]

MOOAR (see also Moore), Abiah, d. Benjamin and Abiah, Nov. 9, 1741.
Andrew, s. Abraham and Martha, July 31, 1777.
Andrew A., s. Jacob and Phebe, Jan. 23, 1806.
Anne, d. Benjamin and Abiah, Aug. 11, 1753.
Benj[ami]n, s. Benj[ami]n, jr. and Hannah, Sept. 3, 1770.
Deborah, d. Joshua and Deborah, July 20, 1777.
George French, s. Andrew A. and Abiah L., Sept. 1, 1835.
Hannah, d. Benj[ami]n, jr. and Hannah, Nov. 6, 1768.
Hannah, d. John, lately deceased, bp. Oct. 26, 1783. C. R. 2.
Hannah, d. Benjamin and Susan, July 16, 1827.
Harriet Abiah, d. Andrew A. and Abiah L., Mar. 3, 1838.
Harriott, d. Jacob and Phebe, Feb. 8, 1811.
Isaac, s. Abraham and Lydia, Feb. 16, 1759.
Jacob, s. Abraham and Martha, Dec. 22, 1769.

MOOAR, Jacob, s. Abraham, la[tely] dec[eased] and Martha, Feb. 19, 1781.
John, s. Abraham and Martha, Apr. 17, 1773.
John, s. Benjamin and Hannah, Aug. 14, 1780.
John, s. Benjamin and Phebe, Mar. 6, 1810.
Joseph, s. Benjamin, jr. and Hannah, Mar. 7, 1777.
Joshua, s. Timothy, jr. and Elezebith, June 3, 1751.
Joshua, s. Joshua and Deborah, Nov. 2, 1778.
Lowis, d. Benjamin and Hannah, May 15, 1773.
Lydia, d. Abraham and Sarah, Aug. 30, 1766.
Lydia Abbot, d. Isaac and Lydia, Aug. 15, 1790.
Martha, d. Abrah[a]m and Martha, Aug. 13, 1771.
Martha, d. Jacob and Phebe, Apr. 15, 1816.
Mary, d. Benjamin and Abiah, Oct. 11, 1755.
Mary, d. Timothy and Elizabath, May 26, 1760.
Mary, d. Benjamin and Hannah, Nov. 24, 1782.
Mary, d. Jacob and Phebe, at Pownal, Vt., May 24, 1818
Nathan, s. Benjamin and Hannah, June 14, 1787.
Nathan, s. Benjamin and Phebe, Sept. 18, 1812.
Phebe, d. Jacob and Phebe, June 30, 1808.
Phebe Dane, d. Jacob and Phebe, May 16, 1813.
Prissey, d. Benja[min] and Hannah, Nov. 16, 1778.
Rebecca, d. Daniel and Martha, Aug. 13, 1735.
Rozina, d. Jacob and Phebe, Mar. 19, 1804.
Samuel, s. Benjamin, jr. and Hannah, Mar. 7, 1775.
Sarah, d. Abraham and Sarah, Mar. 3, 1765.
Sarah, d. Abraham and Martha, July 29, 1775.
Timothy, s. Benja[min] and Hannah, Feb. 5, 1785.
——, s. Daniel and Martha, June 4, 1733.

MOOARE (see also Moore), Abraham, s. Abraham and Lydia, Jan. 15, 1761.
Martha, d. Daniel and Martha, Mar. 8, 1725-6.
Mary, d. Benjamin and Abiah, Dec. 16, 1760.
Priscilla, d. Timothy and Anne, June 12, 1724.

MOOARS (see also Moore), Sarah Abbot, d. Isaac and Lydia, Jan. 1, 1793.

MOOR (see also Moore), Adeline, d. Friend, carpenter, and Tryphena, Feb. 28, 1847.
Anne, d. Timothy and Anne, Apr. 16, 1721.
Asa, s. Daniel and Marth[a], Jan. 15, 1737-8.
Harriet Abiah, d. Andrew A. and Abiah, Mar. 3, 1837.
Timothy, s. Abraham and Prissilla, Sept. 16, 1688.
Timothy, s. Timothy, jr. and Elizabeth, Feb. 14, 1741-2.

MOORCROFT, Thomas, s. William, Oct. 18, 1827.

MOORE (see also Moar, Moare, Moars, Mooar, Mooare, Mooars, Moor, Moores, More), Abraham, s. Abraham and Priscilla, Jan. 11, 1691-2.
Elda, d. Milton and Abigail, June 27, 1848.
Elezebith, d. Timothy [jr. C. R. 2.] and Elezebith, Mar. 8, 1747-8.
Elizabeth, d. William, wool-comber, and Harriet, Apr. 5, 1847.
George, s. Benjamin and Hannah, bp. Oct. 19, 1834. C. R. 3.
Geo[rge] Milton, s. twin, Milton, mechanic, and Abigail, Jan. 31, 1845.
Hannah, d. Benjamin and Hannah, bp. Oct. 19, 1834. C. R. 3.
John Milton, s. twin, Milton, mechanic, and Abigail, Jan. 31, 1845.
Joseph, s. Benjamin and Abiah, Feb. 13, 1745-6.
Joseph R., s. Richard, printer, and Eliza, Sept. 2, 1844.
Mary, d. Milton, carpenter, and Abigail, May 5, 1846.
Mary E., d. Joshua, farmer, and Mary E., Jan. 29, 1845.
[Me]hetebel, d. Benjamin and Abbiah, Nov. 1, 1749.
Oscar L., s. Andrew A., shoemaker, and Abiah, Oct. 12, 1845.
Priscilla, d. Abraham and Priscilla, May 15, 1691.
William Scrnton, s. Richard, bp. Sept. 7, 1834. C. R. 2.

MOORES (see also Moore), Albert S., s. Friend, mechanic, b. Hancock, N. H., and Tryphena, b. Hudson, N. H., July 26, 1849.

MORE (see also Moore), [Benjamin. C. R. 2.] ——amine, s. Timothy and Anne, Feb. 18, 1715-16.
Mary, d. Abraham and Priscilla, Apr. 16, 1695.
Mary, d. Timothy and Anne, July 10, 1718.
Sarah, d. Daniel and Martha, Apr. 20, 1740.
[Timothy, s. Timothy. C. R. 2.] —y and Anne, June 10, 1713.

MORELAND, ——, ch. Mrs. Moreland and Solomon Wood, Nov 6, 1841.

MORFET, William Le Baron, s. David, Mar. 7, 1843.

MORISON (see also Morrison), John, s. Joseph and Peggy, Nov. 3, 1783.
Jonathan, s. Joseph and Peggy, June 20, 1787.
Joseph, s. Joseph and Peggy, June 10, 1781.
Mary Homes [Holmes. C. R. 2.], d. Joseph and Peggy, Feb. 9, 1799.
Samuel, s. Joseph and Peggy, July 30, 1782.
Thomas, s. Joseph and Peggy, Nov. 18, 1785.

MORRILL, Edward T. [Herbert. c. r. 2.], s. Samuel, printer, and Hannah, Dec. —, 1845.
George Henry, s. Samuel, bp. Mar. 31, 1833. c. r. 2.
Samuel S[tilman. c. r. 2.], s. Samuel and Hannah, Oct. 10, 1832.

MORRISON (see also Morison), Charles Herbert, s. Charles G. bp. June 12, 1836. c. r. 2.
Ellen A[ugusta. c. r. 2.], d. Charles [G. c. r. 2.] and Mary M., Sept. 15, 1834.
Matilda Trask, d. Thomas and Sophia, Feb. 6, 1815.
Peggy, d. Joseph and Peggy, Nov. 22, 1779.
Mary E[lizabeth. c. r. 2.], d. Charles [G. c. r. 2.] and Mary M., Dec. 1, 1832.

MORSE (see also Moss), Charles P., s. John C. and Catherine, Sept. 23, 1843.
Charlotte A., d. John C. and Catharine, Aug. 19, 1838.
Darius, s. Merril and Hannah, Sept. 9, 1802.
Frank M., s. Jacob, watchman, Feb. 25, 184[7 or 8].
John Currier, s. Merril and Hannah, Mar. 30, 1804.
Lucy A., d. Jacob W., and Elizabeth, Dec. 10, 1845.
Martha, d. Merril and Hannah, Dec. 29, 1805.
Susanna Currier, d. Merril and Hannah, Oct. 21, 1807.
William B., s. John C. and Catherine, Sept. 14, 1841.
——, twin chn., John H., and Nancy, July 5, 1838.

MORTON, George, s. twin, Charles, spinner, and Nancy, Oct. 10, 1846.
James F., s. Charles and Nancy (Holt), Feb. 21, 1849. p. r. 89.
Robert, s. twin, Charles, spinner, and Nancy, Oct. 10, 1846.

MOSS (see also Morse), Lydia, d. Moses, of Methuen, bp. Sept. 11, 1785. c. r. 2.

MOULTON, Daniel, s. Nat[hanie]ll, bp. Nov. 22, 1741. c. r. 2.

MOUNTGOMERY (see also Montgomery), Anna, d. John, bp. Aug. —, 1781. c. r. 1.

MOWETT, ——, s. Comodore, butcher, and Eliza A., Mar. 29, 1846.

MUCH, Charles Thomas, s. Thomas and Sarah, May 17, 1839.
Frances Ann, d. Thomas and Sarah, Aug. 26, 1837.

MULLEN, Charles M., s. John, manufacturer, and Mary M., Oct. 10, 1845.
Jonathan W., s. John, wool-sorter, and Mary, Dec. 21, 1843.

MUNIGEN (see also Monhagen), Edward Orne, s. Andrew, laborer, and Catherine, Sept. 24, 1844.

MURDOCK, Moses Brown, s. James and Rebekka L., bp. Apr. 16, 1820. C. R. 6.

MURPHY, John, s. Thomas, laborer, and Margaret, both b. Ireland, Mar. 13, 1849.
William, s. Benjamin, laborer, and Christiana, Dec. 31, 1848.

MURRAY (see also Murry), Arthur, s. Arthur, farmer, and Catherine, May 11, 1844.
Beatrix Morrison, d. Walter, bp. Nov. 6, 1842. C. R. 2.
Caroline, d. Charles, flaxcomber, and Margarett, Aug. 7, 1846.
Ellen S., d. Arthur, laborer, and Catharine, Apr. 9, 1846.
Francis C., d. James, cordwainer, and Adeline, Jan. 4, 1846.
James Ramsey, s. Walter, bp. July 4, 1841. C. R. 2.
Mary [Scott C. R. 2.], d. Walter, spinner, and Christianna, Mar. —, 1846.
Robert, s. Walter, manufacturer, and Christiana, Feb. 9, 1844.

MURRY (see also Murray), Hannah, d. Margaret, May 24, 1849.

NASON (see also Neason), Catherine M., d. James and Ruby S. (Kimball), June 19, 1841. P. R. 54.

NEASON (see also Nason), James H[enry. P. R. 54.], s. James, yeoman, and Ruby, Jan. 19, 1847.
John H., s. James, farmer, b. Boston, and Ruby [S. P. R. 54.], Oct. 18, 1849.
Mary E., d. James, farmer, and Ruby [S. P. R. 54.], Dec. 19, 1843.

NEEDHAM, Albert, s. Eben, farmer, and Ellen, Apr. 18, 1845.
Catherine, d. Samuel and Fanny, Mar. 12, 1826.
Charles W., s. Ebenezer and Sally (Wright), May 5, 1838. T. C.
Herietta, d. Samuel and Fanny, Mar. 3, 1828.
Samuel J., s. Samuel and Fanny, Oct. 30, 1819.
Susan E[aste. C. R. 2.], d. Samuel and Fanny, Jan. 23, 1830.
William, s. Samuel and Fanny, Aug. 27, 1821.
——, s. Benja[min] and Nancy, July 21, 1824.

NESS, Joseph, s. James, laborer, and Elizabeth, both b. Scotland, Dec. 13, 1849.

NEWALL (see also Newell), Mary, d. Capt. David, bp. Aug. 30, 1778. C. R. 1.

NEWCOMB, Charles, s. Thomas, Sept. 26, 1818.

NEWELL (see also Newall), Phebe, d. ——, of Charlestown, bp. Nov. 12, 1775. C. R. 1.

NEWMAN, Abby Ann, d. Mark, jr. and Juliet C., Oct. 28, 1833.
Anna D., d. Mark and Abigail, Apr. 1, 1816.
Catherine Dickinson, d. Mark H. and Mary D., Feb. 21, 1836.
Catharine Merriam, d. M., jr., bp. July 6, 1845. C. R. 2.
Charlotte E[lizabeth. C. R. 2.], d. Mark, jr. and Juliet C., Nov. 12, 1831.
Edward A[ugustus. C. R. 2.], s. Mark, jr. and Charlotte, Mar. 7, 1830.
Hannah, d. Mark and Sarah, June 6, 1809.
Hannah Haskell, d. Mark, jr., bp. June 11, 1837. C. R. 2.
Henry Jewett, s. Mark, 2d, bp. Aug. 8, 1830. C. R. 2.
Lucy Sarah, d. Mark, jr., bp. Sept. 16, 1842. C. R. 2.
Margaret Wendell, d. Mark [Preceptor of Phillips Academy. C. R. 2.] and Sarah, Mar. 3, 1801.
Mark, s. Mark ["Preceptor of Phillips Academy." C. R. 2.], and Sarah, July 13, 1804.
Mark H., s. Mark and Sarah, June 9, 1806.
Mark H[askell. C. R. 2.] s. Mark H. and Mary D., Sept. 11, 1833.
Mary D., d. Mark H. and Mary, Aug. 10, 1829.
Mary Dickinson, d. Mark H. and Mary D., Aug. 12, 1831.
Rebecca [Almira. C. R. 2.], d. Mark, jr., cabinet maker, and Elizabeth, Oct. 13, 1846.
Samuel Haskell, s. Mark, jr., bp. Sept. 16, 1842. C. R. 2.
Samuel Phillips, s. Mark and Sarah, June 6, 1797.
Sarah Phillips, d. Mark and Sarah, Mar. 19, 1802.
Sarah P[hillips. C. R. 2.], d. Mark H. and Mary D., Nov. 22, 1838.
Susannah, d. Samuel and Hannah, May 15, 1814.
William John, s. Mark and Sarah, Oct. 26, 1811.

NICHOLAS (see also Nichols), James, s. John, bp. July 1, 1739. C. R. 2.
——, d. James and Anna, Feb.—, 1738-9.
——, s. James and Anna, Mar. 19, 1740-41.

NICHOLLS (see also Nichols), John Edwards, s. John, 3d and Mary, Sept. 15, 1809.

NICHOLS (see also Nicholas, Nicholls, Nicklas, Nickols, Nicoles, Nicolls, Nicols), Andrew Sigourney, s. Nathaniel, bp. Sept. 7, 1834. C. R. 2.
Betsy, d. John, jr. and Nanny, July 26, 1789.
David Horatio, s. Nathaniel, bp. Oct. 4, 1835. C. R. 2.
Deborah, d. John, jr. and Anna, Mar. 31, 1801.
Edward Irison, s. John, jr. and Nanny, May 12, 1787.
Elisabeth, d. Nicholas and Elisabeth, Mar. 27, 1694.
Elizabeth, d. James, bp. Feb. 19, 1738. C. R. 2.
Elizabeth, d. John and Elizabeth, bp. Oct. 18, 1778. C. R. 1.
George W., s. John E. and Sarah, Aug. 30, 1837.
Hannah, d. John and Elizabeth, bp. Oct. 18, 1778. C. R. 1.
Harriet V., d. John E. and Sarah, Dec. 22, 1839.
Harriott, d. John, 3d and Mary, Mar. 4, 1820.
James, s. John, jr. and Nanny, June 14, 1794.
John, s. John and Elizabeth, bp. Oct. 18, 1778. C. R. 1.
John Knox, s. John E. and Sarah, Nov. 19, 1835.
Joseph, s. John, jr. and Nanne, Dec. 12, 1798.
Joseph Alonzo, s. Nathaniel, bp. Sept. 7, 1834. C. R. 2.
Julia Ann, d. John E. and Sarah, Aug. 30, 1832.
Justin Harrison, s. John, 3d and Mary, May 23, 1816.
Justus Willis, s. Nathaniel, bp. Sept. 7, 1834. C. R. 2.
Margarett, d. Nicholaus and Elizabeth, July 30, 1688.
Margarett Silver, d. James and Mercy, July 15, 1817.
Martha, d. John and Elizabeth, bp. Oct. 18, 1778. C. R. 1.
Mary Eliza, d. John, 3d and Mary, Jan. 31, 1813.
Mary F., d. John E. and Sarah, July 14, 1834.
Nabby, d. John and Elizabeth, bp. Apr. 25, 1790. C. R. 1.
Nancy Josephine, d. John E. and Sarah, June 21, 1843.
Nancy Norris, d. John, 3d and Mary, Dec. 6, 1806.
Nathaniel Holt, s. Nathaniel, bp. Sept. 7, 1834. C. R. 2.
Phebe Foxcroft, d. Phillip and Sarah, Dec. 7, 1806.
Philip, s. John and Elizabeth, Mar. 2, 1771.
Samuel, s. John and Elizabeth, bp. Oct. 22, 1780. C. R. 1.
Sarah, d. John and Elizabeth, bp. Dec. 1, 1782. C. R. 1.
Sarah A, d. John E. and Sarah, Apr. 20, 1831.
Sarah Fowler, d. Phillip and Sarah, Aug. 31, 1799.
Susan A., d. Nathaniel, bp. Sept 7, 1834. C. R. 2.
William Watson, s. Nathaniel, bp. Sept. 7, 1834. C. R. 2.
William W., s. John E. and Sarah, Aug. 22, 1841.

NICHOLSON (see also Nickelson), Mary Gould, d. Sarah, Dec. 10, 1805.

NICKELSON (see also Nicholson), Abigal, d. Francis and Sarah, Dec. 2, 1777.

NICKLAS (see also Nichols), Anne, d. James, bp. July 31, 1737. C. R. 2.

NICKOLS (see also Nichols), Benjamin, s. John and Elizabeth, bp. Oct. 7, 1785. C. R. 1.
Betsey Foster, d. Phillip and Sarah, Jan. 26, 1809.
Erastus, s. Philip and Sarah, Sept. 3, 1804.
James, s. James and Anna, May 19, 173[3. C. R. 2.].
Phillip, s. Phillip and Sarah, Apr. 14, 1802.
Samuel Foster, s. Phillip and Sarah, Oct. 27, 1800.
Ruth, d. Nicholice and Elizab[eth], —— [1703].
Sarah, d. James and Anna, Aug. 1, 1731.

NICOLES (see also Nichols), Anna [Hannah. C. R. 2.], d. James and Anna, Oct. 21 [1729. C. R. 2.].

NICOLLS (see also Nichols), Elizabeth, d. Nicholas and Elizabeth, Apr. 26, 1687.
Francis, s. Nicholas and Elisabeth, Aug. 14, 1690.
Hannah, d. Nicholas and Elizabeth, Jan. 22, 1696-7.

NICOLS (see also Nichols), [Dorcas. C. R. 2.], d. James and Anna, Dec. 30, 1735.

NOON, Edward, s. John, laborer, and Caroline, Aug. 20, 1848.

NOURSE, Sarah Elizabeth, d. John I., yeoman, and Mary C., Jan. 15, 1847.

NOYCE (see also Noyes), Abigail, d. Nichalos and Sarah, Nov. 7, 1727.
James, s. [Dr. C. R. 1.] Nichalos and Sarah, Jan. 31, 1731-2.
James, s. Nicholas and Sarah, Oct. 19, 1743.
Mary, d. [Dr. C. R. 1.] Nicholas and Sarah, Nov. 6, 1739.
Nichalos, s. [Dr. C. R. 1.] Nichalos and Sarah, Nov. 29, 1733.
Phebe, d. Nicholas and Phebe, Sept. 22, 1813.
Sarah, d. Nicholass and Sarah, [Sept?] 27, 1735.[bp. Sept. 28. C. R. 1.]
Susannah, d. Nicholas and Sarah, July 21, 1741.
Timothy, s. Nichalos and Sarah, Oct. 23 [1725].
Ward, s. Nichalos and Sarah, Dec. 21, 1729.

NOYES (see also Noyce, Noys, Noyse), Aaron, s. Wadleigh and Phebe, Jan. 27, 1829.
Caroline P., d. Frederick and Hannah, Mar. 31, 1819.
Charles D., s. Frederick and Hannah, May 28, 1832.
Elizabeth, d. Timothy and Sarah, June 18, 1768.
Ellen, d. Frederick and Hannah, Jan. 23, 1827.
Emily, d. Frederick and Hannah, Sept. 25, 1821.
Fanny, d. Frederick and Hannah, Oct. 13, 1814.
Frederick, s. Frederick and Hannah, Apr. 6, 1829.
Hannah, d. twin, Samuel and Hannah, Oct. 11, 1766.
Hannah Varnum, d. Frederick and Hannah, Sept. 28, 1812.
Henry Alfred, s. Wadleigh and Phebe, bp. Oct. 9, 1842. C. R. 3.
Isaac, s. Samuel and Hannah, May 21, 1765.
Josiah M[ilton. C. R. 3.], s. Wadleigh and Phebe, Jan. 6, 1833.
Lydia Jane, d. Frederick and Hannah, July 18, 1823.
Martha Elizabeth, d. Wadleigh and Phebe, bp. July 14, 1839 C. R. 3.
Mary, d. twin, Samuel and Hannah, Oct. 11, 1766.
Mary, d. Timothy and Sarah, Oct. 6, 1770.
Mary, d. Timothy and Sarah, Aug. 15, 1775.
Mary, d. Nicholas and Phebe, Jan. 20, 1804.
Mary Ann, d. Wadleigh and Phebe [A. C. R. 3.], Oct. 22, 1830.
Mary Ann, d. Wadleigh and Phebe, bp. July 14, 1839. C. R. 3.
Mary B., d. Frederick and Hannah, Jan. 1, 1810.
Moses, s. Wadleigh and Phebe, bp. Nov. 22, 1835. C. R. 3.
Nathan [Ballard. C. R. 3.], s. Wadleigh and Phebe, Sept. 29, 1827.
Nicholas, s. Timothy and Sarah, Mar. 21, 1760.
Nicholas, s. Timothy and Sarah, July 5, 1762.
Philip, s. Timothy and Sarah, Aug. 25, 1764.
Sally, d. Aaron, bp. Oct. 13, 1793. C. R. 2.
Sally, d. Nicholas and Phebe, Apr. 24, 1806.
[Samuel. C. R. 1.], s. Nicholas and Sarah, July —, 1737.
Sarah, d. Timothy and Sarah, May 21, 1766.
Sarah, d. Frederick and Hannah, Apr. 26, 1816.
Sarah Ward, d. Dr. Ward and Prudence, May 13, 1792.
Timothy, s. Nicholas and Phebe, Sept. 30, 1801.
Wadly, ch. Aaron, bp. Jan. 10, 1796. C. R. 2.
Ward, s. Nicholas and Phebe, June 20, 1811.
William Gilbert, s. Wadleigh and Phebe, bp. Nov. 12, 1837. C. R. 3.
——, s. Nicholas and Sarah, Sept. 9, 1724.

NOYS (see also Noyes), Mary [Maria. C. R. 1.], d. Dr. Ward and Prudence, Apr. 27, 1794.

NOYSE (see also Noyes), Philep, s. Timothy and Sarah, Jan. 11, 1757.
Philep, s. Timothy and Sarah, Dec. 19, 1757.
Sarah, d. Timothy and Sarah, Mar. 29, 1755.
Timothy, s. Timothy and Sarah, Jan. 7, 1754.

NUTTING, Joseph, s. Richard and Miriam, Apr. 1, 1719.
Phillip F., s. Phillip B. and Mehitable, Oct. 7, 1827.

ODEL, Joseph, s. Joseph and Sarah, bp. Oct. 16, 1768. C. R. 1.
Pamela, d. Joseph and Sarah, bp. Oct. 16, 1768. C. R. 1.
Phebe, d. Wiliam and Phebe, Oct. 16, 1749.
Richard, s. Joseph and Sarah, bp. Mar. 4, 1770. C. R. 1.
Sarah, d. Joseph and Sarah, bp. Mar. 8, 1772. C. R. 1.

O'DONNELL, Martha Ann, d. Daniel, blacksmith, and Jane, both b. Ireland, at Springfield, Oct. 17, 1848. [bp. Sept. 17. C. R. 4.]

O'NEAL, Elizabeth, d. Joseph and Elisa[beth], in Conn., Aug. 1, 1793.

ORDWAY, Daniel, s. Daniel and Deborah, Sept. 17, 1773.
Isaac, s. Daniel, bp. Feb. 12, 1775. C. R. 2.

ORREL (see also Orrell), Sarah Ann, d. John, clothier, and Ann, Feb. 14, 1845.

ORRELL (see also Orrel), Margaret, d. John, spinner, and Nancy, Mar. 23, 1847.

OSGOOD (see also Ossgood), Aaron, s. Hooker and Dorathy, —— [1703-4?].
Aaron, s. Joshua and Mary, Oct. 11, 1760.
Abbiah, d. Timothy, 3d and Phebe, Dec. 13, 1747.
Abigael, d. Josiah and Abigael, Dec. 17, 1730.
Abigall, d. Christopher and Hannah, Aug. 29, 1673.
Abigall, d. Thomas and Susanna, Aug. 11, 1690.
Adeline, d. Peter, farmer, and Rebecca M., Dec. 31, 1849.
Alfred, s. John, Esq. and Hulda, Mar. 7, 1773.
Appelton, s. William and Mary, Mar. 4, 1742-3.
Appleton, s. William and Mary, Dec. 27, 1735.
[Asa. C. R. 1.], s. Timothy, 3d and Phebe, Oct. —, 1744.
Asa, s. Phebe, wid. [Timothy. C. R. 1.], Dec. 22, 1753.

OSGOOD, Asa, s. Asa and Dorcas, bp. Nov. 5, 1780. C. R. I.
Benjamin, s. Hooker and Dorithy, May 20 [21. T. C.; 28. dup.], 1700.
Benjamin, s. Josiah and Hannah, Feb. 24, 1755.
Benja[min] Binney, s. Dr. George and Eliza[beth], Nov. 29, 1790.
Charles Grandison, s. Peter and Susanna Poor, June 4, 1785.
Charles Grandison, s. Capt. Peter, jr. and Hannah, bp. Sept. 20, 1789. C. R. I.
Charles Wesley, s. Peter and Rebecca M., Nov. 14, 1841.
Charlotte, d. Col. John and Hulda, Nov. 27, 1767.
Charlotte, d. Capt. Timothy and Sarah, Feb. 26, 1809.
Charlotte, d. Peter, farmer, and Rebecca M., Nov. 8, 1847.
Charlottee [Emeline. C. R. I.], d. Isaac [jr. C. R. I.] and Charlottee, Dec. 31, 1831. [Dec. 20. P. R. 92.]
Chloe, d. Timothy, jr. and Chloe, Mar. 1, 1766.
Christopher, s. Christopher and Hannah, Aug. 28, 1675.
[Christopher. C. R. 2.] ——phor, s. Ezekel and Rebecca, Jan. 21, 1721-2.
Christopher, s. Ezekiel, bp. Sept. 9, 1750. C. R. 2.
Christopher, s. Samuel and Eliz[abe]th, Apr. 25, 1769.
Christopher, s. Samuel, jr. and Lydia, Apr. 1, 1816.
Clemence, s. John and Mary, Oct. 4, 1678.
Clement, s. John and Mary, Oct. 12, 1680.
Daniel, s. John and Hannah, Jan. 19, 1693.
Daniel, s. Jeremiah and Lydia, Apr. 29, 1737.
Daniel, s. Ezekiel and Mary, May 9, 1755.
Daniel, s. Josiah and Hannah, Apr. 26, 1758.
Darcis, d. Jeremiah and Marcy, Aug. 11, 1748.
David, s. Hooker and Dorothy, Oct. 8, 1698.
[David. C. R. 2.], s. Stephen and Hannah, Feb. 25, 1718-19.
David, s. Isaac and Elisabeth, Oct. 14, 1747.
David, s. Ezekiel and Mary, Feb. 20, 1758.
Dean, s. Samuel and Hannah, July 27, [1714].
Deborah, d. Thomas and Susannah, Feb. 26, 1685-6.
Deborah, d. Timothy and Mary, Apr. 28, 1730.
Dorathy, d. Christoph[er] and Hanna, July 4, 1671.
Dorathy, d. Hooker and Dorathy, —— [1707?].
Dorathy, d. Samuel and Dorathy, Sept. 18, 1745.
[Dorcas. C. R. I.], d. Dea. John and Hannah, Sept. —, 1721.
Dorcas, d. Stephen, jr., bp. Feb. 6, 1732. C. R. 2.
Dorcas, d. Jeremiah and Mary, July 14, 1746.
Dorcas, d. Ezekiel and Mary, Aug. 2, 1759.
Dorcas, d. Sam[ue]ll, bp. Mar. 27, 1763. C. R. 2.

OSGOOD, Dorcis, d. John, jr. and Martha, Mar. 24, 1752.
Ebenezer, s. John and Hannah, Mar. 26, 1685.
Elezebith, d. Samuel and Elezebith, Dec. 17, 1755.
Elezebith, d. John, 3d and Mary, Mar. 1, 1757.
Eliakem, s. Samuel and Dorathy, Aug. 21, 1743.
Elisabeth, d. Isaac and Elisabeth, Apr. 14, 1746.
Elisabeth, d. Joseph, bp. Nov. 8, 1789. C. R. 2.
Eliza [Elizabeth. C. R. 2.], d. Samuel, jr. and Lydia, May 30, 1808.
Elizabeth, d. Hooker and Dorathy, —— [1710.]
[Elizabeth. C. R. 2.] ——th, d. Ezekiel and Rebecah, Aug. 20, 1732.
Elizabeth, d. Dr. George and Eliza[beth], Oct. 24, 1788.
Elizabeth, d. Thomas and Hannah, July 17, 1794.
Enoch, s. Col. John and Hulda, Nov. 7, 1775.
Esther, d. Christopher and Hannah, Oct. 31, 1684.
Ezekiel, s. Ezekiel, bp. Jan. 13, 1712. C. R. 2.
Ezekiel, s. Ezekiel and Mary, June 1, 1747.
Ezekiell, s. Christopher and Hannah, Nov. 5, 1679.
Frances Gayton, ch. Isaac [jr. C. R. 1.] and Charlotte (Adams), Dec. 28, 1829. P. R. 92.
Frederick, s. Samuel, jr. and Lydia, May 28, 1806.
George, s. [Capt. C. R. 1.] Joseph and Margrat, Dec. 1, 1758.
George Ephraim, s. Peter and Sally, July 31, 1833.
George Newton, s. Samuel, bp. Jan. 29, 1832. C. R. 2.
Granvill, s. Capt. Timothy and Sarah, Oct. 25, 1811.
Hanna, d. Christopher and Hanna, Oct. 19, 1668.
Hannah, d. Jo[h]n and Mary, May 30, 1674.
Hannah, d. Thomas and Susanna, Nov. 29, 1679.
Hannah, d. Stephen, Mar. 4, 1701-2.
Hannah, d. Ezekiel and Rebecca, bp. June 1, 1718. C. R. 2.
Hannah, d. Stephen, jr., bp. Feb. 16, 1735. C. R. 2
Hannah, d. Timothy and Mary, July 31, 1735.
Hannah, d. W[illia]m, bp. ——, 1737. C. R. 1.
Hannah, d. Samuel, jr. and Dorathy, Feb. 7, 1747-8.
Hannah, d. John, jr. and Marthe, Dec. 27, 1748.
Hannah, d. Col. John and Martha, Nov. 6, 1754.
Hannah, d. Ezekiel and Mary, Sept. 21, 1761.
Hannah, d. Samuel, jr. and Hannah, Oct. 1, 1773.
Hannah, d. Ens. Timothy and Cloe, Oct. —, 1781. [bp. Oct. 28. C. R. 1.]
Hannah, d. Joseph, bp. May 14, 1786. C. R. 2.
Hannah, d. Capt. Peter, jr. and Hannah, Dec. 23, 1795. [bp. Dec. 28, 1794. C. R. 1.]

OSGOOD, Hannah [Wilkins. C. R. 2.], d. Thomas and Hannah, June 3, 1796.
Harriot, d. Capt. Peter, jr. and Hannah, Mar. 28, 1791.
Harriot, d. twin, John and Elizabeth, Feb. 9, 1812.
Heber, s. Steven and Mary, Aug. 24, 1668.
Henry, s. Lt. Timothy [jr. C. R. 1.] and Sarah, Aug. 14, 1791.
Hooker, s. Hooker and Dorothy, Mar. 26, 1693.
Isaac, s. Timothy and Mary, Aug. 4, 1724.
Isaac, s. Peter and Sarah, Jan. 27, 1743-4.
Isaac, s. Isaac and Elezebith, Nov. 24, 1749.
Isaac, s. Peter and Sarah, July 15, 1756.
Isaac, s. Ezek[ie]l, bp. Nov. 25, 1764. C. R. 2.
Isaac, s. Timothy, jr. and Chloe, Dec. 8, 1771.
Isaac, s. Thomas and Hannah, Jan. 28, 1793.
Isaac, s. Lt. Timothy, jr. and Sarah, Apr. 20, 1793.
Isaac, s. twin, John and Elizabeth, Feb. 9, 1812.
Isaac F[alkner. C. R. 1.], s. Isaac, jr. and Charlotte, Aug. 16, 1824. [Aug. 12. P. R. 92.]
Isaack, s. Stephen and Hannah [bp. Feb. 21, 1714. C. R. 2.].
Isaak, s. Timothy and Deborah, —— [1708?].
Jacob, s. Isaac and Elezebith, Nov. 16, 1752.
James, s. Timothy, jr. and Phebe, Dec. 26, 1749.
James, s. Timo[thy], jr. and Chloe, Nov. 28, 1768.
Jeremiah, s. John and Hannah, Jan. 16, 1687-8.
Jeremiah, s. John and Hannah, July 11, 1691.
Jeremiah, s. Christopher and Sa[rah], —— [1702].
Jeremiah, s. Jeremiah and Lydea, Sept. 12, 1733.
Jeremiah, s. Jeremiah and Lydia, May 16, 1735.
Jerusha, d. Joseph and Mary, Feb. 10, 1719-20.
John, s. John and Mary, Sept. 3, 1654.
John, s. John and Hannah, June 28, 1683.
John, s. Ezekiel and Rebeca, July 4, 1725.
John, s. John, jr. and Martha, Nov. 12, 1750.
John, s. Mr. Joseph and Margret, Nov. 14, 1754.
John, s. Ezekiel, bp. Apr. 3, 1763. C. R. 1.
John, s. Samuel and Elizabeth, Sept. 7, 1765.
John, s. Col. John and Hulda, June 2, 1770.
John, s. Timothy and Chloe, Oct. 25, 1773.
John, s. Dr. George and Eliza[beth], July 12, 1793.
John Adams, s. Isaac [jr. C. R. 1.] and Charlotte, Aug. 29, 1826. P. R. 92.
John George, s. Mr. Joseph and Margret, Aug. 20, 1752.
John Newton, s. Samuel and Martha, Aug. 24, 1825.
Johnathan, s. Hooker and Dorothy, Sept. 16, 1696.

OSGOOD, Jonathan, s. Josiah and Hannah, Sept. 21, 1761.
Joseph, s. Joseph and Mary, Feb. 9, 1712-13.
[Joseph. C. R. 2.], s. Stephen and Hannah, Apr. 11, 1717.
Joseph, s. John and Hannah, Sept. 5, 1718.
Joseph, s. Joseph and Mary, Dec. 10, 1721.
Joseph, s. Peter and Sarah, Dec. 3, 1751.
Joseph, s. Peter and Sarah, May 30, 1758.
Joseph, s. Samuel and Elizabeth, Oct. 5, 1760.
Joseph, s. Joseph, bp. Aug. 17, 1788. C. R. 2.
Joshua, s. Hooker and Dorothy, Sept. 2, 1694.
Joshua, s. Stephen and Hannah, July 17, 1724.
Joshua, s. Joshua, bp. July 17, 1757. C. R. 2.
Joshua, s. Joshua and Mary, July 16, 1759.
Josiah, s. Thomas and Susannah, Mar. 1, 1682-3.
Josiah, s. Thomas and Susanna, May 31, 1688.
Josiah, s. John and [TOTn], —— [1706-7?].
Josiah, s. Josiah and Abigael, Nov. 20, 1732.
Judeth, d. Thomas and Susannah, Feb. 8, 1683.
[Kendal. C. R. 2.], s. Isaac and Elezebith, July —, 1756. [bp. July 11. C. R. 2.]
Liddia, d. John and Mary, Aug. 12, 1661.
Lydea, d. Samuel and Elezebith, May 31, 1754.
Lydia, d. Christopher and Sarah, June 14,. 1694.
Lydia, d. Christopher and Sarah, Sept. 1, 1695.
Lydia, d. Stephen and Ha[nnah, bp. Mar. 9, 1712. C. R. 2.]
[Lydia. T. C.], d. [S]amuel and Hannah, Oct. 20, 1716.
Lydia, d. Jeremiah and Lydia, Sept. 8, 1728.
Lydia, d. Peter and Sarah, Mar. 22, 1760.
Lydia, d. Samuel, jr. and Lydea, Nov. 14, 1809.
Margaret, d. [Dr. C. R. 1.], Joseph and Margaret [Mehitable. C. R. 1.], Nov. 4, 1760.
Mariah, d. Dr. [Dea. C. R. 1.] George and Elizabeth, Jan. 17, 1802.
Martha, d. John, jr. and Martha, May 3, 1747.
Martha, d. Samuel, jr. and Martha, Apr. 9, 1819.
Mary, d. John and Mary, Nov. 27, 1656.
Mary, d. Christo[phe]r and Hanna, July 5, 1665.
Mary, d. Thomas and Susannah, Feb. 14, 1675[-6].
Mary, d. Stephen and Mary, Dec. 23, 1677.
Mary, d. Christopher and Hannah, Mar. 8, 1686-7.
Mary, d. Timothy and Deborah, Feb. 11, 1689-90.
Mary, d. Capt. Christopher and Sarah, —— [1705?].
Mary, d. Dea. John and Hannah, June 10, 1726.
Mary, d. Timothy and Mary, Feb. 21, 1726-7.

OSGOOD, Mary, d. Ezekiel and Rebeca, June 16, 1729.
Mary, d. William and Mary, Sept. 4, 1[730. C. R. 1.].
Mary, d. Stephen, jr., bp. Jan. 2, 1737. C. R. 2.
Mary, d. Ezekiel and Mary, Mar. 24, 1748-9.
Mary, d. Timothy, jr. and Phebe, Mar. 24, 1752.
Mary, d. John, jr. and Martha, Sept. 30, 1753.
Mary, d. Joshua and Mary, Oct. 8, 1754.
Mary, d. John, 3d and Mary, Feb. 24, 1755.
Mary, d. Joshua and Mary, Oct. 15, 1766.
Mary, d. Timothy and Chloe, Aug. 6, 1776.
Mary, d. Jacob and Rhoda, Apr. 21, 1777.
Mary, d. Thomas and Hannah, Oct. 19, 1799.
Mary Augusta, d. Sam[ue]l and Julia, bp. Oct. 22, 1821. C. R. 1.
Mary Loisa, d. Capt. Timothy and Sarah, Oct. 14, 1804.
Mehetabel, d. Jeremiah and Lydea, Mar. 20 [1732. C. R. 2.].
Mehitabel, d. Thomas and Susannah, May 25, 1694.
Mehitabell, d. John and Mary, Mar. 4, 1671. [1671-2. dup.]
Moses, s. Hooker and Dorithy, —— [1702].
Nathan, s. Ezekiel and Mary, Nov. 15, 1756.
Nathaniell, s. John and Hannah, Jan. 6, 1686.
Peeter, s. John and Mary, Aug. 30, 1663.
[Peter. C. R. 1.], s. Peter and Sarah, June 24, 17[45. C. R. 1.].
Peter, s. Capt. Peter, jr. and Hannah, Feb. 4 [1793. T. C; bp. Feb. 10, 1793. C. R. 1.].
Peter, s. Capt. Timothy and Sarah, Aug. 8, 1802.
Phebe, d. Timothy and Mary, —— 26 [bp. May 27, 1733. C. R. 1.].
Phebe, d. Timothy, 3d and Phebe, Apr. 29, 1746.
Phebe, d. Ezekiel and Mary, Mar. 11, 1752.
Phineas, s. Ezekiel and Mary, May 19, 1753.
Phoebe, d. Christopher and Sarah, Sept. 19, 1688.
Priscilla, d. Christopher and Hannah, Apr. 1, 1681.
Rachel, d. Stephen and Hannah, Jan. 7, 1720-21.
Rebeca, d. Jeremiah and Lydea, Sept. 4, 1730.
Rebecca, d. Samuel and Dorathy, Feb. 6, 1739-40.
Rebecca Pickman, d. Isaac, jr. and Charlotte, Feb. 7, 1823. [Feb. 8. P. R. 92.]
Rebecka, d. Christopher and Sarah, May 3, 1692.
Rebekah, d. Dr. George and Elizebeth, Jan. 31, 1796.
Rhoda, d. Joshua, jr. and Rhoda, Jan. 24, 1796.
Rhoda, d. Samuel, jr. and Lydia, Mar. 30, 1814.
Ruth, d. Ebenezer and Rebecka, Oct. 19, 1718.
Samuel, s. Ezekiel and Rebecka, May 29, 1714.
Samuel, s. Samuel and Dorithy, Oct. 6, 1741.
Samuel, s. Peter and Sarah, Feb. 3, 1747-8.

Osgood, Samuel, s. Samuel and Hannah, June 7, 1779.
Samuel, s. Ens. Timothy and Cloe, Nov. 2, 1779.
Samuel, s. Capt. Peter, jr. and Hannah, bp. Sept. 20, 1789. C. R. I.
Samuell, s. John and Mary, Mar. 10, 1664.
Sara, d. John and Mary, Apr. 7, [16]67.
Sarah, d. John and Mary, Nov. 4, 1675.
Sarah, d. Thomas and Susanna, Feb. 6, 1677.
Sarah, d. Christopher and Hannah, Feb. 19, 1682
Sarah, d. Sam[ue]ll and Hannah, —— [1709?].
[Sarah. C. R. 2.], d. Jeremiah and Lydea, Aug. 5, 1729.
Sarah, d. William and Mary, Feb. 11, 1733-4.
Sarah, d. William and Mary, Dec. 4, 1739.
Sarah, d. Jeremiah and Lydia, Apr. 23, 1741.
Sarah, d. Thomas and Sarah, Dec. 3, 1749.
Sarah, d. Peter and Sarah, Feb. 11, 1749-50.
Sarah, d. Samuel and Elezebith, Sept. 14, 1758.
Sarah, d. Samuel and Hannah, Oct. 27, 1778.
Sarah, d. Timothy, jr. and Sarah, Sept. 9, 1789.
Sarah, d. Dr. [Dea. C. R. I.] George and Sarah, Apr. 30, 1804.
Sarah Ann [Noyes. C. R. 2.], d. Samuel, jr. and Lydia, Nov. 14, 1811.
Sarah F., d. Peter and Sally, Sept. 26, 1833.
Sarah F., d. Peter and Rebecca, Apr. 26, 1840.
Solomon, s. Josiah and Abigail [bp. Aug. 1, 1736. C. R. I.].
Steven, s. Steven and Mary, Mar. 1, [16]65.
Steven, s. Steven and Mary, Aug. 16, 1670.
Susanna, d. Thomas and Susannah, Oct. 29, 1692.
Susanna, d. Ebenezer and Rebecka, July 8, 1716.
[Su]sanna, d. William and Sarah, Jan. 5, 1726-7.
Susanna, d. Lt. William and Mary, Apr. 17, 1746.
Susanna, d. Peter and Sarah, Aug. 23, 1754.
Susannah, d. Capt. Timothy and Sarah, Feb. 17, 1795.
Susannah Richards, d. James and Sarah, Dec. 10, 1815.
Thomas, s. Thomas and Susannah, Dec. 17, 1680.
Thomas, s. Timothy and Mary [Phebe. C. R. I.], Nov. 2, 1721.
Thomas, s. Thomas and Sarah, Oct. 28, 1751.
Thomas, s. [Capt. C. R. I.] Joseph and Margaret, Oct. 29, 1756.
Thomas, s. Samuel and Elizabeth, June 11, 1767.
Timothy, s. John and Mary, Aug. 10, 1659.
Timothy, s. Timothy and Deborah, Aug. 16, 1691.
Timothy, s. Timothy and Deborah, Aug. 22, 1693.
Timothy, s. Timothy and Mary [Phebe. C. R. I.], Aug. 26, 1719.
Timothy, s. Timothy, 3d and Phebe, July 27, 1743.
Timothy, s. Peter and Sarah, Mar. 17, 1763.

OSGOOD, Timothy, s. Timothy, jr. and Chloe, July 7, 1767.
Timothy, s. Capt. Timothy [jr. C. R. 1.] and Sarah, Apr. 26, 1800.
William, s. William and Sarah, June 3, 1725.
William, s. William and Mary, Nov. 27, 1740.
William, s. Capt. Timothy and Sarah, Feb. 22, 1797.
William, s. Capt. Timothy and Sarah, Apr. 9, 1798.
William Samuel, s. Samuel and Martha, Apr. 24, 1823.
Zachariah, s. William and Mary, Apr. 30, 1732.
——, ch. [torn] and Deborah, —— [1701].
——, ch. [Sa]muell and Hannah, —— 13 [1702].
——, d. Samuel and Hannah, ——, 1704.
——, ch. Samuell and Hannah, Mar. 16, 1705-6.
——, ch. Hooker and Dorathy, Apr. 5, 1706.
——, ch. [torn]hen and Hannah, Aug. 18, 1709.
——, ch. John and Hannah, Aug. 22, 1710.
——, d. Joseph and Mary, Jan. 13, 1710-11.
——, ch. John and Hannah, July 17, 1712.
——, ch. Ebenezer and Rebecka, Sept. 3, 1712.
——, d. John and Hannah, Aug. 15, 1714.
——, d. Ebenezer and Rebecka, Aug. 16, 1714.
——, ch. Timothy and Mary, Nov. 14, 1717.
——, s. Ezekiel and Mary, Sept. —, 1750.
——, d. Josiah and Hannah, June 4, 1751.
——, s. Josiah and Hannah, Mar. —, 1753.
——, s. Samuel, jr. and Martha, Jan. 28, 1821.

OSSGOOD (see also Osgood), Hannah, d. John and Hannah, June 24, 1699.
Martha, d. Christopher and Sarah, Dec. 14, 1698.
Mary, d. Joseph and Mary, Feb. 8, 1700-1701.
Mehetabel, d. Samuel and Hannah, —— [1711].
Peter, s. Timothy and Deborah, May 31, 1699.
Sarah, d. Timothy and Deborah, Aug. 8, 1697.
Stephen, s. Stephen and Hannah, June 22, 1700.
——, d. Stephen and Hannah, July 8, 1704.
——, ch. [torn] and Mary, Dec. 3, 1704.

OWEN, Morris, s. John, laborer, and Orlous, May 15, 1845.

PACE, Albert, s. Leonard, laborer, and Hannah, Apr. 26, 1847.
Amus Holt, s. David and Nancy, Sept. 29, 1810.
Caroline A., d. Amos, laborer, and Mary J., Apr. 20, 1845.
Elvira, d. Joseph, laborer, and Olive M., Nov. 26, 1843.
Emiline M., d. Leonard, laborer, and Hannah, Sept. 30, 1845.

PACE, Joseph, s. David and Nancy, Mar. 10, 1821.
Lavina, d. David and Nancy, Sept. 6, 1812.
Leonard, s. David and Nancy, July 15, 1816.
Mary E., d. Amos, laborer, and Mary J., Feb. 20, 1849.
Ruby J., d. Leonard, laborer, and Hannah, b. Derry, N. H., Dec. 23, 1849.
Susan Jennings, d. David and Nancy, June 8, 1809.
William, s. David and Nancy, Aug. 12, 1814.

PACKARD, —— [Francis. C. R. 4.], d. Rev. George and Sarah M., Jan. 23, 1844.

PAGE, Benjamin Frost, s. Ashel and Lucy, bp. Apr. 27, 1794. C. R. 1.
Betty, d. Daniel and Hannah, Sept. 15, 1771.
Daniel, s. Daniel and Hannah, Mar. 14, 1760.
Daniel, s. Daniel, bp. Sept. 19, 1771. C. R. 1.
Emarilla, d. Amos H. and Mary Jane, Nov. 6, 1841.
Evelina Elizabeth, d. John O. and Elizabeth, June 19, 1839.
Francis, s. Ashl and Lucy, bp. Apr. 1, 1792. C. R. 1.
Hannah, d. Daniel and Hannah, Apr. 1, 1761.
Hannah, d. Daniel and Hannah, June 18, 1766.
John Augustine, s. John and Elizabeth, bp. Sept. 5, 1841. C. R. 3.
Mary, d. Daniel and Hannah, July 29, 1758.
Mary Ann, d. Rev. Jesse and Anne P., Nov. 30, 1839.
Oliver Hale, s. John and Elizabeth, bp. Sept. 5, 1841. C. R. 3.
Sarah, d. Daniel and Hannah, May 4, 1763.
William Little, s. Rev. Jesse and Ann P., July 1, 1841.

PALMER, Nathan Edward, s. Daniel W., machinist, and Sabea, Mar. 21, 1849.
Sarah Elizabeth, d. Edward, bp. Aug. 15, 1824. C. R. 6.
——, d. M——, May 25, 1824.

PARK, Agnes, d. Edwards A., proff[essor] of theol[og]y, and Mariah E., July 6, 1845.
William Edwards, s. Edwards A. and Maria E., July 1, 1837.
——, d. Prof. E. A., Feb. 23, 1841.

PARKER, Aaron, s. Asa and Sarah, June 2, 1774.
Aaron, s. Jos[eph], bp. Oct. 19, 1777. C. R. 2.
[Abi]gail, d. Joseph and Marth[a], June 13, 1737
Abigail, d. James and Dinah, Sept. 7, 1743.
Abigail, d. John and Abigail, Oct. 15, 1771.

PARKER, Almira, d. Isaac and Polly, Nov. 26, 1793.
Ann, d. James and Phebe, Apr. 9, 1736.
Anna, d. Nathan and Anna, bp. Sept. 13, 1772. C. R. I.
Anna, d. Hincher, bp. Mar. 20, 1785. C. R. 2.
Anna, d. Carlton, of Dracut, bp. Sept. 17, 1786. C. R. 2.
Asa, s. Benjamin and Sarah [Mary. C. R. I.], Sept. 24, 17[29. C. R. I.].
Asa, s. Asa and Sarah, June 30, 1760.
Augusta, d. Isaac and Polly, July 27, 1797.
Benjamin, s. John and Hannah, June 10, 1693.
Benjamin, s. Benjamin and Sarah, Sept. 25, 1730.
Benjamin, s. Asa, bp. Mar. 7, 1762. C. R. I.
Betty, d. Lt. John and Abigail, Feb. 2, 1780. [bp. Feb. 7, 1779. C. R. I.]
Carlton, s. Carlton, bp. June 12, 1791. C. R. 2.
Carlton O., s. Carlton and Mary, June 24, 1822.
Charles, s. Carlton, bp. Dec. 21, 1800. C. R. 2.
Charles S., s. twin, Carlton and Mary, July 13, 1826.
Charles S., s. Stephen H., trader, and Ann M., Oct. 21, 1845.
Charlotte, d. Lt. John and Abigail, Oct. 1, 1789.
Charlotte, d. Isaac and Polly, Dec. 12, 1799.
Clarasa, d. Isaac and Polly, Dec. 2, 1791.
Doalton [Dalton. C. R. I.], s. James and Dinah, Mar. 10, 1739-40.
Dolly, d. Jonathan and Hannah, Jan. 31, 1771.
Dorcas, d. Joseph and Hannah, Feb. 17, 1769.
Dorcas, d. Lt. John and Abigail, Mar. 5, 1781.
Dorcas, d. Moses and Dorcas B., Nov. 6, 1821.
Elbridge, s. Michael, jr. and Fanny, Sept. 3, 1812.
Elezebith, d. Joseph, 3d and Elezebith, July 21, 1758
Elisabeth, d. Stephen and Mary, Dec. 6, 1692.
Elisabeth, d. Carlton, bp. Aug. 9, 1789. C. R. 2.
Elizabeth, d. Nathan and Mary, Jan. 20, 1663.
Elizabeth, d. Nathan and Elizabeth, Aug. 11, 1733.
[Enoch. C. R. I.], s. Asa and Sarah, Sept. [3 or 23?], 1752.
Fanney [Town. C. R. I.], d. Michael, jr. and Fanney, Jan. 27, 1806.
Francis Emily, d. Carleton, bp. Nov. 26, 1834. C. R. 2.
Frederic, s. Michael and Phebe, bp. Apr. 13, 1788. C. R. I.
Frederick, s. Nathan and Anna, Jan. 20, 1771.
George A., s. George H. and Mary L. (Putnam), July 7, 1848.
George H., s. twin, Carlton and Mary, July 13, 1826.
Hanna, d. Nathan and Mary, May 14, 1659.
Hannah, d. Jo[h]n and Hannah, July 22, 1699.
Hannah, d. Peter and Hannah, Dec. 20, 1736.

PARKER, Hannah, d. Nathan and Hannah, Oct. 11, 1738.
[Hannah. C. R. 1.]—nah, d. Peter and Hannah, Apr. 2, 1743.
Hannah, d. Peter and Hannah, Apr. 4, 1747.
Hannah, d. Jonathan and Hannah, Mar. 24, 1758.
Hannah, d. Joseph, jr. and Hannah, Apr. 30, 1758.
Hannah, d. Peter, jr. and Phebe, Feb. 19, 1771.
Hannah, d. Jonathan and Hannah, Jan. 19, 1774.
Hannah, d. Lt. John and Abigail, Jan. 19, 1777.
Hannah, d. Michael and Phebe, Nov. 4, 1779.
Hannah, d. Isaac and Polly, Oct. 6, 1789.
Helen Lucasta, d. Nathan and Mary, June 12, 1838.
Henry Winthrop, s. Stephen H., merchant, b. Methuen, and Ann M., b. Concord, N. H., Oct. 15, 1849.
Hester, d. Joseph and Mary, May 12, 1654.
Isaac, s. Peter and Hannah, Aug. 29, 1749.
Isaac, s. Asa and Sarah, Aug. 18, 1767. [bp. July 26, 1767. C. R. 1.]
Isaac, s. Isaac and Mary, Sept. 18, 1795.
Jacob, s. Joseph and Lydia, June 11, 1772.
James, s. Nathan and Mary, Aug. 14, 1655.
James, s. Jo[h]n and Hannah, Oct. 12, 1696.
James, s. Joseph and Abigail, Mar. 6, 1715-16.
James, s. Joseph and Lydea, Apr. 25, 1724.
James, s. Joseph and Mary, Aug. 8, 1730.
James, s. James and Dinah, Mar. 17, 1741-2.
James, s. James and Phebe, Aug. 30, 1746.
James, s. Joseph and Martha, Apr. 11, 1751.
Jenny, d. Asa, bp. Dec. 16, 1770. C. R. 1.
Jeremiah, s. Asa and Sarah, Jan. 17, 1764.
Jesse, s. James and Phebe, Oct. 28, 1738.
Jesse, s. John and Abigail, Mar. 17, 1775.
John, s. Nathan and Mary, Dec. 20, 1653.
John, s. Joseph and Mary, June 30, 1656.
John, s. John and Hannah, Mar. 28, 1688.
John, s. Stephen and Mary, Apr. 13, 1688.
John, s. Nathan and Hannah, May 19, 1742.
John, s. Jonathan and Hannah, Mar. 16, 1753.
John, s. Joseph, jr. and Hannah, Aug. 15, 1760.
John, s. Lt. Michael and Phebe, Dec. 11, 1789.
John C[rombie. C. R. 2.], s. Carlton and Mary, July 2, 1828.
Jonathan, s. Jo[h]n and Hannah, —— [1707?].
Jonathan, s. Jonathan and Hannah, Mar. 26, 1738.
Jonathan, s. Jonathan and Hannah, Sept. 20, 1767.
Jonathan, s. Hincher, bp. Sept. 28, 1783. C. R. 2.
Joseph, s. Joseph and Elizabeth, Feb. 27, 1681-2.

PARKER, Joseph, s. Joseph and Lydia, Nov. 25, 1700.
Joseph, s. Joseph and Abigail, —— [1712].
Joseph, s. Joseph and Mary, Aug. 24, 1724.
Joseph, s. Joseph and Mary, July 15, 1726.
Joseph, s. Joseph and Martha, Oct. 9, 1735.
Joseph, s. Joseph, jr. and Hannah, May 10, 1756.
Joseph, s. Joseph, 3d and Elizabeth, Apr. 17, 1760
Joseph, s. Joseph and Lydia, June 5, 1770.
Joseph, s. Michael and Phebe, Jan. 18, 1782.
Joseph, s. Carlton, bp. May 12, 1793. C. R. 2.
Josiah, s. Joseph, jr. and Martha, Apr. 19, 1751.
Kindel, s. Carlton, bp. Oct. 13, 1776. C. R. 2.
Lucy, d. Benjamin and Lucy, Sept. 31, 1802.
Lydea, d. Peter and Hannah, Apr. 24, 1752.
Lydia, d. Michael and Phebe, July 15, 1777.
Lydia, d. Michael and Phebe, Jan. 20, 1784.
Lydia, d. Isaac and Polly, Mar. 26, 1788.
Marble, s. Peter and Phoebe, July 1, 1775.
Martha, d. Joseph and Lydia, —— [1708?].
Martha, d. Joseph and Martha, Feb. 28, 1738-9.
Martha, d. Michael and Phebe, bp. Feb. 12, 1786. C. R. 1
Martha E., d. Carlton and Mary, July 30, 1833.
Mary, d. Nathan and Mary, Apr. 14, 1657.
Mary, d. Nathan and Mary, —— [1660].
Mary, d. Stephen and Mary, June 30, 1686.
Mary, d. [torn], —— [1702].
Mary, d. Peter and Hannah, N[ov.] 28, [1734].
Mary, d. James and Phebe, July 3, 1751.
Mary, d. Joseph and Martha, Sept. 2, 1753.
Mary, d. Asa and Sarah, Nov. 3, 1765.
Mary, d. Peter, jr. and Phebe, bp. Apr. 18, 1779. C. R. 1.
Mary Ann, d. Michael and Mehitable, Jan. 15, 1825.
Mary Jane, d. Carlton and Mary, Oct. 15, 1830.
Mary K., d. Carlton and Mary, Dec. 29, 1823.
Mehetebel, d. Asa and Sarah, Nov. 13, 1756.
Mehitable, d. Michael and Mehitable, June 11, 1817.
Michael, s. Joseph, jr. and Martha, Dec. 24 or 25, 1746
Michael, s. Michael and Phebe, Jan. 17, 1773.
Michal, s. Joseph and Mary, Oct. 9, 1728.
Molly, d. Joseph and Hannah, Sept. 7, 1766.
Molly, d. John and Abigail, Mar. 31, 1773.
Moses, s. Isaac and Mary, Nov. 29, 1801.
Nathan, s. John and Hannah, Oct. 6, 1690.
Nathan, s. Peter and Hannah, June 3, 1739.

PARKER, Nathan, s. Nathan and Hannah, July 14, 1740.
Nathan, s. Joseph, 3d and Martha, Oct. 20, 1741.
Nathan, s. Michael, jr. and Fanny, Oct. 5, 1810.
Nathaniel, s. Carlton, bp. Sept. 28, 1788. C. R. 2.
Obadiah, s. Joseph, 3d and Martha, Aug. 1, 1743.
Obadiah, s. Joseph, 3d and Martha, Aug. 16, 1747.
Olive, d. Asa and Sarah, July 27, 1758.
Olive, d. Hincher, bp. Sept. 28, 1783. C. R. 2.
Peeter, s. Joseph and Lydia, July — [1714].
Peter, s. Nathan and Mary, Apr. 3, 1676.
Peter, s. Peter and Hannah, May 28, 1741.
Peter, s. Peter and Phebe, Oct. 17, 1769.
Peter, s. Michael, jr. and Fanney, Apr. 10, 1807.
Phebe, d. Jamesand Phebe, July 12 [1734. C. R. 1.].
Phebe, d. James and Phebe, Dec. 7, 1748.
Phebe, d. Capt. Peter and Hannah, Nov. 14, 1757.
Phebe, w. Benja[min], and d. David and Phebe Mulford, at Long Island, N. Y., June 11, 1762.
Phebe, d. Peter, jr. and Phebe, Apr. 24, 1767.
Phebe, d. Michael and Phebe, Mar. 27, 1771.
Phenihas, s. Joseph, jr. and Martha, Sept. 3, 1745.
Phenihas, s. Jonathan and Hannah, Aug. 15, 1747.
Pheoby, d. Joseph and Lydia, Aug. — [1711].
Phineas, s. Joseph and Marth[a], Jan. 1, 1748-9.
Phineas, s. Jonathan and Hannah, Jan. 10, 1749-50.
Polly, d. Isaac and Polly, Oct. 27, 1786.
Priscilla, d. Carlton, bp. Dec. 31, 1797. C. R. 2.
Rebecca, d. Michael and Mehitable, May 30, 1821.
Rebecca J., d. Nathan, farmer, and Mary, Aug. 1, 1845.
Rebecca Jane, d. Nathan and Mary, July 2, 1831.
Robert, s. Nathan and Mary, Feb. 26, [16]65.
Robert, s. Peter and Hannah, Mar. 2, 1744-5.
Rozena [Rosina. C. R. 1.], d. Michael, jr. and Fanney, Mar. 17, 1809.
Ruth, d. Joseph and Mary, June 2, 1661.
Ruth, d. Stephen and Susannah, Oct. 4, 1695.
Samuel, s. Joseph and Lydia, Feb. 9, 1775.
Samuell, s. Joseph and Mary, Oct. 14, 1659.
Samuel, s. Stephen and [torn], —— [1702].
Sara, d. Nathan and Mary, Apr. 3, 1670.
Sarah, d. Joseph, jr. and Martha, June 22, 1741.
Sarah, d. Asa and Sarah [Jan. –, 1754.].
Sarah, d. Michael and Phoebe, Dec. 11, 1774.
Serena, d. Peter, jr. and Phebe, Aug. 30, 1768.

PARKER, Simeon, s. Peter and Hannah [Mary. C. R. 1.], May 3, 1754.
Solomon, s. Hincher, bp. Sept. 28, 1783. C. R. 2.
Stephen, s. Stephen and Mary, Aug. 17, 1682.
Stephen, s. Stephen and Mary, Oct. 28, 1683.
Stephen, s. Joseph, 3d and Martha, Apr. 17, 1745.
Steven, s. Joseph and M[torn], Mar. 1, 1651.
Susanna, d. Peter and Phebe, June 27, 1772.
Timothy, s. Nathaniel, Feb. 27, 1811. C. R. 1.
Warren S., s. Simeon, butcher, and Fanny, Oct. 5, 1846.
Wiliam, s. Joseph, jr. and Martha, Apr. 4, 1749.
Wiliam, s. Jonathan and Hannah, Mar. 7, 1755.
——, ch. [torn] and [torn]ia, Feb. 14, 1702-3.
——, ch. [torn] and Lydia, Feb. 28, 1704-5.
——, ch. [torn]h and Abigail, Aug. 16, 1714.
——, d. Joseph and Lydia, Jan. 13, 1716-17.
——, d. Benjamin and Sarah, Jan. 29, 1727-8.
——, s. Joseph and Mary, Apr. 25, 1733.
——, s. Jonathan and Hannah, Mar. 13, 1739-40.
——, s. Samuel and Esteher, July 13, 1741.
——, s. Joseph and Marth[a], Jan. 12, 1743-4.
——. s. James, jr. and Dinah, Feb. 28, 1745-6.
——, twin sons, Carlton and Mary, July 13, 1826.
——, twin chn., Nathan, Feb. 24, 1843.

PARSON (see also Pearsons, Persons), Joseph James, s. Joseph and Sally, Feb. 5, 1821.
Mary Eliz[abe]th, d. Joseph and Sally, Dec. 29, 1822.

PASHO, Henry F., s. Henry F. and Nancy, Oct. 10, 1822.
Julia E., d. Henry F. and Nancy, July 6, 1831.

PATTEN (see also Pattin), Stephen Holt, s. Elijah and Elcy, Jan. 19, 1801.

PATTIN (see also Patten), Elijah, s. Elijah and Lydia, Jan. 15, 1774.
Isabella, d. Andrew and Jane, bp. Nov. 10, 1839. C. R. 2.
Jean, d. Andrew and Jane, bp. Nov. 10, 1839. C. R. 2.
Molly, d. John and Molly, Dec. 4, 1773.
Rhoda, d. John and Molly, July 7, 1775.

PATTISON, Mary, d. Peter, bp. May 3, 1741 C. R. 2.

PAYSON, Anna, d. Thomas E[lliot. C. R. 4.] and Hannah [Brown. C. R. 4.], May 12, 1838.
Thomas, s. Thomas E[lliot. C. R. 4.] and Hannah B[rown. C. R. 4.], June 7, 1839.
Thomas, s. Tho[ma]s E. and Hannah B., bp. June 17, 1849. C. R. 4.

PEABODY (see also Pebody), Aaron, s. Capt. John and Mary, Feb. 13, 1777.
Aaron, s. Sam[ue]l and Elizabeth, bp. Oct. 12, 1777. C. R. 1.
Abigail, d. David, bp. June 2, 1765. C. R. 1.
Asa, s. Oliver and Sarah, Apr. 16, 1758.
Asa, s. Lt. Oliver, bp. May 8, 1763. C. R. 1.
Asa, s. Capt. John and Mary, May 17, 1779.
Betty, d. John [jr. C. R. 1.] and Mary, Oct. 27, 1772.
Charles Augustus, s. Charles Augustus and Julia Livingston, of New York City, bp. Aug. 26, 1849. C. R. 4.
David, s. David, bp. —— [1754 or 5]. C. R. 1.
Enoch, s. Lt. John [jr. C. R. 1.] and Mary, Jan. 8, 1775.
Hannah, d. Moses and Sarah, Aug. 9, 1739.
Henry, s. Sam[ue]l and Elizabeth, bp. May 27, 1781.
Huldah, d. John, jr. and Mary, [Ja]n^y 6, 1765.
Jake, s. Sam[ue]l and Elizabeth, bp. June 25, 1780. C. R. 1.
John, s. John, jr. and Mary, Nov. 2, 1766.
John, s. Sam[ue]l and Elizabeth, bp. Oct. 12, 1777. C. R. 1.
Judith, d. David, bp. Feb. 3, 1760. C. R. 1.
Kimball, s. Dudley and Rebecca, bp. Aug. 4, 1793. C. R. 1.
Lydea, d. Moses and Sarah, July 5, 1731.
Moses, s. Samuell and Lydia, —— [1705?].
Moses, s. Sam[ue]l and Elizabeth, bp. Oct. 12, 1777. C. R. 1.
Persis, d. Oliver, bp. Nov. 1, 1772. C. R. 1.
Polly, d. Capt. John and Mary, Nov. 13, 1781.
Rebecca, d. Moses and Sarah, Jan. 5, 1744-5.
Rhoda, d. Lt. Oliver, bp. May 3, 1761. C. R. 1.
Samuel, s. Moses and Sarah, May 6, 1734.
Samuel, s. Moses and Sarah, Sept. 1, 1741.
Sam[ue]l, s. Sam[ue]l and Elizabeth, bp. Oct. 12, 1777. C. R. 1.
[Sarah. C. R. 1.], d. Moses and Sarah, Mar. 31, 1729.
Sarah, d. Oliver and Sarah, Jan. 21, 1756.
Stephen, s. Oliver, bp. June 1, 1766. C. R. 1.
Stephen, s. Oliver, bp. July 1, 1770. C. R. 1.
Thom[a]s, s. David, bp. Sept. 12, 1762. C. R. 1.
Thomas, s. John, jr. and Mary, Oct. 31, 1768.
William, s. John, jr. and Mary, Aug. 12, 1770.

PEABODY, ——, ch. [torn] and Lydia, Feb. 16 [1702-3].
——, s. Moses, bp. ——, 1745. C. R. 1.

PEARL, Benjamin, s. Rich[ar]d, bp. ——, 1727. C. R. 1.

PEARSON (see also Peirson), Amos, s. Jonathan and Abigall, —— 12 [bp Dec. 15, 1734. C. R. 1.].
Bathsheba, d. James and Bathsheba, Aug. 10, 1759.
Charles I., s. George and Sarah, May 8, 1848.
David Sewal, s. Dr. Abiel and Mary, Nov. 7, 1789.
Elizabeth Adams, d. Dr. Abiel and Mary, Mar. 10, 1791.
George H., s. Joseph J. and Dorcas, Oct. 12, 1848.
Hannah, d. Jonathan and Abigaiel, Mar. 12, 1740-41.
Hannah, d. Enoch and Hannah, July 18, 1830.
Harriet Abby, d. Geo[rge], blacksmith, and Sarah J., Aug. 23, 1846.
John, s. John and Rebecca, Feb. 29, 1735-6.
Mary, d. Dr. Abiel and Mary, May 3, 1793.
Mary Holyoke, d. Eliphalet, bp. Mar. 10, 1782. C. R. 2.
Rebecca, d. John, jr. and Abigail, Jan. 4, 1770.
Samuel Moody, s. Dr. Abiel and Mary, Feb. 3, 1800.
Sarah, d. Jonathan and Abigail, May 1, 1739.
Susanna, d. John and Rebecca, July 13, 1740.
Susanna, d. James and Bathshua, Dec. 21, 1760.

PEARSONS (see also Parson), Sarah Jane, d. Joseph and Sally, Sept. 23, 1816.
Thomas Trow, s. Thomas and Lucy, May 10, 1814.

PEBODY (see also Peabody), Oliver, s. Oliver and Sarah, Sept. 2, 1753.
Rebecca, d. John, bp. ——, 1746. C. R. 1.
Stephen, s. John, bp. ——, 1741. C. R. 1.

PEEL, James W., s. William, finisher, and Sarah, Apr. 21, 1846.

PEETERS (see also Peters), Andrew, s. Andrew and Elizabeth, Dec. 9, 1686.
Beamsly, s. Sam[ue]ll and Pheoby, July 3 [1707].
Beamsly, s. Sam[ue]ll and Pheoby, —— [1710].
Hannah, d. Samuel [jr. C. R. 1.] and Mary, Dec. 14, 1730.
John, s. William and Margarett, Oct. 1, 1695.
Joseph, s. Samuel and Phebe, May 25, 1723.
[Phebee. C. R. 1.], d. Samuell and Pheebe, Apr. 16, 1720.

PEETERS, Phoebe, d. Samuel and Phoebe, Aug. 10, 1699-1700.
Samuel, s. Sam[ue]l and Phoeby, Aug. 14, 1697.
Sibbon, s. Andrew and Elizabeth, Feb. 19, 1687-8.
William, s. Samuell and Pheoby, —— [1703].
——, ch. [torn] and Phoeby, —— 26 [1701].

PEIRCE (see also Pierce), Isaac Newton, s. William and Ellen, Mar. 13, 1843.
Harris Cary, s. W[illia]m, bp. Sept. 28, 1845. C. R. 2.
William, s. Sommers and Martha, Mar. 16, 1726-7.

PEIRSON (see also Pearson), Dorcis, d. John and Rebeca, Dec. 31, 1753.
Elezebeth, d. John and Rebeca, July 31, 1748.
Hannah, d. John and Rebeca, Nov. 7, 1751.
Samuel, s. Jonathan and Abigail, Dec. 19, 1743.

PENNINGTON, Mary C., d. John, laborer, b. England, and Roxanna, b. France, Nov. 15, 1849.

PENTECOST, William A., s. William, clergyman, and Mary, both b. England, Nov. 14, 1848.

PERKINS, Dorathy, d. John and Elizabeth, Aug. 27, 1716.
Hannah, d. Timothy and Hannah, Nov. 15, 1720.
Jemina, d. John and Elizabeth, —— [1707?].
John, s. Stephen S. and Mary, Sept. 22, 1822.
Jonathan, s. Timothy and Hannah, Mar. — [1715]
Keziah, d. John and Elizabeth, —— [1710].
Rebecka, d. John and Elizabeth, July 6, 1718.
Ruth, d. Timothy and Ruth, Mar. 11, 1712-13.
Ruth, d. John and Elizabeth, Mar. 15, 17[14].
Sarah, d. Timothy and Hannah, Aug. 20, 1724.
——, d. John and Elizabeth, Mar. 23, 1711-12.
——, s. Timothy and Hannah, Dec. 9, 1716.
——, d. Timothy and Hannah, Oct. 28, 1722.
——, d. Timothy and Hannah, Nov. 1, 1726.

PERLEY, Melvina L., d. Leverett S., machinist, and Phebe F., June 25, 1848.

PERSONS (see also Parson), Hannah Trow, d. Joseph and Sally, Feb. 21, 1818.

PETENGIL (see also Pettengill), Samuel, s. Samuel and Mary, Nov. 24, 1757.

PETERS (see also Peeters, Petters), Andrew, s. John and Phebe Mar. 26, 1744.
Andrew, s. Andrew and Hannah, Oct. 26, 1771.
Andrew, s. John and Elizabeth Farington, Oct. 10, 1807.
Ariel, s. John and Sarah, Jan. 31, 1762.
Benjamin, s. Samuel and Mary, Aug. 25, 1728.
Benja[min], s. Benjamin and Hannah, bp. ——, 1755. C. R. I.
Charlott, d. John and Elizabeth F., Nov. 30, 1810.
Clarisia, d. John and Elizabeth Farrington, Feb. 1, 1809. [Feb. 12. P. R. 63.]
Daniel, s. Andrew and Hannah, Jan. 3, 1778.
Daniel Kimball, s. Daniel and Susanna, June 3, 1807.
Elizabeth, d. Benj[ami]n and Hannah, bp. June 25, 1769. C. R. I.
Emily, d. John and Elizabeth, Nov. 19, 1823.
Frances Louisa, d. John and Susan (Thomson), July 2, 1838. P. R. 63.
Hannah, d. Benja[min] and Hannah, bp. ——, 1753. C. R. I.
Hannah, d. Benjamin, bp. June 1, 1766. C. R. I.
Hannah, d. Andrew and Hannah, Sept. 17, 1781.
Hannah, d. Daniel and Susanna, Oct. 23, 1802.
Hannah K., d. John and Elizabeth F., Dec. 3, 1814.
Henry Adams, s. Ens. Joseph and Mehitable, Aug. 5, 1796.
Jeremy, s. Lt. Joseph and Mehitable, June 14, 1803.
John, s. Samuell and Pheoby, —— [1705?].
John, s. John and Phebe, June 10, 1735.
John, s. John and Phebe, Aug. 7, 1741.
John, s. Andrew and Hannah, Feb. 4, 1774.
John, s. Joseph and Mehitable, Sept. 27, 1797.
John, s. John and Elizabeth Farington, Apr. 22, 1806.
[Joseph. C. R. I.], s. Samuel and Mary, Mar. 23, 1733-4.
Joseph, s. John and Sarah, bp. June 17, 1764. C. R. I.
Joseph, s. [Lt. dup.] Joseph and Mehitable, Jan. 21, 1799.
Loisa, d. John and Elizabeth F., Mar. 11, 1803.
Lydia, d. Samuel and Mary [Hannah. C. R. I.], Mar. 26, 1737.
Mary, d. Samuel and Mary, July 4, 172[2].
Mary, d. Benja[min], bp. Feb. 26, 1758. C. R. 2.
Mehetabel, d. Andrew and Hannah, Mar. 5, 1769.
Mehitable, d. Daniel and Susanna, Feb. 6, 1805.
Naame, d. Benjamin, bp. Aug. 14, 1774. C. R. I.
Nathaniel, s. John and Elizabeth, Jan. 14, 1817. T. C.
Phebe, d. John and Phebe, Nov. 8 [1733].

PETERS, Phebe, d. John and Phebe, May 11, 1739.
Putnam, s. John and Elizabeth F., Feb. 18, 1812.
Rebecca T., d. William, farmer, and Elizabeth P., b. Beverly, Dec. 31, 1848.
Samuel, s. Samuel and Mary, May 30 [1726].
Sam[ue]l, s. Benjamin and Hannah, bp. May 25, 1760. C. R. 1.
Sam[ue]l, s. Benjamin, bp. June 19, 1763. C. R. 1.
Sarah, d. John and Phebe, Dec. 19, 1736.
Sarah, d. John and Phebe, Oct. 24, 1751.
Sarah, d. Lt. Joseph and Mehitable, June 5, 1800.
[Sarah. P. R. 63.], d. John and Elizabeth, May 21, 1821.
Simeon, s. Hannah, bp. ——, 1755. C. R. 1.
Susan [E. P. R. 63.], d. John and Elizabeth, May 27, 1819. [May 28. P. R. 63.]
Susan Elizabeth, d. John and Susan (Thomson), Apr. 19, 1835. P. R. 63.
Susanna, d. Daniel, bp. June 14, 1812. C. R. 1.
Willard, s. John and Eliza[beth] Farington, Jan. 11, 1802.
William, s. Daniel and Susanna, bp. Sept. 16, 1810. C. R. 1.

PETINGGELL (see also Pettengill), [Benjamin. C. R. 1.] ——in, s. Nathaniel and Susanna, Dec. 19, 1734.
Nathaniel, s. Nathaniel and Susanna, Nov. 24, 1724.
Samuel, s. Nathaniel and Susanna, Mar. 16, 173[1-2. C. R. 1.].

PETTENGILL (see also Petengil, Petinggell, Pettingall, Pettingel, Pettinggell, Pettingill), Benjamin, s. Samuel and Mary, Feb. 7, 1762.
Caroline, d. Merrill and Alice, Jan. 25, 1827.
Charles, s. Merrill and Alice, Mar. 13, 1820.
Frye, s. Joseph and Tabitha, Aug. 28, 1774.
George, s. David and Lydia, Oct. 18, 1820.
Harriot, d. Maj. Joseph and Tabitha, bp. Oct. 28, 1781. C. R. 1.
Harriot, d. Merrill and Ellis, June 18, 1830.
John, s. twin, Sam[ue]l and Mary, Dec. 11, 1768. [bp. Dec. 13, 1767. C. R. 2.]
Joseph, s. Joseph and Tabitha, Mar. 6, 1772.
Mary, d. twin, Sam[ue]l and Mary, Dec. 11, 1768. [bp. Dec. 13, 1767. C. R. 2.]
Mary, d. Merrill and Alice, Nov. 17, 1822.
Mary Jane, d. David and Lydia, Jan. 8, 1823.
Peter, s. Samuel and Mary, Aug. 19, 1765.
Susanna Abbot, d. Sam[ue]ll and Mary, Jan. 16, 1770.
Tabitha, d. Jos[eph] and Tabitha, Nov. 22, 1769.
William, s. Samuel and Mary, Aug. 23, 1759.

PETTERS (see also Peters), Susana, d. Daniel and Susana, June 9, 1812.

PETTINGALL (see also Pettengill), Catherine L., d. twin, David and Lydia, Dec. 16, 1827.
Charlotte H., d. twin, David and Lydia, Dec. 16, 1827.

PETTINGEL (see also Pettengill), Frances, d. Maj. Joseph and Tabathy, Oct. 12, 1778.

PETTINGGELL (see also Pettengill), John, s. Nathaniel and Susanna, July 24 [1727].
Joseph, s. Nathaniel and Susanna, Jan. 30, 1721-2.

PETTINGILL (see also Pettengill), Daniel Abbot, s. David, Mar. 4, 1825.
Sarah, d. Joseph and Tabitha, Aug. 29, 1767.

PEVEY, Ester, d. Peter and Ester, Apr. 23, 1728.
Esther, d. Thom[a]s and Mary, bp. May 4, 1760. C. R. 1.
Peter, s. Peter and Ester, Oct. 17, 1731.
Rachel, d. Peter and Ester, Feb. 26, 1725[-6].
Sarah, d. Thom[a]s and Sarah, bp. May 6, 1770. C. R. 1.
Thomas, s. Peter and Esther, Nov. 14, 1736.

PHELPS, Abigael, d. Henry and Abigael, June 10, 1730.
Abigail French, d. Jonathan and Abigail, Oct. 16, 1812.
Ann [Anne. C. R. 2.], d. Thomas and Prudence, July 10, 1748.
Anniss, d. Sam[uel] and [torn], Feb. 22 [1701].
Barsubah, d. Edward and Ruth, May 8, 1692.
Bathsheba, d. Edward and Ruth, Mar. 7, 1695-6.
Belinda Jane, d. Jona[than] and Abigail, Apr. 14, 1817.
Caroline, d. Jonathan and Abigail, Nov. 21, 1813.
Chandler, s. Henry and Mary, Mar. 5, 1786.
Charles W., s. Henry and Eliza (Merrill), Apr. 6, 1843. P. R. 88.
Deborah, d. Samuell and Sarah, —— [1703].
Deborah, d. John and Deborah, Aug. 15, 1742.
Dorcas, d. Isaac and Dorcas, Mar. 24, 1801.
Edward, s. Edward and Ruth, Mar. 20, 1693-4.
Elisabeth, d. Edward and Ruth, Jan. 27, 1689-90.
Elisabeth, d. Thomas and Prudence, May 14, 1735.
Elizabeth, d. Samuel and Sarah, Sept. 6, 1698.
[Elizabeth, d. Joseph. C. R. 2.] ——h and Elizabeth, Oct. 29, 1712.
Eliza[beth] Abbot, d. Joseph,jr. and Rebecca, Feb. 27, 1799.

PHELPS, Elizabeth Abbot, d. Joseph and Rebecca, Oct. 29, 1803.
Elizabeth Holt, d. Jonathan and Abigail, Apr. 5, 1815.
Francis, s. Sam[ue]ll and Hannah, bp. Jan. 17, 1720. C. R. 2.
Francies, s. Francies and Phebe, Aug. 15, 1743.
George, s. Henry and Eliza, Apr. 14, 1838.
Gilson, s. Henry and Eliza (Merrill), Apr. 10, 1836. P. R. 88.
Hannah, d. Edward and Ruth, Nov. 4, 1685.
Hannah, d. Sam[ue]l and Sarah, May 18, 1691.
Hannah, d. Joseph and Elizabeth, May 20 [1715. C. R. 2.].
Hannah, d. twin, John and Sarah, Dec. 22, 1728.
Hannah, d. Thomas and Prudence, May 24, 1741.
Hannah, d. Samuel, jr. and Priscilla, May 5, 1745.
Hannah, d. Joshua and Lois, Sept. 10, 1769.
Hannah, d. Joseph and Abigail, Jan. 18, 1774.
Hannah, d. Thomas and Mary, May 17, 1781.
Hannah H., d. Jonathan and Abigail, Aug. 31, 1824.
Harman, s. Henry and Mary, Dec. 31, 1788.
Henry, s. Samuel and Sarah, Sept. 24, 1693.
Henry, s. Henry and Abigail, Apr. 4, 1732.
Henry, s. Samuel [jr. C. R. 2.] and Priscilla, Sept. 5, 1740.
Henry, s. Thomas and Mary, Mar. 16, 1775.
Henry, s. twin, Henry and Mary, July 15, 1783.
Henry, s. [the late. C. R. 2.] Joshua and Mary, Aug. 27, 1807.
Hermon, s. Chandler and Lydia, May 30, 1816.
Isaac, s. Thomas and Mary, June 21, 1772.
Jacob S., s. Chandler and Lydia, Oct. 14, 1820.
James H[ardy. C. R. 2.], s. Joel and Lydia A., June 1, 1829.
John, s. Sam[ue]ll and Sarah, Sept. 28, 1686.
John, s. John and Sarah, Mar. 12, 1718.
Jonathan, s. John and Sarah, July 22, 1726.
Jon[atha]n E., s. Jona[than] and Abigail, Sept. 24, 1818.
Joseph, s. Sam[ue]ll and Sarah, Feb. 8, 1688-9.
Joseph, s. Samuel and Hannah, Feb. 27, 1723 [-4. C. R. 2.].
Joseph, s. Thomas and Prudance, Apr. 8, 1750.
Joseph, s. Thomas and Mary, Oct. 30, 1783.
Joseph, s. Joseph, jr. and Rebecca, May 3, 1801.
Joshua, s. Samuel [jr. C. R. 2.] and Priscilla, June 25, 1738.
Joshua, s. Joshua and Lowis, Apr. 8, 1774.
Joshua, s. Joshua, jr. and Mary, Sept. 7, 1796.
Joshuah, s. Edward and Rut[h], ——, 1701.
Lois, d. Joshua and Lois, May 24, 1767.
Lydea, d. John and Sarah, July 31, 172[2. C. R. 2.].
Lydia, d. Edward and Ruth, Jan. 16, 1687-8.
Lydia, d. John and Sarah, May 1, 1732.

PHELPS, Lydia, d. Joshua and Mary, Nov. 10, 1804.
Mary, d. Samuel and Hannah, Feb. 14, 1716-17.
Mary, d. Thomas and Mary, Jan. 28, 1722-3.
Mary, d. Thomas and Prudenc, —— 22 [bp. Aug. 25, 1728. C.R. 2.].
Mary, d. Thomas and Mary, Sept. 18, 1777.
Mary, d. Joshua and Mary, Aug. 21, 1802.
Mary A., d. Jonathan and Abigail, May 28, 1822.
Mary E., d. Henry and Eliza, Sept. 25, 1832.
Molly, d. twin, Henry and Mary, July 15, 1783.
Moses S[tuart. C. R. 6.], s. Austin, professor, and Elizabeth, Mar. 16, 1849.
Nathan, s. twin, John and Sarah, Dec. 22, 1728.
Newton Merrill, s. Henry and Eliza, Jan. 14, 1840.
Phebe, d. Thomas and Mary, Feb. 28, 1786.
[Phineas. T. C.], s. Samuel and Hannah, Jan. 11, 1719-20.
Presilla, d. Samuel and Presilla, May 10, 1748.
[Prudence. C. R. 2.], d. Thomas and Prudence, Feb. 18, 1732-3.
Prudence, d. Thomas and Prudence, Dec. 17, 1736.
Robert, s. Edward and Ruth, May 8, 1699.
Ruth, d. Edward and Ruth, June 1, 1684.
Samuel, s. Samuel and Hannah, Feb. 5, 1712-13.
Samuel, s. Samuel [jr. C. R. 2.] and Prescila, Oct. 21, 1736.
Samuel, s. Joshua and Lois, Aug. 15, 1777.
Samuel, s. Henry and Mary, Aug. 9, 1781.
Samuel, s. Joshua and Mary, Feb. 15, 1800.
Samuel G., s. Henry and Eliza, Apr. 10, 1836.
Samuell, s. Sam[ue]ll and Sarah, Nov. 22, 1684.
Sarah, d. Samuell and Sarah, Oct. 16, 1682.
Sarah, d. John and Sarah, July 20, 1715.
Sarah, d. Joseph and Elizabeth [bp. June 2, 1717. C. R. 2.].
Sarah, d. John, bp. July 27, 1746. C. R. 2.
Solomon, s. Thomas and Prudience, Mar. 24, 1743-4.
Solomon, s. Thomas and Mary, Mar. 17, 1770.
Thomas, s. Sam[ue]l and Sarah, Nov. 5, 1695.
Thomas, s. Thomas and Prudence, June 1, 1739.
Thomas, s. Tho[ma]s and Mary, May 25, 1767.
William H., s. Henry and Eliza, Apr. 10, 1834.
——, ch. [torn], July 12, 1706.
——, ch. [torn] and [torn]h, Dec. 15, 1709.
——, d. Jona[than] and Abigail, Aug. 25, 1820.
——, d. Joshua and Dolly, Jan. 23, 1823.

PHILEPS (see also Phillips), Elezebith, d. Samuel and Elezebith, Oct. 18, 1755.
Samuel, s. Samuel, jr. and Elezebith, Feb. 5, 1752.

PHILLIPS (see also Phileps), Amelia, d. twin, John, jr. and Lydia, bp. Feb. 8, 1813. C. R. 1.
Caroline, d. Col. John and Phebe, bp. Aug. 12, 1810. C. R. 1.
Elisabeth, d. Mr. Samuel and Elisabeth, Oct. 31, 1747.
Elizabeth Barnard, d. John, jr. and Lydia, Dec. 17, 1805.
Gorham, s. Hon. John and Lydia, June 24, 1816.
Hannah, d. Mr. Samuel, jr. and Elisabeth, Jan. 20, 1741-2.
Henry, s. John, bp. Jan. 23, 1774. C. R. 1.
James, s. John, bp. Feb. 14, 1768. C. R. 1.
John, s. Rev. Samuel and Hannah, Dec. 27, 1719.
John, s. Mr. Samuel, jr. and Phoebe, Oct. 18, 1776.
John, s. twin, John, jr. and Lydia, Apr. 12, 1804.
Julia, d. twin, Jo[h]n, jr. and Lydia, Feb. —, 1813. [bp. Feb. 8. C. R. 1.]
Lydia, d. Samuel and Hannah [bp. June 16, 1717. C. R. 2.].
Lydia, d. twin, John, jr. and Lydia, Apr. 12, 1804.
Maria, d. twin, Jo[h]n, jr. and Lydia, Feb. —, 1813.
Mary, d. Rev. Sam[ue]ll [and Hannah, bp. Dec. 7, 1712. C. R. 2.].
Mary [Molly. C. R. 1.], d. Lt. John and Elizabeth, July 26, 1777.
Mary Ann, d. Hon. [Col. C. R. 1.] John and Lydia, Mar. 17, 1808.
Na[tha]n[ie]l Gorham, s. John and Lydia, bp. July 7, 1816. C. R. 1.
Patrick, s. Patrick, laborer, and Mary, July 20, 1848.
Phebe Foxcroft, d. John, jr. and Lydia, Dec. 1, 1799.
Rebecca Gorham, d. [Capt. C. R. 1.] John, jr. and Lydia, Aug. 19, 1802.
Samuel, s. Rev. Sam[ue]ll and Hannah [bp. Feb. 13, 1715. C. R. 2.].
Samuel, s. Mr. Samuel, jr. and Elisabeth, Nov. 6, 1743.
Samuel, s. Hon. Samuel, jr. and Phebe, Apr. 30, 1782.
Samuel, s. John, jr. and Lydia, Mar. 8, 1801.
Samuel, s. Sam[ue]l and Sarah A., Sept. 30, 1828.
Sarah Whitworth, d. [Col. C. R. 1.] John, jr. and Lydia, Feb. 18, 1807.
Susan Lowel, d. Hon. John and Lydia, Mar. 5, 1809.
[Theodore. C. R. 1.], s. Mr. Samuel, jr. and Elisabeth, May 2, 1739.
Theodor[e], s. Mr. Samuel, jr. and Elisabeth, Sept. 6, 1745.
William, s. Rev. Samuel and Hannah, June 25, 1722.

PHIPPS, Abbe, d. A. J. and E., bp. Mar. 29, 1846. C. R. 6
Joseph, s. Joseph, jr. and Sarah, bp. June 29, 1777. C. R. 1.

PIERCE (see also Peirce), Ellen [Prentiss. C. R. 2.], d. William and Ellen, Aug. 5, 1839.
George William, s. Jesse and Catherine J., Jan. 14, 1840.
Mary Alice, d. Tho[ma]s S. and Ann B., bp. Feb. 11, 1838. C. R. 4.
Mary E., d. Jesse and Catharine, July 21, 1836.
Thomas Marland, s. Thomas S. and Ann B., bp. Sept. 1, 1839. C. R. 4.

PIERSON (see also Pearson), Abigail, d. Jonathan and Abigail, Mar. 26, 1737.
Bathshua, d. James and Bathshua, bp. July 27, 1760. C. R. 1.
Benjamin, s. twin, Jonathan and Abigail, July 13, 1746.
John, s. John and Rebecca, Aug. 9, 1744.
[Rebecca. C. R. 1.], d. John and Rebecah, May 26, 1733.
Rebecca, d. John and Abigail, bp. Mar. 18, 1770. C. R. 1.

PIKE, Joseph, s. John, cordwainer, and Eliza, Jan. 24, 1846.
William Francis, s. John, shoemaker, and Eliza A., Oct. 11, 1848.

PILLING, Laura A. [Ann. P. R. 80.], d. Edmond, manufacturer, and Belinda, Jan. 12, 1844.

PILSBURY, Solomon Burke, s. Paul P., farmer, and Sarah A. Dec. 14, 1848.

PLATS (see also Platt), Joseph Hale, s. John, bp. July 9, 1780. C. R. 2.

PLATT (see also Plats, Platts), James William, s. John, manufacturer, and Mary, Dec. 22, 1844.

PLATTS (see also Platt), Hannah, d. John and Sarah, July 12, 1778.
John, s. John and Sarah, at Bradford, July 1, 1774.
Sarah, d. John and Sarah, at Hollis [N. H.], June 2, 1776.

POLLARD, Annah H., d. Dustin, blacksmith, and Hannah T., May 24, 1848.
John D., s. Dustin, blacksmith, and Hannah F., May 14, 1845.
——, d. Capt. Geo[rge] and Ann M., Mar. 2, 1838.

POOL, Samuel Reed, s. Eleaser, and Polly, deceased, of Woburn, living with [Rev.] Mr. French, bp. May 12, 1799. C. R. 2.

POOR (see also Poore, Pore), Abigail, d. Daniel and Dorathy, Feb. 10, 1719-20.
Abraham, s. Thomas and Mary, Feb. 23, 1741-2.
Abraham, s. Abraham and Elizabeth, Mar. 8, 1789.
Albert, s. Jonathan, wheelwright, and Catherine, Apr. 30, 1847.
Albert M., s. Jonathan and Catherine, Jan. 2, 1839.
Andrew, s. Daniel, jr. and Sarah, bp. June 24, 1787. C. R. 1.
Ann, d. Thomas and Mary, July 4, 1738.
Anna, d. Lt. Daniel and Hannah, Feb. 28, 1783.
Anna, d. Lt. Abraham and Elizabeth, Dec. 14, 1786.
Arrabella Boynton, d. Benj[ami]n, jr. and Joanna, bp. Fep. 5, 1792. C. R. 1.
Becke, d. Timothy and Mary, Sept. 7, 1748.
Benjamin, s. Samuel and Deborah, Mar. 5, 1727-8.
Benjamin, s. Benjamin and Phebe, Sept. 15, 1760.
Benjamin, s. Benj[ami]n, jr. and Joanna, bp. Feb. 5, 1792. C. R. 1
Bette [Molley. C. R. 1.], d. Jonathan and Elezebith, Jan. 4, 1755.
Bette, d. Ebenezer and Susanna, Dec. 21, 1759.
Betty, d. Peter, jr. and Elizabeth, bp. May 3, 1778. C. R. 1.
Betty Sibson, d. John, jr. and Cloe, bp. Dec. 7, 1783. C. R. 1.
Caleb, s. [Capt. C. R. 1.] Tho[ma]s and Phebe, Mar. 28, 1767.
Caroline, d. John, jr. and Mary, July 18, 1817.
Caroline A., d. John and Mary O., Oct. 30, 1825.
Catharine, d. Capt. Henry and Lydia, June 13, 1819.
Catharine A., d. Capt. Henry and Lydia, Mar. 28, 1815.
Charles, s. Daniel, jr., bp. Feb. 26, 1797. C. R. 2.
Charles, s. Joseph and Mary, Aug. 20, 1801.
Charles A., s. Col. Timothy and Hannah, May 20, 1825.
Charles P., s. twin, Timothy, farmer, and Jane C., Dec. 25, 1843.
Charlotte, d. Daniel, jr., bp. Apr. 12, 1795. C. R. 2.
Cloe, d. John and Cloe, May 14, 1779.
Dane, s. Daniel and Sarah, bp. Jan. 4, 1784. C. R. 1.
Daniel, s. Daniel and Mehitabell, Feb. 9, 1688-9.
Daniel, s. Thomas and Mary, Sept. 21, 1740.
Daniel, s. Jonathan and Elisabeth, July 21, 1746.
Daniel, s. Peter and Sarah, Aug. 4, 1760.
Daniel, s. Daniel, jr., bp. June 9, 1793. C. R. 2.
Daniel, s. Daniel and Deborah, May 28, 1824.
Daniel Adams, s. Daniel and Hannah, Sept. 11, 1778.
Daniel Adams, s. Lt. Daniel and Hannah, Feb. 11, 1781.
Dean, s. Daniel, jr. and Sarah, bp. June 6, 1773. C. R. 1.
Debbe, d. Benjamin and Phoebe, Feb. 2, 1772.
[Deb]orah, d. Daniel and Mehittabel, Oct. 19, 1714.
Dolly, d. Ebenezer and Susanna, Oct. 12, 1772.

POOR, Dorcas, d. Theodore and Sarah, Oct. 13, 1802.
Dorcis, d. Timothy and Mary, Feb. 18, 1757.
Ebenezer, s. Samuel and Deborah, Jan. 16, 1731-2.
Ebenezer, s. Ebenezer and Susannah, Jan. 4, 1758.
Ebenezer, s. Eben[eze]r, bp. Nov. 3, 1765. C. R. I.
Elizabeth, d. Daniel and Hannah, Jan. 4, 1766.
Elizabeth, d. Abraham and Elizabeth, Nov. 16, 1784.
Elizabeth, d. Stephen and Elizabeth, May 23, 1798
Emily E., d. Daniel A. and Emily, Sept. 27, 1809.
Enoch, s. Thomas and Mary, —— 21 [1736. C. R. I.].
Enoch, s. Thomas, jr. and Phebe, Apr. 20, 1765.
Enoch, s. Lt. Abraham and Elizabeth, May 19, 1782.
Fransis, d. Peter and Sarah, Apr. 24, 1758.
Frederick, s. Lt. Abraham and Elizabeth, May 22, 1780.
Frye, s. Daniel and Hannah, Jan. 28, 1768.
Frye, s. Ens. Isaac and Sarah, bp. July 24, 1803. C. R. I.
Gates E., s. Capt. Henry and Lydia, Aug. 13, 1813.
Gayton Morton, s. Samuel and Betsey, Dec. 11, 1841.
George, s. Stephen and Betsy, Nov. 24, 1796.
George, s. Joseph and Mary, Feb. 21, 1809.
George, s. John, jr. and Mary O., Nov. 30, 1812.
George, s. Joseph and Mary, Oct. 12, 1819.
George Horace, s. James and Susan, Jan. 21, 1841. P. R. 60.
Georgiana W., d. Henry, merchant, and Margaret L. W., b. Portland, Me., July 1, 1849.
Hannah, d. Daniel and Dorathy, Feb. 8, 1712-13.
Hannah, d. Jonathan and Elizebith, Oct. 20, 1749.
Hannah, d. Peter and Sarah, Jan. 13, 1754.
Hannah, d. [Capt. C. R. I.] Tho[ma]s, jr. and Phebe, Dec. 4, 1759.
Hannah, d. Daniel, jr. and Hannah, May 19, 1763.
Hannah, d. Daniel, jr. and Hannah, Jan. 15, 1770.
Hannah, Jonathan and Susanna, Aug. 3, 1770.
Hannah, d. Joseph, of Danvers, bp. Apr. 30, 1775. C. R. 2.
Hannah, d. Daniel, jr., bp. June 9, 1793. C. R. 2.
Harriot L., d. Capt. Henry and Lydia, Mar. 13, 1817.
Helen H., d. Jona[than], wheelwright, and Catharine, Sept. 15, 1845.
Helen R., d. Daniel A. and Emily, Dec. 24, 1816.
Henery, s. Joseph and Mary, Dec. 9, 1802.
Henery, s. Henery and Lydia, Apr. 15, 1808.
Henrietta, d. Jonathan and Catherine, Dec. 22, 1839.
Henry, s. John, jr. and Cloe, May 12, 1781.
Isaac, s. Peter and Sarah, bp. Oct. 10, 1762. C. R. I.

POOR, Isaac, s. Peter and Sarah, Oct. 8, 1763.
Isaac, s. Peter and Sarah, Feb. 16, 1765.
Isaac, s. Daniel, 3d and Sarah, Jan. 31, 1771.
Isaac, s. Daniel and Sarah, bp. Jan. 7, 1776. C. R. I.
Isaac, s. Isaac and Lydia, Mar. 17, 1792.
James, s. Benjamin and Phoebe, Dec. 18, 1769.
James, s. Joseph and Mary, Apr. 13, 1813.
Jane C., d. Daniel A. and Emily, Sept. 7, 1814.
John, s. Daniel and Mehitabel, Oct. 30, 1691.
John, s. John and Mary, July 26, 1718.
John, s. John, jr. and Rebeca, Apr. 16, 1754.
John, s. John, jr. and Chloe, Aug. 3, 1777.
John, s. John, jr. and Mary O., Oct. 31, 1811.
John A., s. John, jr. and Mary O., Mar. 4, 1828.
John E., s. Capt. Henry and Lydia, May 16, 1824.
John Tyler, s. Benj[ami]n, jr. and Joanna, bp. Feb. 5, 1792. C. R. I.
Jonathan, s. Jonathan and Elezebith, Mar. 21, 1747-8.
Jonathan, s. Jonathan and Susanna, Oct. 23, 1772.
Jonathan, s. Joseph and Mary, Apr. 23, 1811.
Joseph, s. Daniel and Mehitabell, Mar. 14, 1699-1700.
Joseph, s. Joseph and Rebeca, Apr. 15, 1731.
Joseph, s. Joseph and Rebecca, Apr. 28, 1732.
Joseph, s. Thomas and Mary, July 8, 1747.
Joseph, s. Thomas and Mary, Nov. 7, 1748.
Joseph, s. Lt. Abraham and Eliza[beth], Sept. 19, 1776.
Joseph, s. Joseph and Mary, Mar. 25, 1807.
Joshua, s. John, jr. and Cloe, bp. Aug. 26, 1787. C. R. I.
Joshua, s. John, jr. and Mary O., Nov. 19, 1807.
Joshua M., s. twin, Timothy, farmer, and Jane C., Dec. 25, 1843.
Lemuel, s. Peter and Sarah, Oct. 13, 1772.
Lydea, d. Timothy [and Mary. C. R. I.], July 18, 1751.
Lydia, d. Isaac and Lydia, bp. June 12, 1796. C. R. I.
Lydia, d. Capt. Henry and Lydia, Dec. 18, 1811.
Lydia A., d. Theodore and Sarah, May 17, 1796.
Lydia Ann Maria, d. Henery and Lydia, June 26, 1809.
Lydia Baker, d. Daniel and Deborah, Dec. 11, 1811.
Margaret, d. Daniel, jr. and Deborah B., Sept. 1, 1809.
Maria Louisa, d. Daniel A. and Emily, Nov. 20, 1811.
Mariann, d. Isaac and Lydia, bp. Oct. 8, 1809. C. R. I.
Martha, d. Daniel and Mehitabel, May — [1713].
Martha, d. John, jr. and Mary O., Mar. 26, 1823.
Martha Ann, d. William and Hannah, Oct. 29, 1838.

POOR, Mary, d. Dan[ie]l and Mehitabell, Mar. 26, 1698.
[Mary. C. R. I.], d. Thomas and Mary, Apr. 6, 1734.
Mary, d. Timothy and Mary, Mar. 17, 1745-6.
Mary, d. Thomas, jr. and Phebe, Dec. 23, 1757.
Mary, d. Daniel, jr. and Hannah, Mar. 28, 1772.
Mary, d. Lt. Abraham and Elizabeth, Aug. 17, 1778.
Mary, d. Theodore and Sarah, Apr. 12, 1800.
Mary Ann, d. Joseph and Mary [Mar. —, 1815].
Mehetabel, d. Timothy and Mary, Oct. 15, 1762.
Mehetabel, d. John, jr., bp. Oct. 17, 1762. C. R. I.
Mehitabel, d. Daniel and Mehitabel, Dec. 10, 1693.
Mehitabell, d. Daniell and Mehitabell, Oct. 3, 1690.
Molly, d. Daniel and Sarah, bp. June 3, 1781. C. R. I.
Nathaniel, s. Lt. Daniel and Hannah, Apr. 20, 1785.
Nelson P[arker. P. R. 60.], s. James, farmer, and Susan, July 16, 1845.
Pamela, d. Lt. Daniel and Hannah, Dec. 23, 1787.
Pamela, d. Abraham and Elizabeth, Sept. 8, 1791.
Patte, d. Benjamin and Phebe, Dec. 23, 1758.
Patte, d. Benjamin and Phebe, Feb. 24, 1765.
Persis, d. Ebenezer and Susanna, Oct. 23, 1774.
Peter, s. Daniel and Dorathy, July 9, 1726.
Peter, s. Peter and Sarah, Apr. 20, 1756.
Peter, s. Peter and Elizabeth, bp. Jan. 27, 1793. C. R. I.
Peter, s. Isaac and Lydia, bp. July 20, 1800. C. R. I.
Phebe, d. Benjamin and Phebe, June 24, 1754.
Phebe, d. Thomas, jr. and Phebe, July 3, 1761.
Phebe Varnum, d. Eben[eze]r and Susanna, bp. Dec. 5, 1779. C. R. I.
Polly, d. Capt. Stephen and Mary, Oct. 22, 1807.
Polly O., d. John, jr. and Mary O., Nov. 13, 1805.
[Priscilla. C. R. I.], d. Daniel and Dorathy [Debora. C. R. I.], Jan. 15, 1727-8.
Rebeca, d. John, jr. and Rebeca, Nov. 2, 1756.
[Rebecca. C. R. I.], d. Joseph and Rebeca, July 15, 1728.
Rebecca, d. John jr. and Mary A., Dec. 18, 1813.
Sally, d. Daniel and Sally, May 8, 1779.
Sally, d. Theodore and Sarah, Apr. 9, 1794.
Samuel, s. Daniel and Mehitabel, Nov. 26, 1695.
Samuel, s. Samuel and Deborah, Oct. 8, 1725.
Samuel, s. Benjamin and Phebe, May 30, 1767.
Samuel, s. Theodore and Sarah, Dec. 26, 1797.
Sarah, d. Daniel and Dorathy [Deborah. C. R. I.], Apr. 15, 1732.
Sarah, d. Thomas and Mary, Jan. 3, 1743-4.

POOR, Sarah, d. John, jr. and Rebeca, May 22, 1750.
Sarah, d. Daniel and Hannah, Apr. 27, 1774.
Sarah, d. Abraham and Eliza[beth] [Sarah. C. R. 1.], Aug. 28, 1774.
Sarah, d. Daniel and Hannah, Aug. 20, 1776.
Sarah, d. John, jr. and Cloe, bp. May 27, 1781. C. R. 1.
Sarah, d. Isaac and Lydia, bp. June 3, 1798. C. R. 1.
Sarah, d. Theodore and Sarah, bp. July 7, 1799. C. R. 1.
Sarah, d. Joseph and Mary, May 10, 1804.
Sarah, d. John, jr. and Mary O., July 16, 1809.
Sarah Bond, d. Capt. Stephen and Mary, Mar. 14, 1810.
Sarah J[ane. P. R. 60.], d. James, farmer, and Susan, b. Methuen, Nov. 3, 1848.
Silvanus, s. Ebenezer and Susanna, Mar. 7, 1768.
Stephen, s. Thomas and Mary, Aug. 2, 1735.
Stephen, s. Tho[ma]s, jr. and Phebe, Feb. 16, 1763.
Stephen, s. Abraham and Elizabeth, Feb. 13, 1771.
Stephen, s. Capt. Stephen and Mary, Nov. 15, 1803.
Susa[nna], d. Ebenezer and Susanna, Apr. 4, 1762.
Susanna, d. Ebenezer and Susanna, Nov. 29, 1763.
Susannah, d. Abraham and Elizabeth, bp. Aug. 23, 1778. C. R. 1.
Susannah, d. Joseph and Mary, Mar. 6, 1817.
Susee, d. Thomas and Mary, Nov. 26, 1745.
Theodore, s. Timothy and Mary [Jan?] 24, 1766. [bp. Jan. 26. C. R. 1.]
Thomas, s. Thomas and Mary, July 19, 1732.
Thomas, s. Thomas, jr., bp. Mar. 27, 1774. C. R. 1.
Thomas Baker, s. Daniel and Deborah, Mar. 16, 1818.
Timothy, s. John and Mary, Mar. 30, 1722.
Timothy, s. Timothy and Mary, Aug. 26, 1754.
Timothy, s. John, jr. and Cloe, bp. Sept. 13, 1789. C. R. 1.
Timothy, s. John and Chloe, Sept. 7, 1790.
Timothy, s. Theodore and Sarah, Dec. 1, 1806.
William, s. Ebenezer and Susanna, Aug. 17, 1770.
William, s. Isaac and Lydia, Feb. 11, 1794.
William, s. Joseph and Mary, Oct. 11, 1805.
William, s. John, jr. and Mary, Apr. 27, 1816.
——, ch. Daniel and Mehetabell, July 20, 1709.
——, d. Samuel and Debora, Sept. 1, 1721.
——, d. Samuel and Deborah, Oct. 5, 1723.
——, d. Joseph and Rebeca, Apr. 6, 1726.
——, d. Joseph and Rebecah, Apr. —, 1734.
——, s. Jonathan and Elisabeth, Dec. 10, 1744.
——, s. Jonathan and Elezebith, Oct. 25, 1752.

POOR, ——, ch. Daniel and Deborah, July —, 1819.
——, s. John, jr. and Mary O., Oct. 8, 1819.
——, inf. ch. John, jr. and Mary O., Nov. —, 1820.
——, inf. ch. Sam[ue]l and Betsey, Oct. 13, 1831.
——, d. F. Timothy, farmer, and Jane, Dec. 28, 1845.

POORE (see also Poor), Abraham, s. Thomas and Mary, June 16, 1730.
Daniel, s. Daniel and Dorithy, Apr. 17, 1718.
Dorathy, d. Daniel and Dorathy, —— [1716].
Elizabeth, d. Daniel and Mehetabel, Aug. — [1711].
Jonathan, s. Daniel and Dorathy, Oct. 9, 1724.
Joseph, s. Dan[iel] and [torn], Mar. 29, 1701.
Mehitabel, d. Daniel and Dorathy, Apr. 4 [1714].
Peter, s. Daniel and Dorathy [Deborah. C. R. 1.], June 11, 1730.
Thomas, s. Daniell and Mehetabell, —— [1703].
Timothy, s. Daniel and Mehitabel, Apr. 15 [1716].
——, ch. [torn] and [Meh]etabel, Mar. 10, 1704-5.
——, ch. [D]an[ie]ll and Mehittabell, Aug. 27, 1710.

PORE (see also Poor), Daniell, s. Daniell and Mary, Sept. 5, 1656.
Debora, d. Daniell and Mary, Apr. 18, 1664. [Mar. 18. CT. R.]
Elizabeth, d. Daniell and Mary, Apr. 15, 1661. [1662. CT. R.]
Hanna, d. Daniell and Mary, May 6, 1660.
John, s. Daniell and Mary, Sept. 5, 1658.
Lusy, d. Daniell and Mary, Sept. 28, 1670.
Matthew, d. [*sic*] Daniell and Ma[ry. CT. F.], Nov. 4, 1654.
Prisilla, d. Daniell and Mary, June 22, [16]67.
Ruth, d. Daniell and Mary, Feb. 16, 1665.
Sara, d. Daniell and M[faded], Dec. 28, 1652

PORTER, Eliza Abbott, d. —— and Mary, at Boston, Oct. 29, 1804.
Elizabeth A., d. John and Sarah, at Boston, Oct. 29, 1803.
Sarah Ann, d. —— and Mary, at Boston, Mar. 19, 1802.
Sarah Austin, d. Nathaniel and Sarah, bp. Jan. 22, 1786. C. R. 1

PRAY, Charles B., s. Charles and Sarah, Oct. 18, 1838.
Edward E., s. Seaver, cordwainer, and Susan, Mar. 16, 1848.
John, s. Charles, stabler, and Sarah C., Oct. 26, 1846.
Joseph, s. Charles, livery-stable-keeper, b. Maine, and Sarah C., Sept. 15, 1849.
Mary F., d. Charles, livery-stable-keeper, and Sarah C., May 15, 1844.
Sarah E., d. Charles and Sarah, Sept 10, 1842.

PRENTISS, Nathaniel A., s. Nathaniel A. and Abigail W., Aug. 20, 1840.
Samuel P., s. Nath[anie]l A., and Abigail W., June 3, 1838.

PRESCOTT, Abbott, s. James M., farmer, b. Amesbury, and Lucy, June 1, 1848.
Mary, d. James M. and Lucy, Sept. 2, 1842.
——, s. Abel and Eleanor, Jan. 23, 1820.

PRESTON, Benjamine, s. Jacob and Sarah, —— 20 or 26 [1705?].
[Caleb. C. R. 2.], s. twin, Samuel [jr. C. R. 2.] and Sarah, Apr. 3, 1716.
Elizabeth, d. Samuell and Susannah, Feb. 14, 1682.
Hannah, d. John and Sarah, June 17, 1698.
Isaack, s. twin, Samu[el] and [torn], —— [1711].
Jacob, s. Sam[ue]ll and Susannah, Feb. 24, 1680-81.
Jemima, d. [torn], M— 29, [1701].
John, s. Sam[ue]ll and Susannah, May 1, 1685.
John, s. twin Jo[h]n and Sarah, Mar. 17, 1690-91.
John, s. John and Sarah, June 13, 1692.
[John. C. R. 2.] —n, s. Jacob and Sarah, Jan. 19 [12. T. C.], 1715-16.
Joseph, s. Sam[ue]ll and Susannah, Jan. 26, 1686-7.
Joseph, s. Jacob and Sarah, bp. Sept. 14, 1712. C. R. 2.
[Joseph. C. R. 2.] ——ph, s. Joseph and Rebecka, Aug. 22, 1713.
Joshuah, s. twin, Samuel [jr. C. R. 2.] and Sarah, Apr. 3, 1716.
Levy, s. Samuel and Sarah, Oct. 25, 1696.
Lydia, d. Sam[ue]l and Susannah, Oct. 8, 1690.
Martha, d. John and [torn], Apr. —, 1702.
Mary, d. Samuell and Susannah, Jan. 5, 1678.
Mary, d. Samuell and Sarah, Mar. 31, 1699.
Pheoby, d. twin, Samu[el] and [torn], —— [1711].
Priscilla, d. Sam[ue]ll and Susannah, Mar. 19, 1695-6.
Rebekah, d. John and Sarah, Jan. 23, 1688-9.
Ruth, d. Sam[ue]ll and Susannah, Feb. 7, 1688-9.
[Ruth. C. R. 2.], d. Sam[ue]ll [jr. C. R. 2.] and Sarah, July 25, 1713.
Samuell, s. Samuell and Susanna, Mar. 16, 1672.
Samuell, s. Sam[ue]ll and Sarah, —— [1708?].
Sam[ue]ll, s. Sam[ue]ll and Hannah, bp. — 1728. C. R. 1.
Sarah, d. Samuel and Sarah, Feb. 5, 1694-5.
Sarah, d. John and Sarah, Feb. 26, 1694-5.
Susanna, d. Samuell and Susanna, Mar. 30, 1677.

PRESTON, Thomas, s. twin, Jo[h]n and Sarah, Mar. 17, 1690-1.
William, s. Samuell and Susanna, Jan. 11, 1674.
——, ch. [torn] and Sarah, Oct. 1, 1710.
——, d. Joseph and Rebecka, Jan. 26, 1710-11.

PRIESTLY, William Henry, s. Isaac, drier in factory, and Eliza, [Sept.] 7 [1846].

PRINCE, Albert L., s. Caleb S. and Martha J., Apr. 24, 1834.
Charles Albert, s. Caleb S. and Martha Jane, Mar. 23, 1838.
George Caleb, s. Caleb Strong and Martha Jane, bp. Sept. 11, 1842. C. R. 4.
John L[eonard. C. R. 4.], s. Caleb S., manufacturer, and Martha J., July 12, 1844.
Martha Ann, d. Caleb S., overseer, and Martha J., May 2, 1846.
Mary E[liza. C. R. 4.], d. Caleb S., manufacturer, and Martha J., June 26, 1848.
——, ch. Caleb S. and Martha Jane, Jan. 1, 1836.

PRINDLE, Daniel Smith, s. Eldad, bp. Apr. 22, 1781. C. R. 2.

PROCTER (see also Proctor), Catharine S., d. William S., laborer, and Mary A., Mar. 3, 1846.

PROCTOR (see also Procter), Agnes Jane, d. William, flax-dresser, and Mary Ann, Apr. 22, 1848.
Robert A., s. William and Mary Ann, Dec. 27, 1840.

PULSIFER, Elizabeth F., d. Eben and Sally, Mar. 9, 1834.
George E., s. Eben and Sally, July 12, 1840.
Hannah M., d. Eben[eze]r and Sally, July 15, 1838.
Joseph, s. Eben and Sally, Jan. 30, 1832.
Sarah Ellen, d. Eben and Sarah, Dec. 28, 1835.

PUNCHARD, Ellen, d. adopted, B. H. and Martha L. (Marland), bp. Jan. 2, 1848. C. R. 4.
Sarah Elizabeth, d. adopted, B. H. and Martha, bp. May 30, 1841. C. R. 4.

PURVES (see also Purvis), ——, ch. Mr. ——, Mar. 23, 1822.

PURVIS (see also Purves), Frances E., d. Davidson, manufacturer, and Ann E., Nov. 12, 1843.

PUTNAM, Alfred, s. Alfred and Mary, Aug. 21, 1826.
Caroline Elizabeth, d. Israel and Mary (H.), Aug. 12, 1829. T. C.
Caroline R., d. James and Sarah McKee, Apr. 15, 1831.
Charles E., s. Alfred and Mary O., Mar. 28, 1830.
Charles Simeon, s. Simeon and Abby B., Nov. 29, 1817.
George, s. Israel W., trader, and Hannah L., June 10, 1848.
George A., s. Israel and Mary (Hawk), Aug. 1, 1838.
Harriet M., d. Israel and Mary (H.), June 26, 1831. T. C.
Israel W., s. Israel and Mary, June 22, 1822.
John N[ewton. C. R. 1.], s. Simeon and Abba, Dec. 26, 1822.
Mary Ann, d. Israel and Mary, Mar. 22, 1826.
Mary Louisa, d. Alfred and Polly O., Feb. 16, 1828.
Nancy Jane, d. Israel and Mary, Oct. 13, 1827.
Samuel P. P. F. [Prescot Phillips Fay. C. R. 1.], s. Simeon and Abba, Mar. 20, 1829.
Sarah A., d. Israel and Mary (H.), Aug. 26, 1833. T. C.
Timothy F., s. Alfred and Mary O., June 17, 1832.
William H., s. Israel and Mary, Jan. 12, 1824.

QUAILEY (see also Qualey), John, s. twin, William, laborer, and Catherine, Sept. 26, 1844.
Michael, s. twin, William, laborer, and Catherine, Sept. 26, 1844.

QUALEY (see also Quailey, Quealy), William D., s. William, laborer, Jan. 8, 184[7 or 8].

QUEALY (see also Qualey), Francis J., s. William, trader, and Catherine D., both b. Ireland, Sept. 4, 1849.
Hannah J., d. Edward, moulder, and Ellen A., July 26, 1848.

QUINN, Daniel, s. Daniel, wheelwright, and Catharine, July 7, 1847.

RADCLIFFE, George W., s. Charles O., machinist, and Mary, Aug. 21, 1848.

RAE (see also Rea), Hannah Pope, d. Daniel and Hannah, Apr. 23, 1818.

RALLEY, Hannah S., d. James and Mary, July 16, 1819.
Julia A. D., d. James and Mary, Mar. 9, 1817.

RAMSAY, Agnes, d. Alexander, flax-dresser, and Ann, Jan. 30, 1845.

RASTROW, ——, s. Hannah, wid. James, Jan. 28, 1832.

RAY (see also Rea), Aaron G., s. Aaron G. and Mary, Mar. 2, 1834.
George Leverett, s. William and Harriet, July 17, 1837.
Jacob C., s. Aaron G. and Mary, Sept. 5, 1837. [Sept. 25. P. R. 55.]
John Henry, s. Aaron Gilbert and Mary, Apr. 24, 1836.
Mary Louisa, d. Aaron G. and Mary, Aug. 6, 1839.

REA (see also Rae, Ray), Albert L., s. William, yeoman, and Harriet N., Aug. 1, 1846.
Augustus L., s. William and Harriet N. (Bradstreet), Aug. 1, 1846. P. R. 90.
[Calvin. P. R. 55.], s. Aaron G., farmer, and Mary, Jan. 8, 1848. [Mar. 8. P. R. 55.]
Charles P., s. Jasper, farmer, and Lucy (Woodcock), Mar. 23, 1846.
Daniel, s. Daniel and Hannah, Apr. 12, 1804.
Elizabeth, d. Daniel and Hannah, Apr. 25, 1820.
Ellen E., d. William, farmer, and Harriet, Mar. 5, 1844.
George L., s. William and Harriet, Mar. 18, 1836.
George W., s. Aaron G. and Mary (Chickering), Jan. 9, 1843. P. R. 55.
Gilbert, s. Daniel and Hannah, Aug. 29, 1802.
Horace, s. Daniel, farmer, and Harriet, Sept. 14, 1845.
Jasper, s. Daniel and Hannah, Oct. 30, 1814.
Latitia, d. Daniel, jr. and Harriet, June 6, 1838.
Lucy Adaline, d. Jasper and Lucy (Woodcock), Mar. 27, 1842. T. C.
Mary, d. Daniel and Hannah, Jan. 20, 1801.
Mary E., d. Jasper and Lucy, Nov. 6, 1840.
Milton, s. Aaron G., cordwainer, and Mary, Jan. 9, 1846.
William, s. Daniel and Hannah, Sept. 14, 1808.
William H., s. Aaron G. and Mary (Chickering), June 25, 1841. P. R. 55.
William W., s. William and Harriet N., Apr. 4, 1842. P. R. 90.

READ (see also Reed), Sarah W., d. Joseph W. and Sarah B., Sept. 30, 1838.

REDMAYNE, Martha Elizabeth, d. William, flax-dresser, and Jane, July 25, 1847.
Mary J., d. William, laborer, b. England, and Jane, Nov. 24, 1848.
Mary R[ebecca. C. R. 4.], d. Charles, machinist, and Juliana, both b. England, Sept. 3, 1848.
Thomas S., s. Charles, machinist, and Juliana, both b. England, Nov. 13, 1849.

REECE (see also Reese), James, s. James and Charlotte, bp. Dec. 27, 1836. C. R. 1.

REED (see also Read), William, s. William G., tin-plate worker, and Eliza, July 8, 1848.
——, d. Carlton, Nov. 15, 1826.

REENAN, Sarah Jane, d. John, fuller, and Bridget, both b. England, Apr. 23, 1849.

REESE (see also Reece), William, s. James and Charlotte, Dec. 24, 1837.

REMINGTON (see also Renington), Joseph, s. John and Abigall, Nov. 29, 1654.

RENINGTON (see also Remington), Thomas, s. John and Abigall, Feb. 4, 1655.

RENWICK, Harriet, d. David, finisher, and Mary, Nov. 8, 1847
Thomas, s. David, finisher, and Mary, both b. Scotland, Nov. 5, 1849.

REYNOLDS (see also Runnels), Abby Minerva, d. John and Prudence Harris, Sept. 23, 1834. P. R. 93.
Gayton Osgood, s. John and Prudence Harris, May 28, 1831. P. R. 93.
James Harris, s. John and Prudence Harris, Oct. 23, 1839 P. R. 93.
Prudence Lavinia, d. John and Prudence Harris, Feb. 27, 1837. P. R. 93.
Rebekah, d. William and Rebekah, Apr. 3, 1773. P. R. 93.

RHOADES, Thomas, s. Thomas, flax-dresser, and Elizabeth, May 17, 1845.

RICE, David, s. David and Maria, bp. June 25, 1826. C. R. 6.
Edward, s. David and Elizabeth, Nov. 26, 1812.
[Eliza Ann. C. R. 6.], d. David and Maria, Dec. —, 1720.
[Mary Livingston. C. R. 6.], d. David and Maria, Nov. 11, 1822.
William [Albert. C. R. 6.], s. David and Maria, July 26, 1828.
——, d. David and Maria, Sept. 14, 1818.

RICH, John, s. James and Anna, bp. ——, 1741. C. R. 1.

RICHARDS, Elizabeth Page, d. Thomas and Abigail, Mar 22, 1796.
Simeon, s. Simeon Town and Abigail Richards, July 4, 1798.

RICHARDSON, Abba Ann, d. Caleb, jr. and Hannah, Oct. 1, 1835
Abigal, d. Caleb and Abigail, Oct. 16, 1795.
Adam Clark, s. Parker and Mary O., Jan. 9, 1837.
Albert, s. Joseph and Lucy, Aug. 6, 1840.
Alvan, s. Sam[ue]l S., cordwainer, and Rhoda A., June 4, 1843.
Caleb, s. Caleb, bp. Apr. 14, 1799. C. R. 2.
Caroline, d. Merrill and Sally, June 29, 1828.
Charles, s. Caleb and Abigail, July 22, 1813.
Dexter, s. Merrill and Sally, Nov. 21, 1819.
Elizabeth, d. twin, Caleb and Abigail, Feb. 9, 1806.
Ellen Phillippi, d. Samuel S., cordwainer, and Rhoda Ann, Dec. 31, 1847.
Etta Maria, d. George and Sophronia, Sept. 14, 1847.
Francis, s. Joseph and Lucy, Aug. 14, 1826.
George, s. Caleb and Abigail, Sept. 20, 1810.
George Stevens, s. Caleb, jr., bp. July 3, 1842. C. R. 2.
Georgianna, d. Joseph and Lucy, Nov. 14, 1830.
Hannah Mariah, d. Caleb, jr. and Hannah, Feb. 17, 1834.
Harriot, d. Caleb and Abigail, Aug. 1, 1801.
Henry F., s. Moses and Sarah, July 3, 1835.
John, s. Thomas [Irishman. C. R. 1.] and Elizabeth, Nov. 6, 1730.
John P., s. Parker and Polly O., Nov. 25, 1830.
John S., s. George, carpenter, and Sophronia, Apr. 16, 1844.
Joseph Henry, s. Joseph W., laborer, and Sophia, Sept. 17, 1846.
Lydia, d. Caleb and Abigail, Mar. 3, 1808.
Margaret, d. Caleb, jr. and Hannah, Feb. 13, 1838.
Mary, d. Caleb and Abigal, June 14, 1797.
Mary, d. Parker and Polly O., Apr. 27, 1829.
Mary, d. Parker and Polly, Sept. 25, 1832.
Mary Ann, d. Mark S., tin-plate worker, and Mary A., Sept. 15, 1845.
Merrill Dexter, s. Merrill and Sally, June 20, 1822.
Parkerson [Parker. C. R. 2.], s. Caleb and Abigail, Aug. 13, 1803.
Sarah, d. twin, Caleb and Abigail, Feb. 9, 1806.
Sarah A., d. Moses and Sarah, Nov. 10, 1838.
Sarah F., d. Samuel S., cordwainer, and Rhoda A., Oct. 5, 1845.
Thomas, s. Thomas and Elizabeth, Feb. 15, 17[31-2. C. R. 1.].
Wesley, s. Parker and Polly O., Jan. 26, 1835.
William H., s. Robert, flax-dresser, and Ellen, June 29, 1845.
——, s. Joseph and Lucy, Feb. 5, 1821.
——, s. Joseph and Lucy, July 26, 1722.

RIDDERBUSH, Betty, d. Christopher and Lucy, bp. Oct. 31, 1784. C. R. 1.
Phebe, d. Christopher and Lucy, bp. Sept. 14, 1783. C. R. 1.

RIDLEY, Charles H., s. James, manufacturer, and Minerva, Mar. 14, 1849.

RIX, Sarah, d. Nathaniel and Mary, Dec. 23, 1748.

ROBBINSON (see also Robinson), [Anna. C. R. 1.], d. Dane and Sarah, Jan. 14, 1736-7.
Elizabeth, d. Joseph and Elizabeth, —— [1707 ?].
Elizabeth, d. Ephraim and Hannah, Oct. 17, 1760.
Hannah, d. Isaac and Dorathy, Sept. 27, 1744.
Lydia, d. Dane and Sarah, Dec. 30, 1739.
Mary, d. Joseph [jr. C. R. 1.] and Mehetable, Aug. 3, 1737.
Mary, d. Dane and Sarah, Sept. 11, 1743.
Mehetable, d. Joseph, jr. and Mehetable, Oct. 9, 1742.
Phebe, d. Joseph and Elisabeth [Pheoby. dup.], Nov. 25, 1717.
Susanna, d. Dane, jr. and Sarah, Feb. 18, 1745-6.
——, s. Joseph and Elizabeth, Dec. 22, 1710.
——, ch. Joseph and Elizabeth, June 1, 1713.
——, d. Isaac and Dorathy, Aug. 3, 1742.

ROBERTS, Catherine [Felt. C. R. 2.], d. James and Harriot, Sept. 7, 1826.
Elizabeth, d. Temple and Rebeccah, June 7, 1817.
Harriot K[neeland. C. R. 2.], d. James and Harriot, Dec. 7, 1821.
James Adams, s. Harriet, bp. Jan. 9, 1831. C. R. 2.
John H., s. Shadrach and Mary Ann, Apr. 29, 1819.
Jonathan Herbert, s. David Sands and Sarah Elizabeth, bp. May 30, 1841. C. R. 4.
Lydia Eliza, d. twin, David G. and Sarah Elizabeth, bp. July 7, 1844. C. R. 4.
Mary Ann, d. Temple and Rebeccah, Dec. 16, 1819.
Mary Cate, d. James A., trader, and Mary A., Jan. 17, 1848.
Sarah Elizabeth, d. twin, David G. and Sarah Elizabeth, bp. July 7, 1844. C. R. 4.

ROBINSON (see also Robbinson), Anna, d. Dean and Sarah, Aug. 28, 1734.
Arthur, s. Edward, Feb. 4, 1833. C. R. 6.
Asa, s. Dane and Sarah, Apr. 6, 1732.

ROBINSON, Asa, s. Asa, bp. Feb. 19, 1764. C. R. I.
Dane, s. Dane and [torn], —— [1703-4?].
Daniel, s. Isaac and Dorathy, Aug. 8, 1750.
Daniel, s. John and Sarah, Dec. 14, 1783.
Dean, s. John and Sarah, Apr. 15, 1788.
Deane, s. Joseph and Phebe, Feb. 2, 1671.
Dolley, d. Isaac and Dorithy, Feb. 6, 1746-7.
Dolly, d. John and Sarah, Sept. 3, 1791.
Dorothy, d. Joseph and Phebe, Feb. 21, 1673.
Elezebeth, d. Joseph and Elezebeth, Aug. 7, 17[27. C. R. I.].
Elisabeth, d. Joseph, jr. and Mehetable, Sept. 4, 1746.
Elizabeth Ann, d. John, weaver, and Nancy, Jan. 11, 1848.
Emily, d. Aaron and Sarah, Apr. 29, 1803.
Ephraim, s. Joseph and Elezebeth, Aug. 11 [1723].
Eward A., s. Edward, Feb. 4, 1833.
Fidelia, d. Aaron and Sarah, at Boxford, May 6, 1799.
George S., s. John G. and Mary J., Sept. 21, 1836.
George W., s. Joel and Rebecca, Dec. 18, 1839.
Hannah, d. Joseph and Phoebe, July 6, 1685.
Hannah, d. Dane and Mary, Jan. 29, 1694-5.
Hannah, d. Epharam and Hannah, June 28, 1755.
Isaac, s. Isaac and Dorathy, Apr. 24, 1741.
Isaac, s. John and Sarah, June 21, 1786.
Isaack, s. Joseph and Elizabeth, Sept. –, [1715].
Israel, s. John and Bekky, bp. Apr. 1, 1764. C. R. I.
Jeremy, s. Joseph, jr. and Mehetebel, Aug. 20, 1754.
John, s. Joseph and Mehetable, Sept. 2, 1739.
John, s. Isaac and Dorathy, Aug. 11, 1758.
John, s. John and Sarah, Mar. 16, 1796.
John, s. Aaron and Sarah, Aug. 29, 1796.
Jonathan, s. Isaac and Dorathy, June 25, 1753.
Joseph, s. Epharam and Hannah, Aug. 23, 1751.
Julia Ann, d. John and Mary, July 5, 1838.
Lucy, d. Asa and Margaret, Feb. 6, 1760.
Louisa, d. Joseph, laborer, and Frances, May 19, 1848.
Martha Lovejoy, d. Dean and Eliza F., bp. Oct. 11, 1812. C. R. I.
Mary, d. Dane and Mary, Apr. 22, 1698.
Maximilian, s. Edward, Sept. 21, 1831. C. R. 6.
Mehetabel, d. Dane and Sarah, Aug. 29, 1726.
Naomy, d. Ephraim and Hannah, Mar. 18, 1763.
Nathan, s. Joseph and Mehetibel, Sept. 1, 1734.
Nathan, s. Isaac and Dorathy, Apr. 20, 1756.
Neoma, d. Epharam and Hannah, Apr. 11, 1758.
Phebe, d. Joseph and Phebe, July 21, 1682.

ROBINSON, Peter, s. Asa and Margret, July 27, 1757.
Samuel Grainger, s. Benjamin and Priscilla, Jan. 12, 1808.
Sally, d. John and Sarah, Oct. 16, 1781.
Sarah, d. Dane and Sarah, Mar. 19, 1728-9.
Sarah, d. Epharam and Hannah, May 21, 1753.
Warren, s. John G. and Mary J., Jan. 25, 1838.
William, s. Asa and Margaret, Feb. 2, 1762.
——, s. Elbridge, mechanic, and Eliza F., Apr. 16, 1844.

ROCKIE, Charles J., s. John, manufacturer, and Christie, Nov. 8, 1844.
George, s. John, spinner, and Christiana, Apr. 26, 1847.
Mary J., d. John, weaver, and Christina, both b. Scotland, Apr. 18, 1849.

RODGERS (see also Rogers), ——, d. Fittz William, cabinet-maker and Mary C., Nov. 28, 1847.

ROGERS (see also Rodgers), Sarah, d. Jacob, bp. Jan. 24, 1779. C. R. 1.
Will[ia]m, s. Jacob and Elizabeth, bp. Dec. 7, 1777. C. R. 1.
——, s. Jeremiah, June 27, 1826.

ROLFE, Samuel, s. John, bp. July 6, 1834. C. R. 2.
William James, s. John, bp. July 6, 1834. C. R. 2.

ROSS, Joseph, s. Barney, laborer, and Mary A., May 30, 1849.
Margaret Elizabeth, d. Robert and Mary, bp. Sept. 3, 1843. C. R. 3.
Sarah, d. John and Sarah, Nov. 3, 1720.
Thomas, s. John and Sarah, Oct. 5, 1718.

ROTHWELL, Caroline Helen, d. George and Elizabeth, bp. June 11, 1843. C. R. 4.
Elizabeth, d. George and Elizabeth, bp. June 11, 1843. C. R. 4.
James Henry, s. George and Elizabeth, bp. June 11, 1843. C. R. 4.

RUNLETT, Hannah Elizabeth, d. Joseph C. and Hannah L., Nov. 26, 1839.

RUNNELS (see also Reynolds), Elizabeth [Foster. P. R. 93.], d. John and Prudence [Harris. P. R. 93.], Feb. 11, 1829.
Frederick, s. Enos and Sarah, Feb. 9, 1785.

RUNNELS, John G., s. John and Prudence, May 26, 1831.
Mary [Harris. P. R. 93.], d. John and Prudence [Harris. P. R. 93.], Jan. 16, 1824. [Jan. 19. P. R. 93.].
Rebecca, d. Will[ia]m and Rebecca, Mar. 30, 1769.
Rufus [Anderson Reynolds. P. R. 93.], s. John and Prudence [Harris. P. R. 93.], Feb. 15, 1819.
Stephen, s. William and Rebecca, Oct. 13, 1771.
Stephen, s. Enos and Sarah, Nov. 18, 1782.
William W. B[artlett Reynolds. P. R. 93.], s. John and Prudence [Harris. P. R. 93.], Apr. 9, 1826.

RUS (see also Russ), [Daniell. C. R. 1.], s. Thomas and Sarah, Oct. 6, 1748.
Martha, d. Wiliam and Mary, Nov. 25, 1749.

RUSE (see also Russ), Margaret, d. John and Debora, Apr. 10, 1673.
Mary, d. John and Debora, June 12, 1667.
Sara, d. John and Debora, Feb. 3, 1668.

RUSEL (see also Russell), Abigal, d. Thomas and Abigal, May 12, 1750.
[Abraham. C. R. 2.], s. John, jr. and Hannah, Nov. 7, 1750.
Aquilla, s. James and Lucy, May 1, 1748.
Daniel, s. Lt. Joseph and Hannah, Aug. 21, 1754.
David, s. John, jr. and Hannah, Feb. 8, 1747-8.
Eligah, s. Lt. Joseph and Hannah, Mar. 8, 1756.
Hannah, d. John, jr. and Hannah, Feb. 21, 1754.
Isaac, s. John, jr. and Hannah, May 24, 1752.
Isaac, s. John, jr. and Hannah, Jan. 28, 1759.
[James. C. R. 2.], s. Thomas and Abigal, May 7, 1749.
James, s. Joseph and Hannah, Jan. 7, 1753.
Jonathan, s. Joseph and Hannah, Aug. 14, 1749.
Perikens [Perkins. C. R. 2.], s. Joseph and Hanah, May 7, 1748.
Prudence, d. Robert and Anne, May 27, 1748.
Rachil, d. Lt. Joseph and Hannah, Feb. 23, 1757.
Rhode, d. Isaac and Elezebith, Aug. 23, 1755.
Sarah, d. Robert [sr. C. R. 2.] and Anne, Sept. 13, 1746.
Sarah, d. Joseph and Hannah, Oct. 29, 1750.
Susanna, d. Isaac and Elezebith, Aug. 3, 1757.

RUSELL (see also Russell), Ammon, s. Joel and Sarah, Aug. 20, 1810.
Israel, s. Joel and Sarah, May 17, 1814.

RUSS (see also Rus, Ruse, Russe), Abigall, d. John and Deborah, Feb. 2, 1680.
Anna, d. Thomas and Anna, —— [1702].
Deborah, d. Hezekiah and Deborah, bp. June 22, 1712. C. R. 2.
Deborah, d. John, deceased, and Priscilla, Apr. 30, 1744.
Hannah, d. John and Hannah, Feb. 20, 1695-6.
Johnathan, s. John and Deborah, Dec. 27, 1674.
[Jonathan. C. R. 1.] — n, s. Thomas and Sarah, May 6, 1731.
Joseph, s. John and Deborah, Apr. 7, 1687.
Joseph, s. John and Deborah, May 6, 1688.
Joseph, s. Joseph and Priscilla, — [1710].
Josiah, s. John and Deborah, Jan. 13, 1684.
Phebe, d. John and Rebekah, Apr. 20, 1683.
Phebe, d. William and Mary, Jan. 1, 1747-8.
Simeon, s. Thomas and Sarah, Nov. 24, 1735.
Thomas, s. John and Deborah, June 17, 1677.
Thomas, s. Thomas and Anne, —— [1703].
Unice, d. Deborah and Peter Bridges, May 23, 1766.
W[illia]m, s. wid. Anne, bp. June 15, 1712. C. R. 2.
William, s. William and Mary, Oct. 11, 1745.
——, ch. [torn] and Anna, Mar. 5, 1705-6.
——, d. Hezekiah and Deborah, Dec. 18, 1710.

RUSSE (see also Russ), John, s. John and Debora, Apr. 5, 1671.

RUSSEL (see also Russell), Benjamin, s. John [jr. C. R. 2.] and Hannah, Jan. 28, 1738-9.
Daniel, s. Joseph and Hephzibah [bp. Oct. 17. C. R. 2.], 1742.
Daniel, s. Tho[ma]s, bp. Nov. 12, 1769. C. R. 2.
David, s. John [jr. C. R. 2.] and Sarah, Nov. 11, 1776.
Elizabeth, d. Tho[mas], bp. Jan. 24, 1745. C. R. 2.
Ezekiel, s. Robert, bp. June 10, 1722. C. R. 2.
Gideon, s. William and Sarah, Apr. 1, 1735.
Hannah, d. Joseph, bp. Jan. 13, 1740. C. R. 2.
Hannah, d. Tho[ma]s, bp. Sept. 27, 1767. C. R. 2.
Hephzibah, d. Robert, bp. May 25, 1755. C. R. 2.
Jacob, s. John, jr., bp. Feb. 1, 1761. C. R. 2.
[James. C. R. 2.], s. James and Lucy, Jan. 11, 1741-2.
Jedadiah, s. Robert, bp. Nov. 26, 1752. C. R. 2.
Jeduthon, s. James and Lucy, —— 31 [bp. Feb. 3, 1745. C. R. 2.].
Jemima, d. John, bp. Jan. 28, 1733. C. R. 2.
John, s. John, jr. and Hanah, July 1, 1746.
Jonathan, s. Robert, bp. Apr. 30, 1758. C. R. 2.
Lucy, d. James and Lucy, Sept. —, 1746. [bp. Sept. 28. C. R. 2.]

RUSSEL, Nathanael, s. Rob[er]t, bp. Feb. 3, 1751. C. R. 2.
Pelatiah, s. Peter and Deborah, Dec. 27, 1727.
Phebe, d. Peter, bp. May 16, 1736. C. R. 2.
Precilla, d. Abigal, wid. "three months and ten days after her father's Death," Aug. 2, 1753.
Priscilla, d. James and Lucy, July 5, 1743.
Prudence, d. Rob[er]t and Abigail, bp. July 31, 1720. C. R. 2.
Prudence, d. Robert, bp. Feb. 10, 1760. C. R. 2.
Sarah, d. William and Sarah, Mar. 26, 1740.
[Sarah. C. R. 2..], d. John, jr. and Hannah, July 7 [1742. C. R. 2.].
Thomas, s. Thomas and Abigail, Feb. 12, 1746-7.
Uriah, s. Thomas and Abigail, May 14, 1743.
Uriah, s. Uriah, bp. Sept. 19, 1773. C. R. 2.
William, s. John, jr. and Hannah, Mar. 5, 1743-4.
[torn]nah, d. Corp. Joseph and Hephzibah, Jan. 11, 1739-40.
——, d. Thomas and Phoebe, July 18, 1704.
——, d. Joel, jr. and Polly, July 16, 1827.

RUSSELL (see also Rusel, Rusell, Russel), Abiel, s. Uriah, bp. Mar. 15, 1789. C. R. 2.
Abiel Edwin, s. Abiel and Sally, Feb. 27, 1821.
Abigail, d. Benjamin and Mary, —— [1710].
[Abigail, d. C. R. 2.] Robert and Abigail, Oct. 4, 1717.
Abigail B., d. Thomas and Abigail, Dec. 6, 1812.
Albert C., s. Moses B. and Clarissa (Peters), Aug. 31, 1839. P. R. 63.
Alpheus, s. William and Sarah, Feb. 22, 1737-8.
Ammon, Aug. 20, 1810. P. R. 71.
Amos, s. Joel and Sally, Oct. 9, 1824.
Angelia A., d. Abiel E., trader, and Hannah D., Apr. 29, 1849.
Aquilla, s. James and Priscilla, Sept. 12, 1717.
Benjamin, s. Robert and Mary, June 12, 1677.
Benjamin, s. Benjamin and Mary, July 28, 1763.
Benjamine, s. Benjamine and [torn], —— [1702].
Bethiah, d. Thomas and Bethiah, Jan. 5, 1763.
Betty, d. John, jr., bp. Oct. 7, 1780. C. R. 2.
Chandler, s. Joseph and Hipza[bah], Sept. 20, 1775.
Charles H., s. Charles and Eliza, Sept. 12, 1830.
Cornelia, d. Moody and Fanny, Feb. 9, 1838.
Deborah, d. Peter and Deborah, Apr. 8, 1729.
Dolly, d. John, jr., bp. Sept. 21, 1788. C. R. 2.
Edward, s. John, jr. and Diania, Nov. 23, 1804.
Elijah, s. Joseph and Hepsibah, Nov. 1, 1768.
Elizabeth, d. Robert and Mary, July 16, 1687.

RUSSELL, Elizabeth, d. Thomas and Abigail, Feb. 22, 1818.
Elizabeth K[nights. C. R. 3.], d. Thomas and Abigail, Feb. 9, 1819.
Elizabeth P., d. Joel and Sally, Dec. 16, 1815.
Elvira Hannah, d. Samuel, laborer, and Lydia E., Sept. 20, 1847.
Gardner [Spring. C. R. 3.], s. Thomas and Abigail, Dec. 29, 1815.
Hannah, d. Robert and Mary, June 28, 1679.
Hannah, d. John and Sarah, Dec. 28, 1730.
Hannah, d. [Lt. C. R. 2.] Joseph and Hannah, Oct. 11, 1760.
Hannah, d. twin, Joseph [jr. C. R. 2.] and Hepsibah, May 27, 1761.
Hannah, d. Uriah, bp. Sept. 10, 1775. C. R. 2.
Hannah, d. John, 3d, bp. Sept. 20, 1778. C. R. 2.
Henry Warren [s. Joel. C. R. 2.], Oct. 20, 1820. P. R. 71.
Hephzibah, d. Joseph and Hephziah [bp. June 30, 1734. C. R. 2.].
Hephzibah, d. Jedediah, bp. Nov. 2, 1783. C. R. 2.
Hepsibah, d. Joseph [jr. C. R. 2.] and Hepsibah, June 18, 1756.
Israel, May 17, 1814. P. R. 71.
Isaac, s. John and Sarah, Dec. 3, 1724.
Isaac, s. Isaac and Elizabeth, July 1, 1759.
James, s. Robert and Mary, Sept. 16, [16]67.
James, s. James and Priscilla, —— [1710].
James, s. twin, Uriah, bp. Nov. 2, 1777. C. R. 2.
James, s. Joel and Sally, Apr. 26, 1822.
James W[heeler. C. R. 2.], s. Samuel, farmer, and Lydia, Aug. 20, 1845.
Jedediah, s. Jedediah, bp. Oct. 5, 1783. C. R. 2.
Job Abbot, s. Abiel and Sarah, Mar. 18, 1830.
Joel, s. Uriah, bp. Aug. 31, 1783. C. R. 2.
Joel, s. Joel and Sally, Oct. 10, 1808. [1809. P. R. 71.]
John, s. Robert and Mary, Oct. 14, 1682.
John, s. John and Sarah, June 8, 1717.
John, s. John, 3d and Phoebe, Oct. 10, 1774.
John, s. John, jr. and Diana, May 27, 1800.
John, s. Phillis and John Freeman, Jan. 27, 1816.
Joseph, s. Robert and Mary, Apr. 1, 1671.
Joseph, s. Thomas and Pheob[e], —— [1702].
Joseph, s. John and Sarah, Jan. 8, 1719-20.
Joseph, s. Joseph and Hephzibah, Jan. 9, 1729-30.
Joseph, s. Joseph [jr. C. R. 2.] and Hepsibah, July 8, 1758.
Joseph, s. Lt. John, jr. and Diania, Oct. 13, 1809.
Levi, s. Joel and Sarah, June 23, 1812.
Lizze Abbey, d. Augustine K., shoemaker, and Abigail, Mar. 22, 1849.

RUSSELL, [Lydia, d. C. R. 2.] [Be]njamin and Mary, Dec. 15, 1713.
Lydia, d. Joseph and Hepsibah, May 17, 1764.
Lydia, d. Uriah, bp. Sept. 15, 1782. C. R. 2.
Lydia, d. Uriah and Lydia, Dec. 5 [1785].
Lydia Abbot, d. Abiel and Sally, June 2, 1818.
Lydia Abbott, d. Thomas, bp. Apr. 6, 1834. C. R. 3.
Mary, d. Robert and Mary, Jan. 14, 1661.
Mary, d. Thomas and Phoebe, Feb. 10, 1692-3.
Mary, d. Benjamine and Mary, —— [1705?].
Mary, d. James and Priscilla, Apr. [bp. Apr. 22, 1716. C. R. 2.].
[Mary. C. R. 2.], d. John and Sarah, Feb. 10, 1728-9.
Mary, d. Benjamin and Mary, Oct. 15, 1764.
Moses Abbot, s. Abiel and Sally, Aug. 4, 1824.
Nancy, d. John, bp. Aug. 8, 1790. C. R. 2.
Peter, s. Thomas and Phoebe, Apr. 23, 1700.
Peter, s. Peter and Deborah, Dec. 4, 1732.
Phebe, d. John, 3d, bp. Sept. 8, 1776. C. R. 2.
Phebe, d. Uriah, bp. Jan. 29, 1786. C. R. 2.
Phebe, d. Lt. John, jr. and Diania, Mar. 30, 1807.
Phebe, d. Joel and Sally, Aug. 26, 1818.
Pheoby, d. John and Sarah, June [bp. June 10, 1716. C. R. 2.].
Phoebe, d. Thomas and Phoebe, Jan. 21, 1689-90.
[Priscilla. C. R. 2.], d. James and Priscilla, Aug. 19, 1712.
Priscilla Jane, d. Thomas, bp. May 4, 1834. C. R. 3.
Rachel, d. Peter and Deborah, Nov. 1, 1730.
Rebecah, d. Peter and Deborah, Aug. 29, 1734.
Rhoda, d. Jedediah, bp. Oct. 5, 1783. C. R. 2.
Robert, s. John and Sarah [bp. Jan. 21, 1722. C. R. 2.].
Sally, d. John, jr., bp. Aug. 17, 1783. C. R. 2.
Sally, d. Joel and Sally, Dec. 13, 1806.
Samuel, s. Joel and Sally, Aug. 8, 1820.
Sarah, d. John and Sarah, Apr. 5, 1713.
Sarah, d. Thomas [jr. C. R. 2.] and Sarah, Jan. 2, 1770.
Sarah Ballard, d. Abiel and Sally, Dec. 24, 1816.
Simmeon, s. twin, Joseph [jr. C. R. 2.] and Hepsibah, May 27, 1761.
Theodore, s. Benj[ami]n and Mary, Dec, 6, 1765.
Thomas, s. Robert and Mary, Dec. 16, 1663.
Thomas, s. Thomas and Phoebe, Aug. 13, 1687.
Thomas, s. James and Priscilla, June 18, 1714.
Thomas, s. Joseph and Hephzibah, June 5, 1732.
Thomas, s. Thomas and Bethiah, June 5, 1765.
Thomas, s. Thomas, jr. and Sarah, Feb. 22, 1768.

RUSSELL, Thomas, s. Uriah, bp. Nov. 7, 1773. C. R. 2.
Thomas, s. twin, Uriah, bp. Nov. 2, 1777. C. R. 2.
Uriah, s. Joel and Sarah, July 16, 1805.
Uriah, s. Joel and Sally, Mar. 29, 1831.
Wichelmina, d. Moody, carpenter, and Fanny, May 31, 1845.
William, s. William and Sarah, Dec. 7, 1732.
William, s. John, jr., bp. July 24, 1785. C. R. 2.
William, s. John, jr. and Diana, July 29, 1802.
Williard, s. Thomas and Abigail, July 20, 1814.
——, ch. [torn] and [P]heoby, June 15, 1706.
——, ch. Hannah, at the almshouse, Dec. 27, 1817.
——, d. Thomas and Abigail, Feb. 2, 1821.

SAFFORD, Abraham, s. Abraham and Martha, Nov. 5, 1763.
Elizabeth, d. Abraham and Martha, Nov. 30, 1761.
Hannah, d. Abraham and Martha, Oct. 2, 1769.
Isaac, s. Abraham and Martha, bp. Nov. 1, 1778. C. R. 1.
John, s. Abraham and Martha, Mar. 16, 1766.
Patte, d. Abraham and Martha, May 15, 1759.
Patte, d. Abraham and Martha, Apr. 28, 1760.
Sarah, d. Abraham and Martha, bp. Feb. 16, 1777. C. R. 1.
Theodore, s. Abraham and Martha, Dec. 29, 1767.

SALKELD, Robert Byers, s. Joseph and Mary, Aug. —, 1848. C. R. 4.

SALTER, Helen Josephine, d. Dr. R. H. and Abbie W., bp. June 12, 1836. C. R. 6.

SALTMARSH, Seth, s. Seth, bp. Apr. 12, 1778. C. R. 1.
Susanna, d. Seth, bp. May 13, 1781. C. R. 1.

SANBORN, Catherine H. A. [Harriet Adelaide. P. R. 108.], d. Eastman, dentist, and Mary C., Sept. 17, 1848.
Emma Mary Eastman, d. Eastman and Mary C. L., Mar. 6, 1841.
Francis Gregory, s. Dr. Eastman and Mary C. L., Jan. 18, 1838.
Helen Clara Martha, d. Dr. Eastman and Mary C. L., Sept. 27, 1839.

SANDERS (see also Saunders), Otis, s. Timothy, Feb. 17, 1839.

SANDERSON, Ellen J., d. Adam, spinner, and Ellen, June 25, 1848.
George W[illiam. C. R. 1.], s. Adan, laborer, and Ellen, Oct. 3, 1845.

SARGENT, Charles Horatio, s. Jesse and Hannah, Sept. 21, 1823.
Eliza Sutton, d. Jesse and Hannah, June 6, 1835.
George O., s. Abel, carpenter, Jan. 20, 184[7 or 8].
Hannah Frances, d. Jesse and Hannah, July 5, 1833.
Jesse Granville, s. Jesse and Hannah, Sept. 5, 1837.
Martha Ann, d. Jesse and Hannah, Sept. 13, 1828.

SAUNDERS (see also Sanders), Ann, d. James, flax-sorter, and Ann, both b. Scotland, Aug. 23, 1849.
Caleb, s. Daniel and Phebe, Sept. 4, 1838.
Charles Parker, s. Benja[min] P., blacksmith, and Lavinia, Mar. 22, 1848.
David, s. Daniel and Phebe F., Oct. 6, 1822.
Issabella, d. William, operative, and Elizabeth, Feb. 12, 1845.
James, s. James, flax-dresser, and Anne, May 24, 1845.
James, s. William, flax-dresser, and Elizabeth, Apr. 12, 1847.
Margaret Watson, d. James, flax-dresser, and Ann, Mar. 25, 1847.
Martha, d. Daniel and Phebe F., July 18, 1835.
Martha G., d. Daniel and Phebe F., Dec. 30, 1828.

SAVORY, Jenny, d. William and Lydia, Feb. 10, 1761.
Mary, d. William and Lydia, June 4, 1759.

SAWYER, Bulah, d. Henry and Sarah, May 17, 1734.
Lydia, d. Josiah, bp. Feb. 21, 1768. C. R. 2.
Nehemiah, s. Amos and Betsy O., of Reading, Feb. 8, 1821.
——, s. Henry and Sarah, Oct. 13, 1736.

SCALES (see also Scals), Abigail, d. Oliver and Abigail, bp. Mar. 14, 1756. C. R. 2.
James, s. Oliver and Abigail, bp. Mar. 14, 1756. C. R. 2.
James, s. James and Mercy, May 31, 1765.
Lydia, d. Moses, bp. July 21, 1751. C. R. 2.
Lydia, d. Oliver and Abigail, bp. Mar. 14, 1756. C. R. 2.
Marcy, d. James, bp. Mar. 22, 1778. C. R. 1.
Mary, d. Moses, bp. July 14, 1754. C. R. 2.
Mary Dane, d. Abigail and Sam[ue]ll Chickering, 3d, July 13, 1781.
Moses, s. Moses, bp. July 20, 1760. C. R. 2.
Oliver, s. James and Mercy, Apr. 27, 1767.
Rebecca, d. Moses, bp. Feb. 28, 1748. C. R. 2.
Stephen, s. James, bp. Jan. 3, 1773. C. R. 1.
Susanna, d. Moses, bp. Sept. 18, 1757. C. R. 2.
Susanna, d. James and Marcy, bp. Jan. 15, 1769. C. R. 1.
William, s. James and Mercy, bp. Dec. 30, 1770. C. R. 1.

SCALS (see also Scales), Hannah, d. Moses and Rebecca, Feb. 4 [1737. C. R. 2.].
Hannah, d. Moses and Rebecca, Jan. 29, 1740-41.
Sarah, d. Moses and Rebecca, Sept. 11, 1743.

SCOTT, Archibald, s. Andrew and Janet, Dec. 15, 1828.
Daniel, s. Thomas and Mary, Oct. 22, 1830.
Jesse Morrison, s. Andrew and Janet, bp. July 21, 1839. C. R. 4.
John, s. Thomas and Mary, Mar. 14, 1828.
Joseph, s. Andrew and Janet, bp. July 21, 1839. C. R. 4.
Mary Murray, d. Charles, bp. Nov. 6, 1842. C. R. 2.
Robert, s. Andrew and Janet, July 16, 1830.
Robert, s. Charles, colorer, and Janett, Feb. —, 1844.
William K. [Ritchie. C. R. 4.], s. Andrew and Janett, May 26, 1834.
——, s. Thomas, July 16, 1826.

SEAMORE, Mary Ann Smith, d. Eliza, at almshouse, July 19, 1822.

SEATOWN, Elezebith, d. James and Elezebith, July 13, 1750.

SESSIONS, John, s. Alexand[e]r and Elizabeth, Oct. 4, 1674.
Alexand[e]r, s. Alexand[e]r and Elizabeth, Oct. 3, 1676.
David, s. Samuel and Mary, bp. Aug. 29, 1736. C. R. 1.
David, s. David and Mary, May 11, 1749.
Hettee, d. David and Mary, Aug. 19, 1744.
John, s. Samuel, jr. and Hannah, June 9, 1742.
Joseph, s. Alexand[e]r and Elizabeth, Mar. 28, 1686
Josiah, s. Alexander and Elizabeth, May 2, 1684.
Mary, d. David and Mary, Oct. 30, 1751.
Nathaniell, s. Alexander and Elizabeth, Aug. 8, 1681.
Samuel, jr., s. Samuel and Mary, bp. Aug. 29, 1736. C. R. 1.
Samuel, s. David and Mary, Feb. 11, 1746-7.
Samuel, s. Samuel, bp. Nov. 1, 1772. C. R. 1.
Samuell, s. Alexand[e]r and Elizabeth, Mar. 8, 1679-80.
Sarah, d. Samu[el] and [torn], ——, 1708-9.
Sarah, d. Samuel and Hannah, Nov. 6, 1740.
Timothy, s. Alexander and Elizabeth, Apr. 14, 1678.
Timothy, s. Samuel and Mary, bp. Aug. 29, 1736. C. R. 1.
——, ch. Samuel and Mary, Dec. 19, 1710.
——, s. Samuel and Mary, Aug. 17, 1712.
[torn]y, d. Samuell and Mary, Sept. 6, 1714.
——, s. Samuel and Mary, Jan. 25, 1717-18.

SESSIONS, ——, d. Timothy and Abigail, May —, 1740.
[torn]us, s. David and Mary, —— 21, 1753.
——, d. David and Mary, Sept. —, 1755.

SHACKELTON, Henry W., s. Joseph, laborer, and Tamar, Aug. 5, 1848.

SHACKFORD, Dorcas, d. John and Dorcas, Oct. 22, 1742.
Joshua, s. Joshua and Lydia, Sept. 16, 1736.
[Lydia. C. R. 1.] ——a, d. Joshua and Lydia, Apr. 25, 1738.
[Samuel. C. R. 1.], s. John and Dorcas, Feb. 4, 1731-2.
——, s. John and Dorcas, Sept. 9, 1735.

SHANNON, Everett, s. Daniel F., carpenter, b. Portsmouth, N. H., and Emily, Nov. 1, 1849.

SHAPEL, Catherine, d. Charles, laborer, b. France, and Julia, b. Ireland, Dec. 8, 1849.

SHATOCK (see also Shattuck), Elezebith, d. Joseph and Joanna, Oct. 9, 1749.

SHATTUCK (see also Shatock), Aaron, s. Isaac [jr. C. R. 2.] and Rebecca, June 29, 1800.
Abby Jane, d. John K. and Martha T., Nov. 20, 1841.
Abiel, s. Joseph and Joanna, Nov. 25, 1741.
Abiel, s. Joseph, jr. and Anna, Aug. 8, 1762.
Abiel H., s. Zebadiah, jr. and Sarah, July 30, 1811.
Anne, d. Joseph, jr. and Anne, Oct. 8, 1756.
Alfred, s. wid. Lucy, bp. July 8, 1832. C. R. 3.
Anna, d. Joseph and Anna [wid. Aug. 9. C. R. 2.], Aug. 4, 1778.
Augusta [Porter. C. R. 3.], d. Nathan and Mary, Apr. 22, 1834.
Benj[ami]n, s. Peter, jr. and Lucy, Aug. 26, 1820.
Benjamin Francis, s. wid. Lucy, bp. May 26, 1833. C. R. 3.
Caroline Augusta, d. Samuel and Hannah, Nov. 27, 1838.
Charles, s. Peter and Susanna, May 21, 1815.
Charles Otis, bp. July 13, 1828. C. R. 2.
Charles W[alter. C. R. 3.], s. Joseph, jr. and Hannah, June 13, 1831.
Charles William, s. Charles, cordwainer, and Rozetta, May 24, 1843.
Dorothy, d. Zebediah and Elizabeth, Apr. 14, 1764.
Edward, s. Joseph, jr. and Hannah, June 22, 1837.

SHATTUCK, Elisabeth, d. Joseph and Joanna, Oct. 7, 1743.
Elizabeth, d. Zeb[adia]h and Eliz[abe]th, Dec. 16, 1759.
Elizabeth, d. Joseph [jr. C. R. 2.] and Anna, Sept. 2, 1760.
Emily Elkins, d. Phineas and Rhoda, bp. Dec. 23, 1827. C. R. 3.
Emma A., d. Thomas C., cordwainer, and Salome K., June 16, 1843.
Ezra, s. Samuel and Lucy, May 26, 1799.
Frances Fry, ch. Phineas and Rhoda, bp. Dec. 23, 1827. C. R. 3.
Franklin, s. Peter and Susannah, May 21, 1808.
George, s. Peter and Susannah, June 18, 1801.
George, s. Peter, jr. and Lucy, June 28, 1819.
George Edward, s. wid. Lucy, bp. July 8, 1832. C. R. 3.
George Otis, s. Capt. Joseph, jr. and Hannah, May 2, 1829.
[Hannah. C. R. 2.], d. Joseph and Joanna, July 14, 1729.
Hannah, d. Zebed[iah], bp. Dec. 6, 1761. C. R. 2.
Hannah, d. Joseph and Anna, Sept. 8, 1774.
Hannah, d. Samuel, jr. and Hannah, May 26, 1820.
Hannah C[handler. C. R. 2.], d. Isaac [jr. C. R. 2.] and Rebecca, Sept. 26, 1785.
Hannah Chandler, d. Joseph and Phebe, Aug. 2, 1791.
Harriot B., d. Leonard and Harriot, Dec. 5, 1828.
Harriott, d. Peter and Susannah, Dec. 10, 1805.
Henry, s. Isaac and Rebecca, Feb. 7, 1790.
Henry, s. Henry and Sophia, Nov. 10, 1819.
[Isaac. C. R. 2.], s. Joseph and Joanna, Mar. 24, 1733-4.
Isaac, s. Isaac and Mary, Sept. 12, 1758.
Isaac, s. Isaac and Mary, July 13, 1766.
Isaac, s. Isaac [jr. C. R. 2.] and Rebecca, Nov. 14, 1787.
Jacob, s. Isaac [jr. C. R. 2.] and Rebecca, Aug. 10, 1792.
James M., s. Samuel and Lucy, Feb. 6, 1815.
James Newton, s. Simeon, cordwainer, and Antress, July 7, 1846.
John, s. Zebadiah, bp. Oct. 23, 1768. C. R. 2.
John C., s. Leonard and Harriot, Aug. 15, 1830.
John [H. C. R. 2.], s. Samuel and Lucy, Dec. 16, 1811.
John Kneeland, s. John K. and Martha T., Nov. 22, 1839.
John Thatcher, s. wid. Lucy, bp. July 8, 1832. C. R. 3.
Joseph, s. Joseph and Joanna, Nov. 27, 1731.
Joseph, s. Joseph, jr. and Anne, Nov. 8, 1757.
Joseph, s. Joseph and Phebe, Oct. 18, 1793.
Joseph, s. Capt. Joseph, jr. and Hannah, Apr. 22, 1827.
Josiah N[ewton. C. R. 3.], s. Nathan and Mary F., Oct. 11, 1835.
Leonard, s. twin, Peter and Susanna, Oct. 1, 1803.
Leonard, s. Peter and Susannah, bp. Sept. 24, 1813. C. R. 2.
Leonard G., s. Simeon and Anstice, June 26, 1840.

SHATTUCK, Lucy, d. Samuel and Lucy, May 24, 1801.
Lucy Brown, d. Joseph, jr. and Hannah, Feb. 10, 1834.
Lydia, d. Joseph [jr. C. R. 2.] and Anna, Apr. 27, 1765.
Martha A., d. Nathaniel and Caroline, Mar. 8, 1831.
Martha Ann, d. John and Martha, Oct. 22, 1837.
Martha Jane, bp. July 13, 1828. C. R. 2.
Martha L., d. Sally and Dudley F. Holt, Apr. 13, 1817.
Mary, d. Joseph and Joanna, July 13, 1746.
Mary, d. twin, Isaac and Mary, Aug. 3, 1760.
Mary, d. Isaac and Mary, Feb. 16, 1776.
Mary, d. Joseph, bp. Feb. 18, 1776. C. R. 2.
Mary, d. Nathaniel and Caroline, Mar. 19, 1824.
Mary A., d. Nathan and Mary F., bp. Nov. 7, 1824. C. R. 2.
Mary Ann, d. twin, Sam[ue]l and Hannah, May 10, 1835.
Mary Barnard, d. Samuel, bp. Mar. 29, 1807. C. R. 2.
Mary Emery, d. Phineas and Rhoda, bp. Dec. 23, 1827. C. R. 3.
Nathan, s. Joseph and Phebe, Mar. 4, 1797.
Nathaniel, s. twin, Isaac and Mary, Aug. 3, 1760.
Nathaniel, s. Isaac [jr. C. R. 2.] and Rebecca, Dec. 7, 1797.
Nathaniel, s. Nathaniel and Caroline, Dec. 15, 1826.
Nathaniel B., s. John R., shoemaker, and Martha S., Apr. 2, 1846.
Nathaniel Barnard, s. Samuel and Lucy, Jan. 5, 1809.
Obed, s. Joseph, bp. Nov. 24, 1776. C. R. 2.
Peter, s. Joseph and Anna, Oct. 18, 1772.
Peter, s. Peter and Susannah, Jan. 27, 1797.
Phebe, d. Isaac, bp. July 10, 1763. C. R. 2.
Phebe, d. Zebadiah, bp. Feb. 23, 1766. C. R. 2.
Phebe, d. Abiel and Phebe, Nov. 26, 1786.
Phebe Abbot, d. Joseph and Phebe, Feb. 21, 1807.
Phebe Abbot, d. Nathan and Mary, bp. Sept. 1, 1844. C. R. 3.
Phineas, s. Isaac [jr. C. R. 2.] and Rebecca, Aug. 4, 1803.
Rebecca, d. Isaac [jr. C. R. 2.] and Rebecca, June 18, 1795.
Rebecca, d. Nathaniel and Caroline, June 25, 1828.
Rebecca, d. Sam[ue]l, bp. Aug. 31, 1839. C. R. 2.
Rebecca S., d. Ezra and Rebecca, Oct. 29, 1820.
Ruth Preston, d. Samuel and Lucy, Dec. 22, 1803.
Samuel, s. Isaac and Mary, Mar. 31, 1772.
Samuel, s. Samuel and Lucy, Feb. 25, 1797.
Samuel Edward, bp. July 13, 1828. C. R. 2.
Samuel, s. John K., laborer, and shoemaker, and Martha T., Aug. 22, 1847.
Sarah, d. Joseph and Joanna, —— 9 [bp. Apr. 15, 1739. C. R. 2.].
Sarah, d. Zebadiah and Sarah, Nov. 3, 1782.

SHATTUCK, Sarah, d. Zebadiah, jr. and Sarah, July 13, 1820.
Sarah A., d. Thomas O., cordwainer, and Saloma K., July 5, 1845.
Sarah Ann, d. twin, Sam[ue]l and Hannah, May 10, 1835.
Sarah Foster, d. Nathan and Mary, bp. Sept. 1, 1844. C. R. 3.
Simeon, s. Isaac and Rebecca, Nov. 7, 1807.
Sophia, d. Henry and Sophia, Feb. 23, 1829.
Sophronia, d. Zebadiah, jr. and Sarah, Dec. 27, 1808.
Sukey, d. Peter and Susannah, Feb. 3, 1799.
Susan, d. Leonard and Harriet, Mar. 18, 1834.
Susannah, d. Peter and Susannah, June 30, 1795.
Susannah, d. twin, Peter and Susannah, Oct. 1, 1803.
Thomas Clark, s. Peter and Susannah, Feb. 15, 1813.
Thomas G., s. Peter, jr. and Lucy, June 19, 1830.
William, s. Joseph, jr. and Anna, Apr. 26, 1769.
William, s. Peter and Susannah, Aug. 19, 1810.
William Bradley, s. wid. Lucy, bp. July 8, 1832. C. R. 3.
William M. B. [Milton Badger. C. R. 2.], s. Sam[ue]l, jr. Mar. 18, 1829.
Zebadiah, s. Joseph and Joanna, Oct. 26, 1736.
Zebadiah, s. Joseph, jr., bp. Jan. 27, 1771. C. R. 2.
Zebadiah, s. Zebadiah and Sarah, Mar. 30, 1785.
Zebadiah, s. Zebadiah and Eliza[beth], June 7, 1792.
Zebadiah, s. Zebadiah, jr. and Sarah, June 27, 1816.
——, ch. Samuel and Lucy, Mar. 9, 1796.
——, s. Peter, jr. and Lucy, July 13, 1822.
——, s. Peter and Lucy, July 9, 1824.
——, s. Peter and Lucy, Aug. 25, 1826.
——, s. Henry, Oct. 1, 1826.

SHAW, Joseph, s. George, laborer, and Sarah, both b. England, Dec. 11, 1849.

SHEARMAN (see also Sherman), Mary Jacobs, d. Martial and Hannah, Jan. 24, 1826.

SHED, Charles, s. Jacob and Susanna, June 6, 1807.
Charles O., s. Silas and Polly, Aug. 29, 1829.
Daniel, s. Daniel and Rebecca, Mar. 30, 1736.
David B., s. Peter F. and Mary, June 27, 1828.
Hannah Brown, d. Silas and Patty, Feb. 5, 1824.
Joseph, s. Peter F. and Polly, Mar. 7, 1831.
Lucy, d. Silas and Polly, Apr. 15, 1828.
Martha, d. Silas and Martha, Dec. 26, 1825
Martha, d. Silas and Polly, Jan. 6, 1826.

SHED, Mary, d. Silas and Polly, Dec. 13, 1822.
Peter, s. Peter and Mary P., Aug. 23, 1824.
Peter, s. Peter and Mary, July 8, 1826.
Silas, s. Silas and Polly, May 23, 1820.
Thaddeus, s. Silas and Polly, June 28, 1834.

SHERMAN (see also Shearman), Henry Thatcher, s. Col. Seth and Mary, Nov. 25, 1835.
Mary P. H., d. Seth and Mary, Feb. 19, 1833.
Samuel R., s. Seth and Mary, Apr. 15, 1842.
Seth Martial, s. Col. Seth and Mary, July 5, 1834.

SHERWIN, Hannah, d. Sam[ue]ll and Mary, Sept. 10, 1763.
Maria W., d. Richard and Eunice, Oct. 2, 1815.
Mehetabel, d. Asa and Mercy, Jan. 14, 1770.
Richard K., s. Richard and Eunice, June 6, 1818.

SHIPMAN, Fred[erick] W[illia]m, bp. Sept. 9, 1821. C. R. 2.
Jennett A., bp. Dec. 7, 1823. C. R. 2.
John, s. Degrasse, bp. Dec. 18, 1825. C. R. 2.
Lydia, d. Degrass and Lydia, July 9, 1827.
Mary L., d. Degrass and Lydia, Aug. 23, 1830.
Mary Louise, d. Degrass, bp. May 22, 1831. C. R. 2.
——, s. Degrass, June 15, 1821.

SILVESTER (see also Sylvester), Mary Ann, d. Joshua and Sarah, July 2, 1812.
Nathaniel, s. Joshua and Sarah, May 4, 1807.
Sarah, d. Joshua and Sarah, Apr. 5, 1810.
William, s. Joshua and Sarah, Jan. 10, 1809.

SIMMONS, Charles H., s. Henry H., manufacturer, and Olive T., Dec. 26, 1848.

SIMONDS (see also Symonds), Joseph Franklin, s. Joseph H., cordwainer, and Mary E., Apr. 30, 1848.
Martha Jane, d. Jonas and Martha, Aug. 12, 1823.

SIMONTON, Thomas, s. Samuel and Eleanor, Feb. 12, 1831.
William, s. Samuel and Eleanor, Aug. 29, 1832.

SIMPSON (see also Simson), Charles Augustus, s. Charles, carpenter, and Mary E., June 6, 1847.
Geo[rge] Frederick, s. William and Phebe, Jan. 3, 1840.

SIMSON (see also Simpson), Elizabeth, d. William and Elizabeth, Sept. 12, 1799.
John, s. William and Elizabeth, Oct. 13, 1814.
Lydia Lacy, d. William and Elizabeth, June 13, 1812.

SKINNER, George H., s. Henry and Mary, Dec. 7, 1826.

SLUMMIN, Marian, d. Cha[rle]s F. and Harriot, bp. Sept. 21, 1848. C. R. 4.

SMALL, Amos, s. William and Sarah, Nov. 14 [1733].
Rosetta Jane, d. Joseph S., carpenter, and N. Orelia, May 13, 1846.
William, s. William and Sarah, bp. May 26, 1734. C. R. 1.

SMART (see also Smartt), George M., s. Hugh, laborer, and Jane N., Oct. 12, 1845.
Joseph Alexander, s. Alexander, flax-dresser, and Catherine, both b. Scotland, May 11, 1848.
William W., s. Hugh, flax-dresser, and Jane, Nov. 29, 1843.

SMARTT (see also Smart), Mary Jane, d. Hugh, flax-dresser, and Jane Mins, Aug. 20, 1847.

SMITH, Abigail, d. John and Elizabeth, Feb. 12, 1815.
Agnes F[erguson. C. R. 3.], d. James and Margarett, Aug. 18, 1833.
Albert, s. Henry, farmer, and Mary F., June 18, 1844.
Albert D., s. Rev. Asa D. and Sarah Ann, Aug. 3, 1842.
Andrew, s. George and Mary, July 24, 1781.
Anne C[rawford. C. R. 3.], d. James and Margaret, Aug. 30, 1835.
Anne Leighton, d. Peter and Esther, May 21, 1841.
Benjamin, s. Benjamin and Sarah, Aug. 6, 1740.
Benjamin Franklin, s. Peter, manufacturer, b. Scotland, and Esther H., May 13, 1849.
Caroline, d. William B. and Mary, Mar. 31, 1832.
Cassendana Hazelton, d. Joseph Francis, tailor, and Celia, Dec. 15, 1846.
David, s. Oliver, bp. July 20, 1729. C. R. 2.
Deborah B., d. John and Abigail, Jan. 1, 1824.
Edward A., s. John and Abigail, May 1, 1820.
Elisabeth, d. John and Mary, Feb. 12, 1747-8.

SMITH, Elizabeth, d. Samuell and Sarah, —— [1708?].
Elizabeth C., d. William, woolcomber, and Mary, May 18, 1845.
Elizabeth Foster, d. Thomas and Elizabeth, Mar. 5, 1814.
Elizabeth M[iller. C. R. 3.], d. Peter, manufacturer, and Esther H., Sept. 15, 1845.
Ellen B[artlett. C. R. 3.], d. Peter and Rebecca, May 19, 1833.
Esther M. [Humphrey. C. R. 3.], d. Peter and Esther H., Oct. 19, 1836.
Franklin, s. Darius and Roxana (Brown), Dec. 14, 1833. P. R. 35.
George, s. George and Mary, Apr. 27, 1784.
George F., s. Daniel, carpenter, and Susan, Jan. 12, 1849.
George Henry, s. Darius, machinist, and Roxanna, Aug. 18, 1848.
George T[hompson. C. R. 3.], s. John and Agness, Mar. 8, 1837.
Hannah, d. Samuell and Sarah, ——[1703-4?].
Hannah A., d. twin, John and Abigail, Jan. 24, 1828.
Harriet A., d. twin, John and Abigail, Jan. 24, 1828.
Harriet A., d. Thomas, cordwainer, and Harriet P., Nov. 18, 1844.
Harriet L., d. Darius and Roxana (Brown), May 5, 1829. P. R. 35.
Helen G[avin. C. R. 3.], d. John [2d. C. R. 3.] and Agness, May 17, 1835.
Harriet R., d. Darius and Roxana (Brown), Oct. 22, 1839. P. R. 35.
Henry D., s. Dustin K. and Betsy, Nov. 6, 1821.
Hiram A., s. Darius and Roxana (Brown), May 11, 1831. P. R. 35.
James, s. Peter and Rebecca, bp. Nov. 30, 1828. C. R. 3.
Jane, d. John and Mary, Dec. 9, 1749.
Jannet M., d. John and Agness, Feb. 22, 1839.
Jannett M., bp. July 23, 1826. C. R. 2.
John, s. John and Mary, Apr. 12, 1755.
John, s. John and Abigail, Dec. 20, 1816.
John C., bp. Mar. 5, 1826. C. R. 2.
John H. D., s. Henry and Susan J., of Gloucester, Dec. 10, 1836.
John M[iddleton. C. R. 3.], s. John, 2d and Agnes, Aug. 17, 1830.
John Russell, s. Thomas and Betsey, July 2, 1807.
Joseph, s. Alonzo and Hannah, Oct. 10, 1833.
Joseph W., s. John, 2d and Agnes, Nov. 14, 1831.
Leonard B., s. John and Abigail, Sept. 25, 1818.
Leonard W., s. Rev. Thomas M. and Mary, Aug. 4, 1826.
[Lucretia Ward. C. R. 3.], d. Peter and Esther, Dec. 1, 1839.
Lydia, d. Oliver, bp. May 23, 1736. C. R. 2.
Lydia, d. John and Mary, bp. June 5, 1757. C. R. 1.
Margaret B[yers. C. R. 3.], d. James and Margarett, Sept. 30, 1837.

SMITH, Margaret W[aterhouse. P. R. 57.], d. Thomas and Elizabeth, July 1, 1817.
Martha Ann, d. twin, Edward, spinner, b. England, and Charlotte, Nov. 19, 1848.
Martha Ann, d. John, 3d, stablekeeper, and Sarah A., July 1, 1849.
Mary, d. John and Mary, Sept. 24, 1744.
Mary, d. George and Mary, Sept. 30, 1786.
Mary, d. Peter and Rebecca, Jan. 1, 1831.
Mary A., d. William B. and Mary, May 3, 1830.
Mary Ann, d. Capt. George, of Salem, bp. Aug. 9, 1801. C. R. 2.
Mary Ann, d. John and Abigail, Jan. 13, 1822.
Mary Williams, d. Rev. Asa D. and Mary Ann, Sept. 26, 1837.
Mercy Hanness [Mary Hariss. P. R. 57.], d. Thomas and Betsey, Aug. 30, 1809.
Nancy Emeline, d. John and Mary, bp. Sept. 22, 1822. C. R. 6.
Peter, s. Peter and Rebecca, Oct. 19, 1828.
Peter Dove, s. Peter and Esther, bp. Oct. 23, 1842. C. R. 3.
Phebe Abbot, d. Tho[ma]s and Betsy, Oct. 27, 1811.
Priscilla, d. Samuel and Sarah, Aug. 17, 1715.
Rebeca, d. John and Mary, Nov. 10, 1751.
Rebecca, d. Peter and Rebecca, May 29, 1827.
Samuel E., s. John and Abigal, July 20, 1830.
Sarah, d. Oliver, bp. May 14, 1732. C. R. 2.
Sarah, d. Benjamin and Sarah, Aug. 9, 1743.
Sarah, d. John and Mary, Feb. 16, 1745-6.
Sarah Ann, d. twin, Edward, spinner, b. England, and Charlotte, Nov. 19, 1848.
Sarah E., d. Dustin K.and Eliza[beth], bp. Nov. 14, 1824. C. R. 2.
Sarah Jane, d. John and Abigail, Jan. 6, 1826.
Starlen, s. Benjamin and Sarah, Aug. 22, 1737.
Susanna, d. John and Mary, May 23, 1753.
Susanna Ward, d. Peter, twine manufacturer, and Esther H., Dec. 16, 1843.
Thomas, s. Thomas and Mary, Mar. 13, 1781.
Thomas, s. Thomas and Betsey, Jan. 11, 1805.
Thomas, s. Thomas and Betsy, Mar. 21, 1820.
——, ch. [torn] and Sarah, Apr. 16, 1706.
——, d. Sam[ue]ll and Sarah, Dec. 17, 1710.
——, ch. Samuel and Sarah, June 16, 1713.
——, s. Dustin K. and Betsy, Feb. 24, 1826.

SNELLING, Aaron, s. Asa and Elizabeth, Oct. 16, 1788
Asa, s. Asa and Elizabeth, July 13, 1784.

SNELLING, Betsey, d. Asa and Elizabeth, Feb. 22, 1792.
Charles, s. Asa and Elizabeth, Aug. 10, 1797.
John Haman, s. Asa and Elizabeth, May 19, 1786.
Joseph, s. Asa and Elizabeth, Jan. 2, 1794.
Melinda Smith, d. Asa and Elizabeth, Nov. 23, 1795.
Moses, s. Asa and Elizabeth, June 12, 1790.

SPAFFORD (see also Spofford), Abiah, d. Moody and Dolly, Oct. 31, 1803.
Benj[amin] Holt, s. Moody and Dolly, Nov. 10, 1815.
Farnum, s. Moody and Dolly, Sept. 18, 1797.
Greenleaf, s. Thomas and Rooxbe, Mar, 7, 1770.
Greenleaf, s. Moody and Dolly, Oct. 19, 1805.
Hariot, d. Moody and Dolly, Apr. 11, 1809.
Henry, s. Moody and Dolly, Aug. 2, 1795.
Isaac, s. Thomas and Ruxby, Feb. 1, 1763.
Isaac, s. Isaac and Mehitable, Sept. 20, 1797.
Jacob Farnum, s. Moody and Dolly, Dec. 28, 1801.
Judith, d. Thomas and Ruxbe, Mar. 5, 1759.
Lucy, d. Isaac and Mehitable, Apr. 4, 1793.
Martha, d. Thomas and Ruxby, Feb. 4, 1761.
Mary, d. Thom[a]s and Reuxby, bp. Aug. 31, 1766. C. R. I.
Mary, d. Thomas, bp. May 22, 1768. C. R. I.
Mary, d. Isaac and Mehitable, Oct. 11, 1801.
Mary, d. Moody and Dolly, Mar. 16, 1807.
Rooxbe Moody, d. Moody and Dolly, Sept. 10, 1799.
Solomon, s. Isaac and Mehitable, June 20, 1799.
Sophia, d. Moody and Dolly, Jan. 10, 1789.
Thomas, s. Isaac and Mehitable, Sept. 13, 1795.

SPEAR (see also Speer), Robert, s. Robert, bp. ——, 1741-2. C. R. I.
Sarah, d. Robert and Margaret, bp. ——, 1739. C. R. I.

SPEER (see also Spear), George Reed, s. David and Hepsibah, May 17, 1847. C. R. 4.
Jane Elizabeth, d. David and Hepsibah, Feb. 21, 1845. C. R. 4.

SPOFFORD (see also Spafford), Abby [S. P. R. 72.], d. Henry, yeoman, and Hannah, May 17, 1846.
Carlton, s. Solomon and Catharine, Oct. 19, 1833.
Caroline Cogshall, d. Farnham and Lydia C., Mar. 6, 1843.
Charles, s. Catherine and Solomon, Aug. 27, 1831.
Charles M., s. Henry and Hannah, Mar. 16, 1833.
Clara F., d. William H., laborer, and Fidelia R., Nov. 14, 1848.

SPOFFORD, Dolly, Aug. 18, 1768. P. R. 104.
Dolly Holt, d. Moody and Dolly, bp. Oct. 6, 1793. C. R. 1.
George G., s. Henry and Hannah F., Dec. 10, 1830.
Harriot, d. Solomon and Catherine, May 25, 1829.
John F., s. Henry and Hannah Fuller, Jan. 18, 1841. P. R. 72.
Lydia F., d. Farnham, farmer, and Lydia, Jan. 22, 1846.
Mary Ann, d. Henry and Hannah, Dec. 13, 1834.
Moodey, s. Thomas and Ruxbey, Apr. 19, 1755.
Moody, s. Moody and Dolly, Apr. 1, 1791.
Nathan [J. P. R. 72.], s. Henry, farmer, and Hannah [F. dup.], Feb. 15, 1844. [Feb. 16. dup.]
Orin F., s. Henry and Hannah F., Jan. 20, 1829.
Rebecca J., d. Henry and Hannah Fuller, Oct. 18, 1838. P. R. 72.
Samuel, s. Thomas and Ruxbe, Apr. 26, 1757.
Sarah E., d. Henry and Hannah Fuller, Nov. 6, 1836. P. R. 72.
William H., s. Henry and Hannah F., Aug. 21, 1826. P. R. 91.

SPOILET, ——, s. James and Abiah, June 20, 1817.

SPRAGE (see also Spreag), [Edward, s. C. R. 1.] Edward and Martha, Apr. 25, 1728.
[Elizabeth. T. C.] —th, d. Edward and Martha, Oct. 11, 1721.
John, s. Edward and Martha, Dec. 24, 1724.
[Joseph. C. R. 1.], s. Edward, deceased, and Ma[r]tha, May 18, 1730.
Roger, s. Edward and Martha, Sept. 19, 1726.
William, s. Edward and Martha, Mar. 4, 1722-3.

SPREAG (see also Sprage), William, s. Edward, bp. Mar. 22, 1724. C. R. 2.

STACEY, Sally, d. Capt. Richard and Rebecca, of Marblehead, May 19, 1780. P. R. 107.
William Proctor, s. ——, May 26, 1839. T. C.

STANDLY (see also Stanley), Jacob, s. Jacob and Hannah, Sept. 27, 1759.

STANLEY (see also Standly, Stanly), Charles S., s. S. S., baker, and Ann, Oct. 8, 1845.
Isaac N[ewton. C. R. 2.], s. Silvester and Ann, Oct. 22, 1833.
Louisa A[ugusta. C. R. 2.], d. Silvester and Ann, June 19, 1832.
Mary Ann, d. Sylvester and Ann, May 13, 1830.

STANLY (see also Stanley), Abiel, s. Jacob and Hannah, May 21, 1764.
Mary, d. Jacob and Hannah, May 13, 1762.

STANYAN, John Minot, s. John and Anna, bp. July 6, 1828. C. R. 3.
——, s. John and Anna, Sept. 17, 1826.

STARK (see also Starkes), John S., s. William D., butcher, and Martha H., Sept. 10, 1844.

STARKES (see also Stark), William, s. William, butcher, and Martha, July 11, 1848.

STARKEY, George, s. John, manufacturer, and Lavina, Oct. 22, 1843.
Isabella H., d. John and Lavina, Jan. 19, 1831.
Margaret Ann, d. John and Lavina, Mar. 27, 1829.

STEAL (see also Steel), Rachel, d. Nicholas and Phebe, July 1, 1739.

STEARNS, Ella J[ane. C. R. 4.], d. Charles B., shoemaker, b. Bedford, and Jane, June 16, 1849.

STEEL (see also Steal, Steell], Benjamin, s. Nicholas and Phebe, Jan. 25 [1740-41. C. R. 1.].
Hannah, d. Nicholas and Phebe, Sept. 17, 1743.
Hannah, d. Benj[ami]n and Hannah, Dec. 13, 1768.
Hannah, d. Benj[ami]n and Hannah, Dec. 24, 1770.
Lydia, d. Nicholas and Phebe, Nov. 20, 1745.
[Phebe. C. R. 1.], d. Nicholas and Phebe, Sept. 27, 1735.

STEELL (see also Steel), Elisabeth, d. Nicholas and Phebe, Feb. 21, 1736-7.

STEEN, Rebecca, d. twin, Thomas and Rebecca, Apr. 13, 1841.
Thomas, s. twin, Thomas and Rebecca, Apr. 13, 1841.

STEEVENS (see also Stevens), Abiall, s. Abiall and Deborah, Sept. 16, 1720.
Aron, s. John and Esther, Jan. 19, 1678-9.
Benjamin, s. Joseph and Mary, Mar. 22, 1683-4.
Benjamin, s. John and Esther, Mar. 14, 1684-5.

STEEVENS, Benjamin, s. Joseph and Mary, Mar. 27, 1697.
Benjamin, s. twin, Joshua and Mary, Apr. 26, 1698.
David, s. John and Esther, Sept. 26, 1686.
Ebenezer, s. John and Esther [Hester. CT. R.], Aug. 6, 1683.
Elizabeth, d. Ephraim and Sarah, Aug. 7, 1683.
Elizabeth, d. Nathan and Elizabeth, Oct. 14, 1697.
Elizabeth, d. John and Ruth, —— [1703].
Ephraim, s. Ephraim and Sarah, July 13, 1698.
Hannah, d. Ephraim and Sarah, Nov. 18, 1685.
Hannah, d. John and Hester, July 3, 1688.
Hannah, d. John and Ruth, July 28, 1692.
Hannah, d. Joseph and Elizabeth, —— [1705?].
James, s. Joseph and Mary, Nov. 31 [*sic*], 1686.
John, s. John and Ruth, Sept. 20, 1690.
Johnathan, s. John and Hannah, Apr. 20, 1674.
Joseph, s. Joseph and Mary, June 20, 1682.
Joshua, s. twin, Joshua and Mary, Apr. 26, 1698.
Mary, d. Joseph and Mary, Apr. 2, 1679.
Mary, d. Ephraim and Sarah, Feb. 10, 1693-4.
Mary, d. John and Ruth, Aug. 23, 1695.
Mehitabel, d. Ephraim and Sarah, Sept. 29, 1691.
Mehitabel, d. Ephraim and Sarah, Aug. 31, 1700.
Nathan, s. Nathan and Elisabeth, Sept. 22, 1693.
Priscilla, d. John and Ruth, Aug. 12, 1699.
Ruth, d. John and Ruth, June 1, 1694.
Samuell, s. John and Esther, May 29, 1677.
Samuell, s. Joshuah and [torn], ——, 1702.
Sarah, d. Ephraim and Sarah, Oct. 28, 1681.
Timothy, s. John and Ruth, May 10, 1697.
——, ch. [torn] and Elisabeth, —— 16 [1701].
——, d. Joseph and Elizabeth, —— [170]2.
——, ch. [Eliz]abeth, d. [torn] —— [17]02.
——, d. Abial and Deborah, June 20, 1709.

STEPHENS (see also Stevens), Asa, s. Ebenezer and Sarah, Dec. 14, 1717.
Isaack, s. John [jr. C. R. 1.] and Elizabeth, Aug. 18, 1719.
John, s. John and Elizabeth, Jan. 23, 1717-18.
Joseph, s. Benjamin and Mary, Aug. 2, 1[724].
Mary, d. Nathan and Hannah, Apr. — [1715].
Nathan, s. Abial and Deborah, July 13, 1716.
Phineas, s. Ebenezer and Sarah, May 13, 171[6].
Rachel, d. Nathan and Hannah [Mary. C. R. 1.], Feb. 6, 1719-20.
Susanna, d. Abial and Deborah, Ma[y] — [1718].

STEPHENS, ——, d. Nathan and Hannah, Nov. 20, 1717.
——, ch. Samuel and Elizabeth, Jan. 7, 1717-18.

STEVEN (see also Stevens), Sarah, d. Jonathan, jr. and Martha, July 23, 1803.

STEVENS (see also Steevens, Stephens, Steven), Aaron, s. Amos and Sarah, Oct. 15, 1785.
Abiah, d. Isaac and Mary [bp. June 20, 1746. C. R. 2.].
Abial, s. John, jr. and Lydia, Mar. 24, 1749-50.
Abiel, s. John and Esther, June 4, 1681.
Abiel, s. John and Tabbatha, Oct. 10, 1770.
Abiel, s. Abiel, bp. Oct. 14, 1770. C. R. 2.
Abiel, s. Thomas and Sarah, Sept. 30, 1789.
Abiel, s. Abiel and Permelia, Oct. 1, 1815.
Abigaell, d. Ebenezer and Sarah, Jan. 28, 1720-21.
Abigail, d. Nathan and Hannah, May 18, 1[726].
Abigail, d. Benjamin and Hannah [Abigail. C. R. 1.], Nov. 16, 1763.
Abigail, d. Joseph and Alice, Jan. 1, 1768.
Abigail, d. James and Mary, Mar. 15, 1808.
Abner, s. Daniel and Hannah, May 9, 1760.
Achsah, d. John, 3d and Mary, Jan. 12, 1753.
Alice, d. Joseph and Alice, Mar. 21, 1762.
Amelia, d. Edward and Phebe, Mar. 20, 1805.
Amos, s. Ebenezer, jr. and Joanna, Feb. 22, 1742-3.
Amos, s. Amos and Sarah, Oct. 3, 1767.
Amos, s. Amos and Sarah, Jan. 20, 1771.
Amos, s. Joshua and Mary, May 28, 1798.
Amos, s. Amos and Susanna, Nov. 17, 1812.
Ann E[liza. C. R. 1.], d. Nathaniel and Harriet, July 4, 1834.
Anna, d. Peter, bp. Nov. 10, 1771. C. R. 1.
Anna, d. Peter and Nabby, July 5, 1774.
Aron, s. Jacob and Tabitha, Sept. 3, 1751.
Aron, s. Jacob and Tabitha, July 25, 1757.
Asa, s. Asa and Mehetable, Nov. 30, 1744.
Asa, s. twin, Peter and Nabby, Nov. 5, 1781.
Asenath, d. Jacob and Tabbitha, Mar. 25, 1771.
Augustus, s. Phineas, jr. and Sally, Aug. 30, 1830.
Barney, s. Amos and Susanna, bp. Sept. 25, 1814. C. R. 1.
Bathsheba, d. twin, Isaac and Mary, Feb. 16, 1753.
[Beemsly. C. R. 1.], s. John and Elisibeth, Mar. —, 1734-5. [bp. Mar. 16. C. R. 1.]
Benjamin, s. Benj[ami]n, bp. Oct. 22, 1721. C. R. 2.

STEVENS, Benjamin, s. Benjamin and Mary, May 30 [1726].
Benjamin, s. Nathan and Hannah [Mary. C. R. 1.], Apr. 1, 1729.
Benjamin, s. James and Dorathy, Mar. 27 [1732. C. R. 1.].
Benjamin, s. Benjamin and Hannah, May 14, 1734.
Benj[ami]n, s. Benj[ami]n, jr. and Hannah, Oct. 8, 1766.
Benjamin, s. Benjamin, jr. and Lydia, July 22, 1783.
Benjamin, s. Joseph, 3d and Phebe, Nov. 19, 1797.
Benjamin, s. Abiel and Permelia, Feb. 16, 1819.
Benjamin, s. Simeon, jr. and Jane, Mar. 25, 1835.
Benjamin Franklin, s. Joshua and Mary, Oct. 13, 1802.
Benj[amin] Frye, s. Benjamin and Huldah, Aug. 3, 1839.
Benjamin Mooar [Moses. C. R. 1.], s. Enoch and Hannah, Mar. 10, 1808.
Benjamine, s. John and Elizabeth, June 24, 1656.
Betsy, d. Daniel and Susannah, Dec. 17, 1776.
Betsy, d. Joshua and Mary, Apr. 28, 1805.
Betty, d. Daniel and Hannah, June 15, 1767.
Betty, d. Peter and Nabby, Apr. 21, 1776.
Betty, d. Benja[min] and Hannah, May 14, 1782.
Bimsley, s. Bimsley and Rebeckah, Oct. 24, 1761.
Bimsley, s. Simeon, jr. and Sally, July 20, 1805.
Bimsley O., s. Bimsley and Mary, Oct. 31, 1831.
Caleb, s. Jona[than] [jr. C. R. 1.] and Martha, Aug. 13, 1791. [Sept. 3. P. R. 78.]
Calvin, s. Solomon and Elizabeth, Dec. 24, 1806.
Caroline, d. Dan[ie]l and Sarah, Feb. 12, 1812.
Caroline Augusta, d. Jona[than] P. and Mary F., May 18, 1837.
Catharine, d. Nath[anie]l and Harriot, bp. Apr. 16, 1834. C. R. 1.
Charles, s. Daniel and Susannah, Jan. 9, 1780.
Charles, s. James and Elizabeth, Aug. 31, 1800.
Charles, s. Benjamin and Sukey, Sept. 19, 1829.
Charles L., s. Leonard and Mary, Nov. 9, 1829.
Charles A., s. Daniel C., shoedealer, and Rebecca, June 27, 1848.
Charles A[bbot. C. R. 1.], s. Capt. Nath[anie]l and Harriot, Aug. 9, 1816.
Charles E., s. John, shoemaker, and Hannah, Nov. 1, 1845.
Charlotte, d. Simeon, jr. and Sally, Jan. 20, 1807.
Charlotte, d. James and Elizabeth, Jan. 6, 1809.
Charlotte Augusta, d. Enoch and Augusta, Jan. 20, 1836.
Charlotte Eliza, d. Moses A. and Lydia, Jan. 10, 1838.
Charlotte Elizabeth, d. Warren and Elizabeth, Aug. 6, 1836.
Charlottee Verstille, d. Capt. Phineas and Becca, June 21, 1816.
Clarissa, d. James and Mary, Oct. 27, 1810.
Cloe, d. Jacob and Tabbatha, Dec. 30, 1762.

STEVENS, Cynthia, d. Edward and Phebe, Sept. 10, 1801.
Cyrus, s. Joseph, bp. Sept. 18, 1768. C. R. 1.
Cyrus, s. Joseph and Alice, Sept. 12, 1770.
Daniel, s. Benja[min] and Mary, Feb. 19, 1727-8.
Daniel, s. John and Elizabeth, Jan. 27 [1728-9].
[Daniel. C. R. 1.], s. Benjamin and Mary, May 19 [10. T. C.], 1738.
Daniel, s. Daniel and Hannah, Mar. 28, 1751.
Daniel, s. Benj[ami]n and Hannah, Jan. 2, 1768.
Daniel, s. Joseph and Phebe, Jan. 13, 1803.
Daniel, s. Joseph, bp. Oct. 27, 1816. C. R. 1.
Daniel, s. Daniel C. and Rebecca, Oct. 27, 1839.
Daniel C., s. Samuel and Phebe, Jan. 29, 1813.
Daniel Page, s. twin, Daniel and Sarah [Apr.? 1815].
Darcus, d. John and Elezabeth, Feb. 23, 173[2-3. C. R. 1.].
David, s. John, jr. and Lydea, Jan. 10, 1755.
David, s. Abiel, jr. and Dorathy, May 23, 1755.
David, s. Thomas and Sarah, Feb. 3, 1761.
David, s. Joshua and Hannah, Dec. 23, 1767.
David, s. Abiel, bp. Sept. 16, 1781. C. R. 2.
David, s. David and Sally, July 27, 1785.
David, s. David and Sarah, Oct. 9, 1794.
David Holt, s. —— Stevens, deceased, adopted s. David Holt, bp. Apr. 16, 1797. C. R. 2.
David P., s. wid. Sarah, bp. July 3, 1824. C. R. 2.
Deborah, d. John and Ruth, —— [1710].
Deborah, d. John and Elezebeth, July 4 [24. T. C.], 1721.
Deborah, d. Benjamin and Hannah, Feb. 4, 1726-7.
Deborah, d. John, jr. and Lydia, June 21, 1742.
Deborah, d. Abiel, jr. and Dorathy, Feb. 24, 1757.
Dolly, d. Benjamin [jr. C. R. 1.] and Hannah, Apr. 6, 1777.
Dolly, d. James and Susanna, bp. Nov. 21, 1779. C. R. 1.
Dolly, d. Jonathan and Susanna, Nov. 21, 1779.
Dolly, d. Jonathan and Susanna, Sept. 26, 1788.
Dorathey, d. James, jr. and Sarah, Nov. 16, 1754.
Dorathy, d. James and Dorathy, May 26, 1719.
Dorathy, d. Abial, jr. and Dorathy, Apr. 21, 1751.
Dorathy, d. Benjamin, jr. and Hannah, Sept. 7, 1757.
Dorcas, d. Asa and Mehetable, Nov. 17, 1742.
Dorcas, d. Asa and Mary, July 19, 1781.
Dorcis, d. Capt. Asa and Mehetebel, Oct. 9, 1755.
Easter, d. Jacob and Tabbatha, Apr. 12, 1759.
Eben, s. John F., millwright, and Mary B., Dec. 5, 1849.
Eben Sutton, s. Henry, bp. Aug. 8, 1847. C. R. 1.

STEVENS, Ebenezer, s. Ebenezer and Sarah, —— [1703].
Ebenezer, s. Ebenezer and Sarah, —— [1713-14].
Ebenezer, s. Jacob and Tabitha, Aug. 17, 1753.
Ebenezer, s. Amos and Sarah, bp. Oct. 22, 1769. C. R. I.
Ebenezer, s. Amos and Sarah, Jan. 10, 1774.
Ebenezer, s. Benjamin, jr. and Lydia, Mar. 26, 1787.
Ebenezer, s. David and Sarah, Aug. 25, 1787.
Ebenezer, s. Phineas and Becca, Nov. 20, 1802.
Edward, s. Thomas and Sarah, Jan. 3, 1755.
Edward, s. Thomas and Sarah, Sept. 30, 1768.
Edward, s. Edward and Phebe, Jan. 2, 1799.
Edward Winslow, s. William, lawyer, and Elizabeth B., Sept. 23, 1844.
Edwin, s. twin, Enoch and Hannah, June 17, 1829.
Elbridge Hubbard, s. Enoch and Hannah, Nov. 1, 1810.
Elezebeth, d. Nathan and Hannah, July 2, 1722.
Elezebeth, d. Benjamin and Hannah, Jan. 12, 1722-3.
Elezebeth, d. John and Elezebeth, Aug. 7 [1723].
Elezebith, d. Thomas and Sarah, Nov. 26, 1752.
Elisabeth, d. Benjamin and Mary [bp. July 14, 1734. C. R. I.].
Elisabeth, d. Samuel [and Hepsiba. C. R. I.], May 22, 173[8. C. R. I.].
Elisabeth, d. Isaac and Mary, Mar. 22, 1739-40.
Eliza Ann, d. Daniel C. and Rebecca, Mar. 11, 1837 [*sic.*].
Eliza Watson, d. W[illia]m and E. L. W., at. Belfast, Me., Dec. 22, 1826.
Elizabeth, d. John and Elizabeth, Oct. 21, 1730.
Elizabeth, d. Jacob and Tabbatha, Jan. 15, 1761.
Elizabeth, d. Jacob and Tabbatha, Nov. 19, 1764.
Elizabeth, d. Joshua and Hannah, Sept. 16, 1771.
Elizabeth, d. Bimsley and Rebecca, Sept. 28, 1776.
Elizabeth, d. Ebenezer and Elizabeth, Feb. 18, 1794.
Elizabeth, d. James and Elizabeth, Oct. 31, 1802.
Elizabeth, d. Jonathan P. and Mary, Sept. 7, 1832.
Elizabeth Allen, d. Jona[than], jr. and Martha [Patty. C. R. I.], Apr. 21, 1807.
Elizabeth B[arker. C. R. I.], d. Isaac and Hannah, July 14, 1819.
Ella Amelia, d. Erastus, machinist, and Amelia, Apr. 17, 1847.
Enoch, s. Daniel and Hannah, Apr. 16, 1758.
Enoch, s. Bimsly and Rebeccah, May 27, 1765.
Enoch, s. William and Martha, Oct. 15, 1769.
Enoch, s. Bimsley and Rebecca, Feb. 27, 1779.
Enoch, s. Peter and Susanna, Jan. 16, 1795.
Enoch, s. Edward and Phebe, Nov. 18, 1796.

STEVENS, Enoch, s. Enoch and Hannah, Feb. 23, 1802.
Enoch Otis, s. Abiel and Permelia, bp. Aug. 25, 1833. C. R. 3.
Epharaham [Ephraim. C. R. 2.], s. Isaac and Mary, Nov. 4, 1757.
Ephraim, s. John and Hanna, May 1, 1672.
Ephraim, s. David and Sarah, Feb. 2, 1790.
Ephraim, s. Joseph and Phebe, Nov. 12, 1808.
Esher, d. Samuel and Elizabeth, —— [1711-12?].
Ester, d. Ebenezer and Sarah, June 26, 1723.
Ester, d. Benjamin and Hannah [Feb. —, 1724-5].
Esther Carlton, d. James and Elizabeth, July 6, 1804.
Ezra, s. Peter and Susanna, Feb. 9, 1800.
Fanne, d. Daniel and Hannah, Sept. 17, 1769.
Frances Jeanette, d. William and Elizabeth B., Mar. 11, 1843.
George, s. Benj[ami]n, jr. and Hannah, bp. Dec. 25, 1774. C. R. 1.
George, s. Benjamin and Hannah, Dec. 21, 1775.
George, s. Nath[anie]l and Harriot, bp. Apr. 16, 1834. C. R. 1.
George, s. Isaac N. [N. M. P. R. 20.], cordwainer, and Ruby, Nov. 7, 1845.
George, s. twin, John F., "millerite," June 30, 1847.
George Osgood, s. James, 2d and Lydia, Feb. 10, 1843.
George Watson, s. William and E. L. Watson, at Belfast, Me., Nov. 24, 1832.
Geo[rge] Webster, s. Moses A. and Lydia, Jan. 7, 1840.
Gorham Phillips, s. William and Elizabeth B., Dec. 7, 1841.
Hannah, d. Benjamin and Hannah, Oct. 1, 1720.
Hannah, d. Benjamin and Mary, Aug. 9, 1731.
[Hannah. C. R. 2.] ——ah, d. John, 3d [jr. C. R. 2.] and Mary, Jan. 16, 1743-4.
Hannah, d. Samuel and Hannah, May 22, 1754.
Hannah, d. Timothy and Sarah, Oct. 8, 1756.
Hannah, d. Daniel and Hannah, May 16, 1762.
Hannah, d. Daniel and Hannah, Aug. 19, 1764.
Hannah, d. Peter and Nabby, bp. Oct. 8, 1769. C. R. 1.
Hannah, d. Benj[ami]n and Hannah, Mar. 23, 1770.
Hannah, d. Bimsly and Rebecca, Sept. 29, 1770.
Hannah, d. Benj[ami]n, jr. and Hannah, Jan. 28, 1772.
Hannah, d. James, jr. and Hannah, bp. Aug. 27, 1775. C. R. 1.
Hannah, d. Simeon and Hannah, Mar. 12, 1781.
Hannah, d. Daniel and Susannah, Sept. 5, 1781.
Hannah, d. Jonathan and Susanna, May 5, 1783.
Hannah, d. Abigail, bp. Oct. 26, 1783. C. R. 1.
Hannah, d. Timothy, jr. and Mary, bp. Feb. 13, 1788. C. R. 1.
Hannah, d. Timothy, jr. and Mary, bp. Aug. 11, 1793. C. R. 1.

STEVENS, Hannah, d. Joshua, July 12, 1796. P. R. 73.
Hannah, d. Joseph and Phebe, May 23, 1806.
Hannah, d. Daniel and Sarah, Aug. 18, 1808.
Hannah, d. Phinehas and Rebeca, Aug. 11, 1812.
Hannah, d. Amos and Susanna, bp. Sept. 25, 1814. C. R. I.
Hannah B[rown. C. R. I.], d. Benjamin and Huldah, Apr. 12, 1832.
Hannah L., d. Moses A., machinist, and Lydia, Nov. 28, 1843.
Hannah Peabody, d. Isaac and Hannah, Sept. 24, 1815.
Hannah Shattuck, d. Joshua and Mary, July 12, 1796.
Hannah Varnum, d. Bimsley and Mary N., July 4, 1836.
Harriet Louisa, d. Henry H., manufacturer, and Eliza P., Oct. 10, 1844.
Harriet S., d. Daniel C., cordwainer, and Rebecca, Sept. 20, 1845.
Harriot L[ouisa. C. R. I.], d. Capt. Nath[anie]l and Harriot, Sept. 24, 1820.
Henrietta, d. Jonathan P. and Mary F., bp. June 10, 1838. C. R. I.
Henry, s. Joshua and Mary, Sept. 6, 1808.
Henry H[ale. C. R. I.], s. Capt. Nath[anie]l and Harriot, Apr. 6, 1818.
Henry James, s. James, jr. and Lydia, Feb. 2, 1837.
Hephzibah, d. Samuel and Hephzibah, Feb. 29, 1739-40.
Hepsebeth, d. Thomas and Sarah, Jan. 15, 1757.
Hepsibah, d. Jacob and Tabbatha, Apr. 2, 1769.
Hepzabah, d. twin, Peter and Nabby, Nov. 5, 1781.
Hepzabeth, d. Peter and Nabby, Dec. 4, 1777.
Herman Abbot, s. David and Sarah, Oct. 18, 1802.
Horace Nath[anie]l, s. Capt. Nathaniel and Harriett, Dec. 16, 1837.
Isaac, s. Isaac and Mary, Oct. 13, 1748.
Isaac, s. Jonathan and Susanna, May 10, 1785.
Isaac A., s. Isaac M. and Ruby (Barnard), July 6, 1844. P. R. 20.
Isaac I., s. Isaac and Hannah, Mar. 24, 1818.
Isaac Mooar, s. Jonathan, jr. and Martha, Jan. 21, 1812.
Isaac Winslow, s. W[illia]m and Harriet, bp. June 5, 1836. C. R. I.
Jacob, s. Jacob and Tabitha, Aug. 3, 1755.
Jacob, s. Abiel and Tabitha, Mar. 12, 1776.
Jacob, s. David and Sarah, July 26, 1792.
[James. C. R. I.], s. James and Dorathy, Oct. 17, 1721.
James, s. James, jr. and Sarah, July 14, 1749.
James, s. Jacob and Tabitha, Sept. 20, 1749.
James, s. Daniel and Hannah, Sept. 26, 1752.
James, s. Benj[ami]n, jr. and Hannah, Nov. 12, 1761.

STEVENS, James, s. Benj[ami]n, jr. and Hannah, Feb. 25, 1765.
James, s. James, jr. and Hannah, Apr. 10, 1774.
James, s. Jona[than] and Susanna, Nov. 30, 1777.
James, s. James and Elizabeth, Apr. 3, 1797.
James, s. James and Mary, June 4, 1804.
James [Alexander. C. R. 3.], s. Alexander, flax-dresser, and Ann, Dec. 31, 1843.
Jemima, d. Jonathan, bp. July 8, 1770. C. R. 2.
Jeremy, s. Jonathan and Susanna, Aug. 22, 1781.
Jesse, s. Isaac and Mary, Apr. 3, 1760.
Joanna, d. Asa and Mehetebel, Sept. 23, 1752.
Joanna, d. Amos and Sarah, Dec. 3, 1779.
Johanna, d. Ebenezer and Sarah, Sept. — [1711].
John, s. John and Hanna, Aug. 30, 1663.
John, s. John, jr. and Lydia, Oct. 2, 1747.
John, s. Daniel and Mary, July 1, 1754.
John, s. Christopher and Eliza[beth], bp. ——, 1755. C. R. 1.
John, s. Jonathan and Jemima, Aug. 25, 1764.
John, s. Abiel, bp. Oct. 26, 1766. C. R. 1.
John, s. Amos and Sarah, Aug. 25, 1783.
John, s. Benjamin, jr. and Lydia, May 22, 1785.
John, s. James and Elizabeth, June 6, 1806.
John, s. twin, John F., "millerite," June 30, 1847.
John Abbot, s. Daniel and Susannah, Mar. 29, 1783.
John Farnum, s. Capt. Phineas and Becca, Feb. 1, 1810.
John W., s. William and Eliza L. W., Apr. 13, 1836.
Jonas, s. Benj[ami]n, jr. and Hannah, Feb. 24, 1770.
Jonathan, s. Joshuah and Mary, —— [1705?].
Jonathan, s. James and Dorathy, Aug. 20, 172[7. C. R. 1.].
Jonathan, s. Capt. James and Dorathy, July 2, 1739.
Jonathan, s. James and Sarah, Apr. 8, 1747.
Jonathan, s. Jonathan and Lydia, Aug. 19, 1758.
Jonathan, s. Joseph and Alice, Mar. 23, 1766.
Jonathan, s. Timothy and Sarah, Mar. 19, 1768.
Jonathan, s. Jonathan and Susanna, June 17, 1774.
Jonathan, s. Joshua and Mary, May 6, 1792.
Jonathan, s. Jonathan, jr. and Martha, Mar. 19, 1805.
Joseph, s. John and Elizabeth, May 15, 1654.
Joseph, s. Joshuah and Mary, —— [1710].
Joseph, s. James and Dorathy [Feb.] 26 [1724-5].
Joseph, s. Benjamin and Mary, Dec. 15, 1732.
Joseph, s. Jonathan and Lydia, Jan. 17, 1761.
Joseph, s. Benjamin and Hannah, Nov. 30, 1765.
Joseph, s. Joseph, jr. and Sarah, Apr. 12, 1774.

STEVENS, Joseph, s. Joseph, jr. and Sarah, Oct. 30, 1775.
Joseph, s. Joseph and Phebe, Feb. 20, 1801.
Joseph, s. Joseph, 3d and Phebe, Apr. 8, 1807.
Joseph W[illiam. C. R. 1.], s. Warren, trader, and Sarah J. [Susan. C. R. 1.], Oct. 16, 1845.
Joshua, s. Joshua and Martha, Dec. 31, 1729.
Joshua, s. Joshua and Martha, Mar. 25, 1[734. C. R. 2.].
Joshua, s. Joshua and Martha, Nov. 9, 1740.
Joshua, s. Samuel and Hannah, Jan. 22, 1761.
Joshua, s. Samuel and Hannah, Jan. 8, 1765.
Joshua, s. Joshua and Marah, Oct. 25, 1786.
Josua, s. John and Hanna, July 17, 1670.
Jo[torn]h, s. James and Dorathy, Jan. 25, 1723-4.
Julia M[aria. C. R. 1.], d. Capt. Nath[anie]l and Harriot, Aug. 6, 1823.
Lenard, s. Timothy, jr. and Mary, bp. Apr. 28, 1782. C. R. 1.
Leonard, s. Abiel, bp. June 25, 1785. C. R. 2.
Leonard, s. Amos and Susanna, bp. Sept. 25, 1814. C. R. 1.
Levina, d. Joshua and Mary, May 13, 1800.
Lucretia, d. Daniel and Susannah, Aug. 19, 1785.
Lucy, d. Jonathan, jr. and Martha, May 24, 1796. [May 27. P. R. 78.]
Luse [Lucy. C. R. 1.], d. David, jr. and Abigal, Apr. 13, 1751.
Lydea, d. Jonathan and Lydea, Nov. 15, 1753.
Lydia, d. [torn], —— [1706-7?].
Lydia, d. John and Annice, Dec. 8, 1744.
Lydia, d. John, jr. and Lydia, May 3, 1745.
Lydia, d. Benja[min], jr. and Hannah, Dec. 1, 1778.
Lydia, d. Mary, Mar. 23, 1814.
Lydia Holt, d. John F. and Lydia F., Nov. 2, 1839.
Lydia P[hillips. C. R. 1.], d. William, Esq. and Elizabeth B., May 5, 1840.
Maria, d. Jonathan, jr. and Martha, July 8, 1809.
Maria [F. P. R. 87.], d. John F., millwright, and Mary, Dec. 3, 1844.
Martha, d. Joshua and Martha, Mar. 5, 1732-3.
Martha, d. Joshua and Martha, Oct. 5, 1742.
Martha, d. Abiel, jr. and Dorathy, Dec. 17, 1752.
Martha, d. Joseph and Alice, Dec. 29, 1775.
Martha, d. Joshua and Mary, May 10, 1790.
Martha, d. Jonathan and Martha (Mooar), Feb. 13, 1798. P. R. 78.
Mary, d. James and Dorathy, Jan. 25, 1716-17.
Mary, d. Benjamin and Mary, May 10, 1723.

STEVENS, Mary, d. Timothy and Rebecah, Apr. 5, 1727.
[Mary. C. R. 1.], d. Benja[min] and Mary, Sept. 6, 1729.
Mary, d. Joshua and Martha, Feb. 7, 1730[-31].
Mary, d. Benjamin and Mary, Oct. 29, 1739.
Mary, d. Isaac and Mary, Jan. 19, 1741-2.
Mary, d. Beamley and Rebeckah, Nov. 17, 1759.
Mary, d. Abiel, jr., bp. Dec. 14, 1760. C. R. 1.
Mary, d. Bimsley and Rebecca, May 3, 1767.
Mary, d. Joseph and Phebe, Aug. 28, 1804.
Mary, d. James and Mary, Feb. 13, 1806.
Mary, d. Daniel and Mary, Aug. 20, 1841.
Mary Ann, d. Enoch, jr. and Hannah, Nov. 20, 1819.
Mary Augusta, d. Bimsley and Mary N., Jan. 27, 1834.
Mary Augusta, d. Enoch and Augusta, bp. May 1, 1842. C. R. 1.
Mary Elizabeth, d. Jonathan P. and Mary F., bp. June 10, 1838. C. R. 1.
Mary Frances, d. John F. and Lydia F., Mar. 16, 1836.
Mary Jane, d. Isaac and Hannah, Aug. 5, 1823.
Mary Lister, d. Enoch and Hannah, bp. June 8, 1800. C. R. 1.
Mary Walker, d. Joshua and Mary, Feb. 12, 1785.
Mehetebel, d. Asa and Mehetebel, Nov. 1, 1750.
[Mehitabel. C. R. 1.], d. Benjamin and Mary, May —, 1736. [bp. May 2. C. R. 1.]
Miranda, d. Timothy, jr. and Mary, bp. May 19, 1799. C. R. 1.
Molle, d. Samuel and Hepsebath, Feb. 17, 1754.
Molley, d. Nathan and Mary, Aug. 28, 1746.
Molly, d. Bimsley and Rebecca, July 26, 1774.
Molly, d. Simeon and Prudence, Sept. 10, 1774.
Moses, s. Amos and Sarah, Oct. 10, 1787.
Moses, s. Jonathan and Susanna, Oct. 1, 1790.
Moses T[yler. C. R. 1.], s. Capt. Nath[anie]l and Harriott, Oct. 10, 1825.
Nabbe, d. David, jr. and Abigal, Oct. 28, 1752.
Nabby, d. Peter and Nabby, Jan. 30, 1769.
Nathan, s. John and Hanna, Apr. 5, 1665.
Nathan, s. Nathan and Hannah, Mar. 16, 1723-4.
Nath[anie]l, s. Jonathan and Susanna, Oct. 18, 1786.
Nehemiah, s. Abiel, bp. May 3, 1778. C R. 2.
Oliver, s. Jonathan and Susanna, May 3, 1794.
Oliver, s. Isaac and Hannah, June 22, 1825.
Osgood, s. Amos and Susanna, bp. Sept. 25, 1814. C. R. 1.
Otis Alexander, s. Alexander, operative, and Ann, Apr. 14, 1845.
Pamela, d. Peter and Susanna, July 31, 1797.
Patty, d. Timothy, jr. and Molly, May 15, 1777.

STEVENS, Patty [Sally. C. R. 1.], d. Timothy, jr. and Mary, Apr. 22, 1780.
Patty [Martha. C. R. 1.], d. Jonathan, jr. and Martha, Feb. 18, 1798.
Permelia [Ann. C. R. 3.], d. Abiel and Permelia, Mar. 6, 1817.
Persis, d. Daniel and Susanna, Dec. 1, 1773.
Peter, s. Samuel and Hephzebah, Sept. 24, 1746.
Peter, s. Timothy and Sarah, Nov. 12, 1758.
Peter, s. Timothy and Sarah, Nov. 12, 1763.
Peter, s. Peter and Nabby, July 16, 1770.
Peter, s. Peter and Susanna, June 24, 1787.
Phebe, d. Benjamin and Hannah, May 9, 1729.
[Phebe. C. R. 2.], d. John, 3d and Mary, May 10, 1739.
Phebe, d. Jonathan and Lydea, Mar. 20, 1757.
Phebe, d. Benjamin, jr. and Hannah, Dec. 25, 1758.
Phebe, d. Thomas and Sarah, May 6, 1759.
Phebe, d. Jacob and Tabbatha, Sept. 29, 1766.
Phebe, d. Peter and Nabby [Abigail. C. R. 1.], Nov. 4, 1783.
Phebe, d. Joseph, 3d and Phebe, May 2, 1810.
Phebe, F[rye. C. R. 1.], d. Benjamin and Huldah, Aug. 18, 1834.
Phebe Kimball, d. Thomas and Sarah, July 28, 1787.
[Pheoby. T. C.], d. James and Dorathy, Nov. 30, 1714.
Philip, s. Timothy and Sarah, Feb. 10, 1761.
Phineas, s. James and Mary, Jan. 29, 1813.
Phinehas, s. Nathan and Hannah, Mar. 7, 1730-31.
Phinehas, s. Amos and Sarah, Dec. 3, 1776.
Phinehas, s. Phinehas and Becca, bp. Aug. 3, 1800. C. R. 1.
Pliny, d. [s. C. R. 1.] Peter and Susanna, Dec. 2, 1792.
Prudance, d. Samuel and Hepzebeth, Sept. 29, 1751.
Prudence, d. Samuel and Hepseba, Oct. 10, 1748.
Prudence, d. Simeon and Prudence, Jan. 31, 1767.
Rebecca, d. Bimsley and Rebecca, Jan. 10, 1769.
Rebecca, d. Phineas and Becca [Rebekah. C. R. 1.], May 23, 1805.
Rebecca, d. Daniel C. and Rebecca, Apr. 26, 1835.
Rebecca, d. Daniel C. and Rebecca, Apr. 14, 1837. [*sic.*]
[Rebecka. C. R. 1.], d. Timothy and Rebeca, Sept. 28, 1722.
Rhoda, d. Amos and Sarah, Nov. 11, 1764.
Rhoda, d. Amos and Susanna, bp. Sept. 25, 1814. C. R. 1.
Richard, s. Isaac and Mary, Apr. 28, 1755.
Richard Hazeltine, s. William, lawyer, and Elizabeth B., Feb. 28, 1846.
Ruth, d. Isaac and Mary, Dec. 28, 1750.
Sally [Betty. C. R. 1.], d. Jacob and Tabitha, Dec. 2, 1773.

STEVENS, Sally, d. James, jr. and Hannah, bp. Dec. 30, 1777. C. R. I.
Sally, d. Jonathan and Susanna, Nov. 9, 1792.
Samuel, s. Samuel and Elizabeth, —— [1710].
Samuel, s. Samuel and Hephzebah, May 27, 1744.
Samuel, s. Samuel and Hannah, Apr. 24, 1757.
Samuel, s. Joseph, jr. and Sarah, July 22, 1778.
Samuel, s. Peter and Nabby, Mar. 20, 1779.
Samuel, s. twin, Enoch and Hannah, June 17, 1829.
Samuel Ingalls, s. Thomas and Sarah, July 19, 1792.
Sarah, d. [torn], —— [1706-7?].
Sarah, d. James and Dorathy, Jan. 13, 1729-30.
Sarah, d. Benjamin and Hannah, Aug. 14, 1731.
Sarah, d. Nathan and Hannah [Mary. C. R. I.], Jan. 17, 1733-4.
Sarah, d. John and Lydia, Jan. 29, 1738-9.
Sarah, d. John and Lydia, June 6 [1740. C. R. I.].
Sarah, d. Nathan and Hannah [Mary. C. R. I.], Feb. 1, 1740-41.
Sarah, d. Samuel and Hephzebah, Mar. 22, 1741-2.
Sarah, d. John and Annice, Nov. 25, 1742.
Sarah, d. Isaac and Mary, Mar. 19, 1743-4.
Sarah, d. Thomas and Sarah, Sept. 4, 1750.
Sarah, d. James, jr. and Sarah, Mar. 7, 1752.
Sarah, d. Timothy and Sarah, Dec. 28, 1753.
Sarah, d. Thomas and Sarah, Sept. 8, 1766.
Sarah, d. Simeon and Prudence, Oct. 27, 1769.
Sarah, d. Thomas, jr. and Sarah, Jan. 7, 1776.
Sarah, d. Joseph and Alice, bp. July 2, 1778. C. R. I.
Sarah, d. Joseph and Alice, July 29, 1779.
Sarah, d. Joseph, jr. and Sarah, June 6, 1780.
Sarah, d. Amos and Sarah, Sept. 3, 1781.
Sarah, d. David and Sarah, Apr. 26, 1797.
Sarah, d. Jonathan and Martha (Mooar), July 23, 1803. P. R. 78.
Sarah, d. Capt. Phineas and Becca [Rebecca. C. R. I.], Aug. 26, 1807.
Sarah, d. Simeon, jr. and Sarah, Apr. 26, 1809.
Sarah, d. twin, Daniel and Sarah [Apr.? 1815].
Sarah Ann, d. Isaac and Hannah, Jan. 13, 1822.
Sarah Jane, d. Simeon, jr. and Jane, Sept. 6, 1837.
Sarah Lavinia, d. Moses A. and Lydia, Jan. 2, 1836.
Sarah M., d. Phineas, jr. and Sally, July 16, 1832.
Sarah Maria, d. Phineas, jr. and Sally, Dec. 24, 1827.
Sarah Ward, d. Daniel, carpenter, and Sarah, Feb. 23, 1844.
Sena, d. Capt. James, Feb. 1, 1816.
Serena, d. Joseph, 3d and Phebe, Oct. 4, 1814.

STEVENS, Simeon, s. John and Annis, Oct. 4 [1740. C. R. 1.].
Simeon, s. Asa and Meh[i]table, May 29, 1746.
Simeon, s. Simeon and Prudence, Apr. 9, 1772.
Simeon, s. Simeon, jr. and Sarah, May 8, 1804.
Simon, s. Asa and Mary, June 10, 1779.
Solomon, s. Daniel and Hannah, July 23, 1756.
Solomon, s. Daniel and Hannah, Nov. 2, 1771.
Solomon, s. Amos and Sarah, Sept. 12, 1778.
Solomon, s. Amos and Susanna, bp. Sept. 25, 1814. C. R. 1
Susan, d. Isaac and Hannah, Feb. 24, 1817.
Susan Louisa, d. William and Eliza L. W., at Belfast, Me., Feb. 6, 1830.
Susana, d. Amos and Susana, Nov. 15, 1815.
Susanna, d. John, jr. and Lydea, July 11, 1756.
Susanna, d. Thomas and Sarah, Dec. 3, 1763.
Susanna, d. Daniel, jr. and Susanna, Mar. 1, 1772.
Susanna, d. Joseph and Alice, Feb. 9, 1773.
Susanna, d. Jonathan and Susanna, Dec. 19, 1775.
Susanna, d. Asa and Mary, June 2, 1777.
Susannah, d. Peter and Su[sa]nnah, Sept. 30, 1789.
Susannah, d. Amos and Susannah, bp. June 23, 1816. C. R. 1.
Suse, d. Bimsley and Rebecca, July 29, 1772.
Theoder, s. James and Dorathey, Nov. 30, 1735.
Theoder, s. John, 3d [jr. C. R. 2.] and Mary, May 20, 1750.
Theodore, s. Benjamin, jr and Hannah, Apr. 8, 1760.
Theodore, s. Benj[ami]n, jr. and Hannah, July 12, 1763.
Thomas, s. John and Elezebeth, Aug. 9 [1724].
Thomas, s. Thomas and Sarah, Oct. 10, 1848.
Thomas, s. Thomas, jr. and Sarah, Feb. 17, 1774.
Thomas, s. Thomas Spofford and Lucy, Apr. 27, 1823.
Tho[ma]s. Osgood, s. Benjamin and Huldah, Apr. 19, 1837.
Timothy, s. John and Hanna, Mar. 2, [16]66.
Timothy, s. Timothy and Rebecah, Aug. 15, 1731.
Timothy Chandler, s. Joshua and Mary, Apr. 2, 1794.
Timothy Johnson, s. Pet[er] and Nabby, [Aug.] 30, 1788. [bp. Sept. 7. C. R. 1.]
Uriah Holt, s. Abiel, bp. Oct. 31, 1779. C. R. 2.
Varnum, s. James and Elizabeth, July 27, 1798.
Warren, s. Bimsley and Mary N., Dec. 31, 1838.
Warren C., s. Warren and Elizabeth, Aug. 11, 1838.
Wiliam, s. Asa and Mehetebel, July 7, 1748.
William, s. Jonathan, bp. July 12, 1767. C. R. 2.
William, s. Asa and Mary, Sept. 8, 1775.
Will[ia]m, s. Jonathan and Susannah, bp. Apr. 17, 1796. C. R. 1.

STEVENS, William, s. Jonathan and Susannah, Jan. 21, 1799.
William, s. Joseph, 3d, and Phebe, Mar. 20, 1799.
William, s. Joseph, 3d and Phebe, Aug. 23, 1812.
William, s. Simeon, jr. and Jane, June 4, 1839.
William Frye, s. Joseph and Phebe, Dec. 18, 1810.
William Oliver, s. William and Eliza Leach Watson, at Belfast, Me., Feb. 3, 1828.
Zachariah, s. Joseph and Alice, Nov. 12, 1764. [bp. Nov. 13, 1763. C. R. 1.]
——, ch. [torn] and Sarah, —— 23 [1702-3].
——, ch. [torn] and Sarah, Oct. 4, 1704.
——, ch. [torn] and [torn] beth, Aug. 1, 1706.
——, ch. Nathan and Elizabeth, May 30, 1709.
——, ch. [Ebe]nezer and Sarah, July 15, 1709.
——, d. Abial and Deborah, Oct. 28, 1710.
——, ch. [torn] and Deborah, Sept. 25, 1712.
[torn]iah, s. Samuel and Elizabeth, Nov. 1, 1714.
——, s. Abiall and Debroah, Aug. 25, 1723.
——, s. Ebenezer and Sarah, Nov. 7, 1725.
——, s. John and Elezebeth, Nov. 7, 1726.
——, s. Timothy and Sarah, —— 22 [1752. C. R. 1.].
——, d. Peter, jr. and Lucy, Apr. 6, 1819.
——, d. Capt. James, Jan. 7, 1821.
——, s. Peter, jr. and Lucy, Jan. 31, 1821.
——, s. Leonard and Mary, June 24, 1821.
——, s. Benjamin and Susan, Oct. 18, 1822.
——, s. Leonard and Mary, Jan. 21, 1828.
——, s. Abiel, Feb. 27, 1829.
——, ch. Bimsley and Mary, Dec. 31, 1838.

STEWARD (see also Stuart), Henry s. John, bp. Mar. 8, 1752. C. R. 2.
John, s. John, bp. Apr. 25, 1742. C. R. 2.
Keturah, d. John, bp. Sept. 16, 1744. C. R. 2.
Martha, d. John, bp. Nov. 6, 1757. C. R. 2.

STEWART (see also Stuart), Mary, d. Rob[er]t, bp. July 11, 1725. C. R. 2.
Simpson, s. John, bp. Feb. 5, 1749. C. R. 2.
William, s. John, bp. Aug. 9, 1747. C. R. 2.
William [Henry. C. R. 1.], s. John and Dorcas, July 11, 1831.

STICKNEY, Abigal, d. Abraham and Abigal, May 5, 1783.
Abraham, s. Abraham and Abigail, May 4, 1787.

STICKNEY, Betsy, d. Abraham and Abigal, Apr. 22, 1799.
Catharine L., d. James M. and Catharine B., Dec. 18, 1838.
Charles, s. John and Rachel, Dec. 8, 1784.
Charles, s. John and Lucretia, June 29, 1808.
Charles O., s. Joseph and Lucretia, Dec. 25, 1829.
Eliza L., d. Joseph and Lucy, Aug. 26, 1817.
Ellen A., d. Joseph and Lucebria, July 26, 1837.
Isaac, s. Abraham and Abigal, July 16, 1781.
Isaac, s. John and Lucretia, Jan. 25, 1810.
James M., s. Abraham and Mary, July 5, 1814.
John, s. twin, John and Rachel, Mar. 8, 1777.
John, s. John and Rachael, Aug. 28, 1778.
John, s. John and Rachel, Nov. 15, 1779.
John, s. John and Lucretia, July 6, 1814.
Joseph, s. Abraham and Abigal, Feb. 18, 1795.
Joseph, s. John and Lucretia, July 4, 1816.
Joseph C., s. Joseph and Lucy, Apr. 3, 1819.
Mary, d. Abraham and Abigail, Aug. 25, 1803.
Mary, d. John and Lucretia, Jan. 26, 1805.
Mary L., d. Joseph and Lucretia, Oct. 6, 1825.
Molley [Molly Farnum. C. R. I.], d. John and Rachel, Apr. 29, 1782.
Naama, d. Abraham and Abigail, Oct. 27, 1805.
Rachel, d. twin, John and Rachel, Mar. 8, 1777.
Ruth, d. John and Lucretia, June 29, 1806.
Sarah, d. Abraham and Abigail, May 2, 1785.
Thomas, s. John and Rachel, Apr. 18, 1783.
Thomas, s. John and Lucretia, Apr. 25, 1812.
William, s. Abraham and Abigal [Mar. 9, 1793. T. C.].
Zepheniah, s. Abraham and Abigail, Apr. 22, 1797.
——, twin chn., Lucretia and Joseph Parkhurst, May 17, 1821.

STILDS (see also Stiles), Morris, s. Frank, laborer, and Catharine, Mar. 12, 1846.

STILES (see also Stilds, Styles), Barnard, s. Hezekiah and Hannah, June 28, 1744.
Caroline E., d. twin, William and Eliza, May 23, 1841.
Daniel, s. Ebenezer and Dorathy, July 25, 1715.
Daniel, s. Elijah and Tabitha, Nov. 15, 1821.
David, s. David and Nancy, bp. June 27, 1813. C. R. I.
Dorathy, d. Ebene[zer] and [torn], —— [1705-6].
Dorathy, d. Hezekiah and Hannah, Jan. 29, 1752.
Dorathy, d. Hezekiah and Hannah, Jan. 14, 1755.

STILES, Ebenezer, s. Ebenezer and Dorathy, July 3 [1707].
Edward Gardner, s. Andrew and Phebe, bp. Oct. 29, 1826. C. R. 1.
Farnum, s. David and Nancy, bp. Nov. 27, 1814. C. R. 1.
Hannah, d. Hezekiah and Hannah, Jan. 10, 1738-9.
Hannah, d. Hezekiah and Hannah, Nov. 9, 1753.
Hannah Kimball, d. Andrew and Phebe, bp. Oct. 29, 1826. C. R. 1.
Harmon Perley, s. Andrew and Phebe, bp. Oct. 5, 1828. C. R. 1.
Henry W., s. twin, William and Eliza, May 23, 1841.
Hermon P., s. Andrew and Phebe, Dec. 28, 1827.
Joseph, s. Andrew and Phebe, bp. Oct. 29, 1827. C. R. 1.
Josiah, s. Dorothy, bp. July 11, 1790. C. R. 2.
Loisa, d. Mosses and Mary, July 14, 1811.
Lydia, d. Elijah and Tabitha, Mar. 24, 1814.
Lydia Gray, d. Elijah and Tabitha, July 23, 1812.
Martha Ann, d. William and Eliza, June 9, 1838.
Mary, d. Moses and Mary, Dec. 30, 1808.
Mehetabell, d. Ebenezer and [torn], —— [1703].
Mehetebel, d. Hezekiah and Hannah, Feb. 18, 1757.
Moses, s. Stephen and Hulda, Nov. 19, 1781.
Moses, s. Ezra, bp. Nov. 25, 1781. C. R. 2.
Moses, s. Moses and Mary, Oct. 15, 1813.
[Stephen. C. R. 2.] ——en, s. Hezekiah and Hannah, Dec. 3, 1737.
Stephen, s. Hezekiah and Hannah, Mar. 27, 1741.
Stephen, s. Stephen and Huldah, July 18, 1777.
——, ch. [torn] and Dorathy, Jan. 31, 1710-11.
——, s. Ebenezer and Dorathy, June 16, 1713.
——, twin chn. Moses and Mary, June 2, 1816.
——, d. Elijah and Tabitha, Dec. 29, 1817.
——, ch. Moses and Mary, Jan. —, 1818.

STIMPSON, Elizabeth C., d. Nath[anie]l and Hepzibah, Jan. 12, 1794.

STOKES, Alice, d. John, laborer, and Ellen, both b. Ireland, May 3, 1849. [June 3. dup.]

STONE, Abiel, s. Simon, bp. May 15, 1720. C. R. 2.
Benjamin, s. Hugh and Dorithy, bp. May 2, 1714. C. R. 2.
Daniel, s. Simon and Hester [Esther. C. R. 2.], Feb. 14, 1717-18.
Daniell, s. Hugh and Hannah, Apr. 28, 1677.
Deborah, d. John and Mary, Feb. 16, 1692-3.
Hannah, d. Hugh and Hannah, Mar. 23, 1679-80.

STONE, Hannah, d. John and Mary, Dec. 25, 1691.
Hugh, s. Hugh and Hannah, Aug. 3, 1682.
John, s. Hew and Hanna, Nov. 24, 1668.
John, s. John and Mary, Apr. 10, 1694.
John, s. Simon, bp. May 5, 1723. C. R. 2.
Katharine, d. Hugh and Hannah, May 25, 1674.
Joseph, s. John and Mary, June 23, 1695.
Kezia, d. Hugh and Hannah, April 22, 1686.
Sarah, d. Simon and Ester [Mar.] 16 [1720-21].
Simon, s. Hew and Hanna, Oct. 8, 1671.
W[illia]m Pierce, s. T. D. P. and Phebe, bp. Sept. 19, 1841. C. R. 6.
——, ch. [H]ugh and Dorathy, Dec. 11, 1713.
——, s. Simon and Esther, June 28, 1719.

STOODLEY, Ann Maria, d. Henry, wheelwright, and Ruby [F. dup.], July 18, 1843. [July 19. dup.]
Joseph Edward, s. Henry and Ruby, Apr. 19, 1839.
Ruby, d. Henry and Ruby, Sept. 6 [7. dup.], 1832.
William Henry, s. Henry and Ruby, Aug. 8, 1833.

STOTT, Alfred Sewall, s. Joshua H., cloth dresser, and Adeline S., July 9, 1847.
Elizabeth, d. Thomas, spinner, and Anna, Oct. 6, 1843.
Harriet, d. James, woolcomber, and Ann, May 17, 1846.
John, s. Jonas, laborer, and Maria, Dec. 14, 1848.
John A., s. Joshua, laborer, and Adeline, June 5, 1845.
Lear E., ch. John, spinner, and Mary, Dec. 30, 1848.
Mary A., d. Thomas, spinner, July 8, 184[7 or 8].
Sarah, d. Thomas, manufacturer, and Ann, Apr. 25, 1845.
Sophia D., d. Joseph, soap-boiler, and Isabella, May 10, 1844.
Susannah, d. Thomas, spinner, and Ann, both b. England, Oct. 28, 1849.
Thomas, s. Robert, dyer, and Jane, Oct. 12, 1847.
——, d. Joshua H., factory operative, b. Canada, and Adaline S., Oct. 20, 1849.

STRONG, George E., s. George F., printer, and Mary P., June 28, 1848.

STUART (see also Steward, Stewart), Abigail Clarke, d. Moses and Abigail, bp. Dec. 7, 1823. C. R. 6.
Elizabeth Wooster, d. Moses and Abigail, bp. Dec. 10, 1815. C. R. 6.
James Clark, s. Rev. Moses and Abigail, Apr. 30, 1811.

STUART, John William, s. George, flax-dresser, and Sarah Ann, June 22, 1847.
Martha, d. George, laborer, b. Scotland, and Sarah A., b. England, Sept. 15, 1849.
Mary Ann, d. Rev. Moses and Abigail, Mar. 8, 1821.
Moses Brown, s. Rev. M., bp. Apr. 17, 1814. C. R. 2.
Robert [Boggs. C. R. 1.], s. John and Dorcas, Mar. 14, 1833.
Sarah Cook, d. Moses and Abigail, bp. [bet. 1817 and 1819.]. C. R. 2.
Susanna, d. William, flax-dresser, and Eliza, Apr. 1, 1848.

STYLES (see also Stiles), Hezekiah, s. Hezekiah and Hannah, Aug. 5, 1759.
Huldah, d. Stephen and Huldah, Mar. 21, 1774.

SUGRUA, Cornelius, s. Charles, laborer, and Mary, both b. Ireland, Nov. 8, 1848.

SUTCLIFF (see also Sutcliffe), James Henry, s. Abraham and Mary, Feb. 19, 1843.
Sarah Elizabeth, d. Abraham and Mary Jane, Mar. 20, 1841.

SUTCLIFFE (see also Sutcliff), Susanna, d. Abraham, laborer, and Mary, Nov. 13, 1845.

SWAIN, John, s. John, bp. Apr. 21, 1776. C. R. 2.
Lucy, d. John, bp. Feb. 8, 1778. C. R. 2.
——, s. John, Feb. 10, 1826.

SWAN, Affy, d. Robert and Affy, Sept. 5, 1774.
Almira F., d. Joseph B., laborer, and Sarah J., b. Salem, N. H., July 2, 1849.
Almira Farington, d. Joseph and Mary K., Aug. 16, 1813.
Ann Maria, d. Joseph B., laborer, and Sarah J., July 17, 1847.
Benja[min], s. twin, Robert and Affa, Oct. 7, 1781.
Deborah, d. Asa and Deborah, bp. Apr. 19, 1719. C. R. 1.
Elizabeth, d. Robert and Apphia, Dec. 20, 1779.
Ephraim, s. Ephraim and Sarah, Oct. 12, 1739.
Ephraim, s. Ephraim, jr. and Martha, Mar. 31, 1769.
Fidelia, d. Robert and Susannah, July 25, 1800.
Fidelia R., d. Joseph and Mary K., May 6, 1825.
George W., s. Joseph and Mary K., Apr. 16, 1820.
Hannah, d. Robert and Apphia, Nov. 11, 1777.
Hannah F., d. Joseph and Mary K., Jan. 5, 1822.

SWAN, James, s. Joshua and Sarah, bp.] ——, 1721-2. C. R. I.
Jeremiah, s. Nathan and Lydia [Sarah. C. R. I.], Feb. 27, 1793.
Jerusha Barron, d. Robert and Susanna, May 22, 1791.
John, s. John and Lois, Apr. 15, 1776.
Jonathan, s. Robert and Elizabeth, bp. Sept. 10, 1732. C. R. I.
Joseph, s. twin, Robert and Affa, Oct. 7, 1781.
Joseph B., s. Joseph and Mary K., May 27, 1815.
Joshuah, s. Joshuah and Sarah, —— [1708?].
Louisa, d. Joseph and Mary K., May 24, 1818.
Martha, d. Ephraim, jr. and Martha, Sept. 29, 1771.
Mary, d. Jo[torn], —— [1706].
Mary Ann, d. Joseph and Mary K., May 12, 1812.
Mary E., d. Joseph, teamster, and Sarah J., July 25, 1844.
Phebe, d. Asa and Deborah, bp. —— [1721]. C. R. I.
Rebecca Sheldon, d. Caleb and Sena, Feb. 24, 1817.
Rhoda, d. Robert and Susanna, Dec. 10, 1795.
Rhoda, d. Robert and Susanna, Oct. 29, 1797.
Richard, s. Robert and Elizabeth, July 1, 1691.
Rubia, d. Robert and Susanna, Mar. 24, 1793.
Ruby A., d. Joseph and Mary K., Jan. 16, 1824.
Sally, d. Robert and Apphia, Mar. 20, 1776.
Sarah, d. Ephraim and Sarah, June 13, 1742.
Sarah Jane, d. Joseph W. and Sarah Jane, Nov. 14, 1841.
Sarah Tyler, d. Nathan and Lydia, July 13, 1791.
Susanna, d. Robert and Affa, Apr. —, 1783. [bp. Apr. 6. C. R. I.]

SWIFT, Anna H[artwell. C. R. 2.], d. Nathaniel and Martha J., Sept. 18, 1842.
Cathrine, d. Dr. Nath[anie]l and Sarah, July 6, 1813.
Charles, s. twin, Dr. Nath[anie]l and Sarah, July 25, 1816.
Charlotte H[arris. C. R. 2.], d. Nath[anie]l, jr. and Martha J., July 26, 1839.
George Baker, s. Nathaniel and Sarah, July 30, 1806.
George Francis, s. Nathaniel [jr. C. R. 2.] and Martha, Dec. 10, 1833.
Jonathan, s. twin, Dr. Nath[anie]l and Sarah, July 25, 1816.
Martha Elizabeth, d. Nath[anie]l, jr. and Martha Jane, Feb. 15, 1836.
Nathaniel, s. Nathaniel and Sarah, May 12, 1805.
Samuel, s. Dr. Nathaniel and Sarah, Feb. 21, 1815.
Sarah Frances, d. Nathaniel and Sarah, Nov. 15, 1807.
William, s. Nathaniel and Sarah, Dec. 17, 1809.
William, s. Geo[rge] B., physician, and Mary B., May 28, 1846.

SYKES, John S., s. Thomas, manufacturer, and Elizabeth, Aug. 1, 1848.

SYLVESTER (see also Silvester), Augusta S., d. Joshua and Lucy, Nov. 9, 1816.
Louisa, d. Nathaniel and Lydia, July 1, 1835.

SYMMES, Anna, d. Rev. Will[ia]m and Anna, Apr. 1, 1768.
Charlotte, d. twin, Rev. William and Anna, Dec. 29, 1771.
Converse, s. Rev. William and Anna, July 22, 1770.
Daniel, s. Rev. William and Anne, Oct. 1, 1761.
Elizabeth, d. Rev. William and Anna, Mar. 13, 1765.
Joshua Gee, s. Rev. William and Anna, July 11, 1763.
Lydia, d. twin, Rev. William and Anna, Dec. 29, 1771.
Theodore, s. Rev. William and Anna, May 16, 1767.
William, s. Rev. William and Anna, May 26, 1760.

SYMONDS (see also Simonds), Benjamin, s. Samuel and Caroline, Feb. 25, 1844.
Benjamin Stevens, s. ——, June 18, 1840.
Charles, s. Jonas and Martha, Mar. 8, 1826.
Henry, s. Jonas and Patty, Feb. 17, 1822.
Richard W., s. Samuel, shoemaker, and Caroline, Dec. 12, 1845.
Samuel, s. Jonas and Martha, Nov. 16, 1814.
Samuel P., s. Solomon and Lydia, June 21, 1820.
Sarah, d. Solomon and Lydia A., Aug. 29, 1815.
Warren, s. Jonas and Martha, Oct. 17, 1816.
Willard, s. Jonas and Martha, Oct. 25, 1818.
——, d. Solomon and Lydia A., June 2, 1817.

TAFT, George, s. John and Ruth, Jan. 8, 1833.
——, s. John and Ruth, Sept. 16, 1831.

TANES, Jane T., d. George, laborer, and Janett R., May 23, 1845.

TARPEY, John L., s. Malachi, laborer, and Margaret, both b. Ireland, May 31, 1849.

TATRO, Louis Batton, s. Lewis, cordwainer, and Amelia, at Northfield, Vt., Jan. 17, 1845.

TAWDRY, Mary, d. John, laborer, and Susan, Jan. 18, 1846.
Rosanna, d. John, spinner, and Susan, July 29, 1847.

TAYLOR, David, s. James, laborer, and Elizabeth, Mar. 30, 1846.
Edward J[ohnson. C. R. 2.], s. Rev. John L., clergyman, and Caroline P., Dec. 31, 1847.
Elizabeth Rebecca, d. James and Elizabeth, June 10, 1837.
Harriott, d. John and Sarah, Sept. 18, 1819.
Henry Bethuel, s. Rev. J. L., bp. July 16, 1843. C. R. 2.
James, s. Jonathan and Sarah, Aug. 9, 1831.
John P[helps. C. R. 2.], s. Rev. John L. and Caroline P., Apr. 6, 1841.
Mariah P[helps. C. R. 2.], d. John L., clergyman, and Caroline P., Nov. 1, 1845.
Mary Ann, d. James and Elizabeth, Jan. 1, 1834.
Mary E., d. Jonathan and Sarah, May 27, 1830.
Susanna, d. James and Betsy, Feb. 20, 1841.
Thomas, s. John and Abigel, Apr. 27, 1748.
Thomas J., s. James, laborer, Oct. 11, 184[7 or 8].
——, d. Thomas and Betsy, May 15, 1824.

THAYER, John, s. John C. and Anna, May 31, 1817.
Mary Jane, d. John C. and Anna, Mar. 16, 1815.

THOMAS, Charles Horace, s. Charles and Elsea Maria, Mar. 1, 1842.
Hannah, d. Alexander, bp. Oct. 8, 1775. C. R. 2.
Hannah Drue, d. Nath[anie]l and Zilpha D., bp. Feb. 3, 1839. C. R. 1.

THOMPSON (see also Thomson, Tompson, Tomson), Andrew George, s. Andrew and Mary, Oct. 8, 1833.
Elizabeth, d. John, laborer, and Mary, both b. England, Aug. 12, 1848.
Hannah, d. Mary, bp. Oct. 23, 1796. C. R. 1.
Martha Martin, d. Mary, bp. Oct. 23, 1796. C. R. 1.

THOMSON (see also Thompson), Julia Ann, d. John and Mary, May 2, 1797.
Mary, d. John and Mary, Mar. 3, 1795.
Timothy, s. John and Mary, June 20, 1792.

THORNTON, Benjamin E., s. George J., laborer, b. England, and Elizabeth, b. Scotland, Dec. 1, 1849.
George Washington, s. George and Elizabeth, bp. Apr. 21, 1848. C. R. 4.

THURSTEN (see also Thurston), Hannah, d. Moses and Hannah, Sept. 10, 1744.

THURSTIN (see also Thurston), Shua, d. Moses and Hanah, July 15, 1748.

THURSTON (see also Thursten, Thurstin, Thurstine), Clarisa, d. Stephen and Philomelia, Feb. 26, 1801.

THURSTINE (see also Thurston), Moses, s. Moses and Hannah, July 7, 1746.

TIBBETS, Eben[eze]r, s. Eben[eze]r and Anna, Dec. 22, 1822.

TILER (see also Tyler), Jacob, s. Jacob and Abigaiel, Apr. 5, 1728.
Jeremiah, s. Jacob and Abigail, Aug. 5, 1733.

TITCOMB, Samuel Got, s. Moses and Elizabeth, bp. Sept. 17, 1769. C. R. 1.

TOMPSON (see also Thompson), Benjamin, s. Joshua, Aug. 10, 1740. C. R. 2.
Hannah, d. Joshua, bp. Feb. 26, 1738. C. R. 2.
Susanna, d. Joshua, bp. Sept. 4, 1737. C. R. 2.

TOMSON (see also Thompson), Sarah, d. Martha and Gilbert Putnam, Mar. 3, 1806.

TOWLE, Benjamin F., s. Jonathan, merchant, and Almira, Feb. 9, 1847.
George Emery, s. J., bp. Nov. 28, 1847. C. R. 2.
Martha [Emery. C. R. 2.], d. Jonathan, trader, and Almira, Feb. 4, 1845.
Mary Elizabeth, d. Jonathan [trader. dup.] and Almira E., May 21, 1843.
Rosabella, d. Andrew, manufacturer, and Mary A., Aug. 6, 1843.

TOWN (see also Towne, Towns), Aaron, s. Aaron and Hannah, May 19, 1762.
Aaron, s. Aaron and Hannah, Aug. 25, 1769.
Abiah, d. Peter and Rebecca [Lydia. C. R. 1.], Oct. 19, 1800.
Amos, s. Peter and Becca [Lydia. C. R. 1.], May 28, 1779.

TOWN, Amos, s. Simeon and Olive, Jan. 19, 1801.
Ansel, s. Peter and Sarah, jr., May 20, 1808.
Asa, s. Asa and Mary, July 17, 1761.
Asa, s. Asa and Mary, Mar. 18, 1763.
Asa, s. Asa and Dorithy, Sept. 29, 1793.
Asa Lovejoy, s. Asa, bp. June 20, 1802. C. R. 2.
Benjamin, s. Nathan and Eunice, Feb. 28, 1746-7.
Bette, d. Joseph and Sarah, May 15, 1763.
Charllotte, d. Simeon and Olive, May 4, 1797.
Daniel, s. Peter and Rebecca [Lydia. C. R. 1.], Jan. 8, 1787.
Dorcas, d. Joseph and Sarah, Mar. 3, 1758.
Easter, d. Joseph and Sarah, May 17, 1760.
Elijah, s. Nath[a]n, jr. and Hannah, bp. Jan. 21, 1776. C. R. 1.
Eliza, d. John and Martha, Apr. 7, 1812.
Ephraim, s. Simeon and Hepsibah, bp. Nov. 14, 1779. C. R. 1.
Fanney, d. Peter and Rebecca [Lydia. C. R. 1.], Mar. 24, 1785.
Hannah, d. Aron and Hannah, Jan. 6, 1759.
Hannah, d. Aaron and Hannah, Oct. 21, 1764.
Hannah, d. Peter and Rebecca [Lydia. C. R. 1.], Oct. 12, 1792.
Hariot, d. Simeon and Olive, July 24, 1803.
Harmon, s. Peter and Rebecca [Lydia. C. R. 1.], Jan. 14, 1797.
Harmon, s. Samuel, bp. Oct. 6, 1799. C. R. 2.
Henry, s. Asa, bp. Aug. 26, 1798. C. R. 2.
Hepzibah, s. Simeon and Hepzibah, bp. Sept. 15, 1793. C. R. 1.
Huldah, d. Asa, bp. July 29, 1759. C. R. 1.
Jacob, s. Nathan, jr. and Hannah, bp. Dec. 7, 1777. C. R. 1.
Jacob, s. Nathan, jr., bp. Nov. 26, 1780. C. R. 1.
Joel, s. Peter and Rebecca [Lydia. C. R. 1.], Feb. 17, 1783.
John, s. Nathan and Eunes, Oct. 29, 1751.
John, s. John, bp. Aug. 18, 1776. C. R. 1.
John, s. Nathan and Mary, bp. Mar. 26, 1786. C. R. 1.
John, s. Asa, bp. May 10, 1795. C. R. 2.
John, s. John and Martha, Feb. 20, 1819.
John, s. John and Patty, Aug. 11, 1821.
Jonathan, s. Nathan, bp. Sept. 12, 1790. C. R. 1.
Joseph, s. Simeon and Hepsibah, bp. May 24, 1789. C. R. 1.
Joseph, s. Asa, bp. Mar. 19, 1797. C. R. 2.
Kendal, s. Peter, jr. and Sarah, Mar. 20, 1810.
Levi, s. Simeon and Olive, Apr. 23, 1810.
Lydia, d. Peter and Rebecca [Lydia. C. R. 1.], Mar. 1, 1781.
Martha, d. John and Martha, Aug. 18, 1813.
Mary, d. John and Martha, Nov. 23, 1815.
Molley, d. Asa and Mary, Feb. 8, 1752.
Molly, d. Nathan, jr. and Mary, Apr. 30, 1774.

TOWN, Molly, d. Nathan, jr. and Hannah, bp. July 7, 1782. C. R. 1.
Moody, s. Simeon and Hepzibah, bp. July 24, 1791. C. R. 1.
Moses, s. Aron and Hannah, July 3, 1756.
Moses, s. Nathan and Hannah, bp. Oct. 7, 1792. C. R. 1.
Myranda, d. Peter, jr. and Sally, Aug. 14, 1806.
Nancy Stevens, s. Daniel, jr. and Pamela, Aug. 27, 1837.
Nathan, s. Nathan and Eunis, July 11, 1744.
Nathan, s. Nathan, jr. and Mary, July 29, 1771.
Patty, d. Unice, May 28, 1792.
Peter, s. Nathan, jr. and Unice, Aug. 10, 1749.
Peter, s. Mary and Peter Bridges, Mar. 22, 1773.
Peter, s. Peter and Lydia, Dec. 28, 1774.
Peter, s. Peter and Becca, Nov. 18, 1777.
Phebe, d. Joseph and Sarah [Esther. C. R. 1.], June 17, 1755.
Rebecca, d. Joseph and Sarah, Mar. 23, 1768.
Ruby, d. Simeon and Olive, Aug. 24, 1805.
Ruth, d. Simeon and Hepzibah, bp. Jan. 24, 1796. C. R. 1.
Sally, d. Simeon and Olive, June 27, 1795.
Samuel, s. Samuel and Rachel, bp. Oct. 6, 1793. C. R. 1.
Sam[ue]ll, s. Nathan, jr. and Mary, Mar. 26, 1769.
Sarah, d. Joseph and Sarah, Feb. 20, 1848-9.
Sarah, d. Aaron Fox and Mary, July 15, 1784.
Sarah, d. Peter, jr. and Sarah, May 16, 1812.
Sarah Adams, d. Asa, bp. Apr. 6, 1800. C. R. 2.
Sene [Tryphena. C. R. 1.], d. Peter and Rebecca, Feb. 16, 1789.
Serena, d. Simeon and Olive, Dec. 17, 1799.
Simeon, s. Joseph and Sarah, July 6, 1747.
Simeon, s. Joseph and Sarah, July 31, 1751.
Solomon, s. Asa and Mary, Oct. 8, 1750.
Solomon, s. Asa and Mary, Dec. 9, 1753.
Stephen, s. Nathan, jr. and Hannah, bp. Sept. 12, 1779. C. R. 1.
Stephen, s. Nathan and Hannah, bp. Feb. 15, 1784. C. R. 1.
Sukey, d. Nathan and Hanah, bp. Nov. 9, 1788. C. R. 1.
Symonds, s. Simeon and Hepsibah, bp. Apr. 8, 1787. C. R. 1.
Tryphena, d. Peter and Lydia, bp. Apr. —, 1789. C. R. 1.
Willard, s. Simeon and Olive, Apr. 5, 1808.
Will[ia]m, s. John and Hannah, bp. Nov. 22, 1778. C. R. 1.
——, ch. John and Martha, Dec. 21, 1817.
——, d. Daniel, jr. and Pamela, Jan. 26, 1840.

TOWNE (see also Town), Daniel, s. Daniel and Hannah, Mar. 30, 1805.
George Warren, s. John, jr., teamster, and Susan B., Mar. 31, 1848.

TOWNE, Hannah, d. Daniel and Hannah, Apr. 16, 1803.
Rebecca, d. Peter, jr. and Sarah, June 21, 1814.
Rufus, s. Daniel and Hannah, Jan. 8, 1809.
——, s. William and Tammy S., Mar. 2, 1832.

TOWNS (see also Town), Aaron, s. Nathan and Phebe, July 25, 1734.
Albert, s. Peter, jr. and Sally, Sept. 28, 1804.

TOWNSEND, Charles, s. Charles J. and Mary, Dec. 19, 1832.
Charles Horace, s. Tho[ma]s J. and Elsea Maria, Mar. 1, 1841.
George A., s. Charles J., farmer, and Mary, Nov. 16, 1844.
Henry W., s. Charles J. and Mary, Oct. 24, 1834.
Mary A., d. twin, Charles J. and Mary, July 8, 1840.
Milton B., s. Charles J. and Mary, Aug. 25, 1838.
Rhoda A., d. twin, Charles J. and Mary, July 8, 1840.
Walter N., s. Charles J., laborer, and Mary, June 21, 1848.
William G., s. Nathan and Eliza S., Dec. 6, 1822.
William W., s. Charles J. and Mary, Sept. 19, 1836.

TRASK, Benjamin, s. Benjamin [and Elizabeth. C. R. 3.], June 28, 1831.

TREFRY, Hannah R., d. Samuel, farmer, and Rebecca, Apr. 28, 1844.
John [John Henry Gallison. C. R. 1.], s. Samuel S., farmer, and Rebecca, Oct. 1, 1847.
Mary B[owden. C. R. 1.], d. Samuel S., farmer, and Rebecca, Nov. 6, 1845.

TROW, Abigail, d. Charles and Mary, Sept. 28, 1810.
Amos W., s. William, jr., farmer, b. Tewksbury, and Elizabeth, b. Billerica, Jan. 6, 1848.
Annis, d. Dudly and Annis, Mar. 10, 1800.
Charles, s. Daniel and Hannah, bp. Sept. 6, 1829. C. R. 3.
Daniel, s. Charles and Mary, Oct. 18, 1813.
Daniel L[amson. P. R. 31.], s. Capt. Daniel and Hannah C., Aug. 6, 1818.
Dudly, s. Dudly and Annes, Jan. 3, 1799.
Ephraim Swan, s. John, jr. and Martha, May 14, 1797.
Ephraim Swan, s. John and Martha, Mar. 1, 1812.
Fidelia, d. Lt. John, jr. and Martha, Sept. 20, 1801.
George Abbot, s. Daniel L., shoemaker, and Phebe C., Mar. 1, 1849.

TROW, Hannah, d. Ens. John and Martha, May 3, 1799.
Hannah D., d. Capt. Daniel and Hannah C., June 17, 1820.
Henry C., s. Dudley and Mary, Mar. 26, 1837.
Jerusha L., d. Daniel and Hannah, bp. Oct. 10, 1824. C. R. 2.
John, s. Richard and Sarah, Feb. 4, 1807.
John, s. Charles and Mary, May 27, 1807.
John Fowler, s. Lt. John and Martha, Jan. 30, 1810.
Jonathan Dodge, s. Dudly and Annis, Oct. 16, 1801.
Maria, d. Dudly, bp. June 2, 1805. C. R. 2.
Martha, d. John and Martha, bp. May 3, 1795. C. R. 1.
Martha, d. Daniel and Martha, Mar. 6, 1825.
Martha, d. Daniel and Hannah, Feb. 19, 1826.
Mary, d. Charles and Mary, Oct. 28, 1804.
Mary, d. Dudly and Annis, May 28, 1805.
Mary L., d. Dudly and Mary, Oct. 18, 1834.
Myranda, d. Lt. John and Martha, Jan. 29, 1807.
Patty, d. John and Martha, July 17, 1793.
Richard, s. Richard and Sarah, May 26, 1803.
Sally [Sarah Swan. C. R. 1.], d. John and Martha, June 26, 1795.
Sarah, d. Richard and Sarah, Apr. 13, 1805.
Sophronia, d. Lt. John and Martha, Apr. 21, 1804.
William, s. wid. Hannah, bp. Oct. 11, 1807, a. 12 y. C. R. 2.
Wil[lia]m, s. John and Martha, Feb. 6, 1814.
——, ch. Charles and Mary, Oct. 28, 1809.

TRULAN (see also Truland), Mary Ann, d. Hugh and Sarah, Oct. 21, 1829.
Robert B., s. Hugh, tailor, and Catherine, both b. Ireland, May 15, 1849.
Sarah, d. Hugh and Mary Ann, Mar. 16, 1833.
Sarah D., d. Hugh and Mary A., Oct. 19, 1835.

TRULAND (see also Trulan), John G., s. Hugh and Sally, July 26, 1827.
Sarah G., d. George and Mary, Aug. —, 1828.

TRULL, Alfred, s. Levi and Anna, June 2, 1822.
Asenath, d. Levi and Anna, Dec. 14, 1800.
Caroline, d. Levi and Anna, Apr. 6, 1818.
Charles, s. twin, Levi and Anna, Jan. 23, 1806.
Fredrick, s. Levi and Anna, Mar. 31, 1802.
George, s. twin, Levi and Anna, Jan. 23, 1806.
John, s. Levi and Anna, May 10, 1808.
Levi, s. Levi and Anna, July 22, 1804.

TRULL, Loisa, d. Levi and Anna, May 27, 1814.
Mary, d. Levi and Anna, May 22, 1812.
Nancy, d. Levi and Anna, July 13, 1799.
Sarah, d. Levi and Anna, May 13, 1816.
Sophrona, d. Levi and Anna, June 5, 1810.
Susan Alice, d. Frederick and Sarah, Oct. 11, 1826.

TRUMBAL, James, s. Timothy and Frances, bp. Oct. 18, 1778. C. R. 1.

TUCK, Abby Jane, d. William, factory watchman, and Abigail B., b. Dracut, at Westford, Apr. 6, 1849.
Charles Henry, s. John, 3d, cordwainer, and Sarah Jane, Nov. 22, 1847.
Charles S., s. John and Elizabeth A., Sept. 6, 1837.
[Elizabeth Abbott. C. R. 3.], d. John and Elizabeth, Dec. 10, 1822.
Hannah D., d. John and Elizabeth, Jan. 8, 1820.
Harriet, d. John and Elizabeth A., June 21, 1825.
John, s. John and Elizabeth A., May 25, 1814.
John Albion, s. John and Sarah Jane, bp. Sept. 6, 1840. C. R. 3.
Lydia, d. Joseph and Martha, Aug. 4, 1734.
Martha Ann, d. John and Elizabeth A., Aug. 17, 1834.
Moses Warren, s. John, 2d and Hannah A. (Bailey), July 11, 1836.
Nathan, s. John and Elizabeth A., Mar. 24, 1827.
Parker, s. Joseph and Martha, bp. ——, 1737. C. R. 1.
Sally [Sarah Ames. C. R. 3.], d. John and Elizabeth A., Feb. 4, 1817.
Samuel T., s. John and Elizabeth A., Aug. 15, 1830.
Sarah, d. Joseph and Martha, Apr. 5, 1742.
Sarah Elizabeth, d. John and Sarah, bp. Sept. 3, 1843. C. R. 3.
Simeon F., s. John and Elizabeth A., July 16, 1832.
William, s. John and Elizabeth A., Mar. 20, 1812.
William F., s. John, 3d and Sarah A., Aug. 25, 1840.
——, s. Joseph aud Martha, July 18, 1745.
——, s. John, 3d and Sarah Jane, Jan. 22, 1840.

TUCKER, Asa Holt, s. William, bp. Sept. 17, 1797. C. R. 2.
Catherine E., d. Samuel, yeoman, and Eliza H., Oct. 28, 1846.
George W., s. William, 2d and Hepsabeth (Pearsons), Mar. 16, 1832. P. R. 83.
Hannah H., d. William, 2d and Hepsabeth (Pearsons), Oct. 1, 1827. P. R. 83.

TUCKER, Hannah, d. William, bp. Sept. 17, 1797. C. R. 2.
Hannah H., d. Samuel and Eliza H., Feb. 22, 1840. T. C.
Harriot E., d. Samuel and Eliza, Apr. 29, 1832.
[Louas Jane. P. R. 83.], d. William and Hepzibah, Aug. 18, 1823.
Lydia, d. William and Hannah, Nov. 25, 1796.
Lydia, d. Samuel and Eliza, Nov. 2, 1837.
Mary Ann, d. William and Hepzibeth, Apr. 25, 1817.
Mary R., d. Samuel and Eliza, Jan. 8, 1836.
Phebe, d. William and Hannah, Dec. 29, 1798.
Samuel, s. William and Hannah, Feb. 17, 1805.
Samuel F., s. Samuel and Eliza, Feb. 12, 1834.
Sarah, d. William and Hannah, Nov. 25, 1802.
Stephen, s. William and Lydia, Oct. 6, 1808.
William, 2d [s. William. C. R. 2.], Aug. 10, 1789. P. R. 83.
William H., s. Samuel, farmer, and Eliza H., May 2, 1844.
[William P. P. R. 83.], ch. William, jr. and Hipzabeth, Mar. [26. P. R. 83.], 1820.

TURNBULL, William, s. Thomas, farmer, and Elizabeth, Feb. 18, 1849.

TURNER, Charles Heber, s. Benj[amin], bp. Nov. 24, 1839. C. R. 2.
Edmond, s. John and Sally, Dec. 10, 1822.
James W., s. Abraham Mills and Sally, Mar. 31, 1832.
Leprelate Hamilton, s. Benja[min], bp. Feb. 16, 1834. C. R. 2.
Mary, d. James and Marey, Dec. 15, 1755.
Mary Jane, d. Edmund, manufacturer, and Mary, July 17, 1844.
Newton Lambert, s. Benj[amin], bp. Jan. 1, 1837. C. R. 2.
Priscilla, d. James, bp. Sept. 19, 1773. C. R. 2.
Samuel, s. James, bp. Sept. 11, 1774. C. R. 2.
——, s. William, Feb. [10?] 1843.

TUTTLE, Anna M., d. Nicholas and Hannah, May 10, 1838.
Emma J., d. Nicholas, mason, and Hannah, Jan. 26, 1846.
George Horace, s. Nicholas, farmer, and Anna, Feb. 17, 1844.
Harriet N., d. Hiram, mason, and Harriet N., Feb. 9, 1844.
Hiram O., s. Hiram O., mason, and Harriet N., Feb. 16, 1846.
Josephine, d. John L., carpenter, and Elizabeth, Sept. 16, 1848.
Lewis C., s. Hiram O., mason, b. Effingham, N. H., and Harriet N., b. Ossipee, N. H., Sept. 14, 1849.
Margaret W., d. Nicholas, mason, b. Effingham, N. H., and Hannah W., b. Beverly, Sept. 17, 1848.

TYLER (see also Tiler, Tylor), Abigail, d. Jacob and Abigail, Mar. 1, 1735-6.
Abigal, d. Jacob and Abigal, Nov. 2, 1750.
Abigall, d. twin, Hopestill and Mary, Jan. 4, 1687-8.
Albert, s. twin, Ebenezer, cordwainer, and Mary M., Oct. 31, 1843.
Bethia, d. John and Hannah, Feb. 17, 1691-2.
Betsey, d. Jona[than] and Martha, Mar. 20, 1789.
Charles, s. Parker and Rebeccah, Sept. 8, 1823.
Charles Henry, s. Charles K., barber, and Abby E., Mar. 18, 1846.
Daniel, s. Job and Phebe, bp. Feb. —, 1817. C. R. I.
Ebenezer, s. Moses and Prudence, Dec. 17, 1673.
[Eliza. C. R. I.]beth, d. Jacob and Abigail, Oct. 5, 1721..
Elizabeth, d. Phineas and Elizabeth, Dec. 28, 1778.
George F., s. Moses C. and Susan W., Mar. 26, 1830.
Hannah, d. Phinehas and Elizabeth, Aug. 9, 1775.
Harriot, d. Parker and Rebecca, Mar. 6, 1803.
Harriot, d. Parker and Rebecca, Dec. 30, 1809.
Henry, s. Job and Phebe, bp. Feb.—, 1817. C. R. I.
Herbert, s. twin, Ebenezer, cordwainer, and Mary M., Oct. 31, 1843.
Hopestill, s. Hopestill and Mary, Oct. 26, 1685.
Jacob, s. Jacob, jr. and Abigal, May 27, 1752.
James, s. Hope and Mary, Dec. 28, 1683.
James, s. Moses and Prudence, May 7, 1685.
James, s. Jacob and Lydia, Sept. 6, 1768.
James, s. Job and Phebe, bp. Feb. —, 1817. C. R. I.
Jeremiah, s. Moses and Elenor, Nov. 20, 1755.
Jeremiah, s. Jacob and Lydia, Mar. 23, 1762.
Job, s. Moses and Prudence, Dec. 16, 1675.
Johannah, d. Hope and Mary, Nov. 21, 1681.
John, s. Job and Mary, Apr. 16, 1653.
John, s. Moses and Prudence, Sept. 14, 1669.
John, s. John and Hannah, Aug. 16, 1684.
John, s. Jacob, jr. and Lydea, Jan. 9, 1756.
John Abbot, s. Parker and Rebecca, Oct. 3, 1807.
Johnathan, s. Moses and Prudence, Mar. 3, 1682-3. [1688. T. C.]
Joseph, s. Moses and Prudence, Sept. 18, 1671.
Joshua, s. Moses and Prudence, of Boxford, July 4, 1688.
Leonard, s. Parker and Rebecka, Oct. 20, 1815.
Louisa F., d. Moses C. and Susan W., June 27, 1838.
Lydea, d. Jacob and Lydea, ——, 17[57].
Lydia M., d. Moses C. and Susan, Jan. 30, 1834.

TYLER, Maria, d. Eben B., cordwainer, and Mary M., Sept. ——, 1846.
Mary, d. Jacob and Abigail, Jan. 20, 1738-9.
Mary, d. Jonathan and Martha, Oct. 6, 1781.
Mehitabell, d. twin, Hopestill and Mary, Jan. 4, 1687-8.
Mehitable, d. Phineas and Elizabeth, Nov. 30, 1782.
Mehitable, d. Jonathan and Martha, Apr. 3, 1785.
Moses, s. Moses and Prudence, Feb. 16, 1667.
[Moses. C. R. 1.], s. Jacob and Abigaiel, Mar. 4, 1731-2.
Moses Coburn, s. Parker and Rebecca, May 7, 1805.
Moses O., s. Moses C. and Susan W., Feb 26, 1836.
Nathan, s. John and Hannah, Feb. 17, 1686-7.
Nathaniell, s. Moses and Prudence, Aug. 14, 1680.
Phebe, d. Jacob and Lydia, Apr. 24, 1760.
Phebe, d. Jacob and Lydia, Oct. 13, 1765.
Phineas, s. Phineas and Hannah, [Fe]by. 14, 1765.
Sally, d. Jonathan and Martha, Jan. 28, 1787.
Samuel, s. Phinehas and Elizabeth, Feb. 28, 1773.
Samuel F., s. Parker and Rebecca, July 3, 1826.
Samuell, s. Job and Mary, May 24, 1655.
Samuell, s. Moses and Prudence, May 2, 1678.
Sarah, d. Jacob and Lydea, Sept. 2, 1758.
Simeon, s. Phineas and Elizabeth, Aug. 15, 1771.
Rebeccah, d. Parker and Rebeccah, May 24, 1818.
Robert, s. John and Hannah, July 19, 1689.
Thomas H., s. Eben[eze]r B. and Mary M., Oct. 20, 1832.
Warren P., s. Parker and Rebecca, Feb. 18, 1821.
William B., s. Moses C. and Susan W., Aug. 13, 1831.
William Glanvil, s. Job and Phebe, bp. Feb. —, 1817. C. R. 1.
——, ch. [torn]nathan and Pheoby, June 19, 1709.
——, s. Parker and Rebecca, Oct. —, 1829.

TYLOR (see also Tyler), Alexander S., s. Parker and Rebecca, May 11, 1811.

UMPHRY (see also Humphries), John Albert, s. John, coffee-grinder, b. Bristol, Me., and Aramudo, b. Holderness, N. H., at Lowell, Apr. 2, 1849.

UNDERWOOD, John James, s. Dr. Jonas and Sarah, Dec. 18, 1827.
Susan M., d. Dr. Jonas and Sarah, Mar. 23, 1830.

UPTON, Abiel, jr., s. Abiel and Mary (Jenkins), Apr. —, 1792. P. R. 98.

UPTON, Ābiel, s. Abiel and Molly, Apr. 14, 1802.
Abiel A[ugustus. C. R. 2.], s. George and Eliza, Feb. 25, 1833.
Alpheus A[lva. C. R. 2.], s. Samuel and Lydia, Sept. 7, 1831.
Anna, d. Abiel and Molly, July 30, 1803.
Edward C., s. Abiel, jr. and Abigail, bp. July 24, 1825. C. R. 2.
Edward Wilson, s. Edward C., bp. July 17, 1842. C. R. 2.
Elbridge, s. John B. and Phebe, Dec. 2, 1816.
Eleanor Gustava, d. Abiel, watchman, and Mary, Nov. 11, 1846.
Eliza Ann, d. George and Eliza, Dec. 7, 1827.
Eliza Matilda, d. E. C., bp. Sept. 28, 1845. C. R. 2.
Elizabeth, d. Abiel and Molly, Mar. 9, 1805.
Elizabeth M., d. Carleton, mason, and Elizabeth, June 21, 1845.
George, s. Abiel and Molly, Nov. 10, 1799.
George Henry, s. George, yeoman, and Elizabeth, May 15, 1846.
George W[illiam. C. R. 2.], s. George and Elizabeth, June 2, 1829. [June 8. dup.]
Harriott, d. John B. and Phebe, Apr. 1, 1815.
John Abbot, s. Abiel, jr. and Abigail A., Aug. 5, 1818.
Joshua, s. Tho[ma]s, of Marblehead, b. in Andover, bp. Jan. 11, 1801. C. R. 2.
Margaret, d. Abiel and Molly, June 5, 1809.
Martha J[ane. C. R. 2.], d. George and Elizabeth, June 2, 1831. [June 8. dup.]
Mary, d. Abiel and Mary (Jenkins), Mar. 31, 1789. P. R. 98.
Mary F., d. Abiel, baker, and Mary, July 17, 1843.
Mary Louisa, d. George and Elizabeth, Feb. 19, 1836. P. R. 98.
Samuel, s. Abiel and Mary (Jenkins), Mar. 31, 1796. P. R. 98.
Samuel D[arius. C. R. 2.], s. Samuel and Lydia, Oct. 14, 1828.
——, s. Abiel, jr. and Abigail, Dec. 5, 1820.
——, s. Samuel and Lydia, July 30, 1821.

VALPEY (see also Valpy), Charles A., s. Sam[ue]l G., victualler, and Sarah C., b. N. H., Sept. 22, 1849.
Daniel A. [Daniel Stephan Abbot. P. R. 105.], s. Samuel S. and Elizabeth, Sept. 26, 1820.
Elizabeth [Maria. P. R. 105.], d. Samuel and Elizabeth, Sept. 6, 1825.
Mary Jane, d. Samuel S. and Elizabeth, May 15, 1830.
Sarah E., d. Samuel G., butcher, and Sarah C., Sept. 17, 1843.

VALPY (see also Valpey), Abraham M[artin. P. R. 105.], s. Sam[ue]l S. and Elizabeth, June 9, 1827.
Samuel [George. P. R. 105.], s. Samuel S. and Elizabeth, Apr. [12. P. R. 105.], 1819.

VALPY, Thomas G[ilbert. P. R. 105 ; Kilbourn. C. R. 2.], s. Samuel S. and Elizabeth, July 16, 1832.

VARNUM, John, s. Benja[min], jr. and Hannah, July 9, 1768.

VEZEY, Mariett Maria, d. Oliver, laborer, and Sophronia, Sept. 14, 1846.

VINTON, George, s. George and Eliza, Feb. 5, 1826.

WADDINGTON, Mary Jane, d. Thomas, bp. Aug. 2, 1846. C. R. 4.

WAGH, Margaret, d. Joseph and Margaret, bp. Jan. —, 1731-2. C. R. 1.

WALAND, Elizabeth W., Timothy, laborer, and Ellen, May 28, 1849.

WALDO, Abbie C., d. Jonathan and Loucina, May 28, 1839. T. C.
Elizabeth A., d. Jonathan and Loucina, Mar. 14, 1834. T. C.
Ellen B., d. Jonathan, carpenter, b. Vt., and Loucina, July 6, 1849.
John, s. Jonathan and Loucina, Dec. 20, 1835. T. C.
Joseph Warren, s. Jonathan, carpenter, and Lousina, Mar. 15, 1847.
Mary Frances, d. Jonathan, carpenter, and Louisana, Dec. 16, 1844.
Sarah C., d. Jonathan and Loucina, Oct. 5, 1832. T. C.

WALKER, Abiel, s. Benjamin and Abiel, Mar. 26, 1768.
Benjamin, s. Benj[ami]n and Abiel, Nov. 15, 1763.
Benjamin, s. Abbot and Lydia, Sept. 6, 1801.
Hannah, d. Benjamin and Abiel, July 20, 1766.
Samuel, s. Abbot and Lydia, July 12, 1803.

WALLWORTH (see also Walwork, Walworth, Wolworth), Charlotte F., d. Johnathan and Elizabeth B. (Brierley), May 16, 1840. P. R. 86.
James W., s. Johnathan and Elizabeth B. (Brierley), July 2, 1848. P. R. 86.
Thomas H., s. Johnathan and Elizabeth B. (Brierley), Dec. 12, 1842. P. R. 86.

WALTON, George M., s. Josiah and Mary, Dec. 20, 1822.
Mary D., d. Josiah and Mary, Mar. 14, 1824.
William J., s. Josiah and Mary, July 27, 1821.
——, s. Josiah and Mary, Nov. 29, 1825.

WALWORK (see also Wallworth), John [H. P. R. 86.], s. Jonaathan and Betsey [Elizabeth B. P. R. 86.], Oct. 27, 1841.

WALWORTH (see also Wallworth), Charles Buckly, s. Tho[ma]s and Maiy Ann, Apr. 9, 1833.
Elizabeth M., d. Tho[ma]s and Betsy Holmes, Mar. 13, 1830.
Hannah, d. Thomas and Mary Ann, Sept. 30, 1828.
Mary Ann, d. Tho[ma]s and Mary Ann, Apr. 12, 1830.
Thomas, s. Thomas and Mary Ann, Mar. 12, 1835.

WARD, Ellen M., d. Jonathan W., Mar. 17, 1834.

WARDEL (see also Wardwell), Dameris, d. Thomas and Abigail, Apr. 26, 1737.
Mary, d. Thomas and Abigaile, Mar. 18, 1739-40.

WARDLE (see also Wardwell), Marcy [Mary. CT. R.], d. Samuell and Sara, Oct. 3, 1673.

WARDWEL (see also Wardwell), Abiah, d. William andDorothy, Apr. 22, 1731.
Abigail, d. Eliakim and Ruth, June 27 [1714. C. R. 2.].
[Abigail. C. R. 2.] ——il, ch. twin, Samuel and Return, Feb. 19, 1727-8.
Benjamin, s. Samuel and Return, Feb. 28, 1725-6.
Daniel, s. Daniel and Damaras, Aug. 27, 1776.
David, s. Samuel and Return, Feb. 26 [1724. C. R. 2.].
Ebenezer, s. Samuel and Return, June 8, 173[1. C. R. 2.].
Eliakim, s. William and Dorathy, Jan. 22, 1722-3.
Enoch, s. Daniel and Damaras, Apr. 19, 1778.
Hannah, d. William and Dorathy, July 6, 1721.
Joshua, s. William and Dorathy, Dec. 6, 1728.
Martha, d. twin, Samuel and Return, Feb. 19, 1727-8.
Mary, d. Samuel and Return, Nov. 4, 1720.
Mary, d. William and Dorathy, Feb. 17, 1726-7.
Nathan, s. William and Dorathy, Aug. 15 [1724. C. R. 2.].
Rafe [Ralph. C. R. 2.], s. Samuel and Return, June 27, 1729.
Sally, d. Peter and Dorcas, Aug. 25, 1778.
Samuel, s. Samuel and Return, Sept. 1 [bp. Sept.15, 1717. C. R. 2.].
Samuel, s. Samuel and Return, Feb. 8, 1722-3.

WARDWELL (see also Wardel, Wardle, Wardwel, Wardwill, Wordwill), Abiel, s. Solomon and Bethiah, Aug. 25, 1771.
Abigail Frost, d. Peter, bp. Sept. 3, 1786. C. R. 2.
Albert, s. Simon, jr. and Margaret E. F., Apr. 28, 1840.
Amos, s. Ezekiel and Damaris, July 25, 1796.
Asa Kimball, s. John and Sarah, Sept. 3, 1805.
Augustus F., s. Thomas G., cordwainer, and Mary H., May 9, 1847.
Benjamin, s. Solomon and Bethiah, Aug. 6, 1769.
Benj[ami]n F[ranklin. P. R. 74.], s. Daniel and Lydia, Apr. 17, 1816.
[Bethiah. C. R. 2.] ——ah, d. William and Dorathy, Mar. 17, 1734-5.
Betsey, d. Esther, bp. Oct. 29, 1780. C. R. 2.
Charles, s. Simon, bp. May 17, 1795. C. R. 2.
Charles O., s. Charles and Mehitable, Oct. 9, 1821.
Christopher Andrew, s. Elbridge G. and Lavina, Mar. 22, 1843.
Clara E., d. Charles, cordwainer, and Mehitable, Apr. 14, 1844.
Clarissa, d. Simon, bp. Nov. 13, 1791. C. R. 2.
Cloe, d. Solomon, bp. Sept. 1, 1771. C. R. 1.
Daniel, s. Daniel and Lydia, May 28, 1804.
Delia [Aurilla. P. R. 58.], d. Benja[min] F., housewright, and H. E., Nov. 20, 1845.
Dorcas, d. Jonathan and Rachel, Oct. 21, 1761.
Dorcas, s. Peter and Dorcas, Sept. 29, 1783.
[Dorithy. C. R. 2.] —hy, d. William and Dorathy, Jan. 30, 1715-16.
Dorothy, d. John and Lydia, July 27, 1762.
Edward, s. George and Mary G., Nov. 24, 1829.
Elbridge Gerry, s. Daniel and Lydia, May 30, 1810.
Eliakim, s. Samuell and Sarah, Aug. 17, 1687.
Eliakim, s. Eliakim and Martha, July 24, 1767.
Elisabeth Gage, d. Simon, bp. July 10, 1791. C. R. 2.
Eliza L., d. Joseph and Lucinda, Aug. 31, 1813.
Elizabeth, d. Samuell and Sarah, Sept. 3, 1675.
Elizabeth, d. Ezekiel and Damaras, Apr. 4, 1787.
Ellen, d. John, jr. and Miriam F., May 25, 1838.
Enoch, s. Joseph and Lucinda, Feb. 26, 1821.
Enoch, s. Joseph and Lucinda, Feb. 26, 1822.
Ezekiel, s. Solomon and Bethiah, Oct. 14, 1777.
Ezra, s. Solomon and Bethyah, Aug. 24, 1773.
Fanny, d. Daniel and Lydia, Nov. 5, 1802.
Francis, s. Gideon C. and Joanna, Sept. 7, 1804.
Francis, s. John, jr. and Mary, Nov. 13, 1832.

WARDWELL, Franklin, s. Thomas J., yeoman, and Mary A., Jan. 21, 1847.
George, s. Simon, bp. Aug. 11, 1793. C. R. 2.
George, s. George and Mary, July 10, 1826.
George, s. William W. and Elizabeth, Aug. 30, 1833.
George, s. Tho[ma]s and Mary Ann, June 2, 1835.
George H., s. [twin], Simon, jr. and Margaret E. F., Apr. 18, 1834.
Georgianna, d. Simon, cordwainer, and M. E., Feb. 22, 1846.
Gideon Church, s. Simon, bp. July 10, 1791. C. R. 2.
Gilbert B., s. Simon and Margaret, May 16, 1829.
Hannah, d. Peter and Betty, Feb. 4, 1793.
Hannah B., d. Simon, jr. and Margaret, Mar. 3, 1827.
Hannah Joy, d. Thomas, cordwainer, and Mary, Nov. 10, 1844.
Harriot Morse, d. Daniel and Lydia, Jan. 5, 1801. P. R. 74.
Harriot, d. Josep[h] and Lucinda, Aug. 22, 1823.
Harriot Huse, d. Daniel and Lydia, Jan. 5, 1801.
Henriette, d. Elbridge G., carpenter, and Lavina, July 20, 1847.
Henry, s. Simon, bp. Apr. 29, 1798. C. R. 2.
Henry, s. John and Sarah, Oct. 10, 1799.
Henry, s. [twin], Simon, jr. and Margaret E. F., Apr. 18, 1834.
Hiram H., s. Simon, jr. and Margaret, Oct. 13, 1818.
Isaac, s. Jonathan, bp. Oct. 14, 1753. C. R. 2.
Isaac, s. Peter and Dorcas, July 5, 1780.
Isaac, s. Nathan and Phebe, Sept. 29, 1795.
Jedediah, s. Jonathan and Rachel, Aug. 16, 1770.
Jeremiah, s. Thomas and Abigail, Jan. 6, 1741-2.
Jeremiah, s. Joshua, bp. Jan. 27, 1771. C. R. 1.
John, s. William and Dorathy, Oct. 9, 1719.
John, s. John and Lydia, Mar. 19, 1766.
John, s. twin, John and Sarah, Sept. 7, 1803.
Jonathan, s. William and Dorathy [bp. Dec. 16, 1711. C R. 2.].
Jonathan, s. Peter and Betty, Apr. 29, 1791.
Joseph, s. Joshua and Mary, Jan. 29, 1760.
Joseph, s. Ezekiel and Damaras, July 27, 1784.
Joseph, s. Joseph and Lucinda, Sept. 27, 1829.
Joseph, s. Thomas J. and Mary Ann, Nov. 12, 1839.
Joseph Warren, s. Daniel, bp. Aug. 19, 1781. C. R. 2.
Josephine E[lizabeth. P. R. 58.], d. Benjamin F., carpenter, and Hannah E., July 30, 1844.
Julia Maria, d. Henry, clothier, and Angeline, Oct. 5, 1846.
Justus E[dwin. P. R. 74.], s. Daniel and Lydia, May 28, 1813.
Leonard, s. Gideon C. and Joanna, Aug. 30, 1801.
Louisa Cassendra, d. Benja[min] F., carpenter, and Hannah E., Apr. 3, 1847.

WARDWELL, Lucy Ann, d. Simon, jr. and Margaret, Feb. 9, 1825.
Lydia, d. John and Lydia, June 23, 1760.
Margaret, d. Simon, jr. and Margaret, Oct. 28, 1820.
Margarett E., d. Simon, jr. and M. E. F., Apr. 29, 1838.
Maria, d. Simon and Margaret E., Jan. 9, 1844.
Martha, d. Joseph and Lucinda, Oct. 11, 1832.
Mary, d. Thomas and Abigail, Feb. 3, 1744-5.
Mary, d. Daniel and Damaras, Nov. 28, 1774. [Nov. 29. dup.]
Mary, d. Nathan and Phebe, July 6, 1800.
Mary Adams, d. Joseph and Lucindia, Feb. 4, 1816.
Mary Jane, d. Capt. Geo[rge] and Mary, Nov. 30, 1828.
Mary Maria Morse, d. Daniel and Lydia, June 9, 1808.
Mary Mariah, d. Simon, cordwainer, and Margaret E. F., Jan. 9, 1844.
Mary W., d. Henry and Angeline, Sept. 17, 1837.
Matilda, d. Simon, cordwainer, and Margaret E. F., Feb. 9, 1847.
Moses, s. John [jr. C. R. 2.] and Sarah, at Bradford, Feb. 3, 1790. P. R. 29.
Nathan, s. W[illia]m, jr., bp. Jan. 20, 1740. C. R. 2.
Nathan, s. Nathan and Hulda, Nov. 10, 1765.
Nathan, s. Nathan and Phebe, Apr. 28, 1792.
Nathaniel, s. Simon, bp. July 10, 1791. C. R. 2.
Octavia Susan, d. Dr. Daniel and Sarah, July 8, 1824.
Olive, d. Nathan and Huldah, July 3, 1768.
Oran, s. John and Sarah, Sept. 24, 1807.
Pamela, d. Ezekiel and Damaras, May 6, 1792.
Patty, d. Simon, bp. July 10, 1791. C. R. 2.
Peter, s. Peter and Betty, May 2, 1789.
Phebe, d. Nathan and Phebe, Oct. 18, 1793.
Pheoby, d. William and Dorithy, Oct. 3, 1717.
Rachel, d. Jonathan and Rachel, Nov. 29, 1759.
Rachel, b. Jonathan and Rachel, Dec. 6, 1764.
Rebeckah, d. Sam[ue]ll and Sarah, Sept. 10, 1691.
[Return. C. R. 2.], d. Samuell and Return, Feb. 24, 1718-19.
Rosella, d. Elbridge, carpenter, and Lavina, Nov. 26, 1844.
Ruth, d. Josh[u]a, bp. Nov. 16, 1766. C. R. 2.
Sally, d. Nathan and Phoebe, June 29, 1798.
Samuel, s. Jonathan and Rachel [No]v. 7, 1766. [bp. Nov. 9. C. R. 2.]
Samuel, s. Ezekiel and Damaras, June 15, 1790.
Samuel, s. Joseph and Lucinda, Oct. 16, 1818.
Samuell, s. Samuell and Sarah, Feb. 24, 1676.
Sarah, d. Will[ia]m and Dorathy, June 1 [1714. C. R. 2.].
Sarah, d. John and Sarah, Aug. 31, 1801.

WARDWELL, Sarah, d. twin, John and Sarah, Sept. 7, 1803.
Sarah J., d. Charles and Mehitable, June 5, 1831.
Sarah Jane, d. Henry, manufacturer, and Angeline, Mar. 17, 1845.
Silvanus, s. Thomas and Abigale, June 1, 1746.
Simon, s. Simon and Ruth, Aug. 24, 1803.
Simon Willard, s. Simon, jr. and Margaret, Feb. 15, 1813.
Solomon, s. Thomas and Abigail, Jan. 19, 1738-9.
Solomon, s. Thomas and Abigail, July 14, 1743.
Solomon, s. Solomon and Bethiah, Feb. 3, 1768.
Stephen, s. Ruth, bp. Nov. 3, 1793. C. R. 2.
Stephen H., s. Simon, jr. and Margaret, Oct. 9, 1816.
Susanna, d. Joshua, bp. Sept. 11, 1763. C. R. 2.
Theodore Ames, s. W[illia]m H., bp. Aug. 29, 1847. C. R. 2.
Thomas G., s. Simon, jr. and Margaret, Oct. 13, 1814.
Timothy Osgood, s. Dr. Daniel and Sarah, Nov. 22, 1829.
William, s. Samuell and Sarah, Nov. 9, 1679.
William, s. Thomas G., cordwainer, and Mary H., Aug. 4, 1843.
William H., s. Simon, jr. and Margret, Feb. 13, 1823.
William S., s. John, jr. and Miriam F., Mar. 20, 1830.
William T[heodore. C. R. 2.], s. W[illia]m H., bookseller, and Sophia M., Apr. 18, 1844.
William W., s. William W. and Elizabeth, May 17, 1832.
William Watson, s. Daniel and Lydia, Apr. 15, 1806.
Zachariah, s. Zachariah Frye and Esther, Feb. 18, 1792.
——, ch. William and Dorathy, May 3, 1709.
——, s. William, jr. and Margery, Jan. —, 1739-40.
——, s. Simon, jr. and Ruth, Feb. 8, 1825.
——, s. Charles and Mehitable, Mar. 5, 1826.
——, s. Dr. Daniel and Sarah, Nov. 21, 1828.

WARDWILL (see also Wardwell), Ezekiel, s. Thomas and Abigal, Feb. 15, 1750-51.
Mary, d. Eliakim and Mary, Aug. 28, 1748.

WARE, Galen Edwin Alonzo, s. Galen and Catharine, May 11, 1811.

WARREN, Lucretia, d. "adopted of Mrs. Richard," bp. Dec. 19, 1830. C. R. 2.

WASSON, William, s. John, bp. Aug. 20, 1749. C. R. 2.

WATERMAN, Herbert, s. Rev. Henry and Eliza G., Sept. 10, 1847. C. R. 4.

WATSON, Elizabeth, d. Frederic, flax-dresser, and Agnes R., July 12, 1843.
Sarah Marshall, d. John and Sarah M., June 4, 1843.

WAYLAND, see Waland.

WEBSTER, Abigail Ann, d. John, farmer, and Ellen [Ellena. dup.], Oct. 15, 1843.
Almira Esther, d. John, yeoman, and Eleanor, Nov. 17, 1846.
Henry A., s. John S., manufacturer, and Mary Ann, Oct. 28, 1843.
Lucretia Orpha, d. John, farmer, and Eleanor, b. Dracut, Oct. 27, 1848.

WEEKS, Elizabeth M., d. Luther C., painter, and Martha, at Stoneham, May 10, 1848.

WELCH, Charles A., s. Charles A. and Mary L., b. Boston, bp. Oct. 3, 1847. C. R. 4.
Hannah, d. John and Elinor, Oct. 26, 1766.
John, s. Cornelias, laborer, and Bridget, May 17, 1847.
Joseph, s. John and Elinor, Mar. 26, 1770.
William Henry, s. Robert, machinist, and Hannah, both b. England, Sept. 13, 1849.

WELLS, Albert Newton, s. twin, William H., teacher in the English Academy, and T. S. O., Jan. 26, 1846.
Alfred Ordway, s. twin, William H., teacher in the English Academy, and T. S. O., Jan. 26, 1846.
Smith, s. William H. and Hannah, Apr. 22, 1842.

WENTWORTH, Ann, d. John P. Robinson, engineer, and Betsy, Sept. 19, 1846.

WESCOTT, Frederick, s. Everett, cordwainer, and Emily, Mar. 28, 1845.
John E., s. Everett, cordwainer, and Emily, June 6, 1843.

WESTON, Adoniram J., s. Jacob and Lydia B., Jan. 5, 1838.

WHEELER, ——, d. Capt. Caleb, Dec. 17, 1827.

WHINNEY, Henry s. William and Sarah, May 18, 1828.
Sarah Ann, d. William and Sarah, Oct. 22, 1826.

WHISTON, Elisabeth, d. Increas and Abigail, Sept. 9, 1747.
John, s. Increase and Abigail, Apr. 5, 1743.
Samuel, s. Increas and Abigail, Jan. —, 1744-5.
Sarah, d. Increas and Abigale, Jan. 28, 1741[-2].

WHITCOMB, Eliza A., d. Benjamin, laborer, and Polly, July 5, 1844.
Eliza A., d. Benja[min], laborer, and Polly, July 5, 1845.
Horace, s. Benjamin and Polly, Mar. 27, 1841.
John Newton, s. Benja[min] W., laborer, and Polly, Feb. 14, 1846.
Mary Jane, d. Benjamin and Polly, June 21, 1838.
Sarah Ann, d. John and Ann, bp. June 5, 1842. C. R. 4.
William, s. Benja[min] laborer, b. Mount Holley, Vt., and Polly, b. Claremont, N. H., Mar. 2, 1849.

WHITE (see also Wight), Annah, d. John and Sarah, Sept. 17, 1699.
Charlotte, d. William A. and Sarah L., Apr. 8, 1839.
Elizabeth, d. John and Sarah, Apr. 8, 1688.
George Ann, d. W[illia]m A. and Sarah L., Feb. 8, 1837.
George Holbrook, s. George and Mary Ann, bp. Sept. 3, 1848. C. R. 3.
George N., s. Nathaniel and Hannah, Aug. 24, 1821. T. C.
George P., s. John F. and Sarah M., May 13, 1839.
Issabell, d. Nath[anie]l and Hannah, Jan. 5, 1820.
John, s. John and Sarah, July 7, 1698.
John, s. John and Hannah, Dec. 29, 1780.
Lora Melvina, d. Burnham S., cordwainer, and Mary S., Oct. 28, 1847.
Mary, d. Hannah, "bound to Deacon J. Abbot," bp. June 26, 1726. C. R. 2.
Mary E., d. Burnham S., cordwainer, and Mary, Oct. 2, 1845.
Mary Ellyott, d. Anna, and "Reputed" d. John Ellyot, Apr. 7, 1724.
Peggy, d. Richard Rogers and Nancy, Feb. 1, 1805.
Sarah, d. John and Sarah, Apr. 11, 1694.
——, ch. [torn] and [torn] rah, Jan. 30, 1702-3.
——, s. Mrs. ——, Sept. 23, 1821.

WHITEHEAD, ——, d. Robert and Nancy, Jan. 22, 1839.

WHITEHOUSE, Mary Abby, d. Thomas L., laborer, and Abigail, July 11, 1848.

WHITING, Lucy, d. Adoniram and Lucy F., Aug. 29, 1828.
Patty, d. Oliver and Martha, July 27, 1775.

WHITNEY, Joshua B., s. Joshua B., blacksmith, and Wealthy J. F., Jan. 16, 1848.
Luella Francena, d. Joshua B., blacksmith, b. Dexter, Me., and Wealthy Jane F., b. Derry, N. H., Aug. 28, 1849.

WHITON (see also Whitten), Elizabeth Antonett [s. Benjamin and Clarissa?], bp. May 3, 1829. C. R. 2.
Ethelinda, d. Benjamin and Clarissa, bp. July 11, 1824. C. R. 2.
John F. [s. Benjamin and Clarissa?], bp. Feb. 11, 1827. C. R. 2.

WHITTAKER, Catherine A., d. Lawrence, finisher, and Catharine, Aug. 2, 1845.
James Lawrence, s. Lawrence, manufacturer, and Catherine, Aug. 4, 1846.

WHITTEN (see also Whiton), Benjamin [F. C. R. 2.], s. Benjamin and Clarissa, Mar. 28, 1822.
Charles Francis, s. Benjamin, Nov. 2, 1826.
——, d. Benjamin, Jan. —, 1829.

WHITTIER, Ann Elizabeth, d. Nath[anie]l and Hannah, Aug. 10, 1825.
Daniel, s. Nathaniel and Anna, Feb. 7, 1812.
Edward, s. Nath[anie]l and Hannah, Mar. 16, 1818.
Hannah E[mily. C. R. 2.], d. Nathaniel and Hannah, Oct. 27, 1830.
Joseph, s. Nathaniel and Hannah, Feb. 12, 1822.
Mary Louisa, d. Nath[anie]l and Hannah, July —, 1828.
William, s. Nathaniel and Hannah, Oct. 1, 1834.
——, d. Jona[than] S. and Charlotte P., July —, 1820.

WHITWORTH, Mary Ann, d. John and Ann, Nov. 9, 1830.
——, ch. John and Ann, Sept. 7, 1838.

WIER (see also Wyer), George, s. Charles, flax-dresser, and Catharine, Nov. 13, 1845.

WIGHT (see also White), Hannah, d. John and Hannah, bp. July 11, 1784. C. R. 1.
Nathan Berven, s. John and Hannah, bp. Jan. 14, 1787. C. R. 1.

WILD, Sarah Ann, d. Joseph Benjamin and Louisa, bp. June 4, 1843. C. R. 4.
William Henry, s. Joseph Benjamin and Louisa, bp. June 4, 1843. C. R. 4.

WILEY (see also Willey, Wyley, Wyllie), Benjamin, s. Wiliam and Elezebith, Feb. 3, 1750-51.
David, s. David, bp. Oct. 9, 1791.
Elizabeth, d. William, laborer, and Mary A., July 30, 1844.
George Nathaniel, s. James and Phebe S., Sept. 1, 1837.
James, s. David, bp. Feb. 28, 1790. C. R. 2.
John, s. Rob[er]t bp. June 19, 1743. C. R. 2.
Jonathan, s. Will[ia]m and Sally, bp. Aug. 14, 1791. C. R. 1.
Joseph, s. Sarah, w. W[illia]m, bp. June 21, 1795. C. R. 1.
Lydia Calahan, d. William and Sarah, July 3, 1788.
Wiliam, s. Wiliam and Elezebith, June 1, 1749.

WILKINS (see also Willkins), Abner, s. Abner and Mehitable, Dec. 4, 1784.
Franklin Kimbal, s. wid. Almira, bp. Mar. 29, 1846. C. R. 3.
John Calvin, s. wid. Almira, bp. Mar. 29, 1846. C. R. 3.
Luke Bowns, s. wid. Almira, bp. Mar. 29, 1846. C. R. 3.
Uriah, s. Abner, bp. Nov. 20, 1791. C. R. 2.

WILLEY (see also Wiley), ——, s. Robert and Jane, —— 8, 1743.

WILLIAMS, Frances G., d. William, laborer, and Ellen, Jan. 14, 1849.
George H., s. George H., woolsorter, and Mary A., Apr. 29, 1845.
Isaac Frye, s. Sam[ue]ll and Phebe, Aug. 16, 1764. [bp. May 20. C. R. 1.]
James, s. Sam[ue]ll and Phebe, Aug. 22, 1759.
Mary, d. Sam[ue]l, bp. Aug. 23, 1761. C. R. 1.

WILLKINS (see also Wilkins), Debbe, d. Moses and Deborah, bp. May 26, 1793. C. R. 1.

WILLSON (see also Wilson), Abiel, s. John and Hannah, June 10, 1760.
Abiel, s. Isaac and Hannah, June 10, 1828.
Abigall, d. Joseph and Sarah, at Ipswich, Sept. 13, 1688.
Anna, d. William and Anna, Feb. 20, 1764.

WILLSON, Asie, s. John and Marcy, Dec. 21, 1728.
Charles, s. Dr. Ward Noyes and Dorcas, June 17, 1785.
Chloe, d. John and Hannah, Feb. 9, 1766.
David, s. William and Chloe, Feb. 16, 1799.
Dorcas, s. John and Hannah, Mar. 10, 1762.
Hannah, d. John and Marcy, Sept. 10, 1726.
Hannah, d. John, jr. and Hannah, June 25, 1746.
Henry, s. Isaac and Hannah, Feb. 26, 1834.
James, s. John and Hannah, Dec. 17, 1770.
John, s. Joseph and Sarah, Feb. 23, 1682.
John, s. John and Mercy, —— 2 [1720. C. R. 1.].
John, s. John, jr. and Hannah, June 11, 1742.
John, s. William and Anna, Sept. 18, 1766.
John, s. Joshua and Dorothy, Nov. 1, 1775.
Jonathan, s. Joshua and Dorothy, Aug. 16, 1774.
Joseph, s. Joseph and Mary, June 6, 1677.
Joseph, s. Josep[h], Mar. 20, 1701.
Joseph, s. John and Marcy, Jan. 20, 1721-2.
[Joseph. C. R. 1.], s. John and Marcy, Jan. 17, 1741-2.
Joshua, s. John and Marcy, Oct. 28, 1735.
Joshua, s. John, jr. and Hannah, Feb. 10, 1743-4.
Lydia, d. John and Marcy, Aug. 20, 1737.
Lydia, d. John and Marcy, Sept. 30, 1739.
Mary, d. Joseph and Mary, Feb. 26, 1674-5.
Mary, d. Joseph and Sarah, Dec. 17, 1680.
Mary, d. John and Marcy, Dec. 8, 1731.
M[ehe]tabel [Elizabeth. C. R. 1.], d. John and Marcy, Sept. 18, 1733.
Mercy, d. John and Mary, bp. Feb. 16, 1751. C. R. 1.
Micah, s. Elizabeth, d. John Willson, bp. Sept. 13, 1767. C. R. 1.
Phebe, d. John and Hannah, Dec. 18, 1767.
Sarah, d. Joseph and Sarah, Dec. 31, 1678.
Simmeon, s. John and Hannah, June 28, 1764.
Thomas, s. William and Anna, May 1, 1762.
Thomas Whiting, s. William and Chloe, Jan. 17, 1797.
——, d. John and Marcy, Jan. 3, 1723-4.

WILLSONE (see also Wilson), Mary, d. Joseph and Mary, abt. Sept. 29, 1673. [Dec. 29. CT. R.]

WILSON (see also Willson, Willsone), David, s. Joshua and Doretha, Feb. 6, 1779.
Dolly, d. Joshua and Dorothy [Dolly. C. R. 1.], Apr. 29, 1777.
Elezebith, d. John, jr. and Hanah, May 6, 1748.

WILSON, Enoch, s. twin, Joshua and Dorothy, Apr. 30, 1785.
Frederick, s. Joshua and Dorathy, Aug. 17, 1789.
Hannah, d. Nat[haniel] Lovejoy's wife, bp. —— [1719 or 20.]. C. R. 1.
Hannah Frye, d. Isaac and Hannah, Nov. 4, 1835.
Isaac, s. Joshua and Dorathy, Sept. 29, 1792.
James, s. Joshua and Dorothy, June 27, 1796.
Jeremy, s. twin, Joshua and Dorothy, Apr. 30, 1785.
John, s. John, jr. and Hannah, Jan. 29, 1754.
John Robinson, s. Joshua, jr. and Dolly, Feb. 19, 1814.
Joseph, s. John, jr. and Hannah, Jan. —, 1756.
Joseph, s. Joshua and Dorothy, Aug. 20, 1781.
Joshua, s. Joshua and Dorathy, Apr. 28, 1787.
Marcy, d. John, jr. and Hannah, Feb. 11, 1752.
Mary Ellen, d. J. L., spinner, and Mary Ann, Feb. 28, 1846.
Mercy, d. John and Mercy, Aug. 13, 1717.
Molley, d. John, jr. and Hannah, Aug. 12, 1758.
Samuel, s. Joshua and Dorathy, Apr. 5, 1783.
Sarah, d. John, jr. and Hannah, Mar. 6, 1749-50.
Susan, d. Isaac and Hannah, May 11, 1827.
William, s. William and Anna, May 28, 1760.
William Wylder, s. W[illia]m, bp. Sept. 9, 1798. C. R. 2.
——, ch. [torn] and Marah, Feb. 18, 1702-3.
——, ch. John and Mercy, Jan. 15, 1718-19.

WINCHESTER, Charles, s. Lemuel, bp. Sept. 19, 1792. C. R. 2.
Lemuel, s. wid. Hannah, bp. Aug. 8, 1802. C. R. 2.
Lydia Flint, d. Lemuel, bp. May 12, 1799. C. R. 2.
Rebecca, d. Lemuel, bp. Aug. 28, 1796. C. R. 2.
Samuel, s. Lemuel, bp. Aug. 24, 1794. C. R. 2.
Sarah Ella Maria, d. Wentworth, shoemaker, and Harriet L., Feb. 22, 1849.

WINNING, Adeline, d. Robert, yeoman, and Elizabeth N., July 25, 1846.
Albert, s. Robert, farmer, b. Billerica, and Elizabeth R., Dec. 1, 1848.
Martha Caroline, d. Alexander, farmer, and Mary Ann, Nov. 12, 1843.
Mary Elizabeth, d. Alexander, bp. Feb. 25, 1849. C. R. 2.

WINTHROP, Alexander M., s. Thomas, cordwainer, and Ellen, Dec. 9, 1844.
Helen, d. Tho[ma]s, bp. May 5, 1844. C. R. 2.
Thomas Fergus, s. Thomas, bp. Nov. 6, 1842. C. R. 2.

WISE, Mary Ann, d. John and Mary Eaton, Feb. 18, 1827.

WITHERBEE, Henry S., s. Nahum and Mary, Feb. 8, 1836.

WITHEY, William Henry, s. Richard, dyer, and Ellen W., Oct. 19, 1847.

WOLFENDEN (see also Woolfenden), Anna Cropper, d. Robert and Mary, bp. July 31, 1838. C. R. 4.
Elizabeth Ann, d. Robert and Mary, bp. May 31, 1840. C. R. 4.
Ellen Harrison, d. Joseph, spinner, and Betsy, Sept. 17, 1847.
Ja[me]s Harrison, s. Robert and Mary, bp. Oct. 28, 1838. C. R. 4.
Joshua Hayes, s. Robert and Mary, bp. Oct. 28, 1838. C. R. 4.
Mary M., d. Joseph, laborer, and Betsy, Apr. 20, 1845.

WOLWORTH (see also Wallworth), Henry, s. Tho[ma]s and Mary Ann, Sept. 11, 1837.

WOOD (see also Woods), Abiel, s. Israel and Sarah, Mar. 6, 1767.
Andrew Palmer, s. John and Mary, Aug. 28, 1769.
Bethiah, d. Israel and Sarah, Mar. 7, 1777.
Betsey, d. Moses and Betsy, May 15, 1814.
Betsy Emily, d. Moses and Betsy, in Stark, Me., Dec. 9, 1821.
Daniel, s. John and Mary, Nov. 10, 1767.
David, s. Israel and Sarah, Feb. 1, 1765.
David, s. Lt. Moses and Betsy, Aug. 31, 1816.
Eleanor, d. John and Mary, Mar. 14, 1761.
Esther, d. John, bp. Sept. 24, 1795. C. R. 2.
Hermon, s. John, bp. Dec. 1, 1807. C. R. 2.
Israel, s. Israel and Sarah, Jan. 22, 1763.
Jacob, s. Israel and Sarah, Mar. 30, 1774.
Jesse, s. John and Mary, Apr. 24, 1776.
John, s. John and Mary, Mar. 27, 1764.
John, s. John, bp. Sept. 24, 1795. C. R. 2.
Joseph, s. Israel, bp. Nov. 7, 1773. C. R. 2.
Lucinda, d. John and Esther, Mar. 3, 1796.
Lydia, d. Israel and Sarah, Apr. 21, 1771.
Molle, d. John and Mary, Aug. 7, 1759.
Moses, s. Israel and Sarah, May 16, 1779.
Moses, s. John, bp. July 10, 1803. C. R. 2.
Moses, s. Moses and Betsy, June 13, 1812.
Phebe, d. Nathan and Elizabeth, Aug. 17, 1751. P. R. 17.
Polly, d. John, bp. Sept. 24, 1795. C. R. 2.

WOOD, Richard, s. Israel and Sarah, Mar. 11, 1764.
Richard, s. John and Mary, Jan. 22, 1766.
Sally, d. Solomon and Sally, May 15, 1823.
Samuel, s. Israel, bp. May 19, 1782. C. R. 2.
Sarah [Ralph. C. R. 2.], d. Israel [jr. C. R. 2.] and Sarah, June 7, 1769.
Sarah, d. John, bp. Nov. 10, 1802. C. R. 2.
Susanna, d. Obadiah and Deborah, Nov. 5, 1759.
——, s. Phineas and Betsy, July 22, 1821.

WOODAN, Sarah, d. Joseph, weaver, and Eliza, both b. England, on the ocean, May 22, 1849.

WOODBERY (see also Woodbury), Polly, d. Will[ia]m and Sarah, Mar. 20, 1783.

WOODBRIDGE, Adolphus, s. Benjamin and Rhoda, Apr. 8, 1826. P. R. 73.
Albert W., s. Osgood and Hannah, Sept. 9, 1838. P. R. 73.
Augusta, d. Dudley, jr. and Mary, Mar. 14, 1839.
Benjamin, s. Samuel and Abia, Jan. 7, 1757. P. R. 73.
Benjamin, s. Benjamin and Patty, Nov. 22, 1789.
Benj[ami]n F., s. Benj[ami]n, jr. and Rhoda, Aug. 7, 1819.
Caroline Dorcas, d. Samuel, jr. and Dorcas, Aug. 1, 1822.
[Charles D. P. R. 73.], ch. Osgood and Hannah S., May 26, 1827. [May 19. P. R. 73.]
Clarissa, d. Osgood and Hannah S., Sept. 30, 1829.
Dudly, s. twin, Benjamin and Patty, Sept. 23, 1797.
Eliza, d. William and Mary, Dec. 7, 1828. P. R. 73.
George B., s. Osgood and Hannah S., Mar. 1, 1820.
Hannah B., d. Sam[ue]l, jr. and Phebe B., Apr. 22, 1828.
Hannah Maria, d. Osgood and Hannah, June 27, 1833. P. R. 73.
[Harriet. P. R. 73.], d. Benjamin and Rhoda, July 19, 1822.
Henry Gilmanson, s. Alex[ande]r Allen and Sally, Jan. 29, 1816.
John R., s. Samuel and Dorcas, Mar. 21, 1829.
Joshua, s. Samuel and Abia, Aug. 31, 1771.
Lorenzo L., s. Osgood and Hannah, Apr. 22, 1836. P. R. 73.
Lucretia, d. Dudley, jr. and Mary, July 31, 1832.
Martha M., d. Osgood and Hannah, Mar. 9, 1835. P. R. 73.
Mary, d. Benjamin and Martha, ——, 1786. P. R. 73.
Mary, d. William and Mary, Dec. 5, 1831. P. R. 73.
Nancy, d. Dudley, jr. and Mary, Dec. 18, 1828.
Osgood, s. Benjamin and Patty, Feb. 27, 1792.

WOODBRIDGE, WOODBRIDGE, Patty, d. Benjamin and Patty, Apr. 3, 1792.
Polly, d. Benjamin and Patty, Oct. 29, 1786.
Samuel F., s. Benjamin and Rhoda, Mar. 23, 1824. P. R. 73.
Samuel Gilman, s. Samuel and Abia, July 4, 1768.
Sarah E. B., d. Samuel and Phebe, Aug. 8, 1826.
[Susan B. P. R. 73.], d. Osgood and Hannah, July 8, 1822.
Susannah, d. Benjamin and Patty, Mar. 4, 1788. [Mar. 14. P. R. 73.]
William, s. twin, Benjamin and Patty, Sept. 23, 1797.
William O., s. Osgood and Hannah, July 10, 1824. P. R. 73.
William, s. William and Mary H., Sept. 30, 1826.
——, d. Sam[ue]l and Dorcas, June 15, 1827.

WOODBURY (see also Woodbery), Mary A[lline. C. R. 3.], d. Eben[eze]r, shoemaker, and Mehitable, May 8, 1845.
Mary Elizabeth, d. Richard, shoemaker, and Mary Ann, July 23, 1844.
Moses Eben, s. Eben, shoemaker, and Mehitable, Oct. 9, 1848.

WOODCOCK, Emeline Mary Jane, d. Gideon, coffee-grinder, b. Anson, Me., and Jane, b. Andover, N. H., at Dracut, Apr. 22, 1849.

WOODMAN, Benjamin, s. Joshua and Elizabeth, July 27, 1683.
Dor[o]thy, d. Joshua and Elizabeth, Nov. 13, 1669.
Elizabeth, d. Joshua and Elizabeth, Feb. 6, [16]67.
Johnathan, s. Joshua and Elizabeth, Apr. 1, 1674.
Josua, s. Josua and Elizabeth, Apr. 2, 1672.
Mary, d. Joshua and Elisabeth, Apr. 9, 1690.
Sarah, d. Joshua and Elizabeth, Apr. 9, 1686.

WOODS (see also Wood), Abba Elizabeth, d. Hannah, bp. Apr. 19, 1829. C. R. 6.
Abigail Wheeler, d. Rev. Leonard and Abigail, July 25, 1811.
Catharine, d. Capt. Moses and Betsy, Jan. 1, 1819.
Daniel Bates, s. Rev. Leonard and Abigail, Sept. 20, 1809.
Harriet Newell, d. Leonard and Abi[gail], bp. Dec. 10, 1815. C. R. 6.
Joseph Wheeler, s. Joseph W. [deceased. dup.] and Hannah, Nov. 12, 1827. [Nov. 11. dup.]
Margaret O[liver. C. R. 2.], d. Rev. Leonard and Abigail, Apr. 12, 1813.
Sarah Abbot, d. Rev. Leonard and Abigail, June 18, 1817.
Sophia Walker, d. Rev. Leonard and Abigail, May 12, 1819.

WOODWARD, Sarah, d. Joseph and Sophia, May 21, 1849. C. R. 4.

WOOLFENDEN (see also Wolfenden), Isabella J., d. Robert, weaver, and Mary, both b. England, Jan. 7, 1849.
Mary Alice, d. Robert and Mary, bp. Apr. 16, 1843. C. R. 4.
Rachel E., d. Robert, manufacturer, and Mary, Dec. 8, 1845.

WOOLLEY, Augustus, s. Nathan and Sarah, Dec. 29, 1763.

WORCESTER, Caroline Augusta, d. Eldad and Sarah, Dec. 30, 1821.
Charles, s. Osgood and Phebe, Aug. 26, 1811.
Clark Howard, s. Leonard and Rebecca, bp. Oct. 10, 1830. C. R. 3.
George, s. Capt. Eldad and Sarah, Mar. 21, 1820.
John, s. Osgood and Phebe, Sept. 22, 1814.
Joseph Wise, s. Leonard and Rebecca, bp. Oct. 10, 1830. C. R. 3.
Justin, s. Leonard and Rebecca, bp. Oct. 10, 1830. C. R. 3.
Mark True, s. Leonard and Rebecca, bp. Oct. 10, 1830. C. R. 3.
Sarah, d. Capt. Eldad and Sarah, Sept. 26, 1818.

WORDWILL (see also Wardwell), Daniel, s. Thomas and Abagil, Nov. 18, 1753.
Easther, d. Jonathan and Rachel, June 25, 1758.
Eliakim, s. Eliakim and Mary, Mar. 31, 1750.
Hannah, d. Jonathan and Rachel, Jan. 23, 1756.
Isaac, s. Jonathan and Rachil, Oct. 10, 1753.
Jeremiah, s. Thomas and Abigal, Dec. 6, 1748.
Jonathan, s. Jonathan and Rachil, Mar. 20, 1748-9
Joshua, s. Joshua and Mary, Nov. 2, 1757.
Peter, s. Jonathan and Rachel, Feb. 25, 1752.
Phebe, d. Thomas and Abigal, Mar. 2, 1756.
Simon, s. Eliakim and Mary, May 17, 1752.
Theoder, s. Eliakim and Mary, Apr. 13, 1754.

WORMWOOD, Dorcas, d. Henery and Mary, Dec. 8, 1673.

WRIGHT (see also Write), Abigail, d. Walter and Elizabeth, Jan. 31, 1698-9.
Benjamin, s. John and Hannah, June 22, 1742.
Christopher, s. Walter and Susanna, Nov. 27, 1672.
Dorothy, d. Walter and Elizabeth, July 23, 1688.
Elisabeth, d. John and Hannah, Jan. 25, 1744-5.
Elizabeth, d. Walter and Elizabeth, July 20, 1685.
Elizabeth, d. Samuel, jr. and Elizabeth, Dec. 16, 1775.

WRIGHT, Hephzibah, d. Joseph and Sarah, Oct. 14, 1720.
James, s. John and Hannah, Mar. 21, 1746-7.
John, s. Walter and Susanna, Feb. 10, 1675.
John, s. twin, Samuel and Ruth, July 5, 1741.
[John. T. C.] —— hn, s. John, jr. and Mary, May 3, 1749.
Joseph, s. Walter and Elizabeth, Oct. 28, 1693.
Joseph, s. John and Hannah, Mar. 15, 17[31-2. C. R. 1].
Lydia, d. Samuel and Ruth, at Harvard, May 14, 1737.
Marcy, d. Samuel and Ruth, at Harvard, Mar. 17, 1730-31.
Martha, d. Samuel and Ruth, at Harvard, Dec. —1, 1732.
Mary, d. John and Hannah, Mar. 25, 17[34. C. R. 1.].
Phebe, d. John and Hannah, Feb. 17, 1739-40.
Ruth, d. Samuel and Ruth, at Harvard, Aug. 24, 1729.
Samuel, s. twin, Samuel and Ruth, July 5, 1741.
Sarah, d. Walter and Elizabeth, Mar. 20, 1695-6.
Sarah, d. Samuel and Ruth, at Harvard, Nov. 14, 1734.
[Sarah. C. R. 1.], d. John and Hannah, Jan. 25, 1735-6.
Susana, d. John and Mercy, July 24, 1700.
Susannah, d. John and Hannah, Dec. 14, 1737.
Thomas, s. Walter and Susanna, Mar. 4, 1677-8.
Walter, s. Walter and Susanna, Feb. 12, 1668.
——, s. John and Hannah, Apr. 9, 1726.
——, d. John and Hannah, May 9, 1730.
——, d. Samuel and Ruth, —— 29 [173]9.
——, s. twin, Samuel and Ruth, July ——, 1741.

WRITE (see also Wright), [Elizabeth. C. R. 2.], d. Joseph and Sarah, Feb. 13, 1718-19.
Experience, d. John and Marcy, Aug. 5 [1711].
Hannah, d. Joseph and Sarah, June 20, 1717.
John, s. John and Mercy, Mar. —, 1701-2.
Joseph, s. Walter and Elizabeth, Oct. 20, 1693.
Joseph, s. Joseph and Sarah, Mar. — [1712-13]. [bp. Mar. 7, 1714. C. R. 2.]
Joshuah, s. John and Mercy, July 28, 1716.
Sarah, d. Joseph and Sarah, Aug. 7, 17[15. C. R. 2.].
——, ch. [torn] and Marcy, Aug. 5, 1709.
——, ch. [torn] and Elizabeth, —— [1701].

WYER (see also Wier), Ann, d. Eleazer, of Boston, bp. Dec. 26, 1779. C. R. 2.

WYLEY (see also Wiley), Jane, d. twin, Robert, bp. Apr. 5, 1741. C. R. 2.
Sarah, d. twin, Robert, bp. Apr. 5, 1741. C. R. 2.

WYLLIE (see also Wiley), James, s. Rob[er]t, bp. Oct. 29, 1738. C. R. 2.

WYMAN, Anna, d. Thomas and Hannah, Mar. 7, 1763.
Anna, d. Zebulun and Margaret, Mar. 24, 1763.
Hulda, d. Thomas and Hannah, May 18, 1761.
Mary Frances, d. Daniel, butcher, and Frances, Aug. 27, 1846.
Phebe, d. Joseph, of N. Reading, bp. Sept. 24, 1758. C. R. 2.
Samuel, s. Tho[ma]s and Hannah, bp. Feb. 27, 1763. C. R. 2.

YALDEN, Loisa, d. James and Hannah, July 18, 1804.
Perthenia, d. James and Hannah, Aug. 25, 1801.

YORK, Sarah Ann, d. Isaac and Phebe, Dec. 24, 1816.

YOUNG, David A., s. Peter and Deborah, bp. Nov. 28, 1824. C. R. 2.
Francis Cogswell, s. Rev. Jeremiah [S. dup.] and Harriet F., Dec. 31, 1843.
Hannah S., d. Peter, bp. July 18, 1824. C. R. 2.
John, s. Peter, bp. July 18, 1824. C. R. 2.
Johnson, s. Benjamin, bp. June 24, 1781. C. R. 1.
Sarah, d. William [and Sara Irish. CT. F.], June —, 1659. CT. R.
Susannah, d. Benjamin and Hannah, bp. Nov. 16, 1777. C. R. 1.
——, s. Peter and Debrah, Oct. 20, 1824.
——, d. Peter and Deborah, May 9, 1827.

SURNAMES MISSING

——, Benjamin, s. triplet, [torn], Mar. 12, 1703-4.
——, Colby Cooper, d. [torn] and Polly, ——, [1791 ?].
——, Daniel, s. [torn], —— 25 [1701].
——, Daniel, s. Amos and Hannah, Mar. 5, 1808.
——, Ezekiell, s. [torn], —— [1702].
——, Martha, d. [torn], ——7 [1701].
——, Phebe, d. [torn] —— [1704].
——, Rachel, "gradd. Samuel Farnum by his Daughter Alice," bp. ——, 1737. C. R. 1.
——, Zeb——, s. triplet——, Mar. 12, 1703-4.
——er, ——, ch. ——, July 3, 1707.
——ing, ——ry, ch. ——, ——25 [1701].
——od, ——, ch. [torn], July 13, 1706.

——n, ——, ch. [torn], July 5, 1707.
——, ——, ch. [torn], Apr. 11, 1703.
——, ——, ch. [torn], Apr. —, 1703.
——, ——, ch. [torn], Apr. —, 1703.
——, ——, ch. [torn], May —, 1703.
——, ——, ch. [torn], Mar. 17, 1704-5.
——, ——, ch. [torn], Mar. 19, 1704-5.
——, ——, ch. [torn], Mar. 23, 1704-5.
——, ——, ch. [torn], Mar. 25, 1704-5.
——, ——, ch. [torn], Mar. 30, 1704-5
——, ——, ch. [torn], Apr. —, 1705.
——, ——, ch. [torn], Aug. 3, 1706.
——, ——, ch. [torn], Aug. 30, 1706.
——, ——, ch. [torn], Sept. 2, 1706.
——, ——, ch. [torn], Sept. 12, 1706.
——, ——, ch. [torn], Sept. 12, 1706.
——, ——, ch. [torn], May 14, 1707.
——, ——, ch. [torn], May 26, 1707.
——, ——, ch. [torn], [Jü]ne 1, 1707.
——, ——, ch. [torn], June 22, 1707.
——, ——, ch. [torn], July 14, 1707.
——, ——, ch. [torn], Sept. 13, 1707.
——, ——, ch. [torn], Sept. 30, 1707.
——, ——, ch. [torn], Nov. 29, 1907.
——, ——, ch. [torn], Dec. 3, 1707.
——, ——, ch. [torn], Dec. 4, 1707.
——, ——, ch. [torn], Dec. 17, 1707.
——, ——, ch. [torn], Dec. 24, 1707.
——, ——, ch. [torn], Dec. 18, 1709.
——, d. "Sally Woodbridges Child," Jan. 14, 1816.

INDIAN

"A Pappoose of a Basket Maker from Old Town, Maine," Aug. 27, 1843.

NEGROES

Cato, s. Salem and Rhema, May 26, 1768.
Chandler, Pomp, s. Flora, bp. July 5, 1778. C. R. 2.
Cyrus, s. Salem and Rama, servants [of Rev. Samuel Phillips], bp. Dec 23, 1770, a. 6 w. 2d. C. R. 2.
Dick, s. Joanna, servant of Lt. John Aslebe, Feb. 29, 1726-7.

Dole, Dudly, s. Cesar and Tamer, Aug. 14, 1776.
Dole, Elsy, d. Cesar and Tamer, Apr. 6, 1780.
Elisha, Sarah, d. Lewis and Hannah, Aug. 17, 1813.
Esther, d. Peter and Lydia, ser[va]nts of Joshua Lovejoy, Nov. 19, 1788.
Foster, Peter, s. Lucy, bp. Oct. 20, 1793. C. R. 2.
Freeman, Asa, s. Cesar and Jenny, Apr. 9, 1782.
Freeman, Caroline, d. Cesar and Lydia, June 12, 1803.
Freeman, Charlotte, d. Cesar and Jane, bp. Aug. 7, 1803. C. R. 1.
Freeman, Deborah, d. Cato and Lydia, bp. Aug. 30, 1801. C. R. 1.
Freeman, Dorcas, d. Cato and Lydia, Oct. 31, 1795.
Freeman, Elmiry, d. Cesar and Jenne, May 4, 1794.
Eunice, d. Bristow and Eunice, Dec. 25, 1800.
Freeman, Hannah, d. Cesar and Jenny [June] 11, 1791.
Freeman, Isaac Savory, s. Cesar and Jenny, Apr. —, 1797.
Freeman, Jacob Kimball Holden, s. Cato and Lydia, Apr. 4, 1805.
Freeman, James Honestus, s. Cato and Lydia, Sept. 1, 1793.
Freeman, Jane S., d. Lydia, Aug. 3, 1806.
Freeman, John [Cook. C. R. 1], s. Cesar and Jane, Nov. 22, 1799.
Freeman, Lydia, d. Cesar and Jenny, Aug. 31, 1784.
Freeman, Lydia Ann, ward of Cato, bp. Oct. 6, 1822. C. R. 1.
Freeman, Mahala, d. Cato and Lydia, Dec. 5, 1790.
Freeman, Nathaniel Sherlock Milton, s. Cato and Lydia, Oct. 21, 1802.
Freeman, Peter, s. Cato and Lydia, Jan. 15, 1808.
Freeman, Roccena, d. Cato and Lydia, [Mar.] —, 1792
Freeman, William, s. Cesar and Jenney, Feb. 13, 1787.
Freeman, Zadoc Lew, s. Cato and Lydia, Aug. 5, 1797.
Freeman, ——, William Cesar and Charlott, July 29, 1812.
George, "a Molatto Boy, Servant to the Widow Farnum," bp. ——, 1747. C. R. 1.
George "of Mr. Isaac Blunt," bp. Nov. 15, 1761. C. R. 2.
Green, Joseph, s. Joseph and Anna, June 4, 1815.
Green, ——, ch. Joseph and Anna, Feb. 12, 1817.
Hutchinson, Lyman, s. Peter and Nancy, Apr. 7, 1808.
Jonas, s. Salem and Nancy, bp. Sept. 29, 1776. C. R. 1.
Kate, d. Abraham and Dido, "servants to Mr. Bridges," bp. ——, 1746-7. C. R. 1.
Lucy, ch. ——, bp. July 14, 1771. C. R. 2.
Lydia, d. Peter and Lydia, Late Serv[an]ts of Joshua Lovejoy, Aug. 20, 1787.
Nancy, "maid servant (a minor) to James Parker," bp Feb. 8, 1756. C. R. 2.

Peter, s. [Abraham] and Dido, [servant of —] mes Bridges, Jan. or Feb. 1744-5.
Peter, s. Pomp and Cate, bp. May 16, 1773. C. R. 2.
Pompey, "servant to Tho[ma]s Russel," bp. Nov. 18, 1764. C. R. 2.
Prince, "inf. of Jonathan Cummings jr.," bp. Oct. 1, 1769. C. R. 2.
Rose, d. Abraham and Dido, "Servants to Mr. Martin," bp.——, 1750. C. R. 1.
Russel, Elizabeth West, d. Phillis, Jan. 13, 1814.
Sabina, maid servant to Capt. Gibson, bp. Sept. 11, 1743. C. R. 2.
Salem, Boy, Servant to John and Rebecca Poor, bp. ——, 1747. C. R. 1.
Silas, " of Mr. Isaac Blunt," bp. Nov. 15, 1761. C. R. 2.
Simeon, s. Thomas and Rose, servants to Mr. Oliver Peabody, bp. Nov. 4, 1759. C. R. 1.
Stasie, Gallio, s. John and Gallio Nota, "negro of Mr. Dudley Bradstreet," June 24, 1687.
Thompson, William S., s. Nancy, Mar. 29, 1813.
Titus, ch. "belonging to Capt. Tim[oth]y Holt," bp. Oct. 16, 1763. C. R. 2.
Titus, s. Salem and Rema, Servants of Rev. Jona[than] French, Nov. 24, 1774.
——, ch. Abraham and Dido, ——, 17, 17—.

www.ingramcontent.com/pod-product-compliance
Lightning Source LLC
LaVergne TN
LVHW011159110826
845150LV00006B/1269

* 9 7 8 1 4 2 5 5 7 3 2 0 1 *